"This book makes a unique contribution to Korean Studies because of its social movements' prism. It will resonate well in Korea and will also serve as a good introduction to Korea for outsiders. By providing details on twentieth-century uprisings, Katsiaficas provides insights into the trajectory of social movements in the future. His worldwide field-work experiences and surprising insights into Korea are described well in this book."
—Na Kahn-chae, director, May 18 Institute, Gwangju, South Korea

"In *Asia's Unknown Uprisings*, Katsiaficas continues to develop his unique perspective on social movements that he first enunciated in books on the global insurgency of 1968 and autonomous movements in Europe in the 1970s and '80s. Finally, for the first time in English, we now have a comprehensive overview of the remarkable waves of popular uprisings that have taken place in South Korea in the twentieth century. With this volume, Katsiaficas challenges the Eurocentrism of social movement scholarship and provides a radical reappraisal of the role of mass popular uprisings in contemporary history."
—Eddie Yuen, coauthor of *Confronting Capitalism: Dispatches from a Global Movement* and *Catastrophism: The Apocalyptic Politics of Collapse and Rebirth*

Endorsements for Vols. 1 and 2 of *Asia's Unknown Uprisings*

"In *Asia's Unknown Uprisings*, George Katsiaficas inspires readers with an exciting yet scholarly examination of the rise and interlinking of mass revolutionary waves of struggle. In no way Pollyannaish, Katsiaficas presents readers with an analysis of the successes and failures of these late twentieth-century movements. In view of the phenomenal Arab democratic uprisings begun in late 2010 and early 2011, Katsiaficas's analysis is profoundly relevant in helping us understand how the metaphorical flight of a butterfly in one part of the planet can contribute to a metaphoric hurricane thousands of miles away."
—Bill Fletcher, Jr., coauthor of *Solidarity Divided: The Crisis in Organized Labor and a New Path toward Social Justice*, and BlackCommentator.com editorial board member

"George Katsiaficas is America's leading practitioner of the method of 'participant-observation,' acting with and observing the movements that he is studying. This study of People Power is a brilliant narrative of the present as history from below. It is a detailed account of the struggle for freedom and social justice, encompassing the different currents, both reformist and revolutionary, in a balanced study that combines objectivity and commitment. Above all, he presents the beauty of popular movements in the process of self-emancipation."
—James Petras, author of *The Arab Revolt and the Imperialist Counterattack*

"George Katsiaficas has written a majestic account of political uprisings and social movements in Asia—an important contribution to the literature on both Asian studies and social change that is highly-recommended reading for anyone concerned with these fields of interest. The work is well-researched, clearly argued, and beautifully written, accessible to both academic and general readers."
—Carl Boggs, author of *The Crimes of Empire: Rogue Superpower and World Domination*, and professor of social sciences, National University, Los Angeles

"With a characteristic discipline, which typifies the intellectual fabric of great minds, George Katsiaficas shares a family resemblance with Herbert Marcuse, the greatest revolutionary thinker of the twentieth century. Like Marcuse before him, Katsiaficas imbues us with eros for revolutions and respect for meaningful facts . . . This is a great read by a major thinker, destined to be a classic about the revolutions and passions of the Asian world."
—Teodros Kiros, professor of philosophy and English at Berklee College of Music and a non-resident Du Bois Fellow at Harvard University

"Through Katsiaficas's study of Asia's uprisings and rebellions, readers get a glimpse of the challenge to revolutionaries to move beyond representative democracy and to reimagine and reinvent democracy. This book shows the power of rebellions to change the conversation."
—Grace Lee Boggs, activist and coauthor of *Revolution and Evolution in the Twentieth Century*

"The work of George Katsiaficas reveals the sinews of social revolution—not the posturing of political parties, but the impulse that rises from the grassroots which tap into an ever present tendency in history, that of the self-organization of citizens."
—Dimitrios Roussopoulos, author of *Participatory Democracy: Prospects for Democratizing Democracy*

"The heartbeat of the eros effect only grows stronger in this expansive work, as George Katsiaficas lovingly details the élan vital of do-it-ourselves rebellions, and in places too long ignored. His sweeping account not only helps us take better pulse of and better engage in today's directly democratic uprisings but also charts their direct lineage in revolts waged outside nationalist, hierarchical structures. In fully embracing the complexity, surprise, messiness, cross-pollination, and power of revolutions in which people experiment in forms of freedom together, *Asia's Unknown Uprisings* grasps the promise of a shared future in such egalitarian yearnings."
—Cindy Milstein, Occupy Philly and co-collaborator of *Paths toward Utopia: Explorations in Everyday Anarchism*

Asia's Unknown Uprisings

Volume 1: South Korean Social Movements in the 20th Century

George Katsiaficas

Asia's Unknown Uprisings Volume 1: South Korean Social Movements in the 20th Century
George Katsiaficas
© George Katsiaficas
This edition © 2012 PM Press
All rights reserved.

ISBN: 978-1-60486-457-1
Library of Congress Control Number: 2011906342

Cover: John Yates / www.stealworks.com
Cover Photo: May 18 Memorial Foundation
Interior design by briandesign

10 9 8 7 6 5 4 3 2 1

PM Press
PO Box 23912
Oakland, CA 94623
www.pmpress.org

Printed in the USA on recycled paper, by the Employee Owners of Thomson-Shore
in Dexter, Michigan.
www.thomsonshore.com

to Korea, with love

Contents

I am the People, the Mob

Carl Sandburg

I am the people—the mob—the crowd—the mass.
Do you know that all the great work of the world is done through
      me?
I am the workingman, the inventor, the maker of the world's
      food and clothes.
I am the audience that witnesses history. The Napoleons come
      from me and the Lincolns. They die. And then I send
      forth more Napoleons and Lincolns.
I am the seed ground. I am a prairie that will stand for much
      plowing. Terrible storms pass over me. I forget. The best
      of me is sucked out and wasted. I forget. Everything
      but Death comes to me and makes me work and give up
      what I have. And I forget.
Sometimes I growl, shake myself and spatter a few red drops for
      history to remember. Then—I forget.
When I, the People, learn to remember, when I the People, use
      the lessons of yesterday and no longer forget who robbed
      me last year, who played me for a fool—then there
      will be no speaker in all the world say the name: "The
      People," with any fleck of a sneer in his voice or any
      far-off smile of derision.
The mob—the crowd—the mass—will arrive then.

LIST OF TABLES

LIST OF CHARTS, GRAPHS, AND MAPS

LIST OF ILLUSTRATIONS AND PHOTOGRAPHS

LIST OF ABBREVIATIONS

2MB	Lee Myung-bak, South Korean President, 2008–2013
4.19	April 19, 1960 Student Overthrow of Syngman Rhee
5.18	May 18, 1980 Gwangju People's Uprising
CA	Constitutional Assembly (tendency in social movements)
CCEJ	Citizens' Coalition for Economic Justice (경실련)
CCP	Chosun Communist Party (1945–1948)
CIA	U.S. Central Intelligence Agency
CNU	Chonnam National University (in Gwangju)
DIA	U.S. Defense Intelligence Agency
DJ	Kim Dae Jung, South Korean President, 1998–2003
DJP	Democratic Justice Party
DPRK	Democratic People's Republic of Korea (North Korea)
FKTU	Federation of Korean Trade Unions (한국노총)
FTA	U.S./South Korea Free Trade Agreement
HUSAFIK	History of U.S. Armed Forces in Korea
IMF	International Monetary Fund
IOC	International Olympic Committee
JCS	U.S. Joint Chiefs of Staff
JOC	Young Catholic Workers Organization (Jeunesse Ouvrière Chrétienne)
KBS	Korean Broadcasting System
KC	Korean Constabulary
KCIA	Korean Central Intelligence Agency
KCTU	Korean Confederation of Trade Unions (민주노총)
KMT	Kuomintang Party of Chiang Kai-shek
KPA	Korean People's Army (of North Korea)
KPR	Korean People's Republic
KWAU	Korean Women's Associations United
NCC	National Council of Churches
NCDC	National Coalition for a Democratic Constitution
NDP	New Democratic Party

NFDYS	National Federation of Democratic Youth and Students (민청학련)
NKPD	New Korea Democratic Party
NL	National Liberation (tendency in social movements)
NSL	National Security Law
NWYL	Northwest Youth League
OSS	U.S. Office of Strategic Services
PC	People's Committees
PD	People's Democracy (tendency in social movements)
PSPD	People's Solidarity for Participatory Democracy (참여연대)
ROK	Republic of Korea (South Korea)
SKLP	South Korean Labor Party
SNU	Seoul National University
SOFA	U.S.-ROK Status of Forces Agreement
UIM	Urban Industrial Mission
UMMDR	United Minjung Movement for Democracy and Reunification (민통련)
USAFIK	U.S. Armed Forces in Korea
USAMGIK	U.S. Army Military Government in Korea (1945–1948)
USIS	U.S. Information Service
WB	World Bank
WTO	World Trade Organization
YADM	Youth Alliance for the Democratization Movement (민청련)
YS	Kim Young-sam, South Korean President, 1993–1998

My First Encounter with Korea

IN NOVEMBER 1999, I had an unbelievable first trip to South Korea. Unbeknownst to me, my book on 1968 was in its third printing and had become something of a bestseller. About a week before I left Boston, Lee Jae-won, the book's translator, faxed me some tough questions about Korean interpretations of my concept of the eros effect.[1] Since the English version of the book had been published twelve years earlier, I went back to what I had written, talked with several trusted friends, and prepared as best I could in the limited available time.

From the very first day I was in Seoul, the reception afforded my work was stunning. The major media had already reviewed the book, and now they prepared detailed articles on my thoughts. With reporters and photographers showing up at the hotel, and my publisher arranging a bevy of interviews, I had an opportunity to speak up and make myself heard in a society where social movements continue to be important vehicles of social change. Some of the headlines were: "A Social Revolution Is a Gust of Eros"; "Eros and Imagination Are the Starting Points of Revolution"; "Revolution Is Global"; "Power to the People! Power to the Imagination!" "Eros Is the Instinct of an Anti-Structure Society"; "TV Instigates Indifference to Public Problems," and somewhat erroneously, "The 1968 Revolution in France Is the Origin of Reformism."

On one level, I was bewildered by the intense media blitz and confused by its sudden appearance. One afternoon, when I thought I was on my way to meet a student of Alain Touraine, we arrived, obviously very late by the rush we were in, and found TV cameras waiting. "You have twenty seconds to explain the movements of 1968 to Koreans," a reporter informed me. I composed myself and summarized my take on 1968 ("Internationalism and self-management are the twin aspirations of the global movement of 1968, whether in France or Czechoslovakia, Vietnam or the United States"). When I was finished, I was taken not to meet my acquaintance but to an audience of fifty people waiting patiently for me to discuss

European autonomous movements in the 1970s and 1980s (the subject of another of my books, *The Subversion of Politics*, a Korean translation of which was subsequently published). Although it was satisfying to be so honored and to have my ideas taken so seriously, I am not someone who believes in following leaders, and I hope that dimension of my thinking came through.

Of all the interviews, the newspaper that most interested me was *Hankyoreh*, a daily begun in 1988 (one year after the military dictatorship capitulated to the June Uprising). In order to raise the money to start the paper, sixty thousand people each gave at least 5,000 won (then about $5). The minimum donation was one share, while the most anyone could give was two thousand shares. Altogether, about $5 million was raised. Today the paper owns its own building and publishes six days a week with in-depth news, analysis of events, book and movie reviews, sports, and weather. Most of the writers are from the labor, student, and feminist movements and prominently include a number of journalists who were banned from reporting by previous military dictatorships. The irony of having past punishment turn into credentials for employment never fails to bring a smile to my lips. When juxtaposed to anything in the United States (where family trust funds are behind almost all national movement publications), *Hankyoreh* is light-years ahead. Even when compared to other daily newspapers like *Libération* (France) and *Die Tageszeitung* (Germany), it appears to me that its wider circulation gives it an unmatched popular base.

One of the high points of my first few days was a presentation near Seoul National University at a movement bookstore. People stayed for four and a half hours passionately discussing the eros effect, revolutionary movements, and the future of Korea. At one point, when the slide projector jammed, people spontaneously began to sing movement songs until we had fixed the problem. After the meeting was over, about a dozen of us stayed to have dinner and continue the discussions. We laughed about some of our personal dilemmas and touched on topics like shamanism in Korea and which journals and organizations had been represented earlier. When it was almost time to leave, we sat in a circle. Each person took the time to reflect upon the evening, provide a sense of how they felt about it, and speculate about what they might have said or done differently. As I recall, I said I was honored to be somewhat a part of the movement in Korea, whose activists had long inspired me. As we bid adieu, someone explained to me that this after-party and wrap-up were old Korean customs. I noted how much traditional group life was embedded in everyday reality—an important resource in the construction of a new society, and as I would subsequently learn, one often overlooked in the eyes of foreigners.

After a week in Seoul, I traveled on a train to Gwangju. Originally, my publisher's itinerary had called for me to return to the United States without leaving Seoul, but I had changed the ticket to stay a few extra days. I wanted to visit Gwangju personally in order to get a sense of the meaning and legacy of the 1980 uprising. Although I had insisted that my host not go to any trouble in arranging my trip, they had notified people in Gwangju I was coming. When we arrived, a delegation was waiting at the train station. Before I could orient myself in the city, we met veterans of the uprising, visited a collectively run bookstore that functions as a movement center, went to a reception for Kim Jun-teh, poet of the Commune whose new book was released that day, and met the mayor who informed me that, "Gwangju's young people are all reading your book." "Where am I?" I wondered.

At a forum on the eros effect that evening, I discovered that many people spoke German, and much of the session transpired in that language. The questions here were more intellectual, having to do with rooting the eros effect in the works of Marx. The next day we visited the graveyards in Mangwoldong where martyrs of the uprising are buried. The new cemetery, lavishly funded by the democratic administrations after 1993, has state of the art video displays and a series of monumental sculptures commemorating the events of 1980 (as well as previous episodes in Korean revolutionary history). Most impressive of all was the original cemetery, where bodies of the dead had been unceremoniously dumped by the military in 1980. (Many other bodies were never found.) The next day, at Chonnam National University, once again the issue of activating the eros effect was prominent in the discussions after my talk. I had never previously experienced such a high level of discourse about my own work. The questions asked of me in Korea helped me better understand my own concepts, one of the first times I came to realize that my journeys there were as much about self-discovery as anything else.

The main question I was asked in a variety of forms was this: Is the eros effect simply an analytical construction useful for helping understand revolutionary movements or is it also a movement tactic useful in transforming society. If the latter, "How can the eros effect be activated?" Although I am responsible for uncovering the phenomenon of the eros effect, I could not adequately answer this question. The eros effect is not simply an act of mind, nor can it simply be willed by a "conscious element" (or revolutionary party). Rather it involves popular movements emerging as forces in their own right as hundreds of thousands of ordinary people take history into their own hands. When people identify with insurgent movements and massively rise up, the basic assumptions of a society—the authority of the government, the division of labor, and specialization—vanish overnight. During moments of the eros effect, popular movements not only imagine a new way of life and a different social reality, but hundreds of thousands of people—sometimes millions—live according to transformed norms, values, and beliefs. The conscious spontaneity of people who come together in beloved communities of struggle is a new tool in the struggle for freedom, a contemporary phenomenon often called "People Power."

I discovered the eros effect while pondering my research notes about the synchronicity of worldwide revolts in 1968, and I extended it in my book on subsequent European autonomous social movements. During my research in Korea, I was amazed to learn that the eros effect is similar to what has been called the "absolute community" of the Gwangju Uprising—as well as to the subsequent explosion of People Power in Asia and the Arab Spring of 2011. So smitten was I with the significance of these waves of insurgencies, my effort turned into this two-volume book, *Asia's Unknown Uprisings*. The focus of Volume 1 is twentieth-century Korean social movements, especially the Gwangju Uprising, often from the point of view of citizen participants. My empirical investigations of late twentieth-century uprisings in ten places in South and East Asia provide new historical data on the causes and consequences of contemporary urban insurgencies. On the basis of these Asian experiences, in Volume 2, I provide further insight into the eros effect and an analytical framework within which to comprehend more fully my empirical work.

Gwangju's Universal Meaning

As this book goes to print, more than a decade has passed since I first came to Gwangju and began to study its heroic uprising. In that time, I have become intimately connected to the city and its people. In my adopted Korean hometown, I awoke one afternoon in 2008 as if in a dream. I was in the middle of a public event, speaking about the 1980 uprising to an audience of Koreans. In my own mind, I asked myself between syllables how it is possible that I had anything to tell the people of this city, who themselves had sacrificed so much to accomplish the great event whose history I was discussing. Somehow, I managed to finish the talk without so much as blinking an eye to betray the privacy of my own inner conversation. After the long Q&A, many people approached me and went out of their way to thank me for informing them about their own history. I reflected upon the partiality of experience. Although they had lived through these events, they felt I helped them integrate their own experiences into a larger picture. If this current book can help readers feel a similar entry into a larger view of history than we normally are able to glimpse, I will deem it a success. Few people would choose to devote most of a decade of their life, as I have, to weaving a tapestry portraying at one glance so many individuals' experiences. In my view, the Gwangju uprising's significance is comparable to the Paris Commune of 1871 (a comparison I draw out in Volume 2).

For me, Gwangju has become much more than a locus of political activity or scholarly research. Early in my time there I had a dream that remains quite vivid to this day. I was looking at myself in a large mirror. My body was intact except for one small detail: my face appeared to be Korean. Murmuring a comment to the image, I noted this apparent change and asked: "Have I always been Korean?" "Yes," the image in the mirror replied, and I answered, "Good, now I am home."

Despite my feelings of intimate connection to Gwangju, my understanding of events there was only possible through the patience and wisdom of many people who took the time to explain their experiences and insights. On more than one occasion, people remarked that I was the first foreigner to whom they had ever spoken. What an honor for me! From the moment I arrived in Gwangju in 1999, I was a public figure whose views were well-known because my books had been translated, and I therefore had the privilege to be granted insider status in movement circles. To my delight, I discovered that many of my political insights match well with the experiences and ideas of Gwangju people. To gain an understanding of Korean politics, I am indebted to more than fifty former members of the Citizens' Army (or 시민군) that formed to protect people during the uprising.

Our conversations were recorded and published in two volumes in Korean by Chonnam National University.

The specific point at which I began to write this book was in 2000, when I was invited to return to Korea as the opening speaker at an international symposium on the twentieth anniversary of the Gwangju Uprising. During my second trip to Gwangju, I was once again feted and involved in animated discussions, giving four presentations in nine days. Of all the honors bestowed upon me, at that time none felt greater than being invited to meet President Kim Dae Jung (or DJ, as he is known). After the annual ceremony at Mangwoldong cemetery, I was also invited to a banquet where I was seated at the table next to President Kim and permitted to greet him briefly. (I wished him luck in his meeting the next month with North Korean leader Kim Jong-il.) My table companions included Catholic Bishop Carlos Belo, Nobel Prize cowinner from East Timor. The next evening, I again met Belo over dinner. As we relaxed together, he spoke eloquently about the dearth of scholarly research on democratization movements in Asia and suggested I consider writing about them. "Professor," he politely began, "you've written about European and American social movements. Why don't you write about Asia? We have many movements here as well." With Belo's suggestion, the point of origin of this book can be traced. At the symposium the next day, one of the speakers noted that many histories of Korean social movements are regional, and in private conversation, he reinforced his point by asking me to write a general history of Korean movements. Since I was not bound to any one region of the country, he felt I could tie them all together and discuss their relationship to each other and to the rest of the world.

When I first considered this project, I was unsure I could accomplish it, since I had little or no working knowledge of Korean and knew only a smattering of details about its people's rich history of uprisings. Upon reflection, I realized I was uniquely situated. As an outsider, I would have the freedom to ask questions that might not be asked by Koreans (what Germans call *Gnarrenfreiheit*) as well as to hear answers that might be less encumbered for someone in conversation with a foreigner. In few places other than Korea have social movements accomplished so much in the previous three decades. The Gwangju Uprising was viciously suppressed, but Koreans won the right to direct presidential elections in 1987 by defeating their U.S.-backed military dictatorship. As they continued the process of democratic consolidation, they won legalization of independent trade unions and expansion of civil liberties. They enacted an exemplary form of transitional justice by imprisoning former dictators Chun Doo-hwan and Roh Tae-woo. Cultural changes in everyday life have led to increased rights for youth and women. Although the current conservative administration of President Lee Myung-bak is ominously reversing many of the hard-won gains of previous struggles, South Korea retains a vitality and civility that stands in stark contrast to much the rest of the world.

In 2000, I couldn't imagine that I would devote much of the next decade of my life to this project. Once I had begun, my energies were naturally directed to similar uprisings in nearby countries. I was surprised to find a string of popular insurrections from 1980 to 1992 that transformed the region. Volume 2 of *Asia's Unknown Uprisings* is devoted to people's insurgencies in the Philippines, Burma, Tibet, China, Taiwan, Nepal, Bangladesh, Thailand, and Indonesia. Besides providing a rich indication of the region's popular aspirations, these events shed insight into its recent history. Like Western European autonomous movements after 1968, these uprisings—although centrally formative in terms of the region's subsequent culture and politics—remain largely invisible. Unlike Eastern European insurgencies that overthrew communism in 1989, events in Asia received relatively little attention. As I pondered Asian uprisings' lasting impact during years of research, I became aware not only that the Western mass media often ignored them, but also that the capitalist world system used the democratic wave to legitimize itself—to expand markets, to gain access to people's labor power, and to enrich the economic elite. Included in my expanded comprehension was DJ's own role in disciplining the Korean working class while implementing a neoliberal agenda. The dialectic of liberty and enslavement then became a major theme of my analysis.

Korea's Sea of Blood

My overwhelming sense is that Korea is simultaneously the most civil society I have ever experienced and the most Americanized Asian country I have ever visited. Layered over a traditional Buddhist/Confucian social structure is a highly developed political economy bearing the birthmarks and character of its American protector. While the U.S. military presence is not highly visible, more than a million soldiers wearing one uniform or another remain poised for battle along the Demilitarized Zone (or DMZ) between South and North Korea—a vestigial Cold War partition whose continuing existence scars the region and perpetuates wasteful military spending in the name of security. Historical divisions long since healed in South Africa and considerably thawed since the heady days of the Cold War in Ireland remain a real threat to life on the Korean peninsula. Do progressive Americans have a role to play in ending this ominous stalemate? Clearly we have not done our part in the past fifty years.

Korea was so ravaged that a literal sea of blood was spilled in the twentieth century at the hands of both Japan and the United States. Ruthlessly colonized by Japan, devastated in three years of total war against the United States, and divided for more than half a century, Korea exists in the twenty-first century on the basis of miraculous accomplishments. The North prides itself on being the first country to defeat the United States in a war—and thereby halting centuries of European westward expansion. Traditionally the rice bowl of the entire country, the South has transformed itself from one of the world's poorest nations in 1953 into one of the planet's wealthiest—a member of OECD whose economy surpassed the size of Russia's when the price of oil was low. Per capita income rose from $200 in the early 1950s to more than $20,000 by 2007. In decades, Koreans did what European countries took centuries to accomplish.

Modern Koreans have lived in a whirlwind of happiness and sorrow, of prosperity and poverty, of progressive political movements and reactionary dictatorships. A small country in comparison to its neighbors, Korea's internal communication networks and civil society are extraordinarily well developed, a significant resource in the country's long history of struggles for freedom. Social movements in the South overthrew some of the worst Cold War military dictators. In 1960, Syngman Rhee was compelled to leave the country after his police gunned down dozens of students who protested rigged elections and torture. Park Chung-hee seized power a year later, and ruled resolutely until his assassination in 1979, when his own chief of intelligence killed him for calling upon the military to violently suppress student-led protests in Busan and Masan. After Chun Doo-hwan seized power at the end of 1979, he brutally suppressed the citizens of Gwangju. Like his contemporaries, Chile's dictator Augusto Pinochet and Turkey's military rulers, Chun closely collaborated with U.S. banks and corporations to enhance foreign economic interests in exchange for their support. Overthrown by a popular uprising in 1987, Chun (along with his protégé Roh Tae-woo) was eventually sentenced to prison. With new progressive governments beginning in 1998, South Korea pursued a "sunshine policy" of dialogue and reconciliation with the North for a decade. Despite democratic reforms, South Korea's economy remains ruled by the dictatorship of the neoliberal market, and giant corporations have their way with the country's wealth. A tiny clique of imperial collaborators is firmly in control of the country's conservative mass media, poisoning the atmosphere with half-truths and intentionally distorting reports. Since 2008, New Right ideologue Lee Myung-bak has used the presidency to bulldoze people's hard-won reforms and to roll back democracy.

George Orwell was not entirely wrong when he predicted for 1984 a world of "doublespeak" where "freedom is slavery." What passes today for the "free market" and "neoliberalism" are actually forms of modern slavery. The profit imperative of big corporations compels them to seek new markets and to conquer ever-expanding arenas of investment. By bringing down regional barriers to their penetration, they are able to drive local businesses under and thereby take over profitable local economic activities. In recent decades, entire regions have been subjugated in a far more efficient and profitable manner than classical colonialism could ever have accomplished. Although uprisings in Korea won greater freedoms and voting rights, through the financial crises of 1997 and 2008, enormous profits were extracted from the region in the form of paper transactions, and millions of workers were disciplined by the market to submit to wage reductions, part-time status, and previously unacceptable levels of unemployment.

Acknowledgments

No project of this magnitude could have been completed without the help of numerous other people. Shin Eun-jung tirelessly guided me as no one else has been able to do. More than to anyone, I am indebted to her for astute insights, patient explanations, meticulous research, and loving insistence upon keeping my focus. Na Kahn-chae and Na Il-sung never failed to explain intimate details of Korean history. Won Young-su patiently read and criticized every page of an early draft, and Jordi Gomez offered me his careful eye for detail. Victor Wallis gave generously of his time and offered critical insights to help deepen the scope of my analysis. James Petras, Basil Fernando, Lee Jae-won, and Yoon Soo-jong provided political criticisms that substantially broadened my perspective. My first Korean friend, Paik Nak-chung, helped orient me in my initial steps into Korea. Oh Choong-il has been a great older brother. The women of the May Mothers' House in Gwangju have continuously lifted my spirits and inspired me. Ed Baker, David McCann, Loren Goldner, and Ko Changhoon patiently provided insight and encouragement. Ngo Vinh Long, Yoon Chang-hyun, Lee Jae-eui, and Park Hae-gwang have been gentle and steady companions. Years ago, I promised the late Yoon Young-gyu that I would complete this book. I am pleased to have kept my word. The staff of the 5.18 Institute and Department of Sociology at Chonnam National University, Seoul's Christian Institute, the 4.19 Institute, and Busan Memorial Park was all of great help. In 2001, I was a visiting professor at Chonnam National University, and I was able to return in 2007 courtesy of a Fulbright grant. Thanks to a sabbatical from Wentworth Institute of Technology, I remained in Gwangju until the end of 2009. Besides being based upon scholarly sources, my portrayal of these events is also based upon nearly a hundred interviews with individuals central to this history.

I trust that my insistence upon articulating my own views in the quest for a precise and critical history of Korea's long twentieth century will show how much I owe to scholars whose past endeavors helped make this book possible. Quoting Nietzsche, Bruce Cumings exhorts us to "be honest in intellectual matters to the point of harshness." I trust I do not exceed Nietzsche's limits.

Every scholar depends upon librarians, and I have relied upon the exceptional services of Dan O'Connell, Pia Romano, Amy Lewontin, and the staff at Wentworth Institute of Technology. My students there during eight semesters when I taught about East Asian social movements helped me anticipate significant questions I needed to address. I was also lucky to have younger scholars in my life to inspire and instruct me—especially Eddie Yuen, Markus Mohr, Billy Nessen, Jon Rogers, and Darcy Leach. Kim Dae-sung, Kim Goo Yong, Jin Ju, Lee Mihwa, Kim Su A, Soh Eugene, and Lee Jae-won all graciously helped translate interviews and source materials. I thank my daughters, Dalal and Cassandra, for their understanding and support.

For the most part, I have used common spellings of Korean names. At the end of the 1990s, when the Korean government adopted a new form of transliteration, Kwangju became Gwangju, and a host of other changes occurred that have confused many people. When appropriate, I have used Korean characters directly. Throughout this book, I have used modest estimates of numbers of people involved so as not to exaggerate the events in question. At several junctures, I provide a range of figures based upon previous accounts. My extensive footnotes are meant both as guides for future research as well as indications of my sources. For most readers, they are unnecessary.

My experiences in Asia date to my childhood. I spent much of my youth growing up in the U.S. Army and went to fifth and sixth grades in Taiwan. As an idealistic college student during the Vietnam War, I remember being shocked by the gap between reported facts and the situation I knew. Over the years, I have never seen such a wide variation between what I consider truth and propaganda as I have in relation to Korea—especially with regard to the North. In both the United States and South Korea, media reports are regularly exaggerated, or even downright untruthful. I hope this book contributes to breaking the chains of lies and omissions, which have shackled us for far too long.

August 13, 2011
Cambridge, Massachusetts

NOTES

1 I developed the concept of the eros effect to explain the rapid spread of revolutionary aspirations and actions during the strikes of May 1968 in France and May 1970 in the United States as well as the proliferation of the global movement in this same period of time. As I pulled together my empirical studies, I was stunned by the spontaneous spread of revolutionary aspirations in a chain reaction of uprisings and the massive occupation of public space—the sudden entry into history of millions of ordinary people who acted in a unified fashion, intuitively believing that they could change the direction of their society. From these case studies, I came to understand how in moments of the eros effect, universal interests become generalized at the same time as the dominant values of society are negated (such as national chauvinism, hierarchy, and individualism). See *The Imagination of the New Left: A Global Analysis of 1968* (Boston: South End Press, 1987).

CHAPTER 1

Uprisings and History

What all men speak well of, look critically into; what all men condemn, examine first before you decide.

—Confucius

Heaven rewards the virtuous and punishes the wicked, and does it through the people.

—Gao Yao, twenty-first century BCE

TO MANY OBSERVERS, insurgencies are evil and malignant, best mentioned only in passing or in utter condemnation. "Real" history consists of elite men in polished backrooms whose well-mannered behavior is an ideal to which we all should aspire. Deals made by the rich and powerful, their lines in the sand and signed pieces of paper, give security to the world, while movements against them breed violence and fear.

This book turns that understanding on its head. I see structural imperatives of the existing world system daily breeding war, ecological devastation, and poverty, while movements to qualitatively change those structures are the planet's greatest hope. A few hundred billionaires, giant corporations, and militarized nation-states today feel entitled to squander the vast wealth produced by generations of hard-working men and women. Uprisings are a significant vehicle for ordinary people to change all that.

In the 1890s, Gustave Le Bon compared revolutions to "microbes feeding on decaying flesh." In the early twentieth century, learned Harvard professors Lyman Edwards and Crane Brinton continued Le Bon's prejudiced understanding when they labeled George Washington and Thomas Jefferson "philosopher-killers." While many thinkers reject out of hand such overtly conservative frameworks, contemporary versions of them like Samuel Huntington's notion of the "democratic distemper" of social movements of the 1960s and his embracing the military in poor countries as the "motor of development" have been widely applied by policymakers.

Although long regarded as pathological behavior, uprisings can also been understood as healthy responses to conditions of severe oppression. People's actions are predicated upon the conditions under which they arise. In the case of Asian uprisings in the late twentieth century, economic expansion patterned rising expectations, and people's disappointment propelled insurgencies. Although many observers predict renewed protests with the economic crisis that began in 2008, our accumulated knowledge about social movements indicates that conditions of economic decline give rise to right-wing, even dictatorial, attempts to preserve elite privileges—not to movements that expand the rights of ordinary citizens.

No matter how much economic determinists seek to portray uprisings and social movements as moments in the movement of capital, they are more than Skinnerian responses to socio-economic stimuli. The preponderant power of contemporary governments and corporations tempts us to disregard people's capacity to act autonomously. If the reasons for insurgencies were found mainly in reactions to intolerable circumstances, then understanding upheavals would mean simply studying the social conditions that cause them. Such a reduction of human action to circumstance would thereby leave us in a circle of incomprehension, in which social conditions could be delineated, but not the emergence of social movements seeking to transform them.

In my view, uprisings and insurgencies are not simply reactions but indications of people's aspirations, dreams, and imaginings of better lives. What are those dreams? Why do uprisings occur one day and not years before? Why do they arise simultaneously in place after place with startling rapidity? What are their outcomes? I seek to answer these questions in this book.

Civil insurgencies are key to understanding ascendant dynamics within society—the flowering buds of social change whose blossoming becomes the future. Their long-term effects are often more lasting than decisions made by powerful individuals or elite groups. For far too long, brilliant movement theorists have written magnificent books that delineate their own autobiographical experiences, implying that if only they were in power, things would be different. Academic experts promulgate their unique insights, peddling them as truth when every generalization remains contingent and has less than universal value. Charles Tilly tells us, "Democracy is good for social movements." Yet in both democratic South Korea and Taiwan, social movements suffered great declines when many of their leading members were brought into new administrations after the inauguration of progressive presidents. As movement supporters were disillusioned by the incapacity of the new presidents to accomplish what they had promised, the impetus for change dissipated.

Many social scientists seek universal laws, acting as if history were a great puzzle, whose solution could lead to precise predictive power. One after another, writers repeat the same tired formula that history repeats itself. From Sorokin to James Davies and the J-curve, the quixotic quest for laws of history continues unabated. Looking to the past for guidance in the present, we borrow costumes, vocabulary, and tactics from distant times and places. While there may indeed be cycles in history—the dynastic collapse cycle in China comes to mind—iron laws of behavior are more suited to natural phenomena than to cultural ones. German philosopher G.W.F. Hegel was convinced that "Each period is involved in such peculiar circumstances, exhibits a condition of things so idiosyncratic, that its conduct must be regulated by considerations connected with itself, and itself alone. Amid the pressure of great events, a general principle gives no help. It is useless to revert to similar circumstances in the past. The pallid shades of memory struggle in vain with the life and freedom of the present. Looked at in this light, nothing can be shallower than the oft-repeated appeal to Greek and Roman examples during the French Revolution."[1]

There are no laws of history—and certainly no "iron" ones. Eternally valid generalizations about history may help calm fears and reduce the stress of uncertainty and indeterminacy, but they also hide new possibilities and stifle fresh dreams. They trample on the imaginative capacity of human beings to make something new of ourselves, to act freely, to try new relationships for the first time.

Cherishing the capacity of ordinary people to expand liberty embeds within my history a passionate engagement. Not only do I regard uprisings as healthy and more necessary than ever, I see them as containing a reasonability superior to that of the existing system, as constituting a form of ordinary people's wisdom that exceeds the shortsighted decision-making powers of world corporate and political elites. Turning again to Hegel: "Reason is the sovereign of the world; the history of the world, therefore, presents us with a rational process." In that spirit, I seek to uncover the structure of action and content of ideas contained in the sensuous morality of people's uprisings. Reasonability is uncovered within passionate action undertaken together by thousands of people; this rational process does not conform to Cartesian categories in which the mind and body, thought and emotion, are separated from each other. As Hegel advised, "We may affirm absolutely that nothing great in the world has been accomplished without passion."[2] By portraying the reasonability of popular insurgencies, I hope to assist Reason in becoming a material force in history.

European philosophers of the seventeenth and eighteenth centuries sought to understand the structure of individual thought and to classify it according to its various dimensions and historical unfolding. Using a similar analytical method, we can comprehend social movements as the logical process which unfolds within the praxis of thousands—and sometimes millions—of people as they rise up to change their lives. The inner logic in seemingly spontaneous actions during moments of crisis—particularly in events like general strikes, uprisings, insurrections, and revolutions—constitutes the concrete realization of liberty in history. People's collective actions are the specific character of freedom at any given moment. That is why I expend so much energy analyzing the precise details of uprisings and emergent aspirations, dreams, capacities, and limitations in concrete situations.

Most people would never risk life and limb for superficial reasons; uprisings are therefore indications of heartfelt grievances deeply embedded in human needs and desires, and their unfolding logic reveals the innermost desires of ordinary people. As German philosophers of the eighteenth century sought to uncover the structure and content of European ideas as they emerged in theory, I seek to portray the internal development and aspirations of popular movements as they are revealed in practice. In constructing my narrative of this concrete history, my central interest lies in contributing to a world where ordinary people's wisdom becomes more important than the money of the rich or power of politicians. The unfolding grammar of insurgencies in the late twentieth century is contained within the forms of eros effect, autonomy, and decommodification (establishing relationships based upon motives other than money or power). Taken together, these actions of millions of people embody a sensuous wisdom far superior to that of all existing economic and political elites—whether elected or self-selected.

All too often, historians pay attention to decisions of world leaders while ignoring actions of ordinary people. This book reverses that dynamic. Uprisings involving thousands of people during moments of crisis are my prism of understanding. In my view, uprisings are a great window through which to view essential qualities of society. Moreover, the praxis of insurgencies contains a neglected theoretical value that has yet to be accorded its rightful place alongside individual luminaries of philosophical thinking.

The velocity of social change today is faster than at any other time in history. In the twentieth century, human beings continually demonstrated a capacity to govern themselves without the "help" of political vanguards and almighty leaders. The breathtaking speed with which the Arab Spring unfolded is the latest example of this phenomenon. By portraying the synchronized aspirations-in-action of millions of Asians at the end of the twentieth century, I hope to help make apparent their exemplary role in global political change as a means of orienting all of us in constructing a better future. East Asia's spectacular economic rise (in my view, one of the outcomes of the uprisings) is well known; the accomplishments of civil society in expanding freedom there are similarly impressive. Uprisings of ordinary people are already understood as a significant means of limiting the domination of power-hungry politicians and greedy corporate executives—and they may one day be employed to destroy the system that creates and empowers such elites.

Contemporary technologies and resources give humanity the capacity to create heaven on earth—or its opposite, depending upon how we allocate the vast social wealth bequeathed to us by previous generations. Great wealth and prosperity exist alongside starvation and disease. While a third of humans live well, another one-third is at the edge of disaster. Daily, one hundred thousand people starve to death, and a billion more are on the verge of starvation. Despite decades of focused effort, every day some twenty-five thousand children under the age of five die of easily preventable causes. Wars continually plague humanity. Beginning at the end of World War II, during the "Cold" War, more than ten million people perished as a result of state violence. Should we permit militarized nation-states to unleash wars? Should a few hundred billionaires be allowed to control the majority of humanity's wealth? Should giant corporations be granted leave to destroy the planet?

Human beings have never democratically chosen to live under the yoke of existing world economic and political structures—under militarized nation-states promoting the interests of giant corporations and the superrich. Despite massive attempts to transform these structures, their resilient adaptation, their capacity to blunt and become stronger from every radical insurgency including the 1789 French and 1917 Russian revolutions, is remarkable testament to the need for a global solution to humanity's continuing problems.

Korea's Uprisings

In this book, I portray the unfolding aspirations of thousands of people as expressed through their actions. Even when great periods of discontinuity result from world leaders' decisions to unleash the most terrible weapons at their disposal—as with the Korean War—people's dreams and aspirations remain intact. Koreans' desire for unification and independence transcends the devastation of one of history's most destructive wars. Prior to 1950, tens of thousands of southerners sacrificed their lives in the struggle for those goals; when a new democratic movement emerged in the 1960s, the same aspirations remained squarely at the heart of people's dreams. As the twentieth century began, Japanese colonialism overwhelmed indigenous resistance and seized the peninsula. During the Korean War, as many as five million lives were extinguished from 1950 to 1953. U.S. bombs and artillery destroyed nearly every major city.

Modern Korea's tragic history has a silver lining, however, in an abundance of popular insurgencies. From the Farmers' War of 1894 to the 2008 candlelight protests, Korea's long twentieth century stretches through the March 1, 1919, uprising against Japanese colonial rule, the 1946 October Uprising against the U.S. military government, the 1948 Jeju and Yeosun Uprisings against the nation's division, the 1960 uprising against the Rhee dictatorship, the 1979 Puma Uprising against Park Chung-hee's *yushin* system, the 1980 Gwangju People's Uprising against the Chun Doo-hwan dictatorship, the 1987 June Uprising and Great Workers' Struggle, and the 1997 general strike against neoliberalism. The source of these earth-shaking events is a remarkable capacity for popular action—a gift of Korea's deeply rooted civil society.

Despite the nation's rich and painful history of uprisings, they are seldom adequately addressed in Korean studies. In one of the best English language histories, *Korea's Place in the Sun*, distinguished scholar Bruce Cumings devotes only a page to Gwangju and one paragraph to the June 1987 uprising—two key events that overwhelmed the military dictatorship and won democracy, perhaps for the first time in Korea's five thousand years of history. Moreover, Cumings relates only ten days of the 1987 uprising, from June 10 to 20,[3] when, in fact, people sustained it for nineteen days—from June 10 to 29—and would have continued longer if the dictatorship had not capitulated to their insistence upon direct presidential elections. Cumings also places the Puma Uprising in August and September 1979, when it occurred from October 16 to 18; he tells us that Chun was forced from office in June 1987 (when he finished serving the remainder of his term until January 1988).[4] Inattention to detail may be excused, but Cumings's work reflects a broader sense in which uprisings are not understood as a major variable in the constellation of forces that shaped modern Korea. Martin Hart-Landsberg's insightful book, *The Rush to Development*, offers only a few paragraphs on Gwangju and two sentences on the June Uprising.

This narrative history of twentieth-century Korea through the prism of uprisings is thus a necessary supplement to existing English-language studies. My emphasis on uprisings is part of the stream of *minjung* (or people's) history, one of many convergences of my own work with that of Korean scholars and activists who seek to build bridges from the insurrectionary past to freedom struggles in the future. Uprisings provide a means to understand the continuity in what is generally considered to be a discontinuous century. Every insurgency accelerated major tendencies in the movement's next phase. The 1960 student revolution was a "moment of repentance" for Christians in Korea; after it, they asked forgiveness of their compatriots for having supported the Rhee dictatorship. Thereafter Christians worked incessantly for liberty and social justice. The Gwangju Uprising produced the radical politics of the 1980s, gave us *minjung* art, and taught valuable lessons about the real character of the United States. The 1987 June Uprising and Great Workers' Struggle produced the NGOs and labor unions that carried reforms into the most densely constructed protective barriers of corporate boardrooms and secret backroom deals. Ironically, as NGOs rose in prominence, professionalization and specialization led to the movement's overall decline. One of people's great breakthroughs was to lay the groundwork for increasing women's liberties, which in turn led to middle-school girls' leadership of the 2008 candlelight protests.

Although widely understood as locomotives of history, popular revolutionary movements continue to be denied precise portrayal. In almost every case, histories of Korea center on the lives of "Great Men," framing world events around individuals like Kim Il-sung—or Dean Rusk, Douglas MacArthur, and Park Chung-hee. Even when the individualism of Western society is transcended, descriptive narratives limited to specific organizations and particular networks predominate, which once again understate the role of nameless ordinary people who spontaneously develop their own forms of organization during uprisings. By emphasizing professional organizations—whether communist parties or NGOs—the role of grassroots movements in creating and nourishing them is hidden. The 1894 Farmers' War in Korea is often called the *Tonghak* Rebellion after the organization of its most famous leaders, even though thousands of Korean farmers who fought and died were not adherents of *Tonghak* religion. To borrow an example from nearby Vietnam, histories written in both Hanoi and Washington buried the heroic sacrifice of the people of southern Vietnam and their central role in the defeat of the United States, while emphasizing the role of North Vietnam's communist organization and leadership. Elite theory is present even within insurgent movements' own self-understanding. Many progressive accounts of the civil rights movement are little more than biographies of Thurgood Marshall or narratives of the NAACP's unfolding, stories of Rosa Parks, Martin Luther King, Jr., Malcolm X, or the Southern Christian Leadership Conference—not the millions of ordinary people who struggled and sacrificed to liberate African Americans from Jim Crow racism.[5]

Organizations and Movements

In the twentieth century, during the epoch of corporate capitalism and state socialism, overemphasis of the "Organization Human" superseded the nineteenth century's "Great Man" orientation. Today, we observe the continuing extension of this same principle in both academic studies of social movements and activists' professionalization. When NGOs are understood as the alpha and omega of civil society, specialized organizations become ends in themselves, rather than one dimension of popular movements' self-organization, one aspect of "civil society"—and perhaps not even its most important one. In worst-case scenarios, fetishizing NGOs leads to underestimation of class divisions, co-optation of grassroots aspirations, and emergence of collaborationist strata that blunt the radical impetus of insurgencies.[6] For system change, uprisings are vital; for system maintenance, professional organizations serve well when they become established and gain legitimacy. More often than not, NGOs are vehicles to transform antisystemic insurgencies into engines of reform that strengthen the very structures against which movements arose.

To understand how societies can be transformed, Muthiah Alagappa maintains the need to focus on the totality of civil society, rather than its insurgent protests, since the latter may "obscure the more mundane and less visible functions of civil society in normal times, functions that may be just as crucial as its actions in moments of crisis."[7] By these crucial functions, he refers to a variety of roles professional organizations play, including creation of free public space in liberalization periods, supporting the development of political parties in the transition phase, and making the consolidated system more inclusive. Clearly these are important tasks, yet he does not seem concerned with how uprisings motivate ordinary people to step forward at great personal risk. Nor does he discuss how popular insurgencies inextricably change those involved in them. In the midst of uprisings, new lifelong friendships form, political consciousness is raised, and identities change—all in the time frame of a few days or weeks. In every case, previously subaltern people—minorities, women, and low-caste people—experience new possibilities in their lives and develop leadership skills and networks.

All-too-often, self-defined professional "revolutionary" groups (and individuals) remain loyal to the status quo and abandon—or work against—more radical formations in the streets. We can observe this dynamic in many places, from Korean progressive politicians and their parties, Bangladeshi and Czech democrats, French and Italian Communists, or Filipina and Thai people's organizations. On the other hand, spontaneous actions by tens of thousands of people often throw forth visions that go beyond those that established political parties deem "realistic"; they sow seeds from which new leaders emerge, who challenge the reticence of established figures to help implement people's aspirations. Uprisings are crucibles within which society's ascendant forces are galvanized, they continue to pressure politicians and parties to grant more liberties to ordinary citizens, and their actions generate new forms of organization that reshape existing organizations and institutions.

Capitalism's ability to morph into new forms and strengthen itself through major crises, as it has continually done in the last several centuries, presents a clear need for discovering ways to maintain popular mobilizations as a vehicle for impeding the reintroduction of elite privileges. Even when movement organizations come to power, as many have done, the system is able to withstand—and even benefit from—the new infusion of leaders. Take the case of Nelson Mandela and the African National Congress in bringing neoliberalism to South Africa, or the role of the American Revolution in eventually helping Great Britain to continue to be a hegemonic world power long after its military and economic prowess had declined.

Contemporary historians' inattention to the specific dynamics of uprisings has a variety of causes. Protests and demonstrations are often transitory and unable to preserve their momentum for long periods of time. Yet popular uprisings have grown increasingly able to regenerate themselves—as we can see in new iterations of the 1986 and 2001 People Power protests in Manila, in the importance of Gwangju to the June 1987 Uprising in Korea, and in the recurrence of massive protests in Thailand (1973, 1992, and 2010), Nepal (1990 and 2006), Burma (1988 and 2007), and Tibet (1959, 1989, and 2008). Hundreds of thousands of people internalize lessons learned from previous episodes of insurgencies as they continue to act without the "help" of leaders from above. While professional organizations claiming to "represent" the opposition often strengthen unjust systems through participation in them, insurgencies seldom fail to create new visions for freedom. Time after time, uprisings can be found to strengthen opposition movements; in their immediate aftermath, workers' strikes proliferate, independent media flourish, the number of voluntary associations mushrooms, feminists activate networks, and subaltern groups mobilize to win more rights.

Another ostensible reason behind failures to recognize uprisings' significance is the difficulties that may be imposed upon anyone seeming to challenge established powers by embracing insurgents' views. In societies where scholars and activists enjoy freedom of inquiry, a salient reason for their lack of interest in social upheavals can be traced to a presumption that popular insurgencies lead to totalitarian dictatorships when they succeed and increased repression when they fail—but not to more open societies. Whether the closing of social space is attributed to excessive regime reactions or to uprisings' successful overthrow of existing governments, analysts prefer soft challenges to hard ones. Yet in excluding uprisings from their purview of inquiry, investigators carry ideological assumptions and hold to "iron laws" that perpetuate blind spots rather than illuminating previously unexamined areas. Ideological distortions are especially problematic for Korea because of the vibrant string of uprisings that has animated its recent history.

Classical philosophers believed social conflict was natural and healthy. Immanuel Kant's *Idea for a Universal History* eloquently recognized that "the means employed by Nature to bring about the development of all the capacities of humans is their antagonism in society." More recently, Frances Fox Piven observed the profound impact of conflict and disorder: "The rare intervals of nonincremental democratic reforms are responses to the rise of disruptive protest movements, and the distinctive kind of power that these movements wield . . . Democratic successes flow not from the influence of voters and parties taken by themselves, but from the mobilization of a more fundamental kind of power that is rooted in the very nature of society."[8]

Modern sociologists and political scientists, whatever their different purviews, commonly subscribe to the notion of the "rational" individual actor lying at the core of society. In contrast, the crowd is commonly seen as embodying a form of "contagion," of authoritarian domination and unintelligent action. At worst, academics understand groups through the model of lynch mobs that lead individuals to suspend their individual rationality and act according to debased instinctual passions that only harm others. In contrast to this view, millions of ordinary people who arose in Korea in the string of twentieth-century uprisings are living proof of another dynamic: *ordinary people, acting together in the best interests of the group, embody a reasonability and intelligence far greater than any of today's corporate or political elites.* One does not need to be radical to comprehend the increasing intelligence of the world's peoples and elite corruption and inability to rule properly. Recent observers of technology have penned simple insights that speak volumes: the Internet and the World Wide Web have facilitated "the wisdom of crowds" and "smart mobs."[9] The role of collective intelligence facilitated by social media during the 2011 Arab Spring is too important to overlook.

The intelligence and reasonability of popular uprisings may surprise many people, while a better application of Le Bon's "contagion" theory can be found in the herd instinct of international financial investors, whose panic has resulted in massive sell-offs that overnight ruin economies—as during the Asian Financial Crisis of 1997 or again in the global economic meltdown that began in 2008. Unreasonable investment decisions of greedy "rational" actors who determine what to do with humanity's wealth based on individual self-interest trample on the lives of those without riches; but when the dispossessed rise up, then—and only then—do mainstream commentators speak of disease.

Despite the history of the reasonability of social movements and the rationality of peoples' grassroots decision-making, in the twelve decades since Le Bon formulated his ultraconservative notion of "contagion," mainstream wisdom maintains the parameters of his thinking. The capacity of ordinary people to make intelligent decisions in the interests of humanity is continually underestimated. Even in comparison to democratically elected political leadership (as in the United States) and self-perpetuating economic elites (at the center of corporate power), ordinary people are far wiser.[10] At gatherings like the World Social Forum, people assume the need to abolish nuclear bombs and all weapons of mass destruction, to end wars, and to cure poverty through redistribution of wealth. When was the last time we could hear such gems of common sense come from the mouth of a major political or corporate leader?

Korea's Invisibility

Dwarfed by China, Russia, and Japan—a shrimp among whales—Korea is barely able to compete with its neighboring powers. For much of their history, Koreans expended great resources to repel or accommodate outsiders, while preserving unique native traditions. As part of Asia, Korea is doubly marginalized, for not only is it a small part of a huge continent, but Asia is distant from the centers of Anglo-American world power. Asia's long historical continuity contrasts favorably with the West, where extirpation of ancient state and culture was so deep that Latin all but disappeared and ancient Greek barely survived. In Asia, dynasties came and went, but all conquerors, whether Jurchen, Mongolian, or Manchu, became Chinese, bequeathing Asian cultures a sense of the importance of civilization above state. By contrast, France, Hungary, and England took their names from invading tribes that conquered indigenous people.

For Hegel, history moved from East to West: "In Asia arose the light of spirit, and therefore the history of the world . . . The history of the world travels from East to West, for Europe is absolutely the end of history, Asia the beginning."[11] Hegel traced historical progress through the unfolding of the individual, a process he located in the lives of Socrates, Jesus, and Martin Luther—"Great Men" who sacrificed their own lives for the good of humanity. For Hegel as well as for Kant, history's internal progress led to perfection through the state. Yet today, nearly all states are equipped with technological weapons designed to kill and maim citizens. Liberty and self-government, the most significant political concepts developed from the American and French revolutions, demand the abolition of militarized nation-states armed with weapons of mass destruction—and their replacement with assemblies of activated citizenry (precisely the kind we encounter during uprisings). For us to become "citizens of paradise" living in perpetual peace, we must first comprehend ordinary people—not political parties, organizations, professional politicians, and "Great Men"—as history's most important force.

As a geopolitical construct, East Asia hardly existed before Western powers' domination of the region. Historians' fetishization of individual leaders has contributed further to Asia's marginalization. Although Asian popular movements have emerged in dialectical opposition to elite accommodation of foreign powers, Western versions of history emphasize the role of friendly regimes. By the middle of the twentieth century, U.S. power was so pervasive that it could easily import two residents of New Jersey (Ngo Dinh Diem and Syngman Rhee) to rule over two "new nations" created by American power: South Vietnam and South Korea. In the early 1980s, Kim Dae Jung and Benigno Aquino, popular leaders of vast democratic strata, befriended each other while in exile in Newton, Massachusetts, where each had escaped death sentences from their respective country's system of justice. On at least one occasion, they shared breakfast at Aquino's home.[12] Kim went on to become South Korea's president; Aquino was assassinated as soon as he dared return to Manila. No one could have guessed that their cook that morning—Aquino's soft-spoken wife, Corazon—would herself be pressed into service as head of the Philippine state within a few short years.

Asia's role in European history remains profoundly important. Tracing the empirical history of European insurgencies as recent as 1989, it is apparent that Asian ones predated and inspired them. Asian uprisings were understood by participants in Eastern Europe's 1989 revolutions as vital, even "central to the global movement."[13] Television news reports from China played an especially significant role when Gorbachev visited Beijing in mid-May: "Everywhere in East Europe people were talking about it. Everybody told me: 'without the Chinese, we could not have done anything.'"[14] The horror aroused by Chinese repression of protesters in Tiananmen Square apparently helped to persuade Europe's Soviet leaders (with the notable exception of Ceausescu in Romania) to relinquish power peacefully. The Chinese movement followed forerunners in the Philippines and Korea—both of which (as insurgencies within the U.S. sphere of power) were well covered in China. When Czech president Havel visited Manila in 1995, he paid homage to 1986 People Power: "Your peaceful People Power Revolution was an inspiration to us for our own revolution."[15] (Like many others, Havel was unaware that the Philippine rising of 1986 was led by country's rebellious armed forces who used their firepower on more than one occasion to seize television stations, attack loyalist helicopters, and even the presidential palace itself.)

Contemporary East Asia's migration from the periphery to the center of the world system is commonly understood in economic terms, all the more so since Asia is in the forefront of world economic growth. In a few short decades, economic expansion in Northeast Asia has created a combined behemoth equivalent to those in Europe or the United States. With enormous foreign currency reserves, the region is poised to take the lead in world politics. Decades of Anglo-American attacks on Soviet powers in China and Russia brought violent deaths upon more than ten million people in the Cold War (five million on the Korean peninsula, three million in Indochina, and uncounted more in southern Africa, Central America, Chile, Argentina, and the Middle East).[16] As has been urged by Howard Zinn and others, the casualties at Hiroshima and Nagasaki should also be included in the tally of Cold War deaths. Since Japan offered twice to surrender to the United States before the use of atomic bombs, U.S. nuclear devastation constituted the opening battle of the Cold War, rather than the closing engagement of the Second World War. The huge expenditure of East Asian lives at the hands of U.S. wars in Korea and Indochina served as crucibles of fire, precipitated refugees by the tens of millions, and so thoroughly changed social conditions that unprecedented mobilizations of millions of people erupted to change the direction of their society's trajectory.

For partisans of the U.S. war on communism, people's movements in Eastern Europe stand out as the high point of the Third Wave of democratic revolutions.[17] In the United States, the Tiananmen Square events in 1989 China may be well known, but hardly anyone has heard of the 1980 Gwangju Uprising. Part of the reason is undoubtedly that Western media afforded wide coverage to Chinese communism's internal problems while scarcely covering events within the U.S. sphere of influence. Korea has long been relegated to the margins of American consciousness. *Los Angeles Times* reporter, Frank Gibney, entitled his book on

Korea's giant steps toward democracy in the 1980s a "Quiet Revolution" because he felt it is "something relatively undetected and unnoticed . . . People's images of Korea are still formed by quick television sound-bites of riots in Seoul and flash-backs to the Korean War."[18] But there is even more to Korea's peripheral status, indicated by the Korean War's nickname, "The Forgotten War." The 1950 massacre of hundreds of Korean civilians by U.S. troops at No Gun Ri is known as a "Korean My Lai" (after the 1968 massacre of Vietnamese villagers), even though the My Lai massacre occurred nearly two decades *after* the massacres in Korea. Thus, when the 1980 massacre in Gwangju is called "Korea's Tiananmen," does the nine-year time difference signify an attenuation of U.S. media's Attention Deficit Disorder?

Eurocentrism's Blind Eye

European and American bias against Asia has a long and tragic history. Dehumanization of Asians played major roles in wars that took millions of lives. Without first turning Asians into evil demons of Americans' paranoid fantasies, how else could they be obliterated by the millions? "Gook" was the most common epithet hurled by hundreds of thousands of Americans in Vietnam—but it is actu-ally Korean in origin. I have heard far too many stories from Vietnam veterans about how the first thing they would do on patrol was to "snuff the friendly gook," the South Vietnamese liaison who was suspected of being an enemy agent. In the admixture of racism and militaristic barbarism inflicted upon East Asia by the West, everyone may become dehumanized, but Asians were devastated. Sadly, in the eyes of U.S. policymakers and many others, an Asian life is simply not worth as much as that of an American or a European.

In the Academy Award–winning documentary film *Hearts and Minds*, U.S. General William Westmoreland unashamedly claimed that Asians do not place the same value on human life as Americans. The former commanding general of U.S. forces in Vietnam in 1968, Westmoreland's racism may be easily understood, because bias against Asians was so pervasive among U.S. troops. It is more dif-ficult to rationalize Hanson Baldwin, military editor for the *New York Times*, who called Koreans "the most primitive of peoples," who live where "life is cheap," or Telford Taylor, chief U.S. prosecutor in Nuremberg, who wrote that, "indi-vidual lives are not valued so highly in Eastern mores."[19] When he was Harvard University president, Lawrence Summers (subsequently director of U.S. President Barack Obama's National Economics Council) told an incoming contingent of students that there were close to one million child prostitutes in Seoul in 1970, when in fact, there were scarcely that many children there at that time. Although Summers apologized later for having "misremembered" a statistic, he made no concession about his image of Koreans.[20]

Like Western political leaders, scholars like Max Weber and Karl Marx chas-tised Far Eastern cultures for being despotic and feudal, lacking the ingredients for organizational success, and outside the grand narrative of Western civilization. Max Weber believed the West exclusively knew rational law and rational per-sonal ethics. Most famously, Hegel developed the operative category of Oriental despotism: "The Orientals have not attained the knowledge that Spirit—man as such—is free; and because they do not know this, they are not free. They only know that one is free . . . that One is therefore a despot, not a free man."[21] Over the years, Hegel's formulation has continued to be repeated. In 1956, Zbigniew Brzezinski wrote that in the Orient, "despotic forms of government have been the rule for thousands of years." Nor are anarchists immune from racism against Asians. Gentle and poetic anarchist prince Peter Kropotkin had many virtues, yet one encounters passages in *Mutual Aid* with consternation. His use of "savages" and "barbarians" is curiously antiquated. Moreover in his *Memoirs*, we find oblique, racist references to "Asiatic schemes" as well as mentions of "an Oriental fashion, in an abominable way" and "oriental amusements were looked upon with disgust."[22] I assume that Kropotkin would have outgrown these prejudices, although in his own day, they were seldom questioned. Sadly, they are still alive in Russia as proven by the many public attacks on Asian people.

Communist policymakers in the Soviet Union similarly distrusted Asians. In 1937, under Stalin's orders, some two hundred thousand Koreans living in eastern Siberia near Korea and Japan were deported to Central Asia (Kazakhstan and Uzbekistan) for fear they would support Japan. In the same period of time, many Korean Communists were summarily executed for fear they might be Japanese spies.[23] Even "progressives" like former Czech president Vaclav Havel made racist remarks: Havel off-handedly equated Asia with despotism and Europe with democracy. Jürgen Habermas has also associated Asia with evil during the German "historians' debate."[24] Ernst Nolte's 1986 article had challenged the unique character of Nazi crimes and labeled the Holocaust an "Asiatic" deed perpetrated by Hitler and the Nazis. Nolte attributed their motives to fear of becoming potential victims of Stalin's gulags and class murders—which he also considered "Asiatic." In response, Habermas challenged Nolte's conclusion denying the uniqueness of Nazism's crimes, but he never challenged the "Asiatic" label of these crimes against humanity. Habermas's acceptance of Nolte's term is part of a substantial bias against Asians.[25]

Even among those who celebrate the reasonability of uprisings, does Eurocentrism account for many people's study and adulation of the Paris Commune more than 130 years ago while simultaneously being ignorant of Gwangju's uprising? Lack of interest among many Westerners for Asian history, while rapidly coming to an end, has left a gap between Koreans and Americans. Korean activism may be legendary among U.S. activists (and in Latin America as well after the 2003 Cancun protests against the WTO), but few people could say even one basic thing about it. Images of Molotov cocktails being thrown, of well-organized street protests, or of activists' suicides may appear in the media, but substantial analysis of the movement is seldom available.

Less overt Western claims to superiority are also at work today. Many analysts judge civil society as having originated in Europe and only arriving in Asia in the last few decades. By somehow limiting the definition of civil society to its European form, they exclude Asia's rich history of nonstate social organization, values, and norms. Following Hegel and Kant's understanding of social development in Europe passing through stages from barbarism to feudalism and capitalism, civil society is comprehended as the flowering of the bourgeois individual amid a postfeudal public sphere. When only that model is considered to have produced a "true" civil society, analysts fetishize European individuals and salon culture at the same moment as they deny the existence of Asia's autonomous forms of civil society. (This is not the place to engage in a prolonged discussion of Asian values, but it is worth noting that U.S. cities remain unsafe and dirt-strewn while families disintegrate, at the same time as East Asians far more often enjoy safe and civil public spaces and nurturing family structures.)

Rather than come to terms with some of the advantages of Asian civilization, Westerners all too often impose Eurocentric categories. In so doing, they make the presupposition that Europe's trajectory—especially the phenomenon of individualism—is both universally desirable and applicable. By civil society, Habermas understands solely its appearance in the West (as a "bourgeois public sphere").[26] He creates an eternally valid category from a historically specific phenomenon— precisely what György Lukács considered the chief characteristic of all forms of "bourgeois" thinking.[27]

By idealizing civil society as it developed in the West, contemporary theorists ignore the destructive power of the individual that is institutionalized in corporate capitalism. Rational choice theory preserves this Western model of behavior on the false premise that if everyone aggrandizes his or her own personal interests, the entire society benefits. As an economic principle, the notion of the "invisible hand" powered the creation of postfeudal forms and helped win expanded individual political rights, but today it has turned into its opposite, freeing billionaires to amass even more wealth while billions of people live on the margins. Even those with substantial benefits are impoverished spiritually by corporate "me-first" culture that pervades everyday life. The extension of the idea of the "invisible hand" of the market led to the financial crisis of 2008 and was quickly rejected by those most in favor of it. Massive government intervention across the world was required to avert complete meltdown—practical proof of the futility of this invisible hand in the contemporary world. In the "free market" neoliberal equation, where does the common good exist? In a phrase: it doesn't.

True to Western bias, Habermas also privileges individualistic discourse and elevates certain forms of discourse (those in university lecture halls) over others (such as public assemblies in the streets and demonstrations). From Koreans' point of view, Western "rationalism" is often unreasonable. "In Western philosophy, reason is derived from solitary individuals." However, during the Gwangju uprising, "reason was achieved by human beings who were conscious of being members of the community, not that of individuals."[28]

The Reasonability of Uprisings

Building upon the notion that collective grassroots insurgencies are key factors in social development, the logic of history can be traced within the unfolding reasonability of self-directed actions of thousands of people in revolutionary situations. In broad outline we can observe transitions from protracted wars of the American and French revolutions in the eighteenth century to armed working-class urban

insurrections in 1848; from centralized party-led seizures of power at the beginning of the twentieth century to the diffuse global revolt in 1968. Comparing the
development of movements from 1789 to 1848, and from 1917 to 1968, the multitude's ever-expanding contestation of power in everyday life becomes apparent.
From national independence to freedom from toil and poverty, people's visions
of freedom continually moved forward. Popular struggles became increasingly
self-organized and autonomously intelligent.

"The people make history," little more than an empty rhetorical device in the
mouths of politicians and pundits, came alive in 1968. A wide variety of forms of
protest and political foci emanated from below. The inner tension among differences inside the insurgency, far from being reflective of the global movement's
weakness, showed its diversity, its vibrant inner dialectic of development, dif-
ferentiation, and progression. Free expression of dissonant viewpoints meant
for some observers that the 1968 movements were purely negative. Were there
universal dimensions to what appeared to be contradictory and sometimes even
conflicting issues and tactics? Was there a unifying grammar of liberation that
clustered many aspects of struggle into an overriding logic? Or did the "post-
modern turn" doom insurgency to fragmentation, isolation, and an inability to
challenge the system as a whole?

By carefully assembling fragments of national histories in my book on 1968,
I uncovered the movement's universal meaning and logical structure—previously conceptualized solely in national terms, or at best in the linear addition
of struggles in many countries—in the twin aspirations of self-management and
internationalism, qualities evident in the actions of millions of people during New
Left general strikes of May 1968 in France and May-September 1970 in the United
States. Both these upheavals occurred without the "leadership" of a central committee or the permission of elite groups. Social movements in the 1960s provide
astonishing evidence of the capacity of ordinary people to create participatory
forms of popular power that contest the established system. In May 1968 in France,
the entire country convulsed in near-revolution as organs of dual power sprang
up everywhere from the grassroots. Two years later in the United States, four
million students and half a million faculty declared a nationwide strike in May
1970 in response to the killings at Kent State and Jackson State Universities, the
invasion of Cambodia and repression of the Black Panther Party. Once again,
no central organization brought together this strike—the largest in U.S. history.
Despite the absence of centralized organization (or should I say because of it?),
people were able to formulate unified national demands around *political* issues
and to question the structure of the militaristic system that compelled universities
to be part of weapons research and development. In 1970, U.S. national chauvinism and racism were negated by international solidarity; in place of competition
and hierarchy, cooperation and egalitarianism became people's values; instead of
individual advancement and accumulation of wealth being individuals' primary
concerns, social justice and alleviation of inequality were at the center of people's actions. Although the movement fell short of its long-term goals, it provoked
numerous political reforms and thoroughly transformed civil society.

Since the global revolt of 1968, a string of uprisings swept away East Asian dictatorships and overthrew East European Soviet regimes. Immanuel Wallerstein, Terence Hopkins, and Giovanni Arrighi understood the movements of 1989 as "the continuation of 1968."[29] The wave of Asian uprisings predated events in Eastern Europe and did not flow from decisions made by world leaders to end the Cold War. A New Left impetus for universal liberation was especially evident in the Gwangju Uprising of 1980, which helped set off the chain reaction of revolts and uprisings throughout East Asia. Gwangju's "beautiful community" among the city's citizens is especially noteworthy. Their spontaneous ability to drive out the military; to defend, govern and manage their own affairs; to rapidly organize their Citizens' Army and Citizen-Student Struggle Committee; and to live without crime and competition are legendary. In the liberated city, daily rallies involving tens of thousands of people directly made the most important decisions. Gwangju's participatory democracy illustrates concretely how the New Left's vision of greater democracy, far from being peculiar to Europe and the United States in the 1960s, remains globally central to insurgencies.

In 1871, the Paris Commune arose as the existing National Guard mobilized with a long drum-roll and seized control. In Gwangju in 1980, people spontaneously *created* a Citizens' Army and drove thousands of the best troops of the South Korean military out of the city. Inside liberated Gwangju, as in the Paris Commune, liberty and democracy defined the essential character of people's lives. Crime rates plummeted and cooperation flourished within communities based on love. The erotic energies unleashed by these movements tie people together in intimate ways with more force than years of sharing jobs, taking the same classes, or living in the same apartment buildings are often able to do. Our primal impulses to live in communities based on love and respect for one another, to observe basic notions of peace and justice, create a cathexis that propels continuing insurgency.

In the years after Gwangju, a chain reaction of uprisings swept East Asia. In 1986, the Marcos dictatorship in the Philippines was overthrown in an uprising led by the Catholic hierarchy and key elements of the military. More popularly remembered are the million-plus people who stubbornly stayed in the streets despite being ordered by the army to disperse. Once the bulk of the military defected to the side of the opposition and Marcos left the country, the very words "People Power" were enough to frighten even the most entrenched dictators no matter where in the world they ruled. The Philippine Revolution helped animate the 1987 June Uprising in South Korea, a nineteen-day marathon endeavor in which Christian groups also played a leading role. In this same period, when leaders at the highest levels of government seeking to shift power blocs precipitated regime changes in East Europe, the eros effect in East Asia emanated from an accumulation of experience and street actions by millions of people. As I discuss in detail in Volume 2, other East Asian uprisings of the 1980s and 1990s involved global awareness amid manifestations of New Left attributes such as autonomy, direct democracy and solidarity: Burma (1988), Tibet and China (1989), Taiwan, Nepal, and Bangladesh (1990), Thailand (1992), and Indonesia (1998). In 2011, similar grassroots dynamics were the driving force of the Arab Spring.

The international character of these insurgencies reveals an action-alternative to both Soviet-style state "socialism" and Western capitalism. They prefigure a kind of revolution entirely different than those in the past, which sought to capture national power and centralize control. International solidarity expressed in today's alterglobalization movement has no central organizing point. From below, millions of people have autonomously chosen to make the planet's economic structures their strategic target. Recognizing the global economic system as the root cause of permanent war, systemic starvation and misery, and ecological catastrophe, millions of people around the world focused energies on transforming it. International proliferation of the tactic of confronting elite summits indicates a deepening of popular intuition and intelligence independent of any one group or individual's decisions. From below, millions of people enunciated and acted upon their own understandings.

Directly democratic forms of decision-making and militant popular resistance are intimately woven together in these liberatory movements. The conscious spontaneity and self-directed actions of hundreds of thousands—sometimes millions—of people, is nourished by beloved communities of struggle. People's self-organization is contained within a grammar of autonomy, solidarity, and decommodification. Histories of struggles on various continents and in different countries may seem juxtaposed across unbridgeable divides, but they nonetheless hang together in these qualities and in the connections forged by people as they struggle for peace and justice.

In moments of great love for fellow human beings and for freedom, a form of release occurs which is similar to a traditional Korean shamanistic ritual, or *shinmyong*—a collective feeling of ecstasy when *han* (sorrow, pent-up grief) is discharged. In contrast to Western individualism, Korean culture has bequeathed unique forms of collective emotional vitality in *shinmyong* and *han*, and they remain central to Koreans' self-understanding.[30] Korean social movements spontaneously reproduce moments of *shinmyong* in their eruptions, and people grasp the emotional and erotic core of activism. During my initial visit to Korea, I was struck by how popular my concept of the eros effect had become. On my second visit, as I walked to the inauguration of a new statue of poet-activist Kim Nam-ju in Gwangju Biennale Park, I was approached by a stranger about my age who recognized me with a smile. "Katsiaficas," he said, and before I could respond, he continued, "eros effect!" Those were his only English words.

In the twentieth century, people's capacity to create autonomous organizations dramatically altered the relationship of spontaneity and organization. An example of the intelligence of crowds can be found in people's adaptations of new technologies and tactics. From the grassroots, social movements' energies resonate across national boundaries stimulating "echo effects" with greater velocity and more force than goods and services can be traded. No centralized organization sent out its agents to spread People Power, yet it is a concept whose power resonates in every continent. Without highly paid trainers, insurgent activists adopt new technologies and bring them into the field faster than even the corporate elite can be trained to employ them. By connecting us to each other in new ways, people's adaptation of emergent technologies forms unsupervised collectivities, for which the established forces of law and order are unprepared. We witnessed this phenomenon from the fax machines of 1989 China to cell phones of 1992 Thailand. Even in impoverished and highly repressed Burma, with only a handful of Internet servers in 2007, people used text messaging, blogs, and video imagery to funnel reports out of the country. Despite enormous repression during the Arab Spring, people continued to connect with each other and coordinate actions via social media networks.

Insurgent groups may form and disband, crowds may gather and be scattered, but they leave behind a residue of collective capacity for thought and action that builds upon previous incarnations. Leaders may be killed or imprisoned and tremendous casualties inflicted, but the open expression of dreams and aspirations continues to undermine the system. In the back of their minds, people cherish what they hold dear.[31] This intelligence and intuition of popular movements, the basis of People Power and the eros effect, is one of humanity's greatest resources.

In contrast to insurrections at the beginning of the twentieth century, more recent uprisings have emanated from civil society, not political parties. While conventional wisdom tells us that uprisings belong to the nineteenth century, mainstream media bombard us with apocalyptic visions of the future. As Fredric Jameson quipped, as a result, most people find it easier to imagine the end of the world than the end of capitalism. In the final decades of the twentieth century, however, an enormous wave of change swept the world, overthrowing dozens of dictatorships in a matter of a few short years—and posing the possibility of a radically different social universe. Popular intuition seemed to anticipate forthcoming political upheavals with greater efficacy than many tomes churned out by the academic social movement industry or even by many "Left" presses. Despite common portrayals of quiescent accommodation, struggles of epic proportions today animate millions of people's lives. Latin America is embroiled in arguably the most significant transformation of its political and cultural landscape since Columbus. From the Zapatistas to the communards of Arequipa (Peru) and Venezuela, people's daily lives are being bettered through ballots, protests, and all manners of political activism—including popular insurrections. In addition to overthrowing dictatorships in Tunisia and Egypt, People Power's arrival in the Arab world has forever transformed the relationship between rulers and ruled in the area.

Produced from the accumulation of centuries of movements and experiences, the multitude's wisdom far surpasses that of elites. Would anyone argue that the peace movement is not far more intelligent than the "great" American presidents who make war after war against poor and defenseless countries? Would anyone propose that South Korean military dictators were wiser than the people of Gwangju—who risked life and limb to realize democracy? Who would defend the corporate elite's greed, rather than human need, as the method by which we should make use of the vast wealth our species has accumulated over generations of labor? We can find an alternative use of banks and insurance company assets, we can downsize corporate behemoths and dismantle military might—but only if we believe in the power and wisdom of ordinary people.

Elite Use of Uprisings

While emanating from popular aspirations for better lives, uprisings are also useful to elites. In the last centuries, every attempt to transform the world system has only strengthened it. Both the American and French Revolutions led to intensified imperial conquests. From the Russian Revolution to the Chinese, from May 1968 to Gwangju, insurgent energies have been redirected to revitalize unjust structures of hierarchy and populate them with new elites. The global anti-apartheid struggle brought Nelson Mandela out of decades of imprisonment on Robben Island and into the highest seat of power in the South Africa, but he was compelled to implement neoliberal economic policies that continue to plague the poor. Similarly, East Asian uprisings against dictatorships, even when they included significant forces against capitalism, enabled the IMF and World Bank to broaden their powers. In democratic South Korea, the Philippines, and elsewhere, new administrations implemented neoliberal programs that permitted foreign investors to penetrate previously closed markets and to discipline workforces of millions of people in order for giant corporations and banks to extract greater profits. Mubarak may have been deposed, but the military rulers who followed him in power stabilized the system of Mubarakism.

In *The Shock Doctrine*, Naomi Klein uncovered elite use of economic crises to assert more total systems of control. While economic crises are different than those produced by popular insurgencies, both types of crises have nonetheless been turned into vehicles for system domination and expansion. After the world-wide revolts of 1968 caught everyone by surprise, the CIA evaluated and found ways to use the People Power tactic—as in Ukraine's Orange Revolution. Between 1974 and the mid-1990s, more than sixty countries changed into some form of democracy.[32] Insurgent democratization movements transformed theorists like Samuel Huntington, compelling him to swallow his denunciation of the "democratic distemper" (his idea of the "problem" of too much democracy in the United States as a cause of antiwar protests) and to switch to singing the praises of democracy.[33]

Despite the system's capacity to absorb and even profit from the energies of insurgencies, it would be wrong to judge uprisings simply as failures. Compared to dictatorships, democratic governments, like countercultural spaces, contain new opportunities. Victories in achieving democracy in Korea, ending apartheid in South Africa, mitigating U.S. racism and sexism, and promoting expanded rights for all have created better lives for millions of people—as well as establishing the staging grounds for future struggles. The basic criterion must be whether or not uprisings help improve people's daily lives. To judge social movements by the specific administrations that they leave in their wakes or by their failure to change the entire system would be to condemn all past attempts as well as to disregard liberties and prosperity won. If we are to be realistic, we need to count ways movements have improved people's lives, opened doors for subaltern groups who had previously experienced only closed ones, and won greater freedoms in the everyday lives of ordinary people.

A more cynical reading of uprisings' impact has been inculcated by political scientists' production of a veritable library of books on democratization which emphasize elite-led transitions from authoritarianism, thereby posing the inevitability of elite rule as an iron law whose certainty is the same as that of winter's coming in Boston. Even in cases where the decisive factor in democratization was popular insurgency—as in South Korea in 1987—much of mainstream U.S. literature considers the transitions elite-led.[34]

The Coming Korean Wave

Given Korea's rich history, and more recently Korean activists' exemplary involvement in protests in Cancun and Hong Kong, what will be Korea's future role in the world movement? Although not well known, the series of East Asian uprisings in the last two decades of the twentieth century leaves a legacy that includes the possibility of a global movement against the inhumane system of neoliberalism and war-regimes that today rules over the bulk of humanity's accumulated wealth. Will the cacophony of revolts in East Asia after Gwangju, coupled with new insurgencies in Latin America and elsewhere, lead to a broad and sustained anticorporate and antiwar offensive? To a harmonized global uprising?

In the twenty-first century, as society's velocity of change accelerates, so too must our movement's capacity to adapt to changing circumstances. In the absence of the capability to innovate tactics and targets, revolutions atrophy, or even turn into their opposite (as happened in both the United States and the USSR). Alongside participatory currents, the history of social movements is also the history of popular insurgencies being placated, accommodated, and sold out. Ritualized protests organized by top-down groups with leaders whose faces do not change no longer suffice to bring the "masses" into the streets. Apparently, entrenched elites, like Leninist-style parties, are not needed to transcend the reformism of spontaneously formed movements since these movements are themselves capable of developing a universal critique and autonomous capacities for self-government. Indeed, recent history portrays again and again the conservatism of "Leninist" elites in moments of crisis.[35]

Insurgent European movements since 1968 would not have been possible without the safe haven offered by free spaces at the edges of the commodity system. While it may seem of marginal importance, Asian civil society is a similar resource. Korean civil society in particular sustained a protracted seventeen-year struggle to bring former dictators to justice and was an incredibly significant facilitator of movement mobilization. In these counterhegemonic spaces, people can experience, however temporarily, a break from the incessant imposition of cash connections and arbitrarily imposed forms of domination. With the construction of a transnational civil society unanchored in any state or political party, a new world becomes visible.

Far from being muffled, cries for global change are daily amplified. Largely invisible on CNN and in the mainstream media except for occasional sound bites, millions of activists around the world work incessantly for peace and justice. Even though the second U.S. war on Iraq had not yet started, as many as thirty million people around the world took to the streets on February 15, 2003, to protest its initiation. Called by the European Social Forum, these protests were organized without any central group. While seemingly marginalized, the global movement today involves more activists than at any other point in the historical evolution of our species. As we become increasingly aware of our own power and strategic capacities, our future impact is certain to become more synchronized. Today the multitude of humanity animates our own dynamic, and a tendency we can project into the future is for the activation of a global eros effect, in which synchronous actions erupt across borders of nationality, race, age, gender and language.

Korea's rich history of uprisings is a human resource that has much to offer the rest of the world. Despite their similarities, Korean uprisings have wide variations and comprise differing universes of discourse. While the 1948 Jeju Uprising was centrally organized down to some of its smallest details, the 1980 Gwangju Uprising broke out spontaneously and spread beyond the dreams (or nightmares) of anyone involved. To be sure, both the Gwangju and Jeju uprisings were against the penetration of the Korean life-world by the international megalith—the *Gesamtkapital* of corporate/government power preponderant everywhere today—but their differences reflect the divergence between the Old Left's centralization and the New Left's spontaneity. The 2008 candlelight protests led a new type of movement in which the whole society became a demilitarized space. If lessons from the past are any indication, then movements thrive precisely when they can create such centers of occupation for democratic discussions—as they did through bloody sacrifice in Gwangju's Democracy Plaza. The U.S. civil rights movement helped to eliminate certain forms of racism and brought greater dignity to all. The coming global struggles for economic justice and peace will shape human beings as equals no matter what their national identity.

At the beginning of the twenty-first century, the Korean wave, or *Hallyu*, is one indication of the magnetic attraction and universal appeal of Korean culture. While generally understood as the wild popularity enjoyed by polished productions of television dramas, movies, and music, *Hallyu's* origins lay in the *minjung* (people's) movements of the 1980s, in the sacrifice of thousands of people whose determined resistance lifted the stifling dictatorships imposed by Japan and the United States. Once censorship and fear had been defeated, the loosened creativity and expressive spirit of ordinary people produced great works of art and infused mass culture with a global dynamism crystallized from freedom struggles throughout Korea's long twentieth century.

NOTES

1   G.W.F. Hegel, *Philosophy of History* (New York: Dover, 1956), 6.

2   Ibid., 23.

3   Bruce Cumings, *Korea's Place in the Sun: A Modern History* (New York: Norton and Co., 1997), 387.

4   Bruce Cumings, "Civil Society in West and East," in *Korean Society: Civil Society, Democracy, and the State*, ed. Charles Armstrong (London: Routledge, 2007), 24.

5   A notable exception is Robin Kelley's book, *Race Rebels: Culture, Politics, and the Black Working Class* (New York: The Free Press, 1994).

6   See James Petras, "NGOs: In the Service of Imperialism," *Journal of Contemporary Asia* 29, no. 4 (1999): 429.

7   Muthiah Alagappa, ed., *Civil Society and Political Change in Asia: Expanding and Contracting Democratic Space* (Stanford: Stanford University Press, 2004), 5.

8   Frances Fox Piven, *Challenging Authority: How Ordinary People Change America* (Lanham: Rowman and Littlefield, 2006), 18.

9   See the recent books by nonacademic and nonmovement observers James Surowiecki, *The Wisdom of Crowds* (New York: Anchor Books, 2004) and Howard Rheingold, *Smart Mobs: The Next Social Revolution* (Basic Books: 2002).

10 See, for example, the film *The Battle of Chile*.

11 Hegel, *Philosophy of History*, 99, 103.

12 Interview with Ed Baker, Cambridge, MA, 2007.

13 Edward Friedman, ed., *The Politics of Democratization: Generalizing East Asian Experiences* (Boulder, CO: Westview Press, 1994), 24.

14 Christopher Neck, *Actual* (April 1990); *World Journal*, April 6, 1990, 33. Quoted in Edward Friedman, ed., *The Politics of Democratization: Generalizing East Asian Experiences*, (Boulder, CO: Westview Press, 1994), 54.

15 V.G. Kaulkarnia and R. Tasker, "Promises to Keep," *Far Eastern Economic Review*, February 29, 1996, 22.

16 For a summary of U.S. Cold War actions, see William Blum, *Rogue State* (Monroe, ME: Common Courage, 2000). Blum counted sixty-seven U.S. interventions since World War II.

17 Samuel Huntington, *The Third Wave: Democratization in the Late Twentieth Century* (Norman: University of Oklahoma Press, 1991).

18 Frank Gibney, *Korea's Quiet Revolution: From Garrison State to Democracy* (New York: Walker and Company, 1992), xi.

19 *New York Times*, July 14 and 19, 1950; Telford Taylor, letter to the *New York Times*, July 16, 1950.

20 Stephen M. Marks, "Summers Apologizes for Korea Remark," *Harvard Crimson*, July 16, 2004.

21 Hegel, *Philosophy of History*, 18.

22 Peter Kropotkin, *Memoirs of a Revolutionist* (New York: Dover Publications, 1971), 76, 82, 310.

23 Bruce Cumings, *North Korea: Another Country* (New York: New Press, 2004), 118.

24 Friedman, *Politics*, 14.

25 See the discussion in Jürgen Habermas, *The New Conservatism: Cultural Criticism and the Historians' Debate* (Cambridge, MA: MIT Press, 1990), xvii.

26 Jürgen Habermas, *The Structural Transformation of the Public Sphere: An Inquiry into a Category of Bourgeois Society* (Cambridge, MA: MIT Press, 1989). See also JaHyun Kim Haboush, "Academies and Civil Society in Chosun Korea," in *La société civile face à l'État: dans les traditions chinoise, japonaise, coréenne et vietnamienne* (Paris: École-française d'extrême-orient, 1994).

27 György Lukács, *History and Class Consciousness* (Cambridge, MA: MIT Press, 1972).

28 Choi Jungwoon, *The Gwangju Uprising: The Pivotal Democratic Movement that Changed the History of Modern Korea* (Paramus, NJ: Homa and Sekey, 2006), 134.

29 Giovanni Arrighi, Terence K. Hopkins, and Immanuel Wallerstein, "1989: The

Continuation of 1968," in *After the Fall: 1989 and the Future of Freedom*, ed. George Katsiaficas (New York: Routledge, 2001), 35.

30 For Hagen Koo's discussion of *shinmyong*, see *Korean Workers: The Culture and Politics of Class Formation* (Ithaca, NY: Cornell University Press, 2001), 145–46.

31 Conversations with Basil Fernando on this subject have been enormously helpful.

32 Alagappa, *Civil Society*, 3.

33 See *Asia's Unknown Uprisings Vol. 2*, chap. 1 for a critique of Huntington.

34 See *Democracy in Korea: The Roh Tae Woo Years* (New York: Carnegie Council on Ethics and International Affairs, 1992).

35 For the role of the French Communist Party in May 1968, see my *The Imagination of the New Left: A Global Analysis of 1968* (Boston: South End Press, 1987). For the Italian Communist Party in 1977, see my *The Subversion of Politics: European Autonomous Social Movements and the Decolonization of Everyday Life* (Oakland: AK Press, 2006). See also the discussion of Thailand in *Asia's Unknown Uprisings Vol. 2*.

CHAPTER 2

Korea Enters the Modern World System

The Korean mind-heart is attuned to the spirits that inhabit the nature of all things (bears, crickets, trees, flowers, homes, rivers, mountains), and the ghosts and goblins that walk the night, the shamans who cast spells, the heterodox women who unite mind and body in the writhing incantations of the *mudang* sorcerer. This is the human mind connected to the viscera and the body in touch with its natural environment, and out of it comes superstition, intuition, revelation, insight, madness, wisdom, and above all, freedom. It is the purest Korean tradition, infusing songs, poems, dances, dreams, and emotions; it resists all attempts to excise the senses and bank the fires of passion. It is the Korea that I, as a Western rationalist, know least about.

—Bruce Cumings

KEY DATES IN KOREAN HISTORY

1392–1910	Chosun dynasty
1592–1598	Lee Sun-shin builds turtle ships to defeat Japanese invasion
1866	U.S. ship *General Sherman* burned and sunk near Pyongyang
June 10, 1871	U.S. attacks Korea
1894	Farmers' War (*Tonghak*); indigenous movement defeated
September 15, 1894	Japan sacks Pyongyang
November 21, 1894	Japan massacre at Luushun (Port Arthur)
October 8, 1895	Japanese gang assassinates Korean Queen Min
May 29, 1905	Japan defeats Russia in Russo-Japanese War

July 29, 1905	Secret U.S./Japan Taft-Katsura Treaty recognizes Japanese control of Korea
October 26, 1909	Patriot Ahn Jung-kun assassinates Japanese Prince Ito Hirobumi
1910–1945	Japan officially annexes Korea
March 1, 1919	Nationwide nonviolent uprising against Japanese colonialism
April 10, 1919	Korean Provisional Government forms in Shanghai
May 4, 1919	Chinese movement for independence begins
1929	Wonsan general strike and Gwangju student movement
April 29, 1932	Korean patriot Yoon Bong-gil assassinates Japanese military commander of China
December 13, 1937	Rape of Nanjing begins; more than 200,000 Chinese slaughtered
December 7, 1941	Japan attacks Pearl Harbor
August 1945	United States uses atomic bombs on Hiroshima and Nagasaki
September 2, 1945	Japan surrenders, ending World War II
1945	Victorious Allies "temporarily" divide Korea and Vietnam
1945–1948	U.S. military government in southern Korea
1945–1950	100,000 southern Koreans killed resisting U.S. occupation and division of the nation

ANY HISTORY OF twentieth-century Korea must necessarily convey the proud and gentle spirit of its people, their inner spirituality and passion expressed in everything Korean from Christian rites to shamanistic rituals. For me, to know Korea is to fall in love with its culture and civilization, to experience the communal character of a society that recognizes with humility connections between people. Just ask any of the hundreds of American Peace Corps volunteers from the 1960s that embarked from their homeports to help a devastated land modernize. Their solitary sojourns turned into lifelong commitments. Like Bruce Cumings, nearly all contemporary figures in Korean studies first became acquainted with Korea through government or religious service and became so enamored of the country and culture, they chose to devote their lives to it.

To become intimate with Korea and come to love the land and its people is also to be repelled by some aspects of life there, such as the easy acceptance of hierarchy so central to Confucian ethics and the all-pervasive patriarchal power that subjects women to inferior status. Korea has been called more Confucian than China, a place where even Christians are "Confucians dressed in Christian robes."[1] It is no accident that the yin-yang symbol is an enduring emblem of Korean identity, since the simultaneous existence of contradictory elements is so common. Confucian patriarchy empowers elders and men, especially elevating scholars to high positions vis-à-vis the uneducated, the young and women. Yet within this framework, the very gentleness of Confucian politeness facilitates a ring of public safety that permits young women to walk the streets at all hours without the fear that urban Americans routinely accept as part of daily life.

Koreans have no difficulty recognizing the "white in the black," and they regularly weave sour tastes into sweet dishes. Reported to be among the most brutal soldiers who fought in Vietnam (on the side of the United States), Koreans nowadays go there by the hundreds to find brides.

More than an indication of how the universe appears to most Koreans, the yin-yang identity also refers to the contradictory ways in which Korea's image in the eyes of foreigners is structured. Where many Japanese and Americans referred to them as lazy louts with "no get-up-and-go," *Fortune* magazine had a different assessment in 1977: "Work, as Koreans see it, is not a hardship. It is a heaven-sent opportunity to help family and nation. The fact that filial piety extends to the boss-worker relationship comes as a further surprise to Americans."[2]

Korean young people have carefully delineated roles and spaces within which they can grow to maturity. Everyone is encouraged to do their utmost to develop themselves through education—and the drive to study is so strong that youth are compelled to spend long hours in classrooms, even to sacrifice their Saturdays and vacations. So intent are Korean families on advancing their status by investing in human capital that high school students regularly go home after 10 p.m. and must be back in school with homework ready to pass in before 8 a.m. Corporal punishment remains widely accepted as an appropriate means of discipline.

Despite great changes, Korea's future promise remains constrained within the apparently intractable division of the peninsula. While most South Koreans enjoy prosperity and hard-won democratic liberties, a new conservatism threatens to undermine the political and economic gains for which so many people sacrificed. For the first twenty-five years of its existence, North Korea was a model to which southerners enviously compared themselves. After nearly every building had been destroyed by the United States in the war of 1950–1953, the North's economic advancement was strident and benefited the vast majority, while in the South, former Japanese collaborators, abetted by U.S. authorities, monopolized wealth and power and imposed decades of hardship on ordinary citizens. Since the demise of the Soviet Union, North Korea's economy has stagnated; today, cut off from the traditional southern rice bowl, it can barely feed its own people. In the South, democracy brought with it prosperity for many, and the middle class has grown tremendously.

South Korea's advanced contemporary society contrasts sharply with its recent past. At the beginning of the nineteenth century, the country's decrepit Chosun dynasty could barely manage to feed its people. According to official census figures, the population fell from 7,561,403 in 1804 to 6,755,280 in 1837—more than a 10 percent decline.[3] So difficult was life for many of the poor that a half a million people died from starvation in 1784 alone.[4] In 1872, tens of thousands again died from hunger, but agricultural output grew, and by the end of the nineteenth century, Korea's population climbed to nearly thirteen million.[5]

Tradition and Modernity

In 1853, Japan was forced to permit Western penetration of its economy at the point of U.S. cannons under the command of U.S. Commodore William Perry. For a few decades thereafter, Korea remained proudly independent, until modern Japanese military might, assisted by indigenous collaborationist forces, accomplished what centuries of previous attempts by Japan had failed to do: to seize control of the entire peninsula and use it as a stepping-stone for conquest of the Asian mainland. Centuries of Korean history are full of legendary episodes of resistance to Japanese invasions. Almost every Korean knows the name of Non Gae, who sacrificed her own life to strike a blow against Japanese invaders in the sixteenth century. Blessed with considerable beauty and a talented dancer, she waited for her chance to strike back as Japanese forces entered Jinju in Gyeongsangnamdo. Slyly seducing a leading Japanese general, she wrapped her arms around him—and plunged them both into the river from high up on rocky cliffs. From the army of Buddhist monks who helped repulse the same invasion to Admiral Lee Sun-shin and his turtle ships, which decisively routed the Japanese in every battle they fought from 1592 to 1597, any Korean child can recite accounts of resistance to Japan.

Alongside proud Korean traditions of independence runs a parallel history of servitude and betrayal, of courtly domination by the noble class and ruthless exploitation of the populace. The long history of inequities and deprivation gives Koreans their heartfelt memory of centuries-old wounds. Koreans' soulful presence has no better point of reference than in the concept of *han*, explained by poet Kim Ji-ha as "the *minjung's* angry and sad sentiment turned inward, hardened and stuck to their hearts. *Han* is caused as one's outgoingness is blocked and pressed for an extended period of time by external oppression and exploitation."[6]A theologian expressed it as: "*Han* is the suppressed, amassed and condensed experience of oppression caused by mischief or misfortune so that it forms a kind of 'lump' in one's spirit."[7] Given the terrible conditions most commoners suffered, popular uprisings against the *yangban* (the aristocratic elite) sapped the nobility's strength to resist Japan's continual invasions.

Particularly in the Jeolla region, the southwestern corner of the peninsula long distant from elite centers of power and wealth, marginalization from courtly privileges helped to spawn native cultural forms for free expression of dissidence— and of *han*. Pansori music and masked dance became vehicles permitting performers to release *han*—and to criticize the powers-that-be. In the Wando region of South Jeolla, commoner Jang Bo-go was able to establish a parallel power in the ninth century. The free people of Wando based their lives on egalitarian principles, and they established far-reaching trade links with distant lands, including Japan, China, and the Arab world. Around that same time, Zen Buddhism took hold in Jeolla and took a more radical twist than in its Chinese place of origin.[8] Some grassroots resistance remains the stuff of legends, like Hong Gil-dong, a Robin Hood figure during the Koryo dynasty (around the same time as Robin of Loxley roamed Sherwood Forest).

In 1866, three great world powers sought entry into Korea—all were denied. Neither the Prussian merchant Ernest Oppert, nor the French commander of an Indochina fleet with a squadron of vessels, nor the U.S. warship *General Sherman* were able to break down the doors of the Hermit Kingdom. When they landed,

French troops were defeated; the Prussians exited in haste; and the American ship was burned and destroyed when it ran aground on the Daedong River near Pyongyang. The United States sent a special envoy to protest, but no one would meet him. Washington ordered its Asian warships to invade, and in 1871—the same year as the Paris Commune—twenty-six boats, led by warships *Palos* and *Monocracy*, landed over six hundred troops on Kanghwa Island. Korean forces, although slaughtered to the last man, fought valiantly. After this "Little War with the Heathen," as the *New York Herald* dubbed it, the American expedition commander characterized the courage of the Koreans as "rarely equaled and never excelled by any people."[9] Still, no one would talk with the Americans, and they were compelled to withdraw.

Korean Civil Society's Resilience

For well over a thousand years, only three dynasties ruled the Korean peninsula. While neighboring China saw imperial families rise and fall, and Japan was wracked by warring clans, Korea was relatively stable—as long as foreigners were kept at bay. Many Western scholars insist that Korea has no history of democracy and that civil society there only began in the late twentieth century, assertions contradicted by longstanding autonomous forms of consensual decision-making—and by people's resistance to centralization. Alongside *yangban* tyranny and royal fiat, communal village government worked by consensus. Representatives were also selected to coordinate neighborhood needs, and daily forms of cooperation patterned the tapestry of people's lives. Villagers autonomously shared labor with each other through *dure* (두레), an important and continuing neighborly bond. Folk drama reinforced group ties at the same time as it gave occasion to ridicule the powers that be. Beyond the power of governing authorities to regulate, shamanistic rituals invoked higher powers to sustain and empower people. Villagers' longstanding forms of mutual aid for everything from home repairs and agricultural labor to music, dance, and theater survive to this day in urban Gwangju, where neighbors and friends gather to make *kimchi*, buy fresh oysters at the seashore as part of nonprofit cooperatives, or gather regularly in representative neighborhood councils to locate and solve pressing issues.

Many such traditions remained invisible to the first Americans who came to Korea after the Korean War, especially government functionaries who arrived under the auspices of the U.S. State Department and Peace Corps. One of their teachers was Gregory Henderson, who spent more than eighteen years in Korea or Washington as a chief architect of U.S. policy. Like many of his contemporaries, Henderson simply transposed categories developed to explain feudal Europe and the United States to Korea, where he found "a society lacking in strong institutions or voluntary associations between village and throne; a society that knows little of castle town, feudal lord and court, semi-independent merchant societies, city-states, guilds, or classes cohesive enough to be centers of independent stance and action in the polity . . . a society characterized by amorphousness or isolation in social relations."[10] Some social dimensions identified by Henderson as missing can be located in Korea's past, like Jang Bogo's semi-independent merchant society and the class politics of the farmers' movement (*Tonghak*) at the end of the nineteenth century. His assertion that social relations in Korea are characterized by isolation fails to recognize salient communal features of daily life.

Henderson famously identified the "persistence of the pattern" of the "vortex" of centripetal power sweeping everything toward the center. Although he regards this dynamic as uniquely Korean, similar centralization can be found in France, where power is vested almost exclusively in Paris. Henderson asserted that the pattern of the vortex "in overt form can be detected in the period from 1880 to 1910; its transformation and expansion" could be traced from the late Japanese period to the Americans' first two decades.[11] Thus his "cure" for "homogeneous, power-bent" Korea was U.S. modernization. Curiously he failed to note that this was precisely the period of increasing concentration of capital, and simultaneously when Koreans struggled mightily against Japanese and U.S. power, a true "vortex"—but one propelled by foreign imperial forces.

Henderson well understood that countervailing powers traditionally existed within the Korean state, specifically that a "top council, called *hwabaek*, determined the (nonhereditary) succession to the throne and sometimes exercised a veto over the king's decisions. Reflecting the importance of each element in the central council, discussion was supposed to produce unanimity, and 'it was the custom that any single disagreement brought the termination of the discussion on the specific issue.'"[12] Henderson's description of power would have made any European monarch blush with anger at the notion that any disagreement by a high councilor could end discussion! One can only wonder what Tudor monarch Henry VIII would have been compelled to do with his first five wives.

Henderson neglected to include Confucian means of dissidence like *bibangmok* (the tree where people could hang anonymous notes of protest), *kwondang* (when students of high Confucian academies went on strike to call attention to grievances), and *sinmungo* (the drum which could be beaten to request legal action).[13] For generations before the penetration of modernity, traditional networks wielded power as much through cooperative dissidence as through competitive violence. Precisely this difference with the West is an essential reason why Korean everyday life continues to be so attractive to foreigners and Koreans alike. Koreans know better than most how to thrive and prosper within groups, and excel at simultaneously offering praise and criticism. Even when they immigrate to the United States, Korean small businesses use a unique method of lending money to each other to expand operations. These civil resources are not simply financial. They derive from generations of living with trust for each other in a social system where honorable action and righteous deeds are arguably more important than profitable maximization of individual financial gain.

By 1700, private academies, or *seowon*, where *yangban* studied for civil service examinations to become high-ranking government officials, are thought to have been so widespread that there were more in Korea than in all of China—some six hundred in all. Focused around particular scholars with local followings, *seowon* constituted an important source of a "reasoning public." Autonomous of government control, they were part of a public sphere, or midlevel institution of civil society.[14] Rural scholars often functioned as intermediaries between state and people, and were a vital component of traditional society.[15]

Indigenous political formations were federations and confederations, not only centralized empires. The most significant recurrent problem faced by Korea has been invasions—which have accelerated and reinforced centralization of power. Although dolmen with astronomical inscriptions have been uncovered dating to 3000 BCE, it is widely believed that the first Korean kingdom (*Chosun* or "Land of the Morning Calm") was founded in 2333 BCE on the principle "to live and act for the benefit of all mankind." In the first millennium CE, after four hundred years of Chinese rule were overturned, Korea entered the Three Kingdom period, marked by variations in forms of power and wars between Silla, Baekje, and Goguryeo. The adoption of Buddhism in 384 by the king of Baekje in the eastern part of the peninsula reflected a cosmopolitan outlook. During these centuries, Korea was home to a variety of artistic forms and cultural expressions. When Silla finally succeeded in uniting the peninsula in 677, defeated Baekje nobles sailed south and east to the far coast of Japan, where they established a line of royalty leading to the current emperor of Japan.[16] In the ninth century, a painter whose origins lay in Baekje was lauded as "the first memorable painter in Japan, the first to bring landscape, for example, to the level of dignified art."[17] In subsequent periods, Koreans infused Japanese civilization with advanced knowledge of ceramics and helped propagate the teachings of Buddha.

In response to regional threats from Japan and China, Koreans turned inward, and native traditions flourished. In the early eighth century, woodblock printing was employed for Buddhist sutras, a form of printing continually developed until the monumental publication of the *Tripitaka Koreana* in 1251 using a total of 81,258 woodblocks. Cultural advancements help explain why only three dynasties ruled for nearly 1,500 years preceding Japanese conquest. The peninsula's isolation and shared values conditioned stability and homogeneity—as well as rivalries and revolts. Silla appears to have had a more equitable distribution of land than subsequent dynasties. Having developed out of a dozen walled city-states in the southeast, Silla's power was such that even Jang Bogo's enclave of commoners in the eighth century was ultimately overwhelmed. Silla's capital city, Kyongju, may have had as many as one million residents, and its cultivation of knowledge—including a magnificent observatory and claim to the world's first woodblock book printing—became legendary. In 947, Baghdad-born historian Abdul Hassan Ali bin Hussein al-Masoud wrote that few strangers from Iraq who came there, left. "So healthy is the air there, so pure the water, so fertile the soil, and so plentiful all good things."[18]

In the tenth century, fortified urban areas effectively established some autonomy from Silla, further examples of walled cities Henderson was unable to find. Rebellions weakened Silla internally, leading to the ascendancy of Koryo, whose capital at Kaesong held in its center Songgyungwan, a university with a history of over a thousand years. One of the great artistic achievements of Koryo was its ceramic art, especially its refined celadon; another was masterful Buddhist paintings, only a handful of which remain in Korea. Near the end of the Koryo dynasty, slave revolts became significant. In 1198, a slave leader named Manjok called on his fellows to burn the registers and thereby become the equals of ministers and generals.[19] In 1231, disaster struck Korea in the form of conquest by Mongols. The country was devastated. Thousands of women were abducted, all children older than ten massacred,[20] and starvation became widespread. During the half-century that Mongols dominated the peninsula, they used it as a staging ground for unsuccessful invasions of Japan. Altogether they kidnapped hundreds of thousands of people—one estimate counted as many as two million.[21] Only after the Ming overturned Mongol rule in China were Korea's fighters able to regain control of the peninsula. To preserve Koryo culture, a fifty-volume text was published using moveable metal type in 1234, more than two centuries prior to Gutenberg's printing press.[22]

In 1392, Goguryeo General Lee Song-gye established the Chosun, or Lee, dynasty, and his heirs would hold power until Japan's conquest in the twentieth century. Lee moved the capital to Hanyang (Seoul), propagated neo-Confucianism, and, to safeguard the country, became a vassal of the emperor of China, thereby turning Korea into a tributary state. At the top of the neo-Confucian social order were the *yangban*, nobles who jealously vied for power with each other while excluding commoners from climbing into their ranks. National examinations for rising into the ranks of government were rigorously maintained. A kind of caste system remained extant from Koryo. Nobles were at the top, followed by *jungin* or middle-class people, and commoners (merchants, soldiers, and farmers). At the bottom of the social ladder were *chonmin*—outcasts and slaves—among whose ranks were clowns, *kisaeng* (women entertainers), puppet masters, traveling actors, Buddhist monks and nuns, shamans, and criminals. Unlike American slaves, *chonmin* were generally not owned by one person nor were they bought and sold. Keeping their own communities, they exercised a considerable degree of autonomy in their affairs since they "were almost entirely self-governing, a function they pursued with considerable internal democracy."[23] Lands belonged to the king, who allocated plots to favored *yangban*. As in Koryo, ceramic arts were refined and remain known, even in China, for their superior artisanship. A strong merchant guild, which Henderson calls "the strongest non-governmental organization" during the Lee dynasty was characterized by strong bonds, and members called each other "brother," "uncle," and "nephew."[24]

To be sure, the central power of the Korean state was considerable. Yet countervailing powers of court-based officials who needed increased taxes and rurally based aristocrats who sought to enhance their wealth led to conflicts that limited the expansion of central power.[25] Although the Lee dynasty officially repressed Buddhism, many people remained attached to it, as well as to shamanism and other beliefs frowned upon by Confucian court officials. These subaltern discourses were further strengthened through plays like Chunhyang, the story of Hong Gil-dong, and composition of *sijo* verse.[26] Among the elite, factional fights that lasted more than a century in the fifteenth and sixteenth centuries (the "literati purges") weakened central power.[27] As the dynasty's gentry grew more corrupt and numerous, people's dissatisfaction grew, as did the frequency of revolts.[28]

In 1446 King Sejong, perhaps the greatest monarch in the country's long history, invented and introduced an alphabet that empowered ordinary people both to express themselves in writing and to comprehend texts. While Sejong did not overturn neo-Confucianism, he was not unfriendly to Buddhists—an attitude for which he drew protests from *yangban* students. Sejong's reign was marked by great progress in science and the arts. At the same time China named its emperor "Son of the Heavens" and Japan bestowed the title of "Ruler of the Heavens" on its emperor, Sejong built the concept of "people of the heavens."[29] Under King Sejong the Great, the Korean alphabet was introduced in 1446, the only alphabet native to East Asia. During his reign, he reformed prisons and tax codes, instituted generous maternity leaves for mothers and fathers, built a Jade Hall on palace grounds in which more than thirty scholars were granted permanent privileges to undertake intensive studies, and encouraged scientific breakthroughs. A 1983 Japanese *Dictionary of Science and Technology* counted sixty major world scientific achievements from 1400 to 1450—twenty-nine in Korea, five in China, and twenty-six in the rest of the world.

Five hundred years later, at the end of the Chosun dynasty, many Koreans were little better off than slaves. Rebellions were endemic, as the *yangban* class had grown to number some four million—nearly a third of society—who ruthlessly exploited those remaining below.[30] Taxes were sometimes so intolerable that revolts were predictable. Using Japanese data, Henderson calculated the number of *yangban* in one region as increasing from 7.4 percent in 1690 to 48.6 percent in 1858.[31] So comfortably ingrown was the Lee Dynasty that one eighteenth-century scholar could write: "However, for nearly 400 years since the founding of the present dynasty, our country hasn't had a single ship that traded with foreign countries."[32] China also closed down maritime ventures—despite the promising voyages of Zheng Ho (who Gavin Menzies recently asserted had circumnavigated the globe centuries before Magellan).[33] So great was the threat of land-based invaders in this period that both Korea and China allocated great resources to defense of their cultures from northern horsemen who sought to plunder their riches.

Lee Dynasty records indicate the existence of 360,000 slaves in the late fifteenth century and 370,000 in the late sixteenth. As a result of Hideyoshi's Japanese invasions of 1592–1598, population declined so drastically that male slavery was outlawed in many places. The whole country rose against the invaders, whose troops numbered over 150,000. With an incompetent and corrupt royal court, Koreans organized themselves into "Just Militia," often composed of Buddhist monks, while *chonmin* spearheaded secret societies with names like "Sword Society" and "Kill the Lord." Thanks to Admiral Lee Sun-shin's turtle ships, Koreans emerged victorious, but vast swaths of land were devastated wherever Japanese had been able to land. It took more than a century for farming output to reach pre-1592 levels.[34] In the seventeenth century, Dutch sailors shipwrecked off the coast of Jeju Island were rescued but kept as slaves. When they finally escaped to Japan, they wrote a tale of a country whose customs were harsh and where people's lives were full of drudgery. Their anecdotal account is verified by official records that indicate many people lacked sufficient food during the same time. As the country recovered from the ravages of Hideyoshi incursions, Lee dynasty census data from 1693, 1789, and 1807 put total population at over 7,000,000. (In 1910, the Japanese counted nearly twice as many: 13,300,000).

Many people were compelled to do labor at the bidding of landowners, and their lives were subject to *yangban* whim. In the seventeenth century, scholar Yu Hyong-won wrote that more than 80 percent of Koreans were slaves,[35] a widely questioned assertion on a controversial topic. Widely varying estimates of the number of slaves abound. In one region, Henderson found that slaves decreased from 43.1 percent of population in 1783 to 31.3 percent in 1858.[36] American scholar James B. Palais reinterpreted the same Japanese data used by Henderson and concluded that slaves were about 30 percent of the population. Shikata Hiroshi, the Japanese researcher whose data both Americans reinterpreted, had maintained that only 5 percent were slaves in 1789. Subsequent data analysis is therefore questionable, since the data themselves spoke so differently to the researcher from whom they originated. Another Harvard researcher found a register from a Seoul suburb in which 75 percent of the residents were considered slaves.[37] Palais, nonetheless, was content with the 30 percent figure since that is the same proportion he attributed to the ancient Greece, Rome, and the American South.[38] Palais's analogy to American society and possible inflation of Korean slavery helped to legitimize the "progressive" character of U.S. intervention in Korea. Once again, analogy to the West substituted for rigorous empirical data. Besides being numerically dubious, the status of slaves is also unclear. Henderson maintains that private slaves became "members of the family" and were treated with an attitude "significantly different than that of Americans or Europeans toward slaves."[39]

By the nineteenth century, a series of uprisings shook the society. In 1812, much of northern Korea was seized by armed insurgents around Gasan and held for months before the nobility and king used a scorched-earth campaign to defeat the peasant army.[40] In 1862, destitute farmers in southern Korea around Jinju rose against particularly harsh treatment. Much as during the French revolution of 1789, they burned records of debt, destroyed government buildings, and assassinated particularly corrupt and cruel officials. Although the central government sought immediately to reform the most severe of the *yangban* excesses, the revolt spread throughout the country. The Seoul-based king massacred his subjects to restore order. He especially blamed *Tonghak* founder Choe Che-u, whom he ordered to be publicly beheaded on March 10, 1864. Revolts remained a common occurrence until the end of the Chosun dynasty.[41] Statistics indicate fifty thousand predominantly female slaves at the end of the nineteenth century, despite the abolition of slavery in 1886 and again in 1894.[42]

Internal disorders facilitated the outside world's penetration of Korea. Beginning in 1868, backed by its newfound U.S. godfather, Japan pressured Korea to admit its merchants. Refusing to take no for an answer, Japan succeeded eight years later in getting its currency accepted in some Korean ports along with duty-free trading rights. While these inroads may seem minor, they indicated a loosening of China's centuries-old grip on the Korean peninsula. To protect its merchants, Japan also dispatched a few hundred troops—an ominous portent of things to come. As Japan built its military into a modern fighting force, Korea and China's attempts to preserve their traditional cultures only widened the technological gap. Having already lost two Opium Wars to Britain, China was in no position to check Japan's encroachment, neither on its historic hegemony in Korea or even on its own soil.

Twenty years after the uprisings of 1862, food shortages and excess government expenditures on the military led to a mutiny by soldiers who had received no pay. On July 23, 1882, hungry citizens and soldiers seized Seoul's rice reserves. After a night of deliberations, they attacked the royal palace and Japanese legation. In response, Queen Min asked the Japanese to increase their troop strength in Korea, an act for which she would later pay dearly. The indigenous power structure was so weak that little resistance to increased Japanese presence could be mounted. For their parts, the United States and European powers were quite satisfied to have Japan dominate Korea in order to check Russian interests. Germany welcomed the Japanese presence in Korea, and the United States instructed its officials to refrain from publicly criticizing Japan.

It was said that in 1883, when the first U.S. envoy arrived in Korea, the king, hoping that the United States would come to Korea's aid, "danced with joy" and asked for military advisors. The U.S. government did nothing—although an American company helped electrify Kyongbok Palace.[43] Fully two years before electrification of Tokyo's Mikado Place and Beijing's Forbidden City, Seoul's Kyongbok Palace had one of the most advanced lighting systems already working. Businessman Henry Collbran and Horace Newton Allen created the company known today as Korea Electric Power (formerly Han-Seoung—as Seoul was then called—Electronic Company). Together with businessman Harry Bostwick, they set up streetcars and a commercial electric lighting system. Privatizing HSEC, they raised fares and kept wages minimal. When strikes and boycotts resulted, they requested U.S. troops, before suddenly selling the venture to Japanese interests and profiting handsomely in what became known as the Collbran-Allen Affair.

In 1884, Japan attempted a *coup d'état*, but angry crowds surrounded the palace where they had installed a "progressive" government. "Righteous armies" spontaneously sprang up everywhere to answer Japan's assault on the Korean state. As Japanese businesses and homes were attacked, only with the help of Chinese troops could order be restored. Resistance to domestic despotism and Japanese conquest was widespread. Between 1876 and 1894, at least fifty-two significant large-scale farmers' uprisings occurred; in 1893 alone, more than sixty-five were counted.[44] The first major outbreak culminated in the 1894 Farmers' War, more commonly known as the *Tonghak* Uprising. Despite wide popular support, the ragtag *Tonghak* army was eventually defeated by Japanese troops armed with modern weapons.

Farmers' War of 1894
Through centuries of deprivation and hardship, Koreans learned to create inner worlds to transcend oppression and imagine themselves living freely. Oppressive

laws, such as one forbidding women to remarry if their husbands died, were part of a system that condemned hundreds of thousands of women to poverty and marginalization. While the *yangban* benefited from the resultant pool of surplus labor, ordinary Koreans suffered. By the end of the nineteenth century, as their rulers' powerlessness in the face of Japanese aggression became blatant, Korea underwent a profound social breakdown. The old order disintegrated, and a new one arose in the form of an entirely new religion, an indigenous synthesis of beliefs unique to Korea: *Tonghak*, or "Eastern learning."

Tonghak's cardinal teaching was that human life is the kingdom of God. Regardless of gender, age, and class, all people were considered equally holy. So much did this message resonate with common people that even after founder Choe Che-u had been executed in 1864, farmers continued their revolts using his name and that of his religion. With the Japanese invasion and corrupt local officials vying for power, a great insurrectionary army of farmers emerged. Similar to the Taiping rebellion in China, which established a "Heavenly Kingdom of Great Peace," *Tonghak* sought to create a "Millennium of Peace and Equality." Like Cao Dai in Vietnam, *Tonghak* was a synthetic religion that advocated earthly justice while drawing inspiration from a variety of sources, both secular and heavenly: Buddha, Confucius, concepts of class struggle, humanism, and nationalism.

A humble man, Choe spent his early life as a teacher in a rural area. At the age of thirty-one, he left his home region to live among ordinary people, to observe their misery, and to listen to their life stories. Returning home in 1860, a high fever overtook him, during which a divine voice spoke, telling him heaven resides in every human being. Rising from his sick bed, he began to preach the virtues of an egalitarian society based upon human rights and the divine character of human beings. Choe is said to have jumped and danced after he heard his divine voice, leading some to regard *Tonghak* as an evolved form of *mudang* or shamanism. His primary concern, like all healers, was to deliver people from evil.[45] The idea that God resides in each of us ennobled ordinary people; so centrally important was his egalitarianism that, unlike Taiping leader Hong Xiuquan, Choe Che-u never proclaimed himself a king.

Like many other uprisings, the specific precipitating incidence that set off the Farmers' War appeared to be relatively minor. A local administrator in Jeolla asked farmers to bring wasteland into productive use and offered them tax breaks for their work. After they completed their toil, he taxed them anyway. Hungry and powerless, they neither could nor would comply. Loyal and patriotic subjects, the aggrieved farmers sent four delegates to reach out to the king—whom they were sure would correct the problem. For three days, the four men knelt in front of the palace gates without being granted an audience. Finally King Kojong offered them these words: "Your building of walls, your flying flags, your scattering of leaflets merely stir up the people. Such practices will bring a sea of troubles on Korea and end in war."[46] For the impoverished farmers, long accustomed to degradation from court officials and arrogant exploitation by landowners, the king's insensitive response was the last straw. After all, they believed that "The whole nation is as one, its multitudes united in their determination to raise the righteous

Tonghak forces preparing for battle in 1894. Artist unknown

standard of revolt . . . when all the people can enjoy the blessings of benevolent kingly rule, how immeasurably joyful will we be!"[47]

Facing starvation and shorn of their trust in the royal family, farmers thronged to the leadership of Jeon Bong-jun, rising up by the thousands on January 10, 1894. They captured arms from the government arsenal and reclaimed from royal granaries the food they themselves had grown. Alarmed by news of the insurrection, the king dispatched a Royal Commissioner at the head of an armed column to put it down. Routinely killing farmers they happened upon, the king's men burnt houses of anyone suspected of sympathy for the rebels and raped women unfortunate enough to fall into their hands. In March, however, when *Tonghak* forces advanced, the Royal Commissioner vanished.

Another garrison was sent from Seoul, but on April 23, in a pitched battle in Jangseong, the *Tonghak* forces prevailed. One of their slogans, shouted as they marched behind multicolored banners, was "Repel the West, Repel Japan!" On the twenty-seventh, they occupied the important city of Jeonju, where they established a headquarters in the fortress. Soon all Honam (the entire Jeolla region) was liberated, and the number of *Tonghak* members was estimated at four hundred thousand.[48] Joined by nationalists, scholars, and dissident monks, the movement prepared to march on Seoul.

On June 1, the frightened king secretly asked the Ching emperor for help, but both China and Japan sent in troops. Despite having suffered bloody losses to the king's troops, the farmers remained abundantly patriotic. Not wanting to give foreign powers a reason to remain in Korea, *Tonghak* leaders suspended their plans to march north, relinquished control of Jeonju, and entered into negotiations with the king's representatives. As they negotiated, the insurgents established official Overseer Offices (*Jipgang-sos*) in fifty-three Honam districts, autonomous regional administrative systems symbiotically related to militant struggles.[49] The insurgents' offices functioned to prevent extortion, to protect poor farmers, to abolish class discrimination through equitable land distribution, and to organize armed resistance—grassroots forms of dual power indicative of a robust civil society.

Feigning interest in a peaceful settlement, the government talked of accommodating farmers' demands and fired the governor of Jeolla and a few other officials. In this interim period, the movement found space to articulate its program: burning of slave registers, equitable division of land, ending discrimination against the underclass, appointment of government officials on the basis of merit rather than family, permission for widows to remarry, and punishment of corrupt officials, tyrannical rich, and Japanese collaborators.[50] They also called for an end to the requirement for low-class people to wear the demeaning Pyongyang hat. Most significantly, insurgents demanded prohibition of rice exports to Japan at a time when many Koreans were starving.

While the royal courts hesitated in implementing *Tonghak* demands, Japan made King Kojong virtually their prisoner and engaged Chinese forces in the Sino-Japanese War. As would tragically repeat itself in 1950, regional powers fought each other on Korean soil. Within a matter of a few short weeks, Japan defeated China. On September 16, 1894, Japanese forces sacked Pyongyang. Learning of Japan's victories, *Tonghak* leaders reassembled their forces in Jeongsan on September 18, mobilizing more than 339 regional units with one hundred thousand fighters. They embattled the combined forces of Japan and those of the king in Ugeumchi on October 22, winning the first two engagements. Initiative shifted dozens of times in bloody confrontations over more than two weeks, but ultimately the king's troops—reinforced with Japanese artillery and other modern weapons—routed the poorly armed farmers, whose main weapons were sharpened bamboo spears.

After gaining the upper hand, the Japanese were ruthless in hunting down insurgents. Recent scholarship estimated the number of farmers killed at over fifty thousand—the first in a long line of atrocities carried out by Japan in the twentieth century. Other estimates counted as many as three to four hundred thousand casualties.[51] Movement leaders' heads were put on display in Seoul, their bodies given to the city's dogs.[52] After Jeon Bong-jun was captured, he was brought before a court for judgment. Humbly accepting his fate, he stated that his "sole objective was to remove corrupt officials from office and to expel the Japanese occupation forces."[53] Sentenced to death, he retorted: "Whoever buys and sells people in order to fill their own bellies leads the nation into darkness. Isn't it right to kill such people? You are traitors, whose collaboration with foreign enemies is the ruin of your own country."

Despite their courageous battles, *Tonghak* leaders never sought to overthrow the king—although more radical farmer-warriors in their ranks certainly wanted to. The uprising of farmers was neither controlled by nor called into being by religious leaders alone. Long before the nineteenth century, egalitarian values and class resentment were widely held among farmers, especially in the Jeollas. Leading the country in its quest for progress and independence, the 1894 rising would not be the last time that the Honam poor would bloodily suffer at the hands of the propertied class of Seoul who did not hesitate to use foreign powers to maintain control. The *Tonghak* movement was decimated, but it refused to die, transforming itself into *Chondogyo*, a new name for their religion that made it possible to survive under Japan's rule.

Japan's Conquests

Whether in Asia or Europe, the fate of small, cultured nations like Czechs and Koreans is to be ruled by their less gentle neighbors. Weakened internally by oppressive *yangban* rule and grassroots resistance to it, Korea's civilization was ravaged by foreign conquest in the twentieth century. Once the West had opened Japan and armed its military, the Japanese went from backwater recipient of Korean and Chinese cultural graces to their ruthless conqueror. Equipped with modern weapons and military training, the long inferior Japanese maneuvered themselves in 1910 to capture the Korean prize they had long coveted. In short order, Japan quickly defeated China—by then considerably weakened by foreign penetrations since the Opium Wars beginning in 1839.

In late October 1894, Japan launched a blitzkrieg across the Yalu River into Manchuria. Within a month, they advanced to Port Arthur (known in China as Luushun), gaining firm control of the Yellow Sea. Although reports vary, eyewitnesses claim Japanese troops under General Yamaji Motoharu massacred the entire Chinese population—as many as sixty thousand people on November 21. As regional powers collaborated in China's suffering, Russia, Germany, and Japan divided Chinese territories and patched together a temporary truce. Japan took Taiwan and declared null all previous treaties with China.

Using his new powers as an opportunity to annex Korea, the emperor sent in special teams of ninja. At dawn on October 8, 1895, dozens of well-armed Japanese men—including Harvard-educated Shiba Sirou, Meiji Oligarch Kaoru Inoue, Prime Minister Hirobumi Ito, and Ambassador Goro Miura—planned and carried out the brutal execution of Korean Queen Min.[54] After overrunning Seoul's Kyongbok Palace and gang-raping the queen, the men burned her alive.[55] Tried later for the crime, they were found not guilty due to insufficient evidence—a verdict that would have made any 1950s southern jury in the United States blush with joy. When the murderers returned to Japan, throngs applauded them and the emperor congratulated them. To this day, the government of Japan has yet to apologize.

Amassing capital from its primitive accumulation in East Asia, Japanese domination remains a formidable regional power—one whose economic strength shields its public failure even to acknowledge, let alone apologize for, its twentieth-century barbarity. Massacres that make U.S. bloodletting at Wounded Knee and My Lai pale by comparison have never been properly addressed, not by Japan nor by the international community—but then, neither has the United States been compelled to make amends for African slavery, Native American genocide, nor its savagery in Korea, Vietnam, Iraq, and dozens of other places. Once Native Americans had succumbed to the European onslaught, East Asia became the next American frontier. Although most Americans remain oblivious to it, at the end of the nineteenth century, the United States massacred more than two hunded thousand Filipinos (some estimates say as many as 1.4 million people were killed), another forgotten page in a sad and tragic underside of American democracy, when "Manifest Destiny" and the "white man's burden" continued to animate erstwhile patriots and entrepreneurs in their quest to profit from "progress" and "enlightenment."

Horrible as the slaughter in Korea has been during its twentieth-century "sea of blood," it should be understood as one episode in the ongoing incorporation of noncapitalist lands into the world capitalist system. In East Asia, comparable examples include the carnage carried out in the Philippines at the end of the nineteenth century when the United States seized the country from Spain, in Taiwan in 1947 when Chiang Kai-shek's forces prepared the ground for the Generalissimo's flight from his defeat on the mainland, and on Jeju island in 1948, when the U.S. military government needed a refuge for anti-Communists from northern Korea. Japan's intrusion into Korea bore great resemblance to Europe's "civilizing mission" and American "Manifest Destiny." Racially charged fantasies justified atrocities against Koreans just as they did in Europeans' actions toward Native Americans and Africans.

As Korea entered the twentieth century, Japan replaced China as the region's primary power. Like Koreans who collaborated, Japan saw itself as bringing reform to antiquated structures. Of course, the Japanese emperor exploited Korea's production of rice and its coal and mineral deposits. With no countervailing powers to challenge its military, Japan quickly moved to dominate all of Korea. One of its first measures was to compel Korean authorities to ban men's traditional hairstyle—the topknot. Any male found with long hair tied up on the top of his head was publicly humiliated, arrested, assaulted, taken from his home, and given a proper Western style haircut. Rather than submit, many men took their own lives. Though it may seem trivial, the Japanese offensive against Korean traditions grew in an ever-widening vortex.

For some observers, these events marked "the birth of modern Korea."[56] Japanese authorities established courts in which *yangban* and commoners were equal; they reformed and standardized currency, consolidated the taxation code, introduced science and math into the Confucian examination system, and abrogated the autocratic power of district officials. At the turn of the century, fewer than a dozen Korean cities had populations over fourteen thousand. Seoul's population was only slightly over two hundred thousand—by 1940 it had increased nearly 500 percent and approached a million.[57] Japan's influence meant similar augmentation of transportation and infrastructure—especially railroads—as well as advancement in communication lines, irrigation, public health facilities, trade, and industry.

How much these developments helped raise the quality of ordinary Koreans' lives is a significant question. The railroads were used mainly to grow Japanese industry and transport its troops. Since Japanese landlords confiscated much of the best farmland in the South, thousands of landless farmers roamed the

All over Korea, fighters joined the resistance to Japanese colonization. Photographer unknown

countryside. One estimate placed their number at one-third of the total popula-tion.[58] Starving and homeless, many found their way to Siberia or Manchuria, where they could survive—and fight Japan. Centuries of Korean dynastic stability had conditioned many people to accept authorities, but another current running through Korea's past was resistance to continual Japanese raids.

Convinced of their superiority, Japanese colonial authorities treated indig-enous people with contempt, eventually even banning Korean names and lan-guage in schools. Koreans tried all means at their disposal to find independence: from formation of independence clubs favoring gradual reform, to nonviolent protests and noncooperation, and finally to outright revolt and armed resist-ance. Japan's military superiority over China and, in 1905, its decisive defeat of Russia made it master of the entire region—a status ratified internationally with the secret U.S./Japan Taft-Katsura agreement a few months after Japan humili-ated the Russian Navy at Port Arthur on May 29 and won the Russo-Japanese war of 1905. The United States recognized Japan's right to "establish suzerainty of Korea" in exchange for Japan's assurance not to interfere with U.S. actions in the Philippines. Like the great power agreement to divide Korea in 1945, Taft-Katsura divided the Pacific into spheres of influence, an important precedent to the divi-sion of Korea four decades later. After the Taft-Katsura agreement of July 1905, Japan immediately sent its first Governor-General to Korea, beginning a brutal occupation facilitated by U.S. complicity. These two world powers kept their agreement secret for nearly twenty years because they knew people would have unfavorable reactions. In the same year, Britain renewed its treaties with Japan, by which Japan's "paramount" power in Korea and British rule in India (as well as its interests in China) were mutually recognized.

Korea was compelled to sign a Treaty of Protectorate on November 17, 1905, that granted Japan control of its foreign affairs. While Japan's victory over Russia was an inspiration for patriots in India and elsewhere to fight European imperialism, in Korea it was a day of monumental sadness. The country had no one to help it gain independence. On November 23, Seoul newspaper *Hwang–sung Shimun* expressed the nation's despair: "Is it worthwhile for any of us to live any longer? Our people have become the slaves of others, and the spirit of a nation which has stood for 4,000 years . . . has perished in a single night."

Because of its ethnocentric discrimination against Koreans, Japanese occupation made almost everyone into patriots—except for a small number of imperial collaborators. When a "Righteous Army" led by *yangban* arose to fight Japan's colonization, thousands of people flocked to its banners.

In 1906, separate insurrections captured Hongseong and Chuncheon, and disbanded units of the Korean army began a guerrilla campaign. In response, the Japanese ruthlessly suppressed entire regions, massacring anyone suspected of aiding insurgents and razing whole towns. From 1907 to 1908, the fighting was so intense that official Japanese statistics reported 15,189 insurgents killed, 3,211 wounded, and 1,556 captured. As enumerated in TABLE 2.1, armed resistance crested in 1908.

TABLE 2.1 **Insurgents and Armed Confrontations, 1907–1911**

Year	Number of Insurgents	Number of Encounters
1907	44,116	322
1908	69,804	1,451
1909	27,663	953
1910	1,891	147
1911	216	32
Total	**143,690**	**2,905**

Source: Governor General of Korea, Records of the Subjugation of Insurgents, Seoul: Japanese Garrison Army Headquarters, 1912, Appendix Table 2, as quoted in Brahm Swaroop Agrawal, *Korean National Movement* (Gwalior, India: Jiwaji University Press, 1996), 72.

While bravely fought, the resistance was doomed by the superior firepower of Japan. Some estimates place the number of Korean insurgents killed at twenty thousand out of a population of fifteen million—meaning that more than one Korean in a thousand gave his or her life for the country's independence, a far higher proportion of population than Americans who were killed in World War II.[59]

Although resistance inside the nation's borders was bloodily contained, patriots refused to submit. On October 26, 1909, in Harbing, China, Ahn Jung-kun assassinated Japanese prince Ito Hirobumi—the first Japanese resident-general in Korea and president of Japan's Imperial Council. Although executed for his patriotic act, Ahn is considered righteous across all of Korea today. Faced with an unrelenting guerrilla war and various forms of cultural resistance, Japanese politicians enacted a formal Treaty of Annexation on August 22, 1910. Nonetheless, resistance remained rampant. In the five years from 1911 to 1916, the prison population doubled from sixteen to thirty-two thousand, according to Frederick A. McKenzie, a correspondent with London's *Daily Mail*.[60] In 1918, not even the arrest of 140,000 people could prevent the national uprising.[61] As Japan consolidated its domination, Koreans refused to accept their colonial status and massively protested on March 1, 1919—a day that remains central to Korean history in both North and South.

March 1, 1919: Korean Independence Uprising

Under Japanese colonial rule after 1910, Koreans had no freedom of assembly or association, nor were there autonomous media to convey the will of the people. But using networks of indigenous civil society—including religious groups like *Chondogyo* (then with more than twice as many members as Christians), market days in towns, and word of mouth (*sabaltongmoon*)—the entire country rose up as one.[62] So successful was the mobilization that Japanese rulers were caught completely by surprise. Like the 1968 Tet offensive in Vietnam, a robust indigenous civil society synchronously mobilized the entire country to act in unison without a word being leaked to foreign occupation authorities. Despite severe repression, informal networks tying Koreans together were so remarkably resilient that Japanese authorities were unable to penetrate them. By 1912, newspapers and presses had been shut down and more than 50,000 political arrests made; in 1918, an estimated 140,000 people were arrested to prevent the kind of rising that occurred on March 1.[63]

The *Zeitgeist* of 1919 put independence into the very air people breathed. At the end of World War I, the Versailles Peace Conference promised "self-determination," raising hopes of Koreans, Vietnamese, Indians, and colonized peoples all over the world. In January, when the conference began, a humble Vietnamese named Nguyen Ai Quoc arrived, hat in hand, with hopes of pleading for Vietnamese independence, but he was refused entry and not even permitted to present his petition. Ho Chi Minh, as he later became known, went on to lead his nation to independence by forging an alliance with the only power willing to support anticolonial movements—the Soviet Union. A Korean delegation led by Kim Gyu-sik was also present in Versailles. While admitted, they, too, were refused formal seats as voting delegates. The Koreans were unaware of a secret pact among the United States, Japan, and France to bar discussion of Korean and Indochinese issues. In Korea, the U.S. embassy instructed its representatives, "not to do anything which may cause Japanese authorities to suspect American Government sympathizes with Korean nationalist movement."[64]

Inside Korea, a remarkably unified opposition congealed. Christian, Buddhist and *Chondogyo* leaders all worked together, distributing leaflets and spreading the word of the uprising through their networks. The "driving force behind the March First Movement" was Son Byeong-heui, leader of *Chondogyo*, still a million strong despite systematic Japanese attempts to extirpate the movement.[65] Son spent nearly ten years considering and preparing for the uprising. He first founded a monastery in Seoul and selected five hundred leading *Chondogyo* members from around the country for intensive training. Then he sent secret, mimeographed plans to every parish. Finally, he established a Preparatory Committee and National Headquarters for nonviolent nationwide demonstrations.[66] On December 24, 1918, Son called upon all one million *Chondogyo* members to pray for forty-nine days in order to prepare spiritually for independence. Meeting in a small inner circle, *Chondogyo* leaders resolved to unite with Christians and to present a petition signed by about thirty leading patriots. On February 28, a small group gathered at Son's house and gave final approval for the declaration of independence to be released the next day, two days before Korean King Kojong's funeral (amid rumors he had been poisoned by a Japanese conspiracy). Of the thirty-three leaders who signed the final declaration, three were Buddhist monks, fifteen members were from *Chondogyo*, and fifteen were Protestants.[67]

At 2 p.m. on March 1, 1919, a young student named Jung Jae-yong stood up in Seoul's Pagoda Park and publicly recited Korea's Declaration of Independence. Once the declaration was made public, the thirty-three distinguished signers gave themselves up for arrest from the restaurant where they sat in order to dramatize their strict principles of nonviolence. Jung Jae-yong urged people to march—and march Koreans did—as many as one million people on that day alone. After the initial protests took place at Tapgol Park, the crowd split into three marches. One group set off in the direction of the palace where the body of the king waited burial; another group converged on the United States and French consulates; and the last group aimed at the Colonial Administration Building. As night approached, Japanese civilians joined police in beating nonviolent protesters who remained in the streets.

At the same precise time as the declaration was read all over the country, thousands of people mobilized. Huge demonstrations filled the streets of Wonsan, Pyongyang, Jinnampo, Anju, Jinju, Euiju, and Sunchon, with the same "*Mansei!*" ("Long Live!") chants everywhere.

The next day, protesters appeared in the streets of Kaesong and Yesan; within a week, the movement appeared in Gwangju, Busan, and Taegu—in short, wherever Koreans breathed. Even Koreans in Japan and China mobilized. While estimates of the total number of participants vary widely, no one disputes the fact that this was the largest nationalist movement in Korean history. It is sometimes called the Mansei Movement[68] because demonstrators chanted "*Mansei!*" Some estimates place the number of participants at more than two million people, others at half that. At a minimum, one million people out of a total population of sixteen million participated in demonstrations.[69] Over three months, the total number of protests reached more than 1,500—and occurred in all but nine of Korea's 220 counties.

Despite the pacific character of protests, Japanese colonial troops killed hundreds of people and imprisoned many more. According to official Japanese reports, 533 protesters were killed, 1,409 wounded, and 12,522 arrested between March and December. Koreans counted far more causalities: by the end of May, Japanese repression is said to have claimed 7,509 lives, with an additional 15,961 injured, and more than 46,948 people imprisoned, many with sentences ranging

Women led peaceful nationwide demonstrations for independence on March 1, 1919.
Photographer unknown

from ten to fifteen years.[70] Not surprisingly, official Japanese figures are lower, maintaining 19,525 people were arrested in these protests. Their principal occupations were tabulated in TABLE 2.2.

An official Japanese report claimed at least "20,000 demonstrators have been armed with clubs, kitchen knives and similar weapons," but it is hard to know if this was a mendacious attempt to justify the severe measures colonial authorities took against generally peaceful protesters.[71] Japanese newspapers proclaimed that the "stirring up of the minds of Koreans is the sin of the American missionaries. This uprising is their work."[72] Churches were often involved in the protests,

TABLE 2.2 **Occupations of Arrested People in 1919**

Farmers	10,864
Students	1,936
Unemployed	1,053
Merchants	800
Day workers, servants	744
Businessmen	478
Public service	456
Teachers	419
Inn and restaurant operators	237
Other/unknown	2,538
Total (as counted by Japan)	**19,525**

Sources: Korean Government–General, *The Korean Independence Thought and Movement* (Seoul: Government General of Korea, 1924), 105–6, in Japanese; Brahm Swaroop Agrawal, *Korean National Movement* (Gwalior, India: Jiwaji University Press, 1996), 109. For more tables, see Chong-Sik Lee, *Politics of Korean Nationalism* (Berkeley: University of California Press, 1963), 115–18, and http://www.geocities.com/Tokyo/Towers/5067/ksun.htm#APPENDIX%20H.

but so was every organization of Korean civil society: Buddhists, *Chondogyo*, women's associations, and student groups all mobilized. The protests spread to Manchuria, Russia, and other places where Koreans lived.[73]

Although all the esteemed signers of the declaration were male, women prominently formed the front of many of the marches on March 1. Their underground network *Songjuk-hoe* (Pine and Bamboo Association) had been formed in Pyongyang in 1913. Female participation in the March 1 Movement "revealed a potential strength that had been latent in the traditional society."[74] To consider the astonishing mobilization of a million Koreans on the same day while keeping it secret from Japanese troops and officials is to realize the extraordinary strength of Korean civil society.

Women were central to Korean civil society's lingering power, and their leadership on March 1 was a public display. Prominent women leaders included Kim Maria, Hwang Ae-dok, Yi Song-wan, Chang Son-hi, Oh Sin-do, Park Hyun-suk, and Ahn Kyong-sin—all of whom were jailed. The participation of women students was especially striking, and so was that of many *kisaeng* (women entertainers, called *geisha* in Japan), who refused even to speak to Japanese colonists after March 1. Forming a union, they devoted themselves to traditional forms of art. One of the movement's teenage martyrs, Yu Kwan-sun, became especially well known. After the protests began, she returned to her hometown, Chiryong in South Chuongchong Province. On April 2, she handed out Korean flags and publicly called for independence. A year later, on the uprising's first anniversary, she again called out for the country's independence. For her outspoken efforts, she was arrested. During her trial she refused to remain quiet, instead throwing chairs at the judges and chanting "*Mansei!*" She was later tortured to death. Yu's body was never recovered, although her missionary school claims to have found her in scattered pieces.

One church reported that 2,656 of its members (including 531 women) were arrested in 1919 for actions related to Korean independence. What for some was the "modernization" of police under Japanese colonial rule—their efficient combination and expansion—was a disaster for most Koreans. Within a year after the uprising, the number of police stations rose from 151 to 251, that of substations in the same period from 686 to 2,495.[75] The extent of Japanese repression may be debated but not its barbaric character. There are numerous eyewitness accounts. On April 15, 1919, all the village residents in Jeam-ri (near Suwon in Gyeonggi Province), including at least twenty-nine people, were rounded up in the church. With the doors barred, the building was set on fire, killing them all. In fifteen other nearby villages, more than 317 houses were burned—bringing the total number of killed to hundreds—possibly more than a thousand.[76] For nearly a century, Japan denied that any such Jeam-ri incident took place, but in 2007, proof of a massacre of civilians and its cover-up was found in the diary of the commander of Japanese military forces, Taro Utsunomiya, and published by Japanese newspaper *Asahi Shimbun* and the Korean paper, *Hankyoreh Sinmun*.[77]

Like most uprisings that do not seize control of the government, the March 1 Movement led to increased state repression, but it also deeply affected many people

and paved the way for the next steps in the movement's evolution of forms of organization and contestation of power. A few weeks after March 1, a provisional government of Korea was established in Shanghai representing a wide spectrum of political perspectives; armed groups blossomed in Manchuria and fought a continuous
struggle against Japan; and forms of cultural resistance intensified inside Korea.
Years later, Kim Yong-bock wrote that, "The event of March First Independence
Movement lives in the hearts and minds of the Korean people, and it has become
a permanent historical symbol for them . . . It was the first people's movement in
Korean history, in which an axial transition occurred in a revolutionary way."[78]

In sheer numbers, the proliferation of social movement organizations after
the 1919 uprising is noteworthy. The Japanese Governor-General's own figures
show marked increases in organized groups among youth, farmers, and workers,
as indicated in TABLE 2.3.

TABLE 2.3 **Social Movement Organizations, 1920–1933**

Year	Farmers' Movements	Labor Movements	Youth Movements
1920	0	33	251
1921	3	90	446
1922	23	81	488
1923	107	111	58
1924	112	91	742
1925	126	128	847
1926	119	182	1,092
1927	160	352	1,127
1928	307	432	1,320
1929	564	465	1,433
1930	943	561	1,509
1931	1,759	511	1,482
1932	1,380	404	863
1933	1,301	374	1,004

Source: *The Recent Security Situation in Korea*, 1933, as reported in Kang Man-gil, "Contemporary Nationalist
Movements and the Minjung," in *South Korea's Minjung Movement: The Culture and Politics of Dissidence*, ed.
Kenneth Wells (Honolulu: University of Hawaii Press, 1995), 87.

Yo Un Hyung and Lee Kwang Su, involved in early drafts of the declaration
of independence, were among those who established the Provisional Government
of Korea in Shanghai on April 10, 1919. Syngman Rhee, then living in the United
States and thought to be "the protégé of Woodrow Wilson," was chosen as the first
president. Rhee's authoritarianism led to his being replaced in 1925 by Park Eun-
sik, who was succeeded by Kim Ku the following year. The group encompassed
many different factions of Korea's diverse political scene and even formed a Korea
Liberation Army, which eventually fought alongside Allied Forces in World War
II in China and Burma.

Every uprising simultaneously reveals the essential problems of a social order
and points toward their solution. The problem raised by the March 1 Movement
was international in scope, and Korea's provisional government in Shanghai
served as a stimulus for Chinese students and intellectuals. The victorious Allies

at the Versailles Peace Conference refused China's demand for restoration of territories seized by Germany. Instead, in all their wisdom, the leaders of the world were intent upon ceding those territories to Japan. As soon as that news reached Beijing, several thousand students rallied in Tiananmen Square on May 4. Their call to action, distributed throughout China, included an explicit reference to the Korean uprising of March 1: "The Koreans in their struggle for independence also cried, 'Give us our wish, or give us death.'"[79] Here is direct evidence of how China's May 4 Movement drew inspiration from the courageous uprising of their Korean neighbors. Students began the Chinese movement, which by mid-May turned into a general strike of students in dozens of cities.[80] Workers and farmers across the country quickly joined. As the May 4 Movement intensified, people boycotted Japanese goods in major cities, and succeeded in getting some of the worst collaborators removed from positions of power. From nationalist resistance to Japan, the movement soon changed into one against feudalism with demands including greater civil liberties.[81] The pattern is familiar: students spark popular upheavals for democracy, which, in turn, generate workers and farmers movements that move beyond the immediate demands of the movement's infancy.

Although only uncovered at the end of the twentieth century, the pattern of the international diffusion of protest and the escalating demands made from the grassroots has a long history. One report in 1919 noted: "It is true that the longing for freedom and independence now finding expression in many parts of the world, in Egypt and Ireland in particular, has exercised powerful influence over the ideas and thoughts of many Korean young men and women, who are sufficiently educated to be able to read newspapers."[82]

From Uprising to Armed Resistance

The ferocious repression of the Japanese police made peaceful protests inside Korea impractical. Expatriates found refuge among the hundreds of thousands of ethnic Koreans in Manchuria and Russia, where they linked up with Chinese and Russian revolutionaries.

Impoverished peasants and lumpen carried the fight against the Japanese wherever they could.[83] Some people took inspiration from Ahn Jung-gun's assassination of Prince Ito a decade earlier. On September 2, 1919, Baron Saito, the newly arriving Governor-General, narrowly escaped a bomb thrown at his carriage in Seoul. Soon, however, even secret groups found it extremely difficult to build resistance inside the country. A newly formed national communist labor federation was savagely repressed.

Koreans could not count on any world power for assistance in this period—except for the weak and besieged revolutionary government of Russia. As leader of the new Russian republic, Lenin promised all colonized peoples support for independence. Animated by the victory of the Russian Revolution, many people gravitated toward Lenin, who personally met with Korean communist Lee Tong-hui in January 1921. By that time, not one but several Korean communist parties had been founded. Altogether, a total of thirty-six different communist groups with 3,700 armed members fought alongside the Russian Red Army against White counterrevolutionaries.[84] On April 17, 1925, a new Communist Party of Korea was formed at a secret meeting in a Chinese restaurant in Seoul. In Hawaii, Suh Dae-suk founded a Communist group aimed at liberating the country, one of many outside the country who understood itself as "the Communist Party." When these various groups failed to unite, the Communist International in Moscow decided to dissolve all of them—even the one that had already belonged to the Comintern for two years.

Anti-Japanese Korean freedom fighter in Manchuria in the 1930s. Photographer unknown

Although questions of political organization remained problematic, the urgency of the armed struggle demanded action. Having escaped to Siberia, Hong Bom-do became a battalion commander in Irkutsk and continued the fight against Japan. Within two months after March, Hong led a group of two hundred armed workers, farmers, and youth. Uniting with other groups into the Korean Independence Army in Manchuria, they engaged Japanese army units and killed hundreds of soldiers in major victories before being forced to retreat to Siberia by a massive counterattack. Another group that formed inside China, the Righteous Brotherhood, issued a manifesto, "Declaration of the Korean Revolution" by Shin Chae-ho, which was explicitly revolutionary: "To preserve the existence of the Korean people, the Japanese robbers must be expelled; the only way to expel the Japanese is through revolution." [85] One estimate put the number of insurgents in the border region at more than 160,000 in the early 1930s.[86] Eventually, paranoid of their possible loyalty to Japan, Stalin would order Hong and his soldiers to Kazakhstan as part of a massive relocation of ethnic Koreans.

Anarchists and feminists also emerged within the vibrant spectrum of Korean revolutionaries. Utopian thinker Shin Chae-ho became an enthusiastic anarchist, a doctrine intimately bound up for him with Korean shamanism. Shin was quite radical, declaring that, "The beastly people of the capitalist, imperialist countries are full to bursting with the blood, flesh, and bones of the proletarian *minjung* [people] of all the colonies in the Orient. They torment the proletarian *minjung*, especially those of the colonies in Asia where our *minjung* live under circumstances more miserable than death." In the early 1920s, utopian thinker Cho So-ang founded the Korean Independence Organization dedicated to a "World Family Without States" based on "universal love."[87] Another Confucian intellectual, Park Eun-sik, spoke of international peace through a "Great Unified World Society." Like many other independence-minded Koreans, they could not tolerate life under Japanese rule and moved to Manchuria.

In 1924, the Korean Anarchist Federation formed in China, where they regularly published a newspaper. By 1928, as libertarian tendencies continued to grow, an Eastern Anarchist Federation emerged with participants from Korea, China, Vietnam, Taiwan, and Japan. Japanese teenager Kaneko Fumiko lived in Korea during the March 1 Uprising and was greatly affected. Although only seventeen at the time, she left her Korean family and moved to Tokyo, where she helped organize the Society of Malcontents in 1922 with anarchist Park Yeol.

In the aftermath of the uprising, Japanese colonial policy had to be revised since force alone failed to suppress Koreans' spirit of independence. Dubbed "Cultural Politics," the new policies brought civil police to replace the army and permitted limited freedoms of speech, association, and assembly.[88] Moreover, Koreans themselves were transformed by March 1 and began to assert themselves. One indication of how uprisings liberate people's sensibilities can be found in the "New Women" movement in Korea of the 1920s. Stridently embracing the need for cultural as well as political change, these women advocated free love, free marriage, and an end to patriarchy at the same time as they opposed Japanese imperialism.[89] Using their magazine, *New Women*, to propagate their views, they met with great resistance, in part because of the perception that their beliefs were Japanese-influenced and that they uncritically adopted Western culture. In this period, even women's peaceful acts of patriotism were next to impossible. While many women left to become fighters in Manchuria and China, inside Korea, others formed cultural and educational associations. The first women's labor group, Kyung-Sung Women Workers Union in the Fiber Industry was formed in 1923. Despite ideological differences between socialist and Christian women's organizations—differences mirrored in the movement as a whole—women came together in 1927 to form *Kun-u-hoe*, a patriotic organization devoted to ending gender discrimination, child marriages, prostitution, and wage discrimination against women while advocating choice in marriage, support for women farmers, and freedom of speech, assembly and association. More than forty organizations participated in the first meeting in July 1928; a year later, more than seventy branches sent representatives.[90]

Another strong source of struggle against Japan was the cultural movement: music, art, literature, and theater that exposed "the reality of colonized Korea for its better understanding by the Korean people."[91] Between 1925 and 1938, the Korean Artists Proletarian Federation brought more than a hundred works of literature into existence.[92] While criticized by some for gaining in ideology but losing in art, the group helped prepare the ground for future resistance. In the first half of the 1920s, 234 student strikes erupted against Japanese control of education. The student-led uprising of June 10, 1926, during which two thousand people were arrested on one day, was heavily influenced both by communist groups and by *Chondogyo*, which printed a hundred thousand leaflets for it. Altogether, these various forms of resistance to Japan were expressions of a vibrant oppositional civil society.[93]

In 1919, the Korean bourgeoisie (then almost exclusively merchants and landlords) began to "take a serious interest in modern industry."[94] While most Koreans resisted Japan, budding capitalists sought to benefit from the "modernization" of their country. Evidently one effect of the 1919 rising was a revision of Japanese colonial development policy so that Koreans as well as Japanese were permitted to benefit from the country's economic development. Korean businessmen did not really care about nationalism: they routinely used Japanese police to discipline labor and more or less endorsed the obliteration of Korea's national identity.[95]

Korean workers saw the matter quite differently. In September 1921, five thousand coalminers and dockworkers struck in Busan. After a prolonged strike beginning in July 1923, women working in Kyungseong rubber factories helped form the Korean Labor Federation in 1925. The next year, the Chosun Women Sisterhood Association organized, the first group specifically to organize female farmers and workers.[96] At the time, wages of Korean women were only one seventh of those of Japanese men, although women comprised 60 percent of the industrial work force.[97]

In 1929, a new crescendo of working-class resistance was reached. A three-month long general strike in Wonsan, initiated by transportation workers and dockworkers, ended in bitter defeat for the union, but it indicated people's accumulation of experience and capacity to carry popular forms of resistance to increasingly more sophisticated levels.[98] Female workers in Busan rubber factories also went on strike, as did graphite miners as well as brewery, brassware, and print workers. Later in 1929, a fight between Korean and Japanese high school students on a train from Mokpo to Gwangju turned into an explosion against Japanese colonization. The first phase of the Gwangju student movement involved strikes and protests at nearly two hundred schools with more than 50,000 participants. After several students were arrested as leaders, the revolt intensified even further and spread throughout the country. Altogether the upsurge activated as many as 250,000 students to demand release of imprisoned protesters, autonomy for education, and freedom of assembly and speech.[99] All over Korea, young people surged into the fight. In Jilin, Kim Il-sung was arrested after he enlisted in a secret Marxist group while a high school student.[100]

By August 1929, anarchists in Manchuria had constructed a self-governing zone in Shinmin under the auspices of the Korean Anarchist Communist Federation. Village, district, and area councils all worked together through a decentralized structure called the Korean People's Association that enabled over two million Koreans to meet their own needs.[101] The Korean People's Association declared its aim as, "independent self-governing cooperative system of the Korean people who assembled their full power to save our nation struggling against Japan." The Japanese military mounted a major offensive against them in what has been called the longest battle of the Pacific war. As Japanese attacks grew in intensity, Kim Jwa-jin successful led resistance fighters until his assassination in 1931, possibly by Stalinists. Kim had counseled insurgents to ignore Stalinist assaults and work for independence. Overwhelmed by attacks launched by both Stalin and Japan, the autonomous Shinmin zone was crushed, but insurgents continued to fight. From 1931 to the war's end, as many as two hundred thousand guerrillas were killed in Manchuria.[102]

Koreans remained steadfast in direct actions against Japanese authorities. On January 8, 1932, Lee Bong-chang waited patiently for Emperor Hirohito to leave a parade. He threw two grenades at the carriage, but the first one went wide of the mark, and the second, while accurate, failed to explode. Three months later in Shanghai, Yoon Bong-gil, a disciple of Kim Koo, lobbed a bomb at a Japanese ceremony killing Japanese General Sirokawa Yosinori, overall commander of Japanese forces in China, and wounding many other high-ranking officials, including Mamoru Shigemitsu, the top-hat and tuxedo wearing representative of the emperor who limped aboard the USS *Missouri* to sign Japan's surrender in 1945.

In response to continuing attacks inside Korea, Japan further built up its police force, which reached an average of about twenty-three thousand men between 1920 and 1943—one policeman for every thousand inhabitants.

Although some Koreans were recruited (and would later become prominent officials in 1945 under the U.S. military government), nearly 90 percent of officers and two-thirds of lower-ranking police were Japanese.[103] Police powers were not constrained by injunctions against search, seizure, or arbitrary punishment

On April 29, 1932, Yoon Bong-gil attacked high-ranking Japanese officials in Shanghai.
Artist unknown

of anyone suspected of a crime. Torture and murder of dissidents were common-place and went unpunished. Korea's Japanese Governor-General was appointed directly by the emperor and had absolute authority. From 1942 to 1943, only 400 Koreans had been promoted above the rank of low-level officials, while 48,372 Japanese held such positions—about 120 times as many Japanese as Koreans. Above them were 2,455 high-level administrators, almost none of whom were Korean.[104] So skewed was the power structure that even Japanese civilians were empowered to forcibly seize lands and houses of Koreans without being punished. Japanese landowners emerged as Korea's most significant property owners, and some 90 percent of Korean farmers were reduced to tenancy under which they paid over 80 percent of their harvests to the landowner.[105] In North Jeolla, 85 percent of all households were landless or tenant farmers, and in all of Honam, more than half of all major landlords were Japanese.[106] A Red Farmers Union emerged in the 1930s comprised primarily of small landowners whose livelihood was threatened by the colonial administration. Concerned with encroachment upon village life as well as tax policy, the union formed in at least 32 of the 123 counties of southern Korea.[107]

As the situation of Koreans deteriorated, nearly half of all rice grown was exported to Japan. In 1935, the Japanese Governor-General acknowledged that, "the number of wretched farmers lacking food and searching for bark and grass to eat, had approached one-half of the peasant population."[108] Thousands of young girls were sold into lives of sex work by families too destitute to care for their own children.[109] The impoverishment of Koreans is indicated in TABLE 2.4 in statistics showing nearly a 50 percent decline in consumption of rice under Japanese rule.

TABLE 2.4 **Per Capita Rice Consumption in Korea under Japanese Rule**

Years	Per Capita Consumption	Index
1912–1916	0.7188 sok	100.0
1917–1921	0.6860 sok	95.5
1922–1926	0.5871 sok	81.6
1927–1931	0.4964 sok	69.0
1932–1936	0.4010 sok	55.8
One sok = 4.96 bushel		

Sources: Andrew J. Grajdanzev, *Modern Korea* (New York: Institute of Pacific Relations, 1944), 88; The Statistical Charts of the Korean Economy (Seoul, 1940), 204–7; Brahm Swaroop Agrawal, *Korean National Movement* (Gwalior, India: Jiwaji University Press, 1996), 97.

In this same period of time, rice exports to Japan increased by nearly 400 percent, from an average of 1.5 million sok from 1910 to 1918, to 6.2 million sok from 1921 to 1939.[110] Clearly, Japan was starving Korea to feed its own population. This was not an isolated policy. In northern Vietnam during the winter of 1944–1945, more than a million people starved to death (out of a population of fourteen million), while colonial authorities exported rice to use as fuel in Japan's oil-starved factories.

By the time Japan attacked the United States at Pearl Harbor, it had imported hundreds of thousands of Koreans to serve as laborers for the dirtiest and most dangerous jobs in mines and factories.[111] Thousands more Koreans served as conscripts in the military, and tens of thousands of women (a total of as many as two hundred thousand, half of whom were Korean) were compelled to become sex slaves (euphemistically called "comfort women") for the emperor's legions. A high estimate placed the total number of Koreans shipped to Japan as forced laborers at 7,000,000 from 1937 to 1945.[112] Kang Man-gil estimated the number of those "forcibly mobilized" as laborers at between 1,130,000 and 1,460,000.[113] Others counted the number of Koreans sent by Japanese colonial policy outside Korea at 16 percent of the total population—about 4,000,000 people.[114] In 1945, the U.S. military placed 2,400,000 Koreans in Japan and 1,900,000 in Manchuria.[115] The massive trafficking meant that thousands of victims annihilated by U.S. nuclear weapons at the end of the war were Korean, including about one in seven at Hiroshima—about 20,000 out of 140,000 who perished that day—and thousands more at Nagasaki. So poorly regarded were Koreans by the war's end that they were not allowed to use their names but required to take Japanese ones—even in Korea. Despite all their sacrifices and hard work, Koreans remain forgotten victims. In the twenty-first century, Koreans have yet to be accorded full rights in Japan. They are still not allowed to be buried at many Japanese cemeteries.

When future historians look back on World War II, the bloodiest conflict in a long history of human bloodletting, they may remember it more for the continuing wars in the decades after it than for the peace that it was supposed to bring. Since 1945, more than ten million human beings have met savage deaths inflicted by factory-made killing machines.[116] When pause is given to consider fully the legacy of World War II, it may well be concluded that Adolf Hitler's kind of human beings won. Before Hitler could be nullified, his variety of ethnic cleansing had thoroughly changed Germany; in the succeeding decades, that tactic—along with aerial bombing of cities and use of all manner of new weapons against civilians— became business-as-usual.

In 1945, when U.S. General Douglas MacArthur became *de facto* ruler of Japan, he befriended the Japanese emperor, patronized erstwhile war criminals, and embraced Korean collaborators. Continuing Japan's policy of repressing currents of Korean nationalism, he ordered Koreans to suffer the harsh occupation prepared by the United States for Japan. Japanese nationalism ranks with German Nazism as a great destructive force defeated in 1945, yet in the dialectic of liberation and enslavement, Korea's freedom from Japan would soon see it devastated by war as never before.

NOTES

1   Koh Byong-ik, "Confucianism in Contemporary Korea," in *Confucian Traditions in East Asian Modernity: Moral Education and Economic Culture in Japan and the Four Mini-Dragons*, ed. Tu Wei-ming (Cambridge, MA: Harvard University Press, 1996).

2   George Ogle, *South Korea: Dissent Within the Economic Miracle* (London: Zed Books, 1990), 76. The less complimentary assessment is from Bruce Cumings, *Korea's Place in the Sun: A Modern History* (New York: Norton, 1997), 300.

3   Ingeborg Göthel, *Geschichte Südkoreas* (Berlin: Deutscher Verlag der Wissenschaften, 1988), 9.

4   John K. Fairbank, Edwin Reischauer, and A. Craig, *East Asia: Transition and Transformation* (Boston: Houghton Mifflin, 1976), 322.

5   James Palais, *Views on Korean Social History* (Seoul: Institute for Modern Korean Studies, 1998), 11.

6   Tong Hwan (Stephen) Moon, "Korean Minjung Theology: An Introduction," in *Korean-American Relations at Crossroads*, ed. Wonmo Dong (Princeton, NJ: The Association of Korean Christian Scholars in North America, 1982), 17.

7   Hyun Young-hak in *Minjung Theology* (London: Zed Press, 1983). Quoted in Yayori Matsui, *Women's Asia* (London: Zed Books, 1989), 140.

8   Lee Jae-eui, "Operation Fascinating Vacation," in *The Kwangju Uprising: Eyewitness Press Accounts of Korea's Tiananmen*, eds., Henry Scott-Stokes and Lee Jae-eui (Armonk, NY: ME. Sharpe, 2000), 38.

9   Kim Han-kyo, ed., *Studies on Korea: A Scholar's Guide* (Honolulu: University of Hawaii Press, 1980), 56–61. Quoted in Cumings, *Korea's Place in the Sun*, 98.

10 Gregory Henderson, *Korea: The Politics of the Vortex* (Cambridge, MA: Harvard University Press, 1968), 4.

11 Ibid., 5.

12 Ibid., 22.

13 Chung Chai-sik, "Confucian Tradition and Nationalist Ideology in Korea," in *South Korea's Minjung Movement: The Culture and Politics of Dissidence*, ed. Kenneth Wells (Honolulu: University of Hawaii Press, 1995), 71.

14 JaHyun Kim Haboush, "Academies and Civil Society in Chosun Korea," in *La société civile face à l'État: dans les traditions chinoise, japonaise, coréenne et vietnamienne* (Paris: École-française d'extrême-orient, 1994). See also John Duncan, "The Problematic Modernity of Confucianism," in *Korean Society: Civil Society, Democracy and the State*, ed. Charles Armstrong (London: Routledge, 2002).

15 Cho Hein, "The Historical Origin of Civil Society in Korea," *Korea Journal* 37, no. 2 (Summer 1997).

16   See Wontack Hong, *Baekje of Korea and the Origin of Yamamoto Japan* (Seoul: Kudara International, 1994).

17   Cumings, *Korea's Place in the Sun*, 30.

18   Hermann Lautensach, *Korea: A Geography Based on the Author's Travels and Literature* (Berlin: Springer: 1945). Quoted in Cumings, *Korea's Place in the Sun*, 37. "Masuid" referred to by Cumings is Abdul Hassan Ali bin Hussein al-Masoud, sometimes called the Herodotus of the Arab world.

19   See Lee Ki-baik, *A New History of Korea* (Cambridge, MA: Harvard University Press, 1984), 144, 168.

20   Brahm Swaroop Agrawal, *Korean National Movement* (Gwalior, India: Jiwaji University Press, 1996), 5.

21   "The Mongols in Korea," *Korean Repository*, vol. v, 1898, 133–37 as cited in ibid., 5.

22   For considerable evidence that Korea had movable type long before Gutenberg, see James Gale, *History of the Korean People* (Seoul: Royal Asiatic Society, 1972). In deference to Germans' inventiveness, I would grant that the telephone may indeed have been a German invention.

23   Henderson, *Korea: The Politics of the Vortex*, 53.

24   Ibid., 52.

25   James Palais, *Politics and Policy in Traditional Korea* (Cambridge, MA: Harvard University Press, 1975), 5.

26   See David McCann, *Form and Freedom in Korean Poetry* (Leiden, UK: Brill, 1988). McCann's analysis includes verses by *kisaeng* as part of his exploration of the form's past.

27   Cumings, *Korea's Place in the Sun*, 79.

28   Moon, "Korean Minjung Theology," 17.

29   *King Sejong the Great: The Everlasting Light of Korea* (Pohang: Yong Hwa, 1997), 9.

30   Moon, "Korean Minjung Theology," 16.

31   Henderson, *Korea: The Politics of the Vortex*, 41.

32   Pak Che-ga as quoted in ibid., 380.

33   Gavin Menzies, *1421: The Year China Discovered the World* (London: Bantam Press, 2003).

34   Palais, *Views on Korean Social History*, 11.

35   Bruce Cumings, *North Korea: Another Country* (New York: New Press, 2004), 129.

36   Henderson, *Korea: The Politics of the Vortex*, 41–2.

37   Palais, *Politics and Policy*, 25.

38   Ibid., 34.

39   Henderson, *Korea: The Politics of the Vortex*, 54.

40   For a full treatment of these events, see Sun Joo Kim, *Marginality and Subversion in Korea: The Hong Kyŏngnae Rebellion of 1812* (Seattle: University of Washington Press, 2007).

41   Won Youngsu, "Popular Rebellions and Uprisings in Chosun Period," in *International Encyclopedia of Protest and Revolution: 1500 to Present*, ed. Immanuel Ness (London: Wiley Blackwell, 2009).

42   Henderson, *Korea: The Politics of the Vortex*, 397.

43   G.M. McCune and J.A. Harrison, eds., *Korean-American Relations*, vol. 1, *1883–1886* (Berkeley: UC Press, 1950), 29–114; R.T. Pollard, "American Relations with Korea," *Chinese Social and Political Science Review* 11 (1932): 425–71.

44   Kang Man-kil, "Historical Background of the Gwangju Democratic Uprising," in *History of the 5.18 Democratic Uprising*, vol. 1, ed. May 18th History Compilation Committee of Gwangju City, (Gwangju: The May 18 Memorial Foundation, 2008), 55.

45   Moon, "Korean Minjung Theology," 26.

46   James S. Gale, *History of the Korean People*, 316.

47   Lee Ki-baik, *A New History of Korea*, 284.

48   Henderson, *Korea: The Politics of the Vortex*, 63.

49   *Chondogyo: The Religion of the Cosmos That Blossomed in Korea*, (Seoul: Central Headquarters of Chondogyo, 2005), 95; Kang Man-kil, *History*, 57.

50   Agrawal, *Korean National Movement*, 43.

51   Professor Gatzuo Inoue provided statistics. See *Korea Times*, June 2, 2001, 3.

52   Göthel, *Geschichte Südkoreas*, 14.

53   Agrawal, *Korean National Movement*, 41.

54   Most Japanese remain ignorant of these events, although they were reported on August 24, 2009 in a special Asahi television broadcast. See also Kim Tae-ick, "The Sobering Truth of Empress Myeongseong's Killing," http://english.chosun.com/site/data/html_dir/2009/08/25/2009082500866.html.

55   See Kim Young-Sik, "A Brief History of the U.S.-Korea Relations Prior to 1945," paper presented at the University of Oregon, May 15, 2003, http://www.freerepublic.com/focus/f-news/943949/posts.

56   Cumings, *Korea's Place in the Sun*, 120.

57   Henderson, *Korea: The Politics of the Vortex*, 99.

58   Agrawal, *Korean National Movement*, 95.

59   Agrawal, *Korean National Movement*, 73–74.

60   See McKenzie's 1920 book, *Korea's Fight for Freedom*.

61 · Lee Ki-baik, *A New History Of Korea*, 314.

62   Christine Lienemann-Perrin, *Die Politische Verantwortung der Kirchen in Südkorea und Südafrika: Studien über ökumenischen und politischen Ethik* (München: Kaiser, 1992), 80.

63   Peter N. Stearns, *The Encyclopedia of World History*, 782, http://books.google.com/books?id=MziRd4ddZz4C&pg=PA782&lpg=PA782&dq=date+of+Korean+King+Kojong+death+1919&source=web&ots=Y56Pi8y7uI&sig=eLw_nCmTRFLVF-eG5f76hJ34MCI&hl=en&sa=X&oi=book_result&resnum=5&ct=result#PPA782,M1, accessed December 18, 2008.

64   Quoted in Chae-Jin Lee, *A Troubled Peace: U.S. Policy and the Two Koreas* (Baltimore: Johns Hopkins University Press, 2006), 17.

65   Carter Eckert, *Offspring of Empire: The Kochang Kims and the Colonial Origins of Korean Capitalism 1867–1945* (Seattle: University of Washington Press, 1991), 281.

66   Benjamin Weems, *Reform, Rebellion, and the Heavenly Way* (Tucson: University of Arizona Press, 1964), 70.

67   Lienemann-Perrin, *Die Politische*, 80. Chondogyo officially says there were fifteen of its members, two Buddhists, nine Methodists, and seven Presbyterians. *Chondogyo: The Religion of the Cosmos That Blossomed in Korea*, 107.

68   See Shannon McCune, *The Mansei Movement: March 1, 1919* (Honolulu: University of Hawaii, Center for Korean Studies, 1976).

69   Eckert, *Offspring of Empire*, 45. Shannon McCune reports that of the arrested, (19,525), 13,211 had no religious affiliation, 2,486 were Presbyterians, 560 Methodists, 2,283 Chondogyo, and 55 Catholics (*The Mansei Movement*, 34).

70   See Park Eun-sik, *Agony: Korean History*. Park was second president of Korea's provisional government. Tabulating the fierce repression unleashed by the emperor to punish Koreans, historian Kang Man-gil counted 7,500 citizens killed, 16,000 injured, and more than 46,000 arrested. Kang Man-gil, *A History of Contemporary Korea* (Kent, UK: Global Oriental, 2005), 29.

71   *The Korean "Independence" Agitation* (Seoul: Seoul Press Office, 1919), 17. This

strongly pro-Japanese document is contained in Harvard University's Widener Library Depository.

72   Quoted in Shannon McCune, *The Mansei Movement*, 16.

73   Ki-baik Lee, *A New History of Korea*, 344.

74   Kim Yung-Chung, "Women's Movement in Modern Korea," in *Challenges for Women: Women's Studies in Korea*, ed. Chung Sei-wha (Seoul: Ewha Women's University Press, 1986), 90.

75   Stearns, *The Encyclopedia of World History*, 783.

76   British missionary, Dr. Frank W. Schofield, took photos of the carnage, which were published by the Oriental Relations Committee of the Christian Federation Association as "The Korea Situation" in July 1919.

77   On March 1, 2007, some called for renewed inquiry into the massacre and the colonial government's cover-up.

78   Kim Yong-bock quoted in Lienemann-Perrin, *Die Politische*, 199.

79   Chow Tse-tsung, *The May Fourth Movement: Intellectual Revolution in Modern China* (Stanford: Stanford University Press, 1967), 107.

80   Ibid., 139–44.

81   Nishi Masayuki, "March 1 and May 4, 1919 in Korea, China and Japan: Toward an International History of East Asian Independence Movements," *International Herald Tribune/Asahi Shinbun*, October 29, 2007. Posted on Japan Focus website (http://www.japanfocus.org/) on October 31, 2007.

82   *The Korean "Independence" Agitation*, 15.

83   Cumings, *North Korea*, 114.

84   Göthel, *Geschichte Südkoreas*, 25.

85   Quoted in Kang Man-gil, "Contemporary Nationalist Movements and the Minjung," in *South Korea's Minjung Movement: The Culture and Politics of Dissidence*, ed. Kenneth Wells (Honolulu: University of Hawaii Press, 1995), 33–34.

86   Bruce Cumings, *The Origins of the Korean War*, vol. 1 (Princeton University Press, 1981), 34. (Hereafter Cumings, *Origins*, 1).

87   Kim Gi-seung. "Embracing and Overcoming of Social Darwinism by Confucian Intellectuals in the Early Twentieth Century Korea: The Cases of Park Eun-Sik (1859–1925), Jang Ji-Yeon (1864–1921), Lee Sang-Yong (1858–1931), Sin Chae-Ho (1880–1936), and Cho So-Ang (1887–1958)," *International Journal of Korean History* 2 (2001): 25–40.

88   Kang Man-gil, "Contemporary Nationalist Movements," 3, 11.

89   Insook Kwon, "'The New Women's Movement' in 1920s Korea: Rethinking the Relationship Between Imperialism and Women," in *Feminisms and Internationalism*, eds. Mrinalini Sinha, Donna Guy, and Angela Woollacott (Oxford: Blackwell, 1999), 37–61.

90   Ibid., 96–97.

91   Sohn-Pow-key, Kim Chol-choon, and Hong Yi-sup, *The History of Korea* (Seoul, 1982), 313. Quoted in Lienemann-Perrin, *Die Politische*, 86.

92   Namhee Lee, *The Making of Minjung: Democracy and the Politics of Representation in South Korea* (Ithaca, CA: Cornell University Press, 2007), 270.

93   See Sunhyuk Kim, "South Korea: Confrontational Legacy and Democratic Contributions," in *Civil Society and Political Change in Asia*, ed. Muthiah Alagappa (Stanford: Stanford University Press, 2004), 140–42.

94   Eckert, Offspring of Empire, 27.

95   Ibid., 226. Despite various efforts at reform, Japanese arrogance and hatred of Koreans, while incomprehensible to most Westerners, mitigated attempts to integrate Koreans into Japan's Greater East Asia Prosperity Sphere. One incident in particular might clarify its depth. After a great earthquake struck Tokyo on September 1, 1923, Japanese

mobs armed with bamboo spears and knives hunted down and killed more than six thousand Koreans. Police arrested many others, including anarchists Kaneko Fumiko and Park Yeol. Kaneko eventually died in prison, whether from suicide or murder—the official documents have yet to be made public.

96 Chong-Sook Kang and Ilse Lenz, *Wenn die Hennen krähen: Fauenbewegungen in Korea* (Münster: Verlag Westphälisches Dampfboot, 1992), 77.

97 Hyun-back Chung, "Together and Separately: 'The New Women's Movement' After the 1980s in South Korea," *Asian Women* 5 (Fall 1997): 22.

98 Martin Hart-Landsberg, *The Rush to Development: Economic Change and Political Struggle in South Korea* (New York: Monthly Review Press, 1993), 114.

99 Kyun Moon Hwang in *Contentious Kwangju: The May 18th Uprising in Korea's Past and Present*, eds. Gi-Wook Shin and Kyung Moon Hwang (Lanham, MD: Rowman and Littlefield, 2003), 140; Kang Man-gil, "Contemporary Nationalist Movements," 50.

100 Cumings, *North Korea*, 108.

101 Alan MacSimoin, "Anarchism in Korea," a public talk given in Dublin, September 1991, http://libcom.org/history/1894-1931-anarchism-in-korea.

102 Bruce Cumings, *The Origins of the Korean War*, vol. 2, *The Roaring of the Cataract, 1947–1950* (Princeton University Press, 1990), 346–47. (Hereafter Cumings, *Origins*, 2.)

103 Agrawal, *Korean National Movement*, 87.

104 Ibid., 89.

105 Hart-Landsberg, *The Rush to Development*, 105.

106 Sallie Yea, "Cultural Politics of Place in Kwangju City and South Jeolla Province" in Gi-Wook Shin and Kyung Moon Hwang, *Contentious Kwangju: The May 18 Uprising in Korea's Past and Present* (Lanham: Rowman and Littlefield, 2003), 115–16.

107 Gi-wook Shin, "The Historical Making of Collective Action: The Korean Peasant Uprisings of 1946," *American Journal of Sociology* 99, no. 6 (May 1994): 1601.

108 The Governor General of Chosen, *Thriving Chosen* (Seoul: 1935), 82.

109 David McCann translated folklore that cried out: "Castor-tree, don't bear your beans; the village girls go off as doxies." See "Arirang: The National Folksong of Korea," in *Studies on Korea in Transition*, eds. McCann, et al. (Honolulu: University of Hawaii Press, 1979), 51–52.

110 See also Kang Man-gil, "Contemporary Nationalist Movements," 104–5 for official Japanese estimates of exports of Korean rice.

111 Koreans made up about one-third of the industrial work force in Japan and accounted for more than 60 percent of the most difficult work in mines. Cumings, *Korea's Place in the Sun*, 177.

112 Kang and Lenz, *Wenn die Hennen krähen*, 31.

113 Kang Man-gil, "Contemporary Nationalist Movements," 21.

114 Stearns, *The Encyclopedia of World History*, 783.

115 Lee Ki-baik, *A New History Of Korea*, 48; Henderson, *Korea: The Politics of the Vortex*, 100.

116 In *Rogue State* (Monroe ME: Common Courage, 2000), William Blum counts sixty-seven U.S. interventions since World War II. See also http://www.xs4all.nl/~stgvisie/VISIE/interventielijst.html. Since the end of World War II, the United States has bombed twenty-three nations. (See: Lenora Foerstel and Brian Willson, "United States War Crimes," http://www.globalresearch.ca/articles/FOE201A.html)

CHAPTER 3

U.S. Imperialism and the October People's Uprising

The United States should realize its interest in the maintenance of the British, French, and Dutch colonial empires. We should encourage liberalization of the colonial regimes in order to better maintain them and to check Soviet influence in the stimulation of colonial revolt.

—U.S. Office of Strategic Services, April 2, 1945

The best way to describe southern Korea at present is to state that they are in a powder keg ready to explode upon application of a spark . . . Koreans have not understood why they were not given complete independence and allowed to establish completely their own government within two to three days of the arrival of American troops.

—U.S. General John Reed Hodge, Telegram to MacArthur,
September 13, 1945

CHRONOLOGY	
1910–1945	Japan rules Korea
August 6, 1945	U.S. atomic bomb devastates Hiroshima
August 9, 1945	U.S. atomic bomb devastates Nagasaki
August 15, 1945	Japan surrenders to the Allies
1945	Victorious Allies "temporarily" divide Korean and Vietnam
1945–1948	U.S. Military Government in southern Korea
September 2, 1945	Vietnam's independence proclaimed by Ho Chi Minh

September 6, 1945	Korea's independence proclaimed by Korean People's Republic
October 16, 1945	Syngman Rhee brought to Korea on U.S. military airplane
November 5, 1945	National Council of Labor Unions forms
December 8, 1945	National Federation of Peasant Unions forms
1945–1950	100,000 southern Koreans killed resisting U.S. occupation and nation's division
September 23, 1946	Busan railroad workers begin strike
October 1946	General strike/uprising in southern Korea against U.S. military government
October 2, 1946	U.S. tanks patrol Daegu; martial law declared

HOLLYWOOD ACCOUNTS OF World War II place the United States in the noble position of saving the world from Nazi crimes, of freeing Jews from the Holocaust, and of liberating Asians from Japanese aggression. Yet, the postwar order built by the United States failed to keep promises of self-determination and national independence. In Korea and Vietnam, the United States betrayed its former allies and fought bloody wars against them, extinguishing the lives of millions of people. Even before the war's end, the slaughter of innocents began. Although Japan had offered to negotiate terms of surrender as early as January 1945, the United States nonetheless insisted upon using nuclear weapons.[1] These were warnings to the Soviet Union—the first shots in the Cold War.[2] From 1945 to 1950, as many as a hundred thousand Koreans were killed while resisting the American imperial system in the southern half of the peninsula. Well before the official start of the Korean War in 1950, southern movements showed distinct stages of development: from the creation of a Korean People's Republic (KPR) in 1945, to autonomous workers' unions, farmers' associations, and women's organizations, to a massive general strike and popular uprising in 1946, armed insurrections in Jeju, Yosu and Sunchon in 1948 to stop the division of the country, to the guerrilla campaigns of 1949, and finally, when all else had failed to liberate the country from foreign power, to armed struggle of the entire nation to expel the Americans and overthrow those who served them. In each phase of the movement's development, American imperialism was uninhibited in applying greater amounts of violence to control the situation. In 1945, the United States prohibited the KPR and arrested its leaders. In 1946, they ordered police and U.S. troops to use firepower to break strikes and put down insurgent villagers. In 1948, American officers used right-wing paramilitary youth groups and the newly formed Korean Constabulary to suppress armed insurrections. In 1949, they organized massive suppression campaigns and mandated summary courts of execution to murder thousands of suspected partisans.

Finally in 1950, they called in the full weight of U.S. military power against the Korean people. Bombers flew thousands of bombing sorties from safe-rear areas in Japan that reduced cities to rubble, battleship barrages turned refugee columns into piles of flesh, and summary executions by the thousands were carried out in the name of freedom. To be sure, in all these endeavors, U.S. officials

After the defeat of the Yeosun Uprising in 1948, partisans regrouped and were arrested on Baekwoon Mountain. Photographer unknown

were assisted by Koreans all too eager to reap the benefits of their ties to imperial power—regardless of whether it was Japanese or American.

Japan-U.S. Collaboration

When World War II abruptly ended, geopolitical dislocations in Korea were so severe that Japanese and American forces conducted joint operations to suppress the autonomous People's Committees that sprang up everywhere to govern the country. Even before American troops landed in Korea, preparations were made for collaboration between U.S. "liberators" and Japanese forces. When the first contingent of American troops arrived to take control of Seoul, Japanese police lined the streets to protect them. Acting under U.S. General John Reed Hodge's order to prevent disturbances, they shot and killed two Koreans who came out to cheer the Americans' arrival. At the September 9 surrender ceremony, Hodge announced—to the horror of thousands of people—that all members of the colonial government would remain in power—including the Japanese governor-general.[3] As Korean resistance to the maintenance of imperial power intensified during the early weeks of the American occupation of southern Korea, combined American-Japanese units attacked demonstrations in Busan and elsewhere.[4]

Neither an aberration nor an accident, Japanese-American collaboration remains the chief characteristic of U.S. policy in Asia even under President Obama, involving the United States in a web of pain and unresolved grief from Japanese war crimes. As Chalmers Johnson reminded us, Japan never even acknowledged its deep-seated racism: "even defeat in war did not cause the Japanese to give up their legends of racial, economic, and cultural superiority . . . they never gave up their nationalist and racist convictions that in slaughtering over twenty million

Chinese and enslaving the Koreans they were actually engaged in liberating East Asians from the grip of Western imperialism."[5]

In 2007, the *New York Times* prominently featured a dated photo of then Japanese Prime Minister Abe Shinzo's grandfather, Kishi Nobusuke, playing golf with U.S. President Dwight Eisenhower and President George W. Bush's grandfather, Senator Prescott Bush. The *Times* failed to inform readers that Kishi spent three years in Sugamo Prison as a Class A war crimes suspect for his role in the kidnapping of thousands of non-Japanese laborers during World War II. Neither did the *Times* report that Prescott Bush's companies had worked for the Nazis, a role that brought him censure and fines. That photo speaks volumes about the postwar constellation of power in which the United States was the brightest star. In 2009, Japanese Prime Minister Taro Aso admitted for the first time that his family had used hundreds of Dutch, British, and Australian prisoners as slave labor in their mining company. These revelations came decades after the fact because proper investigations were never permitted in 1945. Within months of their surrender, Germany and Japan quickly changed into America's best friends. The transition occurred with such speed that by 1950, former allies Russia and China were the Cold War enemies of the United States.

Immediately after the defeat of the Japanese, popular anticapitalist and anticolonial movements were extremely powerful at the same moment as the United States had few reliable allies and only weak clients. They were compelled to bring Syngman Rhee to Korea from the United States to serve as president even though he had not set foot there for three decades. The U.S. government had not yet had time to launch its massive anti-Communist propaganda campaign, nor had Senator Joseph McCarthy begun his purges. Faced with a powerful GI movement to return home, the United States needed time to build its imperial domination. The United States therefore made concessions, allowing the Japanese to keep their emperor and not to undergo any kind of denazification. Socialists were briefly allowed in a coalition government, trade unions and the Communist Party were legalized as means to slow down mass struggles. Unfortunately, many leftists (including Korean communists) were caught off guard by the rapid shifts in their status, and they collaborated in popular fronts until the United States gained sufficient strength to toss them like a piece of trash.

Unlike Germany, which was compelled to denazify (albeit superficially), Japan was never made even to acknowledge its criminal actions. Indeed, when he was in office in 2007, Prime Minister Abe Shinzo repeatedly denied Japanese government involvement in the sexual slavery of more than two hundred thousand women during World War II.[6] Instead, he continued to visit Yasukuni shrine, where he paid homage to men normally regarded as criminals and unworthy of respect. Even after the U.S. House of Representatives demanded an apology in 2007, Abe refused.[7] In 2009, the "liberal" and "democratic" Japanese government continued to refuse to apologize,[8] instead maintaining these women were happy to be given "as gifts from the emperor to his loyal soldiers."[9]

With Japan's sudden surrender in 1945, Japanese troops remained in control of much of Asia. The Allies "temporarily" divided Korea and Vietnam to accept formally the transfer of power. The "Big Four" (United States, UK, USSR, and China) agreed to Russia getting control of northern Korea, China of northern Vietnam, the United States of southern Korea, and the UK of southern Vietnam (as far north as the sixteenth parallel, not the seventeenth, the dividing line in 1954 after the defeat of the French). American historians make Korea's division seem whimsical, even accidental. Given minutes to make a proposal to the Russians, U.S. Navy second lieutenant Dean Rusk quickly ascertained that the thirty-eighth parallel was as suitable a point of demarcation as any. When Stalin agreed, the die was cast. Sadly, the issue of unification has not been in the hands of Koreans ever since that fateful day in 1945. The line drawn in the sand at the thirty-eighth parallel was never intended to be permanent, merely a demarcation point for accepting the surrender of the Japanese military authorities who remained in place after the tragedies of Hiroshima and Nagasaki. These imaginary and temporary lines drawn by the victorious forces of democracy would cost the lives of more than five million human beings in two major battles of the Cold War. If the United States had not intervened to divide Korea, the country would have been spared destruction, millions of lives would have been saved, and the country would probably today resemble parts of northeast China.

Even before World War II had ended, the U.S. Office of Strategic Services (forerunner of the CIA) called for the maintenance of colonial regimes in Asia. It was inevitable that indigenous people would refuse to accept that fate, that they would fight backroom decisions made by learned experts in London and Washington whose primary consideration was Anglo-American interests—not those of Vietnamese, Koreans, Cambodians, Laotians, and Chinese.

Near the end of World War II, the United States had agreed in Potsdam that the great powers, "mindful of the enslavement of the people of Korea, are determined that in due course Korea shall become free and independent." Koreans took these promises to heart and organized their own independent forms of government before U.S. troops arrived. Rather than embracing grassroots organs of power created directly by Koreans, the United States suppressed them and instead established a new colonial government—the U.S. Army Military Government in Korea (USAMGIK). Japanese-friendly police officers, judges, and jailers, were all integrated into the Korean support apparatus of the U.S. military government. Many Japanese were never even asked to change their offices in the old Japanese headquarters.

Within weeks of the war's end, the United States enlisted the assistance of Japanese troops against indigenous resistance in China, Vietnam, and Korea—even before the terms of Japan's surrender could be signed. American OSS agent 019, better known by his pseudonym Ho Chi Minh, emerged from the mountains of Vietnam to find himself isolated by the very powers with whom he had fought against Japan. Ho had provided the United States with valuable information on Japanese ships and troop movements during the war. When he learned of Japan's surrender to the Allies, he immediately encouraged his starving people to seize rice stocks, and all over the country, people rose up in a *khoi nghia*, an uprising of the whole people. Thinking he still had the ear of Washington, Ho wrote multiple telegrams to President Truman in 1945 begging him to make Vietnam "a protectorate of the United States like Puerto Rico" (an entreaty made to rid Vietnam of French, British, Chinese, and Japanese occupiers). Ho never received a reply, but allied intentions were clear enough when the British Royal Air Force and Japanese planes strafed and bombed the Viet Minh, chasing them out of Saigon.

While in Korea, Japanese police officials and bureaucrats served the U.S. military government, in China, Japanese troops helped Americans guard Kuomintang railroad supply routes. If any of these facts come as a surprise, it is only because for decades they have been so carefully buried beneath repetition *ad nauseam* of the U.S. role as liberator of Asia. Like Ho Chi Minh, Kim Il-sung had fought on the side of the Allies. As did every Korean farmer who spotted an airplane high in the skies, Kim identified U.S. planes as "good" planes, while Japanese planes were the "enemy." One Japanese police report from November 1944 placed Kim Il-sung near Vladivostok, where he "is preparing to dispatch agents to important points along the Korean-Manchurian border area in order to destroy railroads in coordination with the air raids of the United States Air Force in the same area."[10] A U.S. intelligence source corroborates this information when it wrote that Kim and a few hundred guerrillas under his leadership were in the general area of Khabarovsk where they had gone because of the "threat of extinction" at the hands of the Japanese.[11]

Common sense may tell us that the U.S. architecture of power changed Asia greatly, but the continuities between Japanese and U.S. rule in Korea and Vietnam are more salient than their differences. In the post–World War II transition, Koreans who served Japan as policemen and army officers were quickly integrated into American units, so much so that 80 percent of policemen and government workers simply went from Japanese pay to American pay.[12] The United States took over prisons, military bases, and government offices, including the former Japanese headquarters, which the United States put to the same uses as had Japan—to suppress protests, strikes, and all opposition to its military government. Two years after "liberation," the U.S. military government had actually locked away more political activists than had the Japanese. Whereas there were 17,000 prisoners in 1945, by October 1947 the number stood at 21,458. If there is any doubt who was in charge, "Both police and constabulary were under the high level command of American officers."[13] Moreover, some 85 percent of the police were well known as sadistic torturers and brutal enforcers of Japanese rule.[14]

Japan's Biological Warfare Unit

In the new postwar international order, former Nazi and Japanese officials and Axis collaborators were hired by the United States throughout the world. Instead of facing imprisonment or worse, Nazi intelligence agents, German rocket scientists, and Japanese experts in biological warfare happily became American agents. None of these nefarious transitions is more sinister than United States embracing Japanese biological warfare experts from Unit 731 of the Japanese Imperial Army. While former U.S. allies like Ho Chi Minh and Kim Il-sung became outcasts, erstwhile Japanese war criminals were made into multimillionaire pharmaceutical executives and distinguished professors with American help. In exchange, they provided the United States with valuable technical data gleaned from criminal experiments.

Of all those involved with Unit 731, the most notorious is Colonel Ishii Shiro. Ishii personally oversaw wartime biological weapons experimentation on thousands of prisoners—including American, Chinese, and British prisoners. Never in danger of being punished by the victorious Allies, Ishii received all expense paid junkets to the United States (and during the Korean War to South Korea). For the rest of his life, he was granted honor and prosperity (as were other members of Unit 731).[15] In exchange for the secret details of his research programs, including thousands of slides and dozens of interviews, Col. Ishii and his fellow war criminals were granted immunity in 1946 by General Douglas MacArthur. In 1947, they were again promised protection from all prosecution by high-ranking U.S. government officials.[16]

American POW's who survived Ishii's germ warfare experiments were compelled by U.S. officers to sign affidavits promising to keep secret the details of their imprisonment. They were banned from publicly describing daily injections of germ agents or the murder of hundreds of their fellow prisoners. When the U.S. Congress attempted to investigate Ishii's handiwork, boxes of files detailing Unit 731's activities were mysteriously sent back to Japan by the U.S. military before investigators could peruse them. Subsequently, in a "complete search of HQ files" an aide to MacArthur assured investigators that there was nothing in the files about Japanese biological warfare.[17]

Professor Mori Masataka researched biowarfare for more than a decade, conducting site visits in a dozen parts of China. He concluded that Japan's biowar unit killed more than 270,000 Chinese during the war. Although the United States investigated Unit 731 four times between August 1945 and December 1947, each investigation conveyed immunity to men whose actions were clearly criminal.[18] Rather than condemning Ishii and Co., General Douglas MacArthur was convinced that "Japan's germ warfare research is of great significance to U.S. national security . . . if the U.S. brings them to trial, other countries will learn [their secrets]." After the final investigation, U.S. officer Edwin Hill commented, "We cannot get this information in our labs." As a result, rather than bringing members of Unit 731 to trial as war criminals, the United States protected them to use their expertise.

Looking back, we may wonder why the United States empowered the very same Japanese men who had cost so many soldiers and sailors their lives. Then, as now, one answer can be found in generalized ignorance among U.S. policymakers. High-ranking U.S. government operative Gregory Henderson tell us that when the State Department civil-affairs units arrived in Korea, they had trained for duty in the Philippines (in some cases for Japan) and had "no more than an hour's lecture on Korea."[19] Thrust into world leadership in 1945, President Truman admitted openly he knew "next to nothing" about Asia. His small coterie of Europeanist advisors steered him to fight Communism at all costs—especially in France. That is why former allies in French Indochina like Ho Chi Minh were quickly branded as enemy agents, against whom Japanese troops and planes were brought to bear. Despite a mountain of evidence pointing to U.S. ignorance, it would be wrong to accept that problem alone as the cause of subsequent events. A number of pertinent questions arise: Why was Korea divided and not Japan? After all, the Russians had happily split Berlin even though they alone had captured it. Why didn't the United States rule Japan in conjunction with the rest of the Allies? Behind the scenes, powerful forces were at work, most importantly, the United States' willfulness to impose its own interests on Asia.

United States publicity contrasted markedly with its surreptitious intentions. On March 20, 1946, the United States publicly maintained its support for Korean independence and pledged to cooperate with the Soviets to bring about the country's self-determination. Yet at the same time, a high-ranking U.S. member of the Joint Soviet-U.S. Commission wrote a more forthright confidential memorandum: "In the American view, freedom from Russian domination is more important than complete independence . . . it is not believed to be in the U.S. interests to form a Korean Government which could be granted complete independence in the next few years."[20] Given this policy objective, is it any wonder that the talks of the joint commission quickly broke down?

By January 1947, George Marshall, whose name became an adjective for U.S. postwar reconstruction of Europe, was explicit about Korea's role. He directed his subordinates to: "Please have plan drafted of policy to organize a definite government of So. Korea and *connect up* its economy with that of Japan."[21] The next year, a confidential internal State Department memo from George Kennan, one of the chief architects of the Cold War, was clear about basic U.S. interests: "We have about 50 percent of the world's wealth but only 6.3 percent of its population . . . Our real task in the coming period is to devise a pattern of relationships which will permit us to maintain this position of disparity without positive detriment to our national security."[22] Within the constellation of U.S. imperial planning, Greece and Korea were assigned similar positions as outposts for containment of Communism—and they quickly became arenas within which brutal and bloody conflicts were fought. Despite vastly different cultural and geographic conditions, Greece and Korea's wars involved strikingly similar tactics, which became models for subsequent U.S. "peacekeeping" missions from Vietnam to Iraq.

As they had done on March 1, 1919, Koreans created a broad national consensus that peacefully sought national independence. When the United States ignored their aspirations for independence and instead empowered former Japanese collaborators, mammoth uprisings broke out in 1946 and 1948. No one expected that the slaughter of thousands of people would be the U.S. answer.

Formation of the Korean People's Republic

On September 6, 1945, only four days after Ho Chi Minh declared Vietnam independent, hundreds of independence activists (perhaps a thousand in all) gathered at the Gyeonggi Girls High School and proclaimed the existence of the Korean People's Republic (KPR). Korean tradition of communal action inhibited any one person from proclaiming the republic. As had occurred on March 1, 1919, many different groups together made the proclamation. By consensus, the delegates selected eighty-seven leaders, fifty-five of whom (including both Kim Il-sung and Syngman Rhee) were appointed to the new government's highest body pending general elections. On September 8, the new government's newspaper, *Korean People's Newspaper*, called for the necessity of "a social revolution as a second liberation."[23] Ten days later, the KPR announced its program: "We are determined to demolish Japanese imperialism, its residuary influences, antidemocratic factions, reactionary elements, and undesirable foreign influence in our state, and to establish our complete autonomy and independence, thereby anticipating the realization of an authentically democratic state."[24]

The new government called for lands to be given to those who worked them, "complete emancipation of women," an eight-hour day for workers, an end to child labor, an end to illiteracy, nationalization of major industries and banks, and a major program of rapid industrialization. It promised freedoms of speech, assembly, and religion, and expressed a desire for "close cooperation with the USA, USSR, England, and China" while simultaneously promising to oppose any undue foreign influences. They also promised to advance the cause of world peace.[25]

The KPR platform united a broad spectrum of leaders and reflected the basic ingredients of the kind of government Korean people wanted. Yo Un-Hyoung (여운형), its key organizer, had been part of the Shanghai-based Korean Provisional Government founded in the aftermath of the 1919 uprising. During the early 1930s, Yo spent more than three years in Japanese prisons in Daejon. Once he was released, he launched a daily newspaper in Seoul. In 1944, he anticipated Japan's eventual defeat and founded the underground National Construction League to prepare for Korean independence. By mid-1945, the organization had grown to around ten thousand members.[26] Nearly lynched in October 1946 (during the October rising), he was murdered by rightists in July 1947.

When he first arrived in Korea in early September 1945, U.S. military Governor-General John Reed Hodge insisted the country was a powder keg, but it did not explode then. Rather, the KPR tried time and again to contact Hodge, to work with him, to keep the peace. Hodge knew Koreans wanted independence, and their leaders believed American promises of self-determination. When the U.S. military government conducted an opinion poll of 8,453 Koreans in August 1946, the results were clear. Unification was seen by 71 percent of the respondents as a prerequisite for the formation of a government. Fully 70 percent preferred socialism and 7 percent communism, while only 14 percent favored capitalism, and 8 percent were noncommittal.[27] With 18 percent of the farmland and more than 90 percent of Korea's industrial infrastructure having been in the hands of the Japanese, the basis of a communitarian economy had already been prepared.

While in the eyes of ordinary people, the promise of peace and prosperity was quite clear, Governor-General Hodge pushed ahead with the U.S. plan—he took all former Japanese properties as U.S. property and refused to recognize as legitimate the Shanghai-based Provisional Government and the newly organized KPR, both of which his American advisors (as well as latter-day annalists) discounted without reason. Gregory Henderson subsequently derided Koreans for their "lack of any parliamentary tradition."[28] He claimed that in 1945, "Korea had almost no groups able to establish meaningful platforms and objectives for themselves ... no one knew what to unite around."[29] Bruce Cumings similarly states that, "Within weeks after liberation, it was apparent that Korea lacked the very requisites of political order."[30] Yet, contrary to these assertions, within days of Japan's defeat, Korean people had organized a new government with a clear program and widespread popular support. According to Merrell Benninghoff, a key member of the U.S. occupation authority, members of the KPR "consider themselves the new government; they released political prisoners, and assumed responsibility for public safety, food distribution, and other government functions."[31]

All over the country, People's Committees (PCs) sprang up and operated as a de facto government in all but seven of the 123 counties in southern Korea. Hundreds of PCs arose as if out of thin air. Bruce Cumings wondered, "How is such a phenomenon to be understood? How could it happen so fast?"[32] The explosion of People Power meant that by December 1945, more than 2,546 PCs formed at various levels of villages, districts, counties, cities, and provinces as part of a new government from the grassroots.[33] In addition, more than one thousand new labor unions were formed, giving rise to the National Council of Korean Labor Unions (*Chonpyong*) with over five hundred thousand members.[34] In the northern provinces, the PCs were even more significant since the Russians happily let them manage day-to-day affairs. On October 15, delegates from all over the country converged in Pyongyang and mandated immediate direct elections at the village level, where village elders had selected many delegates. The newly elected local leaders were then to elect representatives to the next level, and so on until a national government would be formed. For decades, anti-Communist ideologues portrayed the northern zone as under the Russian boot despite robust empirical data documenting the PCs democratic self-governing reality.[35] The PCs were vehicles for expression of people's will and desire, of freedom to choose. All sectors were involved in these PCs—except for people who had collaborated with the Japanese. In the sixty-one counties where these PCs governed, they collected taxes, controlled the police; some organized a census and created armed defense units.

Autonomous organizations of workers, women, students, scientists, writers, and farmers emerged from the grassroots and were endorsed by the KPR. By 1946, some thirty-five such broad organizations worked as parallel structures with the KPR through democratically elected national coordinating bodies.[36] These organizations included a Writers' Alliance, Scientists' Alliance, National Women's Union, and Democratic Youth Federation.

On November 5, 1945, within only a few months of Japan's surrender, labor unions united under the umbrella of the National Council of Korean Trade Unions (*Chonpyong*), and a month later, on December 8, 1945, the National Federation of Peasant Unions formed. A few months after its founding, *Chonpyong* had more than half a million members, 223 offices, and 1,757 local unions.[37] In the countryside, farmers formed People's Committees and unions from the grassroots. One estimate was that by November—a scant three months after the Japanese capitulation when the farmers' union first formed at the national level—3,322,937 people belonged to it in 25,288 villages, 1,745 districts, and 188 counties.[38] This remarkable capacity for self-organization demonstrated Koreans' pent-up desire for more power in determining their destiny. Even those who overemphasize the role of communists in forming these groups still acknowledge the overwhelmingly popular character of an "associational explosion."[39] The movement sprang from the grassroots; it was not until September 8, 1945, that Park Hon-yong led a meeting in Seoul to reconstitute the Korean Communist Party. Hoping to enlist U.S. support for Korean democracy, Park met Hodge on October 27, 1945, and advised him to remove pro-Japanese officials. Despite his willingness to meet incoming American officials, Park was continually rebuffed.

Instead of working with indigenous leaders, the United States imported Syngman Rhee, using a plane reserved for Douglas MacArthur. Rhee was introduced at his first press conference by Hodge, who immediately called for new political parties to step forward. Soon, more than fifty political parties registered with the new military authorities. Among them was the Korean Democratic Party, commonly known to represent collaborators seeking to avoid punishment. The party was characterized by U.S. intelligence sources as "composed predominantly of large landowners and wealthy businessmen."[40] Despite—or should I say because of—its own intelligence estimates of this group's character, the United States adopted it as its main liaison. At the same time, USAMGIK refused to cooperate with the KPR, but sent U.S. troops to confront it. One of the first such incidents occurred on October 24, 1945, in Namwon, North Jeolla, when U.S. troops forcibly took control of Japanese property being administered by the Namwon People's Committee.

As Japanese owners and managers left the country to return home, Korean workers took over factories and ran them autonomously. Two months after the Japanese surrender, U.S. officials found forty-two of South Jeolla Province's fifty factories running smoothly.[41] In Jeju and Busan, arriving Americans found that workers' councils were running numerous factories successfully. All over the country, factories quickly resumed production at levels sometimes exceeding those of their time under Japanese control. Altogether, somewhere between one and two million workers were involved in these councils and were one of the most important sources of support for the KPR.[42] Political issues, not just economic ones, keenly activated workers, and they continually went into the streets to express their views. Between August 1945 and March 1947—that is, under the U.S. occupation government—there were at least 2,388 workers' demonstrations involving six hundred thousand people.[43] In factories where Korean owners remained in place, strikes were widespread. On August 31 at a Chongson textile factory owned by the Kim brothers, over a thousand workers went on strike.

Buttressed by the release of more than ten thousand political prisoners from Japanese jails—the first of whom were freed on August 16, 1945—and by the demobilization of fifteen thousand young men from the Japanese army, the new progressive forces in the country constituted a clear majority. This explains why Hodge perceived the situation to be a "powder keg ready to explode." As Hodge moved against the PCs, he used violence once again in Namwon. On November

15, Hodge ordered the arrest of five leaders of the PC. When hundreds protested, at least two people were killed and many injured by American bayonets.[44] Five days later, at the Congress of People's Committees on November 20, 1945, 650 delegates from 25 cities and 175 regions of the South call for the immediate and full transfer of administrative power from the U.S. military government to the People's Committees.

The U.S. response came in December. On the eighth, the military government banned strikes; on the twelfth, the United States outlawed the People's Committees and the KPR, declaring them to be "public enemies."[45] On the eighteenth, Hodge decided to form a Korean Constabulary with a nucleus of Koreans who had served in the Japanese Imperial Army. U.S. officials were convinced that their actions thereby "uprooted" the "popularly based government." [46] Subsequent events would prove the Americans sadly mistaken. Although a U.S. colonel was governor in each province, the PCs held real power. On December 8, 1945, at a Seoul meeting for the founding of the National League of Peasant Unions in which some 239 farmers unions sent 545 representatives, a representative from South Jeolla told how people followed the instructions of the local People's Committee—not the district officials.

Clearly the United States underestimated people's resolve to fight for their country's independence. On March 1, 1946, celebrations of the Korean independence movement built to a bigger action on June 27, when up to half a million people marched in Seoul against the U.S. military government.[47] On May 23, the United States closed border crossings, effectively dividing the country. As they stepped up their campaign against the South's leftists, Park Hon-yong and several key organizers went to the North.

Under the U.S. military government, the country's living conditions deteriorated quickly. Within a year, as Americans expelled workers councils from factories they were running and took control of all Japanese assets away from the KPR, more than a million people could not find work, half of them in the Gyeongsangs.[48] Even among those with jobs, like railway workers, desperate times had descended upon them. Many were unable even to provide sufficient rice for the family dinner table. Inflation sapped the purchasing power of ordinary people. Within a year of American "assistance," the military government estimated that rice was a hundred times more expensive than prior to their arrival. In Seoul, prices rose even more—by 3000 percent, as illustrated in FIGURE 3.1. Another index, using 1936 prices as a base, established a level of 58,305 by 1947.[49]

The shortage of food was not caused by an insufficient amount of rice in the country but by political factors—especially the license given by USAMGIK to police to collect the harvest. Even though the Japanese had starved Koreans for years to extract more rice for themselves, after the arrival of the Americans, rice collections were as bad, or even worse, than under the Japanese. Americans found significant quantities of rice in policemen's homes; in Daegu a warehouse of rice was in the hands of a right-wing youth group.[50] Most importantly, huge amounts of rice were being smuggled to Japan everyday by government agents who sought to enrich themselves.

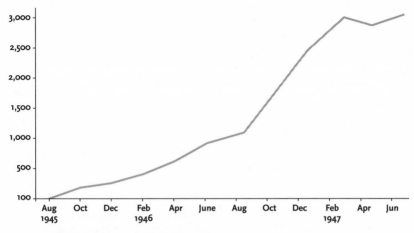

FIGURE 3.1 **Wholesale Prices in Seoul, 1945–1947**

Leading up to the fall of 1946, eighty-one police stations and twenty-three government offices were attacked by local residents unwilling to be strong-armed any longer into quietly accepting hunger, disease, and foreign domination.[51] On August 15, 1946, Hwasun coal miners were fired upon by U.S. troops, and at least seven people were killed. As the unrest continued, tanks and bayonets were used against miners facing starvation with winter approaching.[52] On September 6, the Americans issued arrest warrants for Park Hon-Yong, Lee Chu-ha, and Lee Kang-guk, three key organizers of the Communist Party (조선공산당). Activists in the Gyeongsang region, long a significant force, had already been severely repressed. On August 23, all twenty-eight members of the Yongju PC had been arrested, as had thirty-five people in Bosong. So loud were subsequent cries of torture emanating from the Daegu police station, that reporters dared to inquire the source of them. "Drug addicts," they were told.[53]

To compound the misery people were compelled to endure, a cholera epidemic broke out. By October 1, it had taken nearly ten thousand lives, more than half in the two Gyeongsang provinces. Rather than move resources to help people deal with these emergencies, Hodge and his coterie of officers sent guns to the police and encouraged them to stop protests. Even with new and better arms allotted to them, more often than not, the police could not maintain order, so U.S. troops were assigned to assist them. U.S. Cold War concerns to crack down on dissent lest the Russians exploit it were clearly more important than the everyday needs of ordinary Koreans.

The 1946 October Uprising: From General Strike to Farmers' Revolt

During the Vietnam War, as the United States pulverized "free-fire zones" with more bombs than dropped by all sides during World War II, Henry Kissinger famously remarked that, "all societies have their breaking points." His tragic misunderstanding of history would cost the lives of tens of thousands of U.S. soldiers and many times that of innocent Vietnamese. Breaking points may well

TABLE 3.1 **Cholera Reports as of Midnight, October 1, 1946**

Province	Total Cases	Total Deaths
North Kyongsang	4,896	4,025
South Kyongsang	2,744	1,277
North Jeolla	2,380	1,591
Gyeonggi	1,232	775
South Chuongchong	1,103	636
Jeju	741	390
South Jeolla	734	429
Kangwon	354	187
North Chuongchong	296	134
Seoul	242	83
Total	**14,772**	**9,527**

Source: HQ, USAMGIK, Department of Public Information, press releases, October 4, 1946. Item Number 8 as reported in Thomas H. Lee, "The Origins of the Taegu Insurrection of 1946," (Thesis, Harvard University, 1990), 55.

exist, but if they do, it is not to submit to superior force, no matter how powerful it may be, but to rise against oppression—if not today, then tomorrow or the next day. The indomitable human spirit, easily calmed by a modicum of comfort and regulation, refuses to remain quiet in the face of intolerable situations, highest among which are hunger and disease, precisely the conditions brought to Korea by American "liberation." It should not then have come as a surprise when the entire zone under the control of the U.S. military government rose up less than a year after the Japanese surrender.

The 1946 October Uprising was the most significant armed popular movement since *Tonghak*. Official U.S. Army history called it "out-and-out revolt in South Korea."[54] For journalist Mark Gayn, then in Korea, the events marked "a full-scale revolution, which must have involved hundreds of thousands, if not millions of people."[55] If not for U.S. Army intervention, the uprising would have toppled the Seoul administration and instated the KPR as the sole government. By the time the shooting stopped, hundreds of ordinary Koreans had been killed and thousands more wounded and arrested. Kang Man-gil counted over 300 dead, more than 3,600 missing, 26,000 wounded, and 15,000 arrested.[56] Gi-wook Shin estimated that about 1,000 people and 200 police were killed, and 30,000 citizens arrested.[57] *Chonpyong* reported more than 11,000 of its members had been arrested. Tallying up the exact number of casualties is no easy matter since estimates vary so widely. American OSS agent Stewart Meacham counted 500 dead in two months (including 59 Daegu police) and a total of 8,000 arrests, of which 5,540 were in the Gyeongsangs alone. At least sixteen people were sentenced to death.[58] Ingeborg Göthel reported that altogether, as many as 7,000 people were killed and 22,000 patriots languished in prison by the summer of 1947.[59]

Amazingly, no U.S. casualties occurred—remarkable testament to the self-discipline and organization of the protests. The PC leadership still retained hopes the Americans would see the light of day and hand over power to the KPR, so they passed the word not to kill U.S. soldiers—and people listened. No greater testament to the incipient government's legitimacy can be given than the remarkable discipline exhibited as insurgents nationwide refrained from attacking Americans. At the same time, hatred of the police ran so deep that even the hospitals in Daegu refused to treat them and did not—until ordered to do so at the point of U.S. gun barrels.

The uprisings should have spelled the end of Hodge's rule as governor-general of Korea since his policies had clearly failed. Yet American power firmly backed him, especially after he sent a telegram to MacArthur on October 28 pointing to "evidence" that the Russians were poised to invade the South after the harvest.[60] Whether or not U.S. commanders believed that the Russians were coming, their troops fought like they were already in such a war. The American director of the Department of Transportation, whose position situated him to hear nationwide reports, characterized the U.S. role: "We went into that situation just like we would go into battle. We were out to break that thing up and we didn't have time to worry if a few innocent people got hurt. We set up concentration camps outside town and held strikers there when the jails got too full. It was war. We recognized it as war. And that is the way we fought it."[61]

Without U.S. troops, the KPR would have been swept back into power. U.S. suppression of the uprisings was centrally coordinated, but the insurgencies, all in support of the KPR and the PCs, spread spontaneously. What began as a strike by railroad workers became a general strike and then turned into an armed rural insurrection of proletarianized farmers.

The uprising began on September 23, 1946, when some eight thousand railroad workers in Busan stayed home and declared a strike for higher wages, daily pay, job security, and larger rice rations.[62] Nearly all the city's students immediately joined the strikers. That afternoon, a thousand railroad workers in Daegu also went out. The next day, railroad workers in Seoul, Daejon, Daegu, Incheon, Gwangju, and Sunchon—at least thirty thousand in all—walked off their jobs. Significantly, Busan workers' innocent demands were transformed into a political strike against U.S. occupation. National demands were formulated, calling for an immediate end to the terror inflicted by the USAMGIK, release of political prisoners, higher rations of food, and dismissal of all government and police workers who had collaborated with Japanese colonialism. Most importantly, they also called for land reform, nationalization of industry, and the transfer of power to the People's Committees.[63]

Chonpyong called for a general strike, and very soon, over 250,000 workers (some sources say as many as 330,000) went out on strike—chemical workers, textile workers, communications, print workers, and farmers. Across the country, citizens rallied around the strikers, who were joined by even right-wing unions. Students boycotted the lectures of reactionary professors, and many others went on strike to support the workers. In Seoul, 295 companies experienced strikes in which nearly 50,000 workers and students participated (30,000 laborers, 6,000 office workers, 16,000 students, and 300 professors). While the leadership of the KPR, PCs, and workers' and farmers' unions were significant, this movement was nothing short of a new March 1 rising of the whole people. Everywhere people stopped whatever it was they did on a daily basis to participate in a nationwide movement for independence and justice. In all the major cities, people went into the streets by the thousands to protest. As a general strike ensued, some two million people took part. It was a massive action against the division of the country, the retention of reactionary, pro-Japanese forces by the USA, and hunger.

With hunger rampant, rice was a central focus of protests. A petition to General John Reed Hodge requested a minimal rice ration per person—a demand repeated by all strikers. In the beginning, protests generally remained peaceful, except at Seoul's Yongsan Station, where two police and two strikers were killed in a sudden confrontation that was only quieted through 1,400 arrests.[64]

On the morning of October 1 in Daegu, a group of three hundred people, including many women and children, marched in front of City Hall to demand higher rations of rice. As in many parts of Korea, Japanese administrators remained there to work for the Americans. The USAMGIK also rehired former police officers, even those whom had been driven from office as a result of their brutality during the Japanese occupation. Police were the only ones legally allowed to carry firearms. In a city where the radical Left was well organized, the U.S. military government ruled Daegu as though they were in a "hostile country."[65] Try though they did, the Americans were unable to dismantle the Daegu PC.

Leading this fifth demonstration against hunger in Daegu was a large women's contingent from the Chosun Communist Party (CCP). The number of protesters swelled to about a thousand. Some time after people began to disperse, several thousand students, chanting slogans against U.S. imperialism, assembled in solidarity with striking workers, about five hundred of whom remained at the protest. Police moved in to disperse the crowd, and in the ensuing scuffles, at least one worker was shot and killed.

The next day, thousands of people—led by students from the region's medical school—walked peacefully in a makeshift funeral procession. They stopped at the central police station, where a lone U.S. major, John Plezia, kept them from going inside. As soon as Plezia left to inform his superiors about the standoff, the young crowd surged inside and captured dozens of policemen (including the chief) as well as firearms and ammunition. In intense fighting, at least thirty-eight police and forty-eight protesters were killed and sixty-three others injured.[66] U.S. intelligence reports described what happened next: "For a number of hours, Daegu was under mob rule. Roaming bands of rioters attacked outlying police stations under cover of the general disorder in front of the main police station. Policemen were attacked and killed in their homes. Homes of military government officials (Koreans) and of police officials were wrecked by rioters."[67]

Once the police had been overpowered, U.S. troops of the Sixth Infantry Division were called in to enforced martial law. While U.S. tanks asserted their control over the city, the turmoil spread to outlying towns and districts in North Gyeongsang Province, and from there to other parts of the country. On October 3, some ten thousand people overpowered the police in Yeongcheon. During the two days in which residents controlled the town, they executed especially vicious police, ruthless landlords, and pro-Japanese officials. Without the arrival of U.S. troops, the town would have remained in the hands of insurgents for even longer.[68] In Pohang and Gyeongju, demonstrators burned government buildings and homes of the very rich. USAMGIK declared martial law. In Jeonju, police fire killed twenty people—including many women and children.[69] On October 6, a report claimed more than sixty people were shot dead in Daegu.[70] In Kaesong, at least twenty demonstrators were killed by police gunfire. Henderson tells us the number was more likely double that.[71]

People in Gyeongju, Pochong, Waegwan, Gimcheon, and Uiseong were able to seize significant amounts of rice and to destroy tax records. A short distance north of Daegu in Naksong-dong Tabu, two thousand people, none of them armed with firearms, took over the police station on the morning of October 3. They overran a warehouse where local produce had been taken by the government, and more than 100 bags of rice and 1,335 bags of wheat were divided up among people. In Sonsan on October 5, a crowd with stones attacked rice stores guarded by U.S. troops, and two people were killed by U.S. gunfire.[72]

All over the South, people rose up and were suppressed by American troops and tanks. U.S. reinforcements were rushed in from Seoul to restore order. In reports back to Hodge, American officers noted disturbances in more than sixty other towns and villages in North Gyeongsang. By October 6, Hodge declared martial law throughout all of North Gyeongsang Province.

The next day, fresh upsurges were reported throughout South Gyeongsang Province. In Jinju on October 7, four civilians were killed when U.S. troops opened fire on a crowd seeking rice. In Masan, police and forty U.S. troops opened fire on a hungry crowd of six thousand, killing at least eight people and wounding dozens.[73] One American sergeant wrote President Truman a personal letter to make sure the chief executive knew the situation. In his words: "Our entire battalion patrolled that town all day (Masan) with dead bodies lying all over the streets, and we kept our machine guns blasting."[74] Later on October 7, two protesters were killed in Namji, near Masan. After 24 policemen and strikers were killed in Busan in a confrontation on October 9, U.S. troops reinforced the police. In Hadong near Busan, hundreds of farmers with bamboo spears attacked police over a three-day period. One of the group's leaflets explained, "It is not that we hate the police, but that we are ready to die for the independence of the fatherland . . . Let us transfer all power to the people."[75] On October 11 in Ungcheon, police and U.S. soldiers killed at least five citizens. Further to the north in South Chungcheong and Gyeonggi-do, the U.S. Seventh Infantry Division stepped in when police were unable to maintain control. Other places where U.S. troops were involved in the suppression of the 1946 movement include Uiryeong, Kaesong, Paekchon, and Hapdeok. While this list of U.S. interventions seems extensive, it is by no means complete.

The fighting spread to nearby Yeongcheon county, where ten thousand people seized power and killed about twenty people maintained in power by USAMGIK. People had never been permitted to publicly express grievances against former Japanese collaborators, and the U.S. military government permitted no mechanisms of legal retribution, so direct action increasingly became the vehicle to enact a modicum of justice. Thousands of people in Uiseong took over the county government, and in Waegwan, two thousand people overran the police station, killed the chief, and wrecked homes of Japanese collaborators. In Hwanjung, four hundred people took the warehouse and helped themselves to rice, while others burned records of rice and grain collections.[76]

On October 8, after two weeks of strikes among the country's railroad workers, negotiations began between workers' representatives and the USAMGIK's Department of Transportation officials. *Nochong*, a yellow union (a union that is loyal to the employers) that had formed on March 10, 1946, with U.S. encouragement, called on strikers to return to work and publicly offered to settle the entire strike—at the same time as *Chonpyong* leaders had either been arrested or were being hunted by the police. On the day negotiations began, about a thousand Daegu railroad workers returned to their jobs. Two weeks later, the USAMGIK announced an agreement providing increased rice rations and better pay, as well a few other benefits.[77] Against the wishes of imprisoned and underground *Chonpyong* leaders, *Nochong* unionists worked collaboratively with USAMGIK to conclude the strike. With its new legitimacy in the eyes of the country's American rulers, *Nochong* quickly became the leading force in the union movement.[78] By June 1948, *Nochong* could count 448 unions and 108,239 members in its ranks, while *Chonpyong*, which at its high point counted 1,194 branches and nearly 500,000 members, included only 24 unions and barely 5,000 members.

Urban workers may have returned to their jobs, but in the countryside, the flame of uprisings continued to burn out of anyone's control. In Haenam on October 11, 54 farmers were killed and 357 arrested, while the police suffered ten killed, along with 28 other rightists.[79] On October 17, disturbances were reported in South Chungcheong Province, and U.S. troops intervened in Myeongcheon, Yesan, and Hapdeok. From the Gyeongsangs, the movement spread to South Jeolla, where remarkable numbers of people rose up against the government in two-thirds of all counties during the first half of November—one estimate was that sixty-five thousand participants were involved.[80] By October 31, the unrest spread to almost all of South Jeolla, where it continued until late November. In the first two weeks, more than fifty towns there experienced riots, the majority led by farmers armed with hoes, spears, clubs, rocks—anything they could find to fight the police. In Naju on October 31, thousands of people marched; two U.S. C-47 cargo planes buzzed the crowd. When they refused to disperse, soldiers of the Twentieth Infantry opened fire, killing ten people. A telephone operators' strike in Mokpo was similarly dispersed: U.S. troops drove wildly through the crowd, injuring many. In Imsong, police fired into a protest of six hundred people. In Hwasun on the same day, three thousand miners, in a march that included hundreds of starving women with young children, set off in the direction of Gwangju to protest their unemployment and hunger, but they were turned back by U.S. forces led by Col. Peake. The next day, police in Youngsanpo killed five people when some three thousand protesters advanced on the police station.[81] On November 3, police killed five people who had helped burn grain collection records in Hwanjung. Police killed at least twenty people in Puan, Naju, and Hampyeong.

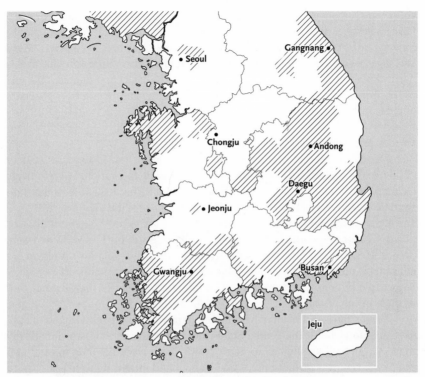

FIGURE 3.2 **Uprisings from September to December 1946 in Southern Korea**
Source: Cumings, *Origins*, 1:353.

On November 4, Col. Peake and at least a dozen U.S. soldiers went back to Hwasun from Gwangju to arrest the leaders of the miners' strike. When they attempted to take five prisoners away, more than a thousand people blocked the road and destroyed two U.S. Jeeps. The convoy then simply drove through the crowd, killing three people and injuring thirty-three.[82] On November 20 in Joseongri, police killed six people.

By the time it had run its course, the uprising had become national in scope. In eight weeks, more than 214 insurgent groups launched attacks in the American zone. Of these incidents, at least 35 involved more than a thousand people.[83] By the end of the year, people in forty counties—comprising 30 percent of the southerners—had risen up. From October 1 to November 20, U.S. Army Intelligence tabulated at least 214 protests—including 140 in both Gyeongsangs and 59 in South Jeolla.[84] Sociologist Gi-wook Shin estimated that 2.3 million people took part in the uprisings, and he observed that, "Although the urban strike initiated the action, peasants transformed the strike into a major uprising . . . By the end of 1946 some forty counties, or about 30 percent of South Korean counties, witnessed peasant uprisings."[85]

While the movement spread spontaneously across the country, in many cases, people's actions were remarkably similar. Besides meting out justice to former Japanese collaborators, attacks focused on destroying records of rice collections, much as they had in rural areas during the French Revolution, when farmers systematically burned records of debts that had trapped their families for generations.[86] According to official U.S. sources describing the Jeollas: "Mobs [sic] destroyed all official records that they could get their hands on, and this is particularly true of rice and grain collection records. In fact in some cases the sole purpose of attacks on police stations and city halls seems to have been to secure and destroy these records."[87]

Causes and Consequences of the October Uprising

Some analysts, searching for the causes of the uprising, focused on hunger, cholera, unemployment, and other socio-economic indications. Surely these were major issues, particularly the cholera epidemic that took at least ten thousand lives. (Although clearly significant, Cumings seems not to be aware of this.) The high rate of joblessness and terrible inflation sapped everyone's purchasing power—except those who positioned themselves close to the USAMGIK and were paid in U.S. dollars. Structural explanations of motivations for uprisings are convenient, but they can also be a means of avoiding more difficult questions. Why would hundreds of thousands of people rise up and risk their lives as well as those of their families?

The terrible conditions of hunger and deprivation Koreans suffered in 1946 were atrocious, but if the United States had facilitated mechanisms for solving them, through allocating resources to health and food rather than to arms and police salaries, it is questionable—and in my mind, highly doubtful—that hardship alone would have led to the kind of desperate actions people took. Clearly economic motivational factors were present, but I can imagine a scenario in which rice shortages were mitigated by sharing, rather than exacerbated by hoarding and profiteers who sold rice to Japan; where cholera was solved by focusing medical attention on it and allocating resources to improve sanitation conditions; and where unemployment was resolved through job sharing, encouraging workers' self-management, and cooperating with communal councils that had sprung up to run factories. From this perspective, the fundamental underlying cause of the bloodshed was U.S. policy, especially its refusal to support the grassroots initiatives like the KPR and PCs.

One needs also to consider the legacy of Japanese colonization—and not only as it was reflected in dire living conditions of millions of ordinary people. The basic problem that the uprising sought to solve was that Koreans were overwhelmingly opposed to continuing rule by Japanese collaborators, that people did not want their country divided, that they did not want any foreign power—Russian or American—to control their destiny. Without acknowledging the primacy of this concern, all other expositions of the uprising's causes turn into studied ignorance. In 1946, U.S. imperial interests came first—no matter what the cost—and hundreds of Korean patriots sacrificed their lives trying to prevent the American version of Japan's suppression of indigenous resistance at the beginning of the twentieth century. In the 27 years since 1919, thousands of people surpassed the strict nonviolence of the March 1 Uprising.

For Cumings, the "Autumn Harvest Uprising" was "a last, massive attempt by the PCs and the groups associated with them to seize power in the provinces."[88] While the KPR and PCs did their utmost to, as Cumings puts it "seize power in the provinces," they were defeated, but only by heavily armed U.S. troops who never hesitated to open fire when they felt the slightest provocation. In Cumings's words: "With railroad and communication facilities largely in American and right-ist Korean hands, and with a national police network that could be mobilized on a countrywide basis to deal with what were, after all, regional uprisings, the denouement was all but determined."[89] Curiously, he leaves out mention of U.S. troops in his assessment of the balance of forces. Yet U.S. troops were the one critical factor that prevented regional uprisings from holding onto and consolidating power bases from which they could have surrounded and overwhelmed the major cities—including central authority in Seoul. Without U.S. intervention, Koreans would have settled their own disputes with far less of the violence than ensued. Cumings's omission of American power is integral to his subsequent portrayal of the Korean War as a civil war, rather than a war for national independence. His assertion that this was a "last" effort on the part of the PCs to seize power in the South is also factually incorrect. As we will see, PCs resurfaced in the 1948 Yeosun revolt, and once again in 1950 at the start of the Korean War.

While Cumings's trailblazing work was initially welcomed among progressive Koreans when it appeared, subsequent Korean commentators are less laudatory. Based upon previously unpublished data, Jung Hae-gu criticizes Cumings's work on the October Uprising on a number of levels. In Jung's estimation, he did not properly understand the role of preexisting anti-Japanese networks in the uprisings. His failure to portray continuity in the Korean patriotic movement prevented Cumings—and many subsequent researchers as well—from seeing desire for national independence and freedom from foreign control as central motivating concerns.

Cumings considered the October Uprising to be a peasant movement, calling the events the "Autumn Harvest Uprisings." Such a characterization, Jung tells us, minimizes the importance of workers' strikes that were central to the uprising's origins. Once the upsurge had begun, all manner of citizens participated, including significant numbers of students who played important roles. Cumings does not provide a framework of analysis for considering why the entire society participated—including even conservatives—leading him once again to miss the *political* character of the insurgency. Cumings could not comprehend the national and international aspirations of the movements that gave them more than a local character.[90] By separating workers' strikes and student movements from the provincial uprisings, and then analytically constructing the uprisings according to province, Cumings bifurcates the movements into component parts without grasping their significance in their entirety. The spontaneous proliferation of the uprising throughout the Gyeongsang provinces and then into South Jeolla and across the country reveals how much ordinary people's desires resonated with the opportunity to enact some immediate measure of justice and fight for Korean independence. Although it spread like wildfire, the movement had very similar aspirations wherever it appeared: elimination of Japanese collaborators, especially brutal police; administration of the country and public security in the hands of the PCs; and resistance to the U.S. military government.

Finally, Jung points to Cumings's use of the term "rebellion" to describe the movements. While Cumings notes that some Americans saw the uprisings as "a full-fledged revolution," he asserts they were a rebellion because "revolution was denied to peasants who lacked the organization necessary to depose their masters."[91] Rebels seek to rise against something or someone, but deep in their psyche, they cherish their opponent and do not seek to transcend it. Not wanting to overthrow power, they fail to envision alternatives. Yet in 1946, the PCs and KPR had already been established as viable vehicles for self-government of Koreans. If previous performance of the KPR is any indication, they would have continued to equitably distribute food, free prisoners by the thousands, support workers' councils in the factories, and call upon indigenous institutions of civil society to govern amicably. Apparently, Cumings discounts the tremendous capacity of self-organization demonstrated by people's actions, their discipline in withholding attacks on U.S. troops, and the precise targets they attacked, like rice collection records. The leadership of PCs, the KPR, and CCP all comprised multiple levels on which organization was strong and capable of articulating unified actions. If there are criticisms to be made of the KPR and Left groups, they should begin with their naïve belief in U.S. promises of self-determination, in their attempts to reason with intransigent U.S. imperial masters who would spare no effort to impose American interests. The very fact that the KPR and organized groups discouraged people from attacking American soldiers testifies to their failure to comprehend the reality of the conflict with which they were engaged. If U.S. troops had been sent home in coffins, the American public may have learned of Koreans' desire for independence, rather than being led to believe in their willingness to be subjugated.

For Cumings, when the upsurge ended, "the forces of the Left had been the biggest losers. The successful suppression of the uprisings marked a turning point in the strength and visibility of the Korean National Police. The forces of order in the South now dealt with a deeply intimidated peasant population."[92] Clearly, with hundreds of activists killed and thousands more wounded and imprisoned, a severe blow had been struck to Korea's independence movement. Like a law of the jungle, increased state repression follows every defeat of insurgency. After October, activists by the thousands were imprisoned, while many more were forced underground or took to the mountains.

Cumings's description of the 1946 October Uprising reflects disdain for Koreans' aspirations for independence. He continually uses "mob" and "rioters" to describe citizens while "rightist allies" and "American tactical troops" seek to "restore order" and "rescue police."[93] He quotes statement after statement of protesters who "refuse to be a nation of traitors"; who "don't want our country to be a colony of the U.S."; who aimed to bring justice to Japanese collaborators; and whose demands often were simply, "Return the Korean government to the People's Committees!" Yet, contrary to his own empirical data, he calls the movement "inchoate" and "apolitical"; in his view, "no organization capable of channeling and utilizing the social force that Korean peasants represented existed."[94]

The form of the uprising showed how much people's self-understanding had grown since 1919. Like the March 1 Movement, people initially went peacefully into the streets as supplicants seeking national independence. Yet in 1946, new forms of organization were created from below—the KPR, PCs, and a host of village, factory, and urban councils under the umbrella of national groups. Various Left and popular front type groups constituted another level of the self-organization of insurgency. Moreover, tens of thousands of people took up arms to defend their rights. This unfolding of the people's aspirations and actions represents a historical process through which Koreans congealed into the subjects of their own future.

Since at least the beginning of the twentieth century, revolutionary movements have been understood to go through many stages. Rather than create a framework for all movements, I seek here to grasp the historical contours of the 1946 October Uprising in the actions of hundreds of thousands of people. Their self-organization and revolutionary forms of dual power, the transitions from urban strikes to rural uprisings and from peaceful protests to armed insurrections reveals innovative capacity far superior to the dull repetition of routine crystallized in governments and political parties. In the historical progress from 1919 to 1946, we see the growing self-awareness of Koreans and the potential for a liberated country that could have served as a model for much the rest of the world. If the United States had not massively destroyed the peninsula from 1950 to 1953, Korea would have become an inspiration to others, a shining example of how people's self-government could move a country forward.

That uprisings unfold in relation to each other is one of the great lessons that empirical studies verify. In 1946, a workers' strike precipitated a series of rural insurrections. In a subsequent chapter, a different dynamic will become apparent in 1987, when widespread democratization protests created an opening for the largest strike movement in Korean history. Whence they originate can be elusive, but that one act of insurgency leads to many more is abundantly clear.

Faced with continuing resistance to its rule, U.S. policymakers realized they had no choice but to withdraw from Korea, and they did so by 1949. That decision was one positive outcome of the 1946 uprising. However, as would subsequently be repeated in South Vietnam and Iraq, U.S. operatives created a "new nation" with an indigenous government armed with massive quantities of the best weapons available. To sustain their Frankenstein state in southern Korea, American advisors recommended the creation of a new Korean Constabulary (KC), which they pieced together from remnants of forces that had fought for Japan. Fully 90 percent of KC officers had served the emperor before they served the United States. The rank-and-file, however, were completely different: many of the enlisted men were opposed to continuing U.S. governance of Korea. In the aftermath of U.S. suppression of the 1946 uprising, so widespread was anti-U.S. sentiment that Alan Millet estimated that at least five KC regiments had "substantial Communist cells."

Evidently, the experiences gleaned from the sacrifices of 1946 stiffened the resolve of hundreds of thousands more activists to continue the struggle. As we will see, on the island of Jeju and in the mainland port cities of Sunchon and Yeosu, the capacity of ordinary people to enact forms of self-government was far from intimidated.

NOTES

1   Walter Trohan, "Japs Asked Peace . . . Roosevelt Ignored M'Arthur Report on Nip Proposals," *Chicago Tribune*, August 19, 1945. See http://www.ihr.org/jhr/v06/v06p508_Hoffman.html.

2   This thesis was initially put forward in a 1965 study by Gar Alperovitz, *Atomic Diplomacy: Hiroshima and Potsdam* (London: Pluto Press, 1994). See also Howard Zinn, *Passionate Declarations* (New York: HarperCollins, 2003), 24–26.

3   Martin Hart-Landsberg, *Korea: Division, Reunification, and U.S. Foreign Policy* (New York: Monthly Review Press, 1998), 71–72. Also see his excellent *The Rush to Development* (Monthly Review Press, 1993).

4   Cumings, *Origins*, 1:290.

5   Chalmers Johnson, *Nemesis: The Last Days of the American Empire* (New York: Metropolitan Books, 2006), 76.

6   This is the number used in Germany. See, as one example, Jai Sin Park, "Arbeiterinnenbewegung in Südkorea," in *Dritte Welt: Frauen Bewegung in der Welt*, Band 2, eds. Autonome Frauenredaktion (Hamburg: Argument Sonderband AS 170, 1989), 205; in the United States, the figure used is often one to two hundred thousand. For example, see Miriam Ching Yoon Louie, "*Minjung* Feminism: Korean Women's Movement for Gender and Class Liberation," in *Global Feminisms Since 1945*, ed. Bonnie G. Smith (London: Routledge, 2000), 131.

7   See Martin Fackler, "No Apology for Sex Slavery, Japan's Prime Minister Says," *New York Times*, March 6, 2007.

8   Not only does the Japanese government refuse to apologize, but also in my experience, even raising the issue angers many Japanese people. In 2007, I witnessed many Harvard colloquia where Japanese graduate students angrily refused to let the issue be discussed, claiming it was irrelevant.

9   The phrases are taken from Japanese Professor Aiko Ogoshi, "How Can Philosophy Respond to Modern Antigones?" World Conference on Philosophy roundtable, Seoul National University, August 4, 2008.

10   Cumings, *Origins*, 1:36.

11   U.S. Intelligence Summary, North Korea, no. 30, February 16, 1947. Note that more than eighteen months before the founding of a government in northern Korea, U.S. intelligence reports refer to it as though it were a separate country.

12   Cumings, *Origins*, 1:166.

13   USAF in Korea, "SK Interim Gov Activities" *U.S. Military Government in Korea* 33 (June 1948): 394–95.

14   Henderson, *Korea: The Politics of the Vortex*, 85.

15   For further information on U.S./Japanese biological warfare see Hal Gold, *Unit 731: Japan's Wartime Human Experimentation Program* (Tokyo: Yenbooks, 1996); Sheldon H. Harris, *Factories of Death: Japanese Biological Warfare, 1932–1945, and the American Cover-Up* (London: Routledge, 1994); and Stephen Endicott and Edward Hagerman, *The United States and Biological Warfare* (Bloomington: Indiana University Press, 1998).

16   Harris, *Factories of Death*, 118.

17   *New York Times*, December 27, 1949, 16.

18   See Gold, *Unit 731*.

19   Henderson, *Korea: The Politics of the Vortex*, 124.

20   Quoted in *History of the U.S. Armed Forces in Korea* (HUSAFIK), vol. 2 (Seoul and Tokyo: U.S. Office of the Chief of Military History: 1947, 1948), 154–55, 238–39.

21   Quoted in Cumings, *Origins*, 2:35.

22   George F. Kennan, "PPS/23: Review of Current Trends in U.S. Foreign Policy," *Foreign Relations of the United States*, vol. 1 (1948).

23   Göthel, *Geschichte Südkoreas*, 50.

24   Kyung Cho Chung, *Korea Tomorrow* (New York: Macmillan, 1956).

25   Hart-Landsberg, *The Rush to Development*, 121.

26   Yi Tong-hwa, "Yo Un-hyong and the Preparation Committee for the Reconstruction of the Nation," *Korea Journal*, November 1986, 42.

27   U.S. State Department, *The Foreign Relations of the United States*, vol. 6, 561–63. Quoted in *For the Truth and Reparations: Jeju April 3rd of 1948 Massacre Not Forgotten*, ed. Hur Sang Soo (Seoul: BaekSan Publisher, 2001), 76. See also "Paramilitary Politics under the USAMGIK and the Establishment of the Republic of Korea," http://www. ekoreajournal.net/upload/html_20030820.org/HTML43212.

28   Henderson, *Korea: The Politics of the Vortex*, 119.

29   Ibid., 130.

30   Cumings, *Origins*, 1:99.

31   Ibid., 145–46

32   Ibid., 271.

33   Ibid., 273.

34   Kang Man-gil, *History of Contemporary Korea*, 329–30.

35   Cumings, *Origins*, 1:393–95.

36   See Kim, "South Korea," 141 (see chap. 2, n. 93).

37   Sunhyuk Kim, *The Politics of Democratization in Korea: The Role of Civil Society* (Pittsburgh: University of Pittsburgh Press, 2000), 26.

38   Quoted in Gi-wook Shin, "The Historical Making of Collective Action: The Korean Peasant Uprisings of 1946," *American Journal of Sociology* 99, no. 6 (May 1994): 1602.

39   Kim, "South Korea," 26.

40   Cumings, *Origins*, 1:93.

41   Clive Hamilton, *Capitalist Industrialization in Korea* (Boulder, CO: Westview Press, 1986), 21, as cited in Mi Park, *Democracy and Social Change: A History of South Korean Student Movements, 1980–2000* (Bern: Peter Lang, 2008), 50.

42   Martin Hart-Landsberg, *The Rush to Development*, 18.

43   Koo, *Korean Workers*, 26.

44   Cumings, *Origins*, 1:312; A different account is contained in Shin, "The Historical Making of Collective Action," 1604. Shin counted fourteen thousand protesters and attributed three deaths to police gunfire. Other account place the date as November 17. All agree these killings were the first by U.S. troops since 1871.

45   Cumings, *Origins*, 1:197.

46   Henderson, *Korea: The Politics of the Vortex*, 127.

47   Göthel, *Geschichte Südkoreas*, 53.

48   Cumings, *Origins*, 1:377.

49   Kang Man-gil, *History of Contemporary Korea*, 327.

50   Cumings, *Origins*, 1:379.

51   Shin, "The Historical Making of Collective Action," 1604–5.

52   *Joongang Ilbo*, October 10, 1999; *Mal* (January 1989); interview with Lee Young-il, Yosu, August 2, 2003.

53 Heo Man-ho and Lee Changhee make this point in reference to the work of Chong Hae-gu. See "October First Incident of 1946 in Daegu: State-Building, Democracy and Human Rights," in *Democracy and Human Rights in the New Millennium*, International Symposium on the 20th Anniversary of the Kwangju Uprising Program (Gwangju: May 18 Institute, 2000), 73.

54 Thomas H. Lee, "The Origins of the Taegu Insurrection of 1946," (Thesis, Harvard University, 1990), 96.

55 Mark Gayn, *Japan Diary* (New York: William Sloane Associates, 1948), 388.

56 Kang Man-gil, *History of Contemporary Korea*, 184.

57 Shin, "The Historical Making of Collective Action," 1606 gives similar figures. See Cumings, *Origins*, 1:379.

58 Ogle, *South Korea*, 11.

59 Göthel, *Geschichte Südkoreas*, 9.

60 Cumings, *Origins*, 1:548.

61 Quoted in Ogle, *South Korea*, 11.

62 Lee, *The Origins of the Taegu Insurrection*, 77; Cumings, *Origins*, 1:352.

63 Göthel, *Geschichte Südkoreas*, 54; Cumings, *Origins*, 1:354.

64 Lee, *The Origins of the Taegu Insurrection*, 77.

65 Heo Man-ho and Lee Changhee make this point in reference to the work of Chong Hae-gu in *Democracy and Human Rights*, 53–54.

66 Heo Man-ho and Lee Changhee, *Democracy and Human Rights*, 64; Cumings, *Origins*, 1:356.

67 HUSAFIK, G-2 Weekly Summary No. 56, from September 29 to October 6, 1946, October 11, 1946, as cited in Lee, *The Origins of the Taegu Insurrection*, 83.

68 Lee, *The Origins of the Taegu Insurrection*, 84.

69 Henderson, *Korea: The Politics of the Vortex*, 146.

70 Göthel, *Geschichte Südkoreas*, 54.

71 Henderson, *Korea: The Politics of the Vortex*, 146.

72 Lee, *The Origins of the Taegu Insurrection*, 86–87.

73 Ibid., 90.

74 Letter from Sergeant Savage to President Truman, April 1947 about events in 1946 September railroad strike.

75 Cumings, *Origins*, 1:362.

76 Shin, "The Historical Making of Collective Action," 1606.

77 Lee, *The Origins of the Taegu Insurrection*, 78.

78 "Narrative History of the Department of Labor" as quoted in Lee, *The Origins of the Taegu Insurrection*, 79.

79 Cumings, *Origins*, 1:365–66.

80 Ibid., 1:366.

81 Lee, *The Origins of the Taegu Insurrection*, 94.

82 Cumings, *Origins*, 1:361–5.

83 Lee, *The Origins of the Taegu Insurrection*, 96.

84 Ibid., 15.

85 Shin, "The Historical Making of Collective Action," 1606.

86 See Peter Kropotkin's remarkable two-volume history, *The Great French Revolution, 1789–1793*.

87 "Jeolla-South Communist Uprising of November 1946," December 31, 1946, U.S. 6th Infantry Division Headquarters, in XXIV Historical File as cited in Cumings, *Origins*, 1:366.

88 Cumings, *Origins*, 1:352.

89 Ibid., 380.

90   정해구, *10월인민항쟁 연구*, (서울: 열음사, 1988), 10–12.
91   Cumings, *Origins*, 1:351.
92   Cumings, *Origins*, 1:380–81.
93   Ibid., 358–59 alone contain six references to "rioters" and "mob."
94   Ibid., 357.

CHAPTER 4

Against Korea's Division: Jeju Uprising and Yeosun Insurrection

The formation of a separate government in south Korea will not facilitate the twin objectives . . . of national independence of Korea and the withdrawal of the occupying troops.
—United Nations Temporary Commission on Korea, January 1948

Without massive infusion of U.S. aid, the Republic of Korea could not survive.
—CIA National Intelligence Estimate, late 1948

CHRONOLOGY	
February 28, 1947	Massacre of Taiwanese by Chinese allies of U.S. (10,000+ killed)
March 1, 1947	U.S. orders police to fire on peaceful gathering in Jeju: six killed, dozens wounded
March 10, 1947	500 people arrested for strikes against USAMGIK on Jeju
March 1, 1948	More than 2,500 arrests at gathering on March 1 Commemoration
March 1948	More than 10,000 arrests
April 3, 1948	Simultaneous attacks on police and government offices in Jeju
1948–1954	Jeju massacre: over 30,000 killed
May 10, 1948	U.S.-organized elections in southern Korea
August 15, 1948	Proclamation of the Republic of Korea in Seoul
September 9, 1948	Proclamation of the Democratic People's Republic in Pyongyang

October 20, 1948	Fourteenth Regiment mutinies in Yeosu; Sunchon and Gurye also controlled by revolutionaries
December 1, 1948	National Security Law passed
1950–1953	Korean War: more than five million people killed
March 31, 1952	International Association of Democratic Lawyers charges U.S. with waging biological warfare

AFTER THE OCTOBER Uprising, lessons were drawn on both sides. For patriots for whom national independence was paramount, the struggle had reached a new stage in the southern part of the country: more centralized organization was needed to realize genuine independence. A Workers' Party had been established in Pyongyang in August 1946—well before the October Uprising—and on November 23, some 585 people gathered in Seoul to form the South Korean Labor Party (SKLP).[1] Progressive forces regrouped with a sharper and more radical core. In their minds, the masses' spontaneous reaction to the killing of hundreds of hungry protesters had been proven insufficient to bring down the government. Centralized national organization was what was needed, so they united their small parties—the Chosun Communist Party, the People's Party, and the New Peoples Party—to form the SKLP.

American policymakers were no less clear in their assessment of the situation—the Rhee government was so weak that on its own, it would not have been able to survive more than three months. Without U.S. support for Rhee, he would have passed into obscurity, probably in his U.S. home. Since patriots like Kim Ku would have insisted upon retaining Korea's unity, the country would not have had a major war in 1950.

Rhee and his American backers were intent on dividing the country, and they began to do so by 1946, when they closed the DMZ to cross-border transit. By mid-1947, the U.S. military government made even radio contact with the North illegal, a prohibition that created difficulties for the SKLP to communicate with its northern sister organization. Loosely structured, the SKLP was forced underground. As it systematically set up its branches all over the South, it did so with a dubiously conceived chain of command. Inside the American-created Korean Constabulary, for instance, where the party quickly found thousands of supporters, separate lines of intraparty communication were established for officers and enlisted men in the same units. Officers remained in contact with SKLP headquarters in Seoul, while enlisted men reported to regional party leadership, a separation of command structure that would prove fatally flawed in Yeosu within a year. Despite his paltry attempts in 1945 to persuade U.S. officials to jettison their Japanese police and officials, Park Hon-yong rose to become party leader. Soon an inner struggle ensued between his followers and those of Kim Il-sung—a clear sign of the growing distance between the southern party and its northern counterpart.

The October 1946 Uprising convinced SKLP leaders that people were ready to rise again, and they moved to organize more systematic actions. When a new strike of railroad workers erupted in January 1947, bloody confrontations between the indigenous labor unions and the newly formed *Nochong* (the yellow union endorsed by the United States) left hundreds dead and thousands in prison. While organized rightists attacked strikers, a general offensive of U.S. troops and police killed hundreds of union leaders—many of whom were summarily executed. Thousands more unionists were imprisoned without trials in the same dungeons built by Japan, now even more efficiently managed by the U.S. military government.[2] Refusing to be intimidated, *Chonpyong*, the All Korea Labor Council, initiated a series of strikes from March 1947 to May 1948. Beginning on March 22, 1947, strikes in fifteen cities drew participation from more than twenty thousand industrial workers.[3] Declared illegal in early 1947, *Chonpyong* ceased to exist by 1949.[4] In August 1947, its central office was closed down by USAMGIK and more than a thousand of its supporters were arrested.[5]

In March 1947 and again prior to August 15, police under the direction of USAMGIK arrested thousands of activists to prevent demonstrations from occurring. Military governor Hodge specifically banned any celebration of August 15 Liberation Day except the one he organized.[6] In Jeonju, when people gathered in defiance of the ban, police arrested 150 demonstrators, while U.S. fighter planes buzzed other celebrants.

While American repression grew more brutal in the South, on the northern side of the thirty-eighth parallel, Russian forces disarmed Korean soldiers of the Chinese Eighth Route Army as they crossed the border in their walk home. Perhaps as many as thirty thousand battle-hardened veterans of the anti-Japanese and anti-Kuomintang wars returned to liberated Korea. For many, Russians no less than Americans were suspected of having their own national interests at heart. To many people's surprise, rather than ignoring or repressing the People's Committees as the Americans were doing, the Soviets recognized their legitimacy and encouraged them to continue taking care of people's everyday needs. At the end of the war, after some Soviet soldiers committed rapes and treated people as conquerors, Communist discipline was quickly imposed. In January 1946, the newly arriving Soviet military attaché instituted the death penalty for any soldier raping a woman, and troops became better behaved. Cumings tells us the initial number of incidents was exaggerated by the United States.[7] By 1946, factory output in the Soviet zone was greater than at the war's end. While cynics would later say the PCs were turned into instruments of Kim Il-sung's rule, many northerners tell a different story, insisting they retained a great deal of autonomy—until 1950, when the war obliterated the cities and turned Kim Il-sung into the Great Leader needed to save Korea from the absolute ruin to which U.S. bombs and firepower reduced it.

With liberation from Japan, thorough agrarian reform in the northern zone distributed land to those who farmed it. Some 95 percent of all land was confiscated without compensation and distributed to farming families, 70 percent of whom benefited directly from the new government's program.[8] Poor tenant farmers suddenly found themselves living in more stable conditions. Anyone with the slightest allegiance to Japan was dealt with harshly, causing many who had collaborated with the emperor to go immediately to the South, especially former large landowners whose estates were turned into cooperative farms for former tenants. With land reform and other social welfare measures, Kim Il-sung's Workers' Party enjoyed enthusiastic support in the North—and among many in the South as well. While the October Uprising engulfed the South, Bruce Cumings noted that, "North Korea, by contrast, was an island of tranquility."[9] When war did come to the North—as Syngman Rhee promised it would from the day he arrived in the South—northern farmers were fighting for their own land.

As early as June of 1946, Rhee advocated the formation of a separate government in the South to try and hold onto power. Convinced he could not survive any challenge, whether from conservatives like Kim Ku or Marxists Like Kim Il-sung, the United States enabled Rhee to disregard the national integrity of Korea, pushing through a resolution at the United Nations calling for separate elections in the southern part of the country to form a new government. In January 1948, the UN convened an eight-country Temporary Commission on Korea that visited Seoul to ascertain the viability of the U.S. proposal. Much to the dismay of the United States, the commissioners' majority opinion was against the formation of a separate republic in southern Korea.[10] Undeterred, the United States beguiled the UN's Interim Committee (since the General Assembly was not in session) into proceeding with the elections.

To protest the U.S./UN partition of Korea through separate elections in the South, the SKLP called for a general strike to begin on February 7, 1948. The week before it was scheduled to begin, Kim Il-sung called Korean Communists to action: "Among our party members, there must be no leisurely and luxurious life. We must be so active that we feel dead if we have no work to do." Southerners responded vigorously with strikes and sabotage. After a brass band began playing "The Internationale" in Busan, rail and telegraph lines were cut. A twelve-car train was wrecked, and saboteurs put fifty locomotives out of action. Scattered clashes with South Korean police and rightists resulted in the deaths of forty-seven strikers and 1,500 arrests.[11] At the height of the three-day wave of resistance, a group calling itself the General Strike Committee for South Korea demanded that both the United States and the UN Commission (there to prepare UN-supervised Korean elections) get out. A letter to Governor-General Hodge made clear the demands of the strike: they wanted the right for Koreans to form their own government without foreign interference—whether from the United States, USSR, or UN. While repression had greatly disrupted communications among groups in the South, many participated in the general strike starting in February to "stop the division of the nation" through the May 10 elections.[12] In North Jeolla on February 25, proindependence protesters and police clashed, leaving five police and twenty-seven protesters dead.[13]

Jeju April 3 Uprising

In 1945, not even the most cynical New Yorker would have entertained the suggestion that American soldiers and sailors would soon be responsible for the massacre of tens of thousands of islanders in the Pacific. Yet that is precisely what happened on the matrifocal island of Jeju, a volcanic, palm-tree lined oasis off the southern coast of Korea. Jeju's people were as surprised as anyone by U.S. policy—and the brutality with which it was enforced. Like most Koreans, they had called American warplanes "righteous" and Japanese planes "enemy." Not only did U.S. bombs help weaken the invaders, but when American planes wrecked the emperor's transport ships, rice often washed ashore to feed starving islanders.

Jeju has a long tradition of self-governing villages, in which women divers' associations were a kind of living anarchism for centuries.[14] Although the United States labeled Jeju a "Red Island," it was actually "more strongly tuned with the spirit of independence and autonomy than any other ideologies."[15] Separated from the mainland by a hundred miles, they developed their own dialect and customs. "No thieves, no gates, no beggars" they proudly proclaimed. Women divers in Jeju were at the center of a matrifocal culture stretching across a wide range of coastal Korea. Working through forms of consensual decision-making, in which older divers had ultimate say in the event of a group's inability to reach unanimity, they lived in a system of direct democracy for decades. So independent were Jeju women divers that they rose up in 1901 and 1933 against Japan. In Hadori village from January to April 1933, 1,700 women divers insisted upon women's power through communal decision-making, including the right to set the prices of their products. Because of fierce resistance, the Japanese were unable to place a police station in the village: "Why do we need a police box," asked the residents "and be forced to live under outsiders' rules, when we live peacefully and autonomously?" As the revolt spread, the Japanese governor fled the island.[16]

In Hyun Ki-Young's novel, A Wind Riding Island, the protagonist Kim Si-Jung related that: "The society of women divers who live by harvesting sea products is the very archetype of an ideal community that humanity has dreamed of: an equal society built on shared property and management of a sea farm. A Commune has this feature: Within the community no power exists through which one person rules others. Individuals are part of a community helping each other in adversity as nature's children, independent beings, and autonomous beings who don't fall under the yoke."[17]

In their anarchism, islanders had been influenced by Lao-Tzu, not Bakunin or Kropotkin. Lao-Tzu's China was full of war and instability, yet in every direction for fifty miles from his village, peace was preserved. He believed in pacifism and a moral authority based upon the order of nature. Since self-government flowed organically in communal life, he far preferred it to rule by politicians. His notion of "a small country and small population" fit perfectly with Jeju village life.[18] Here lies a positive kernel of all Korean regionalism—the impetus to local autonomy and self-government in contradistinction to centralized power and its centripetal vortex. By 1948, islanders' affinity for anarchism had been channeled into communism for two reasons: Japanese repression of the independent villages and the success of the Soviet revolution, including its kind treatment of northern Koreans.

Under Japanese rule, seventy-two factories in chemical or manufacturing had been established on the island. Within days of Japan's surrender, all seventy-two of these enterprises were taken over and run through workers' self-management.[19] As in the rest of Korea, U.S. military authorities arrived and took charge of "enemy asset management." Control passed to the Americans. On September 23, 1945, five days before the arrival of the first Americans, a PC formed with wide public support. By the end of the month, they had selected Ahn Se-hoon as governor. For nearly three years, the PC ruled Jeju peacefully, even building 27 schools.[20] In contrast to the rest of southern Korea, the island was at peace. On November 9, 1945, when the American military government first arrived, its initial assessment was that the People's Committee was "the only party on the island, and to all extents and purposes, the only government." Even as late as October 1947, U.S. occupation commander Governor-General John Reed Hodge told a group of visiting congressional representatives that Jeju was "a truly communal area that is peacefully controlled by the People's Committee without much Comintern influence."[21]

By late 1946, the SKLP had established itself as the core leadership within the Jeju PC and gradually persuaded or compelled all other tendencies to follow its leadership. Military and political committees were organized on the county, town, and village levels in strictly hierarchical relationships to each other. (For a detailed view of this structure, refer to FIGURE 4.1.) Mass organizations under the direction of the SKLP were also established, including a women's group, a farmers' cooperative, fishermen's guild, consumers' club, labor union, teachers' guild, and cultural association. Within the party, action groups for propaganda, finance, logistics, intelligence, and organization were developed.

In August 1946, the U.S. military government designated Jeju as a separate province. With its ties to South Jeolla severed, control of the island's government passed from the U.S. Fifty-Ninth Battalion directly to Hodge's headquarters. Hodge quickly appointed a new conservative governor and dispatched right-wing police to Jeju. Lying at a sea crossroads between China, Japan, and Korea, the island occupies a strategic regional position. In October 1946, an AP report

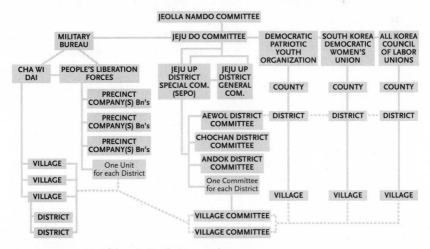

FIGURE 4.1 **Structure of the Jeju South Korean Labor Party**
Source: "Report on South Korean Labor Party, Cheju Do," Report to Colonel R.H. Brown, Commanding Cheju Do, June 20, 1948. Provided by April 3 Institute, Jeju.

compared it to Gibraltar in the Mediterranean, and in 1947, Rhee promised to permit the United States to build an enormous base there. In October 1949, the U.S. embassy spoke of Jeju's "extraordinary strategic value."[22]

After the October 1946 Uprising on the mainland, when U.S. troops had become directly involved in killings of civilians, tensions on Jeju rose considerably. Previously considered a place where top American brass could relax and enjoy hunting expeditions, the island's situation abruptly changed when islanders gathered to commemorate Korean Independence Day on March 1, 1947. A crowd of at least fifty thousand islanders (some say many more) assembled at North Elementary School, the largest peace demonstration in the island's history.[23] When the crowd spilled over into city streets, American troops ordered Korean police to open fire. When the shooting stopped, at least six people lay dead with many more wounded. Dozens of people were arrested.[24] A week later, over a thousand people protested the continuing detention of the arrested. Police again fired on the crowd, this time killing five people. Faced with outrageous use of force, all schools, offices, and businesses went on strike. Altogether, over 160 public agencies joined the strike. Some police, soldiers, and a Coast Guard band joined in the protests—as did many conservatives. Besides the immediate release of the arrested and compensation for their injuries, the strike demanded punishment of police who had killed people, firing of Japanese collaborators among them, and reconvening of the U.S.-Soviet Joint Commission (the body then handling Korean affairs whose talks had broken down). Elsewhere in Korea, U.S. sources reported that sixteen people were killed and twenty-two seriously injured during March 1 celebrations.[25]

By March 10, in at least 176 places, islanders used peaceful work stoppages to protest the bloodshed. The police who opened fire on March 1 were outsiders under U.S. orders, sent by Hodge after he severed Jeju from its longstanding status as part of South Jeolla Province. With the situation spiraling out of control due to American machinations, the U.S. governor-general sent more right-wing police to the island. Five hundred strike leaders were arrested, sixty-six native policemen were dismissed, and right-wing mainlanders were brought in as replacements. In protest, the governor resigned.

Many of those arrested were savagely beaten; at least three young men died from torture, as discovered when their badly deformed bodies were pulled from a river on March 16. Rather than arrest the police responsible for the torture-murders or stop the violence, the Americans put 328 citizens on trial in military courts, with at least one American judge helping to convict 158 on charges ranging from unlawful meetings, violating American military laws, and planning strikes. Hundreds more right-wing police were shipped to Jeju. The most brutal of the new arrivals were eight hundred or more members of the Northwest Youth League (NWYL), anti-Communist refugees from northern Korea. These unpaid murderers lived off the spoils of war, raping and murdering their way from village to village, subjecting hapless islanders—particularly defenseless women—to tortures and humiliations that make Peckinpah movies seem tame. Promised land in exchange for services, many eagerly complied with the orders of their American masters.

By the end of the year, at least 2,500 people had been arrested; many were subsequently tortured to death.

American intelligence routinely referred to Jeju as a "Red Island." U.S. reports estimated by 1948 that some sixty thousand people (perhaps 20 percent of the population) were members of the SKLP and that altogether some eighty thousand islanders could be considered sympathizers or active supporters.[26] Although the Jeju People's Liberation Army of the SKLP only had about four hundred core members (and half as many rifles), some four thousand locally organized self-defense forces supported them—mostly armed with hoes, swords, spears, shovels, and rakes. U.S. Colonel Rothwell Brown analyzed U.S. and Korean military interrogation records of four thousand islanders and estimated the size of the SKLP at sixty thousand or more, but he considered them, "for the main part, ignorant, uneducated farmers and fishermen."[27] "Two weeks are enough to quash the revolt," he assured his superiors. Significantly, the SKLP on Jeju was composed almost exclusively of islanders while Koreans working with the American Military Government were predominantly mainlanders.

On March 14, U.S. intelligence reported that a general strike had broken out in Jeju in response to the police killings. Strike support was so overwhelming that even 75 percent of the USAMGIK employees were involved. More than 95 percent of all public officials and workers joined the strike, including 41,211 people from 166 public offices and civic organizations. Participation was so widespread that police sent from the mainland were needed to operate the power plant. By March 20, the entire police force in Mosulpo had joined the strikers. At the same time in Daegu (on the mainland), thousands of students were on strike. In early 1947, while the USAMGIK collected 69 percent of its stated rice quota in all of southern Korea, it collected only 1 percent in Jeju, where grain requisitions were five times higher.[28]

International comparison with the Taiwan uprising and massacre of February 28, 1947, (the day before police opened fire in Jeju) is needed in order to uncover the source of the terror. Both Syngman Rhee and Chiang Kai-shek were best friends of the United States in fragments of larger nations suddenly declared to be "new nations" by policymakers in Washington. Although thousands of years of history testified to the unity of Korea, the peninsula was being divided to suit U.S. imperial needs for bases and bulwarks. American aggression was justified by Cold War exigencies to beat back a perceived Communist threat. To establish a safe rear area to which Chiang and his Kuomintang (KMT) could escape from their coming defeat in China, U.S. ships transported Chiang's army across the sea to Taiwan. As soon as Chiang's troops arrived in force, they massacred tens of thousands of islanders—whose corpses were thrown into the sea or left in the fields to rot.[29] Their only "crime" was to assert their right to govern themselves. Evidently Rhee and his American handlers learned valuable lessons to apply to Jeju as they watched the extirpation of the indigenous Taiwanese power structure.

Resistance inside Korea was more systematic and protracted than Taiwanese had been able to mount. With the approaching partition of Korea through separate elections in the South, the SKLP's call for a nationwide strike for February 7,

1948 resonated widely. Resistance was most vocal on Jeju, where protests included running battles with police in many places. [30] On March 1, 1948, police arrested 2,500 young people protesting the coming partition election, and again many youth were tortured. At least one body was subsequently pulled from a river. Unauthorized rice taxation in 1948 was five times the 1947 level—on an island so poor that wooden tools were used because metal was so rare. As a cycle of repression and resistance widened, the SKLP made preparations to end the reign of terror by seizing control of the island.

At midnight on April 3, 1948, the signal for coordinated insurgent attacks appeared: 89 fires on top of extinct volcano craters lit up the night. At 2 a.m., simultaneous attacks involving as many as 3,500 people were launched against the Northwest Youth League and eleven of the island's twenty-four police stations. Altogether perhaps fifteen former Japanese collaborators and policemen were killed. Organized as a People's Army with at least thirty members of each district comprising a battalion, and battalions grouped into regiments, the insurgents explained their actions through a newspaper they widely distributed.

The American response was swift and draconian: another U.S.-armed regiment was imported from Busan, and an additional 1,700 police were sent in. Between late March and mid-May, ten thousand people were detained. The government continually reinforced its garrison, as attacks and counterattacks mounted in intensity. Insurgents retreated to their bases in villages, caves, and the forests on Mount Halla, the extinct volcano whose mammoth presence looms over the island. On April 29, the provincial governor and a majority of the local constabulary in Daejong-myun went over to the side of the guerrillas, leading to a bloody battle. [31]

The United States ordered the commanding officer of the Ninth Regiment of the Korean Constabulary, Kim Ik-ruhl, to conduct a "scorched earth" policy, but instead, Kim hammered out a three-point peace agreement with guerrilla leader Kim Dal-sam. Although U.S. officials ostensibly arrived on April 29 to help implement the agreement, the treaty was scuttled by the massacre of partisans who had surrendered and returned to their homes in Orari. The police perpetrated these killings, but through a fabricated report the United States blamed them on insurgents. U.S. Colonel Mansfield had originally approved the peace treaty, but hope for a negotiated settlement faded when the U.S. military provincial governor, General W. Dean, vetoed it. [32] Since the governor of the island had joined the guerrillas, Dean needed to find new administrative personnel willing to collaborate with the American occupation government. First, the United States sought to purge SKLP sympathizers from the ranks of their assistants. Lt. Moon Sang-gil was summarily executed in Seoul, as were three sergeants on Jeju. After he had arrested four thousand civilians in two weeks, Colonel Rothwell Brown was asked about his feelings. He replied simply that his "mission was to suppress the uprising."

During the week leading up to May 10 elections, armed guerrillas fought police in at least sixty-three towns; they also attacked three government buildings. When elections finally were staged, voter turnout on Jeju was lowest in all

The population of Jeju Island was displaced under the rule of the U.S. military government in 1948. To take this photo, refugee children were assembled. Photographer unknown

of Korea. So abysmal was participation that the two seats in the new national assembly reserved for Jeju were simply left vacant. Women's League members had campaigned to prevent people from voting, and thousands of residents went to the mountainside the night before to avoid being taken to the polls at gunpoint. Half of all election officials did not even show up, requiring auxiliary police dressed in Japanese uniforms to supervise polling places.

All over the island, attacks intensified and continued for months. On May 12, to prevent infiltration from the mainland, the USS *Craig* took up position patrolling the waters around Jeju.

The guerrillas seemed to have the upper hand. On June 18, Colonel Pak Chingyong, commander of the government forces, was shot and killed by one of his subordinates. On June 27, U.S. reports indicated that two Coast Guard vessels were taken over by "Communist mutineers who murdered captains and took vessels to

The USS *Craig* was one of many U.S. ships to blockade Jeju in 1948. Photographer unknown

North Korean ports."[33] By the end of the year, Jeju police reported over a hundred battles and six thousand arrests, and U.S. sources put the number of fatalities at more than five thousand.

As soon as the new government of South Korea proclaimed its existence on August 15, new President Syngman Rhee stepped up the campaign against Jeju insurgents. All over the island, trees and bushes were uprooted, lands cleared, houses burned, and collective punishment for villages meted out—but still the resistance grew. On August 25, underground elections to support Korean unification were held. In the northern part of the country, people voted for 210 seats, while even more, 360 in all, were selected by regionally elected representatives in the South. American sources report that 25 percent of Jeju islanders voted in these clandestine elections, while the guerrillas claimed a turnout of 85 percent.[34] (Communist sources in the North noted that 77.52 percent of all South Korean voters took part in the exercise.) After the elections, 1,002 delegates (including Kim Dal-sam and five others from Jeju) gathered in the northern city of Haeju to cast their votes for the Korean People's Assembly.

With the proclamation of the Democratic People's Republic (DPRK) in Pyongyang on September 9, Korea had two governments, each claiming sovereignty over the entire peninsula. Among many major differences, one stands out with regard to Jeju: a U.S. general was the island's military governor until August 15, 1948, but even afterward, secret agreements signed on August 24 gave the U.S. operational control of the ROK national police and armed forces until June 30, 1949.[35] In September, General William Roberts, then chief U.S. military officer in Korea, told ROK Prime Minister Lee Bum-suh in no uncertain terms who was in charge: "As you know, operational control of the Korean Constabulary still rests with the Commanding General, USAFIK, and it is of paramount importance, therefore, that all orders pertaining to operational control of the Constabulary be cleared with the appropriate American Advisor, prior to publication."[36]

Under the U.S. military government, bloodletting in Jeju began that would kill more than thirty thousand people out of a total population of about three hundred thousand. (Some estimates place the number of people killed closer to seventy thousand.) [37] Many more were wounded; women were systematically raped; at least a hundred thousand people were forcibly relocated to "protected" enclaves along the coast; and 70 percent of the islands' homes were destroyed. Altogether, about 119 soldiers and an additional 119 police were killed from 1948 to 1954, testimony to the relatively pacific character of the people's resistance. As Kim Dong-choon put it: "The technical advisors estimated the number of armed guerrillas at about 500, the number of victims killed at over 30,000. Who prompted the military to conduct such an unique and irrational operation?"[38]

U.S. forces were directly and indirectly involved in turning the whole island into one giant killing field. Ultimately, since command was in the hands of a U.S. general under the secret protocols, U.S. responsibility is paramount. U.S. aircraft were used for intelligence gathering, although reports of bombing and strafing have not been verified. Washington supplied right-wing forces with ample munitions, transportation, and encouragement, especially members of the Northwest

Youth League who, with U.S. support, took over the island's police force and newspapers. Hundreds of NWYL members became rich through their campaign to exterminate the locals, steal their lands, and appropriate their wealth. On November 17, with the active knowledge and collaboration of the United States, martial law was declared. Some eighteen warships provided by the United States to blockade the island bombarded defenseless villagers with 37 mm canons.[39] Despite U.S. responsibility, there was never even a public event in the United States about the Jeju massacre until a Harvard University conference in 2003. No American political figure has ever acknowledged, let alone apologized for, the atrocities perpetrated on Jeju. A succession of ROK dictatorships and local right-wing gangs so intimidated the population that it was not until 1988 that the first public talk about the uprising and massacre could be held.

The uprising's coordinated assaults at midnight on April 3, 1948, reveal the centrally organized character of the uprising. As noted, the PC was the island's de facto government from 1945 to 1948, and islanders were overwhelmingly united behind it. The SKLP's leadership was widely accepted. The synchronized beginning of the upsurge on April 3 indicates central organization and control, a tactic in the tradition of Old Left armed insurrections.[40] Of the major leaders, only Kim Dal-sam made good an escape to North Korea, where it is said he personally informed Kim Il-sung of the tragedy befalling the island. In the South, the SKLP's hopes for persuading Americans to cooperate with Korean independence were finished. With the continuing massacres, any illusions about U.S. benevolence were bloodily extinguished. The only possible recourse was all-out partisan warfare.

Yeosun Insurrection

The news of the Jeju massacres may have been suppressed in the United States, but in northern Korea, it is said that Kim Il-Sung shed tears when he heard the news. The slaughter no doubt motivated him to rescue his fellow Koreans. Southerners had already used the weapons of unions, general strikes, and rural seizures of power to protect Korea's unity and independence—but far superior U.S. firepower enforced American imperial will. After the defeat of Japan in World War II, the dialectic of liberation and enslavement consigned Koreans to a new occupation. While brutally imperialist, the Japanese had built industries and cities, railroads and roads—all of which the Americans would destroy in the name of freedom. Faced with massacre after massacre of unarmed protesters, southerners reluctantly began an armed struggle. After the suppression of the October 1946 Uprising, guerrilla units formed in earnest. What other possibility remained but to fight for independence?

The last great popular upsurge by southerners opposed to the country's division began unexpectedly in October 1948, when the Fourteenth Regiment of the Korean Constabulary in Yeosu was ordered to Jeju to help suppress the uprising. Thousands of soldiers mutinied, killed their officers and former Japanese collaborators, seized control of at least six counties around Yeosu and nearby Sunchon (hence the name "Yeosun") and made good their escape to Giri Mountain—where they established bases for an ongoing guerrilla war. The Yeosun mutiny marked the high point of southerners' resistance to the division of Korea. Insurgents hoped to activate the entire country to oppose the U.S.-imposed regime that had partitioned the country, and they nearly succeeded. The United States sent in nearly all troops under its command, coordinated a massive counteroffensive, and bloodily retook Sunchon and Yeosu. In the aftermath of the uprising, thousands of people were executed, the army was purged of leftist elements, and a National Security Law was promulgated making it a capital offence to collaborate with the DPRK.

According to U.S. documents, there was "no known indication of mutiny or revolt in the ranks of the Korean Constabulary prior to 19 October."[41] U.S. intelligence reports had noted that Constabulary recruits from Busan had visited Jeju during May (after the uprising began) and advised insurgents not to attack the Constabulary, which included many people sympathetic to a unified country, but rather to focus on the rightist-dominated police. For more than a year, right-wing police employed continuously since the days of Japanese colonial control and members of the mainland Constabulary had fought with each other, at times with fatalities.[42] On May 1, 1948, the Fourteenth Regiment was formed—less than six months before they mutinied. After authorities in Seoul discovered that as many as half of its members might be sympathetic to the SKLP, the regimental commander was arrested along with other officers, and they were sent to Seoul to await trial for subversive activity.[43] On October 16, as they waited to board a waiting transport ship bound for Jeju, sergeants known to be members of the SKLP (or at least opposed to Rhee's government) met to discuss what, if anything, they should do. Three ideas emerged: hijack the ship to North Korea, join the insurgents in Jeju, or take over Yeosu.

On October 18, an unsuccessful assassination attempt was made on Rhee.[44] The next day, the ROK president flew to Japan to meet MacArthur. That night, while the men of the Fourteenth Regiment waited to depart for Jeju, they were issued new M-1 carbines and granted a short respite before boarding ship. As they relaxed, sergeant Chi Chang-soo rose and called on them to fight for justice—not to kill fellow Koreans on Jeju who wanted only national unity and independence. Forty men immediately went over to his side. They rushed the ammunition warehouse, seized more weapons, and gathered more recruits. Soon, nearly the entire regiment of about two thousand enlisted men resolved to oppose deployment to Jeju and to fight for a unified Korea.

Meeting resistance from their officers, they killed as many as twenty, sparing one, Kim Gi-hoe, who claimed to be sympathetic.[45] More than likely, fifteen of the officers they killed were clandestine members of the SKLP, as would later be claimed by Lee Hyun-sang, commander of all guerrillas in the South. (As noted earlier, enlisted men reported to the South Jeolla provincial party leadership, while officers made contact with the national party apparatus in Seoul—when it was possible to do so.) It is unclear if SKLP national or regional officials had advance knowledge of the mutiny. Apparently, officers who were members of the SKLP attempted to stop an uprising for which they were not prepared, whether thinking that the time was not right or believing that orders should have come down from party headquarters.

Taking as many of the new weapons as they could carry, the mutineers headed to downtown Yeosu. By the time they arrived, their ranks had swelled to almost 2,500. As people cheered, they hoisted the DPRK flag. Spontaneously, citizens began assembling across the street from the former headquarters of Admiral Lee Sun-shin.[46] Some five thousand of the town's fifty thousand citizens gathered to see what was happening.[47] As word spread that Yeosu was liberated and the country would be reunified, celebrations immediately broke out. The Fourteenth Regiment issued a statement explaining that they couldn't go to Jeju because they would have had to kill "our own Korean People. From now on, we are soldiers of the people." They also stated their main aim was to "protect the country against foreign imperialism" and to "obtain the real independence of Korea."[48] Supported by the vast majority of the citizens and armed with new and better weapons than those used by the police, they quickly took over the entire city.

In the newly liberated public space, women read a declaration of immediate nullification of all ROK laws and their replacement with those of the DPRK. Proclamations announced that land was to be redistributed on an equitable basis. Japanese collaborators, particularly brutal policemen, and rightists were to be tried by people's tribunals. Assembling on the streets of downtown Yeosu, six hundred SKLP members were armed by the insurgents. The administrative power of Yeosu was placed in the hands of the old People's Committee backed by the insurgent military. The head of the PC was Song Uk, principal of the girls' middle school, and its members were the same respected citizens as had served on it in 1945. A newspaper was published promising to defend the new Korean People's Republic and repeated its program: redistribution of land, an immediate purge of Japanese collaborators, and opposition to division of the country. In one decisive blow, the Fourteenth Regiment restored the banned citizens' council, and the group immediately reinstated the program for which people had already rallied.

Before the uprising, prices for basic food like rice had risen nearly 500 percent. (Eight kilos of rice had increased in stores from 2,368 won to 11,192.) The restored PC immediately lowered the price. As armed insurgents roamed the city, many former Japanese collaborators were summarily executed. At least one railroad policeman was also killed—but not the local rich. Kim Young-jun, richest man in Yeosu and owner of a shoe factory, was executed by a young people's tribunal, but not for his wealth—for giving Japan an airplane. People also took his factory and gave the white shoes it produced to the poor. Everywhere people marched to spread the news of liberation. U.S. sources spotted "a group of twenty-four people carrying a red banner at the gate" at Yeosu Leper Colony. U.S. intelligence continued: "Even the students of Middle School, Marine School, and Girls' Middle School are armed."[49]

Having taken Yeosu, the insurgents decided to capture nearby Sunchon. At 10 a.m. on October 20, a train carried four hundred armed insurgents to Sunchon.[50] Firing their guns into the air as they made a grand entrance, they were quickly joined by the city's military forces. Sunchon's police, however, massed on the city's north side. At 7 p.m., after a daylong battle in which four hundred police were killed, insurgents controlled Sunchon.[51] Several thousand citizens restored the People's Committee. Tribunals were quickly instituted, and former Japanese collaborators were executed. Many more policemen were also killed, probably around a hundred.[52] In the words of U.S. intelligence reports, a "large proportion" of the people supported the people's tribunals, and middle-school students "avidly joined in the assaults on the police."[53] At the same time, two U.S. officers, Greenbaum and Mohr, who happened to be caught up in the scene, were safely escorted away from public view. One report claims they were ensconced in the nearby house of a missionary. In any event, the self-discipline of people in not killing the Americans would not be reciprocated. U.S. officials knew they were fighting a war, while ordinary Koreans still harbored hope that their U.S. "liberators" could be persuaded to grant them independence.

In an attempt to expand the area controlled by their People's Republic, insurgents divided armed units into three sectors—Namwon, Gwangju, and Gwangyang. They quickly took Gurye and reached Pulgyo, Goheung, Boseong, and Gokseong.[54] In Gwangyang and Boseong, citizens spontaneously formed people's courts—and in Gurye, which Cumings described as "not radical at all" the DPRK flag flew everywhere and people's courts were set up.[55] According to U.S. reports, the rebel column was marching and singing the "Red Flag Song" when two thousand insurgents attacked Gurye. American intelligence complained, "Civilians too damn active" and reported insurgents in Namwon, Jangheung, Goheung, and Hadong.

On the night of October 21, ROK units intercepted a top-secret communication from the insurgents in Sunchon to their comrades in Gwangju with details of a plan to seize control of all of Honam (North and South Jeolla Provinces). The Fourteenth Regiment was to take Namwon, Jeonju, and Iri, while the Fourth Regiment, based in Gwangju, after seizing Mokpo and Gwangju, would link up with the Fourteenth in Iri.[56] When scattered fighting was reported in Gwangju, a U.S. report said about five hundred men of the Fourth Regiment "seem to be cooperating with the rebels." The North Korean flag was reported flying over Gwangyang by two different sources.

So serious was the situation that USAMGIK headquarters sent a letter to Captain James Hausman, the lead U.S. combat coordinator on the ground in Korea (and self-described "father of the South Korean Army") telling him, "The fledgling ROK government is tottering and Yeosu must be retaken immediately at all cost."[57] Hausman took his assignment to heart. He personally directed ten of the ROK's fifteen Constabulary regiments to encircle and retake the insurgent cities one at a time—no matter what the cost to the population. Too young to enlist, Hausman had joined the military under false pretences by using his brother's name. Here was his opportunity to make something of himself.

On the same day the Russians were pulling out all their troops from the North, U.S. officers were coordinating suppression of peoples' movements in the "independent" South.[58] U.S. documents reveal micromanagement of KC troop movements including such details as the number of men loaded in Kunsan to go to Gwangju and specific amounts of canned goods and gasoline shipped from one city to another. In the Jeollas, the uprising was successful because it was so popular, and it was suppressed only through superior firepower provided and supervised by Hausman and an elite group of U.S. officers. With only one exception, all the Korean commanding officers who directly took orders from Americans had served in the Japanese military. Most were graduates of Manchurian Bong-Chun Military Academy, where they were specifically trained to hunt down Korean partisans.[59] As Cumings summarized, "The commanders who actually subdued the rebels were Americans . . . even though the Occupation had ended and the United States had no mandate to intervene in Korean internal affairs."[60] Secretly, the United States had secured Rhee's agreement for U.S. control of the ROK military—something which Rhee was quite willing to grant given the weakness of his support among people in the South—including within his own army. In late 1947, American diplomat Gregory Henderson believed the ROK forces "were still so badly trained and under-equipped as to not justify rational estimate of capacity to resist attack."[61] Rhee had U.S. cargo planes to move troops and materials as needed, U.S. weapons by the boxcar, U.S. spotter aircraft to provide intelligence, and U.S. personnel to coordinate his offensives. Why did he need support among ordinary Koreans?

After two days of intense fighting, Sunchon was taken on the morning of October 23. The attack on Yeosu began that same morning at 9:40 a.m. and lasted until October 27. U.S. officer Minor L. Kelso described "setting up mortars above Yosu . . . setting much of the town on fire."[62] For two days, warships also rained heavy shells on the city, killing many civilians. A Coast Guard vessel with 37 mm cannons was sent to Yeosu from Incheon. Among the insurgents, a hundred schoolgirls, armed with vintage Japanese rifles, held the waterfront on October 25. On October 27, they helped repel a second amphibious landing, bravely holding firm despite fire from warships at 10 a.m.[63] Hausman described "house-to-house fighting" before the city was completely overrun at 2 p.m. on October 27. The wharf and fishery areas were razed, and fully one-fourth of the city was burnt completely. Although the entire population was rounded up, only a few men of the Fourteenth Regiment were captured, no more than ten uniformed insurgents and sixty-three in all. The rest fought their way out of the encirclement and made their way to Giri Mountain.

After hundreds of people were killed defending the city, a grisly massacre took place, calmly observed by U.S. officers. One U.S. report told how "the Korean Constabulary was shooting wildly." All the citizens were rounded up in the elementary school. Korean police, many of them wearing their old Japanese uniforms, took horrific vengeance.[64] The worst was former Japanese army sergeant Kim Chong-hwan, "Tiger Kim," as U.S. officers nicknamed him, who used his samurai sword to decapitate many prisoners. U.S. reports concluded that, the main objective was the "sacking and raping of now over-powered Yosu. Doubtless this proceeded as their wildest dreams would have it."[65] Anyone with white shoes was fingered for death (since they were wearing the free shoes distributed by the PC), as was anyone with rough hands, since it meant they were a factory worker, fisherman, or poor farmer. Students and youth were also targets of the murderous Constabulary.

On December 6, 1948, American journalist Carl Mydans published details of these atrocities in *Life* magazine. Mydans described how five thousand arrestees were "beaten with bars, iron chains, and the butts of rifles."[66] Dozens of summary executions took place, and an additional 866 death sentences went through what the United States called "proper channels." Near Mansangri Beach on October 27, more than 125 people were executed and their bodies left for others to find and bury. In Ho-Myong Dong, an additional hundred people were slaughtered. In Gurye, at least 188 farmers were executed upon the arrival of the suppression army (what people called the Korean Constabulary).

Cumings considered the terror of Tiger Kim and the slaughter perpetrated by U.S.-led forces in Yeosu as "not a slaughter of innocents."[67] In his view, the "revolutionary terror of the rebels met its opposite as loyalists took their awful retribution."[68] Clearly the number of people slaughtered differed by an order of magnitude—hundreds were killed by the insurgents versus thousands by the United States and KC. We will never have an accurate count of the number of individuals who perished as a result of the uprising and massacre. Out of a total population of about 100,000 in Yeosu, Sunchon, Gwangyang, Gurye, Posang, Pulgyo, and Goheung, the ROK government claimed 7,000 killed; the North Koreans: 2,326. In 2002, scholar Kim Deug-Joong surmised about 10,000 deaths, a number also used by Lee Young-il of the Yeosu Research Institute.[69] Scholar Lee Chaehun estimated that 2,000 of the 4,700 soldiers involved in the insurrection were killed.[70] A total of at least 2,591 were imprisoned as a result of the uprising. Surviving captives thought to have been insurgents were transported to Daejon prison—including 300 from Jeju and 1,300 from Yeosun. (In all probability, they were all executed in the mass killings in Daejon supervised by U.S. officers as North Korean troops advanced south in the early days of the Korean War.) Among the casualties in 1948, we also should count many unknown refugees who fled the fighting and became victims of the government's subsequent blockade of food in a vast swath on Giri Mountain.[71]

Although "Hausman's boys" killed thousands of civilians, his responsibility—and that of the United States—has yet to be acknowledged by U.S. authorities. Instead, Hausman is recorded in U.S. accounts of this period as a heroic figure, joining a long list of men like Jeffrey Amherst, George Custer, Ithiel de Sola Pool, and William Westmoreland who gained accolades for their participation in extermination campaigns. For his "efficiency" in "planning and execution of the suppression of Yeosu Uprising," Hausman would receive the U.S. Legion of Merit citation. (In 1981, he would receive an additional medal of recognition for his years of service from Chun Doo-hwan.) Despite clear knowledge of thousands of casualties, U.S. policymakers remained undeterred in their support for Rhee and Korea's division.

Systematically combing the vast wilderness of Giri Mountain, U.S. advisors led thousands of Korean troops on search and destroy missions. Anyone captured was deemed an insurgent. Rounded up, these hapless people—many of them refugees from the intense fighting—were subject to the "justice" the United States brought to Korea. By the end of November 1948, 1,714 people had been tried in military courts, and 866 received death sentences. Describing the retribution faced by captives during the long campaign on Giri Mountain, one U.S. soldier

Corpses of massacred insurgents after the U.S.-led suppression of the Yeosun Uprising.
Life magazine

penned some unforgettable lines: "Weeding out is a simple process. Summary and Special Courts, appointed by regimental commanders, try and award death penalties. A good Summary Court Officer can handle sixty to seventy cases in the morning and supervise the executions in the afternoon. If ammunition is scarce, bamboo spears work quite efficiently. It is necessary, however, to make a number of thrusts and is quite tiring on the soldiers. The soldiers are a tireless lot though."[72] Most of the corpses were burned and ashes scattered—an affront

Two U.S. officers display the captured flag of the Fourteenth Regiment after the suppression of the Yeosun Uprising. *Life* magazine

to generations yet to come when we remember the importance of reverence of ancestors in Korea. Kim Gi-hoe, the officer spared by the Fourteenth Regiment when they first mutinied, became a partisan leader on Giri Mountain. After he was killed and beheaded, U.S. Capt. James Hausman kept his severed head in a five-gallon gasoline can in his office.[73]

Consequences of the Insurrection
The Yeosun insurrection represented a qualitative leap in the tactics of South Korea's movement for national integrity and independence. Not only did militancy escalate, but the class character of the insurrection, strikingly represented by the enlisted men's leadership, helped win them broad regional support. By weaving together anti-imperialism and class struggle, and by affirming the unity of Korea, the content of the uprising was revolutionary and nationalist. The massacre in Jeju had made the futility of even small group resistance apparent since, in tactics reminiscent of Nazi actions in Greece, the whole island had been ravaged in response to guerrilla attacks. By seizing control of an entire region, the insurgents hoped to overthrow the government—an objective they came close to accomplishing.

U.S. intelligence estimated that the "fledgling ROK government is tottering" and corroborated the views of the leaders of the uprising who believed they could spark a last great battle for liberation of the country. As the insurrection unfolded, the United States believed a "nationwide rebellion" had been planned. American intelligence reported that "the communist cells tried to start a rebellion at Daegu and did kill a few loyal officers but the situation was brought under control in a matter of hours. It is hard to say what might have happened if the communists [*sic*] had succeeded in pulling a nationwide rebellion, as planned."[74] In 1948, the CIA estimated that about 10 percent of the population of the South—about two million people—belonged to SKLP organizations. Of that number, ten thousand were classified as "cadre" and another six hundred thousand as "activists."[75] If the organization had succeeded in coordinating actions among its members, would the United States have bloodily had its way in 1948? In retrospect, we know that the uprising was not planned in advance, as indicated by the difficulties SKLP members had in communicating with each other. The harsh repression in the South severely limited all forms of communication among patriots, leaving activists isolated and needing to take initiative on their own.

For Cumings, the actions taken in Yeosu were misguided: "Basically it was a rebellion by military officers who didn't want to go to Jeju to suppress the rebels. I thought it was kind of a foolish rebellion because they didn't know what they were doing."[76] For him the uprising was "spontaneous and poorly-planned . . . a last-ditch stand born of both outrage and futility, taken on the spur of the moment with little hope of success."[77] (He is mistaken when he maintains "military officers" were the ones who took action, since enlisted men were the central force.) As in his analysis of the 1946 October Uprising, Cumings fails to distinguish rebellion and revolution. In the understanding of Jean-Paul Sartre: "The revolutionary wants to change the world; he transcends it and moves toward the future, toward an order of values which he invents. The rebel is careful to preserve the abuses from which he suffers so he can go on rebelling against them . . . He does not want to destroy or transcend the existing order; he simply wants to rise against it."[78] According to Sartre's criteria, Yeosun was not a rebellion, far from it. A rebellion only reacts against unjust authority. A revolution seeks to establish a new order—and this was precisely the character of Yeosun. PCs were restored, people's tribunals meted out harsh justice, the flag of the DPRK was flown, and people's goals of independence and unification were clearly subversive of the order so desperately maintained by the United States. The banks in both Yeosu and Sunchon were robbed—not to line the pockets of the "rebels"—but to fund their People's Republic. People believed North Korean troops would arrive to link up with the insurrectionary government. If they considered the Rhee government legitimate and the uprising's goal had been only to secure greater justice within it, then rebellion would be an apt term, but the insurgents aimed to establish a completely different system. If it had been a mere rebellion, the insurgents would have lain down arms once it was clear they had been defeated in Yeosu. In fact, they fought their way out, attacking Gurye on October 25, and holding it during that night.[79] Led by Kim Gi-hoe, they burned the police station on the twenty-sixth before moving on to Giri Mountain. On November 5, Gurye was again attacked. As fighting continued, on November 19, Constabulary forces led by U.S. offices killed two hundred insurgents and captured five hundred more.

Trained in the North's cadre schools and one of the key leaders of the southern Party, Lee Hyun-sang believed the uprising was a "crime against the Party" since it was not authorized by Pyongyang. Nonetheless, he helped guide many surviving fighters to Giri Mountain and stayed with them.[80] In evaluating the

Yeosun Uprising, I am reminded of Rosa Luxemburg's preference for the superiority of the worst mistakes of a truly democratic workers' movement in comparison to the best dictates of a party's central committee. With historical hindsight, 20–20 vision is easy to maintain, but seldom can people accurately judge
in the heat of battle what the outcome will be. In such moments, as Marcuse
tells us, "Only he who commits the desperate act can judge whether the price
he is bound to pay is too high—too high in terms of his own cause as a common
cause. Any generalization would be ambivalent, nay profoundly unjust: it would
condemn the victims of the system to the prolonged agony of waiting, to prolonged suffering."[81] If the communications network of insurgent forces had been
better, or if other regiments had mutinied, or if the United States had not resolved
to save Rhee—an endless number of ifs could be added here—the outcome may
have been favorable to Korea's patriotic forces. Refusing to go to Jeju and massacre their fellow Koreans, the men of the Fourteenth Regiment acted in the best
traditions of freedom. Once they had made their fateful decision, they had little
choice but to follow through.

The unfolding of the movement in the southern part of the country continued in logical progression: from establishment of the KPR and the PCs; to massive
public protests, strikes by workers, and rural seizures of power; and finally to the
establishment of armed revolutionary dual power in entire regions. Defeated only
through massive firepower directed by the United States, the movement refused
to accept defeat and continually moved to higher levels of struggle. Between the
Yeosun insurrection and what U.S. historians consider the outbreak of the Korean
War on June 25, 1950, guerrilla warfare became of necessity the anti-imperialist
movement's tactical approach.

With the severe brutality suffered in Jeju and Yeosun, the resistance stiffened. Between November 2, 1948 and January 30, 1949, three mutinies occurred
in the ranks of the Sixth Regiment in Daegu.[82] In the same month, British sources
reported three thousand arrests in Gwangju. On December 20, a nineteen-hour
battle near Naju involving two hundred rebels inflicted severe losses on ROK
troops. Guerrillas were strongest in South Jeolla, where four separate forces, each
with a hundred armed partisans and thousands of supporters, continually gathered strength as they disabled telegraph and railroad lines.

On January 3, 1949, two hundred insurgents attacked the outskirts of Jeju
City. They managed to set City Hall on fire and destroy all the records inside. Their
offensive embarrassed the government of Rhee, and he stepped up the extermination campaign. Four more battalions of his army were assigned to Jeju. Soon
more than 70 percent of the villages were burned, and the interior of the island
was essentially depopulated, except for the upper parts of Mount Halla. More
than one in three islanders were forced to live in a fenced government camp along
the coast (a model for the subsequent "strategic hamlet" program in Vietnam).
Nonetheless, incessant guerrilla attacks left only small coastal areas safe for U.S.-
backed forces. In April, the island was nearly completely overrun by partisan
forces that emerged from their bases on Mount Halla. Rhee visited Jeju and personally ordered a "scorched earth" policy. Results were rapid. Partisan leader Kim

TABLE 4.1 **Statistics Related to Guerrilla Activity in Southern Korea, 1949**

Month	Guerrillas	Incidents	Enemy Casualties
April	16,257	482	716
August	44,200	759	1,203
September	77,900	1,184	2,104
October	89,900	1,330	2,415
November	77,900	1,260	2,213

Source: Yi Sung-yop, "The Struggle of the Southern Guerrillas for the Unification of the Homeland," *Kulloja* (January 1950), 21, as reported in Cumings, *Origins*, 2:273. Casualties refer to enemies killed and wounded.

Min-sok was imprisoned and beheaded; Lee Tok-ku was killed and his mutilated body crucified in front of the new city administration building on June 7, 1949.

Despite the massive application of force, resistance grew throughout Korea. In the spring of 1949, the SKLP launched a major guerrilla offensive. As portrayed in TABLE 4.1, the number of guerrillas in southern Korea grew from 16,257 in April 1949 to 89,900 in October—falling to 77,900 by November.[83]

Even among Rhee's troops in the KC, mutinies continued. On May 4, 1949, two battalions of the Eighth Regiment walked across the thirty-eighth parallel and joined the armed forces of the DPRK. In August, the SS *Kimball B. Smith*, a U.S. merchant ship leased to the ROK, defected to North Korea with all its crew, who took with them three American advisors.

On Giri Mountain, dozens of executions monthly continued until at least July 1949. U.S. naval ships patrolled the coasts of South Korea, and U.S. planes provided daily intelligence reports to the ROK. U.S. officers continued to supervise former Japanese army officers in the campaigns to encircle the guerrillas. Nonetheless, by the end of the summer of 1949, "the guerrillas operated in large areas of southern Korean and appeared quite formidable. Therefore the Americans decided to step in directly, and inaugurate a major winter suppression campaign. Beginning in the late fall of 1949, it lasted almost down to the outbreak of the war."[84]

Japanese trained police and army officers proved invaluable to U.S. rule in Korea and would form the core of the ROK's political infrastructure for decades to come. U.S. operatives were keenly aware of their importance to American administration. On August 2, Hausman personally intervened with Syngman Rhee to save the life of future dictator Park Chung-hee. Park had been an intelligence officer in the Japanese army and sought to capture or kill Kim Il-Sung. In 1948, although involved in the Yeosun Uprising, he turned on his comrades. His subordinate officer, Kim Jeong-sok, captured at the same time as Park, was executed. For the next three decades, Hausman remained the most important U.S. military liaison in Korea. He was no doubt quite pleased when his protégé became military dictator of the ROK in 1961.

Without U.S. agents continually correcting Rhee's blind decisions, it is doubtful the ROK would have survived. After two U.S. consuls came to Gwangju to assess the situation, partisans set a clever ambush and killed twenty-five police. Government forces evacuated villages and built walls of sand bags around police stations. "Each police box resembles a medieval fort," reported the Americans. In

Gurye, local officials believed 90 percent of the citizens were "Communist." After Yeosun, the guerrillas had apparently made many new converts there.

On September 29, the chief of the U.S. Korean Military Assistance Group reported that, "Guerrilla activities and operations within the Provinces of Jeolla Pukto, Jeolla Namdo, and Kyong Sang Namdo are increasing in scope and extent." State Department officials reported that the "government has lost control outside the cities and larger towns." In October, hundreds of guerrillas were reported at Muju and Jinju. Later that month, about seventy guerrillas facilitated people's courts where about four thousand farmers from forty-six villages harshly punished "evil landlords" and carried out land reforms. U.S. intelligence in Tokyo called a wide swath of the Jeollas from Namwon through Giri Mountain to Sunchon and around to Mokpo "the guerrilla stronghold in the ROK, with the guerrillas in nearly complete control of South Jeolla province."[85] Elsewhere, there were reports of PCs being reestablished and heavy guerrilla recruitment from villages.

FIGURE 4.2 provides a picture of where guerrillas were most concentrated.

This insurgency was no North Korean infiltration, as Syngman Rhee insisted. In April 1950, American intelligence surmised, "almost 100 percent of the guerrillas in the Jeolla and Kyongsang Provinces have been recruited locally." As the guerrilla struggle intensified, Rhee's American advisors encouraged him to create an elite force of fifty thousand men extracted from the national police and charged with "systematic eradication of all guerilla and rebel activities in South Korea." Despite the intense campaign against them, around a thousand insurgents were able to survive until 1950—when they linked up with advance elements of the Korean People's Army (KPA).[86] In fact, in Mokpo and Gwangju, partisans rose up before the KPA arrived. In one case, four thousand textile workers stoned their factory's owner, drove him away, and took over production themselves.[87]

National Security Law and the Rhee Dictatorship

Within two months of the demise of Yeosu, Rhee's government came under strong U.S. pressure to crack down on sympathy for the North. In response, they passed a National Security Law, modeled on Japanese law, which mandated the death penalty for anyone acting on behalf of the government in Pyongyang. In its first year, police used their expanded legal authority to arrest 188,621 people under NSL provisions.[88] The army was purged at the same time as recruitment and arming of paramilitary right-wing groups was accelerated. The U.S. was so pleased with the performance of the NWYL on Jeju that its members were given new uniforms and sent to Yeosu and Sunchon to have their way with the citizenry. Rhee established a new paramilitary National Student Defense Corps in 1949, which Namhee Lee compared with Hitler's youth organization.[89]

While the Yeosun insurrection was a tactical defeat after which strong blows were dealt to movement personnel and organizations, it also served to convince the United States that Rhee's government was in dire straights. A few weeks afterward, a CIA National Intelligence Estimate, "Prospects for the Survival of the ROK" concluded, "without massive infusion of U.S. aid, the ROK could not

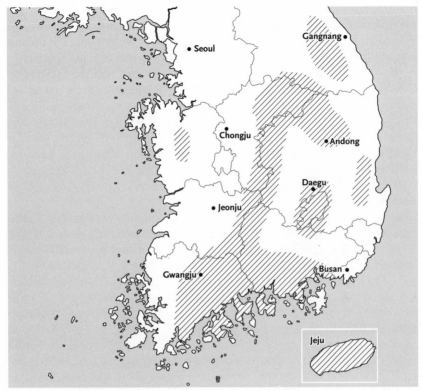

FIGURE 4.2 **Guerrilla Strongholds, 1949**
Source: Cumings, *Origins*, 2:270.

survive."[90] Secretary of State Dean Rusk was convinced that the ROK would fall in three months if it were not delivered economic aid.[91] A year afterward, in October 1949, massive amounts of American supplies flowed into the country. In the CIA's assessment, "The ROK is wholly dependent on U.S. economic and military aid for its survival."[92]

Rhee's iron fist targeted even moderate nationalists like Kim Kyu, who had become president of the Shanghai-based Korean Provisional Government after Rhee was impeached. Although a staunch anti-Communist, Kim vowed never to accept the country's division. On June 26, 1949, he was assassinated, an act subsequently traced to Rhee's orders. Rhee closed down newspapers, purged the army, and arrested as many as a thousand politicians in one month. He found a mainland corollary to his "scorched earth" policy in an Orwellian-entitled "National Guidance Alliance" (보도연맹 or *Bodoyonmaeng*) that required hundreds of thousands of people to register with the police. Assured of their safety only if they reported to ROK officials, anyone who had been involved in civil organizations after 1945 faced imprisonment. With the stroke of his pen, the dictator made membership in the National League of Peasants' Unions or the Women's League—broad patriotic civic groups founded after Japan's defeat—into criminal offenses carrying a potential death penalty.

To implement his new measures, Rhee nearly doubled the number of police. When the United States officially turned over control of the police to Rhee in 1948, they counted thirty-four thousand police. By the end of the year, their number stood at sixty thousand.[93] U.S. sources placed the number of political prisoners in the American military government's jails at more than twenty-two thousand in mid-1947—nearly twice as many as under the Japanese—but Rhee far surpassed even that number. By the end of 1949, his jails were overflowing with thirty thousand prisoners, approximately 80 percent of whom were thought to be Communists.[94] At the same time, only one of the hundreds of Koreans officially deemed "traitors" to the Japanese in 1945 was in prison, while many others sat as judges and sentenced patriots to death.

Korean War

In few wars in history has a country been as devastated as Korea was in three short years from 1950 to 1953. The light-hearted U.S. television comedy series *M*A*S*H*, so popular in the United States for years, failed to portray the utter devastation Korea suffered in what Americans routinely refer to as the "Forgotten War." In 2003, I visited massacre sites in both South and North Korea and met survivors of U.S. air raids, witnesses of biological weapons being deployed, as well as people who had been wounded, lost parents, and seen their children killed. It was terribly traumatic for these people to rehash these horrible stories, yet it meant so much to them because I am an American. The "Forgotten War" remains very much remembered in Korea. As a group of us returned to Pyongyang from Sinchon, my bus buddy was Tran Trong Giap, a Vietnamese delegate to the commemoration of the fiftieth anniversary of the armistice. As we rode away from the area, Tran told me, "The Korean War was the most barbarous war in history. We had two or three My Lais in Vietnam, but there were too many massacres here and the United States killed thousands, not hundreds."

In and around Sinchon, we had heard testimony and visited the site of a gruesome killing spree in an area controlled by the United States on October 17, 1950. In fifty-two days, more than 35,000 people were slaughtered, including 8,000 children and 400 teachers. At the bridge over the Sok Dang River, more than 2,000 people were tied up—sometimes in groups—and thrown into the water to drown. Even more horribly, 1,200 people were burned to death in an ice storehouse. Seeing the marks scratched into the black, sooty walls and ceilings by human beings trying to escape the burning inferno was an eerie, terrifying experience. The Sinchon Museum reminded me of the Holocaust Museum in Washington, D.C. As I walked past piles of victims' shoes, eyeglasses, hair, and personal belongings, I felt simultaneous rage and horror, disbelief and anger.[95]

Despite the prevailing view that the United States liberated and enlightened Korea by overturning Japanese colonial rule, the sad postwar reality was that a U.S. military government imposed America's imperial will through massive force. Acting in its own Cold War interests to create bulwarks against perceived Russian expansionism and the "domino effect" of the Chinese revolution, the United States ultimately partitioned both Korea and Vietnam into two states.

When Koreans refused to go quietly in the night, the United States used its military superiority to destroy the entire peninsula.

In the first few weeks of the war, the North pushed southward, and in a few weeks had seized the entire peninsula except for encircled remnants of ROK and U.S. forces in a corner of the peninsula's southeastern tip dug in along the Naktong River around Busan. Kim Il-sung's first radio address after the war broke out called for the reinstatement of the People's Committee in areas abandoned by the ROK and United States. All over the country, people did just that. On June 27, people elected a fifteen-member PC in Yonbaek. Within a month, similar elections took place in hundreds of villages—and elected delegates chose representatives for townships, then counties, and finally for provincial level governing authorities. The PCs of 1945 apparently had much more staying power than is generally understood.

If not for massive U.S. airpower launched from Japan, all of Korea would have been captured by the seasoned fighters of the DPRK amid popular support that greeted them as liberators. Without the U.S. Air Force and Navy, the war would have ended in a few weeks at the most, with the North victorious. If the United States had allowed Koreans to settle their own differences—or, speculating widely—if Roosevelt had lived another year and accepted Korean independence—the peninsula would have been spared utter devastation, and millions of lives would have been saved. Today, unified Korea would probably be a prosperous hub of northeast Asia. If the United States had seen fit to treat it as a most favored nation, Korea would likely be as prosperous today as Japan. Certainly North Korea, the most industrialized part of East Asia outside Japan in 1945, would not be anywhere near its currently impoverished state. Mired in continuing conflict with the United States (which still refuses to sign a peace treaty with the DPRK to replace the cease-fire agreement of 1953), the North has suffered terribly from more than half a century of blockade, financial embargo by world institutions, continual intrusions and feigned attacks, demise of its major benefactors in Russia, and poor decisions made in the midst of natural disasters.

Of course, most American and conservative South Korean commentators portray the war as caused by a Communist invasion—but no one has ever answered the question: how can Koreans invade themselves? Even if we accept June 25, 1950 as the starting date of the war, considerable doubt exists about who attacked whom on that date. Rhee had always promised to control the entire peninsula, and his generals continually ordered major incursions across the DMZ. In 1949 alone, the DPRK counted 2,617 attacks across the thirty-eighth parallel in which hundreds of their soldiers were killed. Moreover, lest we forget, the war started long before June 25, 1950. In the five years before it, under the U.S. military government and the Rhee regime, more than a hundred thousand patriots in the South were killed.[96] Holger Heide estimated the number at twice that.[97] Severing this "little" war from the "real" Korean War serves to blame North Korea for the conflict.

The DPRK claims the South attacked across the thirty-eighth parallel on June 25 and the North responded. Both sides agree that as DPRK soldiers pushed southward, ROK and U.S. troops panicked and fled, leaving an open field. U.S. accounts do not contest the panicky retreat. Indeed, the Pentagon has reluctantly confirmed reports from this period of U.S. troops' massacres of unarmed and clearly marked refugee columns composed of innocent civilians fleeing the fighting (as at No Gun Ri). Standing in remarkable contrast to systematic U.S. attacks on civilians from land, sea, and air, North Korean soldiers were mostly disciplined and refrained from wanton attacks. After the victory of the Chinese revolution in 1949, many fighters returned home to Korea, where they formed the nucleus of the KPA. Years of experience fighting alongside Chinese Communist forces against Japan had steeled tens of thousands of Korean veterans, who brought with them legendary skills and discipline when they repatriated in 1949 and 1950. Cumings estimated that 80 percent of the officers of the KPA had served in China and more than 100,000 soldiers had battle experience there.[98] China's Fourth Field Army, the crack unit of the People's Liberation Army, never lost a battle; it alone was said to have had some 145,000 Koreans within its ranks. Almost none of the soldiers who had fought against Japan from inside China went over to the U.S. side—although nearly all former officers who had served in the Japanese military did. Apparently it did not matter which imperial master these collaborators served, as long as they were paid handsomely for their expertise.

Channing Liem, ROK ambassador to the UN from 1960 to 1961, revealed that U.S. policymakers were instrumental in abetting Rhee's nefarious plan to conquer the North. According to Liem, former U.S. Secretary of State John Foster Dulles met Rhee on June 18—only a week before the war began. Dulles told him, "If he was ready to attack the Communist North, the United States would lend help through the UN" but to be sure to "persuade the world that the ROK was attacked first." Secretary of State Dean Acheson was "quick to blame the war on North Korea regardless of the evidence."[99] Independent journalist I.F. Stone wrote a weighty indictment of U.S. manipulation of the UN and the media at the beginning of the war.[100] Bruce Cumings concluded his monumental *Origins of the Korean War* by finding it impossible to determine who began the war. Years later, Cumings—foremost American expert on Korea for decades—conclusively "proved" the Korean War was a civil war: "Koreans know this war in their bones as a fratricidal conflict."[101] Clearly, Cumings speaks of a small sample of Koreans.

In 1980, Cumings questioned the conventional view that North Korea was solely responsible for instigating the war. Yet today, reading Cumings's insistence that the war was "civil and revolutionary" in character and his refusal to name the United States—the only outside power that bombed cities and killed so many civilians—as the main responsible party appears to absolve American imperial ambitions for the cause of so many deaths. Cumings's loyalty is evident in his naming Dean Acheson, one of the men most intimately involved with perpetuating the war, "the greatest of postwar secretaries of state."[102] Acheson was the U.S. "architect of Korea policy from the important transition point in early 1947 to the momentous American intervention in 1950." Yet rather than take him to task for the suffering and deaths he caused, Cumings praises him—even takes the subtitle of Volume 2 of his study—"The Roaring of the Cataract"—from

Acheson's description of how he felt in 1950, as the United States "grasped for world leadership amid the regression of the British empire."[103] Continuing in the same vein, Cumings heeded the friendly advice he received from Dean Rusk that documents are less important in writing history than "ongoing discussions of all sorts, hardly any of them recorded for posterity."[104] Perhaps that helps explain why Cumings regards the Greek Civil War as occasioned by the Soviets, not as commonly understood in Greece, as by the UK and United States—while Stalin and Communists, remaining faithful to agreements with Churchill, sold out indigenous independence fighters.[105]

By excluding in advance the simple explanation of the war as one of national liberation, Cumings fundamentally disagrees with the point of view of millions of Koreans, nearly all of whom in 1945 held desires for national independence and integrity of Korea foremost in their hearts. The fervent desire for Korea's unity and autonomy is what made millions of people ready to sacrifice their lives and fortunes. In 1950, the United States denied that aspiration; today few U.S. accounts grant it visibility. Rather, as Cumings tells us, North Korea "occupied" South Korea; the United States assisted the Rhee government,[106] and the United States "retrieved it from oblivion in the summer of 1950."[107]

Considering the war's outcome rather than its origins, Cumings considers the verdict mixed: "For the Truman Cold War liberal, Korea was a success, 'the limited war.' For the MacArthur conservative, Korea was a failure: the first defeat in American history . . . so we need another verdict: a split decision—the first Korean War, the war for the South in 1950, was a success. The second war, the war for the North was a failure."[108] By evaluating the war on the basis of U.S. views, Cumings continues to disregard Koreans' viewpoint. The Cold War rendered Koreans invisible as the United States and the USSR fought each other. In my view, the killing of five million Koreans and the destruction of their homeland was an unnecessary tragedy for which the United States is primarily responsible.

The key to the brutal repression of Korea is the victory of the Chinese revolution in 1949 and U.S. fear of the proliferation of anticolonial revolutions in Asia (the "domino effect"). American Cold War strategy dictated the sacrifice of millions of Korean lives—and subsequently millions of Indochinese as well—in order to encircle China and contain its revolution. Subsequent American obfuscation of its genocidal role in Korea covers up world-historic U.S. imperial savagery. Making alliances with ruthless dictators and colonial powers throughout the world, not just Korea, the United States launched hot wars to roll back the advance of Third World revolutions in Asia, Africa, and Latin America. The United States overthrew democratically elected leaders like Iranian Premier Mohammad Mossadeq (1953), Guatemalan President Jacobo Árbenz (1954), Brazilian President João Goulart (1964), and Chilean President Salvador Allende (1973), all of whom were sacrificed to American imperial ambitions—this is but a partial list of only the most visible among millions of victims of American "liberation."

Facts exist in a context, and within the above context, the debate about the start of the Korean War vanishes into irrelevance. The war "started" the day the United States intervened against grassroots People's Committees, the moment it occupied Japanese military bases and restored and defended Japanese collaborators and all exploiters willing to serve whichever colonial power would protect their property interests. In its uninhibited willingness to apply force when needed, U.S. strategic goals never changed. Circumstances changed in 1945, when victory over Japan brought U.S. corporate interests into a collision course with powerful popular movements, necessitating a genocidal solution. Within the imperialist metropoles, illusions on the Left about Roosevelt and Stalin facilitated the tyrannical project by giving time and space to the United States to prepare the restoration of despotic domination, whether in Greece or Korea.

To dwell on the origins of the war is an insufficient means to evaluate it. As Kim Dong-choon notes in his remarkable book, "It is high time to break through the fixation on the beginning of the war, on which traditional as well as revisionist schools remain caught, in order to enact a fundamental paradigm shift."[109] In his view, it is more important to evaluate the war's character in order to seek ways to finish with its continuing impact in Northeast Asia more than half a century after its "end." While the United States has long since made peace with Vietnam and with North Korea's Chinese allies, it still maintains a state of war with Pyongyang. In order to uncover the roots of this continuing conflict, the most important question that needs to be asked concerns the war's character: was it a civil war or one of national independence against imperialist intervention?

If it was a civil war, then who are the equivalents to Lee and Grant, to Stonewall Jackson and William Tecumseh Sherman? Whether we seek an answer in South Korean or U.S. histories, movies, and public monuments, we inevitably come across U.S. generals, not Korean ones: MacArthur, Ridgeway, and Walton Harris Walker (after whom a Sheraton Hotel and Casino in Seoul are still named). The prominence of U.S. generals in the Korean "civil" war is no accident, since Syngman Rhee gave United States complete operational control of ROK troops through the Daejon Agreement of 1950. (The Combined Forces Command continues to this day.) What kind of independence is it when President Rhee signed the Daejon agreement of 1950 handing over control of all South Korean armed forces to the United States?

Rhee did not bring MacArthur to Korea to help with the war; MacArthur brought Rhee to Korea from the United States on one of the U.S. military planes reserved for MacArthur's personal use. Less than three months after the "North Korean surprise attack," MacArthur assembled a fleet larger than D-Day's Normandy invasion force, and, on September 15, he landed at Incheon, easily retaking Seoul while North Korean troops were still busy instituting land reform in the South. MacArthur then brought Rhee back to Seoul a second time, handing him the reins of power as Rhee cried with joy. In 1950 he again presented him as leader of a government in Seoul after retaking it from the North Koreans.

Prominent U.S. scholars compare Greece's Peloponnesian Wars to the Korean War, using an analogy to the autonomous city-states of Athens and Sparta to comprehend North and South Korea. If we seek precedents in ancient Greek history, it seems more realistic to compare the United States to Persia based upon size considerations alone. Then as now, foreign imperial interests attracted some indigenous fighters to cross over to the invaders' side. During the invasion by Xerxes, some Greeks fought on the side of Persia (as did others when Alexander brought the war to Asia a generation later). If we follow the logic of the "civil war" characterization, we could imagine that if Persia had conquered Greece, extant history might characterize Persian assistance to peace-loving Greeks who rose against the militaristic Spartans who had seized Thermopylae. Alternatively, consider that if the British had controlled half of the United States after 1789 (when the U.S. Constitution was approved), would historians today refer to the "First American Civil War" beginning on July 4, 1776?

The question of whether the disaster that befell Korea should be understood as a civil war or one of national independence can also be answered by inquiring why the United States has continued its economic embargo of North Korea for more than half a century. If the conflict was indeed a civil war, then the United States should have long since ceased to be involved. How then do we account for decades of U.S. encirclement and isolation of the North, for tens of thousands of U.S. troops remaining in Korea for more than half a century, and for continuing U.S. operational control of South Korea's military? Over the years since the 1953 armistice, at least ten U.S. planes, including an EC 121 spy plane, have been shot down by the DPRK. From 1976 to 1993, U.S. "Operation Team Spirit" threatened invasion and nuclear war. According to the DPRK, every single day for decades, U.S. warplanes capable of dropping nuclear weapons approached the thirty-eighth parallel and, at the last minute, veered off, making the possibility of a U.S. nuclear attack a daily reality. After the capture of the USS Pueblo in 1968, U.S. negotiators apologized for its invasion of DPRK territorial waters and pledged in writing never to do so again, yet the DPRK reported hundreds of subsequent American naval intrusions into its territorial waters. In the 1980s and 1990s, North Korea counted more than 7,900 provocative acts per year, and the United States admitted daily high-altitude surveillance flights over North Korea.

U.S. Massacre of Civilians

In the United States, when the Korean War is remembered—as in the Korean War memorial in Washington, D.C., or any number of Hollywood movies and television productions like *M*A*S*H*—it is portrayed as a military conflict, of soldier vs. soldier. Yet for the people of North Korea, the war meant that every city and nearly every town was completely destroyed by bombs and artillery.

I heard first-hand from one survivor, Choi Gee-ok, of the horror of cleaning up corpses in Pyongyang after U.S. napalm and aerial bombardment left scores of people in her immediate vicinity maimed beyond recognition. The horrific destruction meant only two blocks of buildings in all of Pyongyang remained standing when the shooting stopped. Nearly every major dwelling in North Korea was completely destroyed by bombs and artillery, and about one in four persons living in them was killed. The United States used over six hundred thousand tons of armaments and five times the amount of napalm on Korea as was used in all of World War II.[110] American forces deployed chemical and biological weapons and bombed dams and dikes—actions considered "war crimes" when the United

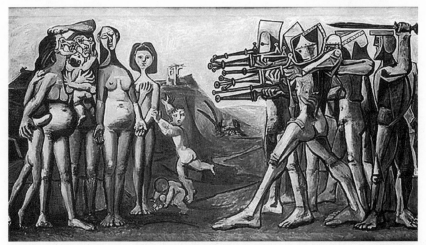

Massacre in Korea. Like many other artists, Pablo Picasso opposed the slaughter of civilians during the Korean War.

States convicted Nazis in Nuremberg—and when U.S. troops invaded across the thirty-eighth parallel, civilian massacres were commonplace. U.S. bombing of hydroelectric stations was so thorough that besides damaging dams that provided 75 percent of water for agriculture and killing thousands of civilians, even Pyongyang was flooded. The battleship USS *Missouri* fired on Seoul when the North occupied it, turning civilians into bloody unrecognizable body parts. Beginning with President Truman's press conference on November 30, 1950, the United States continually threatened to use nuclear weapons. By the time a truce was agreed in 1953, some five million lives had been sacrificed on the altar of the anti-Communist crusade.[111]

Of all the tactics that speak to the war's genocidal character, none to me is more significant (and less reported) than U.S. biological war against North Korea. Cumings does not choose to clarify it. I have already discussed U.S. protection of members of Japanese biological warfare Unit 731. Developed by criminal experimentation on POW's, Col. Ishii and his team's knowledge—as well as some of their specific germ agents—were subsequently used by the United States hundreds of times in its war against the DPRK, especially in the period from January to June 1953, in other words, near the end of the war when the United States realized it could not win a military victory. The War Museum in Pyongyang contains vials of infected insects as well as still labeled U.S. bombs that were used to drop them. Smallpox powder was spread in residential areas as early as 1951, and in 1952, at least ten kinds of germs and pests were disseminated by twenty kinds of bombs, especially on traffic and railroad lines leading to China. North Korean prisoners exchanged on April 7, 1953, were found to have been infected with the plague.[112]

The United States developed its biological weapons beginning in 1947, when Fort Detrick, Maryland, became the center of U.S. germ warfare. In fiscal years 1951–1953, the United States spent more than $345 million on biowar research, money used by the United States to build the weapons it deployed during the

Korean War.[113] U.S. policymakers were unashamed in advocating criminal use of banned weapons. Less than a week after the official outbreak of war in Korea, the Earl Stevenson Commission issued a report advocating biological warfare's use. During the war, the U.S. Air Force acknowledged that Unit 406 in Yokohama, Japan needed twenty thousand white mice per month, and samples of plague, cholera, anthrax, typhoid, and dysentery were made available to them. Although U.S. media did not report it, U.S. biowar was known in many parts of the world. On March 31, 1952, the International Association of Democratic Lawyers issued a report charging the United States with war crimes in Korea—including biological warfare—and in 1953 an International Scientific Commission confirmed that biological warfare had been used.[114]

In the war's aftermath, the cover-up of U.S. biowar was accompanied by fabrications of North Korean brainwashing of U.S. prisoners—claims kept alive by Hollywood adaptations of *The Manchurian Candidate*. As late as 1958, so eager were U.S. authorities to cover up its use of biological weapons that the Eisenhower administration charged three journalists with sedition for reporting U.S. germ warfare. Although the U.S. government denies to this day that it used biological warfare against North Korea, a mountain of evidence weighs against the United States—so much so that scientist George Wald, a Nobel Prize Laureate, concluded in 1979 that the United States had indeed used them. More recently, many more materials have surfaced that document U.S. germ warfare.

To be sure, the Korean War was fought against civilians with brutalities on all sides. The South Korean government estimated that leftists killed 129,000 police, members of paramilitary groups and their families, former Japanese collaborators, and pro-American citizens.[115] But the numbers by the United States and its allies are nowhere nearly equivalent. The North Korean government estimates 172,000 citizens killed in the forty-day U.S. occupation around Sinchon alone. In 1999, Pulitzer Prize winning journalists Charles Hanley and Martha Mendoza uncovered the No Gun Ri massacre of as many as four hundred refugees by retreating U.S. troops in 1950. Once that story became known, investigators uncovered dozens of other similar massacres soon after June 25. For half a century, a succession of U.S.-backed military dictatorships repressed any discussion of the massive killings from 1945 to 1953. Activists disappeared and reports vanished. Documents went missing from U.S. archives. Finally, after Koreans won democracy, a slow reevaluation began.

In 2008, the South Korean Truth and Reconciliation Commission found 1,222 instances of mass killings from 1950 to 1953, with at least 215 of these involving U.S. troops or airplanes massacring unarmed civilians. At Cheongwon in central Korea, up to seven thousand people were slaughtered.[116] In the first weeks of the war, as North Korean troops rapidly moved south, thousands of prisoners held by the Rhee regime were executed. Tens of thousands of registered members of the "National Guidance Alliance" were killed in cold blood during the first weeks of the war.[117] In Daejon, some 1,800 prisoners, many of them captured during the suppression of the Yeosun and Jeju uprisings, were executed in a massacre that lasted three days as truckloads full of captured "enemy" were brought to

Hundreds of prisoners, many of them captured insurgents from Yeosun and Jeju, were executed at the start of the Korean War in 1950. One of the children of a man killed here later showed the author a copy of this photo—but with U.S. officers in the background (a detail cropped out of the publically available version). Photographer unknown

Yangwul, on the outskirts of the city. According to witnesses, at least two Jeeps with American army officers watched the killings.[118] Only in 2008 did news of the Daejon massacre get covered in the *New York Times*—more than half a century after it occurred. In 2002, I visited Daejon and was shown a very familiar photo by the surviving son of one of the executed prisoners. I recognized the photo except for one major difference: his photo, wrinkled and aged, had a U.S. officer watching the prisoners about to be executed. In all the versions of the famous photo carried in U.S. media, the American had been cropped out of the frame.

To be sure, American allies in South Korea continue to assert their own autonomous role. In 2008, after the conservative Lee Myung-bak government took office in Seoul, it immediately began to dismantle the country's Truth and Reconciliation Commission and closed the official investigation of the massacres in Jeju. Under the Lee administration, breakthroughs in accurately reporting history are being reversed. Yet, like Pandora's box, once the truth of past atrocities became known, it will be impossible to pretend they never happened.

In the war's immediate aftermath, recrimination bitterly divided Koreans, even among former comrades in North Korea. Blamed for the failure to liberate the South, DPRK deputy Prime Minister Park Hon-yong was executed for having met with U.S. officials, and southern guerrillas, abandoned by the DPRK in their armistice agreement, were subsequently made into nonentities. As in Vietnam, where Ngo Vinh Long documented how Hanoi's official histories marginalized southern guerrillas in accounts of victory over the United States, North Korean accounts routinely neglect southern patriots like Lee Hyun-sang and Nam Bu-gun, both of whom were executed by the Rhee regime.

Although the United States covered up its massacres of civilians in South Korea until the twenty-first century, the Pentagon still refuses to accurately or fully report them. For decades, the government insisted that then U.S. ambassador, John Muccio, never approved attacks on refugees. After the 1999 revelations about No Gun Ri, the United States reiterated its position that there was no official approval of such massacres. Yet scholars subsequently discovered a letter from Muccio in which he informed Assistant Secretary of State Dean Rusk that it had been decided to implement a policy to shoot approaching refugees.[119] Under the judgments made in Nuremberg, that act is considered a war crime. The Pentagon had excluded that letter from materials it handed over to investigators. Similarly, after the U.S. Air Force claimed it never had a deliberate policy of strafing and bombing refugees, the 2002 BBC documentary, *Kill 'Em All*, revealed documents ordering pilots to "shoot all refugees."

So little did U.S. policymakers value Korean lives that, alongside their use of biological weapons (omitted from Cumings's voluminous work), they nearly used atomic weapons as well. On December 9, 1950, MacArthur requested permission for discretionary use of atomic bombs, and in April 1951, the United States came close to dropping them.[120] The long history of U.S. nuclear threats against the DPRK continued through Eisenhower's decision to use nuclear weapons in 1953.[121] After the armistice, the United States continued its war for over fifty years through threats of nuclear war, continual penetration of the airways and waters of North Korea, and a stifling economic blockade. "Honest John" nuclear artillery was brought to South Korea in 1957 and when the neutron bomb was developed, it was deployed there. In 1975, Secretary of Defense James R. Schlesinger publicly stated that the United States would not hesitate to use tactical nuclear weapons then stationed in South Korea in the event of renewed conflict.[122] Under President Carter, more than seven thousand nuclear devices were removed from South Korea, and in the early 1990s, Operation Team Spirit was suspended, but other nuclear war exercises continue. Today, the United States remains poised to devastate the DPRK. In March 2003, the United States deployed a dozen B-52 bombers and an equal number of B-1s to the U.S. Pacific territory of Guam, moving U.S. nuclear bombs within range of the DPRK. To be sure, hundreds—some say thousands—of other U.S. nuclear weapons are today targeted on North Korea.

Although the armistice agreement of 1953 banned economic sanctions, even international law has not stopped the United States from constraining DPRK trade, financial transactions, and almost all areas of its economy. Beginning with the Trading with the Enemy Act and Export Administration Act of 1950 through the Foreign Assistance Act of 1975 and the Export Banking Act of 1988 (forbidding loans to North Korea), the United States has continually sought to break the North Korean system. Altogether more than a hundred thousand articles have been banned by the United States from being exported to North Korea. Airplanes, trucks, computers, and semiconductors are all included in the ban as are cosmetics, face powder and bicycles. Although the Clinton administration took steps to lift the sanctions, Bush and Obama sternly reinforced them. Today, finance, trade, fixed investments, transportation, and postage—all branches of the economy—are subject to U.S. restrictions. The direct cumulative effects of U.S. economic warfare are estimated to be in the hundreds of billions of dollars. Indirectly, when one factors in the continual U.S. military threats and the therefore necessary defense expenditures of the DPRK, the United States has bullied a small country into economic crisis—and then mobilized the international mass media to blame the victim. Whether or not the leadership of the DPRK has made mistakes in economic management, the cumulative effects of more than half a century of U.S. economic warfare have been devastating.

Given the history of U.S. intervention in Korea after World War II, it should come as no surprise that U.S. media seldom report any of the above U.S. actions but instead clamor about Pyongyang's nuclear weapons program and missiles. As the Korean War became a vehicle for Japan's growth, regarded by Premier Yoshida as a "gift of the gods," continuing tensions in Northeast Asia and exaggeration of the North Korean threat today helps sell U.S. antimissile systems and boosts its armament industry.

In my own experience, I have never seen as much distortion of truth as I have encountered in South Korea. Major newspapers routinely report items about North Korea that have no basis in fact. Often, Japanese media are the source of disinformation and rumor. In 2003, Professor Toshimitsu Shigemura of Waseda University in Tokyo maintained that North Korean leader Kim Jong-il died and had been replaced in public by body doubles.[123] In 2008, Japanese media claimed Kim was on his death bed. Although there was little evidence to substantiate that claim, Western media propagated it far and wide. Another piece of common distortion in the U.S. media was the report of a missile launch over Japan in 1998. The news was widely covered and helped lead to Bush's famous "Axis of Evil" speech. In fact, as North Korea maintained all along and was subsequently, but quietly, confirmed by the CIA, an attempted satellite launch was made—not a missile. Anyone with the most rudimentary knowledge of high winds and geography could have surmised that a rocket propelling a satellite from North Korea would, of necessity, pass over Japan. Even progressive American experts on Korea are not exempt from *ad hominem* attacks on the North. Although sympathetic to the liberal wing of the State Department's effort to normalize relations with North Korea, in 2006 Bruce Cumings wrote that Pyongyang's "policy for half a century has been to pile lie upon lie, exaggeration upon exaggeration, even when it would be more convenient and helpful to tell the truth. But that is what we have learned to expect from Communist regimes."[124] While North Koreans pride themselves on being the first to defeat the United States, they still suffer from their nation's division system. Vietnam's outright victory over the United States and subsequent reunification of the country leaves a very different reality there. Once the USSR disappeared in 1990, many conflicts in the world were settled—but Korea remains the alpha and omega of anti-Communist stubbornness.

Since U.S. imperial leaders were never made to admit responsibility for the tragedy in Korea, they went on to devastate Southeast Asia a decade after the Korean War. Ironically, when South Korea's economic miracle took off because of the U.S. war, new insurgent forces were created who rebuilt movements for justice and independence.

NOTES

1 Cumings, *Origins*, 2:238.
2 Hagen Koo, "The State, *Minjung*, and the Working Class in South Korea," in *State and Contemporary Society in Korea*, ed. Hagen Koo (Ithaca: Cornell University Press, 1993), 134–35.
3 Göthel, *Geschichte Südkoreas*, 55; Cumings, *Origins*, 2:304.
4 Byoung-Hoon Lee, "Militant Unionism in Korea," 163.
5 Kim, *Politics of Democratization*, 27.
6 Cumings, *Origins*, 2:241.
7 Ibid., 1:482.
8 See Gi-wook Shin, *Peasant Protest and Social Change in Colonial Korea* (Seattle: University of Washington Press, 1996), 174.
9 Cumings, *Origins*, 1:xxv.
10 Joyce and Gabriel Kolko, *The Limits of Power: The World and United States Foreign Policy, 1945–1950* (New York: Harper and Row, 1972), 314, 321–2. Quoted in Hart-Landsberg, *Korea*, 85.
11 *Time*, February 23, 1948.
12 Gang Jeong-gu, "Overview of Genocides Before and After the Korean War," in *Forum: Civilian Massacre*, Program of the 24th May Commemorative Event (Gwangju: May 18th Memorial Foundation, 2004), 170.
13 John Merrill, "The Jeju-do Rebellion," *Journal of Korean Studies* 2 (1980): 163.
14 Clarified for me by Hyun Ki-Young in an interview on April 29, 2002 in Jeju.
15 Hyun Ki-Young, "Marginal Spirit Freeing Itself from the Mainstream," in *The Role of Jeju Island for World Peace in the Twenty-First Century*, Conference Proceedings of the 2nd Conference on the Jeju April 3rd Uprising (Jeju National University, 2002).
16 Interview with Ko Chang-hoon, Jeju, February 16, 2007.
17 Hyun Ki-Young, "Marginal Spirit," 3.
18 Ibid., 5.
19 Yang Jungs-lim, "Toward the History of Resistance Beyond the Memory of Massacre," *Reconciliation Beyond Memory, Program of the International Conference on the 60th Anniversary of the April Third Uprising* (Jeju: 4.3 Research Institute, 2008), 335.
20 See Ko Changhoon, "The International Context of the Jeju Sasam Uprising," *The Islander*, June 2003.
21 Bruce Cumings, "The Question of American Responsibility for the Suppression of the Jejudo Uprising," in *For the Truth and Reparations: Jeju April 3rd of 1948 Massacre Not Forgotten*, ed. Hur Sang Soo (Seoul: BaekSan Publisher, 2001), 17–18.
22 강준만, 한국현대사 산책 2 (서울:인물과 사상사, 2004), 209–10.
23 Chang-sung Hyun, in Hur, 26.
24 James West, "Jeju April 3rd Martial Law: Was It Legal?" in *For the Truth and Reparations: Jeju April 3rd of 1948 Massacre Not Forgotten*, ed. Hur Sang Soo (Seoul: BaekSan Publisher, 2001), 63; John Merrill writes that only one person, a child, was shot and killed that day ("The Jeju-do Rebellion,"154). According to other U.S. documents, on the afternoon of March 1, 1947, police fired into an "unauthorized parade and meeting of about 1,000 people." They killed six civilians; another subsequently died from his wounds. ("U.S. troops assisted in dispersing the crowd." G-2 Periodic Report HQ 6th INF DIV 19001, no. 500, March 2, 1947.
25 Merrill, "The Jeju-do Rebellion"; U.S report of March 14, 1947 (courtesy of 4.3 Institute).
26 U.S. intelligence cited in Merrill, "The Jeju-do Rebellion," 157.
27 Cumings, *Origins*, 2:254.
28 Bruce Cumings, Speech at Harvard University, April 25, 2003.
29 While the exact number of killed will never be known, estimates range from ten

thousand to over a hundred thousand. On April 1, 1947, seven Taiwanese associations estimated the number slaughtered at fifty thousand. For discussion of Taiwan's February 28 Uprising see Lai Tse-Han, Ramon Myers and Wei Wou, *A Tragic Beginning: The Taiwan Uprising of February 28, 1947* (Stanford: Stanford University Press, 1991), 158. See also *Asia's Unknown Uprisings Vol. 2* (Oakland: PM Press, 2012).

30 See Merrill, "The Jeju-do Rebellion," 162–65.

31 Merrill counted three thousand guerrillas on Mount Halla (*Korea: The Peninsular Origins of the War*, [Newark, NJ: University of Delaware Press, 1989] 68).

32 Merrill has a different version. He claims Colonel Pak Chin-gyong's attempts to persuade the guerrillas to surrender failed, after which the new government offensive began. See "The Jeju-do Rebellion," 174–75.

33 Document provided by 4.3 Research Institute, 390.

34 Merrill, "The Jeju-do Rebellion," 177. U.S. intelligence estimated 25 percent of the Southern rural population might have voted; the North put the figure at 77 percent of eligible voters participated.

35 Cumings, "The Question of American Responsibility," 15.

36 Quotation from Jeju 4.3 Museum.

37 Estimates of the number of people killed range from range from 15,000 (the lowest of U.S. figures at the time) to 80,065. See Christian Institute for the Study of Justice and Development, *Lost Victory: An Overview of the Korean People's Struggle for Democracy in 1987* (Seoul: Minjungsa, 1988), 8. In a 1949 report to the American authorities, South Korean officials said 27,719 islanders had been killed, close to the North Korean figure of 30,000 or about 10 percent of the islanders. Some estimates place the number killed as high as 80,065, or more than 25 percent of the population. Seong Nae Kim, "Lamentations of the Dead: The Historical Imagery of Violence on Jeju Island, South Korea," *Journal of Ritual Studies* 3, no. 2 (Summer 1989): 252. In 1949 discussions with U.S. intelligence officials, the governor of Jeju privately told his American superior that 60,000 had been killed out of a population of 400,000, 40,000 had fled to Japan, and more than 39,285 homes had been destroyed.

38 Dong-Choon Kim, *The Unending Korean War: A Social History* (Larkspur, CA: Tamal Vista Publications, 2009), 175.

39 Yang Han Kwon, "The Truth About the Jeju April 3rd Insurrection," *For the Truth and Reparations: Jeju April 3rd of 1948 Massacre Not Forgotten*, ed. Hur Sang Soo (Seoul: BaekSan Publisher, 2001), 4.

40 Based on U.S. Counter Intelligence Corps (CIC) sources, Cumings concluded that the guerrillas were not centrally commanded but "operated in mobile units (kidong pudae) eighty or a hundred strong that often had little connection with other rebels. This, of course, was one of the elements that made the movement hard to suppress." U.S. sources were wrong about so many dynamics in Jeju, and their guess that autonomous fighting units were the enemy was incorrect. Units engaged in hit and run tactics when trying to reach safety in the open terrain of Jeju or when attacked, but that does not necessarily imply their autonomous organization. See "The Question of American Responsibility," 21.

41 MBC produced a remarkable series of documentaries in 2001 called "Now the Truth Can Be Told." One of them focuses on the Yeosun uprising. Producer Lee Chaehun reported in 1999 that Jung Gi-soon, a member of the Women's League inside liberated Yeosu in 1948 whose two sisters and brother were murdered by the U.S.-backed forces when they retook the city, still had qualms in 2001 about being interviewed for the documentary because of the National Security Law. See Lee Chaehun, "It's Time to Speak Out—The Insurrection of Yeosu 14th Regiment," in *Forum: Civilian Massacre*, Program of the 24th May Commemorative Event (Gwangju: May 18th Memorial Foundation,

2004), 146. See the report from Kwangju of October 20, 1948, by Captains Hausman, Reed, Treadwell and Frye. Finally, in January 2009, Korea's Truth and Reconciliation Commission issued a report that at least 439 civilians were massacred in the Yeosun incident.

42   Cumings, *Origins*, 2:261.

43   Cumings believes these arrests "may have set the events in motion." See *Origins*, 2:260.

44   Merrill, "The Jeju-do Rebellion," 179–80.

45   안재성, 이현상:평전 (서울: 실천문학사, 2007), 245.

46   On April 14, 1592 in the waters off Yeosu, Admiral Lee's fleet destroyed more than 400 Japanese ships in a decisive defeat of Japan's expansionism.

47   Based solely on U.S. and North Korean documents, Cumings estimated that two thousand people gathered in downtown Yeosu. Cumings, *Origins*, 2:260. The MBC documentary used both U.S. and ROK documents, as well as oral testimonies of eyewitnesses in South Korea to construct their narrative in which five thousand people gathered.

48   Merrill, "The Jeju-do Rebellion," 179–80.

49   From Chronology: October 18, 1948 to November 1, 1948 (RG 407/270/5516 Entry 427 File# 306), 26.

50   "Short History of the Yosu Campaign," G-2 Section, Hausman Archive, Box 7.

51   Merrill, *Korea: The Peninsular Origins of the War*, 106.

52   That is the approximate number of police corpses found after the city was retaken. At the time when the city was in insurgent hands, Korean police sources reported five hundred of their members had been killed in Sunchon.

53   Cumings, *Origins*, 2:262.

54   Interview with Lee Young-il, Yeosu Institute, December 14, 2001.

55   Cumings, *Origins*, 1:296.

56   Documents provided by Yeosu Research Institute, marked "2400–21 October," 10.

57   Letter from headquarters to Hausman cited in "My Earliest Memories in Korea," Harvard University Hausman archive, Yenching Library, Box 9.

58   *Time*, November 1, 1948, 18.

59   Lee Young-il, "The Truth about 'Yo-Sun Incident' and 'Massacre of Civilians,'" in *Forum: Civilian Massacre*, Program of the 24th May Commemorative Event (Gwangju: May 18th Memorial Foundation, 2004), 180.

60   Cumings, *Origins*, 2:264.

61   Henderson, *Korea: The Politics of the Vortex*, 149.

62   Minor L. Kelso, letter of June 12, 1995, in Harvard University, James H. Hausman Archive, Box 7.

63   Merrill, *Korea: The Peninsular Origins of the War*, 111.

64   Keyes Beech, *Tokyo and Points East* (Garden City: Doubleday, 1954), 139.

65   "The Yeosu Operation Amphibious Phase," 8.

66   In 1968, twenty years after the U.S.-supported massacres in Yeosu, Carl Mydans and Shelley Mydans published *The Violent Peace*, providing further details of Yeosu atrocities.

67   Cumings, *Origins*, 1:263.

68   Ibid., 265.

69   Interview with Kim Deug-Joong, Seoul, June 12, 2002. Hong Young-gi estimated a range of seven to ten thousand killed. Interview, Gwangju, May 23, 2001.

70   Chaehun, "It's Time to Speak Out," 148.

71   Gang Jeong-gu, "Overview of Genocides Before and After the Korean War," in *Forum: Civilian Massacre*, Program of the 24th May Commemorative Event (Gwangju: May 18th Memorial Foundation, 2004), 170.

72 Unsigned letter to General Mullins, HQ 2nd Army in Fort Meade from Liaison Office KMAG, dated July 28, 1949.

73 Hausman's typed autobiography is in his Harvard archive, Box 9.

74 "The Truth About the Yeosu Incident," marked "from Carbon Copy loaned to Capt. R.K. Sawyer by Major John P. Reed, Ward E2, Fitzsimmons AH, Denver Colorado," 3. Box 726 RG 319 Records of the Army Staff, 2–3.7A AE.

75 Cumings, *Origins*, 2:238.

76 Cumings in MBC film about the Yeosun Uprising from the series, *Now the Truth Can Be Told*.

77 Cumings, *Origins*, 2:263.

78 Jean-Paul Sartre, *Baudelaire* (New York: New Directions, 1967), 51–52.

79 James Hausman, "History of the Rebellion of the 14th Constabulary Regiment," Harvard University Hausman archive, Box 7, Folder 5.

80 안재성, 이현상 평전 (서울:실천문학사, 2007), 255–56.

81 Herbert Marcuse, *Counterrevolution and Revolt* (Boston: Beacon Press, 1972), 52.

82 Kang Man-gil, *A History of Contemporary Korea*, 188.

83 Yi Sung-yop, quoted in Cumings, *Origins*, 2:272–73.

84 Cumings, *Origins*, 2:289.

85 Ibid., 400.

86 Interview with Lee Young-il, Yeosu, December 14, 2001.

87 Cumings, *Origins*, 2:687–8.

88 Cumings, *Korea's Place in the Sun*, 343.

89 Lee, *The Making of Minjung*, 88.

90 Hausman archive, Box 9.

91 Göthel, *Geschichte Südkoreas*, 63.

92 Cumings, *Origins*, 2:385.

93 Henderson, *Korea: The Politics of the Vortex*, 143.

94 Hart-Landsberg, *Korea*, 77.

95 U.S. responsibility for the Sinchon Massacre is a debated topic in South Korea. Right-wing thugs who lost properties because of the Workers' Party land reform were also involved in the Sinchon orgy of blood. Apparently, holocaust denial is not limited to German atrocities during World War II.

96 Northern estimates of the number of Southerners killed before June 25, 1950, ranged up to one million. The most brutal of the massacres perpetrated under the U.S. military government was on the island of Jeju, where upward of thirty thousand people were killed (though some estimates place the number closer to seventy thousand).

97 Holger Heide, *Die Erzeugung individueller und kollecktiver Überlebungstrategien als Voarraussetzung für die kapitalistische Entwicklung. Das Beispiel Südkorea* (SEARI Institut für sozialökonomische Handlungsforschung, Universität Bremen: 1997), 3.

98 Cumings, *Origins*, 2:362–63.

99 Channing Liem, *The Korean War: An Unanswered Question* (Albany, NY: Committee for a New Korea Poloicy, 1993).

100 I.F. Stone, *The Hidden History of the Korean War: 1950–1951* (1952; repr., Boston: Little, Brown, 1988).

101 Cumings, *North Korea*, 6.

102 Cumings, *Origins*, 2:42.

103 Ibid., xviii.

104 Ibid., 12 and xviii.

105 Ibid., 39.

106 Ibid., 667.

107 Cumings, *Korea's Place in the Sun*, 299.

108 Cumings, *North Korea*, 4.

109 Dong-Choon Kim, *Der Korea-Krieg und die Gesellschaft* (Munster: Wesphalisches Dampfboot, 2000), 30. My translation from the German. The book's English version is *The Unending Korean War: A Social History* (Larkspur, CA: Tamal Vista Publications, 2009).

110 *New York Times*, August 18, 1952.

111 Chung Dae-hwa, "Reevaluation of the Korean War: Its Genesis, Process and Conclusion," *Social Science Journal* (Busan National University) 13, no. 21 (December 1995): 55 (in Korean) counts North Korean losses of 3 million people (out of a population of 10 million; South Korean losses were put at 2 million out of a population of 20 million; Chinese losses at 1 million; U.S. losses at fifty-four thousand). Among Chinese killed was Mao Zedong's son. Other estimates are 3 million out of a population of 30 million, including 1 million innocent in South Korea. The PBS video, *Pacific Century: The Fight for Democracy*, uses the number of 4 million. The very fact that numbers are off by a million or more is an indication of how bloody the war was—and how indiscriminately Koreans lives were sacrificed. David Halberstam gives much lower numbers: 33,000 U.S. soldiers, 415,000 South Korean, 1.5 million North Korean and Chinese troops. See his *The Coldest Winter: America and the Cold War* (New York: Hyperion, 2007). Dong-Choon Kim estimates 1.3 million South Korean soldiers and civilians killed, 2.5 million North Korean, an additional 650,000 refugees from the North who were killed in the South, and of course Chinese and American troops (*The Unending Korean War*, 216).

112 This and other atrocities are well documented in Alan Winnington and Wilfred Burchett's *Plain Perfidy: The Plot to Wreck Korean Peace* (Peking: published by the authors, 1954). Leading up to, during and after the armistice negotiations, the U.S. side repeatedly violated its previous agreements. This book constitutes one of the most eloquent expositions of U.S. crimes—ranging from medical experimentation on prisoners to biological warfare. A more recent exposé of U.S. germ warfare is Endicott and Hagerman's *The United States and Biological Warfare*. Wilfred G. Burchett, *Again Korea* (New York: International Publishers, 1968) is an indispensable source on the DPRK's early history.

113 Endicott and Hagerman, *The United States and Biological Warfare*, 48.

114 International Scientific Commission on Biological Warfare in Korea and China, *Report*, 1952.

115 Gang Jeong-gu, "Overview of Genocides Before and After the Korean War," 174.

116 Choe Sang-hun, "Unearthing War's Horror Years Later in South Korea," *New York Times*, December 3, 2007, A9.

117 Gang Jeong-gu, "Overview of Genocides Before and After the Korean War," in *Forum: Civilian Massacre*, Program of the 24th May Commemorative Event (Gwangju: May 18th Memorial Foundation, 2004), 170. In the same volume, Seo Jung Seok uses the higher number of three hundred thousand in his article, "*Kookminbodoyeonmang*, Massacre of the member of National Guidance Alliance and its responsibility," 186. Cumings repeats the U.S. embassy's estimate of seventy thousand people, but the numbers used in South Korea are much higher (*Korea's Place in the Sun*, 223).

118 Alan Winnington, "United States Belsen in Korea," *Daily Worker*, London, August 9, 1950 (Cumings, *Origins*, 2:699). In 1999, at the same time as I was shown a photo of a U.S. officer standing behind the Korean executioners of young prisoners, bound and kneeling about to be killed, (the officer was removed from photos released) . . . I was given a photocopy of Winnington's article.

119 Charles J. Hanley and Martha Mendoza, "Letter on Korean War Massacre Reveals Plan to Shoot Refugees," *Washington Post*, May 30, 2006, A4.

120 Cumings, *Origins*, 2:750. See 747–52 for excellent documentation and U.S. considera-
     tion of use of nuclear weapons. Curiously, he omits any substantive discussion of bio-
     logical weapons.
121 On May 19, 1953, Eisenhower's decision to use nuclear weapons was supported by the
     Joint Chiefs of Staff and General Omar Bradley. Fortunately, he did not implement
     that decision.
122 Lee Chae-Jin, *A Troubled Peace*, 76.
123 Choe Sang-hun, "Speculation on North Korean Leader Thrives in Factual Vacuum,"
     New York Times, September 20, 2008.
124 Cumings, *North Korea*, 76.

CHAPTER 5

The *Minjung* Awaken: Students Overthrow Rhee and Park

On the way home from school,
Bullets flew through the air
And blood covered the streets.
The lonely discarded book bag
Was as heavy as it could be.
I know, yes, we all know
Even if Mom and Dad say nothing
Why our brothers and sisters were bleeding.

—Elementary school pupil, April 1960

The evil influence of political power has swallowed up the people's right of fair elections, which constitutes a minimum requirement of democracy. The knavish railings of ignorant despotism have trampled down all remaining hopes of freedom of speech, assembly, association, and thought. With an overpowering joy and happiness, we are now lighting up the torch of freedom. Behold! We are proud to toll freedom's bell that will shatter the stillness of the Dark Age.

—South Korean student declaration, April 19, 1960

CHRONOLOGY	
March 15, 1960	Rhee claims 90% of vote in rigged elections; police kill Masan protesters
April 11, 1960	Corpse of student Kim Ju-yol, killed in Masan protests, discovered by fisherman
April 11, 1960	More than 40,000 Masan citizens protest

April 18, 1960	Six thousand Korea University students insist Rhee take responsibility for Masan killings
April 19, 1960	Student-led protests in Seoul; 186 killed by police gunfire; buildings set afire in Busan
April 25, 1960	Professors lead march of 100,000 to National Assembly
April 26, 1960	Syngman Rhee resigns
July 29, 1960	Parliamentary elections; Second Republic established with Chang Myon as Prime Minister
May 12, 1961	Meeting planned for students from North Korea and South Korea to approve reunification
May 16, 1961	Military coup d'etat overthrows Chang Myon government
1961–1979	General Park Chung-hee military dictatorship
1964 to 1965	3.5 million people participate in protests against Korea–Japan Treaty
June 3, 1964	Martial law declared in Seoul; Japan Treaty approved as is dispatch of 20,000 troops to Vietnam
November 13, 1970	Chun Tae-il commits suicide to protest dire conditions of garment workers
August 10, 1971	Gwangju (Gyeonggi Province) riot about inadequate housing infrastructure
April 22, 1973	Joint Easter service against Park's *Yushin* draws 100,000 participants
April 9, 1975	Eight members of the government-fabricated "People's Revolutionary Party" executed
March 10, 1978	Women workers fired from Dongil Textile disrupt yellow labor union rally
August 11, 1979	Police arrest 170 workers during YH Company labor strike; Kim Kyung-suk is killed
October 4, 1979	Kim Young-sam expelled from National Assembly
October 16, 1979	Busan University students march; army called out, 400 people arrested, 600 injured
October 18, 1979	Martial Law declared in Busan; Masan protests break out: 10,000+ in streets
October 20, 1979	Martial Law declared in Masan
October 26, 1979	Park Chung-hee assassinated by his own KCIA chief
December 12, 1979	Chun Doo-hwan military coup
April 21, 1980	Hundreds of miners in Sabuk clash with police
May 14, 1980	"Seoul Spring": 70,000 students march for democracy; 900 strikes by workers
May 15, 1980	100,000 students march in Seoul; leaders agree to stop protests
May 16, 1980	Torchlight parade for democracy in Gwangju
May 16, 1980	U.S. releases ROK 20th Division for dispatch to Gwangju

WHEN PRUNED, SOME varieties of trees wither and die. Others grow back stronger than ever. The same may be true of peoples. Koreans responded to the severity of Japanese colonization and the devastation of the U.S. war by rebuilding with reinvigorated strength. The cunning dialectic of history meant that the Korean War's extermination of old social structures nearly wiped out the *yangban* aristocracy and prepared the grounds for the emergence of the *minjung*—the new subject-object of Korea's history. Comprised of the vast majority of people—excluding very rich landlords and industrialists, former Japanese collaborators, elite military men and police officials—*minjung* became the name for the cross-class social force that overthrew decades of U.S.-backed dictatorships and shaped southern Korea into an egalitarian and prosperous society.

In both North and South Korea, governments drew upon their impressive human resources, especially the civil society produced by five thousand years of culture, to reconstruct quickly and efficiently after the devastation of war. Korea's recovery made it the envy of many Third World countries wishing to emulate its rise from rags to riches. One of the world's poorest countries in 1953, Korea grew at "miraculous" rates for three decades. Although the North today lags far behind, in 1980, the two Koreas were roughly equivalent economically. South Korea continues its fabulous development from one of the world's poorest countries to one of its wealthiest—OECD member with the world's thirteenth-largest economy and a substantial high-tech sector. Its modern infrastructure, efficient public transportation, and safe social spaces make the United States and much of Europe seem archaic. Gross National Product (GNP) is more than one hundred times what it was in the 1950s—having increased from $200 per person to more than $20,000 in 2008 (before falling back slightly during the financial crisis that began that year). As a sign of how the country has grown, the average male today is fully five inches taller than his 1961 counterpart.

Although it now seems unlikely, the North may even have outpaced the South in economic growth until 1978. At the time, many people maintained that it was superior in people's satisfaction with government and economy as well.[1] Che Guevara visited North Korea in the mid-1960s and described it as a model for what Cuba should become. Australian journalist Wilfred Burchett and British economist Joan Robinson both admired the North for its progress. Land reform was thoroughgoing and comprehensive, and millions of families still own their own land. Although it retains substantial technological sophistication, a number of factors combined to impoverish the country: decades of confrontation with the United States and the ROK in the aftermath of an armistice—not a peace treaty—at the end of the war in 1953; systematic U.S. economic blockade of material goods and financial services; collapse of Pyongyang's main trading partner, the USSR; poor decisions made by high leaders; and devastating droughts and floods. Korea's division into two states—named the "division system" by Paik Nak-chung—enervates the nation's dynamism and eats away at its soul. In both North and South, the existence of an "enemy" regime claiming the right to rule the entire peninsula means limited political freedom and enormous sacrifices. Precious resources are diverted into unnecessary military expenditures. In both

Pyongyang and Seoul, as paranoia, hatred, and fear run wild, an elusive need for national security poisons government decisions.

During the Cold War, as in West Berlin and Taiwan, massive U.S. aid was distributed to build South Korea into a model for the "superiority" of American capitalism (as opposed to Communism). In Korea, U.S. benefactors maintained elite rule by promoting former Japanese collaborators into high positions of power in the American imperial order. The result was a harshly regulated system that strictly compelled millions of people to decades of backbreaking toil in exchange for meager rewards. Aided by the United States and Japan, the South Korean economy grew at astonishing rates, with GNP increasing an average of 9 percent or better from the 1960s into the mid-1990s. Millions of laborers paid for economic progress through a world record-setting industrial accident rate, a six or even seven-day workweek, and a centralized decision-making apparatus that restricted political inputs to a few men's ideas.

In this context, Syngman Rhee thrived, able to convince his supporters in the United States to grant him enormous sums of money and considerable leeway as the "frontline" of their Cold War. In 1953, foreign assistance was well over 14 percent of GNP (reaching 22.9 percent in 1957). Throughout all of Rhee's tenure as president, foreign aid was a substantial portion of the total government budget.[2] Between 1953 and 1963, the ROK was the beneficiary of what Alice Amsden called a "unique" amount of foreign aid as the United States sustained three-fourths of South Korea's total investment.[3] By the end of the 1950s, five-sixths of all economic inputs were from direct U.S. grants. Dependence on America meant that in 1961, more than half of all consumer goods were provided by U.S. aid.[4] Even though the United States annually provided some $100 per capita to the country, corruption was rampant, and thousands of people scavenged daily meals in garbage dumps. Extreme poverty compelled many others to work in dangerous and dirty jobs. U.S. Army bases nightly brought in truckloads of young Korean women to service the soldiers.

While Rhee relied on the United States for his base of support, behind American largesse and military might stood the ROK armed forces—at six hundred thousand men, the country's most powerful institution. Rhee had ceded sovereign control of the military to the United States, which only abetted his machinations in power. Whenever he requested action from his American caretakers, he received an affirmative answer. Rhee increasingly ruled with an iron fist, and his murderous grip on power turned thousands of patriotic citizens into victims of persecution. Running on a platform of peaceful reunification of Korea, moderate politician Cho Pong-am received two million votes in the 1956 election as the candidate of the Progressive Party. Subsequently accused of being a North Korean spy, Cho was arrested in 1958 and executed in 1959.

Rhee and his team of advisors directed industry to produce for the domestic market in line with their policy of import-substitution. Using the model of Japanese *zaibatsu*, they organized family-owned conglomerates (like Hyundai, Daewoo, and Samsung) at the core of the country's economy, a legacy still central to South Korea's industrial and financial organization. As economic development between 1948 and 1960 demanded more off-line workers, the number of colleges in Korea doubled (from thirty-one to sixty-two), and the number of college students nearly trebled (from 24,000 to 97,819), with a great proportion of students concentrated in Seoul. Although Korea's GNP was less than one-tenth of England's, it had more college students per capita, and Seoul was "one of the largest educational centers in the world."[5] The country's secondary schools experienced a similar surge in growth. In August 1959, an autonomous labor federation formed—the Korea Trade Union Council—which explicitly opposed the yellow Federation of Korean Trade Unions' (FKTU) ties to government. The new democratic union signed up more than 160,000 workers in its first year.[6]

While great discontinuity is evident between the endeavors to expel the United States before the war and the popular movements after it, the size and spirit of South Korea's continuing grassroots insurgencies remained undiminished.

4.19: Students Overthrow Syngman Rhee

Rhee's disdain for ordinary Koreans finally became his undoing. In 1960, he was driven from power and compelled to return to the United States, where he had lived for decades, by a popular uprising led by students. In elections on March 15, 1960, Rhee and his cronies shamelessly stuffed ballot boxes or stole them from neighborhoods known to be opposition strongholds. When the official vote tally was announced, Rhee claimed an overwhelming mandate for himself and for his handpicked vice presidential candidate, Lee Ki-bung, a notorious and corrupt crony. Weeks before citizens went to the polls, many people suspected that the results had already been decided. In Daegu on February 28, high school students had gone into the streets to warn of Rhee's plot to extend his rule, and 120 people had been arrested. As soon as the election results were announced on the evening of March 15, a contingent of ten thousand students led a huge march in Masan, which converged on City Hall and demanded fresh elections. Police immediately attacked, killing eight students and wounding 123 more. As he always did, Rhee called the protests "Communist inspired." Before the situation spiraled out of control, U.S. commanding General Carter Magruder approved Rhee's request to send in elite Korean marines to quiet the citizenry. Undeterred by the army, similar outbursts occurred in Pohang, Daejon, Suwon, Osan, and Jeonju. Organized groups of professors, journalists, and lawyers made public statements in support of protesting students.

On April 11, a fisherman discovered the bloated body of sixteen-year-old Kim Ju-yol in the sea near Masan. The young teenager from Namwon, a freshman at a Masan commercial high school, had been hit in the eye by a tear gas canister. Police claimed he was a Communist, a charge "proven" by papers linking him to North Korea found in his pockets (which many people believed had been planted). Both the murder and the cover-up detonated a huge explosion. Immediately, 40,000 protesters gathered, and by evening, an estimated 140,000 people had viewed his corpse.[7] As people refused to remain quiet, once again police resorted to force and killed many demonstrators. Sporadic demonstrations by high school students in several provinces refused to let the Rhee regime continue its unreasonable use of violence to impose its will.

Police viciously attacked student protests in 1960. Photographer unknown

In his arrogance, Rhee continued to believe unbridled force would compel Koreans to submit. On April 18, gangsters in Seoul attacked a protest by Korea University students near Dongdaemun. Using chains and metal rods, members of the Anti-Communist Youth Corps mercilessly beat unarmed students. Police witnessed the beating of students but did nothing to stop it, perhaps because the chief of presidential security had summoned the goons to stop the protests.[8] In response to the attack, students from seven Seoul universities called for an all-out mobilization the next day. On April 19, thousands of students took to the streets of Seoul. By the time they approached the presidential palace, their ranks had swelled to as many as a hundred thousand people.[9] For the first time, students found massive support for their demonstrations among the general public. During the march, some students chanted, "Let us destroy communism by getting our democracy right!"[10] Here was an early indication of what would become the global New Left's opposition to dictatorships of both the Communist and capitalist variety, of a gut-oriented intuition of freedom that cared little for the ideology of governments that unnecessarily limited it.[11]

At the presidential palace, the massive crowd demanded to see Rhee. They were answered when palace guards opened fire, killing at least twenty people in the first volley. Remarkably, students fought back, refusing to be intimidated by clubs and guns.

They regrouped and spontaneously formed small action teams that destroyed the headquarters building of Rhee's Liberal Party as well as that of the Anti-Communist Youth Corps, the editorial offices of the government newspaper, and five police substations.[12] Protesters burned houses belonging to Rhee's high-ranking subordinates, wrecked City Hall, and attacked dozens of other buildings linked to Rhee and his party.

Even elementary school students participated in the April 19, 1960, uprising.
Credit: *4.19 Revolution Photo Book* (Wounded and Deceased Families, 2000).

Throughout the country, thousands of elementary and high school students mobilized, especially in Incheon, Jeonju, Mokpo, and Daegu. In Gwangju on April 19, high school students demanding new elections surged downtown. Organizers sent runners to visit every school in the city, and as soon as the initial protests occurred, the number of people swelled to 15,000—1,500 of whom were from Chosun High School.[13] Police and firemen fired water laced with red dye but failed to disperse demonstrators. Unpaved roads provided plenty of rocks for ammunition to fight back. Throughout the night, the battle continued as protesters controlled the streets. In Busan, protesters set fire to many government buildings.

Before the violence ended, gunfire on "Bloody Tuesday" had claimed dozens of lives.[14] In Seoul alone, more than a hundred people were killed and over a thousand wounded. Ultimately, martial law was declared, the army was called out, and a 10 p.m. curfew was strictly enforced. Remarkably, the army did not open fire. General Song Yo-chan ordered his troops not to shoot, and soldiers and students reportedly shouted to each other, "We are brothers!"

The next day, college students massively mobilized. For seven consecutive days, there were major demonstrations in Seoul. On April 24, as the entire country appeared to reject the "honesty" of the elections, Vice-President-elect Lee Ki-bung publicly declared he would not accept office. He and his family subsequently committed suicide. On April 25, some 258 university professors gathered at Seoul National University and issued a message proclaiming that, "Student Demonstrations are the Expression of Justice!" They marched through the city to demand Rhee's resignation as well as those of the nation's Chief Justice and speaker of the National Assembly. By the time they arrived at the National Assembly, more than a hundred thousand people were with them, and people

The army sided with citizens to overthrow Syngman Rhee in 1960.
Credit: *4.19 Revolution Photo Book* (Wounded and Deceased Families, 2000).

listened intently as professors announced a fifteen-point declaration. This event was significant for many reasons, not least because it marked the first time in Korean history that professors as a group had entered the struggle against tyranny. The spontaneous gathering of so many people was unprecedented in a society where dictatorships had ruled for so long. Higher education in Korea had expanded, but there were fewer than a hundred thousand college students in the entire country and scarcely more than a quarter million in high schools, numbers that fail to account for central role of universities and high schools in overthrowing the government.[15] Positioned centrally in the cities and afforded great respect in the world's most Confucian society, students and teachers detonated a widespread social explosion.

People took full advantage of their newly found freedom to act—space created by the sacrifice of so many lives. After the gathering at the National Assembly, some fifty thousand protesters attacked Vice President Lee Ki-bung's house. Placing his elaborate furnishings on the street to be photographed, people proceeded to burn them before demolishing the house.[16] Their message was clear: not only must Rhee go, so must his entire administration. Evidently, the massive outpouring of antigovernment sentiment and the capacity of people to act despite deadly police violence convinced the United States publicly to support Rhee's departure. A note delivered to the ROK embassy in Washington made clear his American handlers thought it was time for him to go. Rhee would never have been able to become president without U.S. backing, nor was he able to remain in power without American support. On Friday, April 26, the U.S. ambassador and General Magruder personally paid Rhee a visit to ensure that he would to step down. They offered him the same means of transportation back to the United States that had been provided him in 1945 to bring him to Korea: a U.S. military aircraft. Shortly after the U.S. officials had left, Rhee announced his resignation and boarded a U.S. military plane bound for Hawaii.

Immediately, joyful gatherings suddenly cropped up everywhere. Thousands of arrested students were released, and police withdrew from public view. Students now directed traffic on city streets and took over many police stations. All over the country, as they swept the cities clean of the debris left behind from their hard-won victory, young people proudly stepped into positions of authority amid public acclaim. With the army in the streets, raucous celebrations transpired—spontaneous and joyful expressions of hope for the future of democracy.

The success of the uprising in winning power surprised everyone—most of all those who had been at the center of organizing it.

Decades of pent-up grievances were suddenly possible to discuss in public. As one observer described it: "The April revolution was a giant social revolt . . . The students . . . touched off a general revolt in society. The people revolted against the government. The young revolted against the old. In many schools, students revolted against their teachers. In some government ministries, junior civil servants revolted against senior civil servants. In a more serious vein, some eight lieutenant colonels revolted against some generals, requesting that the army be cleared of corrupt elements."[17]

When the dead were identified and totaled, they numbered 186.[18] At least forty-six of those people were high school students (seventh to twelfth grades), and the vast majority of those killed were less than thirty years old. An additional six thousand people had been injured.

TABLE 5.1 **Age of People Killed in the April Uprising, 1960**

Age	Number
15 or younger	11
15–19	92
20–24	49
25–29	11
30 or over	17
Unknown	6
Total	**186**

Source: So Baek O. ed., *Uriga koroon kil* (The Path of Our Life) (Seoul: 1962), 341, cited in Chong Lim Kim, ed., *Political Particpation in Korea*, 159.

Evidently, a new generation had moved to the center of Korean political life. By 1960, more than half of all South Koreans were nineteen years old or younger. In a highly literate society, youth's newly found powers derived from more than their numbers: Confucian ethics accorded students great respect as well as a need among ordinary citizens to protect them. Concentrated on campuses with room to reflect amid the idealism of youth, students' passionate involvement in politics would soon sweep the world in the global revolt of 1968. Korean students inspired others around the world. Newspapers reported that protesting students in Turkey bowed their heads to show respect to their counterparts in Korea. U.S. activist Tom Hayden, one of the main authors of the Port Huron Statement, the founding document of Students for a Democratic Society (SDS), remembered his feelings when he first heard the news from Seoul: "I was exhilarated when I saw young people our age overthrow the dictator Syngman Rhee. Through that movement, I learned the history of the Cold War for the first time. Those events challenged our naïve belief that our parents were fighting for a free world. I can tell you that movement helped inspire SNCC [the Student Nonviolent Coordinating Committee] and the black movement in the South. Two days after Syngman Rhee's forced resignation, SDS held its first meeting."[19]

Japanese colonialism and the Korean War had destroyed the sources of the traditional Left, and although class struggle currents subsequently emerged, it appears the 4.19 Movement was completely democratic and antidictatorial. Korean students clearly expressed political affinity with the global New Left when they articulated their aspirations by chanting, "Democracy in Politics, Equality in Economy." The professors who led the April 25 demonstration were also harbingers of new social forces that would appear globally in struggles during the 1960s. Dubbed the new working class by Serge Mallet, proletarianized professionals and white-collar employees increasingly play a significant role in social movements. As an especially privileged sector, professors are easily co-opted by being handed plum positions and held in high status.[20] Significantly, farmers, industrial workers, and rural dwellers were marginal to the national movement that overthrew Rhee. Indications of the new social landscape constructed after the Korean War's devastation also included the increased capacity of ordinary people to organize themselves without central control, to rise up against entrenched power and overthrow it. The absence of entrenched opposition leadership may have facilitated the movement's success. As Sungjoo Han understood: "the demonstrating students and masses did not have an organized leadership of their own. Although leaders of the Democratic Party later claimed that they were largely responsible for touching off the protest movements, their actual leadership within the demonstrating masses was not present. Ironically, this absence of clearly definable leadership may have contributed to the early abdication of Syngman Rhee."[21]

Outside his coterie of pro-Japanese Koreans, Rhee had no real base of support. When the time came to rally around him, no one did, not even the United States—which would repeatedly sacrifice discredited regimes (Trujillo, Diem, and Pinochet) to install elected civilian regimes that would continue to defend American interests while significantly deradicalizing and dividing revolutionary upsurges.

Social Movements in the Second Republic

On July 29, 1960, a few scant months after the student revolution, elections swept the Democratic Party into the leadership of the Second Republic. Emboldened by their newfound power, students grew increasingly visionary and militant. Student power was so strong, they even organized talks aimed at reunification with North Korean students at Panmunjom. Alongside demands like lower tuition and a cultural break with their elders, students continued to lead the entire society.

The uprising's success led to an upsurge of movements among many different sectors of the population and ushered in a vibrant new realm of possibilities. Street mobilizations remained significant vehicles of political participation. In the first year after Rhee was sent home to the United States, some 2,000 demonstrations involved around a million people. The military would later release an estimate that an average of 3,900 people took to Seoul's streets every day. Many protests demanded stiffer penalties for ex-Rhee officials, reunification of the country, and a declaration of permanent neutrality.[22]

Hundreds of labor disputes suddenly occurred, involving 340,000 workers. Wage increases of 15 percent to 50 percent were won, and 315 new unions created, including among teachers, bank employees, and journalists.[23] On June 14, 1960, about 400 Samsung workers went on a hunger strike, demanding the reinstatement of 152 fired colleagues, an end to an illegal lockout by Samsung, and for the company to respect existing law.[24] On July 4, police were called in to evict the sit-in, and the struggle ended without success. To this day, Samsung still has no union. The country's unemployment rate stood at 28 percent, a major problem for fifty-one thousand demobilized soldiers and tens of thousands of college students who finished their studies at the end of 1960.

Led by the Democratic Party after the July 29 general elections, the new Chang Myon government immediately instituted freedom of the press. The second republic's bicameral legislature functioned with greatly reduced presidential powers. Under the new regime, hundreds of police officials who had remained since the days of Japanese occupation were fired, and police chiefs who had ordered their men to open fire of unarmed protesters were punished. Nonetheless, most of Rhee's midlevel officials remained, and Chang showed little interest in qualitatively changing institutions. Although he initiated an investigation of the massacre on Jeju, Chang closely consulted the United States, especially CIA station chief Peer de Silva, on nearly all major decisions.[25] At the same time as protesters continued to call for even more extensive punishment of politicians and police authorities responsible for the use of violence against the movement, the new government came under increasing pressure to clamp down.

Buoyed by their newly found powers, students organized themselves into a force that sought to alter Korea's division into two states. The Student Federation for National Unification and left-wing trade unions together demanded immediate reunification. Simultaneously, a coalition of seventeen parties and organizations campaigned against the U.S.-Korea economic accord. Seeking to initiate direct discussions with their counterparts in North Korea aimed at reunifying the country, students set a date for a joint meeting, and a large rally in Seoul called on the government to support the talks. On October 8, 1960, after many defendants charged with the April shootings were found not guilty in the absence of a special law, students who had been wounded during the uprising occupied the empty National Assembly building.[26]

After April 19, students and ordinary citizens were energized as never before. Decades later, activist Kim Gun-tae explained that, "Since 1960, street protests became a tradition in Korea politics."[27] On November 28, sixty members of the Student Christian Federation were arrested in the Christian Broadcasting System building. When a new repressive law was proposed, a significant all night protest remained in the streets on March 22, 1961. Time and again, uprisings are crucibles that temper activists, hardening them to lead the next phase of struggles. The 1960 revolution transformed Christians from ardent supporters of the regime—as they had been under Rhee—to some of the most important opponents of dictatorship. As one Christian publication put it, "The April 19th Student Revolution was the moment of repentance for the Korean Church."[28] The National Council of Churches was even more explicit: "The church finally opened its eyes to see what was going on, and opened windows to see the dawn of a new day . . . The nation has achieved a revolution, fought against tyranny . . . The Christian papers which were so eloquent until the eve of the revolution have suddenly turned into silence."[29]

In the euphoria of democratic renewal, street mobilizations became an everyday occurrence. Once they had overthrown Rhee, students' belief in their autonomous power led them to intensify their initiative to reunify the country. They proposed a joint North-South conference that would create a confederation whose highest body would be composed of an equal number of representatives from North and South, an idea personally considered by Kim Il-sung. For Koreans, with tens of thousands of families divided by the nation's partition, reunification was a heaven-sent prospect, but not for the United States, whose next war against Communism, this time in Vietnam, was just beginning.

Four days before the scheduled student meeting in Panmunjom, a small coterie of U.S.-backed officers, with leading roles played by Park Chung-hee and other former members of the Japanese army, seized control of the government.[30] As the *coup d'état* unfolded at midnight on May 16, 1961, the army moved into cities with force.

At 3:30 a.m., Chung Myon telephoned Magruder for U.S. troops to put down the coup, but the United States refused the government's request. The next day, although the United States retained operational control of South Korea's military, Park moved two full divisions into Seoul without getting Magruder's approval. Although defenders of the United States maintain there is no known evidence of prior U.S. knowledge of the coup, James Hausman (leader of the U.S. campaign to suppress the Yeosun Insurrection in 1948 and self-described "father of the South Korean army") claimed to have had advance knowledge.[31] Twenty years after the coup, Hausman was honored by U.S. military commander General John Wickham with a "Meritorious Civilian Service Award." The citation carried the following words: "Through his close personal relationship with President Park, he was able to persuade the military junta to take actions which eased the apprehensions of U.S. officials, and his comprehensive understanding of the background and aspirations of newly emerged military leadership enabled him to convince U.S. officials at a national level that under this leadership, the Republic of Korea

Former Japanese officer Park Chung-hee led a military *coup d'état* in 1961 and ruled until 1979.
Photographer: Kim Cheon-gil

would move forward in a manner that would enhance the U.S. position in Asia."[32] Remembering that Hausman had personally intervened with Rhee to save Park's life in 1948, we can only guess how much Park was indebted to him in 1961.

The day after the coup, a "revolutionary committee" of thirty generals and colonels pledged to return power to civilians. In their first acts, coup leaders arrested two thousand political leaders, including Chang Myon. They quickly purged more than thirteen thousand government officials and armed forces officers, and closed forty-nine of Seoul's sixty-four newspapers.[33] Cracking down on freewheeling urban youth culture, they used stiff penalties, corporeal punishment, haircuts, and imprisonment to impose cultural conformity. The day after Park's coup, the investigators of the 1948 Jeju massacre were arrested. The dictatorship clamped down on all investigations of past atrocities, so any public hint of the Jeju massacre would have to wait until 1978 when Hyun Ki-Young published his short story, "Aunt Suni."[34] Only in 1999 would the U.S. slaughter of hundreds of unarmed refugees at No Gun Ri in 1950 first be reported. Nearly half a century would pass before dozens more such massacres were allowed to be discussed in public.

Park Chung-hee Dictatorship

A former intelligence officer in the Japanese army, where he was known as First Lieutenant Okamoto Minoru (also called Takaki Masao), dictator Park Chung-hee ruled with an iron fist. Under his regime, people's hopes for expanded democracy and national reunification were suppressed brutally by a surfeit of state violence. Lovers' letters complaining privately of the regime's repression became used to imprison citizens. When no such innocuous "evidence" could be found, police simply conjured it, sending thousands of innocent people to prison in Kafkaesque fashion. Unlucky victims were executed after charges against them had been fabricated.

As ruthless as he was in punishing anyone who disagreed with him, Park also had a vision for the country. Basking in an aura of nationalist pride, he articulated a plan for a prosperous and harmonious Korea. His economic policies may have relegated millions of people to lives of unending toil with few immediate gains, but he promised rewards for future generations, words that carried deep meaning to many people as they daily experienced deprivation and hardship. Before he was done, he would promulgate a *"yushin"* or revitalization system modeled on Japan's Meiji restoration. In the process, he would assume powers for himself not unlike those of a Japanese emperor. Park fashioned himself Korea's Napoleon—the inheritor of the mantle of the April revolution who, in his own words, would lead the nation "in a great reform movement" to realize "the national ideals as demonstrated by the April 19 and May 16 revolutions." Under the auspices of his regime's "revolutionary court," five people were executed on December 21, 1961: the head of Rhee's presidential security guard who had ordered police to open fire in 1960, the leader of the gang that had then so viciously attacked students, and Rhee's minister of home affairs—but also a publisher of a newspaper that advocated reunification as well as a leader of the Socialist Party. Wealthy industrial magnates were paraded through the streets of Seoul wearing dunce hats and ridiculed for profiteering from people's suffering.

Park's military regime embarked upon an ambitious development program to catch up with the North through a "great leap forward in economic growth."[35] Although initially hostile to corrupt leaders of *chaebol* (huge family-owned businesses that cornered pieces of South Korea's economy) who had gorged themselves at the ox of Rhee's import-substitution policies, Park famously made a deal with the country's richest citizens to collaborate on a new export-industrialization strategy. Together, they soon negotiated a deal to construct a new industrial city in Ulsan and embarked upon a host of other projects.

U.S. Secretary of State Dean Rusk received glowing reports from his ambassador in Seoul that Park was moving "with lightning speed, and by and large in the right direction."[36] Park had the wily assistance—some would say "direction"—of U.S. advisors, including W.W. Rostow, a coterie of MIT technocrats, and Harvard professor Samuel Huntington, who hailed the military as a "nation-builder." Among Koreans, Kim Jong-pil was one of dozens of military men who collaborated with Park. Some thought Kim was the "real brains behind the coup." Park's nephew by marriage, Kim founded the Korean Central Intelligence Agency (KCIA) with U.S. help on June 13, 1961—less than a month after the coup.

Park's grandiose scheme required enormous amounts of money, but he had only limited domestic sources. As much as he squeezed workers and devalued the currency to stimulate exports, he still needed far more capital. Between 1953 and 1962, U.S. aid funded 70 percent of Korea's imports and 80 percent of its fixed capital investments—about 8 percent of its GNP.[37] Once the United States needed its monies to fight the war in Vietnam, however, it began to cut back. In order to find new international sources of money, Park endorsed a key U.S. proposal: closer ROK ties with Japan. As soon as Park had seized power, the United States began to pressure him to normalize relations with Japan. As early as October 1961, KCIA chief Kim Jong-pil and a veritable river of high-level diplomats shuttled between Tokyo and Seoul. In November, Dean Rusk (using personal letters from President Kennedy to both Japanese Prime Minister Ikeda and Park) arranged a meeting between Park and Ikeda, after which Ikeda told Rusk it was only a matter of time before a new treaty would be signed.[38]

While Harvard and MIT professors suggested and U.S. policymakers pressured, Park's chosen means to raise capital did not resonate well with the general public, but instead aroused considerable turmoil. Staunch domestic opposition to normalization prevented a treaty from simply being finalized. Park narrowly won elections in 1963, but by March 1964, when news of the treaty being negotiated became public, protests quickly involved as many as eighty thousand students. On March 24, the target of student protests was clear. At Seoul National University: "Death to Japanese Imperialism!" they screamed. The next day more than a thousand Korean university students went into the streets, and within a few days, students in Gwangju, Iri, Daejon, Busan, and elsewhere also mobilized. In some cases, they nearly took control of government offices.[39]

On June 3, 1964, Park declared martial law in Seoul and dismissed dozens of professors and students. The U.S. Combined Forces Commander approved the release of two combat divisions to suppress the protests.[40] Despite thousands of students threatening to storm the Blue House (the presidential residence), Park rammed the treaty through the rubber stamp legislature of the Third Republic. When the opposition went on a hunger strike to protest the treaty, the ruling party took one minute to ratify it, and at the same time, it also approved sending twenty thousand troops to Vietnam to fight on the side of the United States. In exchange for normalization of relations, Japan paid $300 million in grants (for which Park indemnified Japan for all its previous actions) and made available another half a billion dollars in loans.[41]

Immediately, militant protests were rekindled. Some fifteen thousand students launched a march on the Blue House and, at one point, out-battled the police.[42] This time the universities were occupied by the military and closed. One estimate placed the number of people who participated in protests in one form or another at three and a half million from March 1964 to September 1965. On June 22, 1965, more than two hundred church leaders publicly came out in opposition to the treaty. The Association of Christian Mothers initiated a one-million-signature petition drive against it—a monumental feat they accomplished in two short weeks. The government's violent response to Christian activism only further widened the distance between Park's regime and the people it ruled.

Sensing an opportunity to channel public sentiment against the Communist enemy as well as a second avenue to raise capital, Park immediately offered thousands more troops for deployment to Vietnam. Despite scattered student protests, war with Vietnam proved less controversial than his settling of accounts with Japan. Park's movement of troops was so fast, that according to figures released by the U.S. State Department, there were more South Korean soldiers fighting in southern Vietnam in 1965 than North Vietnamese.[43] South Koreans soldiers were widely reported to be even more brutal than their U.S. counterparts. At the end of 1969, some 48,000 ROK military personnel were stationed in Vietnam, and by the time they completed their withdrawal in 1973, some 300,000 veterans had fought there. ROK casualties included 4,960 dead and 10,962 wounded.[44] Wars provide experiences for military officers who go on to inflict future casualties. Lieutenant No Ri-Bang served in Jeju in 1948 and went to Vietnam. Future dictators Chun Doo-hwan and Roh Tae-woo served together in Vietnam, before brutally ruling South Korea after Park's assassination in 1979.

The economic benefits of military intervention in Vietnam were extraordinary. From 1965 to 1970, the South Korean government received $1.1 billion in payments—about 7 percent of GDP and 19 percent of foreign earnings.[45] More than eighty Korean companies did lucrative business in Vietnam—from transportation to supply, construction to entertainment—from which the country accrued another $1 billion for exports to and services in Vietnam. Secret U.S. bonuses paid to Park's government for Korean soldiers who fought in Vietnam totaled $185 million from 1965 to 1973. When we add all these funds to the $1.1 billion in direct payments, the total U.S. allocations to Park's regime amounted to about 30 percent of the ROK's foreign exchange earnings from 1966 to 1969.[46] Altogether U.S. aid to South Korea totaled $11 billion by 1973—more than to any other country except South Vietnam—some 8 percent of worldwide U.S. military and foreign monies.[47] Regimes friendly to the United States in Japan, Taiwan, the Philippines, and Thailand also benefited greatly from the tidal wave of dollars that flooded the region during the Vietnam War.

By the mid-1970s, Park's economic plan and new export strategy paid dividends. Just over 2 percent of economic output when Park seized power, exports rose to 16.5 percent of GNP in 1972 and to 30.8 percent four years later.[48] Nearly three-fourths of all exports went to the United States and Japan. GNP grew at an annual rate of 8.45 percent from 1961 to 1970; from 1971 to 1980, annual growth rate was 7.8 percent. As illustrated in TABLE 5.2, per capita GNP increased rapidly.

TABLE 5.2 **Per Capita GNP in South Korea, 1961–1988**

Year	Per Capita GNP in U.S. $
1961	$88
1970	$289
1980	$1,592
1988	$4,040

Sources: Hagen Koo, *Korean Workers: The Culture and Politics of Class Formation* (Ithaca, NY: Cornell University Press, 2001), 30; Chae-Jin Lee, *A Troubled Peace: U.S. Policy and the Two Koreas* (Baltimore: Johns Hopkins University Press, 2006), 3.

While his plan to build heavy industry went forward, Park's rule grew increasingly repressive. As major benefactors of Park's *yushin* system, *chaebol* did not support democratization. Modeled on Japan's Meiji restoration, the *Yushin* period (1972–1979) was characterized by enormous powers being concentrated in Park's hands. Using emergency decrees to stifle dissent, he built up the *chaebol* as never before. From 15.1 percent of GNP in 1974 to 30.1 percent in 1978, the top ten *chaebol*'s total sales accounted for 55.7 percent of GNP in 1981.[49]

Even prior to *yushin*, Park's rule grew so repressive that Koreans who were able to leave the country could not escape his long reach. In 1967, dozens of Koreans living in Europe and the United States were kidnapped and taken back to Korea by the KCIA. Two of them were professors of political science, who were eventually convicted under the NSL and executed.[50] (Taiwanese émigrés to the United States faced similar fates in this period. It is no wonder given that both Park and Syngman Rhee considered themselves staunch allies of Chiang Kai-shek and mandated school curricula in which South Korean children were taught they were fighting Communism alongside their "blood brothers in Taiwan.")

On June 8, 1967, Park's party won 130 of 175 seats in elections for the National Assembly, but as soon as the count was announced, people began to protest their accuracy. On June 9, when eight thousand students from seven universities demonstrated, Park closed their universities. On June 14, more than fifteen thousand high school and college students took to the streets. Attacked by police, they fought back. Ultimately, 50 colleges and 186 high schools were closed before Park felt secure. To hold final examinations, universities were allowed to reopen on July 3, but sixteen thousand students refused to take their exams and instead took to the streets. In three days of new actions, more than six hundred students were arrested.[51]

New focal points for action were autonomously generated from the grassroots. Two years later, students again mobilized, this time against the proposal to amend the constitution and allow Park to run for a third term as president. When Park did run in 1971, seven hundred students formed "observation teams" and reported widespread irregularities in the voting. Although Kim Dae Jung won more than five million votes—44 percent of the total and 58 percent in Seoul—Park emerged as the winner. In October 1971, well-organized protests against compulsory military training for all college students were stopped only when troops occupied seven Seoul universities for a week. They arrested 1,889 students, registered 12,000 others for military service, disbanded seven student governments, banned 14 publications, barred 74 student clubs from meeting, and expelled 177 students (all of whom were inducted immediately into the military).[52]

Try as they may, students were unable to generate the kind of popular sentiment against Park which they had used to topple Rhee. While their 1960 uprising was spontaneous and generally well received by a sympathetic public, the 1971 movement confronted an apathetic public, in part because it was orchestrated by "deliberate leadership assumed by student government."[53] In the unfolding progression of student politics, the 1971 movement was far more radical than its 1960 counterpart, and it was also distant from ordinary people's concerns. While the 1960 movement had despotism as its enemy, in 1971, a number of issues were woven together in the movement. On March 22, 1971, one statement from students declared:

> In our own country, we are ruled by an antidemocratic, antinationalistic group, which, contrary to the wishes of the people, attempts to build a

fascist system, which negates the democratic goals of freedom and justice. Externally, it is leading us to political and economic subjugation to the foreign powers . . . This group suppresses the just expression of people's discontent by the blanket imposition of uncritical thinking and by arousing a sense of crisis. Furthermore, the hard labor and exploitation of the working masses and peasants is justified in the name of modernization . . . We now proclaim that we are prepared to lead a struggle to halt once and for all the scheme to impose compulsory military training on the students. We hereby appeal to every single student in our school and schools throughout the country to join with us in this critical movement, which is being carried out as a part of our larger democratic and nationalistic struggle.[54]

The thick rhetorical style indicates the ideological character of the group. It would appear that the spontaneous movement of 1960 spoke in far more accessible language and was far more successful than the more well-organized groups in 1971. This will not be the last time we make this observation. As we will see when we explore subsequent uprisings, the outcome of spontaneous and massive occurrences is often far better than deliberately planned ones. One of the great accomplishments of these years of activism was the formation of "*chaeya*" opposition, a movement scene of displaced and dispossessed activists that congealed into an extraparliamentary force and kept pressure on the government (literally, "people staying in the field"). Park had been able to ride on the backs of subaltern groups, but they slowly began to organize against him.

The Urban Poor

With the "miracle on the Han River," Seoul's population grew from 2.5 to 8 million people in the two decades to 1980. For many people, the "miracle" meant they were forced to squat in plank villages (or *panjachon*). In 1964, as Seoul's phenomenal growth was just getting started, one estimate put the number of illegal shacks at 50,000, with an average of more than seven people per unit.[55] By 1968, the number stood at 233,000 shacks, with a total of at least 1,270,000 inhabitants.[56] When the government developed plans for the land upon which people had built their homes, they simply sent in police and thugs to clear people out— often in the middle of the night. Time after time, fights broke out. In one case, rather than allowing their town to be razed, 1,000 residents faced off against 300 police and heavily armed thugs. They put up a strong fight, but after more than 300 citizens were injured, they watched as their homes were reduced to rubble. In the first three years after Park's coup in 1961, some 25,000 households were cleared.

Of the new units that were hurriedly constructed, a large building at the Wawoo Apartments collapsed on April 8, 1970, killing three residents and construction workers. Dozens more people were injured. The mayor's resignation did little to placate people's fears—to say nothing of the growing housing shortage. Two weeks after the Wawoo Apartment collapse, thirty-five representatives of ten districts founded the Federation of Self-Managed Associations of

Seoul Citizens Apartments.[57] After supplications to the guardian spirit of Wawoo Mountain, they immediately began organizing. On June 15, 1971, some three thousand people—mainly housewives and senior citizens—rushed into Seoul City Hall. They demanded immediate repairs of their buildings and withdrawal of the city's order for them to pay off their apartments or face eviction. Taken by surprise, the mayor complied.

On vacant land just outside Seoul in Gwangju (a different Gwangju than the one in South Jeolla), thousands of urban poor, evicted from shantytowns in the city, were unceremoniously dumped "like garbage" with no running water, no electricity, and no sewage system. The government planned hundreds of factories capable of employing 450,000 people, and construction moved at breakneck speed. By 1971, the number of residents had grown from 6,000 to 300,000 in just three years. Speculators moved in, and the city turned its back on previously evicted shantytown dwellers who had high hopes for a fresh start in their newly found homes. Negotiations broke down. Hungry and tired, residents called for a meeting with Seoul's mayor for 11 a.m. on August 10. By 10 a.m., 50,000 people were waiting. When no one came to meet with them by 11:45, the local branch office of City Hall was attacked and set afire. Screaming about their hunger and pain, the crowd charged hundreds of riot police, completely devoured the melons on a truck that happened to pass by, and gathered themselves to march on Seoul. Even though it began to rain, fighting with police went on for hours. At 5 p.m., the mayor announced his unconditional acceptance of their demands.

After Gwangju, the urban poor were better cared for. As is often the case after militant actions, organizations were produced with longer-term strategic visions. A few weeks after the Gwangju riot, the Seoul Metropolitan Community Mission was formed by prominent Protestant leaders, among them Reverend Park Hyung-kyu. Focusing on shantytown organizing, the group helped build community hospitals and clinics, get tax relief for small businesses and the poor, stop evictions, and create schools. They also built churches and converted many people to Christianity.

A new wave of progressive churches spawned the Urban Industrial Mission (UIM), whose activists worked tirelessly for social justice. While continuing to battle evictions, they began organizing labor unions. In the fours years from 1968 to 1972, some forty thousand workers in a hundred enterprises were brought into their organizations.[58] As church activists came into contact with the *minjung*, their lives were forever changed. As Tong Hwan (Stephen) Moon expressed it: "Yes, we had read about the liberation theologies coming from North and South America. We had argued about Western political theologies. But it was not until we heard the desperate cries of the *minjung*, listened to their deep yearning for justice, discovered the dynamic power hidden in them, and witnessed the growing maturity of those who had given themselves to a noble cause, that our whole perspective was transformed."[59]

Minjung theology soon became a significant force in Korea's movement. The UIM created eighty groups in twenty different companies, all working toward a just society, not simply an end to dictatorship. [60] They worked "believing that the suffering of Christ himself in history is that of the poor and working masses, and in the conviction that sharing in events where people suffer can bring about mission or salvation, UIM workers have held to an eschatological faith in a right-eous, equal and peaceful society where the Rule of God is actualized."[61] Christian *minjung* theologists were expelled from universities and seminaries, freeing them to be exposed to the struggles of people. From the young workers who barely could feed their families, to the widows of movement martyrs and parents of imprisoned and tortured students, they discovered in the lives of ordinary Koreans dynamics that "made the Bible a new book to us."

International influences in the early formulation of *minjung* theology were also important. C.S. Song from Taiwan had significant influence, as did Martin Luther King, Jr.[62]Although *minjung* theology in Korea developed first within Protestant churches, it was also greatly influenced by Latin America's theol-ogy of liberation.[63] In 1968, after Cardinal Kim Su-Hwan became head of Korean Catholics, the church's involvement in progressive political causes grew increas-ing overt. Although Christians played significant—some would say central—roles in democratization movements, they remained a minority. Census figures put their numbers at 20 percent of the population in 1985 (4.61 percent Catholic and 16.05 percent Protestant). The number of Buddhists was put at slightly less—19.94 percent of the population.[64]

Chun Tae-il and the Struggle Against *Yushin*

Of all the workers being squeezed by Park Chung-hee's drive to build the economy, none were more exploited and subjected to harsher conditions than thousands of female textile workers. In the area around Pyong Hwa (Peace) market, some twenty thousand girls aged twelve to seventeen labored sixteen hours a day—often seven days a week—in dusty decrepit attics whose ceilings were so low they could not stand up. For all that toil, they barely made enough to cover their bus fare to work, and had only two days off per month. Yet many felt lucky to find work at all, and parsimoniously saved what little they could to send home to their families.

No one is born to work in a factory, and the transition is often full of trauma. Lee Chong-gak remembers her first day on the job, January 8, 1966: "The cotton dust looking like falling snow, and the roaring noise from the machines as big as houses felt like it would pierce my eardrums; it was really like hell. I learned how to work that day. So many of the words used on the floor were Japanese, I could not understand. Because it was so noisy and hard to hear, the supervisor taught me as he glared and yelled; he was just like the grim reaper. To get the 70 won a day, we clenched our teeth and learned the ropes."[65]

Although a Labor Standards Law mandated an eight-hour workday, employ-ers routinely required much longer hours. Many workers suffered injuries due to sleepiness, and illnesses were almost always punished with dismissal rather than being treated with medical care. Under these conditions, a young activist named Chun Tae-il emerged from within the ranks of the workers. With a few friends, Chun formed a group—the Fools' Organization—to challenge the harsh conditions of the economic "miracle." They repeatedly sent letters to the government office in charge of enforcing legal code and reported illegal conditions at Peace Market, especially the flagrant violation of the eight-hour day, the one day/week holiday, and the government's ban on night work for employees under eighteen years old. For his efforts, Chun was fired many times, but he persisted. Finally, unable to alter the dreadful working conditions, Chun Tae-il publicly committed suicide on November 13, 1970, to call attention to the desperate plight of workers. "Observe the Labor Standards Law!" he shouted as he died.

In 1963, the self-immolation in Saigon of Buddhist monk Thich Quang Duc played a huge role in galvanizing opposition to South Vietnam's U.S.-backed president, Ngo Dinh Diem. Chun Tae-il's death by fire similarly had an enormous impact on labor activists and the antidictatorship movement in Korea. So fearful was the regime of his memory that riot police were called in to prevent his coffin from being carried out of his workplace. The government offered money to the family if they would keep the funeral quiet, but they refused. As word of his sacrifice spread, two SNU students committed suicide. Other students organized a public commemoration. Marching with his photo, they promised to "follow in his footsteps." In the aftermath of Chun's suicide, dozens of night schools for workers were organized, where subjects ranging from Korean language to politics were freely available.

Park's export-oriented economic development plan brought the regime much needed capital, but in the early 1970s, as the Vietnam War dragged on, inflation led to an economic crisis. Park's response was to declare a state of national emergency and promulgate the 1972 *Yushin* Constitution that gave him practically unlimited powers. Under it, he alone appointed one-third of the National Assembly and was guaranteed unlimited presidential terms. When whispers of dissent were heard, Park dissolved the National Assembly, and sentenced Kim Dae Jung (who had received 44 percent of the vote in the 1971 elections) to a long prison term after having him kidnapped from a hotel room in Tokyo. Kim was one of the lucky dissidents. Around the same time as he was imprisoned, SNU Professor Choi Chong-kil was killed after he fell (or, as most believe, was thrown) from a KCIA building three days after being summoned there.

Besides its frightening political implications, *yushin* also signified a transformation of the accumulation regime—from one relying on light labor-intensive production (like textiles and electronics) to heavy industry. Park's prolonged campaign to develop capital-intensive factories began with his borrowing vast sums on the international capital market so he could launch his Heavy and Chemical Industry Plan. This second phase of import-substitution and export deepening led to the sudden build-up of industrial enterprises like shipbuilding and automobile production.

Opposition to Park's unilateral decisions was widespread. On April 22, 1973, a joint Easter outdoor service drew a hundred thousand people. During the worship, placards calling for democracy and freedom of the press prominently appeared. In June, priests who had organized the event and their students were arrested, and many were severely beaten. As Christians mobilized to protect their leaders, the campaign against *yushin* intensified. In November 1974, Ham Seok-heon organized the National Congress for the Restoration of Democracy, founded on strict principles of nonviolence. By March 1975, with fifty local branches, he issued a Charter for a Democratic People, in which he justified resistance to all forms of obstruction of democracy.[66] A petition campaign collected more than a hundred thousand signatures calling for reform.

Undeterred by protests, Park Chung-hee enacted Emergency Decrees 1 and 2, banning all anti-*yushin* activities. He ordered the imprisonment of the petition-drive coordinators, including Reverend Park Hyung-kyu and about 140 others. By this time, the spectrum of movement organizations included groups like the Young Catholic Workers Organization (*Jeunesse Ouvrière Chrétienne*, or JOC) who advocated autonomous unions and the National Federation of Democratic Youth and Students, or *Minchonghanyon*, a student organization whose "People, Nation, Democracy Declaration" called for structural transformation of society.[67] At the same time as Reverend Moon Ik Hwan called for reunification, students being sentenced to prison sang "We Shall Overcome," folksinger Kim Min-gee gave renditions of Bob Dylan songs, and many activists read the works of Herbert Marcuse and C. Wright Mills.

On April 13, 1974, hundreds of students took to the streets of Seoul against *yushin*, but 1,224 were quickly arrested and accused of being aided by North Korea.[68] Emergency Decree 4 made it a crime punishable by death to refuse to attend classes or even to utter the name of dissident groups. After dozens of professors were fired, they formed the Council for Fired Professors. Fired journalists formed the Tong-A/Chosun Committee for Struggle, and blacklisted writers created the Writers' Council for Freedom to Write. By making their punishment into a badge of honor, the dissident movement slowly helped legitimate protest in a society where honor means so much—in stark contrast to many parts of the world where cash, not personal standing in the eyes of one's community, is king.

In early May 1974, the KCIA stunned the country when it announced it had broken up a Communist conspiracy to overthrow the government by an organization called the People's Revolutionary Party (PRP). Thousands of people were arrested, and hundreds sentenced to long prison terms, including former ROK President Yun Po Sun and Catholic bishop Chi Hak Soon.[69] We know today that the entire "conspiracy" was fabricated by the KCIA, but at the time it was a deadly serious matter for millions of Koreans—all the more so when eight of the arrested "PRP members" were executed, secretly hanged on April 9, 1975, while their families waited outside Soedaemun prison to visit them. Some of the bodies were cremated without the consent of the families. In one case, the widow of Song Sang Jin watched in horror as riot police stopped her husband's funeral, snatched his body, and took it to a crematorium. Thirty years later, under a new democratic government, the PRP executions were found to have been improper and the men innocent. Court records were found to have been falsified to indicate the suspects admitted to working for North Korea, when, in fact, they all insisted they did not. In 2007, after the families were compensated by the Noh Moo-hyun government, they used the monies to initiate a foundation for social justice.

In late 1974, as Park continued to clamp down, he ordered all newspapers to stop publishing anything about student demonstrations or church criticisms of *yushin*. *Donga Ilbo* daily newspaper, a symbol of independent reporting since the 1920s, refused to follow the order. To set an example, the KCIA pressured advertisers to cease their patronage of the paper. Overnight, about 80 percent of revenues dried up. When it appeared that the paper would go under, Kyungdong Presbyterian Church in Seoul took out a full-page ad. Soon, thousands of ordinary people did the same. Taxi drivers, doctors, and mine workers all bought small spaces. Nine girls working in a textile mill expressed the nation's sentiments best when they said: "Better to stand and die than bow your head and live."[70] Park could not let the public platform for protest continue. He sent in police and a large group of thugs to evict *Donga Ilbo* workers.

On February 15, 1975, Reverend Park and others imprisoned for their petition drive were finally released. Students then demanded full reinstatement of released professors and students. Thousands marched, but with no progress in sight, one student, Kim Sang Jin, committed suicide on April 11, 1975.[71] The government's response was to cremate his body before a funeral could be held, close all universities, and arrest over two hundred students while disciplining hundreds more.

The struggle against *yushin* called for many people to suffer losses in their personal welfare. No one was called upon to sacrifice more than hundreds of thousands of young working women, whose suffering and struggles preconditioned the emergence of the *minjung* as the subject of social transformation. In the unfolding logic of the development of the democratization movement, women's labor activism in the 1970s made substantial contributions. They promoted an opposition consciousness with expanded notions of human rights and democracy, and they helped consolidate opposition groups. The *minjung* identity that was at the heart of the movement originated in great part in the suffering of female factory workers and the rallying of scores of groups that came to their assistance. As Miriam Ching Yoon Louie understood, "the *minjung* movement fused with women workers' struggles in a synthesis process which simultaneously politicized women workers' struggles while giving the cross-class *minjung* movement its working-class orientation."[72] After ten years of participant observation, George Ogle also concluded that the struggles of young women factory workers transformed peoples' consciousness and laid the groundwork for the labor movement of the 1980s. Besides being midwives of the Korean democracy movement,[73] these struggles became a model for similar movements that subsequently emerged in Southeast Asia.[74]

Women as Midwives of the *Minjung*

As Korea industrialized in the early twentieth century, women were at the center, comprising 61 percent of factory workers in the 1930s.[75] With Park Chung-hee's aggressive program of export-led development involving labor-intensive industries, hundreds of thousands of young girls had been enticed to move to urban centers, where they were concentrated in workshops that seemed never to close.

In the United States, a similar process had occurred earlier in the century in places like Lowell and Lawrence, where the Bread and Roses strikes had brought unions and a modicum of justice to women's work.

In Korea, union membership grew from 150,000 in 1961 to 500,000 a decade later, but these unions were company (or "yellow") unions that catered to men, even though big industrial worksites employed about 500,000 women in 1970. The number of female industrial workers grew to 1,090,000 by 1978 and to 1,862,000 by 1987—40.5 percent of all industrial workers.[76] These "Kong Soonie" (the equivalent of Rosie the Riveter in the United States) were enormously important to the Korean miracle, accounting for almost two-thirds of all exports in the early 1970s.[77] Patterns of late marriage in Korea left single women especially vulnerable to low-wage and long-shift work. From 1961 to 1982, more than 60 percent of Korean women between twenty and twenty-four years old were single, compared with less than 10 percent in India and about 40 percent in Thailand.[78] For the most part, these women workers were concentrated in textile, fiber, clothing, and electronics industries, often in free trade zones where unions were illegal and the daily wage was only 500 won (at the time one dollar was 480 won). Men were paid double that amount. As Korea urbanized, more than five million women were wage-earners in 1975,[79] and women workers moved to the forefront of the trade union movement.

On the university campuses as well, women were increasingly self-confident and conscious of the need to build their own autonomous centers. In 1975, a Declaration of Women as Human Beings was published: "The goal of the women's liberation movement is cultural revolution and human liberation. We reject limited reforms originated from men's political consideration, merely aiming at enhancing women's status. We deny every idea of oppression and hierarchy. In a larger perspective, our aim is to establish a community based on the liberation of the whole of humanity, including not only women but also men."[80] At Chonnam National University, women also began to organize autonomously. Im Chun-hee organized a women's research group around issues of equality, abolition of sex discrimination, and women's participation being increased. In the engineering college, there were not even any female toilets.[81]

In 1976, at *Dongil* Clothing Company, while hundreds of women yearned for union help, male workers loyal to the company held a closed-door meeting to select a yellow union leader. After years of trying to integrate the union, women had enough—they broke down the door and occupied the room. After three days, the riot squad came to evict them, but about seventy women took off their clothes and formed a human barricade to prevent police from attacking them. Women then spent months organizing for union elections, and at 6 on the morning they were scheduled, female workers and union leaders who had been up all night preparing the ballot were assaulted by male workers and company goons with huge buckets of feces. Hundreds of female night–shift workers were smeared with excrement to prevent them from voting, and the attackers even forced some into people's mouths. More than one hundred of the women were fired, but they refused to submit. On March 10, 1978, thousands of people attended the FKTU "labor day" event at Jangchung Sports Stadium commemorating the organization's founding. Thousands more watched the live broadcast. Suddenly seventy-six women began chanting, "Resolve the Problem of *Dongil* Textiles!" Police and FKTU thugs attacked the women three times, sending most of them to the hospital with severe injuries, but the women had made their point. On April 1, another 124 women were fired, and the FKTU published a national blacklist with their names so they could not find employment elsewhere. In response, more than twenty-five women sat in at the headquarters of the FKTU and demanded reinstatement. Although they lost their jobs, they continued to struggle for justice though hunger strikes, protests at official ceremonies, and speaking prominently at an Easter sunrise service attended by hundreds of thousands of people.[82] During a nationally televised workers' ceremony, they interrupted and spoke eloquently about how they "were unable to eat shit to survive." For years they persevered. As late as May 13, 1980, hundreds of women from *Dongil* protested once again at the FKTU.

The courage of the *Dongil* women helped stimulate a dialogue with the new women's studies program at Ewha Women's University. As trade union women and college students interacted, the movement began to address unspoken issues and to strategize future actions. In August 1979, at least four thousand young women textile workers lost their jobs at YH Company when the Korean-American owner moved it overseas rather than accede to union demands. The ensuing drama profoundly affected the country. Seeking help, about 170 workers sat-in at the opposition New Democratic Party's headquarters, and the government sent in hundreds of riot police who assaulted them. In the melee, dozens of people, including opposition politicians and journalists, were injured, and one young woman, Kim Kyung-sook, was killed. To protest the police violence, New Democratic Party (NDP) leader Kim Yong-sam and other party members conducted an eighteen-day sit-in at their own headquarters.

Women's activism resonated with other dissident streams in a process of mutual amplification. Cries for an end to *yushin* were everywhere to be heard, but no one in the ruling party seemed to be listening. On June 27, 1978, eleven professors from CNU issued an open letter calling for democratic reforms. They were summoned to police headquarters and detained. When hundreds of students protested, police invaded the campus, arresting and beating students without any real concern for legality. For three days, protests continued. On July 5, police prevented three hundred people from the National Alliance for Democracy from meeting at Seoul's Christian building. In national elections in December, the NDP, running on a platform of democratic reform and an end to *yushin*, received more votes than Park's party.

Farmers were also compelled to make known the severity of their situation, particularly as urbanization meant family farms were rapidly disappearing. Government promises to farmers, like those to workers, remained fiction more often than not. In South Jeolla's Hampyeong County, sweet potato farmers, organized by the Catholic Farmers Association, protested openly against the government's failure to buy all of their crops at agreed prices. On April 22, 1977, some six hundred farmers gathered at Kyerimdong Church in Gwangju to call for adequate pricing and democratization of government agricultural associations.

After waiting futilely for appropriate measures to be taken, they finally used their harvested potatoes to blockade highways and local roads. In May 1978, the *yushin* regime backed down and agreed to keep their promise.

All over Korea, small groups resisted by many different means, including the formation of book clubs. In 1978, a "good books union" was founded in Busan and soon had two hundred members. Like the "jazz clubs" in Czechoslovakia under Soviet rule, informal small group venues provided occasions to freely express opinions and perspectives as well as an opportunity to meet like-minded people. The Busan club would produce activists who would lead the city for more than a decade of struggles. Reading about the Catholic Medellin conference of 1968, Song Gi-in was so impressed by liberation theology that he became a Catholic priest/activist. Arrested more than forty-eight times by the KCIA, he nonetheless continued to use the safe haven afforded by the inner sanctum of the church to lead discussions and hold meetings. Although then an obscure labor lawyer, president-to-be Noh Moo-hyun was also a member of the "good books union." Soon, a nationwide network emerged that not only utilized a shared curriculum list but also kept people in the loop as far as news of the movement against *yushin*.[83]

For his public support of YH workers, Kim Young-sam was expelled from parliament, as were all elected NDP representatives. Parliamentary representatives loyal to Kim Dae Jung also resigned in solidarity. On September 4, 1979, dozens of students protesting *yushin* were arrested in Daegu, and by the end of the month, thousands of students in Seoul were in the streets demanding greater freedom. It would be in Busan, however, where the movement's final blow against *yushin* would be struck. Unwittingly, the YH struggle escalated into the final crisis of *yushin*—the Buma Uprising (named for its explosion in Busan and Masan)—and the end of Park Chung-hee.[84]

Buma Uprising

In Busan, Kim Young-sam's home region, many people demonstrated against the NDP's expulsion, but Park arrogantly believed he could forever impose his will through force of arms. After students mobilized, he called out the army and declared martial law. The protests' sudden popularity surprised everyone—especially the students who initiated them, such as Lee Chin-gol who wrote an anonymous anti-*yushin* leaflet on October 15. Since it meant certain prison if he were seen handing it out, he and a few friends surreptitiously scattered about 90 copies in rest rooms, corridors, and empty lecture rooms at Busan National University.[85] The handbill called on people to gather at 10 a.m. the next day at the campus library to protest *yushin*. Unbeknownst to him, Chung Kwan-min also produced a similar hand-printed leaflet. The next morning, Chung rose from his seat in an economics seminar and called on his fellow students to join him: "Classmates, let's go out and fight for democracy!"

As he strode out the door, a few students followed him, and they all shouted for others to come along. By the time they reached the front of the library, a hundred students had joined. They sang the national anthem and *minjung* songs, and within a few minutes, two hundred or more students were gathered. Chung rose and read his leaflet verbatim. Conservative professors and undercover police tried to stop them, but people moved to another part of campus. A long line of students was in motion. As the group passed a building—any building at that explosive moment—their ranks swelled. Within an hour, there were a thousand, then two thousand—until finally about four thousand students gathered, out of a student body of less than ten thousand.

Chung tried to lead part of the group off campus through a gate near the high school, but police pushed them back. Spontaneously, people retreated and then simultaneously divided into smaller groups to break out of campus through each of the three gates. Police again dispersed Chung's group—this time with tear gas. Hundreds gathered at the library to discuss what to do. At another gate, several thousand were almost able to break through, but police erected barriers to keep them on campus, and they retreated to a soccer field. When the police stepped onto campus, students responded with stones and erected a barricade with basketball backboards. They then pushed through police lines and headed downtown—nearly 10 miles away. Some took buses, while the majority kept together and marched. As they proceeded to walk several miles downtown, citizens they happened to encounter applauded the students, plying them with soft drinks, snacks, and money.[86] Thousands more people swelled their ranks, and the local populace protected them. Activist Kim Ha-gi told me that a friend of his ducked into a supermarket while being pursued by police. The owner quickly lowered the shutters and stepped outside. When police arrived, he simply said, "No cousin, no one is inside." The police moved on to search elsewhere.

At 3 p.m., the procession reached downtown Nampodong (site of the 1960 protests that began the uprising to overthrow Syngman Rhee). At least thirty thousand people gathered.[87] The police divided the crowd into small groups, but by 5 p.m. people were able to regroup as the national anthem was played and the flag was lowered. "Normally we students disliked the Korean national anthem, but that day we sang it with gusto," explained Kim Jong-ho.

As soon as the ritual concluded, people surged ahead, and police attacked, but by then it was too late for the police to have their way. People overturned police cars and burnt out substations, and the crowd commanded the streets until dawn. "All over the city, small groups huddled together, traded information, planned, dreamed, and for the first time in years, spoke openly about their dreams."[88] Prostitutes applauded them, as did people in hotels, giving the youth a feeling of being the heroes of a "ticker-tape parade" as they shouted, "Destroy *Yushin*!"; "End the Dictatorship!"; and "Reinstate Kim Young-sam!" Shopkeepers shared apples and bread. The poor and lumpen joined the street actions, and at one point, they led people to the tax office and set it on fire. More than a dozen police vans were attacked. Despite a midnight curfew and the presence of the army, many students stayed downtown. By 1 a.m., eleven police boxes had been destroyed.[89] By the time dawn came, four hundred people had been arrested and six hundred wounded.[90] Without leaders and using a minimal amount of violence, protesters had defied one of the world's most feared dictatorships. Everyone who heard about it took note.[91]

At 10 a.m. the next day, Donga University students organized a new protest. Close to the city center, they led a peaceful assembly from their campus to the downtown area. Once again, local people overwhelmingly supported the students, giving them money, food, and water. Sustained by their supporters, the protesters continued into the night. More militant members of the group set upon buildings symbolizing Park's rule and set them to the torch. By 9 p.m., two television stations (KBS and MBC), a district revenue office, and other government offices had been destroyed—including twenty-one police substations. Altogether in the two days of protests, there were 1,058 arrests and probably an equal number of wounded.[92] U.S. embassy reports claimed 12,000 people had attacked two television stations and repeated newspaper figures of 800 arrests and seventy-nine police injured.[93] By the early morning hours of October 18, martial law had been declared in Busan, and army units were in position around City Hall and broadcast stations. Classes were cancelled at all major universities. As one activist related, "Anyone who looked like a student was arrested and beaten, so we all went home." A small demonstration was easily broken up.

Busan may have been pacified, but the protests spread to neighboring Masan, where once again student demonstrators drew widespread support and stimulated a grassroots citizens' uprising.[94] Assembling at Masan's April 19 Memorial, over a thousand students from Kyongnam University marched downtown around 5 p.m. and fought their way to the ruling Democratic Republican office. Organizers had carefully timed their mobilization so people would be near the Export Processing Zone, which employed many working-class citizens.[95] When the march appeared, thousands of people joined to attack Park Chung-hee's party office and eighteen other public buildings—although they spared the hospital and other buildings not tied to the hated *yushin* regime. Faced with a growing uprising, the government extended martial law to Masan, and the army arrested 238 citizens. To keep the city quiet, 1,500 armed soldiers patrolled the streets.

In the four days of the Buma Uprising, at least 1,563 arrests were made, around a third of whom were students.[96] While only a four-day event, the Buma Uprising was a life-altering experience for many young people who tasted the freedom of the streets for the first time. That struggle generated men and women who went to lead movements in the future. Several, like, Park Kye-dong, went on to become elected members of the National Assembly. Another activist, Noh Moo-hyun, went on to become president of the country. Writer Kim Ha–gi went onto a life of activism. Arrested and tortured during the South Jeolla Gwangju Uprising for throwing leaflets supporting the insurgents from a Busan rooftop on May 19, 1980, he wrote about the June Uprising in 1987 while imprisoned. As he told me, Buma was the turning point in his life. For him, it was "like the French Revolution, where the people supported the movement. We had always been disappointed before, but this time, the civil revolution really happened. It was as if the dead returned to help the living." He had helped Chung distribute the seminal leaflet that began the October 16 beginning. Like Kim, Chung was also sent on a trajectory of years of activism by his Buma experiences. After helping run a social science bookstore for years, he became a labor activist.

The main outcome of Buma was the assassination on October 26 of Park Chung-hee by his own chief of intelligence, Kim Jae-kyu. While sadness and shock were the media reactions, many people celebrated. Thousands of political prisoners were released, suspended student governments were reinstated, and 793 students expelled for Buma activities, in the words of a U.S. official, "returned to campus as heroes."[97] Park had ruled with an iron fist for almost two decades, and the country palpably breathed more easily once his grip was gone. Hopes for restoration of democracy and civil liberties were high.

Even before Park's rule ended, Korea had changed enormously. When he seized power, Korea was overwhelmingly an agrarian, rurally based country, but within twenty years, it had become an urban industrial society. What took a century in Europe happened in two short decades in Korea. The number of households with televisions in 1979 was more than thirteen times as many as in 1970.[98] Despite *yushin's* strictly enforced puritanical morality, the sexual revolution was catching on, American fashions from the 1960s and 1970s were popular, young men grew long hair faster than police could cut it, and women insisted on wearing miniskirts even though police shamelessly harassed them.

Chun's 12–12 Coup and the Seoul Spring

Amid the swirl of events unleashed by the end of the dictatorship, a tiny coterie of thirty-eight army officers under the leadership of Chun Doo-hwan and Roh Tae-woo seized control of the military on December 12, 1979. They arrested dozens of ROK officers and killed at least four servicemen guarding the military headquarters building. A few high-ranking officers escaped through tunnels across the street to the U.S. bunker, where they huddled with CFC Commanding General John Wickham. In the U.S. command bunker in Yongsan, ROK Minister of Defense, No Che-hyon, and Chairman of the Joint Chiefs of Staff, Kim Chong-hwan, began to order troops into Seoul to confront Chun, but Wickham urged them to wait until dawn.[99] By the time the sun rose, Chun had moved armored units to key positions and his control of the military was a *fait accompli*. A few days later, Chun called on both Wickham and the U.S. ambassador, William Gleysteen. After the meeting, Wickham checked his files and discovered that Chun had given him the exact same message that Park Chung-hee had sent to Gen. Magruder: We're "going to clean up corruption, and return to the barracks. Trust us; watch what we do and you will be proud of us someday."[100]

Despite the coup, many people continued to be optimistic about the country's future. An interim government with a weak president was the façade of decision-making, but behind the scenes, Chun and the military remained firmly in control. On February 19, Kim Dae Jung was released from house arrest and embarked on a speaking tour, regularly drawing crowds of fifty to a hundred thousand as he called for democracy. Universities that had been closed down after Park's assassination were allowed to reopen in March, and previously forbidden student councils reconvened. In Gleysteen's estimation, "The odds of a dangerous disruption, such as a military coup or massive student/worker uprising do not seem high."[101]

Although Park was gone, martial law remained in force, making protests illegal, but they occurred with increasing regularity, especially among workers. From January to May 1980, nine hundred strikes were counted, particularly by miners, textile workers, machinists, and pharmaceutical workers—more strikes than had occurred during seven long years of *yushin*.[102] Textile workers in Peace Market won a 28 percent raise, and bank and financial employees won a 15 percent retroactive pay raise after a sit-in strike.[103] In Busan, Tongguk steel mill workers militantly confronted management; even within the FKTU, a reform movement emerged. On April 21, about seven hundred miners in Sabuk, dissatisfied with the 20 percent raise their union had negotiated and afraid of reprisals, overwhelmed a police box and used the arms they took to seize control of the mine. Promising to fight, they stood their ground until a new agreement was reached on April 24.

On May 2, an emergency student assembly at SNU convened with ten thousand of the school's thirteen thousand students. At this forum, while many people expressed a variety of opinions, the group ratified the Student Association's decisions to abandon opposition to military training in order to focus instead on a full-scale political struggle for an end to *yushin*, removal of martial law, and guarantee of basic labor rights. Students marched to the university main gate, where they burned Chun Doo-hwan in effigy.[104] At Sungkyungkwan and Sogang universities, student councils passed similar resolutions. Soon, across the country, twenty-seven student governments joined the campaign for a national struggle, and they quickly became mobilizing vehicles for planned May 14 and 15 demonstrations in Seoul. The U.S. embassy translated the call issued by students: "The tasks remaining before us now are to repel the foreign power completely which supported the dictatorial regime in the past twenty years, liquidate the comprador bureaucrats and business groups . . . and accomplish self-reliance in the economy, correcting the dependent economic structure distorted by the remnants of the *yushin* system."[105]

On May 9, Gleysteen met with Chun in the very same "safe house" where Park had been killed. In preparation for the meeting, Gleysteen promised Washington that he would not "in any way suggest that the U.S. government opposes Korean government contingency plans to maintain law and order, if absolutely necessary by reinforcing the police with the army."[106] True to his word, he reminded Chun that "the government had to be ready to maintain law and order."

At noon on May 14, at least seventy thousand students from thirty-four universities rallied in downtown Seoul. At the same time, Gleysteen met with acting president Choi Kyu-hah in the Blue House, where the American ambassador made it clear that the United States "would interpose no objection" to the use of special forces troops against student demonstrators.[107] Returning to his office, Gleysteen observed student demonstrators jump over the low wall around the U.S. embassy when their march was broken up. In his words, police used so much tear gas that "our building was choking with pepper gas." So concerned was Gleysteen with Iran—where student militants continued to hold dozens of Americans hostage in the U.S. embassy—that he noted the event several times in his messages to Washington. Later that day, other students visited *Dongil* union activists then occupying the FKTU building. Besides expressing solidarity, students explained the details of Chun's 12–12 coup and asked the workers to participate in their demonstrations. Thinking it would undermine their struggle to reform the FKTU, the workers asked students to vacate the building.[108]

The next day, Gleysteen observed an assembly he estimated to be 80,000 students take an even more militant stance when police attacked them. Others counted the crowd at more than 100,000 students at Seoul Station (some estimates ran as high as 150,000).[109] Gleysteen noted that several armored pepper gas trucks were burned—but also that the protesters did not stop the first Miss Korea contest in Korea being held right across the street from the embassy at Sejong Cultural Center.[110] Tens of thousands of people surged toward the Blue House, but their leaders made a decision to turn the protests back into the city. The next day, the anniversary of Park Chung-hee's military coup, the government warned of military action if demonstrations continued, so student leaders decided to call off protests. When more than a hundred student leaders from fifty-five universities met to discuss the situation further at Ewha's Women's University, police swooped in and arrested ninety-five of them. The rest were able to dash to safety.

On May 16, Wickham released the ROK Twentieth Division from U.S. operational control after "consulting with his own superiors in Washington" and agreed it could be dispatched to Gwangju.[111] That night, fifty thousand people rallied by torchlight at the square in front of Province Hall in Gwangju. Vowing to continue the struggle against dictatorship, they promised that if the universities were closed, they would assemble at 10 a.m. on May 18 in front of the main gate at Chonnam National University. While in the rest of Korea, students decided to stop their protests, in South Jeolla they refused to be intimidated by the new dictatorship. Although the country was ready for democracy—some said it was "overripe"—Chun would hear nothing of it, and his U.S. supporters stood squarely behind him. The stage was set for a major confrontation.

NOTES

1   Published CIA data reported that until 1978, North Korea was ahead of South Korea in GDP per capita.
2   *History of Korean Finance for Forty Years* (Seoul: KDI, 1991), 157.
3   Alice H. Amsden, *Asia's Next Giant: South Korea and Later Industrialization* (New York: Oxford University Press, 1989), 43; Lars Lindstrom, *Accumulation, Regulation, and Political Struggles: Manufacturing Workers in South Korea* (Stockholm: Stockholm Studies in Politics, 1993), 37.
4   Christian Institute for the Study of Justice and Development, *Lost Victory*, 13.
5   Henderson, *Korea: The Politics of the Vortex*, 170.
6   Kim, *Politics of Democratization*, 34.
7   Interview with Paik Han-gi, Masan, October 29, 2009.
8   Sungjoo Han, *The Failure of Democracy in South Korea* (Berkeley: UC Press, 1974), 29; Henderson, *Korea: The Politics of the Vortex*, 175.
9   Göthel, *Geschichte Südkoreas*, 73, and Park, *Democracy and Social Change*, 65.
10   Lee, *The Making of Minjung*, 106.
11   See my book, *The Imagination of the New Left: A Global Analysis of 1968* (Boston: South End Press, 1987), especially chap. 2.

12   Göthel, *Geschichte Südkoreas*, 73.

13   Interview with Kim Ye-Hyan, 4.19 Institute, Seoul, December 13, 2001.

14   Sungjoo Han, "Student Activism: A Comparison Between the 1960 Uprising and the 1971 Protest Movement," in *Political Participation in Korea: Democracy, Mobilization, and Stability*, ed. Chong Lim Kim (Santa Barbara: Clio Books, 1980), 145.

15   Kang Man-gil, *A History of Contemporary Korea*, 318.

16   Park, *Democracy and Social Change*, 65.

17   H.B. Lee, *Korea: Time, Change, and Administration* (Hawaii: East-West Center, 1968), 119. Quoted in Amsden, *Asia's Next Giant*, 42.

18   See Han, "Student Activism," 159; Interview with Kim Ye-Hyan, 4.19 Institute, Seoul, December 13, 2001. Other reports provide a variety of figures: Lee Chae-Jin reports 115 killed and 730 injured (*A Troubled Peace*, 43). In *Korea on the Brink: A Memoir of Political Intrigue and Military Crisis* (Washington D.C.: Brassey's, 2000), John A. Wickham, Jr., claims 142 students were killed (231); Gleysteen asserts that when students marched on Rhee's residence to protest the rigged elections, some 200 were killed by his guards (9); Göthel reports 183 dead and 6,259 wounded (*Geschichte Südkoreas*, 76); finally a church source tells us 185 students or citizens were killed (*Lost Victory*, 14).

19   Tom Hayden made these remarks in Gwangju during a speech at the International Conference Commemorating the 30th Anniversary of the Gwangju Uprising in May 2010.

20   Recent evidence indicates the possibility of collaboration between protesting professors and the U.S. embassy.

21   Han, *The Failure of Democracy in South Korea*, 32.

22   Wonmo Dong, "University Students in South Korean Politics: Patterns of Radicalization in the 1980s," *Journal of International Affairs* 40, no. 2 (Winter 1987): 234; Henderson, *Korea: The Politics of the Vortex*, 179.

23   Koo, *Korean Workers*, 135; Han, *The Failure of Democracy in South Korea*, 178–93; Göthel counted 485 disputes with 340,000 participants (*Geschichte Südkoreas*, 77).

24   Dae-oup Chang, ed., *Labor in Globalizing Asian Corporations: A Portrait of Struggle* (Hong Kong: Asia Monitor Resource Center, 2006), 11.

25   Cumings, *Korea's Place in the Sun*, 344.

26   Kang Man-gil, *History of Contemporary Korea*, 202. Also see Hart-Landsberg, *The Rush to Development*, 135.

27   Interview with Kim Gun-tae, Seoul, August 2, 2008.

28   *Democratization Movement and the Christian Church in Korea during the 1970s* (Seoul: Christian Institute for the Study of Justice and Development, 1985), 23.

29   *Korean Church: History and Activities* (Seoul: National Council of Churches in Korea, 1990), 32.

30   Cumings, *Origins*, 1:175.

31   Cumings, *Korea's Place in the Sun*, 349.

32   Harvard University Yenching Institute, Hausman archive, Box 7, page 3 of the citation.

33   Cumings, *Korea's Place in the Sun*, 351.

34   Hyun Ki-Young, *Aunt Suni*, trans. Song Jong Do (Seoul: Kak Press, 2008).

35   Amsden, *Asia's Next Giant*.

36   Cumings, *Korea's Place in the Sun*, 319.

37   Thomas W. Robinson, *South Korea's Political Development in the 1980s* (Department of State, External Research Contract 1724–32012) August 25, 1983; Hart-Landsberg, *The Rush to Development*, 44.

38   Cumings, *Korea's Place in the Sun*, 319.

39   Göthel, *Geschichte Südkoreas*, 151.

40   Cumings, *Korea's Place in the Sun*, 355.
41   Martin Hart-Landsberg, Seongjin Jeong, and Richard Westra, eds., *Marxist Perspectives on South Korea in the Global Economy* (Burlington, VT: Ashgate, 2007), 212.
42   Hart-Landsberg, *The Rush to Development*, 167.
43   See the discussion in the volume I edited, *Vietnam Documents: American and Vietnamese Views of the War* (Armonk, NY: M.E. Sharpe, 1992), 63.
44   Chae-Jin Lee, *A Troubled Peace*, 55, 70.
45   Cumings, *Korea's Place in the Sun*, 321.
46   Hart-Landsberg *The Rush to Development*, 147–48.
47   Han Sung-joo, "Korean Politics in an International Context," in *Korean Politics: Striving for Democracy and Unification*, ed. Korean National Commission for UNESCO (Elizabeth, NJ: Hollym, 2002), 620.
48   Eugene Kim, "Emergency, Development, and Human Rights: South Korea," *Asian Survey* 18, no. 4 (April 1978): 371, http://www.jstor.org/stable/2643400, accessed on July 23, 2008.
49   Hart-Landsberg, *The Rush to Development*, 191.
50   Lindstrom, *Accumulation, Regulation, and Political Struggles*, 74.
51   *Democratization Movement and the Christian Church in Korea during the 1970s*, 18–19.
52   Sungjoo Han, "Student Activism: A Comparison Between the 1960 Uprising and the 1971 Protest Movement," in *Political Participation in Korea: Democracy, Mobilization, and Stability*, ed. Chong Lim Kim (Santa Barbara, CA: Clio Books, 1980), 153.
53   Ibid., 154.
54   Ibid., 148.
55   Erik Mobrand, "Struggles Over Unlicensed Housing in Seoul, 1960–1980," paper presented at the IPSA Fukuoka, 2006.
56   *People's Power, People's Church: A Short History of the Urban Poor Mission in South Korea* (Hong Kong: Christian Conference on Asia, 1987), 41.
57   Ibid., 35–36.
58   *Democratization Movement and the Christian Church in Korea during the 1970s*, 40.
59   Moon, "Korean Minjung Theology," 13.
60   Lee, *The Making of Minjung*, 224.
61   Quoted in Lienemann-Perrin, *Die Politische*, 159.
62   Interview with Oh Choong-il, 2006.
63   Hyug Baeg Im, "Korean Christian Churches in Democratization Movement," in *Democratic Movements and Korean Society: Historical Documents and Korean Studies*, ed. Sang-young Rhyu (Seoul: Yonsei University Press, 2007), 111–12.
64   Donald Baker, "The International Christian Network for Korea's Democratization," in *Democratic Movements and Korean Society: Historical Documents and Korean Studies*, ed. Sang-young Rhyu (Seoul: Yonsei University Press, 2007), 134.
65   "Story of Lee Chong-gak," in Park Min-na, *Birth Of Resistance: Stories of Eight Women Activist Workers* (Seoul: Korea Democracy Foundation, 2005), 31.
66   Sungsoo Kim, "The Democracy Movement and NGOs in South Korea," The Second Peace Island School, Jeju National University, August 2008.
67   Chulhee Chung, "Structure, Culture, and Mobilization: The Origins of the June Uprising in South Korea," (PhD dissertation, SUNY Buffalo, 1994), 92.
68   Presidential Truth Commission on Suspicious Deaths of the Republic of Korea, *A Hard Journey to Justice* (Seoul: Samin Books, 2004), 131.
69   George Ogle, *Liberty to the Captives: The Struggle Against Oppression in South Korea* (Atlanta: John Knox Press, 1977), 94–95.
70   Ibid., 101.
71   Ibid., 51.

72 Louie, "*Minjung* Feminism," 418.

73 See Nam Jeong-Lim, "Women's Labor Movement, State Suppression, and Democratization in South Korea," *Asian Journal of Women's Studies* 8, no. 1 (2002): 71–95.

74 Chung, "Together and Separately," 24.

75 Ibid., 21.

76 Kang and Lenz, *Wenn die Hennen krähen*, 45.

77 See Walden Bello and Stephanie Rosenfield, *Dragons in Distress: Asia's Miracle Economies in Crisis* (San Francisco: Food First Books, 1990), 25; Hart-Landsberg, *The Rush to Development*, 181.

78 Bello and Rosenfield, *Dragons in Distress*, 28.

79 Seungsook Moon, *Militarized Modernity and Gendered Citizenship in South Korea* (Durham, NC: Duke University Press, 2005), 71. "Economically active women" includes both employed and unemployed women looking for work.

80 Quoted in Mikyung Chin, "Self-Governance, Political Participation, and the Feminist Movement in South Korea," in *Democracy and the Status of Women in East Asia*, eds. Rose J. Lee and Cal Clark (Boulder, CO: Lynne Rienner, 2000). Ok Jie Lee wrote that "manipulation of gender relations has been one of the important ways of maintaining effective control of workers." See her "Labor Control and Labor Protest in the South Korean Textile Industry" (PhD dissertation, University of Wisconsin, Madison, 1990).

81 Interview with Im Chun-hee, December 21, 2001.

82 Jeong-Lim, "Women's Labor Movement," 77.

83 Interview with Kim Ha-gi, Busan, October 31, 2009.

84 Prior to the Korean government's change of the transliteration system from Hangul to English, Busan was known as Pusan. "Puma Uprising" referred to both Pusan and Masan. Since the change, the same uprising is sometimes renamed the Buma Uprising.

85 Interviews with Ko Ho-sok, Chung Kwan-min, Song Gi-in, Kim Jae-kyu, Kim Jong-ho, Busan, May 30–31, 2001.

86 May 18 Gwangju Democratization Movement Materials, Gwangju City May 18 Historical Materials Compilation Committee 광주광역시 5–18사료 편찬위원회, 5–18 광주 민주 화운동자료총서), December 17, 1997, VII: 405. (Hereafter GDMM).

87 Gi-wook Shin puts the number at fifty thousand (*Peasant Protest*, 117). A Yushin spokesperson described the demonstrations as involving only three thousand students and "hoodlums," by which he meant young men who hang around the port.

88 Interviews with Kim Ha-gi, Busan, May 30, 2001.

89 May 18th History Compilation Committee of Gwangju, *The May 18th Gwangju Democratic Uprising* (Gwangju: May 18th Memorial Foundation, 2001), 73.

90 Shin and Hwang, eds. *Contentious Kwangju*, xiii.

91 Interview with Cha Sung-hwan, Busan, October 31, 2009.

92 *Democratization Movement and the Christian Church in Korea during the 1970s*, 109.

93 GDMM VII: 395, 407.

94 Cha Sung-hwan, 참여 노동자를 통해서 본 부마항쟁 성격의 재조명 (unpublished doctoral dissertation, Busan National University Political Science Department, 2009).

95 Interview with Yoon Won-chol, Masan, October 29, 2009.

96 May 18th History Compilation Committee, 75; The U.S. embassy reported a slightly higher figure of arrests at 1568 arrests reported on November 29. GDMM VII: 69. Although the protests occurred in October, Cumings curiously states they occurred in August and September of 1979 ("Civil Society," 23).

97 GDMM VIII: 495. Ominously the U.S. secretary of state's office twice requested the names of these students for indexing. GDMM VIII: 680.

98 Lee, *The Making of Minjung*, 151.

99 Mark Peterson, "Americans and the Gwangju Incident: Problems in the Writing of History," in *The Gwangju Uprising*, ed. Donald N. Clark (Boulder, CO: Westview, 1988), 57; Wickham acknowledged that some of his U.S. officers also wanted to stop the coup.

100 Ibid., 58.

101 GDMM, VIII: 550, March 12, 1980.

102 Stephen Haggard and Robert Kaufman, *The Political Economy of Democratic Transitions* (Princeton: Princeton University Press, 1995), 87. Also see Lee, "Militant Unionism in Korea," 164. Labor Administration reported the number of labor disputes rose from 105 in 1979 to more then 700 by April 24, 1980, almost seven times the number reported in all of 1979. See Chung Sangyong, Rhyu Simin, et al., *Memories of May 1980: A Documentary History of the Kwangju Uprising in Korea* (Seoul: Korea Democracy Foundation, 2003), 64. Some figures are even higher: 1011 disputes and 745 strikes. From 5–18 관련 논문과 작품 영역 및 저술 사업: 2001. 5–18 20주년 기념 학술연구ㄴ업 연구소위 (Gwangju: 전남대학교 5–18 연구소: 2001) hereafter *Essays*, 58, and Ahn Jean, "The socio-economic background of the Gwangju Uprising," in *South Korean Democracy: Legacy of the Gwangju Uprising*, eds. George Katsiaficas and Na Kahn-chae (London: Routledge, 2006), 45.

103 GDMM, VIII: 701.

104 Sangyong, Simin, et al., *Memories of May 1980*, 64.

105 GDMM, IX: 129.

106 William H. Gleysteen Jr., *Massive Entanglement, Marginal Influence: Carter and Korean in Crisis* (Washington, D.C.: Brookings Institution Press, 1999), 114–15.

107 Ibid., 118.

108 Sangyong, Simin, et al., *Memories of May 1980*, 53; interview with Won Young-su, Gwangju, 2009.

109 Shin and Hwang, eds., *Contentious Kwangju*, xiv, Park, *Democracy and Social Change*, 71, and Won Youngsu in *Facts on File* say over one hundred thousand. Cumings maintains that "hundreds of thousands of students and common people flooded the streets of Seoul." See also "The Northeast Asian Political Economy," in *What Is in a Rim?*, ed. Arif Dirlik (Lanham, MD: Rowman and Littlefield, 1998), 132.

110 Gleysteen, *Massive Entanglement*, 119–20, incorrectly named it the Miss Universe contest.

111 United States Government Statement on the Events in Gwangju, Republic of Korea, in May 1980. Articles 49.

CHAPTER 6

Gwangju People's Uprising

In this absolute community, citizens confirmed their greatness, blessed each other, and experienced an absolute liberation from all social bondages and constraints. At this moment, many citizens were plunged into such an extreme ecstasy that they would not have minded dying right then and there, and the struggle changed into a festival.

—Choi Jungwoon

The resulting autonomous minjung community, with its warm bonding among citizens and self-controlled order, demonstrated the beauty of human love that blossomed in the midst of fierce resistance.

—Rev. Park Hyung-kyu

CHRONOLOGY	
May 15, 1980	100,000 people protest in Seoul
May 16, 1980	Torchlight parade in Gwangju
May 17, 1980	Martial law extended to Jeju; Seventh Special Warfare Brigade sent to Gwangju
May 17, 1980	Nationwide police roundup of activists
May 18, 1980	Paratroopers occupy Chonnam National University (CNU)
May 18, 1980	CNU students clash with paratroopers and go downtown; fights break out
May 19, 1980	Gwangju citizens rise up; more troops arrive; tanks, flame-throwers used
May 20, 1980	Taxi and bus drivers lead a 200-vehicle demonstration around 6:30 p.m.

May 20, 1980	MBC television station burnt at 9:50 p.m.
May 20, 1980	Military fires first shots at Gwangju Station: two people killed
May 21, 1980	KBS television station burnt at about 4:30 a.m.
May 21, 1980	Tax office burnt at 10:19 a.m.
May 21, 1980	Asia Motors workers help deliver dozens of vehicles to the resistance
May 21, 1980	Military opens fire on Kumnamno at 1 p.m.
May 21, 1980	Militia forms and begins to shoot back at 3:20 p.m.
May 21, 1980	Military driven out of Province Hall at 5:30 p.m.
May 21, 1980	Buddhists bring Buddha's birthday celebration meal to the city
May 22, 1980	Protests spread to Mokpo, Naju, Hwasun, Haenam, and throughout South Jeolla
May 22, 1980	First rally takes place, approves trading guns for prisoners
May 22, 1980	White House meeting decides to suppress the uprising
May 23, 1980	More than 100,000 people gather for deliberations in Democracy Plaza
May 23, 1980	Settlement Committee trades 200 guns for thirty-four prisoners
May 23, 1980	Secret military agent steals detonators for dynamite
May 24, 1980	Settlement Committee tries to sabotage citizens' assembly
May 25, 1980	Citizen-Student Struggle Committee formed
May 26, 1980	"March of Death" of prominent citizens stops tanks from entering the city
May 26, 1980	USS *Coral Sea* rumored to be coming to rescue Gwangju
May 26, 1980	U.S. Ambassador Gleysteen asked to intervene, refuses to respond
May 27, 1980	Military retakes city

ARCHIMEDES ONCE DECLARED, "Give me a fixed point, and I can move the earth." Historically speaking, the Gwangju People's Uprising of 1980 is such a fixed point—the pivotal moment around which dictatorship was transformed into democracy in South Korea. Years afterward, its energy continues to resonate across the world. For those whose dreams of freedom remain unfulfilled, Gwangju's history provides a glimpse of free societies of the future and inspiration to endure the long journey ahead.

Forged in the sacrifices of thousands, the mythical power of the Gwangju People's Uprising was tempered in the first five years after 1980, when the dictatorship tried to cover up its massacre of at least 164 people.[1] After the Gwangju Commune had been ruthlessly crushed, the news of the uprising was so subversive that the military burned an unknown number of corpses, dumped others into unmarked graves or ocean waters, and destroyed its own records. To prevent word of the uprising from being spoken publicly, thousands of people were arrested, and hundreds tortured as the military tried to suppress even a whisper of its murders. In 1985, thousands of copies of the first book about the Gwangju Uprising were confiscated and its publisher and suspected author arrested.[2] Despite the military's censorship, the tragedy was revealed in poems, paintings, short stories, woodblock prints, plays, novels, and songs.

Korean civil society is so strong that when the facts of the military's brutal killing of so many of its own citizens and subsequent suppression of the facts finally became known, the government quickly fell. As Lee Jae-eui put it: "The reason why the Korean people could overcome that terrible violence so quickly in 1987 was because of Gwangju's resistance."[3] President Chun Doo-hwan and his military government may have won the battle of May 1980, but the democracy movement won the war—seven long years later.

The dialectical negation of military dictatorship is the Gwangju People's Uprising, a shining example of the rapid spread of revolutionary aspirations and actions, of a community of love created in the heat of battle. The spontaneous chain reaction of people coming to each other's assistance, the erotic occupation of public space, and the loving embrace in which the city united nearly everyone in it were one of the twentieth century's clearest expressions of the capacity of millions of ordinary people to govern themselves beautifully and with grace. In few places have so many been able to act with such unity. Universal interests became generalized at the same time as preexisting values (class divisions, hierarchy, and possessiveness) were reversed.

Sociologist Choi Jungwoon developed the notion of the "absolute community" to describe the collective energy which arose among Gwangju people as they battled the brutality of the paratroopers and drove the military out of the city: "In this community, there was no private ownership, other people's lives were as important as one's own, and time stood still. In this community, discriminations disappeared, individuals were merged into one, and fear and joy were intermingled. Distress at the end of one world coexisted with confusion at the beginning of a new world, in which emotion and reason were reborn . . . the intuitive nature of human dignity does not lie in the act and the result of pursuing individual interests and social status, but can be found in the act of recognizing a value larger than individual life and dedicating oneself to attaining it."[4]

Although many activist groups played significant roles in the uprising, at one point even forming an incipient revolutionary government, the people of Gwangju directly governed themselves. They were the ones who drove the military out of the city; they constituted the prime movers of this entire historical event. As the immovable movers, they rallied to defeat thousands of elite South Korean troops pulled off the DMZ. In liberated Gwangju, people freely cooperated with each other in ways we normally only dream of. The nightmare of military brutality and the dream of love simultaneously coexisted. As has been said before: "It was the best of times, it was the worst of times."

As monumental as the courage and bravery of the people in Gwangju were, their capacity for self-government is the defining hallmark of their revolt. In my view, it is the single most remarkable aspect of the uprising. Daily rallies of tens of thousands of people debated and took action about the key issues facing citizens. People's capacity for self-organization that emerged spontaneously, first in the heat of the battle and later in the direct-democratic governing of the city and the final resistance to the military's counterattack, is mind expanding.

The Uprising Begins

On May 14, 1980, in Seoul, when more than seventy thousand people joined in a student demonstration, a huge outpouring of sentiment against the dictatorship was also reported in many other cities, including Gwangju, Busan, and Masan.[5] The next day, more than a hundred thousand citizens assembled at Seoul Station in an even bigger show of support for democracy. While many people believed the time to overthrow the military had come, student leaders buckled under pressure from the government when it warned of dire consequences if protests continued. Student organizers decided to suspend actions scheduled for May 17 and 18. They hoped the military might end martial law and accede to the will of the country. Instead, Chun Doo-hwan clamped down, sending thousands of combat troops to all the large cities, especially to Gwangju, where on May 14, students at Chonnam National University (CNU) had broken through the riot police cordon enveloping their campus. Playing on media stereotypes that depict Jeolla people as thieves, gangsters, and subaltern, the military used regional prejudices as a tool to stigmatize Gwangju's citizens.

At 7 p.m. on the night of May 15, a small group in Gwangju gathered secretly to discuss their situation.[6] Yoon Han-bong was convinced a "sea of blood" was about to be unleashed on the city. He read the signs: Gwangju's proud democratic spirit, on one side, opposed by ruthless men who had seized power in Seoul. He warned fellow activists to get rid of incriminating photos and letters and to check the location of arms. He predicted hundreds of people would be killed, that the movement would take over South Jeolla's Province Hall and defend it as a way to rally the country and build international support. Yoon and the others were members of a national organization still being formed, People's Unity for Democracy and National Reunification.[7] On May 19, farmers were coming to commemorate their victory two years earlier in the Hampyeong sweet potato struggle,[8] and Yoon and Chung Yong-Hwa thought an uprising could grow out of those celebrations.[9] Yoon called his contacts in Daegu, Seoul, Busan, and Masan, wrote public statements for national and international audiences, and talked of the lasting political effect of fighting to the end. He believed the country would not tolerate a second *coup d'état*, like Park Chung-hee's 1961 takeover that led to nearly two decades of dictatorship. Yoon was sure people's mood in 1980 was far different, and certain that the opening session of the National Assembly scheduled for May 20 would condemn any domestic military action. With the country's interim president, Choi Kyu-hah, in the Middle East, Yoon thought there was a window of five or six days to prepare the uprising so it could be "systematic." While he was uncanny in his predictions that night, well ahead of his timetable, thousands of paratroopers were dispatched to Gwangju.

On May 16, while the rest of South Korea remained quiet, some fifty thousand students from nine universities in Gwangju rallied at the fountain in front of Province Hall, renamed it "Democracy Plaza," and marched through the city in a torchlight procession. Gwangju's students had a wealth of activist experience, gleaned most recently from a 1978 struggle to defend academic freedom. Their sixth sense told them to prepare for the worst, so they agreed that evening that no matter what happened, they would gather on the morning of May 18 at the front gate of CNU. On the night of May 17, military intelligence personnel and police raided dozens of homes across the city, arresting as many leaders of the movement as they could find. Activists not picked up went into hiding. At least twenty-six of the movement's national leaders (including Kim Dae Jung) had already been rounded up. According to one observer: "The head of the movement was paralyzed."[10] Another wrote that the "leading body of the students' movement was in a state of paralysis."[11]

With the approval of his superiors in Washington, U.S. General John Wickham, commander of the Combined Forces Command (CFC) of ROK and U.S. troops, had released seasoned paratroopers, and Chun immediately ordered them to Gwangju. The same army units had crushed movements in Busan and Masan less than a year earlier. In the interim, many had been shown an American film on how to suppress demonstrators that advocated bashing collarbones with new clubs, just like the ones they were issued. In case people ran away, the film depicted troops opening fire.[12] Once these troops reached Gwangju, they terrorized the population in unimaginable ways, savagely maiming and sadistically humiliating citizens.

In the first confrontations on the morning of May 18, paratroopers' specially designed clubs broke heads of defenseless students who were sleepily trying to reach classes. As demonstrators scrambled for safety, they regrouped and headed downtown. That morning, students spontaneously organized themselves—first by the hundreds and then by the thousands—to march in protest of the occupation of their city by police and freshly arrived units of the army. Angry and ready to fight back, they surrounded and captured forty-five riot police at Sansutong Junction. For a time, people debated what to do with their captives. They soon decided to set them loose, but immediately after they were released, paratroopers viciously attacked: "A cluster of troops attacked each student individually. They would crack his head, stomp on his back, and kick him in the face. When the soldiers were done, he looked like a pile of clothes in meat sauce."[13]

The first man killed was deaf. Unable to hear the soldiers coming, he paid with his life—but he was not alone. Bodies of the injured were piled into trucks, where soldiers continued to beat and kick them. As students continued to regroup, soldiers used bayonets on them and arrested dozens more people, many of whom were stripped naked and further brutalized. One young child who witnessed these events asked her parents when *their* army was coming. Another child, having been taught political values at a tender age, screamed that Communists had taken over the army. One soldier brandished his bayonet at captured students and screamed at them, "This is the bayonet I used to cut forty VC women's breasts [in Vietnam]!" On the protesters' side, some yelled, "Let's get rid of the *yushin* remnants and drive away Kim Il-sung, too!"[14]

The city's entire population was in shock from the paratroopers' overreaction. The paratroopers were so out of control that they even stabbed to death the director of information of the police station when he tried to stop them from brutalizing people.[15] Despite severe beatings and hundreds of arrests, students tenaciously fought back. For the first time in modern Korean history, Molotov cocktails were used to counter the superior firepower of the military. Throwing teams were organized behind Nokdu bookstore. Despite confusion over how to make and use the gasoline bombs, people kept coming back for more, and others joined in preparing them. Soon a pepper spray vehicle was in flames.[16]

The next day, people from all walks of life dwarfed the number of students among the protesters. From that moment on, students did not play the key role in street actions.[17] This spontaneous generation of a people's movement transcended traditional divisions between town and gown and was one of the first indications of the generalization of the revolt. When working people began to participate, the paratroopers again resorted to callous brutality—killing and maiming people whom they happened to encounter in the streets. Even cab drivers and bus drivers seeking to aid wounded people were stabbed, beaten, and sometimes killed. Some police officers secretly tried to release captives, and they, too, were bayoneted.[18] When the police chief refused to order his men to fire on protesters, he was taken away and tortured in Seoul. Even General Chung Oong, commander of the Thirty-First Division, refused to order his troops to open fire. Temporarily in command of an additional two battalions of Special Forces on May 18, Chung was called three times and told to send his units into combat in the city. Three times he demurred, claiming police were enough. Privately, he referred to the military's operation as one of "collective slaughter."[19] (Disgraced at the time and arrested a year later, he went on to become a popular Jeolla politician and was elected to parliament in 1989.) Although there were some who were ashamed of their units' behavior, most soldiers willingly complied with orders to attack. So eagerly did many paratroopers employ brutal tactics, citizens widely believed they must be on drugs.

Remarkably, instead of running away, people stood their ground. They fought back with stones, baseball bats, knives, pipes, iron bars, wood beams, sharpened bamboo, and hammers against eighteen thousand riot police and over three thousand paratroopers. No one brutalized individual policemen, but instead focused on paratroopers who killed and maimed. So callous were the military that they even used flamethrowers on citizens around 3 p.m. on May 19. Nonetheless some paratroopers who were captured were released unharmed—but disarmed. Citizens were not so lucky. Fighting continued throughout the night of May 19. As Choi noticed: "Despite the paratroopers' atrocities—the kind that had completely emptied downtown Busan in about ten minutes in 1979—in Gwangju, demonstrators surfaced again a little later, the number of them increased the next day, and finally a majority of citizens were united as one in resistance." Describing the motivation of people, Choi continued, "The key to this absolute community was 'love'—in other words, a human response to noble beings . . . the struggle at the moment was an exciting self-creation."

On the morning of May 20, after a mutilated corpse was discovered, many people gathered at Daein market to discuss their options. Female vendors rolled

In the midst of battle on May 20, 1980, when the army seemed to be gaining the upper hand, Gwangju's transportation workers led citizens in a massive counterattack.
Photographer: Hwong Chong-gun

rice balls to help keep up people's strength and encouraged them to continue. By the afternoon, tens of thousands of people assembled on Kumnamno Avenue, the heart of downtown, as if at a funeral. They sang, "Our wish is national reunification." A newspaper called the *Fighters' Bulletin* (투사회보) appeared for the first time with accurate news—unlike the official media. Before long, the military attacked, and paratroopers' clubs broke more heads. Soldiers again used flamethrowers against demonstrators—this time at Sobang Rotary at about 2:30 p.m. Several people were instantly incinerated.[20]

People refused to submit. At 5:50 p.m., as the brutality and resistance continued, a crowd surged over a police barricade. When paratroopers drove them back, they reassembled and sat on a road. They then selected representatives to try and split the police from the army.[21] It was difficult to hear each other, so someone began to collect money to buy a megaphone. Soon, there was more than enough money. In the evening, the march swelled to over two hundred thousand people (some say three hundred thousand) in a city with a population of seven hundred thousand. The massive crowd unified workers, farmers, students, and people from all walks of life, but spirits were low as a result of the killings. Defeat seemed inevitable. Suddenly, nine buses and over two hundred taxis with horns blaring arrived in a procession on Kumnamno. People joyously fell in behind the vehicles.

Taxi drivers had spread the word among themselves to assemble at Mudeung Stadium. Express bus drivers formed at the front of the convoy. All over the city, people stopped whatever they were doing to join the surge. Barmaids arrived, as did shoeshine boys, waiters, and deliverymen. The transport workers' unity rallied the entire city. Here was the city's working class arriving to lead citizens at their moment of gravest need. When defeat hung in the air and the smell of death frightened everyone, transport workers heroically galvanized renewed resistance. Their jobs had taken them all over the city, and they had seen, perhaps more than anyone else, the extent of the slaughter. As they drove toward the military's lines, risking their lives and cars, they hoped to "take the lead and break though the army obstruction line in order to reduce the victimization of citizens."[22]

One citizen's account, published immediately after the uprising, captured the moment: "The ones who didn't join in, who didn't witness the firmly united citizens, can't understand this feeling of liberation. They could have seen the tears on the faces of the young men, who devoted themselves to defend democracy. Their chests were splattered with blood. They shouted the slogans with bloody bands around their heads, until their throats got sore. Our beloved neighbors, young and innocent children, and even housekeepers were now joining the parading cars . . . People who couldn't get on the cars brought rice wrapped in seaweed and drinks . . . They wanted to give eggs, bread, cokes, milk, and juices to the demonstrators. Stuffing all the food into a box, an old man was not able to lift it up. I lifted it up and put it into a car that I just stopped. I could read the resolution to struggle to the death on their faces. Housekeepers who couldn't prepare food brought buckets of water, offered it to them to drink, and cleaned up their faces. Some citizens ran along with the vehicles . . . It was a struggle of blood and love to share lives with others: a man who tapped a participant's back to cheer, a pharmacist who brought out medicines and drinks, and the crowd who did their best, clapping and cheering."[23]

Once again, the paratroopers viciously attacked, and this time, the whole city fought back. As some people threw stones and Molotovs, others tried to cut a path through the military's lines with sticks. Using massive amounts of tear gas, the paratroopers stopped the convoy about 70 feet from their skirmish lines. Drivers in the front were beaten and bayoneted, but people in the rear surged forward. After twenty minutes of vicious hand-to-hand fighting, people broke away to regroup and then counterattacked. Their ranks were filled by newly arrived citizens rallied by loudspeaker trucks circulating in the city. A bus broke through the lines behind the paratroopers and ran into the fountain. Another bus made it through to the police lines. After the driver jumped out because of tear gas shot inside, it struck hard—killing at least one policeman. Out of the mist of tear gas, like an apparition, about fifty white-clad farmers with hoes and bamboo spears appeared—was it a mirage of *Tonghak* fighters or was it real?

Nearly two hundred thousand people were by now fighting for control of Kumnamno Avenue, attacking Province Hall from all sides. The battle raged for more than three hours with burning vehicles continually being pushed into the army blockade.[24] People nearly overwhelmed the Sixty-First and Sixty-Second Battalions. Although the army attacked repeatedly, people stood their ground, and the evening ended in a stalemate at Democracy Plaza only after the military used M-16 rifle fire to stop attacks.[25] In moments of rest, strangers embraced each other as if they were the closest of friends. For Choi, this is the moment when the absolute community formed: "This was a community whose members over-came fear of violence and personal shame through reason and courage. Citizens braving death gathered to join forces after recognizing and congratulating each other for being real human beings. The human dignity pursued by citizens was objectified by mutual recognition in encounters with other dignified human beings. In this absolute community, citizens found their identities as human beings, and they were reborn."[26]

Unable to take control of Province Hall, the crowd shifted its attention away from the barricaded paratroopers on Kumnamno and besieged the Regional Labor Office, MBC television station, and train station. At about 10 p.m., troops from the Thirty-First Provincial Division, mainly South Jeolla natives, announced through loudspeakers, "We are not harming you people. We are just moving out. Please make way!" They were allowed to depart without incident—the crowd's wisdom understood the sincerity of the soldiers. Later it was learned that Special Forces had parachuted into their headquarters and detained their commander, Chung Oong, for refusing to follow orders. Chung and Yoon Hung-jong, the province's martial law commander, were both sacked.[27]

The state-controlled media failed to report killings that occurred right under their noses. Instead, false reports of vandalism and minor police response were the news they fabricated. After the nightly news again failed to report accurately the army's brutality, thousands of people surrounded the MBC television build-ing. Soon the management of the station and the soldiers guarding it retreated, and the crowd surged inside. Unable to get the broadcast facility working, people torched the building. The crowd targeted other buildings quite intelligently. Some people shouted, "Taxation for the common good, not for buying weapons from the United States to kill our own people!" Hundreds of people responded: "At 1:00 in the morning, citizens went in flocks to the Tax Office, broke its furniture, and set fire to it. The reason was that taxes, which should be used for people's lives and welfare, had been used for the army and the production of the arms to kill and beat people. It was a very unusual case to set fire to the broadcasting stations and tax office while protecting the police station and other public buildings."[28]

At the Tax Office, a debate broke out before people torched it. Some people insisted that tax money belonged to all the people so there was no need to burn the building. Others insisted the government used the money to kill people in Gwangju. Once the point was made, about two thousand people surged inside. In the building's basement, a grisly discovery was made: a high school girl's corpse with her breast slashed.[29] Taking the body for proper burial—as well as several bundles of carbines—they torched the building. During the next two days, as the building continued to smolder, it was so hated that no one even attempted to put the fire out.[30] A similar debate broke out when another group gathered at the telephone building. This time they decided not to burn it. Besides the Tax Office, two television stations, the Labor Supervision Office, Province Hall car depot, and sixteen police boxes were burned down.

In the streets around the train station, the battle grew especially intense. One soldier described how he was part of an eighteen-man patrol ordered to go from Chonnam National University a short distance to the station. After their first attempt failed because of stiff resistance, they retreated back to the university. They rearmed themselves and fell into formation behind a truck. An M60 machine gun mounted on it continually fired at buildings as they moved forward. A Major threatened from behind: "I will shoot you to death if you retreat." When they finally reached the station, soldiers were "ceaselessly shooting." He observed one sergeant get killed when he was run over by a truck. The abandoned bodies of about twenty blood-drenched citizens lay in the streets.[31] On the other side, people related that when soldiers fired M-16s into the crowd, killing many in the front ranks, others climbed over the bodies to carry the fight to the army. With incredible fortitude, the people prevailed, and the army beat a hasty retreat back to CNU. Troops also opened fire at the Tax Office and Chosun University, where three thousand demonstrators led by three buses set out to free arrested people from the gym. When tear gas failed to disperse them, hand grenades were also used.[32]

May 21: The Fighting Intensifies

Early on the morning of May 21, people found two corpses at the train station. Loading them onto a pushcart, they went downtown. Exhibiting the grisly evidence of the military's crimes, they urged people to take control of Province Hall, the only place outside the university encampments where paratroopers remained. By 9 a.m. that morning, more than a hundred thousand citizens gathered on Kumnamno. People selected four representatives, including Chun Ok-ju, to go and speak with the governor. Another small group shouted that somebody should go to Asia Motors and bring vehicles. A few dozen people went off, but came back with only seven (the exact number of insurgents who knew how to drive).

At the Asia Motors plant (now KIA), workers at the mammoth factory had just put in an all-nighter because of the heavy volume of orders. On the morning of May 21, union organizer Park Tae-bong, curious about the gunfire he heard, rode his bicycle to the train station.[33] He was shocked, on Buddha's birthday, to find burnt out hulks of cars. He saw at least twenty jeeps with soldiers bustling about. Returning to the factory, he observed citizens from the rally approach and ask workers to open the gate. They readily agreed, and at least twenty vehicles were delivered. Protesters left with some of the vehicles and returned later for the rest. Over the next few days, they were given new buses, jeeps, at least one 2.5-ton truck, and armored personnel carriers—in all, at least 414 new military vehicles were in the hands of the uprising.[34] (After May 21, except for guards and management, the factory of 1,700 workers stopped production.) When protesters informed the workers of the fighting, many immediately joined the insurgency. Later, another vehicle demonstration was formed, this time with new armored cars made by the same people who now drove them. Cruising the city, the column rallied the populace; other drivers headed to neighboring villages to spread the revolt.

Communal meals were prepared in the streets and public buildings of liberated Gwangju.
Photographer: Hwang Chong-gun

A few minutes before 11 a.m., Governor Jang Hyong-tae finally appeared in a hovering police helicopter above Kumnamno. He promised that all paratroopers would soon depart. Unbeknownst to him, division commander Chung Oong had been stripped of his command, and his replacements had already decided to commence "riot cleanup operations." Remaining in the streets, people continued singing and cheered each other on. At least five different leaflets appeared among the demonstrators. The *Fighters' Bulletin* called for college and high school students to assemble by school at different points in the city and for neighborhoods to assemble feeder demonstrations, all of which were to converge on Province Hall. The crowd swelled, and it seemed like the entire city was together in the streets. Trucks brought bread and drinks from the Coca-Cola factory: "The city was no longer under government control. The people of Gwangju were building a commune, but the price for the new system was their blood. The morning of May 21 saw a new sight on the street corners. Meals were prepared for demonstrators on the street, at all the busy intersections.

Women stopped the appropriated vehicles to offer food to the occupants. Street and market vendors, some of the main eyewitnesses to the government's brutality, organized food distribution. Hundreds of housewives fed the demonstrators on Kumnamno. Nobody drank . . . this unity fed the fighting spirit of all the rebels."[35]

At exactly 1 p.m., loudspeakers around Province Hall blared the national anthem. Everyone stopped. Without warning, gunshots pierced the already thick atmosphere. For ten minutes, the army indiscriminately fired volley after volley, killing at least fifty-four people and wounding over five hundred more.[36] In most cities, people would have run away, given up, and gone home, but Gwangju people responded with strength and vigor. Without anyone telling them to do so, people formed action teams and raided police and National Guard armories.[37] Others braved rooftop snipers to pull the wounded to safety. At CNU, insurgents assembled in two groups to free imprisoned citizens. At the front gate, forty thousand people tried to surge through at the same time as ten thousand others converged at the back gate. As happened downtown, troops opened fire, killing many (including a pregnant woman from the neighborhood) and wounding more. The resistance was so strong that paratroopers again used grenades.

As news of the shootings spread, people flocked to defend their community. Like the Minutemen of Concord and Lexington, the miners of Hwasun, textile workers of Naju, farmers of Hampyeong, and fisherman of Haenam rallied to fight back without anyone telling them to do so. They seized weapons, piled into vehicles, and headed to Gwangju. People simply called them "our" army. They soon called themselves *shimingun* (시민군), or Citizens' Army—a term slightly, but significantly, different from that for the North Korean Army, *inmingun* (인민군), or People's Army.

Gwangju people's capacity for self-organization while under fire was a great advantage over the centrally commanded military. Park Nam-son told me that when five hundred armed people heard through wireless reports at the Red Cross Hospital that the army was at the river, many simply went there, hid themselves, and ambushed the troops. They were "organized voluntarily—without leaders." Soon they created an information clearinghouse to coordinate their fighting power. Within twenty-four hours, Park "naturally" emerged as a leader whose directives many people followed, and his group was one of many that formed that day.[38]

Perhaps the most colorful band of the autonomous fighters became known as the "SWAT Team," a name they took from the U.S. television show and painted on the side of their vehicle. On May 21, as volunteers surged forward, about a dozen young men came together and resolved to fight to the death. Each wrote his name and family's address on a piece of paper and put it into their pocket. With the help of the workers at Asia Motors, they reinforced a twenty-four-passenger minibus with steel sheets—the kind used to cover holes in roads. In addition to each person's own rifle, they loaded their armored vehicle with a light machine gun, grenades, and two boxes of TNT. Using their radio, they moved from battle to battle, reinforcing the local militia and helping drive the military back from each point of engagement.[39] On May 22, they fought near Mudeung Library.

Other teams raided police substations and gathered arms for the fight. Many people reported that police cooperated with the insurgents against the military and opened their offices and armories to the people.[40] Some took off their uniforms and joined the fighters. Hwasun coal miners brought large quantities of dynamite and detonators.[41] Women textile workers drove to Naju, where they captured rifles and ammunition and brought them back to Gwangju. Similar arms seizures occurred in Changsong, Yonggwang, and Tamyang counties.[42] In all, up to five thousand people seized arms that day.[43]

As the entire city mobilized, everyone found a place in liberated Gwangju. Skeptical of reported paratrooper atrocities he heard from a temple worker's son, Buddhist monk Song Yon went downtown to buy supplies for the celebration of Buddha's 2,603rd birthday. Finding himself in the midst of wounded and crying people, he helped bring many to hospitals. Ultimately, he cancelled the birthday event at Jungshim Temple, on the edge of the city where Mudeung Mountain gently rises to its heights, and brought all the food downtown to Kumnamno to share with the fighters and people. At midnight on May 21, he went back to the temple to celebrate simply. He felt it was "not a Buddhist's place to turn his back on Gwangju's people but to work for justice with them."[44]

Autonomously, armed groups assembled at two staging areas. At 3:20 p.m., a hastily assembled militia began firing back at the paratroopers. As people joined in, a relentless assault was mounted. Apparently the long-held Confucian tradition, so valued in Korea (as we saw during the 1894 Farmers' War), of never rising with arms against a Korean government was suddenly transcended by thousands of people. As the first armed groups counterattacked with carbines and M-1's, hundreds of unarmed citizens followed closely behind. When an armed fighter fell, someone else picked up the weapon and continued to attack. They quickly carried the battle from the Gwangju Post Office to Province Hall, where the army barricaded themselves behind vehicles plundered from the streets. Others attacked paratroopers at the regional labor office behind Province Hall, on Riverside Road, off Chungjangno, and around Chonnam National University Medical School and Hospital.

As gunfire from the battle at Province Hall could be heard, citizens swarmed into Yu-tong Junction and Gwangju Park. Hundreds of volunteers listened to a reserve army officer as he offered instructions on the best use of arms and helped to form fighting units. More than a dozen other reserve officers stepped forward from among those who had assembled to review quickly the proper handling of weapons. People accepted them as tactical leaders. While some people received arms training for the first time, many others had already completed their mandatory military service. "The militia was mainly made up of workers from the construction sites, small workshops, or shoeshine men, rag pickers, street vendors, waiters, or menial workers. There were many high school boys in uniform and middle-aged men wearing their reserve army uniforms."[45]

At 4 p.m., while citizens were organizing in Gwangju Park, other fighters ambushed thirty vehicles carrying the Thirty-Fifth Battalion of the hated Seventh Airborne Brigade. They had prepared their trap well. When they opened fire from both sides of the road to Hwasun, the military forces quickly retreated. Three of their vehicles were left overturned, and one paratrooper was killed. Six wounded soldiers withdrew to Junam village, leaving behind one of the drivers and many drivable vehicles.[46] The military used helicopters with machine guns to try and control the streets; at least one helicopter was shot down.[47] So many people were wounded by machine-gun fire from a helicopter that Buddhist activist Lee Kwang-young formed a medical corps to help evacuate them to a hospital. Despite clearly marked uniforms with red crosses on white hospital gowns, snipers on the rooftop near the Grand Hotel killed most of the crew. (Lee was left critically wounded and in need of a wheelchair for the rest of his life.)

Around 4:15 p.m., captured machine guns were brought to bear on Province Hall (where the military still held out).[48] An intense crossfire from fighters on the roof of the CNU Hospital and the Chon-il Building made the military's position in Province Hall untenable.[49] While on a scouting mission in a helicopter, the commander of the Sixty-First Regiment concluded that firing from snipers around Province Hall made his mission impossible.[50] So intense was the resistance that the military decided to withdraw from the city. About twenty thousand experienced troops were in the area—but they were no match for the mobilized citizenry. Hiding behind armored vehicles as they wildly fired .50-caliber machine guns, paratroopers covered their retreat from Province Hall and moved to fortified positions at Chosun University. By 5:30 p.m., the army completed its retreat from Democracy Plaza. When the fighters who had assembled at Gwangju Park finally arrived at Province Hall a few minutes later, many wept with joyous relief when they discovered that the military had already withdrawn.[51]

By 8 p.m., armed citizens controlled the city. Cheering echoed everywhere. Although their World War II weapons were far inferior to those of the army, people's bravery and sacrifices proved more powerful than the technical superiority of the troops.

Liberated Gwangju: The Power of Love

Alongside the unity of the city, regional loyalties—long the cause of division and strife in Korea—became less important than the struggle for democracy. On May 21, the *Chonnam Newsletter of Democracy* proclaimed: "Let us actively participate in the struggle for democracy, remembering that what we want is not to blur our goal under the spell of regional animosity, nor do we want indiscriminate destruction but autonomous action based on the democratic spirit."[52] The suspension of regionalism is another indication of the universal appeal of the revolt—an appeal not confined to Jeolla or even to Korea. Alongside conscious rejection of regionalism was international solidarity: The Chosun University Committee for Democratic Struggle referred Gwangju to Vietnam: "In the city of Gwangju, just being young is a crime, and the young are condemned to be crippled for life or killed . . . Alas, the genocide of unarmed people in Vietnam is being repeated upon our own people."[53]

Dubbed the absolute community, the organic solidarity of participants in the Gwangju Commune embodies what I consider to be humans' instinctual need for freedom—grasped intuitively—an unconscious need that was sublimated into collective expression during the uprising. The sudden emergence of hundreds of thousands of people occupying public space; the spread of the revolt from one district to another in South Jeolla; the intuitive identification of hundreds of thousands of people with each other and their simultaneous belief in the power of their actions; the self-organization of the Citizens' Army; and the suspension of normal values like competitive business practices, criminal behavior, and acquisitiveness are all dimensions of what I call the "eros effect."

In the latter part of the twentieth century, high rates of literacy, the mass media, and universal education have forged a capacity in millions of people to govern themselves far more wisely than any tiny elites ensconced in power. As Karl Marx pointed out long ago, one of the most important products of factory-based industry in the nineteenth century was a disciplined working class accustomed to collective endeavor and dependent upon each other for their welfare. Such a capacity, Marx believed, would contribute to the proletariat's capacity to lead society forward. In a similar vein of thinking, we can observe that people today are well versed in the practices of collective participation in mammoth events and huge institutions. One unintended side effect of these spectacles of contemporary society is precisely the recognition of our collective presence in each other's lives. Public space is scandalously underutilized and mistreated by existing institutions precisely because their power depends upon degradation of citizens' collective intelligence.

With its traditional civil society intact, Jeolla's marginalization turned into a valuable resource insofar as it was uncorrupted by consumerist acquisitiveness and capitalist competition. The heritage of oppression and discrimination suffered by Jeolla people constituted avenues for people's unity and solidarity; poverty meant people had little to lose; cooperation and communalism remained unspoiled matter-of-fact facets of their human condition. In the absolute community of the Gwangju Uprising, people's capacity for self-organization and self-discipline is beyond the belief of many North Americans, unaccustomed as we are to even the most rudimentary forms of civil behavior in public spaces.

In comparison to the Paris Commune of 1871, one observes a far-greater capacity for self-government among ordinary people in Gwangju in 1980. While in Paris, the National Guard and their officers defected *en masse* to the Commune, the people of Gwangju organized their own Citizens' Army from below, and then expelled thousands of crack troops whose modern U.S.-supplied weapons were no match for the power of the people. Such a courageous mobilization went far beyond the drum rolls of the Parisian National Guard as they assumed control of Paris from the absent and disgraced government of France. Despite this significant difference, there are remarkable ways in which the two events converge. Within the zones liberated by the emergence of armed resistance from below, a number of similar dynamics arose, including spontaneous emergence of popular organs of democratic decision-making; near absence of criminal behavior; suspension of hierarchies of class, power, and status; and genuine solidarity and cooperation among the citizenry.

In 1980, United States officials saw the matter quite differently. On May 19, Wickham received a phone call from Secretary of Defense Harold Brown asking for his personal assessment. Wickham tersely replied: "Officials cite the evidence of Communist influence in student demonstrations and escalating demands . . . They do not want another Vietnam . . . We must recognize the reality of control by Chun . . . The only issues are the speed of consolidating power and the form in which it takes place."[54] All two hundred U.S. personnel in Gwangju were evacuated to Seoul by plane, and all U.S. aircraft at Songjongri were redeployed. On

May 21, Gleysteen cabled to Washington: "The massive insurrection in Gwangju is still out of control and poses an alarming situation . . . a large mob has gained temporary run of the city." Again, the difference in opinion is startling: Choi finds an absolute community, and Reverend Park Hyung-gyu found a community within which love blossomed where U.S. officials found Communist-influenced mob rule. Ah, elite "intelligence" at work again!

In the liberated city, the power of the mobilized people led to a form of direct democracy that far surpassed the "normal" functioning of the city.[55] From the evening of the twenty-first until the morning of the twenty-seventh, liberated Gwangju was in the hands of its citizens. Spontaneously formed groups organized all essential services, including defense of the city and negotiations with the military for more coffins, release of prisoners (some of whom were already being viciously tortured),[56] and for a peaceful solution to the conflict. Without planning, people began to gather around Province Hall. Without anyone's orders, hundreds of people simply came out of their homes, brooms in hand, and swept away rubble and discarded ammunition casings. Using heavy equipment, workers from Asia Motors cleared burnt out vehicles. Some high school girls organized a suburban intelligence system to inform the Citizens' Army of troop movements.[57] Other young women stepped forward and gathered the corpses. They washed them and laid them out in a martial arts hall across the street from Province Hall for family members to identify them. Members of several groups that had produced leaflets came together and published a daily newspaper. Artists made wall posters, and people with cooking skills created communal kitchens in public. Members of theater groups, skilled in the art of public speaking, helped organize daily rallies; others prepared defensive measures, patrolled the streets and perimeter, and sought to spread the struggle to outlying areas. Without any central commander or central committee, a new division of labor emerged naturally. Altogether, as grassroots energies multiplied, some fifty (or about six every day from May 18 to May 27) written manifestos, open letters, statements, leaflets, and newspapers were freely distributed by a wide variety of groups.[58]

Once the fighting was over, markets and stores reopened for business. No banks were looted, and robbery, rape, or theft hardly occurred—if at all. Foreigners freely walked the streets. Indeed, Baptist missionary Arnold Peterson reported that his car, flying an American flag and with a large sign reading "Foreigners' Car," was cheered by people in the streets.[59] While coffins, food, gasoline, and cigarettes were in short supply, dozens of people cooked communal meals, and no one went hungry. All over Gwangju, people embraced each other, cared for grieving family members, and healed the wounded. The whole city came together like an extended family with people calling each other with familiar forms and suspending the use of normal hierarchical language. Happy to be alive, some shared cigarettes with their newly found comrades in arms, an act remembered by many as symbolizing in an important way the communal experience.[60] Storeowners who still had cigarettes often sold—or gave away—only one pack at a time (to be fair to everyone). The Citizens' Army quickly developed a system for rationing gasoline and attempted to procure more coffins. Blood was in short supply at the hospitals, but as soon as the need became known, people flooded in to donate, including barmaids and prostitutes, who publicly insisted that they, too, should be permitted to donate.

A professor at a Gwangju university who remained anonymous for his own safety wrote: "The citizens, who used to buy up everything in sight no matter what the price, shared their daily necessities. Merchants who used to be impatient and charge high mark-ups didn't raise prices at all. Citizens participated, offering tobacco, pajamas, food, and drink . . . No infamous crime, which might have been expected, was committed, the armed citizens undertook no robbery of money from defenseless banks. They did not harm any of the resident aliens in Gwangju."[61]

So powerful was the unifying energy of the uprising that all religions were drawn into it. The YMCA and YWCA became focal points for activists. Catholic priest Cho Cheul-hyun remained with the insurgents in Province Hall until the final morning. In June 1980, the Roman Catholic priests of Gwangju Archdiocese described the communal spirit of citizens: "While the army cut off communication with the outside and no necessities or food were provided, no one made undue profits by buying things up or being indisposed to sell things. Without knowing when the situation was going to end, people shared their food with each other. As the number of patients who got shot increased and blood was needed, the number of citizens who donated blood skyrocketed . . . Gwangju citizens swept the scattered stone, glass and fragments of tear gas canisters; doctors and nurses moved patients from the city while risking getting shot; bus and taxi drivers protected young people without thinking about their own lives; juvenile vagrants and abandoned children were more virtuous than ever before."[62]

From below, people consolidated the Citizens' Army as hundreds of fighters patrolled the city and kept constant guard against the expected counterattack. Others organized several "settlement committees." As the city's resistance congealed, the military continually attempted to infiltrate troops. Sporadic gun battles broke out around the outskirts of the perimeter citizens defended around the clock. Alongside the Citizens' Army, neighborhoods organized self-defense teams to guard against army incursions. Everyone coordinated the city's defense through telephone contact with Province Hall, and fighters used radios captured from the military to track the army.

Small teams facilitated the uprising's inner self-organization: its newspaper, rallies, internal debates, and media relations. One group of activists met every day at 10 a.m. at Nokdu bookstore. (Nokdu, or "mung bean," was *Tonghak* leader Jeon Bong-jun's nickname, given to him for his small stature.) Yoon Sang-won, Chong Hyun-ay, and many other younger activists held impassioned discussions. Behind the store, they made Molotovs, and militants continually came by to replenish their supplies. Once the military had been driven out, their group grew too big, and they moved their meeting venue to the YWCA and later to Province Hall. They distributed black ribbons, worked on the *Fighters' Bulletin*, and helped with the rallies—as when they prepared the effigy of Chun Doo-hwan to burn on May 24. Kim Sang-jib went to CNU and found a modern bus equipped with a loudspeaker. He brought it downtown and delivered it to the group for their use.

The diverse group of activists who converged at the YWCA created an energy center that brought together many different organizations, among them Wildfire or *Dulbul*, (a night school for workers), Clown or *Kwangdae* (an activist theatrical troupe), all-female Pure Pine Tree Society or *Song Baek Hoe*, the National Democratic Workers' League, and Artists' Council for a Free Gwangju. Members of these groups suspended whatever it was they had been doing and threw themselves into the popular upheaval. Altogether, five teams formed at the YWCA—posters, daily bulletin, money collection, rally coordination, and cooking. Many people worked without sleep. As there were no printing presses, hand printing and mimeograph machines were kept running day and night.

The Artists' Council had been hard at work on an exhibition planned for September, but once the uprising occurred, they all focused their energies on producing hand-drawn posters and street art.[63] Working in a studio under the courthouse near Mudeung Mountain, they labored all night. Using rubber pads from executive desks, Hong Sung-dam made his first block prints. His later woodblocks, some of them reprinted in this book, have become world famous and continue to symbolize the uprising. Although he had made tickets for Clown productions with smaller pads and larger posters for Dulbul night school, he had never done complicated block prints before May. During the Uprising, he ended up making posters in the YWCA. In this way, the uprising sowed the seeds of what subsequently became known as Minjung art.[64]

Song Baek Hoe provided many female activists with an autonomous forum to work together. The group arose from the need to help families of imprisoned activists cope with the difficulties of visiting loved ones and maintaining families' welfare. It rapidly became a vehicle for helping to direct the overall movement's direction during the uprising, especially since so many longtime activists had been arrested or gone into hiding. After owner Kim Sang-yoon was arrested, Nokdu bookstore remained open—and played a vital role in the movement's presence—largely because of *Song Baek Hoe* activist Chong Hyun-ay.

Clown played a key role in organizing the first rally at Democracy Plaza. Their public speaking skills enabled them to help focus people at the appointed times and to maintain continuity in discussions. Once the rallies began, Clown members facilitated deliberations while they themselves wrote and sang songs, sent messages to soldiers, and performed skits on stage. One key member, Kim Sun-chool, had been among activists released from prison after Park Chung-hee was killed. In February 1980, Clown's opening performance at Gwangju's YMCA, "Exorcism of a Pig" (돼지 풀이), satirized the plight of farmers before an audience of more than two thousand people. The atmosphere was described by one performer as passionate, "like a boxing match." Afterward, people mingled "ecstatically" and the buzz of animated conversations went on for hours. They brought the play to villages and towns with the help of the Catholic Farmers' Union. After torchlight performances, farmers would take the stage and play traditional instruments. Kim referred to the countryside tour as having provided a "stage of eros" and "liberation from darkness."[65] Although Clown was a provincial group, members of several Seoul theater groups who saw them perform praised them as superior. To prepare a new play, "Chronicle of Han" (dealing with emotions of separation of North and South Korea), they opened an office near Province Hall, and practiced in the YWCA until May 17. Of their twenty members, more than half were students. When they gathered for a scheduled rehearsal on May 18, they observed first-hand the violence of the paratroopers and immediately joined the protests.

The core members of Wildfire (*Dulbul*) workers' night school were centrally important in the publication of the *Fighters' Bulletin*. Using their office several miles west of Province Hall as workspace, members played an important role in bringing radical ideas to the broad spectrum of activity in liberated Gwangju. Yoon Sang-won had given up a lucrative bank job in Seoul and secretly returned to help with *Dulbul*, where he taught workers fundamental skills from reading to mathematics and politics. Such night schools were a national phenomenon, which helped forge the country's movement for years to come. In the early days of the uprising, some Clown members produced a folded tabloid containing up-to-the-minute news. At least four other groups also autonomously published and circulated information sheets, including high school students from Wolsandong, CNU's *Voice of the University*, and *Dulbul*. On May 19, all these groups merged into the *Fighters' Bulletin*, which became liberated Gwangju's daily newspaper and principal source of reliable reports.[66] Originally five thousand copies, by its ninth issue, it published at least twenty thousand, and perhaps as many as thirty thousand. Many people read it on the walls around the city, where it was prominently posted for all to see. Its tenth issue was prepared but could not be distributed before the military's final onslaught.[67]

In the heat of the moment, a structure evolved that was more democratic than previous administrations of the city. The uprising's overwhelming popular support meant an end to previous marginalization of movement groups in the city's political life. In this process of ordinary citizens moving to the center of the city's life, people's spontaneous actions were crucial.

Liberated Gwangju's Direct Democracy

Instinctively, the people of Gwangju recognized Democracy Plaza as their spiritual home, and they assembled there every day by the tens of thousands. Popular assemblies were a unique feature of the Gwangju Uprising, its crowning achievement. During almost all other people's uprisings, government repression effectively prevented citizens from peacefully gathering.

The capability to assemble peacefully by the thousands, to enact a form of participatory democracy, was a right won through the blood of too many friends and neighbors. When people had won control of cities in the past, as in the Yeosun Insurrection of 1948 where leaders made decisions through People's Committee's, general assemblies were less central to providing direction to the movement than were organizations. Gwangju's seven rallies in five days became the setting for a new kind of direct democracy where everyone could have a say. Members of the Citizens' Army "took the results of the rallies and planned and implemented the people's decisions." Park Nam-son went to every rally, as did

Gwangju citizens governed themselves through direct democracy after driving the army out of the city. Credit: May 18 Memorial Foundation

all fighters who could leave the front lines. They listened carefully and followed the wishes expressed by people.[68] Tens of thousands of people participated in this unique form of deliberative democracy.

The central space in the city's geography, Democracy Plaza sat at the foot of the main downtown street, Kumnamno, where it ran directly into South Jeolla's Province Hall. The fountain in the middle of a traffic rotary formed at the intersection of three major streets and a bundle of smaller ones made a perfect stage, particularly since there was no front and back but rather a circular spatial configuration. During the rallies, adjoining rooftops packed with people tiered around encircled throngs below. People sang and cried, applauded and booed, shouted approval, witnessed tearful accounts, and watched playful skits dramatizing scenes from the fighting. Everyone listened intently when news reports and political analysis were relayed, and a broad popular insight into the political situation in the country was galvanized—a form of collective wisdom that continues to guide Gwangju.

People from all walks of life gathered at Democracy Plaza and stepped to the microphone—farmers, workers, homemakers, students, priests, monks, seniors, shoeshine boys, gangsters, and waitresses all addressed the citizens. Even though the rallies were huge, anyone who needed to speak was able to express heartfelt needs. Amazingly, with hundreds of thousands of participants, there were no fights, no violence—although disagreements were sometimes intense. As an example of how much existing social divisions were transcended in the liberated city, leaders of the two major gangs in Gwangju, the Obi and Hwasun, stood before the assembled citizens and promised to "cooperate with the struggle."[69]

Discursive formation of popular will, a feat dreamed of by philosophers, became reality through these daily rallies. A poem's inspired lines give some feeling for how much the rallies meant:

The day when the pepper fog and tear gas stopped.
People came from the Mujin plain.
All democratic citizens: intellectuals, laborers, and farmers.

People gathered in front of the fountain of the provincial capital.
People tried to touch the fountain.
Sitting on the lawn, hugging each other
Exchanging smiles with each other

There is no song as beautiful as this,
The song we all sang together.[70]

As Lee Jae-eui described it: "The fountain was now the center of unity. All walks and classes of people spoke—women street vendors, elementary school teachers, and followers of different religions, housewives, college students, high school students, and farmers. Their angry speeches created a common consciousness, a manifestation of the tremendous energy of the uprising. They had melded together, forging a strong sense of solidarity throughout the uprising. For the moment, the city was one."[71]

The rallies corresponded to the ideal speech community discussed by German philosopher Jürgen Habermas.[72] In this discourse, everyone was equal, and all could enter public space; disagreement and debate were uncensored, the debate was political and highly moral, and the context was rooted in the vital needs of the lives of citizens. The space in liberated Gwangju was as close as reality has come to Habermas's ideal-typical public sphere.

How do we explain this sudden solidarity, this emergence of a new form of bonding between people? How do we understand the suspension of normal values like competitive business practices and individual ownership of consumer goods and their replacement with cooperation and collectivity? The process of merging into what Jean-Paul Sartre called a "fused group" is complicated and involves emotion, intuition, and spirit—not simply reason. Chong Hyun-ay explained, "the group unconscious made it happen . . . collective unconscious. People said we can't accept a surrender, so we'll come back every day until our feelings of mortification [억울함] are lifted."[73] Sociologist Choi Jungwoon found that the "key" to this "holy, supernatural experience" was "love . . . the intuitive nature of human dignity does not lie in the act and the result of pursuing individual interests and social status, but can be found in the act of recognizing a value larger than individual life and dedicating oneself to attaining it."[74]

As has often been said, the Gwangju Uprising was an indispensable tool in the creation of South Korea's democracy. The rallies were its crucible—where people's determination to be free was democratically galvanized and steeled. After experiencing the wisdom and love of their community, never again could

Gwangju citizens burned an effigy of Chun Doo-hwan at one of their rallies.
Photographer: Na Kyung-taek

people go back to dictatorship. Democracy Plaza became the center of gravity where people congregated, joined work teams, found the latest news, looked for family members, and heard about the shortage of blood—in short, it was where the heart of liberated Gwangju beat, where the city lived and breathed. Naturally there were disputes, particularly as people began to discuss how to resolve the dire situation in which they found themselves, but as these disputes were settled, intelligent decisions were made, such as to buy prisoners' freedom from the military in exchange for weapons, but not to surrender all weapons. Specific demands were first formulated into the general will as these rallies, the most important of which were compensation for victims, a government apology, and imprisonment of Chun Doo-hwan.

I asked Chong Hyun-ay about the improvised character of the gatherings: "Yes," she replied, "direct democracy was prepared. We prepared the stage, microphone, and posters, but the people made it happen. What people said mattered. That's why they participated. Their demand for compensation took years, but we won it!" People came by the thousands. Many neighborhoods had assembly areas at the rallies and sat together, while other contingents arrived together. People made the rallies happen; they spontaneously assembled and created slogans on big character posters. The reason why such a diverse cross-section of people was able to speak at the rallies was, at least in part, because the group organizing the rallies made a conscious effort to be inclusive. As Lee Jae-eui tells us, "the activist groups decided to reserve time for speakers from all walks of life. They expanded the content of the rallies to include not only speeches, but also poetry readings, songs, the burning of government officials in effigy, and short plays."[75]

The rallies were a time for exchange of opinions, but they were also a place for education. Some people did not know who Chun Doo-hwan was, so a brief history of his coup and his military background were prepared. Most importantly, people shared each other's sorrows and dreams, a public openness and sharing with the community of one's innermost feelings that made these rallies so authentic. Many people spoke of the "collective unconscious" as significant to the uprising. As one member of the Citizens' Army remembered, the "rallies gave us the determination to fight."[76]

Altogether there were seven gatherings, as detailed in TABLE 6.1.

The rallies embodied an interactive decision-making process in which the citywide assembly had final power over all major questions, and smaller groups carried out those decisions. The latter would send messages, announcements, and, when appropriate, dispatch representatives to the rallies to help keep people informed of fresh developments and to share new information. Suggestions were written down and posted all over city. Ideas from rallies became programs, like blood donations and collection of necessary supplies, as well as strategic directions for the movement, like imprisonment of Chun and compensation for victims of government violence. Popular self-discipline was strengthened when people were reminded not to destroy public facilities like telephones. Vital information like supermarket options and hospital availability was shared. At many of the rallies, thousands of dollars for the settlement committees and other working groups was quickly raised through donations. When there were no more coffins for the dead, donations were immediately made. People stood up and collected money, and soon more coffins were delivered from funeral homes. When it was announced at a rally that blood was needed, people rushed to the hospitals to donate. The rallies approved trading some guns for prisoners; when trucks were needed, people were dispatched to bring them from Asia Motors, and when proper clothes for the dead were sought, they suddenly appeared.

Choi Jungwoon discounts the significance of the rallies. Once armed citizens took control of the city, he believed the absolute community became a memory: "These demonstrations sprouted from a unique political situation; it is wrong to take them as a direct democratic system as in Greece . . . These rallies followed a preplanned script, but citizens remembered the absolute community's atmosphere and sometimes volunteered to stand on the podium to pour out their bitterness."[77] He continued, "The rallies were not where rational discussions took place to solve problems in reality, but where they comforted each other and soothed each other's wounds."[78] Lee Jae-eui, who was present for many of the rallies, disagrees unambiguously: "These rallies were a form of direct democratic process, through which the popular will could be irrefutably expressed."[79] In the final analysis, whether these rallies were direct democracy or preplanned scripts is an issue that should be decided based upon what actually transpired at them. Perhaps one day researchers will conduct an extensive conversation analysis based upon transcripts made from recordings.

The first rally occurred spontaneously on the morning after the defeat of the military as people came to Democracy Plaza to learn the latest news and check on the situation. Around 6 a.m. on May 22, hundreds of people milled around inside Province Hall. As the morning passed, people with loudspeakers called on citizens: "Let's clean up the streets" or "Armed citizens, go to Gwangju Park." By 9 a.m. about a thousand armed fighters had gathered in Democracy Plaza. By 11 a.m., about forty thousand people had convened around Province Hall. Eight CNU professors convened a meeting in the Boy Scout office. In the Deputy

TABLE 6.1 **Rallies in Liberated Gwangju**

Date	Time of Rally	Number of People	Topics/notable events
May 22	Afternoon	30,000–40,000	Huge meandering discussion
May 22	5–7 p.m.	100,000+	Homage to the dead; Citizens' Settlement Committee announced results of negotiations; Vice-Governor Chung chaired; eight negotiators introduced; Chang Hyu-dong "give up weapons"—jeered; Kim Jeong-bae took mic and was cheered when he declared the need for resistance. CSC backed off stage. Leaders of the two major gangs in Gwangju—Obi and Hwasun—addressed the rally and declared cooperation with the struggle.
May 23	10 a.m. 11 a.m. 11:30 a.m. 3 p.m.	50,000 50,000–100,000 150,000 100,000+	"First Citywide Rally" scheduled for 3 p.m. but began at 11:30 a.m. because people came and began it; Kim Tae-jong presided; Donations of Love for the Injured collected; 1 p.m.: Kim Chang-gil returned with thirty-four prisoners exchanged for 200 rifles; Kim also brought a secret army explosives expert who removed detonators; Student Settlement Committee: Decision to collect arms—2,500 guns collected (50 percent of the 5,400 seized).
May 24	2:30–6 p.m.	100,000	"Second Citywide Rally": crowd against CSC—people demand details; CSC refused to allow use of sound system; unplugged rally loudspeakers; no electricity so tear gas truck used; Chun effigy burned; 7 p.m. SSC meeting: Yoon Sang-won and Jeong Hae-jik criticized Kim Chang-gil. Afterwards YWCA meeting. After that at Posong Construction Company.
May 25	3–7 p.m.	50,000	"Third Citywide Rally": Demand for SC to resign; local problems discussed. 9 p.m. Kim Chang-gil left Province Hall. Citizens-Student Struggle Committee formed
May 26	10:30 a.m.	30,000	"Fourth Citywide Rally": demand for "new government of national reconciliation"; 30,000 people marched to cordons and called for "direct democracy." Military helicopter circled overhead, dropped leaflets.
May 26	3 p.m.	30,000	"Fifth Citywide Rally": Organizers announced that the military would soon attack; demonstration of 6,000 led by high school students.

Governors' office, so many people raised such a wide variety of issues that the meeting quickly tapered off. Around the fountain, without anyone taking charge, people began animated discussions, sometimes aided by students with megaphones, but soon groups became too large for everyone to hear each other. After a list of the dead was read from a platform created by covering the fountain, people gathered around and listened to each other pour out accounts of the previous days of fighting in various parts of the city. Later the discussion turned to what course of action people thought was appropriate.

While these public discussions were taking place, a privately convened Citizens' Settlement Committee (CSC) resolved to negotiate on behalf of the city. Led by Vice Governor Chung Si-chae and composed mainly of high-profile politicians, religious leaders, business owners, and professionals, they dispatched representatives to meet with the military high command, with instructions to convey the following principles:

1. No further military intervention.
2. Release of all arrestees.
3. Acknowledge the excessive use of force.
4. No reprisals.
5. Amnesty for all participants in the uprising.
6. Compensation for the deaths.
7. A promise to disarm if the above conditions were met.

The group's negotiations with military commanders lasted until about 3 p.m., and the CSC succeeded in gaining the release of 848 prisoners. Many people, however, questioned whether the self-selected character of the CSC and its elite composition meant that the group did not represent all citizens. Another group composed mainly of senior antigovernment activists convened at Namdong Cathedral, and soon a core group was continuously meeting there. In Democracy Plaza, many people expressed the need for better organization of the discussions and a more open form of decision-making.

Shortly after 5 p.m., approximately a hundred thousand people filled the plaza. The rally began with an opening ceremony paying homage to the dead. With Vice-Governor Chung Si-chae chairing, CSC members introduced themselves and announced their seven points of negotiations and results obtained.[80] People cheered when they heard of the release of prisoners and also when the CSC expressed the hope "to prevent bloodshed and maintain order." The assembled throng was quite happy to hear that the martial forces commander had personally expressed regret at the excessive violence of troops. Flush with victory, people also feared renewed fighting, a palpable possibility everyone hoped to avoid. Emboldened by the cheering, CSC negotiator Chang Hyu-dong stepped forward and declared that "weapons must be collected and returned, and public security must be entrusted to the martial law command." Immediately people began objecting. Boos turned into loud jeers, and shouts filled the plaza: "We oppose the humiliating negotiations!" "Punish Chun Doo-hwan!" and "Cancel martial law!" The CSC backed off the stage.

The assembled citizens overrode the authority of the city's most respected elder citizens, including the province's vice governor, whose preplanned script called for citizens to disarm. Rather than submit to representative government, the direct democracy of the gathering expressed through people's heartfelt shouts and actions held sway. In this one moment, citizens asserting their right to decide for themselves what to do with their lives revolutionized the situation.

People rejected the CSC's negotiators for many reasons—their own belief that the military would ruthlessly slaughter them once again was widespread, as was the sentiment that the city should gain justice before giving up their arms. Clown leader Kim Tae-jong witnessed the moment when the negotiating group reported to the rally and advised that people "should disarm as soon as possible and wait for the Governor's apology." While people booed, "Some of the citizens rushed up to the podium, took away the microphone, and gently shooed the settlement committee members. While watching it, I came to understand what Gwangju citizens truly wanted."[81]

After the jeering stopped, student Kim Jeong-bae mounted the stage and took the mic. Citing the example of Sobuk miners who had won their struggle in April only by refusing to surrender their arms—and who were brutally attacked after they did so—Kim was cheered wildly as he declared the need for continuing resistance. Many citizen-soldiers watching from rooftops shot their guns in the air to express approval. The vast majority of people were clearly in agreement.

Here is a concrete case in which the wisdom of ordinary people surpassed that of the city's political elite. Citizens' capacity to interpret the Sobuk miners struggle was not accidental but an indication of how popular intuition has great comprehension of political developments. At the rallies, two visionary demands emerged: imprisonment of Chun Doo-hwan for his crimes against them and compensation for the wounded, imprisoned, and families of those killed—not only for the families of the deceased, as the CSC had maintained.

Gwangju's direct democratic form far surpassed the republican government of the 1871 Paris Commune, where about 230,000 citizens voted in elections for ninety representatives. Inside liberated Paris, winning candidates included fifteen supporters of the enemy government and nine citizens against that government but also against the Commune's seizure of power.[82] Moreover, the newly elected Commune representatives were not the only power to be reckoned with: "The Republican Central Committee [neighborhood associations that favored democracy rather than monarchy] acted as a shadow government."[83] In addition, high-ranking officials of the National Guard also gave orders to their units. Sometimes, military commanders in the field received three sets of conflicting orders. The Commune's elected government was practically powerless, rivaled in military affairs by the Central Committee of the National Guard and diminished in political power by the Republican *arrondissement* associations. Meeting behind closed doors, elected officials debated their differences and were often unable to act decisively—thereby depoliticizing the people of Paris. The passivity of the crowd was evident in the ceremony the day after the election when two hundred thousand people attended the announcement of the results and watched the installation of the new government at the Hotel de Ville (City Hall). Unlike the free flowing gatherings at Democracy Plaza in Gwangju when everyone had a voice, people in Paris were spectators as their representatives were sworn in. Then they simply left.

During the entire period of liberated Gwangju, alongside the huge rallies—sometimes during them, but always before and after them—small groups caucused, committees formed, and people formulated proposals and brought them to the next rally. A veritable beehive of activity took place. The interaction between the popular assembly and small groups strengthened each other in a mutually amplifying dynamic of expanding democracy. The rallies helped to propel the process of self-organization forward.

Testifying years later about his personal experiences in the uprising, Professor Song Gi-sook recounted how he and Professor Myeong Lo-geun were approached at the initial gathering at the fountain and asked to gather activists and create a headquarters to "lead an effort to cope with the situation."[84] People were concerned that the past histories of members of the CSC indicated that they were not going to lead the struggle forward but to sell it out. Song Gi-sook was against taking any action, but he went along with Myeong. Holding a bullhorn given to him by a student, Myeong began to speak: "Please choose five representatives from Chonnam National University and Chosun University students respectively." He continued: "Though paratroopers are now driven out, the Citizens' Army is bewildered and in the middle of confusion with no headquarters. A Citizens' Settlement Committee has already formed and went to Sangmudae with settlement conditions, but it cannot control the Citizens' Army. This whole thing was started by students, and they should take a lead in straightening things out. Let's go into the provincial government building and organize a Student Settlement Committee." With that, Professor Myeong led people to the front gate of Province Hall, where members of the Citizens' Army, wearing backward protective helmets taken from riot police, tensely kept guard. After a long day of fighting the military on the outskirts of the city, Park Nam-son had created a "Situation Room" on the first floor at about 11 p.m. to serve as a kind of coordinating place for fighters. The ten student representatives were allowed to enter the building and escorted into the administrative office, where an eyewitness described the scene as "complete chaos." Finally, students went into the empty Boy Scout office and made it their space.[85] They formed a Student Settlement Committee with Kim Chang-gil as chairperson and Kim Jeong-bae as vice chair. Neither was known as a student activist.

The Uprising Spreads
From its epicenter in Gwangju, the uprising quickly spread to Hwasun, Naju, Hampyeong, Youngkwang, Gangjin, Muan, Haenam, and Mokpo—in all to at least sixteen other parts of South Jeolla.[86] Without anyone ordering them to do so, hundreds of people carried news of the events in Gwangju to friends and families. Armed insurgents also systematically sought to canvas outlying areas to bring as much food, arms, and ammunition into the surrounded city as they could get through the military cordon. The rapid proliferation of the revolt is

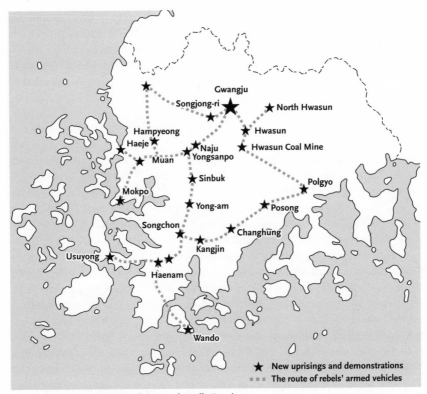

FIGURE 6.1 **The Uprising's Path in South Jeolla Province**
Source: Lee Jae-eui, *Kwangju Diary*, 96.

another indication of people's capacity for self-government and autonomous initiative. Hoping to bring the uprising to Jeonju and Seoul, insurgent convoys were repulsed by troops blocking expressway, roads, and railroads leading out of South Jeolla. Having been defeated inside the city, the military's efforts became focused on preventing people from entering and leaving it. Helicopter gunships wiped out units of armed demonstrators from Hwasun and Yonggwang counties trying to reach Gwangju.[87] Troops also ambushed citizens from Gwangju leaving the city. If the military had not so tightly controlled the media and restricted travel, the revolt may well have turned into a nationwide uprising, as some people hoped—and as U.S. officials and their Korean allies feared.

On May 21, four express buses full of fighters from Gwangju arrived in the port city of Mokpo, heartland of Kim Dae Jung's supporters. As word spread, citizens quickly gathered at the train station to learn the news. Of the 120 fighters, only about 30 had firearms; the rest were armed with sticks. Many wore masks. Television had been cut off for two days and people poured into the streets to hear the news. By 4 p.m., twenty thousand people gathered. As sun set, with no military in sight, people attacked City Hall, emptied police stations of weapons, and destroyed the interiors of KBS and MBC—neither of which had broadcast truthful accounts of recent events. Over 1,600 weapons were gathered from the empty police stations. Soon, thousands of people and about eighty vehicles assembled at the train station to form a Mokpo Citizen's Committee with veteran activist An Chol named chair by acclamation. The army was still nowhere in sight.

On May 22, armed demonstrators attacked police boxes, the KCIA branch office, and the District Tax Office, seizing arms and destroying records. All schools in the city closed, and citizens thronged downtown. At 2 p.m., the first citizens' rally for a democratic constitution began.[88]

On at least three nights, there were torchlight processions. To protest the arrest of Kim Dae Jung (DJ), their favorite son, one hundred thousand people marched, and there were five consecutive days of rallies for a democratic constitution.[89] On May 26, at least thirty thousand took part.[90] The Citizens Committee effectively controlled the city; even after the fall of Gwangju, on May 28 and 29, tens of thousands of people took to the streets shouting slogans like "Pay the price of bloodshed in Gwangju!" When the military finally arrived, at least fifty-six activists were arrested and taken to Sangmudae prison.

Farmers from Hampyeong were in Gwangju at Bukdong Catholic Church on May 18 for the second anniversary celebration of their victory in the sweet potato struggle. As Suh Kyong-won left the church, he was horrified to see some paratroopers beating unarmed youths and making them kneel while others forced young female students to take off their clothes.[91] Returning to Hampyeong, he gathered youth around him, and raided the local police station for firearms. Although police were inside, they did not resist him, either because of their feeling Gwangju merited saving—or because they were intimidated by the young gangsters among Suh's group. With a truck full of onions, a box of carbines, and some ammunition, they set off to gather more recruits but were seized by police before they could make good their plan to go to Gwangju. In Jeonju, people took over City Hall, but police soon drove them out. In Naju, about thirty fighters from Gwangju joined with local people and seized a thousand rifles and fifty thousand rounds of ammunition. In Gangjin, clashes with police and the military left many wounded, while in Jangheung, hundreds of people turned out to welcome demonstrators who arrived. In Hwasun town on the morning of May 21, about two hundred insurgents arrived. Together with miners, they took four boxes of dynamite and about a hundred detonators from nearby sites and delivered them to the insurgency. In both Jeonju and Iri, police were reported to have joined the demonstration.[92]

Haenam people responded especially heartily to the uprising. Citizens rallied every day, and some fought the army with guns. After a female student returned home with news of the shootings in Gwangju, people quickly gathered. Members of the Citizens' Army arrived from Naju. They crashed a car through a wall in the police box and took carbines and ammunition. A procession of seventy-three vehicles formed to go to Gwangju with Park Haeng-sam chosen as convoy leader. Park had been arrested in 1960 during the uprising that overthrew the Rhee dictatorship, and many younger people were his students, so his selection was easily agreed. Each vehicle then selected a coordinator. Three trucks were sent to Nampyeong, but they were attacked, with people in two of the trucks killed. The third made it back to Naju, where the exhausted occupants slept in the deserted police office after being fed by local people. The convoy arrived in Gangjin, where people decided they needed to rediscuss their plan. More than a thousand people soon gathered at a nearby middle school. Setting off once more with even more people and cars, the convoy stopped to rescue a student trapped beneath an overturned tractor. As they made their way to Gwangju via back roads, military units supported by a helicopter near the airport stopped them. The Air Force officers who spoke with them expressed surprise at their having made it so far, especially with so many arms. As they negotiated, the fighters observed that airplanes had been moved to other airports and surmised it was because they were fearful of being captured by the uprising. Faced with an array of overwhelming force against them, about 150 to 200 fighters allowed themselves to be taken away. They were released on May 22.[93] Those who were not captured headed away from Gwangju and split into small groups. On the night of the twenty-second, the military ambushed one group at Ulsuljae with machine guns and grenades, killing many people. While government records claim three dead, people involved insist seven were killed and that helicopters took away their bodies.[94] On May 23, many of the exhausted people in the convoy ate breakfast in Naju. They were ambushed approximately three kilometers from Haenam. Two buses carrying students came under heavy fire, and at least one person was killed.

One armed group from Haenam made its way to Wando. Using a loudspeaker, they called on people to assemble, and within one hour, more than a thousand people gathered in support of the uprising. Even police joined and helped collect forty guns. A pastor led a group on an express bus to Sunchon, where people were enthusiastic in their support of the uprising.[95] Evidently, they did not take further action. Perhaps the memory of the brutality suffered by the citizens in 1948 during the suppression of the Yeosun Uprising lingered in people's minds.[96] In Muan, the main police station and several neighborhood boxes were raided for arms.

The uprising spread so quickly in South Jeolla for a variety of reasons. Chonnam's communal and egalitarian tradition has a long history full of episodes of struggle against overwhelming odds. The region's radical politics is nourished from a number of sources and exists alongside a distinct regional culture, such as *pansori* (a kind of deep-throated blues/opera), *minjung munhak* (literary populism), traditional Korean painting, and *talchum* masked dance.[97] Marginalized from Park Chung-hee's economic development along the Seoul-Busan corridor, by 1978, GNP in Gwangju was only 75 percent of the national average. Agriculture accounted for 38 percent of South Jeolla's output, far more than the 18 percent national average. In 1980, land ownership in Jeolla was highly concentrated, a legacy of the Japanese occupation. By 1942, more than half of all paddy land belonged to large landlords; in North Jeolla, 85 percent of all households were landless tenants or semitenants. Cumings found an inverse relation between rate of tenancy and revolt in 1946; by 1980, this relationship may have changed.

Significantly, one in seven people in Gwangju was a college or high school student in 1980—about 110,000 students in all. As Jang Sang-yong expressed it, "Gwangju was not simply the seat of Province Hall, but the center of education in Honam. Gwangju students were a bridge with blood ties that linked the city with small and medium sized cities and rural areas in the vicinity."[98] Although rural population had halved from 55 percent of population in 1965, students remained linked to their ancestral homes. The migration from the countryside meant that more Jeolla people were considered working class, possibly as many as 46.6 percent in 1980, but only 2.0 percent of regional workers had jobs in large factories in 1975, and 2.3 percent in 1981, while 55.2 percent of Jeolla's industrial laborers were employed in agriculture and forestry in 1986.[99] Surplus agricultural products from the United States flooded the market, as a result of which the Jeolla economy, dependent as it was on agriculture, was collapsing.[100]

Besides economic marginalization, Jeolla people also suffered widespread discrimination and stereotyping. National TV comedy shows made fun of them by labeling them crooks, thieves, lumpen, and gangsters. So pervasive was the feeling that people were culturally and politically subaltern, many residents considered themselves an internal colony. From 1960 to 1980, the population of Honam decreased rapidly, a fact noted in Gleysteen's cables to Washington. He also took great pains to remind his superiors that many Honam people lived in Busan and Seoul, another factor that could have contributed to the uprising becoming nationally activated. Jeolla's proletarianized farmers, working class and lumpen, all congealed with progressive students into a fighting force whose composition by class was arguably as important as its regional orientation. The failure of other Koreans to act decisively led to the isolation of the uprising and allowed the military to concentrate all its forces.

Citizens' Committees in Conflict

Inside liberated Gwangju, alongside joy with the fighting's end, confusion reigned everywhere. At least three different settlement committees formed, and over ten different groups moved into Province Hall.[101] The emergence of grassroots organizations appears to have happened quite naturally. The process was transparent to everyone and open to all. Even the government at one point publicly referred to the uprising as "community self-rule." Province Hall remained at the center of the city's political life, but a completely different set of people was involved as autonomous groups took over abandoned offices. Inside its cavernous structure, there were sufficient spaces for everyone.

Small groups began to find other meeting venues as well. Working groups formed and regularly held discussions in Namdong Cathedral, the YWCA, and in at least one Protestant church. At about 10:30 a.m. on May 22, a group of eight evangelical pastors congregated to appraise the situation. One of them was Arnold Peterson, an American Baptist missionary who happened to be in Gwangju. He later remembered: "The consensus of their feeling is summed up in the phrase 'This cannot be.' It was unheard of that the citizens of a city should rise up and throw off their government with no conscious planning and leadership."[102] There may have been no leadership in place when the uprising began, but the crucible of the fighting produced many resolute enemies of the military.

The first two settlement groups to form were the Citizens' Settlement Committee (CSC) and the Student Settlement Committee (SSC). The CSC, formally known as the May 18th General Citizens' Settlement Committee, consisted of about twenty people: priests, pastors, lawyers, businessmen, professors, and politicians. Prominently represented by Ch'oe Han-yong, a respected anti-Japanese activist and Archbishop Yoon Gong-hui, they formed only hours before the SSC came together at the rally on May 22. Unlike the CSC, the tempestuous origins of the SSC involved many people who had not previously been introduced to each other. Both groups attempted to find a way to quickly end the uprising. On the twenty-second, the military released 848 people after negotiations with the CSC, and on May 23, with the approval of the popular assembly at Democracy Plaza, the SSC returned two hundred guns to the army and was able to secure in exchange the release of an additional thirty-four prisoners.[103]

Armed groups occupied offices in the Situation Room on the first floor while settlement groups met in separate quarters on higher floors. Occasionally joint meetings were convened. On May 23, Park Nam-son organized guard duties and required passes to enter the building after several incidents involving very suspicious characters. Many militants inside the building at first refused to even entertain the notion of a student settlement committee—preferring simply to "fight until death" for democracy and dignity. Patiently Professor Song Gi-sook prevailed, and soon the SSC began taking care of funerals and medical care, alternative media, management of the dozens of vehicles under the control of the citizens, and weapons collection. The CSC negotiated with the military—and so did the SSC. Sometimes the two groups issued joint statements, but they also worked at cross-purposes. Often the settlement groups conflicted with the YWCA group, people meeting at Namdong Cathedral, or the Citizens' Army. This polycentric symphony of autonomous organizations accepted major decisions cleared through the forum of citizens' general assemblies. Cacophony to some, melody to others, liberated Gwangju embodied genuine democracy at its best—something like New England town meetings or New Left general assemblies at the Sorbonne in May 1968 Paris and the Greek theater at the University of California, Berkeley in May 1970.

The volatile character of the rally on May 22—when the CSC attempted to persuade people to surrender but met a groundswell of opposition—convinced many people of the need to organize the rallies better to deal with the apparent ease with which prominent individuals could assert their own decisions and change the city's direction. As Lee Jae-eui recalled, "People were frustrated with the lack of continuity in discussions. That is why Yoon Sang-won and Park Hyo-son decided to get a microphone and have a more systematic rally the next day."[104] A core group drawn from members of *Dulbul* night school, *Kwangdae* theatre troupe, and *Nokdu* bookstore formed to help craft daily rallies. The group naturally arose from the need expressed by many people at and after the rally that evening.

At about 6 a.m. the next morning, May 23, hundreds of high school and middle school students, perhaps seven hundred in all, cleaned the city's streets, while teams from the Artists' Council put up big character posters announcing the "First Citizens' Rally to Defend Democracy." That same morning, union organizer Park Tae-bong drove from Asia Motors to Province Hall, where he was given a small receipt with a stamp authorizing him and eight others to clear from city streets burnt out buses and cars, debris, and abandoned vehicles. Like many people inside liberated Gwangju, Park went about his work with utmost respect for the city and its citizens. He was not paid for his efforts and was not required to clean up the wreckage of the fighting but did it of his own free will.

Earlier that same morning, U.S. authorities convened a meeting at the White House (at 4 p.m. on May 22, or about 6 a.m. on the twenty-third in Korea). This

Hidden Face Unmasked by Hong Sung-dam. Woodblock print 294x405 mm. 1983

extraordinary meeting to discuss Korea included Secretary of State Edmund Muskie, Deputy Secretary of State Warren Christopher, Assistant Secretary of State for East Asian and Pacific Affairs Richard Holbrooke, National Security Advisor Zbigniew Brzezinski, CIA Director Stansfield Turner, Defense Secretary Harold Brown, and former Seoul CIA Station Chief Donald Gregg. All had been briefed by Gleysteen's confidential cables, in which the U.S. ambassador wrote: Gwangju "turned completely into a scene of horrors. . . . Rioters were reported firing on helicopters overhead." Gleysteen claimed "rioters" were "looting" and shooting after having "seized 238 vehicles, about 3,500 firearms and 46,400 rounds of ammunition."[105] Whether Gleysteen's misinformation was due to his own misinterpretation of the situation or his reliance on false reports fed to him by the South Korean military, the White House meeting came to "general agreement that the first priority was the restoration of order in Gwangju."[106] They approved the suppression of the uprising and simultaneously the June visit to Seoul by John Moore, president of the U.S. Export-Import Bank, in order to arrange U.S. financing of mammoth ROK contracts for expansion of the Seoul subway system and for Westinghouse to build a new nuclear power plant.[107] On May 23 in Seoul, shortly after the White House gathering, in a meeting with Korean Prime Minister Park Choong-hoon, Gleysteen acknowledged that "firm anti-riot measures were necessary."[108]

Meanwhile, the "First Citywide Rally" in Gwangju was scheduled for 3 p.m. on May 23, but by 11:30 a.m., at least fifty thousand citizens had gravitated to Democracy Plaza, and their numbers increased to two or three times that by noon. The "agora" forum—families identifying the dead, others caring for bereaved relatives, and high school girls collecting "Donations of Love" for the injured— preempted organizers' plans. With as many as 150,000 citizens in attendance, the rally began hours earlier than scheduled. While refusing to surrender all weapons, people approved the exchange for some guns for as many prisoners could be freed. Was it intuitive knowledge of the White House meeting that brought rally presider Kim Tae-jong to say in his opening speech, "Democracy in this country is not just given. It is to be won with bloodshed and struggle."?[109] People's enthusiastic response meant many in attendance understood the stakes of their struggle.

In this moment, Kim Chang-gil, leader of the newly formed SSC, arrived at the rally bringing with him released prisoners he had traded for guns. Evidently, the goodwill Kim Chang-gil enjoyed from all sides for his efforts had a dark side to it. Unbeknownst to anyone, he also brought a secret military explosives expert with him, whom he guided to the basement of Province Hall and helped remove the detonators vital to the explosives Hwasun miners had delivered. Not until days later would the Citizens' Army discover the treachery. (Kim Chang-gil visited the military encampment in Sangmudae on May 22, 23, 25, and 26 and made ample use of a special hotline that had been set up.[110])

We may forgive the Citizens' Army for their lax security at that moment. The group had yet to formally organize. On this, the second day of liberated Gwangju, those in Democracy Plaza were all paying attention to the rally—and were especially relieved to see so many of their friends and fellow citizens released from the military's detention. Many other militia members were still patrolling the

Activists collected weapons in liberated Gwangju on May 24. Photographer: Hwang Chong-gun

outskirts of the city, where the fighting was still intense. Less than an hour after Kim arrived with the freed prisoners, insurgents shot down a reconnaissance helicopter in Baekwundong in the southwest.[111] Around the same time, two young female textile factory workers and nine militia members were ambushed in Chunam village in Chiwon-dong—all were killed. Later, a minibus with 18 people on board was ambushed in the same area. Three people survived the initial onslaught. Two men were summarily executed, but Hong Kum-sook survived and later testified about it.[112] (Several of the corpses were dragged into a nearby village and buried in unmarked graves—where they remained until 1987.)

At the rally's end, after people sang, "Our Wish is National Unification," many people yielded to SSC requests to give up their weapons. Evidently, the prisoner release convinced many citizens of the dictatorship's intention to settle peacefully. Still, after the SSC systematically canvassed neighborhoods and militia members on the front lines, they managed to collect only 2,500 of the estimated 5,400 weapons in people's hands.[113] An "elaborate psychological war was being fought to split the citizens of Gwangju," [114] and Kim played a central role in it. All over the city, unknown persons slashed school bus tires, and loudspeaker equipment was destroyed.

That night, heated discussions took place inside Province Hall. Kim Chang-gil argued that rallies were unnecessary and demanded they be stopped. He believed all weapons should simply be returned to end the situation peacefully. Although fresh vegetables had been brought into the city by tractor, other supplies were running short. Promising that the military would not take reprisals,

Kim made a persuasive case and convinced most settlement committee members of the wisdom of his ideas. While the SSC was meeting at Province Hall, a few blocks away at the YWCA, activists gathered to prepare the next day's rally. Their attention turned to the need for a citywide funeral. Waiting in line as groups of five hundred at a time were admitted, thousands of people had already visited Sangmu Martial Arts Studio to view the corpses of the city's martyrs.[115] Despite prolific amounts of incense, the severe stench made some people's noses bleed. People felt the failure to arrange a proper funeral was one sign of the settlement committee's incompetence. Activists feverishly worked through the night to prepare poetry, skits, songs, and an effigy of Chun for the next day's rally.

The next morning, the military announced in radio broadcasts that people surrendering weapons would not be arrested. Around Democracy Plaza, leaflets announced the CSC's "success" in negotiations: the military admitted excessive force had been used and promised to release all but 79 of its 927 prisoners, to compensate the families of those killed, to provide medical attention for the wounded, and not to retaliate against anyone once peace was restored. Before the rally that day, the CSC passed a resolution calling for the unconditional return of all weapons. Many people brought their firearms to Province Hall, where activists collected them.

Soon debates broke out. "Why should we abandon seventy-nine citizens to unknown fates?" "How do we know the military will keep those promises?" "Why won't the government openly apologize?" These and other such questions were commonly overheard among clusters of citizens as they earnestly discussed their options. At the same time as the SSC was making assurances of the military's kind intentions, people remembered the massacres in Junam village the day before. Posters appeared critical of CSC "defeatism." As one militant told me, "The Sobuk miners struggle had shown us that if we disarmed and negotiated, soldiers would come and kill."[116]

Around 2:30 p.m., somewhere between fifty and a hundred thousand people gathered in Democracy Plaza, but the rally could not begin because the CSC refused to allow people to use the sound system in Province Hall.[117] Since military agents had systematically destroyed so much of the city's other amplification equipment, it was unclear if the rally could continue. A KBS union leader, caring little that his company's building had been burnt, told organizers where to obtain a sound system. Soon, new—and better—equipment helped people converse again in the open-air assembly. Although it had taken some time, people patiently waited. When the rally finally began, Yoon Sang-won and others revealed the settlement groups' opposition to rallies and their decision to return weapons. People asked for specific details from negotiators and turned against the settlement committees when they would not elaborate on their discussions with the army. People were not content to simply leave their fate in the hands of a few people but wanted to participate in the process of making decisions and to know the tenor and tone of negotiations. In response, the CSC unplugged the new loudspeakers. They hoped to prevent criticisms from escalating and gathering even more public support. The sound system was plugged back in, but members of the CSC—now dubbed the "surrender faction"—kept unplugging it.[118] They hoped to short-circuit direct democracy and substitute their own vote for the popular will of the assembly.

Once again the city's working class came to the rescue: an electrician stepped forward and hooked the sound system up to a tear gas truck that had been delivered by workers at Asia Motors. As the assembly continued its deliberations, some people demanded the CSC be dissolved. Activists were cheered when they called for action to stop the settlement committee's "conspiracy with the military for an unconditional surrender." A heavy rain began, and many people scattered to find shelter. A speaker from the platform cried out, "This rain represents the tears of the spirits of democracy who were killed grievously and cannot lie in peace." People returned to their seats and closed their umbrellas. In the pouring rain, they heartily approved a draft of an "Appeal to the Nation's Democratic Citizens." At the end of the rally, people's high spirits were raised even further when an effigy of Chun Doo-hwan was burned.

After the rally, activists gathered at the YWCA meeting to discuss how to proceed. News arrived that during the rally, paratroopers opened fire on children swimming in a reservoir in Chinwoldong, killing twelve-year-old Pang Kwang-bom. More than ever, they were certain that the army could not be trusted. Meeting for the first time earlier that afternoon, Yoon Sang-won and Park Nam-son resolved to work together. Although Park was central to the operation of the Situation Room and the Citizens' Army, he had not participated in any settlement committee until joining forces with Yoon. The divisions between activists who wanted to surrender and those who refused to submit became so great that the two sides could barely speak, particularly after the CSC kept dismantling the sound system. Nonetheless, later that evening, the SSC convened a meeting inside Province Hall. Many activists joined the discussion, during which Yoon Sang-won and Jeong Hae-jik harshly criticized Kim Chang-gil and the "surrender faction." After midnight, the SSC was reorganized, and Park Nam-son, although not a student, became a member.

On the morning of Sunday, May 25, the rain stopped. The already tense atmosphere inside Province Hall became suddenly much worse when Chang Kye-bom doubled over, claiming he had been stuck with a poison-needle (a weapon thought to be used by North Korean agents). Although later shown to have been fabricated, the "poison needle incident" heightened everyone's anxiety. Already tight security at Province Hall was stepped up. Settlement committee members already wore star pins to gain entry (as well as to collect weapons throughout the city), and new ID cards with seals were issued.

Rally organizers reached out to seek the advice and support of a diverse cross-section of citizens. They arranged a meeting with members of the Namdong Cathedral council of distinguished citizens at 10 a.m. in the YWCA, where they asked the entire group to help plan and coordinate the rallies, but the Namdong group refused to get involved in the assemblies—although after caucusing later, they decided to participate in settlement committee meetings in Province Hall.

Beginning at 3 p.m., the "Third Citywide Rally" drew fifty thousand participants. From outlying districts, people reported on the military's activities and requested help in dealing with local problems. A city damage report began to be taken by various eyewitnesses discussing the extent of the military's destructive actions. The number of people killed was said to be 209—of whom 40 had yet to be identified. At least 1,790 people had been wounded—520 critically. More than 2,000 people were missing.[119] Carefully crafted statements like "Letter to the People" and "Why We Had to Pick Up Guns" were read. Once again, many citizens called for the resignation of the settlement committees.

The Struggle Moves to a More "Systematic" Level

At 7 p.m. on May 25, an emotional meeting began on the third floor of Province Hall. Yoon Sang-won had helped to merge forces from the YWCA with those inside Province Hall, so the conversation included both sides of the issues debated at the assemblies. Many SSC members argued strongly that all weapons should be turned over to the army, but militants refused to consent to what they considered "surrender." They felt that such an act would betray the dead, and signal the entire country that the dictatorship was acceptable. If people would fight to the end, they believed that sooner or later, Koreans would demand justice for Gwangju and win democracy in the process. As soon as the meeting began, government radio broadcasts announced that "hard-liners" had taken over Province Hall. By 9 p.m., Kim Chang-gil resigned from the group and left, leaving the militants in charge.

At 10 p.m., a new leadership group formally took control of Province Hall. Calling itself the Citizen-Student Struggle Committee (CSSC), the group developed a multifaceted structure delineating areas of responsibility and assigning individuals to take care of specific tasks. Chung Sang-yong was selected as overall leader because he was the oldest person in attendance. Former SSC vice chair Kim Jeong-bae became chair. The new CSSC immediately convened an all-night meeting. They decided to try and bring the city back to "normal" as soon as possible, hoping to reopen government offices, media, and unarmed police stations, get the city's buses operating as normal, create a rice reserve at City Hall, and reopen long distance telephone lines. Most importantly, they agreed to reorganize the Citizens' Army by creating new "Mobile Strike Forces"—rapid response units— and assigned people to make sure all perimeter outposts were supplied and vigilant. The CSSC Publicity Department organized four working clusters: one to drive vehicles with loudspeakers through the streets to make announcements; another to publish the daily *Fighters' Bulletin*, posters, and other materials; a third to raise funds and encourage people to donate blood; and finally a group to organize daily rallies. Planning controlled access to Province Hall, rationed fuel, registered vehicles, and requisitioned supplies. Civil Affairs dealt mainly with casualties; Distribution arranged for funerals. At several funeral parlors, Kim Jeong-bae signed his name and promised to pay later for coffins.

At the nucleus of a dedicated constellation of people whom the city increasingly relied upon to guide the uprising stood Yoon Sang-won, one of the remarkable individuals of the battle of Gwangju—and certainly the most remembered. In the aftermath of the carnage, no one's courage and intellect shines brighter than his. After the shootings at the huge rally on May 21 (when the military opened fire

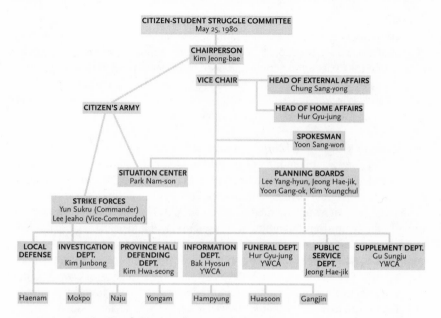

FIGURE 6.2 **Organization of Citizen-Student Struggle Committee**
Source: Na Kahn-chae and George Katsiaficas, *The Gwangju Uprising and the Paris Commune: Preliminary Research* (unpublished)

on over two hundred thousand people), Yoon personally led one of the assaults to procure arms, and he was also involved in the group that took control of armored personnel carriers at Asia Motors Company. In the intense atmosphere of military snipers firing on public areas, endless meetings, daily mass rallies, and occasional skirmishes, Yoon emerged as the "only one who had a strategic view."[120] By making an alliance with Park Nam-son, Yoon brought together several disparate streams: working-class fighters, students, and movement activists. The CSSC became the focal point for continuing armed resistance. They successfully outmaneuvered conservative settlement committee members and pointed the uprising in the direction of its origins: demanding a democratic government. Significantly, Yoon and many of his colleagues had previously participated in a study group about the Paris Commune with poet Kim Nam-ju.[121] Refusing to place his name at the titular head of the council, Yoon was named CSSC "spokesperson," and he spoke eloquently at a May 26 press conference.

In the dialectic of spontaneity and organization, it was clearly the popular movement's impulses that held sway in Gwangju. From the outside, organizational charts and key activist accounts may seem important, but what really mattered was the massive participation of citizens. The schematic chart of the CSSC does not indicate the daily assemblies as the highest decision-making body. Indeed, some people questioned how much influence the leadership had over specific fighting units and work teams. Kim Tae-chan, leader of Strike Force 7, told me, "The leadership didn't influence people all that much."[122] Kim Jeong-bae informed me "local defense was not controlled by the CSSC."[123] As significant as the role of Yoon Sang-won and the CSSC may have been, he and his small organization never put themselves above the popular movement. Once the self-selected settlement committees tried to prevent direct-democratic gatherings from occurring, citizens had no choice but to reconstitute alternative leadership that reflected popular will to continue the struggle, not to surrender.

Many of the militants who fought the army used their own initiative rather than following the suggestions of any leaders. On May 22, for example, Park Nae-pung refused to head to Yongsangpo as Province Hall thought he should. Instead he went to Hwasun train station with four others, where they were able to procure arms for themselves and return to Gwangju.[124] This particular case of individual initiative ended well, yet the lack of strategic organization cost the communards dearly. The *Fighters' Bulletin* called for people to "occupy KBS [television station] to let our reality be known to the whole country through broadcasting."[125] During the fighting, however, the crowd torched the place. If people had better coordination, would they have been able to broadcast news of the uprising to the rest of the country? Would a nationwide uprising have then occurred? Clearly, strategic leadership both in Gwangju and the nation was needed to overthrow the government.[126] Without national organization, Gwangju remained isolated, and the military was able to concentrate its firepower on one city. In hindsight, clarity is possible, but options were limited in the heat of battle.

In the final analysis, the fact that the Gwangju Uprising was not centrally organized made the continual regeneration of its leadership from below both possible and necessary. Moreover, popular intuition that the uprising was not centrally planned is another level of explanation for why Korean people universally identified with Gwangju. The dictatorship insisted that it was linked to North Korea and tried to suppress its history, but popular intuition came to grasp people's resistance as a yearning for freedom, as a city's popular response to the ruthless violence of the military dictatorship.

Military Organization

Armies are notoriously brutal, but the fighters who became liberated Gwangju's Citizens' Army were models of responsibility. People dubbed them "our army" or "our allies" (as opposed to "the army" or "our enemy.") As their trucks passed, citizens offered them food and drinks, showered them with joyful greetings, offered them money, and held up their children to inspire the fighters. The city's young men and women protected the citizenry, and the people, in turn, took care of them. Without any indoctrination and none of the military madness that elicits monstrous behavior in armies around the world, the fighters behaved in an exemplary fashion. Unafraid to impose a new type of order based on the needs of the populace, they disarmed middle school and high school students, an action for which the *Fighters' Bulletin* took responsibility.[127] The Citizens' Army served the popular will directly as formulated at the rallies. From the very first day of liberation, disagreements surfaced, but they were discussed and resolved. Although many of the fighters went without sleep multiple nights in a row, there was no looting, no pillaging, and no banks were robbed.

The militia picked up guns to fight, but people considered them nonviolent—or even antiviolent—since they stopped the violence of the paratroopers. Catholic priest Cho Cheul-hyun testified about the "peaceful nature of the Citizens' Army, who only fought soldiers in self-defense. They hurt no people but protected them. Even when they captured four policemen, they were unharmed and later released."[128] During my interviews with them, several militia members recalled releasing unharmed soldiers they had overpowered. One case in particular remains in my memory. A captured young soldier began to cry when people told him he would be released. The militia members asked him what was wrong. He insisted that if he returned to his unit without his M-16, he would be severely beaten. The fighters deliberated and then returned him his gun—but not his ammunition. Park Nam-son remembered that after several soldiers scouring for food were caught, he received a call from the head of the military. In response to a request to release them, the fighters agreed to do so and, once again, graciously allowed them to keep their weapons—but not their bullets.[129]

By way of contrast to such honorable and kind behavior, the U.S. ambassador and dictatorship whipped up stories of "mass hysteria" and spread rumors of atrocities "including executions and people's tribunals."[130] Much like Gustave Le Bon's frenzied condemnation of revolutions in 1890, Gleysteen sought to create an atmosphere of vindictive behavior. Exaggerations and fabrications of executions transmitted by Gleysteen to Washington added further fuel to the raging fire of paranoid hubris rampant among the coterie of officials who gathered at the White House on May 22 and made U.S. policy the suppression of Gwangju's commune.

Numerous eyewitness accounts provide examples of how remarkably the whole city came together: "In spite of the complete absence of an official peace and order system, Gwangju citizens maintained peace and order perfectly. Though so many firearms were in the hands of citizens, no incident took place due to it. Even financial agencies or jeweler's shops in which crimes are apt to happen in ordinary times were free from any criminal act."[131] As they became more formally organized into a political-military force, the CSSC instructed all civil servants, including the disarmed police, to return to their posts; they took charge of gasoline distribution, traffic control, and information coordination; and they organized resistance to the impending counterattack—all without a centralized authority giving people orders from above—whether from a Supreme Commander or central committee. The interactive process involving direct democratic general assemblies and a consensual based CSSC (including hundreds of fighters in the Citizens' Army) was an indication of the wisdom of ordinary people in the twentieth century. This concrete example of how human beings chose to govern themselves when freed from the military power of the dictatorship indicates the possibility of much more democracy than that embodied in ritualistic elections of politicians with few real differences. Although nearly every movement leader had been arrested or gone into hiding, people autonomously organized themselves, defeated the military, and then governed themselves through consensus and participatory democracy.

These dynamics are reflected even in the organization of the armed resistance. All through the night of May 21, self-organized armed teams fought (and defeated) the military—and skirmishes continued all during the next day. Teams formed loosely. Autonomously constituted mobile patrols carried out the normal functions of police and emergency rescue teams. On May 22, as word spread to assemble at Gwangju Park, seventy-eight vehicles lined up, volunteers painted them with numbers, and they were assigned to patrol one of seven parts of the city to guard against the coming counterattack. Regional defense forces also assembled naturally. As the army probed the city's defenses, organization became tighter.[132] The government's own reserve army system mobilized from the grassroots in some neighborhoods, and people themselves sometimes chose to wear their old uniforms as part of new fighting units. They selected officers and duties, and disarmed underage fighters.[133] One unidentified man gathered fifty or more fighters in Province Hall when they were needed to fight. In another case, Kim Hwa-seong pulled together five teams of five people each on May 22, showed them cars to take and gave each team a radio, captured riot police helmets, and raincoats, before he dispatched them off to patrol the city. Teams dispatched from downtown reinforced local reservists in neighborhoods, complete with team leaders and weapons. Initially grouped into six twelve-member teams, the neighborhood of Hagun-dong's fighters grew to twelve teams including a headquarters.

From May 20 to 22, five attempts were made to free prisoners held in the penitentiary on the outskirts of the city. Nearly 2,700 people, including 170 political prisoners—among them poet and fighter Kim Nam-ju—were incarcerated there, and the army made it a strong point of their defensive positions. At 12:20 p.m. on May 21, hundreds of fighters, prisoners' families, and citizens gathered around the prison. At 3 p.m., using three vehicles, they stormed the prison but were driven back after hand-to-hand fighting. At 7:30 p.m., nine vehicles including two armored cars were mobilized, but the military beefed up its forces with heavy weapons and held the prison. Altogether in these attacks on the prison, at least eight people were killed and seventy wounded.[134] People captured during the battles were later tortured, and the dead buried in unmarked graves.

As the militia moved from using Molotovs to machine guns, new questions of organization and coordination emerged. Early on May 23, citizens captured two army spies after a shootout. The men were taken to Province Hall and interrogated by the Investigations Bureau—a self-selected group that many people felt had been infiltrated, perhaps even controlled, by the police.[135] How could people deal with such a problem? With teams issuing fuel-rationing cards and passes for cars, while others called in on walkie-talkies from patrols, Province Hall was a hub of activity. The critical point made time and again by participants was the importance of popular decisions arrived at through direct democracy—whether by groups of fighters who gathered at such critical moments, or for "big decisions," by the general assembly of citizens during the daily rallies. Yoon Gi-hyun felt that if the uprising had a limit, it was because leaders made mistakes, but he insisted that people who fought with guns didn't do anything wrong.[136]

Although many of the teams of fighters were composed of people already acquainted with each other or even coworkers and friends, anonymity played a vital role in sustaining the continuing capacity of new people to step forward.

Lee Jin-kyong related how when ID cards and people's names were used, the anonymity of the uprising was lost, and the character of the insurgency changed.[137] So flexible were relationships during the formation of the absolute community that when citizens gathered in Gwangju Park on May 22 to receive arms and training, Lee Jae-eui collected ID cards. When people objected, Lee reconsidered and found their objections reasonable, so he returned the cards.[138] Within such dynamic interactions, trust played a significant role, and authority could easily be manipulated. With heightened vigilance because of infiltration, very often a student ID card from a local university sufficed to gain entrance to Province Hall. Kim Chang-gil showed his CNU card to enter and thereafter became the leader of the SSC. As such distinguished citizens stepped forward to "lead" the city, they injected an element of conservatism.

As Park Nam-son remembered, older people formed settlement committees, while younger ones did the fighting. After May 22, he was worried that too many people were armed so he insisted that many give up their weapons. On the twenty-second, Park named the office in Province Hall where fighters congregated the "Situation Office" to portray the urgency of the tasks there and personally took charge of coordinating armed resistance. As a central command emerged at Province Hall, most autonomous fighting units were integrated into teams that eventually turned into the Mobile Strike Forces. They still retained a feeling of equality. Among these fighters and with the people of the city, the informal declension of Korean was used, "People were comfortable with each other and thought of others as equals, even if they were older or younger."[139]

After the CSSC was organized on May 25, Park remained central to the creation of the Mobile Strike Forces that crystallized coordinated armed resistance.[140] When it was agreed to bring the city's life back to normal, he made arrangements for police and city officials to return to work; when police began to patrol the city on their own initiative, he quickly brought them under control of the Citizens' Army. Mobile Strike Forces organized by the Situation Room around noon on May 26 included more than a dozen teams each with six or seven fighters, a Jeep, and a radio.[141] The groups had a clear command structure and were totally committed to fighting the army. Following a formal swearing-in ceremony, each fighter was given a clean uniform and headgear, taken from riot police. Each team selected a leader, identified by an airborne beret, and chose a team nickname like Steamed Bun, Tiger, and White Bear. Everyone wrote their team number and nickname on their helmets. That evening, when they waited to wage their last stand in and around Province Hall, none of the members broke away, and to this day, their participation is a great source of pride.

Class Dynamics in the Uprising
The transformation of the SSC into the CSSC reflected the leading role played by the working class. Although students had sparked the uprising, they were unable to continue to be its leading force. Many of them melted away as the fighting grew intense. While students like Kim Chang-gil led the "surrender faction," others remained vital to the uprising's continuation. Once the city rose up in arms,

students were no longer the leading force—rather working class and lumpen were the core of the armed resistance. As Choi Jungwoon put it: "As soon as the citizens were armed, the working classes occupied honored seats, not some insignificant corner."[142] What began as a student-led struggle spontaneously metamorphosed into a struggle of the whole city. By the end of the uprising, lumpen became one of the militia's main constituencies. They were the most reliable under fire and unafraid of police or the army.

Few commentators have noted the importance of the lumpenproletariat, yet many participants I interviewed took great pains to put them at the center of militant resistance. Park Nam-son remembered, "gangsters, thieves, and beggars shared one common mind against the military . . . among the Citizens' Army, lower class people fought the best." Both Yoon Young-kyu and Jeong Hae-jik emphasized the role of the lumpen.[143] "When other people told us to get out, prostitutes, restaurant workers and poor people gladly hid us."[144] Several members of the SWAT team at the uprising's beginning and many of those who remained in Province Hall on the morning of May 27 were lumpen. The involvement of marginalized people—prostitutes who insisted on donating blood, unemployed or underemployed men, shoeshine boys, and orphans—is noteworthy. Organized criminals were also part of the uprising of the whole people. The public pledge made by gang leaders was indicative of the lumpen's broad participation. Lee Jae-eui reported that while many citizens surrendered their firearms to the CSC on May 22, "Workers and members of the underclass, however, would not abandon their guns."[145] More radical than the students, these militants hoped to spark a nationwide uprising to overthrow the dictatorship—and they were willing to die trying to restore democracy in one fell swoop. They demanded qualitative changes in Korean politics—not only the lifting of martial law, release of all prisoners, and a caretaker government, but the resignation of Chun Doo-hwan and full democratization.[146] Arnold Peterson reported that on May 21, "In a conversation I had with

TABLE 6.2 **Occupations of Citizens Killed during the Gwangju Uprising**

Occupation	Number of People	Percent
Manual laborer	50	30.3
Student	30	18.2
Office worker	19	11.5
Self-employed	12	7.3
Service worker	9	5.5
Housewife	4	2.4
Farmer/Fisherman	4	2.4
Soldier	2	1.2
Other	35	21.2
Total	165	100.0

Sources: Jong-chol Ahn, "The Citizens' Army during the Kwangju Uprising," in *Contentious Kwangju: The May 18th Uprising in Korea's Past and Present*, eds. Gi-Wook Shin and Kyung Moon Hwang, (Lanham, MD: Rowman and Littlefield, 2003), 20; Kim Byung-In, "The Gwangju Democratic Uprising and Citizens' Social Movements," in May 18th History Compilation Committee of Gwangju City, *History of the 5.18 Democratic Uprising*, vol. 1 (Gwangju: The May 18 Memorial Foundation, 2008), 157.

TABLE 6.3 **Occupations and Age of Citizens Arrested during the Gwangju Uprising**

The martial law authorities arrested at least 1,740 people during the uprising. They released 1,010 either as a result of negotiations with the insurgents (who were able to secure the release of people in exchange for weapons on three occasions) or because those arrested were not deemed to be "hard-core." Of the 730 "hard-core" people detained and "being interrogated," the military released the following profiles:

High school and university students	153
Unemployed	126
Factory workers	83
Other industrial workers	79
Drivers	55
Farmers	47
Shopkeepers	47
Salespeople	44
Office workers	37
Others	59

More than half of the above were workers (387, or 53 percent).
More than 21 percent were students.
More than 17 percent were unemployed.
By age:
42 percent (315) were under twenty years old.
42 percent (315) were in their twenties.
11 percent (77) in their thirties.
Nearly 4 percent (28) were forty years old or older.

Source: *AMPO*, September 1980.

Pastor Chang, he was careful to emphasize that the ones who seized guns were not students. Instead they were young jobless and working men."[147]

I have already mentioned the Hwasun coal miners and women textile workers. There are numerous other examples of working-class leadership to which one can point. Besides the vital role of transport workers, factory employees at Asia Motors cooperated or joined with the Citizens' Army. Small workshops and many workplaces emptied out as people became part of the uprising. One study concluded that "largely factory workers" fought to the end in Gwangju because nineteen of the thirty people in a sample of those arrested listed their occupations as factory workers.[148] The small size of the sample makes the conclusion unreliable, but other evidence abounds of how Gwangju's uprising was centrally a proletarian struggle. The exodus from the rich neighborhoods marked the exit of those with money from the beleaguered city.[149] In 1988, the Catholic Gwangju Diocese Peace and Justice Committee found that more than 70 percent of the injured and families members of the dead identified themselves as working class (41 percent were unemployed at the time of the survey, compared with 24 percent in 1980.)[150] Analysis of citizens killed by the military also reveals their working class backgrounds.

Similar extrapolation can be made from government arrest statistics of "hard-core" insurgents. High school and college students were the largest single category but when factory workers and "other industrial workers" are added together, they became the largest single category of those arrested. More than half of all arrested citizens were "working-class." The overwhelming majority (84 percent) were twenty-nine years old or younger.

Women and the Uprising

Once the uprising broke out, women were central to the life of the liberated city and the absolute community, especially as the main force organizing the daily rallies at Democracy Plaza.[151] A handful of women carried carbines, and some were responsible for gathering bottles and fuel to make Molotov cocktails. (Women were suspected less when they gathered bottles or filled containers with fuel.) In a few cases, they threw firebombs.[152] Women were also primarily responsible for posting big character posters and in the publication and distribution of the *Fighters' Bulletin*. They organized the blood donation drives, food preparation, gathered and washed the bodies of the dead, tended to the wounded, and consoled bereaved families.

A cluster of activists called themselves the Women's Bureau and centrally organized the rallies, operated the public address systems, and did much of the office work. Many of these activists had begun working together in December 1978, when they organized *Song Baek Hoe* (Pure Pine Tree Society) to care for political prisoners and their families, especially activist wives and sisters of arrestees. Chong Hyun-ay, its first president, was a key Gwangju activist during the uprising. As the paratroopers began to arrive in the city, she called acquaintances in Jeonju, Busan, and Seoul before long-distance phone lines were disconnected. She carried a gun, made and used Molotovs, and helped provide overall political direction within activist circles. After May 27, she was arrested and held with about seventy other women. At twenty-eight years old, she was the oldest of these prisoners, who included many middle school and high school girls.

High school girls played an important role in demonstrations, especially on May 19 when girls at both Chungang and Gwangsan Girls' High Schools autonomously organized protests.[153] The next day, many housewives and older women took to the streets as participants in the militant protests. Some carried toothpaste and wet towels to help mitigate effects of tear gas, while others broke sidewalk blocks to help make weapons; a few were on the front lines of the street fights. Women participated in great numbers in militant marches—sometimes as many as one-third of the activists involved in street-actions were females. Among citizens killed by the military, at least fourteen were women.

Despite the heroic participation of women in all facets of the uprising, it appears that within movement organizations, they were often confined to "normal" roles and modes of behavior.[154] With the notable exception of Chun Ok-ju, whose eloquence and poise positioned her to be the best known of the orators that canvassed the city in loudspeaker trucks, it was almost always men who rode in the commandeered vehicles of the Citizens' Army. Women were mainly involved in traditionally defined female roles: making *kimbab* and serving food in public kitchens, managing the donations of blood and money, and caring for the wounded and dead. It appears this division of labor appeared "organically" rather than having been based on anyone feeling excluded.[155] Im Chun-hee felt women's exclusion was "avoidable"—a patriarchal division of labor did not have to happen.[156] As an indication of the extent to which the Gwangju community came together, even prostitutes fought the military and insisted on making blood donations. On one occasion, when a doctor tried to stop them, one woman replied: "Our lives are dirty but our blood is pure." She felt "revived" since formerly she was regarded as "low and dirty."[157] The remarkable solidarity of liberated Gwangju was a brief taste of a genuinely free society, yet within that communal liberation, women's roles were not dramatically transformed—nor is it realistic to think they could be in such a short period of time.

When it came to formal leadership positions, women were often excluded and too often subservient to men. The reorganization of the resistance inside Province Hall on May 25 did not include one woman among the leadership positions. On the night of May 26, when it was apparent that the military was poised to reenter the city with overwhelming force, women and young fighters were asked to leave Province Hall by the male leadership (including Yoon Sang-won). More than a few women disobeyed this order and remained for the final battle, but nearly all women left.[158] Several reasons existed for women being asked to leave, the most practical of which was that nearly all men had military training from which they had learned how to use weapons—skills few women had a chance to acquire.[159] Although a few women did carry guns during the halcyon days of liberated Gwangju, they were the exception: generally men carried the guns and women's participation was limited to noncombatant roles—a mirror of the patriarchal division of labor of society at large.

After the uprising, many of the female activists who carried guns during the uprising continued to work tirelessly for justice, some around women's issues.[160] In 1981, women spontaneously confronted Chun Doo-hwan when he appeared on the streets of Gwangju. Although many female activists had been abducted by police and dropped off in isolated areas miles from Gwangju to prevent them from organizing protests, their vociferous public opposition caused Chun to beat a hasty retreat.[161]

The Final Days

At dawn on May 26, more than a dozen tanks crushed militia barricades on the outskirts of the city and began to rumble toward Province Hall. When they heard the news, seventeen distinguished citizens, including members of the CSC, were in the midst of an all-night meeting. They resolved to embark on what became known as "The March of Death" to stop the tanks. Heroically underway for an hour, they drew hundreds of others with them. When they found the tanks, they sat down in the street to stop them from advancing. They told an army general that he would have to kill them first if his troops wanted to attack the city. Their courageous sit-in protest raised people's spirits and delayed the military's final assault.

Hearing from loudspeaker trucks that the army was entering the city, about thirty thousand people gathered around the fountain in Democracy Plaza. By 11:30 a.m., when the rally convened, news of the "March of Death" filled people

Encouraged by the United States, the South Korean military crushed the Gwangju Uprising.
Photographer: Na Kyung-taek

with hope that the military might yet listen to reason. That morning, a large poster had been prominently displayed announcing that the U.S. aircraft carrier *Coral Sea* had entered Korean waters. Wiser heads silently understood it as an ominous portent, but many people believed that the Americans were coming to assist their struggle for democracy. At the rally, the new CSSC leadership read the "Resolution of 800,000 Gwangju Citizens" in which they promised to fight to the end. They called for a democratic government of national salvation, a demand that went far beyond asking the military to apologize for their transgressions, or for the dictatorship to promise not to punish people. This new strident demand reflected the uprising's original aims—to overturn martial law and to establish democracy. At the end of the rally, hundreds of high school students chanted "We Refuse to Return Weapons!" and led a march through the city.

That afternoon, Yoon Sang-won held a press conference for foreign correspondents. Using flip charts, he answered questions from journalists for the *Asian Wall Street Journal*, *Le Monde*, the *Baltimore Sun*, the *Sunday Times* (UK), *Asahi* (Japan), NBC, UPI, and several Korean papers.[162] He publicly asked U.S. Ambassador Gleysteen to mediate a peaceful solution. Gleysteen subsequently was told of Yoon's request via telephone, but he refused to respond.[163] So distorted was U.S. intelligence that on May 25, 1980, Secretary of State Muskie cabled: "The situation in Gwangju has taken a rather grim turn ... the moderate citizens' committee has lost control of the situation and the radicals appear to be in charge." While that information was accurate, he then repeated the same erroneous charges that, "Peoples courts have been set up and some executions have taken place. Student demonstrators have been largely replaced by unidentified armed radicals who are talking of setting up a revolutionary government."[164] The next day, May 26, 1980, Gleysteen wrote to Washington that: The situation in Gwangju "took a sharp turn for the worse. There were reports of vigilante groups, recovery by radicals of weapons turned in earlier, and even of people's courts and executions."[165]

It soon became clear that the end of the uprising was near. At the final rally around 3 p.m. on May 26, the CSSC solemnly announced that reliable intelligence reports indicated that the military would massively assault the city the next morning. Freeing anyone of obligation to remain and fight, they asked all those willing to die for democracy to remain. Buddhist monk Song Yon rose and addressed the citizens gathered at the fountain. Encouraged by leaflets that noted how people of all religions had participated in the struggle, he proclaimed, in the name of the Association of Korean People's Buddhism: "Buddha's heart today, as a step toward the restoration of the tradition as the people's religion which has shared in the long history of our nation, the bitterness and happiness together with the Korean people, urges twenty million Buddhists to actively participate in the grand movement for national democratization which aims at the people's liberation from the bonds of oppression, self-complacency, foreign interference, and untruth. We herewith fully regret our past flaws, our lack of cooperation and our indolence as bystanders, and we march under the flag notifying being together with each other so that we can live together and die together with people, and arm ourselves with the determination of establishing law and justice in our society."[166]

A helicopter hovered overhead and dispersed leaflets announcing the imminent crackdown on the city. Still people remained. Although the rally had ended, no one left. Suddenly, a high school girl sang beautifully "Our Wish Is National Reunification." Although the military reported that only "hooligans, rag-pickers, and rioters" remained, a demonstration of about six thousand marchers set off to the cordons where the March of Death had stopped the tanks. When the march reached the edge of the city, the number of people had swelled to about thirty thousand.[167] They screamed at the army to leave and vowed to defend the city to the end. Marching back to Province Hall, hundreds of people prepared for a desperate last stand. Besides fighters already organized into teams, about 150 others remained after the rally, determined to fight to the end. They included eighty people who had completed military service, sixty youth and high school students, and ten women. All were integrated into the ranks of the Citizens' Army.

That evening, armed paratroopers were able to abduct Chun Ok-ju, and she was subsequently tortured terribly. In Province Hall, the settlement faction again appeared and called for return of all weapons. Reappearing again, Kim Chang-gil joined the ongoing meeting in Province Hall and told people it was no use to stay. Finally, frustrated with continuing attempts to sap people's resolve, Park Nam-son entered the meeting on the second floor. Brandishing a revolver, he demanded that anyone who didn't want to fight leave the building immediately. Kim Chang-gil quickly departed.

With those people willing to sacrifice themselves left in peace, a melancholic quiet took hold. More than one member of the Citizens' Army told me that as they waited for the final assault, they found time to doze for the first time in days. As the night grew late, Yoon Sang-won personally insisted that high schoolers return home so they could survive and continue the struggle. After many protests and with tears in their eyes, many younger militants departed—although some refused or secreted themselves into parts of the building where they remained.

On the night of May 26, families of soldiers stationed near Gwangju, informed the resistance fighters that the military was beginning to move. Small units of fighters were dispatched to various strategic points in the city. About a hundred people held the YWCA and smaller groups were positioned in the YMCA, Kyerim Elementary School, at Yu-dong Junction, Tongnimsan, the Chonil Building, CNU Medical School, Sobang Market, and Hak-dong. Altogether more than five hundred fighters were poised to defend the city.[168] Some three to five hundred people readied the defense of Province Hall.[169] Although most women departed, there were around ten who remained to fight until the end.[170]

With U.S. encouragement and support, dictator Chun mobilized some twenty thousand elite troops and took back the city on the morning of May 27. At 4:30 a.m., the battle raged at Province Hall. While a column of tanks advanced down Kumnam Avenue, Special Forces attacked the building from the rear with grenades and machine guns.

During the assault, Yoon San-won was killed by a blast so powerful that when his body was recovered, it had been partially burnt. Kim Jeong-bae related that at least seventeen people were killed inside the building. Among the casualties

Many corpses were unceremoniously buried in Mangwoldong Cemetery on the outskirts of Gwangju. Photographer: Kim Nyung-man

was Chairperson of the Buddhist Student Union, Kim Dong-soo. At 6:30 a.m., the building was in the hands of the army. They roped together the remaining fighters, kicking and beating them as they led them away. Garbage trucks were brought in to dump many corpses on the outskirts of the city.

Despite their bitter defeat that day, Gwangju citizens fought on. They refused to accept the military's victory that morning as the final act of their struggle. From their prison cells in Sangmudae, where they were packed by the dozens into cells built for a few people, prisoners loudly sang the national anthem every morning. When they were brought before military tribunals, rather than pay attention to the proceedings, they sang movement songs, threw chairs at the judges, and roundly cursed Chun and the dictatorship. They organized hunger strikes to obtain books and family visits, and plotted their movement's next steps. For the next seventeen years, they continued, until finally they won exactly what the rallies at Democracy Plaza had demanded: Chun Doo-hwan and his collaborators were sent to prison, the government apologized, and citizens were compensated for their losses.

Over the years, Gwangju became the watchword for democracy—the primary symbol of and inspiration for Korean freedom struggles. Gwangju has a meaning in Korean history that can only be compared to that of the Paris Commune in French history and of the battleship *Potemkin* in Russian history. Like the Paris Commune, the people of Gwangju spontaneously rose up and governed themselves until they were brutally suppressed by indigenous military forces abetted by an outside power. And like the battleship Potemkin, the people of Gwangju have repeatedly signaled the advent of revolution in Korea—from the 1894 Farmers' War and the 1929 student revolt to the 1980 uprising. Independent of Cold War divisions, both the DPRK and ROK praise the people's uprising. In this sense, Gwangju provides a point of unity across what often appears to be an unbridgeable political divide.

Let's go this way together
Written by poet Kim Nam-ju from prison on a milk carton, smuggled out and secretly distributed.

Let's go this way together
gathering comrades in struggle.
It's much better for us to be three,
but let's not go separately even though we are two.

Let's go this way together.
Let's not say, "You, come later" going ahead.
Let's not say, "You, go ahead" staying behind.

If we are ten or a thousand, ten or a thousand, let's go shoulder to shoulder.
If there are mountains across fields (*uhgiyeocha**) let's help climb them.
If there are fierce waves of sea (*uhgiyeocha*) let's help cross them.

Let's go this way together,
that we should someday climb mountains and cross water.
Let's go this way together,
let's hurry to go this way; the sun is setting down to the west.

After the sun sets, in the dark,
if you fall down, I'll come to help you get up.
If I fall down, you'll come to help me get up.

The wild way having thorns, that someone should go,
what the heck, if we can't continue to go,
let's go after taking a rest, leaning on painful legs together.

uhgiyeocha: sounds that people make to encourage each other.
Translated by Ahn Byoung-sun and Shin Eun-jung

NOTES

1   We will never know how many people were killed. Many bodies were never found, and many of the missing were never accounted for. In 1980, Asia Watch estimated that over two thousand were killed. The South Korean government's official number used to compensate the families of the dead is 164 people. In 1980, the Chun regime claimed 191 people, including 46 soldiers, were killed and an official U.S. briefing team that visited October 30–31 reported 2,522 killed. May 18 Gwangju Democratization Movement Materials, Gwangju City May 18 Historical Materials Compilation Committee 광주광역시 5-18사료 편찬위원회, 5-18 광주 민주화운동자료총서), December 17, 1997, X: 626, 363. (Hereafter GDMM). Gwangju city statistics count over 2,600 people as having died in May 1980, exceeding the monthly average by 2,300 (Christian Institute for the Study of Justice and Development, *Lost Victory*, 30). Gwangju city's death statistics from 1976 to 1983, revealed on the floor of the National Assembly, were an average of 45 people per year from tuberculosis and 151 from "sudden, unnatural deaths" from 1976 to 1978. Both these numbers increased by 2,197, leading to the conclusion that slightly more than three thousand people died during the uprising (See Nicholas D. Kristof, "For Victims of Korea's Ugly Years, A Time to Savor," *New York Times*, December 5, 1995, 3; Tae Yang Kwak, *The Gwangju Massacre and the Politics of Mythmaking* [Chicago: University of Chicago, 1997], 46–49). Ahn Jong-chol, who worked for both the Gwangju city government and national government in Seoul, believes the best numbers are five hundred killed and over three thousand wounded. Once democracy was established in Korea, the government's compensation board awarded money to people who could prove impact. They announced 246 dead, 3,549 arrested, 64 missing. These numbers do not include people like Park Kwan-hyun, leader during the uprising of CNU student government who died of a hunger strike in prison in 1982. Nor do they include many people who simply vanished, or those killed whose families did not want to register with the government. Many eyewitnesses have testified bodies were secretly buried, and others report secret sea burials. Yoon Young-kyu told me that the Mudeung Orphans Center was practically empty after the uprising, and even though it had been previously overflowing, no one made an effort to locate the missing children (interview with Yoon Young-kyu, Gwangju, April 10, 2001). Finally, an application was filed in 2010 to make the uprising part of UNESCO's

world heritage sites in which the following statistics were given: 165 citizens and 27 soldiers were killed in and around Gwangju. Seventy-six people went missing, 3,383 were injured, and 1,476 were arrested. In addition, 102 people later died due to injuries incurred during the events.

2　Lee Jae-eui, *Kwangju Diary: Beyond Death, Beyond the Darkness of the Age* (Los Angeles: UCLA Asian Pacific Monograph Series, 1999). This is the single best primary source in English and I highly recommend it.

3　Other English language sources I have relied on in my research include a collection of foreign journalists' accounts, *Gwangju in the Eyes of the World* (Gwangju Citizens' Solidarity, 1997), an enlarged edition was subsequently published as *The Kwangju Uprising: Eyewitness Press Accounts of Korea's Tiananmen*, edited by Henry Scott-Stokes and Lee Jae-eui (Armonk, NY: M.E. Sharpe, 2000). The above quote is from an article by Bradley Martin, in *The Kwangju Uprising*, 94. Also helpful was *The May 18 Gwangju Democratic Uprising* (May 18th History Compilation Committee of Gwangju City, 1999). Arnold A. Peterson's essay, "5:18 The Kwangju Incident," is contained in 아놀드 A. 피터슨, 5.18 광주사태 (서울: 풀빛, 1995). Last but not least, I have benefited greatly from the May 18 Institute's translation of documents and personal testimonies in 2000 (hereafter referred to in the footnotes as *Documents*). These were available in digital format. In some cases, I have tried to make the translations flow more easily.

4　Choi Jungwoon, *The Gwangju Uprising: The Pivotal Democratic Movement that Changed the History of Modern Korea* (Paramus: Homa and Sekey Books: 2006), 85, 131. In 2003, I met Professor Choi, and he expressed his surprise at the ways in which my concept of the eros effect matched the results of his own empirical investigation into the Gwangju Uprising. His book was translated into English in 2006. After I read it, I couldn't have agreed more with his comparison of our work.

5　Ralph N. Clough, *Embattled Korea: The Rivalry for International Support* (London: Westview Press, 1987), 126.

6　Yoon Han-bong and I discussed this meeting at length in my interview with him on October 29, 2001. As he recalled, five of the eight people at the meeting that night became key activists in the uprising who helped organize the Citizen Student Struggle Committee. One of the people in attendance was Yoon Sang-won. Like many other well-known activists, Yoon Han-bong escaped from the paratroopers' initial invasion. He made his way to the United States, where he organized Young Koreans United with more than a dozen chapters. Also see his book, 윤한봉, 운동화와 똥가방 (서울: 한마당, 1996).

7　Yoon Sang-won was slated to be the Gwangju coordinator.

8　In 1978, farmers in Hampyeong (less than an hour's drive west of Gwangju) piled their sweet potatoes on the roads after the government failed to make good on its promise to buy their harvest. With the help of the Catholic Farmers' Association and popular support, the farmers won their struggle.

9　Interview with Chung Yong-hwa, June 19, 2002.

10　Lee Jae-eui, *Kwangju Diary*, 41.

11　*The May 18 Gwangju Democratic Uprising*, 121.

12　Choi, *The Gwangju Uprising*, 76.

13　Lee Jae-eui, *Kwangju Diary*, 46.

14　Lee, *The Making of Minjung*, 106.

15　*Documents*, 79.

16　Choi, *The Gwangju Uprising*, 95.

17　*The May 18 Gwangju Democratic Uprising*, 127; Choi, *The Gwangju Uprising*, 110.

18　*Documents*, 113.

19　Interview with Chung Oong, Seoul, December 4, 2009.

20   Choi, *The Gwangju Uprising*, 114.

21   Lee Jae-eui, *Kwangju Diary*, 64.

22   Chung Sangyong, Rhyu Simin, et al., *Memories of May 1980: A Documentary History of the Kwangju Uprising in Korea* (Seoul: Korea Democracy Foundation, 2003), 64.

23   *Documents*, 119. Originally published by the Japanese Catholic Association for Peace and Justice.

24   Chung, Rhyu, et al., *Memories of May 1980*, 194.

25   Lee Jae-eui, *Kwangju Diary*, 69.

26   Choi, *The Gwangju Uprising*, 116–17.

27   Lee Jae-eui, *Kwangju Diary*, 70.

28   *The May 18 Gwangju Democratic Uprising*, 138.

29   Interview with Na Il-sung, Gwangju, December 17, 2001; Lee Jae-eui, *Kwangju Diary*, 112.

30   Interview with Kim Kyol, Gwangju, June 14, 2001.

31   Chung, Rhyu, et al., *Memories of May 1980*, 199.

32   Ibid., 201.

33   Interview with Park Tae-bong, May 31, 2002.

34   Na Eui-Kap, "Processing the Gwangju Democratic Uprising," in May 18th History Compilation Committee of Gwangju City, *History of the 5.18 Democratic Uprising*, vol. 1 (Gwangju: The May 18 Memorial Foundation, 2008), 248.

35   Lee Jae-eui, *Kwangju Diary*, 72.

36   May 18 Research Institute, "Manifestos and Declarations" in *Materials Related to the Gwangju Uprising* (Gwangju: Chonnam National University, 1998), 2–126. History-17. 5–18 관련자료의 영어 번역: 5–18 20주년 기념 학술연구사업 연구소위 (Gwangju, 전남대학교 5–18 연구소, 2000).

37   The firing began at 1:00 p.m. sharp on the afternoon of May 21, and at 2:30 p.m. weapons and ammunition were commandeered from the Sampo Branch office of Naju police station, and police boxes at Youngkwang, Keumsung, and Suan. The first groups of armed protesters began firing back at 3:20. Arnold Peterson relates that "at about 2:00 p.m. some of the citizens captured the military arsenal in the town of Hwa Soon, just south of Gwangju. From that time on many of the citizen fighters carried guns" ("5:18 The Kwangju Incident," 44).

38   Interview with Park Nam-son, May 11, 2001.

39   Choi, *The Gwangju Uprising*, 220; 광주오월민중항쟁사료전집, 한국현대사사료연구소 (서울: 풀빛, 1990), 504–7. Once the city was liberated, the team never became a formal part of the structure that emerged in Province Hall. Most members were disarmed by May 26, although some were integrated into the mobile strike units of the Citizens' Army.

40   See, for example, Christopher D. Yoon, "The Kwangju Democratization Movement: U.S. Role During the 1979–1980 Period: Its Impacts and Ramifications," (Master's thesis, Yonsei University, 1994), 21.

41   *The May 18 Gwangju Democratic Uprising*, 143.

42   Lee Jae-eui, *Kwangju Diary*, 77.

43   Choi, *The Gwangju Uprising*, 162.

44   Interview with Song Yon, Seoul, November 30, 2001. Song Yon later founded a Buddhist organization for human rights, Min Tong Yon in Seoul, and went on to help lead June uprising as one of the member groups of the *Kukbon*.

45   Lee Jae-eui, *Kwangju Diary*, 77–78. The movie version of these events, *Operation Fascinating Vacation*, has a middle-aged reserve office become commander of the militia and almost single-handedly defeat the military as he fires a machine gun. Needless to say, the plot transformed the entirety of the uprising from one of

collective-inspired resistance and communal self-government into a "Great Man" version.

46   May 18 Research Institute, "Manifestos and Declarations," 4–24.

47   Interviews with Lee Kwang-young, May 28, 2001, and Lee Jae-eui, April 15, 2008; Linda Lewis, *Laying Claim to the Memory of May: A Look Back at the 1980 Kwangju Uprising* (Honolulu: University of Hawaii Press, 2002), 34.

48   Chung, Rhyu, et al., *Memories of May 1980*, 240–41.

49   GDMM, IV: 82. Others maintain the LMG were never fired. See *Memories*, Sangyong, Simin, et al., *Memories of May 1980*, 241.

50   May 18 Research Institute, "Manifestos and Declarations," 4–7.

51   Chung, Rhyu, et al., *Memories of May 1980*, 246.

52   *Documents*, 67.

53   Quoted in Shin and Hwang, *Contentious Kwangju*, xix.

54   Wickham, *Korea on the Brink*, 130–32.

55   Here in my view is a weakness of Choi Jungwoon's analysis. He believes the absolute community ends once the citizens took up arms to drive the military out of the city and thus excludes the five days of liberation from being worthy of inclusion on the absolute community. "In liberated Gwangju, the absolute community showed cracks and ultimately disintegrated when citizens returned to their daily lives." (See *The Gwangju Uprising*, viii and 126–27).

56   *Documents*, 43.

57   Ahn Jong-chul, "The Citizens' Army During the Gwangju Uprising," in Shin, *Contentious Kwangju*, 14.

58   For a list of these various statements, see Park Chan-Seung, "Manifestos, Statements and Newspapers on the Gwangju Democratic Uprising," in May 18th History Compilation Committee of Gwangju City, *History of the 5.18 Democratic Uprising*, vol. 1 (Gwangju: The May 18 Memorial Foundation, 2008), 392–97.

59   Peterson, "5:18 The Kwangju Incident," 47.

60   *Documents*, 11–12.

61   *Documents*, 113.

62   *Documents*, 127.

63   Interview with Hong Sung-dam, Watertown, MA, October 16, 2003.

64   Japanese and American scholars have claimed that Minjung art's origins are in Japan. See the discussion in Chapter 8.

65   Interview with Kim Sun-chool, Gwangju, May 20, 2003.

66   See Kim Young-khee and Han Sun, "The Gwangju People's Uprising and the Construction of Collective Identity: A Study of the *Fighters' Bulletin*," in *South Korean Democracy: Legacy of the Gwangju Uprising*, eds. George Katsiaficas and Na Kahn-chae (London: Routledge, 2006), 96–112.

67   Chung, Rhyu, et al., *Memories of May 1980*, 323.

68   Interview with Park Nam-son, Gwangju, April 23, 2008.

69   Choi, *The Gwangju Uprising*, 74.

70   Signed by Congregation for the Democratization of Chonnam Province, *Documents*, 58.

71   Lee Jae-eui, *Kwangju Diary*, 105.

72   See his book, *Communication and the Evolution of Society* (Boston: Beacon Press, 1984).

73   Interview with Chong Hyun-ay, July 14, 2008.

74   Choi, *The Gwangju Uprising*, 128, 131. For Choi, the absolute community dissipates once citizens defeated the military (272–73). Choi undervalues the effects of the rallies in liberated Gwangju and pays more attention to the period prior to them.

75   Lee Jae-eui, *Kwangju Diary*, 118.

76   Interview with Chun Yong-ho, Gwangju, June 4, 2008.

77 Choi, *The Gwangju Uprising*, 210–11.

78 Ibid., 212.

79 Lee Jae-eui, *Kwangju Diary*, 117.

80 Chung, Rhyu, et al., *Memories of May 1980*, 253; Lewis, *Laying Claim*, 28.

81 Gwangju City, *Library of Data for the May 18 Gwangju Democratization Movement* vol. v (Gwangju, 1997), 353, as reported in Choi, *The Gwangju Uprising*, 185.

82 Alain Plessis estimates that the number of voters at 230,000 out of 470,000 people who were registered. See *The Rise and Fall of the Second Empire 1852–1871* (Cambridge: Cambridge University Press, 1987), 171

83 Roger L. Williams, *The French Revolution of 1870–1871* (New York: W.W. Norton, 1969), 90, 122, 130.

84 This incident is described in *Documents*, 9–10.

85 Lee Jae-eui, *Kwangju Diary*, 107, says there were fifteen representatives.

86 *The May 18 Gwangju Democratic Uprising*, 164; *Documents*, 72.

87 Lee Jae-eui, *Kwangju Diary*, 137. Interview with Na Il-sung, December 17, 2001.

88 Chung, Rhyu, et al., *Memories of May 1980*, 258.

89 *Documents*, 105.

90 Interview with Lee Sung-sok, October 15, 2001.

91 Interview with Suh Kyong-won, October 20, 2001. During the 1987 June Uprising, he was a representative of the farmers in the *Kukbon*.

92 *Documents*, 61.

93 Interview with Park Haeng-sam, May 16, 2001.

94 Interview with Kim Pyong-yong, Yang Hae-do, Han Kyong-jin, and Yoon Shik, Haenam City Hall, April 21, 2008. They insisted soldiers killed seven people, although the government counted only three. Two of the participants saw bodies airlifted away by helicopter.

95 Ibid.

96 Ahn Song-rae raised this issue at the May Mothers' House, Gwangju, January 12, 2009.

97 See Yea's "Cultural Politics of Place in Gwangju City and South Jeolla Province," in *Contentious Kwangju*.

98 Choi, *The Gwangju Uprising*, 140.

99 *Essays*, 64–65 (see chap. 5, n. 102).

100 *Essays*, 61.

101 Interview with Yoon Young-gyu, December 18, 2001.

102 Peterson, "5:18 The Kwangju Incident," 49.

103 Lewis, *Laying Claim*, 29, 33; Choi, *The Gwangju Uprising*, xvii, 184.

104 Interview with Lee Jae-eui, April 15, 2008.

105 GDMM IX: 219. (80Seoul 006522). The figures given by ROK Command HQ also went on to delineate among the vehicles eighty-nine jeeps, fifty trucks, forty wreckers, forty buses, ten dump trucks, and eight tear-gas-firing jeeps that had been commandeered. *Kwangju Uprising: Eyewitness Press Accounts*, 82.

106 See Gleysteen, *Massive Entanglement*, 135.

107 Tim Shorrock's groundbreaking articles in 1996 were based on documents he obtained individually known as the Cherokee Files. The more than three thousand pages of documents obtained by the city of Gwangju provide an even more detailed understanding of U.S. policymakers' actions and thinking in this period. See Tim Shorrock, "Debacle in Kwangju: Were Washington's cables read as a green light for the 1980 Korean massacre?" *Nation*, December 9, 1996, http://base21.jinbo.net/show/show.php?p_docnbr=20896.

108 GDMM IX: 235: 80Seoul 006610.

109 Choi, *The Gwangju Uprising*, 15.

110 Interview with Kim Chang-gil, October 25, 2001.

111 Lee Jae-eui, *Kwangju Diary*, 112.

112 Lewis, *Laying Claim*, 35–37.

113 Chung, Rhyu, et al., *Memories of May 1980*, 316; Choi estimated the number of arms returned at 4,000 guns and 1,000 grenades (*The Gwangju Uprising*, 195). Lee counted the total number of arms seized by the militia as 2,240 carbines, 1,225 M-1 rifles, 57 pistols, dozens of M-60 machine guns, 2 light machine guns, many hand grenades, 46,400 rounds of ammunition, 4 boxes of TNT, 100 detonators, 5 armored vehicles, and many army jeeps, trucks, radios, and gas masks. Also see Lewis, *Laying Claim*, 27.

114 Chung, Rhyu, et al., *Memories of May 1980*, 317.

115 American anthropologist Linda Lewis and her mother waited in line forty minutes to attend a session of the ten minute memorial service. See Lewis, *Laying Claim*, 50.

116 Interview with Jeong Hae-jik, April 23, 2001.

117 Chung, Rhyu, et al., *Memories of May 1980*, 327 says fifty thousand. Lee Jae-eui, (*Kwangju Diary*, 120) states the number as one hundred thousand.

118 Interview with Jeong Hae-jik and Na Il-sung, April 30, 2008; interview with Chun Yong-ho, June 4, 2008.

119 Lee Jae-eui, *Kwangju Diary*, 129.

120 Chun Yong-ho quoted in *Kwangju in the Eyes of the World*, 88. At the beginning of May, Yoon had agreed to become a regional staff person for the National Democratic Workers' League, slated to launch on May 22. Once the uprising broke out, he threw himself into it.

121 Interview with Chun Yong Ho, November 29, 1999.

122 Interview with Kim Tae-chan, November 22, 2001.

123 Interview with Kim Jeong-bae, November 27, 2001.

124 *Documents*, 31.

125 *Documents*, 68.

126 See Lee's analysis as well as the insightful criticisms written two years after the uprising by the Gwangju Citizens' Movement for Democracy (*Documents*, 133). In my view, such organization needs to be decentralized for many reasons, chief among them being the ease with which centralized organizations are decapitated. For more discussion, see chapter 5 of *The Imagination of the New Left*.

127 *Fighters' Bulletin*, May 23, *Documents*, 71.

128 May 18 Symposium, November 23, 2001.

129 Interview with Park Nam-son, April 23, 2008.

130 GDMM IX: 323–24.

131 *The May 18 Gwangju Democratic Uprising*, 174–75.

132 Choi, *The Gwangju Uprising*, 218–19.

133 Lee Jae-eui, *Kwangju Diary*, 126.

134 May 18 Research Institute, "Manifestos and Declarations," 4–26; Sangyong, Simin, et al., *Memories of May 1980*, 278.

135 See Lee Jae-eui, *Kwangju Diary*, 103, 115, 133.

136 윤기현 testimony in 박병기 엮음 , 5.18연구소 자료총서 3, 5.18항쟁 증언자료집 3 (2003) 전남대학교 출판부, 136.

137 In 2008 at a Seoul conference on 5.18, Lee Jin-kyong showed how those who fought for liberation in Gwangju were the core of those who didn't favor settlement, while those who did not fight favored settlement. 이진경, 조원광. '단절의 혁명, 무명의 혁명' "5.18정신"을 다시 생각한다-새로운 성찰적 시각에서.

138 Interview with Lee Jae-eui, April 2008.

139 Interviews with Oh Kyong-min, April 25, 2001, and Gu Song-ju, October 3, 2001.

140 In December 2008, I was honored to be invited to a dinner meeting of former fighters.

Despite the passage of more than 28 years, during which enormous political differences surfaced among them, they still retained a strong solidarity. In a sense, one could say that remnants of the "absolute community" still exist, that the bonding of 1980 galvanized an eternal feeling of community.

141 Lee Jae-eui, in *Kwangju Diary*, says thirteen teams (133). Park Nam-son told me there were about twenty teams. See also Sangyong, Simin, et al., *Memories of May 1980*, 355; and Choi, *The Gwangju Uprising*, 221.

142 See the discussion in Choi, *The Gwangju Uprising*, 126–27, 132, 163.

143 Interviews with Jeong Hae-jik, October 1, 2008, and Yoon Young-kyu.

144 Interview with Jeong Hae-jik and Na Il-sung, Gwangju, April 30, 2008.

145 Lee Jae-eui, *Kwangju Diary*, 107.

146 *Fighters' Bulletin* No. 5, May 23, *Documents*, 71.

147 Peterson, "5:18 The Kwangju Incident," 44.

148 Shin, *Contentious Kwangju*, xix, 23.

149 Lee Jae-eui, *Kwangju Diary*, 72.

150 Linda Lewis and Ju-na Byun in Shin, 55.

151 First pointed out to me in interview with Chong Hyun-ay, October 28, 2001.

152 Interviews with Oh Kyong-min, Jung Hyang-ja and Im Chun-hee, and Chong Hyun-ay were essential to my understanding of these dimensions of the uprising.

153 Jang Ha-Jin, "The Gwangju Democratic Uprising and Women," *History of the 5.18 Democratic Uprising*, 1:465.

154 Discussions with Dr. Kang Hyun-ah were very helpful in understanding this issue.

155 See Jang, "The Gwangju Democratic Uprising and Women," 471–473 for discussion.

156 Interview with Im Chun-hee, December 21, 2001.

157 Anonymous interview (name withheld for privacy), November 7, 2001.

158 In an interview on October 28, 2001, Chong Hyun-ay reported that she met ten women who had been arrested in Province Hall while she was imprisoned at Sangmudae after May 27.

159 See Kang Hyun-ah, "Women's Experiences in the Gwangju Uprising: Participation and Exclusion," in *South Korean Democracy: Legacy of the Gwangju Uprising*.

160 Kim Myung-hye, "Family Life and Women's Participation in Social Movements in Gwangju," *Korea Journal* 41, no. 4 (Winter 2001): 74–94.

161 Jang, "The Gwangju Democratic Uprising and Women," 466.

162 Journalists' recollections are contained in a highly readable book, *The Kwangju Uprising: Eyewitness Press Accounts of Korea's Tiananmen*, edited by Henry Scott-Stokes and Lee Jae-eui (Armonk, NY: M.E. Sharpe, 2000). See especially Bradley Martin's chapter, "Yun Sang Won: The Knowledge in those Eyes," for his account of Yoon Sang-won's press conference.

163 Choi, *The Gwangju Uprising*, 199.

164 GDMM IX: 254. (80State 138557).

165 GDMM IX: 257. (80Seoul 006660).

166 May 18 Research Institute, "Manifestos and Declarations," 2–14.

167 Lee Jae-eui, *Kwangju Diary*, 136.

168 See the chart in Chung, Rhyu, et al., *Memories of May 1980*, 360–61.

169 Interview with Chung Sangyong, October 17, 2001.

170 Interviews with Gu Song-ju, October 10, 2001, Chung Sangyong, October 17, 2001, Chong Hyun-ay, October 28, 2001.

CHAPTER 7

Neoliberalism and the Gwangju Uprising

U.S. businessmen are cautious over the long-term stability of
the ROK but less concerned over democratic development. If the
military leadership can develop an apparently stable structure and
reinvigorate the economy, then U.S. business and banking circles
will be prepared to go back to business as usual.
> —William Gleysteen, U.S. ambassador to Korea, June 6, 1980

We would like to have a complete democracy with full and open
debate, free press, and elected leaders. The Koreans are not ready
for that.
> —Jimmy Carter, U.S. president, August 21, 1980

CHRONOLOGY OF U.S. INVOLVEMENT IN THE GWANGJU MASSACRE	
February 1979	Secretary of State Vance cabled U.S. Ambassador Gleysteen that U.S. goals were to gain a "maximum U.S. share of economic benefits from economic relations with increasingly prosperous South Korea."
October 26, 1979	Park Chung-hee assassinated.
November 4, 1979	U.S. embassy in Iran seized by students: sixty-six U.S. diplomats and citizens held until January 1981. (In January 1979, the Iranian revolution overthrew the Shah.)
November 29, 1979	U.S. Ambassador Gleysteen: "Yet, there have also been ample reminders that this society of garlic and pepper eating combatants has not changed its basic nature. Dissident elements and some of the political opposition,

	grooved over decades into extremist patterns by confron-tation with authority, have rejected the acting govern-ment's proposed scenario for reform and reiterated their extremist demands for immediate dismantling of the *yushin* system."
December 8, 1979	Cable from Assistant Secretary of State Richard Holbrooke to Gleysteen: "nobody wants another Iran"; tell Christians they "should not expect long-term support"; in early November, Holbrooke blamed potential polarization on a "handful of Christian extremist dissidents."
December 12, 1979	Chun Doo-hwan seizes power.
December 25, 1979	Soviets invade Afghanistan.
February 1980	The United States knew Chun had mobilized Special Warfare Command troops, trained to fight behind the lines in North Korea, to repress dissent in Gwangju.[1]
April 16, 1980	Sec. Vance cable: "great satisfaction over the many positive developments."
May 8, 1980	U.S. Defense Intelligence Agency (DIA) reports to the Joint Chiefs of Staff (JCS) that that the Seventh Special Forces Brigade (responsible for worst brutalities in Gwangju) "was probably targeted against unrest at Chonju and Gwangju universities."
May 8, 1980	Gleysteen to Washington, D.C.: reports ROK Special Forces moved "to cope with possible student demonstrations."
May 9, 1980	Gleysteen meets with Chun Doo-hwan in same safe house where Park Chung-hee was assassinated: United States does not oppose South Korean "contingency plans to main-tain law and order, if absolutely necessary, by reinforcing the police with the army."
May 9, 1980	State Dept. and DIA cables: United States gives proper approval to Chun to use military on student demonstrations.
May 10, 1980	Dep. Sec. of State Christopher to Gleysteen: "We should not oppose ROK plans to reinforce the police with the army."
May 16, 1980	U.S. Commanding Gen. Wickham releases Twentieth Division from U.S. operational control after "consulting with his own superiors in Washington."
May 19, 1980	Wickham to D.C.: "The only issues are the speed of con-solidating power and the form in which it takes";[2] goes to DEFCON 3 alert.
May 21, 1980	Gleysteen to D.C.: "The massive insurrection in Gwangju is still out of control and poses an alarming situation"; "large mob has gained temporary run of the city"

May 21, 1980	DIA officer: "U.S. decision to release ROK OPCON forces for riot duty in Gwangju had greatly increased the anti-American mood."
May 22, 1980	Gleysteen to D.C.: Gwangju "turned completely into a scene of horrors . . . Rioters were reported firing on helicopters overhead."[3]
May 22, 1980	U.S. DOD spokesperson: Gen. Wickham "has accepted and agreed to the request by the Korean government to allow the use of certain selected Korean armed forces under his operational control in operations to subdue the crowds."
May 22, 1980	White House meeting approves suppression of Gwangju (fear of general uprising against the military): "there was general agreement that the first priority was the restoration of order in Gwangju"; simultaneously approves visit to Seoul by John Moore, president of U.S. Export-Import Bank, to arrange financing of Seoul subway construction and nuclear power plant.
May 23, 1980	Gleysteen calls for "firm anti-riot measures" in visit to acting ROK PM; he noted that: "we are doing all we can to contribute to the restoration of order, citing the statement issued in Washington and our affirmative replies when asked to 'chop' CFC forces to Korean command for use in Gwangju."[4]
May 23, 1980	U.S. State Department spokesperson Hodding Carter announces that the Carter administration "has decided to support the restoration of security and order in South Korea while deferring pressure for political liberalization."
May 24, 1980	U.S. asks ROK to postpone suppression of Gwangju until arrival of USS *Coral Sea*.
May 25, 1980	Secretary Muskie cables: "The situation in Gwangju has taken a rather grim turn." According to his sources: "the moderate citizens' committee has lost control of the situation and the radicals appear to be in charge. Peoples courts have been set up and some executions have taken place. Student demonstrators have been largely replaced by unidentified armed radicals who are talking of setting up a revolutionary government."[5]
May 26, 1980	Gleysteen to D.C.: Situation in Gwangju "took a sharp turn for the worse. There were reports of vigilante groups, recovery by radicals of weapons turned in earlier, and even of people's courts and executions."[6]
May 26, 1980	Gleysteen asked to mediate by Gwangju spokesperson; declines.
May 27, 1980	ROK Army retakes Gwangju.

June 21, 1980	Deputy Secretary of State Warren Christopher to Holbrooke: Chun needs "implementation of sensible economic policies."
April 1982	Wickham accused by Christian leaders in Korea of making speech referring to the Koreans as "lemming-like" who will follow any leader.
June 19, 1989	State Department White Paper: United States "did not know in advance that Special Forces were being sent to Gwangju."
December 1995	Special Law on Gwangju Uprising
March 11, 1996	Chun Doo-hwan and Roh Tae-woo trial begins (initial verdict August 26; final verdict in April 1997).
1996	Survey finds 82.5 percent Gwangju people believe United States was involved; 50.8 percent for the rest of South Koreans. Further, 44.5 percent want U.S. apology; 21.8 percent think United States should pay reparations.
May 18, 2002	Jimmy Carter and seven other U.S. officials found guilty by a Peoples Tribunal of crimes against humanity for violation of the civil rights of the people of Gwangju.
October 11, 2002	Jimmy Carter wins Nobel Peace Prize; Nobel Committee praised Carter's decades of "untiring effort to find peaceful solutions to international conflicts, to advance democracy and human rights, and to promote economic and social development."

CONTEMPORARY SOUTH KOREAN anti-Americanism appeared after the Gwangju Uprising—and for good reason. The U.S. government aided and actively abetted Chun Doo-hwan in suppressing the uprising and helped stabilize his government afterward. In 1980, popular intuition in South Korea sensed the role of the United States. If the exact reasons were not immediately apparent, U.S. support for Chun was clear enough.

The rationales for U.S. encouragement of the suppression of the Gwangju Uprising are commonly understood in terms of national security—avoiding a "second Iran" (where American hostages and the U.S. embassy were still held by radicals in May 1980), preventing the debacle of "another Vietnam" (which had "fallen" only five short years earlier), repelling a possible North Korean threat, responding to the Soviet invasion of Afghanistan on December 25, 1979, or stopping the threatened nationwide uprising against the military that loomed in 1980. My reading of thousands of pages of official U.S. documents clarifies that the chief perceived threat articulated by the U.S. government in 1980 was none of the above—but rather of a capital flight by U.S. investors who worried that the ROK government might prove unstable after Park Chung-hee's assassination and the uprising in Gwangju. To mollify U.S. banks, U.S. officials needed to demonstrate regime stability in 1980, and they did so by endorsing Chun's dictatorship.

In a phrase, the United States subordinated the human rights of Korean people—and its own professed concern for human rights—to the economic interests of American corporations. As in Chile in 1973 and Turkey in 1980, a neoliberal accumulation regime was imposed through the mechanism of a military coup. The suppression of Gwangju was thus a part of global implementation of U.S. economic policy, and Chun's attempt to suppress the truth about the massacre also involved hiding the economic process at work.

The Economic Transition

The recession of 1979 ushered in a new post-Keynesian era in the global economy. Stagflation—high unemployment with high inflation—required different economic policies than those developed to deal with the Great Depression. In 1979, as the U.S. recession intensified and unemployment rose, interest rates skyrocketed above 20 percent amid double-digit inflation. Half a century of an inverse relationship of unemployment and inflation gave way to a new dilemma posed by their simultaneous coexistence. Once President Ronald Reagan took office, he began to demolish decades old government programs and to privatize anything and everything. Phrases like "Reaganomics" and "trickle-down" or "supply-side" economics were used for these new policies; in retrospect, these were early formulations for what is today regarded as neoliberalism—or a market-based, globally oriented economy (in contrast to a Keynesian state-guided, developmental one). Sometimes referred to as neoclassical economics, neoliberalism harks back to an earlier period of capitalist accumulation during which government involvement was minimized as the "free market" and "invisible hand" were preeminent—except when the need arose for military intervention on behalf of business and commercial interests. Modern neoliberalism's attacks on social programs considers government spending wasteful, but like classical liberalism exempts military expenditures—in fact, the modern version insists the military be expanded as rapidly as possible since the contemporary economic behemoth depends so centrally on war and weapons production.

Beginning in 1983, when Ronald Reagan was throwing money into a military buildup greater than that of any previous U.S. president, he did do so as a part of a "crusade" to foster free market democracies through the "magic of the marketplace."[7] Beginning with the Reagan-Thatcher era, neoliberal policies axing government social programs for ordinary citizens reigned supreme until the 2008 economic crisis threatened to engulf the capitalist system. Only then did mammoth government expenditures come to the assistance of giant banks and corporations all over the world—along with a pittance for the poor. Like a flying buttress, these emergency measures prop up an inherently unstable main structure, a global financial architecture that systematically goes from crisis to crisis.

In 1979, economic crisis undermined Park Chung-hee's developmental state, through which the ROK had nurtured indigenous *chaebol* and sheltered much of its economy from foreign firms and global market forces. Park's campaign to develop heavy industry relied upon monetary expansion, and the resulting inflation meant an 18 percent rise in consumer prices in 1979, a 30 percent increase

TABLE 7.1 **Korea's Economic Performance, 1978–1991**

	1978	1979	1980	1981	1982	1983	1984	1985	1986	1987	1988	1989	1990	1991
Inflation	14.5	18.3	28.7	21.3	7.2	3.4	2.3	2.5	2.8	3.0	7.1	5.7	8.6	9.7
GDP Growth	11.0	7.0	-3.3	6.9	7.4	12.1	9.2	6.9	12.3	11.8	11.4	6.1	9.0	8.4
Real Wages	20.8	10.9	-4.4	-1.6	4.6	5.9	9.1	4.8	2.7	13.6	10.6	18.8	-1.1	na

Sources: World Bank; IMF; Stephen Haggard and Robert Kaufman, *The Political Economy of Democratic Transitions* (Princeton: Princeton University Press, 1995), 84, 92, 237.

in 1980. With the economy's output falling and real wages declining, 1979 and 1980 marked Korea's worst economic performance since the Korean War. At the same time, the global oil crisis drove up the cost of imports, and the country's exports slowed. In April 1979, Park Chung-hee announced an economic stabilization plan and requested IMF assistance after the second oil shock rocked the Korean economy, but his assassination prevented any major policy shift.[8] The handwriting was on the wall: the global economy necessitated the dismantling of the developmental state. As indicated in TABLE 7.1, the ROK's economy contracted in 1980 for the first time in a decade. Ominously, international investors became circumspect about loans.

As early as September 11, 1979, Gleysteen had come to the conclusion that some kind of transition was urgently needed: "The present predicament of the Korean economy suggests that 12 and 16 percent growth rates to which we have gotten used in Korea overstrained the capacity of even this hard-working society and resulted in a number of structural imbalances. As the focus shifts to expensive capital-intensive industry, and the competitive advantage of labor-intensive industry passes to other countries, Korea will need to pay more attention to economic and financial soundness than to growth for growth [sic] sake. Korea would be well advised to seek cooperative relationships with American and other foreign firms."[9] In 1980, the Korean economy's significance for the United States was substantial. In Gleysteen's words, "In our preoccupation with the security relationship, we should not forget that economic and commercial ties have taken on an enormous importance over the years. In 1979, Korea was our thirteenth largest trading partner, absorbing about $4.2 billion in U.S. exports, while accounting for $4.1 billion in U.S. imports."[10]

So troubling was the economy that on May 30, 1980, three days after the army bloodily retook Gwangju, Gleysteen wrote an article for *Nation's Business*, the national magazine of the U.S. Chamber of Commerce, and he did not even mention the uprising. Instead, he spelled out U.S. plans for Korea's economy: "The next crucial step in the country's economic development—liberalization of the economy from tight central control to a greater reliance on market forces—is one which has been accepted in principle and is being pursued as conditions permit." His language explicitly named the need for a shift from "central control" to "market forces" (that is, to neoliberalism). By linking the onset of "economic liberalization" and the ascendancy of "market" forces to the 1980 massacre in Gwangju, Gleysteen brought a whole new understanding to the meaning of the suppression of the Gwangju Uprising: it marked the bloody beginning of the imposition of a neoliberal accumulation regime onto Korea.

Origins of Neoliberalism

Contrary to the idea that neoliberalism began in the 1990s, its origins lie in the 1970s. After Chile's bloody coup of 1973, economist Milton Friedman made that country his test case, and it soon became an example of what David Harvey called "pure neoliberal practices after 1975." Nobel Prizes in economics were awarded to Friedrich von Hayek in 1974 and Milton Friedman in 1976, thereby legitimating monetarist neoliberal thought. In 1973, John D. Rockefeller III penned his famous lines calling for a "New American Century" in which the world would benefit from global free trade if only governments would stop interfering.[11] With such rhetoric of "freeing" people from onerous government, he advocated rolling back government social programs, which had been enacted in response to the Great Depression.

By recycling petrodollars deposited by oil producers in New York banks, David Rockefeller (one of John's four brothers) and his associates moved aggressively to lend money to developing countries, trapping them in credit markets from which they could not escape. Debt is a key means by which neoliberalism traps countries in a web of dependency and external control. In this venture to expand operations, New York bankers won active support from the U.S. government. From 1980 to 2002, the debt of the developing world rose from $580 billion to $2.4 trillion. As David Harvey put it: "The New York investment banks had always been active internationally, but after 1973 they became even more so, though now far more focused on lending capital to foreign governments. This required the liberalization of international credit and financial markets, and the U.S. government began actively to promote and support this strategy in the 1970s."[12]

Korea was no exception. In the first four years of Chun's government, the country's foreign debt more than doubled, giving South Korea the dubious distinction of fourth place among the world's debtor nations behind Argentina, Brazil, and Mexico.[13]

TABLE 7.2 **South Korean Foreign Debt, 1975–1987**

Year	Foreign Debt ($billion)
1975	8.46
1976	10.53
1977	12.65
1978	14.87
1979	20.29
1980	27.17
1981	32.43
1982	37.08
1983	40.38
1984	43.05
1985	46.76
1986	44.51
1987	35.57

Sources: Economic Planning Board, Bank of Korea; Martin Hart-Landsberg, *The Rush to Development: Economic Change and Political Struggle in South Korea* (New York: Monthly Review Press, 1993), 146.

In 1979, "a dramatic consolidation of neoliberalism" occurred in both the U.S. and UK (then under Margaret Thatcher).[14] Immanuel Wallerstein dated neoliberalism's origin to this period.[15] Latin America expert James Petras dated "the first phase of neoliberalism" there to the 1970s and to 1980 in Turkey. The first phase of neoliberalism "took place shortly after military coups" and was accompanied by "massive corruption, crisis, deepening inequalities, and the emergence of a kleptocratic state."[16]

In the latter part of the twentieth century, neoliberal policy functioned as a vehicle for the penetration of economies by U.S. financial interests, as much as for industrial ones. Pulling Korea along into the "New American Century," U.S. policymakers turned their backs on political liberalization at the same moment as they elevated U.S. economic interests to the top of Korean priorities. The key event was the White House meeting at 4 p.m. on May 22 when top decision-makers agreed to suppress the Gwangju Uprising and have Chun agree to U.S. funding for expansion of Seoul's subway system and for Westinghouse being awarded a contract to construct a nuclear power plant (as mentioned in the previous chapter). At the same time as they sanctioned the suppression of the Gwangju Uprising, they simultaneously authorized the June visit to Seoul by John Moore, president of the U.S. Export-Import Bank to make these arrangements so Chun would award such contracts to U.S. firms, rather than to Japanese ones. At the end of 1980, Japanese investments were 53.7 percent of accumulated foreign investments in Korea while those from the United States comprised only 20.4 percent.[17] Like decades later in Iraq, U.S. economic interests were seldom in the public spotlight, but buried beneath security concerns.

The United States encouraged Chun to provide stability for business reasons, and Chun stepped up his dictatorial measures. The month after the uprising, thousands of government workers and employees in state-owned enterprises were summarily fired, as were hundreds of officials from Korea's banking sector, including at least 230 economic officials at the rank of director-general or above. Also summarily fired were more than ninety high-ranking police officials whose loyalty was uncertain. Soon, the new military authorities dismissed 1,819 employees in state-owned enterprises, including 39 presidents or vice presidents, 128 members of boards of directors (an astonishing 22.5 percent of the nationwide total),[18] and an additional 431 officials from Korea's banking sector. On June 6, 1980, Gleysteen telegrammed Washington with an assessment of the public mood in Korea that echoed Gen. John Reed Hodge's analogy to a volcano in 1945: "The current situation is very analogous to Mount St. Helens. There have been two serious eruptions, the students in Seoul and the citizens in Gwangju, and a thin lava dome composed of strong military control, extreme caution, and a degree of emotional exhaustion has been formed. How long this will hold, given the continued subterranean rumblings in the society, is by no means certain."[19] In the same telegram, the U.S. ambassador candidly assessed U.S. businessmen's lack of concern with democracy and the need for stability, after which "U.S. business and banking circles will be prepared to go back to business as usual."[20] To help allay investor fears, Chun dined on June

13, 1980, with leaders of the American Chamber of Commerce in Korea, including the president of 3-M and representatives of Bank of America, Dow Chemical, and Gulf Oil.

That summer was long and hot for embassy officials as they scurried to get the new regime approved. On August 2, the largest U.S. banks (Bank of America, Chase Manhattan Bankers Trust, Chemical Bank, Hanover and Citibank) hesitated on future medium- and short-term loans. Korea Electrical Company could not obtain commercial loans for nuclear power plants 7 and 8. Chun again moved even more harshly against his opponents, ordering forty-six thousand people to be taken into custody, more than half of whom were either sent to "purification" camps (삼청교육대 or "Samcheong Education Camps"), the front lines, or jail. The official total of people sent to these reeducation camps reached 67,055. At least fifty-two people died in these camps; hundreds more died early deaths due to the brutality they suffered in them; and 2,768 reported physical disabilities due to their harsh treatment.[21]

Satisfied with Chun's capacity to provide stability, U.S. investors flocked to Korea. The centerpiece of investor approval of the new regime came on September 22, when the *New York Times* ran a photo of David Rockefeller shaking hands with a smiling Chun. Three days later, the government announced new policies relaxing foreign investments and permitting non-Korean ownership of everything from land to companies. Common to all neoliberal regimes is repression of the labor movement, and Chun excelled in this effort, sending thousands to jail and tens of thousands more to "purification camps." As a consequence, the number of unions fell precipitously from 6,011 before May 1980 to 2,618 by the end of the year.[22] Even with the unions decimated by December, Chun made it illegal to go on strike without government authorization.

New labor laws made regional and district unions illegal. All 109 regional offices of the FKTU were shut down, over four thousand regional branch offices abolished, and hundreds of officials driven out. At Peace Market, the Cheonggye Garment Workers' Union (created after Chun Tae-il's death in 1970) was declared illegal because it only existed in Seoul; twenty-one leaders went for help to the Asian-American Free Labor Institute, an AFL-CIO organization. When the director refused to assist them, they took him hostage and barricaded the office. Around midnight, police broke in and arrested all the unionists—except for two union members who jumped from a window to their deaths.[23] Even though Korean factory workers already suffered one of the longest workweeks in the world, its length in manufacturing was extended from an average of 53.1 hours per week in 1980 to 54.5 by 1986.[24] Unions were systematically destroyed, and the industrial accident rate skyrocketed. Following the Japanese model of exporting labor, Chun's economic development scheme sent more than 293,000 men overseas to work—more than a quarter of the entire male workforce in manufacturing.[25]

A cold-blooded dictator whose favoritism enriched his family and friends, Chun quickly amassed a huge fortune. His younger brother's connections to the Yakuza in Japan through the mafia of Korea[26] joined a long string of Japanese collaborators rising to the highest levels of power in South Korea: Park Chung-hee,

Chun, and since 2008, Lee Myung-bak (born in Japan)—all beholden to imperial masters there and in the United States.

The method to Chun's madness was that the more he enacted dictatorial measures, the better the Americans liked him since they believed he could provide them with the stability needed to maintain a favorable investment climate. At the same time as he ordered tens of thousands of people arrested, the more the United States drew him closer, the more he enriched himself and his collabora-tors—all of whom became enormously wealthy. His younger brother, or "little Chun," had strong ties to Korean gangs. Officially, he was put in charge of rural public works programs—at least until the murder with fish knives of four rival gang members (after which he took up a position at Harvard's Kennedy School of Government).[27] Estimates of money his family is still hiding exceed hundreds of millions of dollars. In 1997, Korean courts ordered Chun to repay 220 billion won (then approximately $200 million).[28] Chun pleaded poverty, claiming he had less than the equivalent of U.S. $300 to his name. Chun gorged himself at the ox of Korea's economy, amassing a family fortune that approached (some say sur-passed) a billion dollars.[29] As he did so, he compliantly implemented economic policies favorable to U.S. investors. When growth finally resumed, the rates of real wage increases were much lower than even under Park Chung-hee.[30]

Relying upon the active guidance of a set of pro-U.S. technocrats, including his closest American associate, CIA station chief Robert G. Brewster, his "liberali-zation" measures delighted foreign investors. Lest international investors again panic, Chun even reined in his attempt to execute Kim Dae Jung. Chun's regime was cut from the same cloth as Pinochet's Chile (guided by Milton Friedman and the "Chicago boys") and Turkey's military regime of the 1980s (which also befriended U.S. businessmen as it attacked the labor movement). Like these other U.S.-backed dictatorships that imposed neoliberal accumulation regimes, Chun installed men friendly to American business interests in place of Park's old developmental-state Koreans. Chun's people paved the way for Korea's integra-tion into and subordination to the ranks of developed nations, and like military governments in Chile and Turkey "did not leave power until they had made exten-sive adjustments in the economy and deep changes in the structure of the political system."[31] By making Korea's economic recovery contingent upon foreign inves-tors and an increasingly internationalized capital market, Chun set a course that led straight into the disastrous financial crisis of 1997 and economic problems that continue to plague Korea.

Despite the change in the U.S. administration after the elections in 1980, the White House continued its approval of the new dictatorship in Korea. In appre-ciation of his solid support from U.S. backers, Chun commuted Kim Dae Jung's death sentence, lifted martial law, and was invited to visit Nancy and Ronald Reagan—all within a forty-eight-hour period.

As one of the first foreign heads of state to visit Reagan's White House, Chun was greeted in an elaborate ceremony, understood in Korea as a highly visible endorsement of his regime, even though he had not yet been officially elected president under the country's new constitution.

U.S. President Ronald Reagan greeted South Korean dictator Chun Doo-hwan in the White House in 1981. Credit: May 18 Memorial Foundation

U.S. Support for Suppression of Gwangju

If uprisings are a prism through which to glimpse essential (though normally hidden) contours of the social landscape, the Gwangju Uprising provides a visceral case in point, as it reveals in stark outline U.S. economic interests, thereby contradicting decades of public U.S. promises of support for human rights. Popular intuition comprehended U.S. support for Chun, and anti-Americanism immediately swept South Korea. At the time, U.S. officials complained that they were being falsely accused of support for Chun, yet in the intervening years, documentary proof of the accuracy of people's intuition has been uncovered in internal memoranda of the U.S. government. My primary sources are official U.S. cables and communications, thousands of pages of which were released to the city of Gwangju under the auspices of the Freedom of Information Act.[32]

Although U.S. officials and Chun all justified their actions as responses to North Korea, internal government documents make clear that there was little or no North Korean threat to peace during the Gwangju Uprising. Rather than blaming North Korea for the 1980 uprising (as the Chun Doo-hwan government did), U.S. documents indicate a far more accurate understanding of the problems caused by Chun's new military regime. Indeed, Gleysteen noted how the dearth of accurate information in the South Korean media during May 1980 turned many people into regular listeners of Radio Pyongyang: "The Gwangju incident has increased the ability of the North to gain listeners for its propaganda broadcasting . . . In light of the paucity of information in the ROK media, the North became the sole source for many here [in South Korea] of news from that area. These new listeners may well continue to tune their radios to Pyongyang in the privacy of their rooms after midnight."[33] Activist Lee Yang-hyun confirmed to me that he evacuated Gwangju when the fighting began but returned after hearing on Radio Pyongyang that the military had been driven out of the city.[34] If anything, U.S. documents indicate the possibility of *improved* relations with North Korea in this time period, not a stepping up of the latter's subversive activities in the South. In its weekly status report on September 13, 1980, the State Department cabled the U.S. embassy in Seoul that "North Korea continues to signal a desire to expand contacts with us . . . to 'build a rainbow bridge' between the United States and North Korea, which 'spans the past troubled relations to a future of good friendly relations.'"[35]

Buried beneath decades of public tensions between the United States and the DPRK, the successful imposition of U.S. economic interests on a subordinate ROK has been overlooked as a factor in U.S. support for Chun in 1980—and in the sustenance of subsequent South Korean anti-Americanism. As is their mission, U.S. officials working out of the embassy in Seoul clearly understand their goal as facilitating the interests of U.S. investors and corporations; the more they have succeeded in this endeavor, especially when it is perceived to be at the expense of South Koreans' human rights and economic well-being, the greater subsequent anti-American sentiment has become. U.S. documents reveal a close degree of coordination between government officials and businessmen, particularly in August 1980, when this collaboration approached surprising synchronicity. Embassy officials were acutely aware of the need to demonstrate regime stability in South Korea in 1980; regime stability left the United States with little choice but to endorse Chun's rule and to agree in advance with his suppression of the Gwangju Uprising.

U.S. coordination in this period is impressive. A few hours after the extraordinary White House gathering on May 22 that approved suppression of the uprising, on May 23, 1980, in Seoul, Gleysteen requested and was granted a meeting with Korean Prime Minister Park Choong-hoon, in which the U.S. ambassador acknowledged that "firm anti-riot measures were necessary."[36] That same day in Washington, State Department spokesperson Hodding Carter announced publicly that the Carter administration "has decided to support the restoration of security and order in South Korea while deferring pressure for political liberalization."[37] When the choice between human rights and U.S. investors' needs had to be made, the United States sacrificed human rights.[38] President Carter was even more explicit: he told CNN television on May 31 that security interests must sometimes override human rights concerns.[39]

U.S. economic interests are not simply those of transnational capital in general, nor are interests of U.S. corporations identical with investors based in France, Germany, or Japan. In 1980, the expression, "export-subsidy war with Europe and Japan," was recited recurrently in U.S. documents. France was in close pursuit of nuclear power contracts for reactors 9 and 10,[40] and the U.S. embassy worried that the contracts for these multi-billion-dollar projects might be awarded to French companies—as they eventually were. Gleysteen also called for attention to German (Siemens) pressure on a looming telecommunications contract for which the stakes were enormous: "The American job potential for this job alone is close to 30,000 man-years."[41]

Financing the huge capital expenditures for nuclear power plants was what U.S. Export-Import Bank (Eximbank) President John Moore's June 1980 visit was intended to facilitate. The burgeoning and militant anti-nuclear-power movement in the United States had curtailed all new orders for domestic plants, and South Korea became a convenient solution to the problem of Westinghouse's surplus production capacity. Already, the ROK was Eximbank's biggest borrower. Bechtel had written Korea Electric Company's loan applications to Eximbank.[42] Westinghouse and the nuclear industry stood to gain tens of billions of dollars in contracts for nuclear power plants 7 and 8 alone. Less than a week after the slaughter in Gwangju, Moore went to Seoul to lobby for Westinghouse. In their June 3 meeting with Prime Minister Park, Moore and Gleysteen assured the PM that even though noncompetitive contracts had been awarded to U.S. firms, "Korea had received the best product at the best price from the United States."[43] Within two weeks, arrangements were finalized for more than $600 million in loans to Chun's regime. Soon thereafter, Japan also arranged very favorable terms on a much larger $4 billion loan to Chun.[44] At that time, Japan's aid was more than 12 percent of Korea's net external debt and more than 5 percent of its GDP. These assistance packages from the United States and Japan essentially guaranteed Chun's regime its existence—and Korea's dependency on imperial finances.

In this same period, California and Gulf Coast agribusiness wanted to unload their surplus of medium grain rice to Korea—imports the ROK desperately needed because of the terrible harvest in 1980. Just before the sale of 644,000 tons went through, California farmers raised the price by $100/ton, netting them an extra $64 million. The Rice Millers Association evidently tried but failed to convince embassy officials to help raise the price even more than the $100/ton above the record price of that time.[45] Korea needed at least a million more tons of rice, and the U.S. embassy did its best to convince them to accept disliked Gulf rice.[46] Embassy documents note that the American Home Insurance Group and Pan American Airlines were also lobbying hard for access to Korean markets.

Investor Panic and Chun's Rising Star
On June 3, 1980, the same day that Moore and Gleysteen huddled with the prime minister, General Chun Doo-hwan forced the national mineworkers' union president, Choi Chong Sop, to resign. Choi was known to the U.S. embassy as "one of the FKTU's more independently minded national union leaders." The official reason for Choi's dismissal was his embezzling money on overseas trips, but he had also supported a dissident union faction of the Sobuk miners who had taken up arms against the government in April. By the end of 1980, as Chun destroyed more than half the country's unions, he dismissed 17 of the 21 leaders of national unions.

Comparisons to Park Chung-hee are appropriate—although there are significant differences. For the United States, Park was often a thorn in the side, but Chun quickly became an American lapdog. Park had a strategic vision for

Korea and refused to buckle under U.S. pressure on numerous occasions. At one point he moved precipitously toward reunification. In the early 1970s, he even embarked upon a secret program to develop his own nuclear weapons.[47] So annoyed with Park was President Carter when he came into office that he scheduled the complete withdrawal of U.S. troops from Korea. The contrast with Chun is immediately evident.

Faced with Chun's new military regime, international investors initially hesitated. On June 21, 1980, Deputy Secretary of State Warren Christopher wrote to Richard Holbrooke (then Assistant Secretary of State for East Asian and Pacific Affairs) that Chun needs "implementation of sensible economic policies." On July 11, Christopher cabled Seoul that U.S. bankers were in a titter about Korean political dynamics: "We have been informed by one of the large U.S. banks that during the visit of Bank of Korea Governor Shin this week, Shin was given a blunt message. Shin was informed by the U.S. bankers that if Korea did not get its political house in order swiftly then it would be exceedingly difficult to get necessary funding beyond this year."[48] Nine days later, the press reported that 431 officials from Korea's banking sector had been fired.

In early August 1980, the largest U.S. banks still had not decided Chun was their favorite. Chun again moved even more harshly against his opponents. The same day that these bankers' reluctance became evident, the State Department noted in a classified telegram: "Having already purged the KCIA, arrested major political figures and fired more than 5,000 senior and middle grade officials, South Korean military authorities turned their attention to other areas this week." Businesses, unions, the media, universities, and especially the streets were targeted in a series of comprehensive "cleansings." More than 10 percent of the members of the National Assembly were arrested or forced to resign. An additional 835 people were barred from politics. Political parties were abolished and new guidelines for them created. Even the Korean Traders Association was hard hit, with sixty-one executives and employees compelled to submit their resignations. Gleysteen noted with equanimity that import "associations contain their share of deadwood, and as with other sectors the purge could therefore have its beneficial aspects."[49] The "deadwood" Gleysteen referred to was the leftover bureaucracy of Park Chung-hee's national developmental state.

Chun's trimming of the "deadwood" was not enough to placate American investors' doubts; he moved on to some heavy pruning, shutting down 172 periodicals by canceling their registrations.[50] Every remaining newspaper, radio and television station, and wire service was assigned a Chief Emergency Planning Officer, and about two thousand journalists were required to attend three-day "reorientation" programs. Even after all this, newspapers and mass-media companies were consolidated and banned from advertising. The Christian Broadcasting System was particularly hard-hit, having already accepted more than $100,000 for ads that the government decreed could not be aired—nearly bankrupting the company.

Moving to consolidate his power and guarantee the stability demanded by U.S. businessmen and embassy officials, Chun continually intensified repression, which he packaged for public consumption as aimed at "hooligans and gangsters." In public places, police summarily cut the hair of men found with long hair, and more than 14,900 such cases were referred to courts. Even the courts came under attack: Chun replaced five Supreme Court justices who inexplicably resigned on August 9.[51] Hundreds of professors were detained and interrogated, and the embassy guessed 100–150 would be forced to resign. (The actual number was many times that.[52]) Previously reinstated students and professors were all expelled. College presidents and deans were not exempted. "Self-purification" committees were created in religious organizations; over three thousand employees of state-owned industries and banks were fired; and more than four hundred journalists and six hundred elementary and high school teachers lost their jobs.

History's irony meant that the more successfully Chun's "purification" program dismantled unions and jailed labor leaders, driving down wages and compelling the country to work harder, the more the pressure built. By 1987, when the dam broke, greater militancy characterized the irresistible tide of unionization, and wage increases produced robust economic growth.

Choreographing Regime Change

On August 8, 1980, the U.S. embassy noted that the ROK would probably get the international credit it needed if "the streets and campuses stay quiet."[53] Noting that one smaller U.S. bank president "wanted to eliminate all exposure in this country as soon as possible," the embassy repeated the essential condition that the government must keep the "streets and campuses quiet." Early that same morning, Wickham had breakfast with Chun, after which he had arranged to be interviewed by *Associated Press* correspondent Terry Anderson and *Los Angeles Times* reporter Sam Jameson.[54] In remarks he later claimed were supposed to be attributed to a "high-ranking source of the U.S. forces in Korea," Wickham announced that the United States "has decided to support" Chun Doo-hwan as South Korea's next president.[55] He indicated that President Choi (who remained as a figurehead) might soon be replaced by Chun and that the United States "would have little choice but to support Chun" if he were to become president.[56] Within twenty-four hours, banner headlines in Seoul and lead articles around the world blared the story of the U.S. commanding general having endorsed a Chun presidency—precisely the kind of reassurance U.S. investors needed to hear.

Both Wickham and Gleysteen were conveniently absent from Korea when the ensuing uproar peaked, the former to attend a meeting of the worldwide U.S. commanders-in-chief in Virginia, the latter to participate in the first Aspen Institute seminar on Korea "with a spectrum of highly articulate businessmen" (including Warren Christopher's law partner). After Wickham's public endorsement of Chun, he was ordered to wait in Hawaii before returning to Korea. Gleysteen was kept busy providing New York bankers with a "reassuring long-term view of Korean developments." On August 21, President Carter added insult to injury when he told a press conference that: "We would like to have a complete democracy with full and open debate, free press and elected leaders. The Koreans are not ready for that."[57] Compare with Japanese colonial administrator, Nitobe Inazo, who claimed in 1919: "In all humility, but with a firm conviction that Japan is a steward on whom devolves the gigantic task of the uplifting of the Far East, I cannot think that the young Korea is yet capable of governing itself."[58]

Sometimes history takes pity on those seeking clarity amid the muddle and confusion of rapidly changing events. In the case of Korea in 1980, with all its upheaval and turmoil, the month of August stands out as an exceptionally revealing moment. Chun Doo-hwan has been called a gangster by many people for a variety of reasons—and not only for his vast repressive measures or the hundreds of millions of dollars he embezzled. As I brought together my research notes, the inescapable conclusion was that Chun's consolidation of power was so closely coordinated and synchronized with top Americans that his choreographer must have watched the movie *The Godfather* and borrowed from it the elaborate orchestration of Michael Corleone's synchronized killing of all his family's enemies while he was in church.

With both Gleysteen and Wickham out of the country that month, Chun took care of all his business. August began with constitutionally sanctioned President Choi Kyu-ha in the Blue House. Wickham endorsed Chun for president and left Korea the next day.[59] On August 14, Kim Dae Jung's trial began. Two days later, acting president Choi resigned. After getting himself promoted to four-star general, Chun quit the military—so he could be elected president as a civilian. On August 27, the Electoral College did exactly that. President Carter's congratulatory letter to President-elect Chun couldn't have put U.S. priorities better: "As you assume your responsibilities as president of the Republic of Korea, I want personally to assure you of our desire to maintain the basic economic and security interests of both of our nations."[60] The next day, Gleysteen returned, and, with Richard Holbrooke's personal approval, Wickham was also allowed back. Business as usual was the order of the day.

A day later, Gleysteen huddled with Chun, seeking to rein in the government's attempt to execute Kim Dae Jung lest international investors again panic. On September 2, Gleysteen happily noted, "The new line-up should tend to reassure international business interests."[61] Four days later, Secretary Muskie telegrammed that a "steady stream of businessmen and bankers continues to flow," concerned about Korea's stability.[62] As the embassy hustled through loan approvals, Westinghouse Board Chairman Robert Kirby visited Seoul and described "recent Korean developments and Westinghouse's prospects in euphoric terms."[63] On September 22, David Rockefeller's visit led to Chun's new policies permitting 100 percent foreign ownership of companies, 100 percent repatriation of funds invested from abroad, and foreigners' ownership of land.[64]

Christopher noted with glee that "the embassy has been making every effort to protect the interests of U.S. investors" and to "protect Korea's reputation as a favorable business climate." With Chun firmly ensconced in power, the United States ratcheted up the pressure on the ROK—not to liberalize the political system (as the citizenry desperately needed)—but to open up its markets and banks. When Chun's Finance Minister visited the United States in early October, he was pressured to provide greater access to the Korean market by American insurance companies.

As major beneficiaries of Park's *yushin* system, the *chaebol* did not support democratization. Under Chun's "liberalization" they also benefited, because as Alice Amsden tells us, "Liberalization contributed to a rise, not a decline, in economic concentration."[65]

Streamlining the *chaebol* to move toward more capital–intensive industries, many went bankrupt while others sold off shares to affiliated companies. Chun forced a merger of Korea's automobile industry under Hyundai and shipbuilding under Daewoo. Two weeks later, he reshuffled his cabinet. As opposition to Chun mounted at places like Wonpung Textile and Control Data Korea, he pushed through more punitive labor laws and then opened more markets to surplus U.S. products. In the subsequent beef price crisis, thousands of Korean farmers massively demonstrated, demanding compensation for their losses and opposing American demands to further open the agricultural market.[66] In December 1980, Chun purged thousands more professionals. He had proclaimed a new constitution that gave him more power then even Park had enjoyed under *yushin*. On October 27, he dissolved the National Assembly, outlawed all political parties, and banned freedom of speech and assembly. He also changed the name of the KCIA to ANSP (Agency for National Security Planning) while increasing its power.

By making the country's economic recovery contingent upon short-term foreign loans and an increasingly internationalized capital market, Chun and his advisors changed Korea's economic trajectory away from the national developmental state of Park Chung-hee. They pointed the country instead toward integration into international financial structures, whose instability in 1997 devastated Korea's economy during the East Asian financial crisis. Capital markets were greatly liberalized, as were regulations governing banks and trade. In 1983, the regime revised the Foreign Capital Inducement Law, removing nearly all restrictions on profit-taking and capital flow out of the country.[67] In October 1985, an import-liberalization was adopted lifting restrictions on over six hundred items, and a number of other concessions were made to the United States on issues of intellectual property rights and liberalization of regulations of U.S. banks and insurance companies. In the spring of 1987, measures designed to increase U.S. imports by more than $2 billion were announced.

Foreign investment in Korea, a little more than half a billion dollars in the five years from 1977 to 1981, jumped to that much *every year* by 1985.[68] In the view of economic analysts from the German firm, Bertelsmann Stiftung, "South Korea's transformation to market economy was already accomplished by the middle of the 1980s."[69] As the World Bank explained: "Overall, the liberalization of Korea's external sector is proceeding smoothly and deliberately . . . The Korean Government's intervention in the financial sector seems to have been quite distortive, especially in the latter half of the 1970s . . . The financial liberalization efforts since 1980 have greatly improved various aspects of financial allocation."[70] With regard to trade, the report was glowing: "Korea's liberalization program is very much on track, and government merits unequivocal high marks for its effective implementation."[71] Published in March 1987, the report also mentioned that wages for Korean production workers were about one-tenth of those in the United

States. The Christian Institute for the Study of Justice and Development published statistics for 1985 and 1986 that indicated more than 80 percent of Korean workers received less than their own government's minimum cost of living for a four-person family,[72] a clear indication of the storm brewing in the factories that would hit with full fury in 1987. Chun's policies liberalizing trade dramatically helped foreign businesses capture the Korean market. Automatic approval for imported items rose from 68.6 percent of the total in 1980 to 91.5 percent in 1986; the average tariff was 24.9 percent in 1980—by 1990 it had fallen to 11.4 percent.[73]

To be sure, there were conflicts between Chun and the U.S. administrations, but these were relatively minor. Both the Carter and Reagan administrations pressured Chun not to execute Kim Dae Jung, and Chun complied with the embassy's single-mindedly making "every effort to protect the interests of U.S. investors" and to clear out the "distortive deadwood"—that is, the remnants of Park Chunghee's national developmental state. When we contrast American actions with those of Korean civil society in this same time, the discrepancy between Korean and American priorities offers some explanation for the appearance and proliferation of anti-Americanism.

Wisdom of the *Minjung*

Marginalized from Korean economic development by Park Chung-hee, South Jeolla Province was in crisis long before the 1980 uprising. Income was less than three-quarters of the meager earnings in the rest of the country, and imports of surplus agricultural products from the United States created a "state of desolation" for small farmers.[74] By 1980, so many people had left the region that there were a million Jeolla natives in Seoul alone—a fact reported by Gleysteen in his musings about the possibility of the democracy movement spreading after the Gwangju Uprising had been suppressed.[75]

Well aware of the region's economic problems, the United States nonetheless aggressively pursued its material interests without paying attention to the basic economic needs of Chonnam residents—after having trampled on their aspirations for democratic liberties. Although most observers have framed Gwangju's movement solely within the boundaries of political reform, citizens' concerns for economic fairness are noteworthy. During the uprising, economic grievances were part of the spectrum of demands raised, and afterward, economic concerns remained central. In a manifesto released by "Residents of Chonnam Province" on the first anniversary of the uprising, the group called for the truth about the massacre to be known and punishment of those responsible—but also for better prices for farmers' produce, free trade unions, and a free press. The statement went on: "Foreign businesses continue to expand their market share with the help of the military regime. The economic occupation of the Korean market, as well as unreasonable foreign investment, should be stopped in order for the Korean economy to be less dependent on foreign influences."[76]

The United Family Members of the Defendants in the Gwangju Hearings (the set of trials of hundreds of arrestees) bitterly named a specific American family: "we remember the actions of Secretary Haig and others, including David

Rockefeller, head of one of the most influential families in the United States, who, acting before the blood had even dried in Gwangju, was the first American business leader to visit President Chun."[77] On March 10, 1982, the Korean Catholic Justice and Peace Commission decried "indiscriminate introduction of foreign produce" and the "country's drop in self-sufficiency for farm produce."[78] A few months later, on the uprising's second anniversary, the Gwangju Citizens Movement for Democracy published a pamphlet, "What Should We Learn From the Gwangju Uprising?" Decrying the "conglomerates selling out the wealth of the nation," the group criticized their own lack of leadership; it called on students to "continue to stage demonstrations as an avant-garde of change" and workers to continue to organize unions.

The wisdom of these ad hoc groups and their concern for the welfare of ordinary citizens contrasts sharply with the powerful U.S. embassy "making every effort to protect the interests of U.S. investors." While their economic concerns were evident, political acumen was not lacking in these activist groups' discourse: the Families of the Imprisoned enunciated a sophisticated understanding of international politics: "When they experience resistance from students, the government should not intimidate the people with talk of the fall of Vietnam nor brag about having the support of the U.S. government. The fall of Vietnam was caused by the absence of democracy and the corruption of the system."[79] On the uprising's sixth anniversary, the Manifesto of the Chonnam Branch of the National Council for Democratization noted that the U.S. government is "more concerned with its own interests than with the interests of the people of Korea." The group concluded: "The Gwangju Uprising taught us that only united people power can win in the end."[80] They vowed to continue to fight for direct presidential elections. As is now legendary, Gwangju centrally inspired the June Uprising of 1987, which won that very demand.

The relationship between politics and economics is so complicated and historically changing that no one has yet been able to formulate laws or equations that have the consistency and accuracy of the laws of physics. The best we can do is to understand specific contexts and provisionally attempt to project into the future on a very limited basis. After the Gwangju Uprising, Gleysteen attempted his own prognosticating: he continued to believe that many Koreans "will opt for order over liberalization if order is accompanied by economic rewards."[81] Koreans had a different set of priorities: a poll conducted in early June 1987 indicated that the vast majority of self-identified Korean middle-class citizens, an astonishing 85.7 percent, supported the idea that: "We should promote human rights even if it delays economic growth."[82]

When the June Uprising broke out, Chun had already outlived his usefulness to the United States, and his American uncles quickly disavowed him—as they have done to erstwhile imperial collaborators from Ngo Dinh Diem and Rafael Trujillo to Manuel Noriega and Saddam Hussein. It would take another fifteen years of struggle for Chun to be brought to justice, but Gwangju people were equal to the task, refusing to rest until they had brought to light the truth of the uprising—and U.S. reasons for suppressing it.

NOTES

1   Tim Shorrock, "Debacle in Kwangju: Were Washington's Cables Read as a Green Light for the 1980 Korean Massacre?" *Nation*, December 9, 1996, available at http://base21.jinbo.net/show/show.php?p_docnbr=20896.

2   Wickham, *Korea on the Brink*, 132.

3   May 18 Gwangju Democratization Movement Materials, Gwangju City May 18 Historical Materials Compilation Committee 광주광역시 5–18사료 편찬위원회, 5–18 광주 민주화 운동자료총서), December 17, 1997, IX: 219 (Hereafter GDMM). State Department document number 80Seoul 006522.

4   GDMM IX: 234. (80Seoul 006610).

5   GDMM IX: 254. (80State 138557).

6   GDMM IX: 257. (80Seoul 006660).

7   For discussion of these oft-quoted phrases of the Reagan presidency, see "The Crusade of the Democratic Globalists," Tom Barry, http://americas.irc-online.org/am/161; For years, President Reagan invoked this latter phrase, so much so that it has become commonly used in a variety of contexts. See Reagan's Radio Address to the Nation on United States-Soviet Relations, September 29, 1984, available at http://www.presidency.ucsb.edu/ws/index.php?pid=40457. Also see "The Evil Empire," President Reagan's Speech to the House of Commons, June 8, 1982, available at http://reagan2020.us/speeches/the_evil_empire_2.asp.

8   차성환, 참여 노동자를 통해서 본 부마항쟁 성격의 재조명 (unpublished doctoral dissertation, Busan National University Political Science Department, 2009), 122.

9   GDMM VII: 206: 79Seoul 013832.

10   GDMM IX: 304–5: 80Seoul 006921.

11   John D. Rockefeller III, *The Second American Revolution* (New York: Harper & Row, 1973). For insightful discussion see F. William Engdahl, "The Financial Tsunami: The Financial Foundations of the American Century," http://www.globalresearch.ca/index.php?context=va&aid=7813.

12   David Harvey, *A Brief History of Neoliberalism* (Oxford: Oxford University Press, 2005), 28.

13   *Korea: Managing the Industrial Transition* vol. 1 (Washington, D.C.: The World Bank, 1987), 164. Also see Songok Han Thornton, "The 'Miracle' Revisited," *New Political Science* 27, no. 2 (June 2005): 166.

14   Harvey, *A Brief History*, 22, 74.

15   2008 radio interview, http://www.againstthegrain.org/.

16   "Turkey and Latin America: Reaction and Revolution," http://www.dissentvoice.org/2007/09/turkey-and-latin-america-reaction-and-revolution/.

17   Kim Jei-Ahn, "Economic Background of the Gwangju Democratic Uprising," in May 18th History Compilation Committee of Gwangju City, *History of the 5.18 Democratic Uprising*, vol. 1 (Gwangju: The May 18 Memorial Foundation, 2008), 131.

18   GDMM IX: 632: 80Seoul 009434.

19   GDMM IX: 346: 80Seoul 007266.

20   GDMM IX: 348: 80Seoul 007266.

21   *Agence France Press* on August 21, 1995, reported the deaths of 397 others due to their treatment at these camps. They also reported a lower number of total inmates: over 38,000. The number to be arrested was allocated in advance for each region, so police simply rounded people up, including people with tattoos, until the official total reached 67,055. Some 7,500 were sentenced to two years' imprisonment even though they had not been convicted of any crime. See the report of the Presidential Truth Commission on Suspicious Deaths of the Republic of Korea, *A Hard Journey to Justice* (Seoul: Samin Books, 2004), 221.

22 Koo, "The State, *Minjung*, and the Working Class," 148.

23 Cumings, *Korea's Place in the Sun*, 379.

24 Koo, "The State, *Minjung*, and the Working Class," 48–49.

25 Hart-Landsberg, *The Rush to Development*, 195.

26 First pointed out to me in an interview with Rev. Park Hyung-kyu, Seoul, June 4, 2001.

27 See Selig Harrison, "Is South Korea Going to be the Next Philippines?" *Washington Post*, January 25, 1987.

28 http://news.naver.com/news/read.php?mode=LSD&office_id=079&article_id=0000100034&section_id=102&menu_id=102.

29 On Chun and Roh Tae-Woo's fortunes, see Wickham, *Korea on the Brink*, 185–86, 189.

30 Haggard and Kaufman, *Political Economy*, 42.

31 Ibid.

32 In addition to GDDM primary source, Gleysteen and Wickham's memoirs were also helpful, as were World Bank reports.

33 GDMM IX: 355: 80Seoul 007266.

34 Interview with Lee Yang-hyun, June 23, 2001.

35 GDMM X: 401: 80State 244450.

36 GDMM IX: 235: 80Seoul 006610.

37 Donald N. Clark, ed., *The Kwangju Uprising: Shadows Over the Regime in South Korea* (Boulder, CO: Westview Special Studies on East Asia, 1988), 13.

38 The Carter administration's priorities were other than human rights concerns not only in Korea, but in other countries, including Cambodia (where the United States supported UN recognition of Pol Pot's ousted Khmer Rouge government for fear of alienating China—despite Khmer Rouge responsibility for millions of deaths); Iran (where Carter approved the Shah's request for crowd-control equipment, including tear gas); and Argentina (where Carter announced an end to the arms embargo on the military dictatorship). Although there were notable forces advocating a consistent application of human rights criteria to U.S. decisions (notably Patricia Derian, then Assistant Secretary of State for Human Rights Affairs), Richard Holbrooke, Assistant Secretary of State for East Asian and Pacific Affairs, held sway. In his view, the difference between Derian and himself "was that she was myopically fixed on human rights as the only plank in American foreign policy while he had to be concerned about America's security and economic interests." See Victor S. Kaufman, "The Bureau Of Human Rights During The Carter Administration," *The Historian*, September 22, 1998, http://www.highbeam.com/library/docfree.asp?DOCID=1G1:53461483&ctrlInfo=Round20%3Amode20b%3AdocG%3Aresult&ao. Ronald Reagan nominated Elliott Abrams to replace Derian as Assistant Secretary of State for Human Rights and Humanitarian Affairs.

39 Gleysteen, *Massive Entanglement*, xx, 65, 148.

40 GDMM VII: 634: 79State 297698; VIII: 430: 80Seoul 001900.

41 GDMM VII: 308: 79State 255196; GDMM VII:320: 79State 260763.

42 Peter Hayes and Tim Shorrock, "Dumping Reactors in Asia: The U.S. Export-Import Bank and Nuclear Power in South Korea, Part 2," *Ampo* 4, no. 2 (1982):16–23.

43 GDMM IX: 341: 80Seoul 007261.

44 Hart-Landsberg, *The Rush to Development*, 223–24.

45 GDMM X: 805: 80State 329118.

46 GDMM X: 536: 80State 276967.

47 Gleysteen, *Massive Entanglement*, 14.

48 GDMM IX: 583: Department of State telegram, 11July80 State 182038; also quoted in the sidebar to Tim Shorrock, "Kim Dae Jung and the American Challenge," originally in *Hankyoreh Shinmum*, January 1, 1998.

49 GDMM IX: 681: 80Seoul 009828.

50   GDMM X: 30–1: 80State 204864.
51   Jerome A. Cohen and Edward J. Baker, "U.S. Foreign Policy and Human Rights in South Korea," in *Human Rights in Korea: Historical and Policy Perspectives*, ed. William Shaw (Cambridge, MA: Harvard Council on East Asian Studies, 1991), 211–12.
52   Interview with Ed Baker, Cambridge, MA, June 16, 2006.
53   GDMM X: 65: 80Seoul 010189.
54   Wickham, *Korea on the Brink*, 155.
55   For the text of the article, see Sam Jameson, "U.S. Support Claimed for S. Korea's Chon, but State Dept. Disavows Military Official's Remarks on Presidency," *Los Angeles Times*, August 8, 1980, B18–19, For an account of Wickham's endorsement of Chun, see Scott-Stokes and Lee Jae-eui, *The Kwangju Uprising*, 39.
56   Wickham, *Korea on the Brink*, 156. Gleysteen's book, written in close collaboration with Wickham after the two had been summoned to the ROK's National Assembly, incorrectly has the date of the breakfast a day earlier. In his remarks published in the *Los Angeles Times*, Wickham also said that Chun had come to power "legitimately" and, like Park Chung-hee, Chun intended on being president for life—to wear the purple "right into the grave." See Jameson, "U.S. Support Claimed for S. Korea's Chon."
57   Wickham, *Korea on the Brink*, 163.
58   Stefan Tanaka, *Japan's Orient: Rendering Pasts Into History* (Berkeley: University of California Press, 1993), 248.
59   Before the Gwangju uprising, when Wickham had also been conveniently absent from the country, he left his Korean Deputy Commander, Bae Sok-chu, to approve the release of troops to Chun's command. A special issue edition of *Dong-A Ilbo* later reported that he left because "he knew the massacre in Gwangju was going to happen." Special Issue: *A Thorough Investigation of American Forces in Korea* (철저해부 주한 미 군) 1990, as quoted in Yoon, "The Kwangju Democratization Movement," 46.
60   Gleysteen, *Massive Entanglement*, 165–66.
61   GDMM X: 326: 80Seoul 011457.
62   GDMM X: 360: 80State 237970.
63   GDMM X: 438: 80State 250900.
64   Christian Institute for Social Justice and Democracy, *The Power of Transnational Corporations in Korea* (Seoul: Christian Institute, 1981), 13.
65   Amsden, *Asia's Next Giant*, 136.
66   Sangyong, Simin, et al, *Memories of May 1980*, 399.
67   *Korea: Managing the Industrial Transition*, 2:205.
68   *Korea: Managing the Industrial Transition*, 1:169.
69   "South Korea Country Report," http://www.bertelsmann-transformation-index. de/132.0.html?L=1.
70   *Korea: Managing the Industrial Transition*, 2:81, 105, 107.
71   Ibid., 1:74 as quoted in Amsden, *Asia's Next Giant*, 134.
72   Christian Institute for the Study of Justice and Development, *Social Justice Indicators in Korea*, (Seoul: 1988), 55. A resource center sponsored by a consortium of protest groups, the web site of the CISJD (한국기독교사회문제연구원) is: http://www.jpic. org/introduce/books.php.
73   Sung-Hee Jwa and Jun-Il Kim, "Korea's Economic Reform," in *The Politics of Democratization and Globalization in Korea*, eds. Chung-in Moon and Jongryn Mo (Seoul: Yonsei University Press, 1999), 259.
74   In 1980, the average annual income per person in Gwangju was 461,451 won as compared to 619,037 nationally. *Hard Journey*, 209 (see chap. 5 n. 68). Also see *Essays*, 61 (see chap. 5, n. 102).
75   GDMM IX: 352: 80Seoul 007266.

76   May 18 Research Institute, "Manifestos and Declarations," 2–126. The book has a Korean title: 5–18 관련자료의 영어 번역: 5–18 20주년 기념 학술연구사업 연구소위 (Gwangju, 전남대학교 5–18 연구소, 2000).

77   United Family Members of the Defendants in the Kwangju Hearings, "A Letter to President Reagan," in *A Declaration of Conscience: The Catholic Church and Human Rights*, ed. Japanese Catholic Council for Justice and Peace (Maryknoll: Orbis Books, 1983), 131.

78   Ibid., 364.

79   May 18 Research Institute, "Manifestos and Declarations," 2–129.

80   Ibid., 2–139.

81   GDMM IX: 352: 80Seoul 007266.

82   Published in June 1987 in *Hanguk Ilbo*. See *Korea Under Roh Tae-Woo: Democratization, Northern Policy and Inter-Korean Relations*, ed. James Cotton (Canberra: Allen and Unwin, 1993), 88.

CHAPTER 8

The Gathering Storm

Without love, or honor, or even a name to pass on
One's whole life to push forward, a fervent pledge
Our comrades are gone, and only a banner waves;
Until a new day dawns, let's never sway.
Although time goes, mountains and streams know
Awakening, we call out, a fervent battle cry
I'll go on ahead, and you, the living, follow!
I'll go on ahead, and you, the living, follow!

—"A March for My Beloved"
(Gwangju commemorative song)

CHRONOLOGY	
May 18–27, 1980	Gwangju Uprising
August 16, 1980	Acting president Choi Kyu-hah resigns
August 27, 1980	Chun Doo-hwan selected as president by appointed electoral college
December 9, 1980	U.S. Information Service (USIS) office in Gwangju set on fire
January 28, 1981	Chun is first foreign head of state to visit Reagan White House
March 18, 1982	USIS in Busan set on fire
October 23, 1982	Kim Dae Jung is released from prison and goes to the United States
September 22, 1983	USIS in Daegu attacked by bomb
April 13, 1984	Students from fifty-five campuses protest for greater university freedom
October 24, 1984	More than 6,000 police occupy Seoul National University

November 3, 1984	Student leaders from forty-two universities form national coalition at Yonsei University
February 12, 1985	National Assembly elections: opposition wins more votes than ruling party
April 16, 1985	Daewoo Motors workers go on strike
April 20, 1985	350 workers occupy Technology Center at Daewoo Motors
May 17, 1985	More than 38,000 students militantly protest in Seoul, demanding truth of Gwangju
May 23, 1985	U.S. building in Seoul occupied by students; public hearings on Gwangju demanded
May 29, 1985	Alleged author of book about Gwangju arrested
June 24, 1985	Guro walkout by women's workers
August 1, 1985	Group of 401 writers demands freedom of expression
November 22, 1985	Council of People's Artists established
December 2, 1985	Students in Gwangju occupy USIS, demand end to U.S. pressure to open Korean markets
March 1, 1986	More than 125 Catholic priests in Seoul hold simultaneous services for justice
April 28, 1986	SNU students Lee Jae-ho and Kim Se-jin commit suicide, shouting, "No to Nuclear Weapons!"
May 20, 1986	SNU student Lee Dong-su burns himself to death, shouting, "U.S. Imperialists, Go Away!"
October 28, 1986	Students hold meeting; 1,219 arrested at Konkuk University in Seoul
May 3, 1986	Militant action in Incheon; 129 arrests
May 9, 1986	More than 152 Buddhist monks call for democracy
January 14, 1987	Park Jong-chol tortured to death
February 7, 1987	Police arrest 799 demonstrating against torture
February 18, 1987	Korean Women's Associations United formed
April 13, 1987	Constitutional debate suspended by Chun Doo-hwan

Days of Light, Years of Darkness

Chun's suppression of the Gwangju Uprising left a permanent scar on his regime, a bloody birthmark that became people's most lasting memory of the Fifth Republic. As the truth of the massacre became known, Chun's rule lost any sense of moral righteousness—disaster for any ruler, but a fatal flaw in the world's most Confucian society. Although the dictatorship's iron fist came down forcefully, it could not suppress the truth of the uprising since the citizens of Gwangju never gave up their struggle. Only a few days after the slaughter on May 27, hundreds of people being held in cells barely fit for animals were put on trial. Refusing to be intimidated, they threw chairs at the judges in the military tribunals and sang movement songs rather than listening to their pronounced sentences. While much of the rest of South Korea remained in the dark about their sacrifices and suffering, they consoled themselves and built up networks to continue the struggle.

For years, the military suppressed the facts from being known, but ultimately, desperate and isolated initial actions turned into a storm of dissent. The endeavor for the truth to be known took many forms. To awaken the nation to the massacre's unknown history, many people sacrificed their lives. Student Kim Ui-gi jumped from the Seoul Christian Building on May 30, 1980—only three days after the military bloodily retook Province Hall—proclaiming the need for people to learn the truth of the Gwangju Uprising. The next night, "Bloodthirsty Killer Chun Doo-hwan" was painted in red on electric poles throughout downtown Gwangju. On June 2, the *Chonnam Maeil Sinmun* newspaper featured a poem, "Gwangju! Cross of Our Nation!" by Kim Jun-tae, in which Gwangju's persecution and sacrifice was compared with that of Jesus. Shortly thereafter, the newspaper was forced to close down. When the *Gwangju Chonnam Ilbo* resumed publication on June 2, it featured a series of articles entitled "Mt. Mudeung Knows!" headlined in extra large fonts. On June 9, worker Kim Jong-tae set himself afire to publicize the truth. Exactly a year after the massacre of May 27, SNU student Kim Tae-hoon committed suicide to protest censorship of Gwangju's history.

Even when bereaved family members sought to eulogize their loved ones, they faced arrest and persecution—as happened a year after the uprising, on May 18, 1981, when fifty members of bereaved families were arrested after a memorial ceremony in Mangwoldong Cemetery. It took two years for the families of the victims to assemble in one large group, and five long years passed before the first book about the uprising appeared. Lee Jae-eui, whose book—*Beyond Death, Beyond the Darkness of the Era*—became the first written history of the uprising, recounts in the introduction the precautions he took in writing it, and he published it under a pseudonym in May 1985.[1] The suspected author was immediately arrested, and the military destroyed thousands of copies, but small print shops continually made more. Within a year, hundreds of thousands were in circulation, passing from hand to hand like a hot potato. It was rumored even Chun Doo-hwan was in possession of an illegal copy.

Today it may be possible to discuss the uprising in glowing terms, extolling its victory over the forces of darkness, but in the same breath we should remember the thousands of victims—families torn apart by the loss of loved ones, decades of mothers' and fathers' grief at the loss of children, children growing up without parents, physical injuries that lasted for decades, and psychological wounds that left some confined for years and many more unable to live their lives to full potential.[2] Increasingly, victims pointed at U.S. support of Chun as the cause of their—and the country's—continuing problems.

After the Gwangju Uprising, essential features of Korea's political landscape were forever transformed: blind faith in the United States was replaced by anti-Americanism, and militant anti-government protests replaced moralistic appeals for justice. An indication of the latter is that Molotov cocktails became standard fare for street actions after Gwangju. People came to understand the objective of their struggle as overthrowing a U.S.-backed form of fascist dictatorship (rather than one-man military rule), and they also developed their sense of the subjects of resistance as the *minjung* (the masses of ordinary people) rather than prominent personalities within the opposition.[3]

South Korean Anti-Americanism

After 1980, anti-Americanism overnight developed into a significant problem, one that simply won't disappear. Before Gwangju, the vast majority of South Koreans believed the United States was a great friend that would help them achieve democracy. Even during the uprising, the point of genesis of contemporary anti-Americanism, a rumor was widely believed that the aircraft carrier USS *Coral Sea* entered Korean waters to aid insurgents against Chun Doo-hwan and the new military dictatorship.[4] Once it became apparent that the United States supported Chun and encouraged him to suppress the uprising (even requesting that the military delay the reentry of troops into the city until after the *Coral Sea* had arrived), anti-Americanism in South Korea emerged with startling rapidity and unexpected longevity.[5]

In Koreans' memory, a string of less-than-complimentary public statements by U.S. officials also helped fan the flames of anti-American feelings. On November 29, 1979, U.S. Ambassador Gleysteen uttered his famous remark referring to Korea as a "society of garlic and pepper eating combatants." In 1982, U.S. Ambassador Richard L. Walker told a reporter in South Carolina that Korean students and intellectuals were "spoiled brats" for whom workers had no sympathy, and "a highly placed U.S. military official," widely believed to have been General John A. Wickham, Jr. (then serving as commander of U.S. and UN forces in Korea), made a statement in which he referred to Koreans as "Lemming-like."[6]

Within two years of the suppression of the Gwangju Uprising, arsonists attacked United States Information Service (USIS) offices in Gwangju and Busan. In September 1983, a bomb exploded in front of the American Cultural Center in Daegu. On May 23, 1985, the USIS library in Seoul was occupied for three days until all seventy-three students inside were arrested. The May 1986 riot in Incheon had distinct anti-American overtones, and on the twenty-first of the same month, a U.S. center in Busan was again set on fire. During the 1987 June Uprising, U.S. reporters complained that people screamed "Yankee Go Home!" when they tried to cover the demonstrations.

The longer the U.S. government actively abetted Chun Doo-hwan, the more South Korean anti-Americanism increased. As American policymakers realized that the best way to secure markets and resources of East Asian countries like the Philippines, Taiwan and South Korea for American businesses was to foster democracy rather than supporting corrupt and unpopular dictators, a new ambassador was sent to Seoul—James Lilley, longtime CIA operative with years of experience promoting reforms in Taiwan.

As much as the United States was detested, Chun and his coterie of American agents found it impossible to appear in public without elaborate precautions. By chance, Chong Hyun-ay happened to be present when the dictator made an unannounced daytime visit to downtown Gwangju on March 10, 1982. She quickly mobilized about twenty people who were standing nearby and compelled Chun to beat a hasty retreat.[7] Chun was so fearful of Gwangju people that he stayed that night outside the city in a private guest house (*minbak jib*) in Tamyang. To mark his overnight stay, he presented the town with a plaque, but residents took it to Mangwoldong Cemetery and installed it at the threshold of the entrance so everyone entering could step on it—a more polite form of insult than the shoe-throwing journalist George H.W. Bush met in Baghdad, but a Korean equivalent. Months later, Chun again attempted to visit Gwangju, but he was spotted by several young men who jumped into their cars and chased him and his security entourage onto an expressway.[8]

Where garbage trucks had dumped bodies after the slaughter on May 27, the obscure resting place of Korea's martyrs became a Mecca of the democracy movement, with such great presence by 1983 that the government tried to move the bodies to separate locations. Offering the equivalent of about $10,000 and expenses to each family, they organized a Regional Development Commission with the participation of high-level government bureaucrats, professors, rich citizens, and even the Gwangju Chamber of Commerce. Concerned family members immediately alerted the community, and an around the clock vigil was maintained. After one attempt to remove bodies was stopped, angry citizens marched on the commission chair's house and harshly protested. On the fourth anniversary of the uprising, May 18, 1984, about eighty people were arrested in Gwangju, and in Seoul, students from twelve colleges demonstrated.

On the fifth anniversary of the uprising, mothers whose sons or husbands had been killed staged a spirited protest in downtown Gwangju. They hung banners from the sixth floor of the Catholic Center on Kumnamno and chanted through a loudspeaker, "Chun Doo-hwan Resign Now!" and "Don't Hide the Truth!" Soon police came, arrested and beat them, but they never gave up.[9] Their indomitable spirit motivated the entire citizenry. At the heart of the absolute community, their continuing resolve fueled the entire country's will to fight.

In all Korea, Gwangju became the watchword for democracy. On May 17, 1985, coordinated protests at eighty colleges and universities involved some thirty-eight thousand students who called for the truth about the killings to be made public.[10] A week later, seventy-three Seoul students occupied the U.S. Information Service building for three days and demanded an apology from the U.S. government for its role in the slaughter. This strategic choice by activists bore great fruit, for afterward the Gwangju Uprising became a national topic of public debate. As the dictatorship and the United States continued to stonewall, people grew increasingly bold, even desperate. On August 15, as protests continued, Hong Ki-il burned himself to death on Gwangju's main street because of the failure to reveal the truth.

Through years of harsh conditions, Gwangju remained central to the growing discontent with Chun, as people refused to submit. A secretly administered poll by a pro-government newspaper *Kyunghyang Sinmun* from May 15 to 19, 1985, noted that more than 65 percent of all respondents were dissatisfied with the Chun government; the numbers were much higher for those in their twenties (73.6 percent) and college graduates (85.7 percent).[11] According to the Christian

Institute for the Study of Justice and Development, more than 80 percent of Korean workers received wages less than the estimated minimum cost of living.[12] On May 16, 1986, about two thousand relatives of people killed during the uprising publicly protested on Geumnam Street after a mass at Namdong Cathedral. The next day, university students across the country held protests to commemorate Gwangju. On May 20, SNU student Lee Dong-su burned himself to death shouting, "U.S. Imperialists, Go Away!"

During these years of darkness, international support was a critical element encouraging the indigenous democracy movement. On its first anniversary of the uprising, more than five hundred people from Korea, Japan and about a dozen other countries gathered in Japan for an Emergency World Assembly for South Korean Democracy. Concerned that Kim Dae Jung may be executed, more than five million signatures were gathered in Japan for his safety. In the enthusiasm of DJ's celebrity, Félix Guattari, better known for his understanding of microdynamics than of macropolitical structures, embraced France's new socialist government as a "turning point in history," and called DJ a "real friend" of those struggling to end capitalism.[13] If he had lived to see DJ come to power in 1999 and severely repress the workers of South Korea, he no doubt would have phrased himself differently. German media had extensively covered the Gwangju Uprising. Unlike their American counterparts, they reported carefully and analyzed fully the implications of its suppression. Christian associations there made substantial contributions to the movement, including moral and financial support.[14] From some one percent of South Koreans at the end of World War II, by 1987, Christians accounted for almost 25 percent.[15] While Protestants were most active, Catholic Church activists had influence in Asia that became a considerable force in democratization. Surprisingly, the YMCA and YWCA—often considered conservative institutions in the United States—became resources for social movements to mobilize against authoritarian regimes.

History's cunning produces new opportunities, even where disaster strikes. In the dialectical unfolding of social movements, every uprising produces the conditions and actors for the next phases of struggle. As previously existing categories of social status and wealth are destroyed, plowed under by the fertile movement of people's imaginations and labor, new ones emerge to supplant them—not merely replacing them mechanically but developing afresh with new aspirations and tools. What is critical here is the formation of a new social subject—the *minjung*—in the period after Gwangju. In the early 1980s, while Chun grappled with his own illegitimacy, the *minjung*—grassroots people of all classes—created itself as the subject-object of Korean history. Much as György Lukács envisioned the proletariat to be the subject-object of European history, a dream never realized, the *minjung* became the object produced by Gwangju as well as decades of previous struggles and simultaneously the subjects of a democratic and egalitarian order. Formed in the crucible of the Gwangju Uprising, the *minjung* identity consolidated itself through art, imagination, and struggle. Neither the worker-peasant alliance of communism nor the elite Confucian literati, the *minjung* was a synthesis of all the people, excluding only the superrich and their friends in the dictatorship. Emerging full-grown from the bloody sacrifice of Gwangju, the *minjung* constituted nothing short of the crown of creation of five thousand years of Korean history.

Rise of the *Minjung*

In movement circles, the Gwangju insurgents' deaths had an electrifying effect. By 1985, nearly all activists began referring to Gwangju as the "5.18 *Minjung* Uprising" (5.18 민중항쟁)—not as the Gwangju "riot" or "incident," words used by the government to denigrate the event. As the main force of the uprising, *minjung* became a means to unite all downtrodden, oppressed, marginalized, and have-nots in the budding extraparliamentary national movement—all who fought for democracy and economic equality: workers, students, farmers, urban poor, journalists and writers, religious people, youth, women, *chaeya* activists, the professional middle-class, progressive intellectuals, and artists. Composed of the stems for the words for democracy (민주주의 or *minjujuhui*) and nation (민족 or *minjok*), *minjung* (민중) carried both those meanings forward by uniting everyone against the tiny economic and military elite.

Today, various understandings of *minjung* exist. For Namhee Lee, it is an analytic concept without historical grounding.[16] For Kenneth Wells, it was a concept belonging to "populist idealism."[17] Choi Jungwoon understood it as part of the empirical history of Gwangju: "The emergence of the *minjung* was a product of this absolute community."[18] Choi claims the word was "invented" on May 19, 1984, by the Youth Alliance for the Democratization Movement (YADM or 민청련),[19] but the term was used in the *Independence News* (*Tongnip Sinmun*) in the 1890s, and Shin Chaeho used the word in 1923 to describe the leading constituency of independence in his "Declaration of the Korean Revolution."[20] Pacifist Han Seok-heon used "*minjung* democracy" to describe the goal he sought.[21] In 1974, the short-lived National Federation of Democratic Youth and Students (NFDYS or 민청학련) issued a declaration of *Minjung, Minjok, Minjujuhui* (People, Nation, Democracy) that called for "structural transformation of society."[22] In 1980, on the twentieth anniversary of Syngman Rhee's overthrow, SNU students used the word *minjung* in their final resolution.

The concept of *minjung* provided continuity among generations of social movements in Korea like nothing else, and this dimension of its meaning is of paramount significance. South Korea's intense anti-Communism was more than the National Security Law's prohibitions and draconian punishments but had become embodied in everyday forms of visceral rejection of the "red complex," including imagery and even vocabulary emanating from Pyongyang. While North Korea spoke of the people (인민 or "*inmin*") as the basis of revolution, *minjung* provided an alternative conception of movement constituency that strikingly boxed off the democratic antidictatorial struggle from the great popular national and social revolutionary struggles of 1945–1955. Since it cut across economics, politics, and united a broad spectrum of people, *minjung* was decidedly not a Marxist term. Many people could lay claim to it, including Christians, who boldly declared, "The will of the *minjung* is the will of God." While the dictatorship liberally used anti-Communism to tar nearly all its opponents with the brush of "enemy agents" linked to Pyongyang, it was unable to use that smear against Christian activists—since their belief in God automatically exempted them from charges of being godless communists. As a new interpretive frame, *minjung* theology helped form a hegemonic bloc comprised of the vast majority of people.

Only after Gwangju did the *minjung* acquire their status as the new force that would change the country. In the invigorated universe of discourse, both the vocabulary and grammar of movement activism was transformed. Underground and illegal discussion circles proliferated—especially on college campuses—and a variety of perspectives emerged concerning the character of the Gwangju Uprising.[23] A central part of a transvaluation of movement goals and self-understanding after the Gwangju Uprising, the *minjung* arose as the force that could overthrow the U.S.-backed dictatorship and systematically democratize the country. The *minjung's* multiple strands gave it strength and resilience.

In 1980, there was little discussion of class struggle and anti-imperialism nor did robust ties exist between movement activists and workers or farmers. While it called for "structural transformation," NFDYS did not advocate class struggle but democratic, anti-dictatorial struggle. They did not mention anti-imperialism, anti-capitalism, or call for class struggle.

As the lessons of Gwangju were assimilated, much of the reticence to oppose U.S. imperialism and to engage in class struggle against the capitalist enemy vanished. The Gwangju Uprising had been a break in the form of social movements but not in content. While people had picked up guns to drive the army out and governed themselves through direct democracy, they also flew the ROK flag, and many people believed the USS *Coral Sea* had come to help them. In his final press conference, Yoon Sang-won had asked the United States for assistance.[24]

Soon after the suppression of the uprising, anti-Americanism emerged with a vengeance. Student movements in the 1980s, especially after 1985 (the year that started the so-called "great debates" on "social formation of South Korea" or CNP debate—C for Civil Democracy, N for National Democracy, and P for People's Democracy), began to use strident vocabulary like anti-imperialism, anti-capitalism, and class struggle more frequently, and, as I discuss below, to engage in militant struggles around these exact themes. (PD was the newcomer on the scene, first appearing around 1987). The lack of national organization that led to the terrible isolation of Gwangju and allowed the state to concentrate all its firepower on one city indicated for many people the need for leadership as well as for theory capable of winning the struggle against the U.S.-backed dictatorship.

A final dimension of the *minjung's* importance can be located in cultural transformations. Park Chung-hee had banned Western styles like the miniskirt and long hair as part of his campaign to block the 1960s counterculture and revolts from entering Korea, but *minjung* culture became a counterculture rooted in Korean tradition, a subaltern counterpublic sphere that stimulated fresh "imagination, sensitivities, and perspectives" and helped foster "horizontal expansion of movement circles" to laborers, churches, and the new working class.[25] Subaltern discourse encompassed the entire "middling group" (as Han

When office workers joined the 1987 uprising, they were dubbed the "necktie brigade."
Photographer unknown

Sang-jin named off-line office workers, sales personnel, low level administrators, and proletarianized professionals), including many college graduates who became "vertically" integrated into government and workplaces. As we will see, this stratum became one of the central constituencies of the June 1987 *Minjung* Uprising. Dubbed the "necktie brigade," thousands of proletarianized office workers helped sustain and broaden the impetus for democratization. For Han Sang-jin, the countercultural influence was widespread and became a direct precipitating factor in the June Uprising.[26]

Détournement Carlos Latuff 2003, http://fcoo.deviantart.net/images/large/indyart/photo/The_Coca_Cola_
series_final.gif

Similar to Situationist transformations of mainstream advertisements and cultural values (détournement), *minjung* culture took traditional scripts and altered them to reflect a new radical mood. While activists in the United States needed to invent a "life culture" to oppose the legacy of slavery and genocide within American "death culture," Korean students were able to draw heavily from their own history.[27] Elite SNU students presented the traditional drama of Chunhyang with the twist that instead of righteous court officials who rally to rescue the protagonist, it is peasants—in much the same way as in Im Kwon-taek's subsequent movie. So great was people's faith in the *minjung* that in an entirely separate script, the mandate of heaven was replaced by the mandate of the people. As time went on, the new subaltern culture presented narratives in which the main protagonists were female factory workers who went beyond the bonds of company and family to embrace revolution.[28] The effects of this liberated cultural space—beyond the power of the dictatorship to repress and beyond the scope of the market to turn into profits—was an important means of liberating peoples' dreams and desires from the yoke of this-worldly constraint.

Artists and *Minjung* Counterculture

With the dictatorship's repression, the role of artists in creating the *minjung* is especially important, and *minjung* art became one of the best-known dimensions of the many forms in which the movement appeared: *minjung* history, *minjung* theology, and *minjung* literature all appeared as the movement permeated the entire society. So important was art that one observer commented, "Never before in the peninsula's history, or perhaps anywhere else for that matter, has art played such a prominent role in a nation's drive to democratization."[29] An integral part of the Gwangju Uprising, producing posters and helping to organize the mass rallies, artists were on the front lines "with paintbrushes in their hands instead of guns." They had a profound impact on the movement—and their experiences in it changed their work. Seldom have collaborative works been produced with more power than that evoked by the Artists' Council for a Free Gwangju in "The Eye of Yoon Sang-won." In dynamic color and expressive composition, the uprising's political panorama unfolds in a monumental canvas. From prostitutes giving blood to DJ's prison uniform, the eye of Yoon Sang-won, gently shielded by a shamanistic dancer, forms the centerpiece and focal point. This piece, like many others, helped create a new kind of Korean art, based upon people's experiences rather than imitations of Western formalism. In the words of Choi Jungwoon: "The bloody experience of the uprising triggered artistic and cultural movements and social science research. I dare say that until then Korean art, culture, and scholarship merely copied Western models."[30]

Minjung artists bypassed the formalistic specialization of the academy in both the means of exhibition and content of their work. Dramatically portraying real world problems using new forms like expressionist woodblocks and oils, they drew inspiration from traditional papermaking and bamboo flutes, from the swirling energy of ecstatic dance and stoic contemplation of Nature. In the West since the Russian Revolution, art's political engagement is often viewed as a reduction of aesthetics to politics, of beauty to instrumentality, but Korean artists' social involvement appears to have enhanced the integrity of artistic production.[31]

The origin of *minjung* art was traced by Frank Hoffmann to Japanese artist Tomiyama Taeko, whom he believed did the "first *Minjung*-like images." Tomiyama was a friend of Kim Gi-ha, and her images of the murders in Gwangju, "Pieta of Kwangju," were important expressions of solidarity. Borrowing her juxtaposition of figures and titles from Western art, her style came from her study of Käthe Kollwitz and German expressionism. She also admired David Siqueiros, and this "same group of artists informed the first generation of Korean *Minjung* artists."[32] Hoffmann's view was repeated in Germany.[33] My interviews with Korean artist Hong Sung-dam provide evidence to the contrary. Hong laughingly explained to me that because of censorship, he had never been able to see anything by Kollwitz before 1985—years after he had already produced his own images. When he first saw Kollwitz's work, he happily and immediately recognized their great similarity. For his woodblocks, he found early inspiration in Chinese artist No Shin. During the 1980 uprising, Hong produced posters and block prints using rubber desk pads, and these were possibly the first *minjung* prints. In a follow-up email, Hong described the origin of *minjung* art as "spontaneous autogenesis": "We didn't have models or examples . . . We thought and drew what reality called for . . . *Minjung* art developed from practice."[34]

Reinvigorated by their involvement in the *minjung* movement, Korean artists broke free from pedantic emulation of Western forms so beloved in the academic world of painting. They adapted traditional Korean forms like calligraphy and injected subversive elements into indigenous forms of shamanism, *pansori*, masked dance, *pungmul*, and drumming—helping to build a counterculture of struggle—and not just for the middle class. Theater group *Kwangdae* toured the Jeolla countryside, performing at night to villagers who then joined in for festive dance and music. They were part of a veritable movement of theater activists who used traditional popular (*maddangguk*) dramas synthesized with modern elements to create plays of struggle.[35]

Together with other artists, the Gwangju Artists' Council brought together a "Party for the Year 2000" in November 1980. Optimistically conjuring a time and space after the dictatorship's demise, every piece in their first exhibition was confiscated by the military. Unable to get gallery space, they moved to a riverbank for the "health of art" and aimed to relieve the pain and suffering of victims of May 18. They proclaimed: "To restore human dignity, artists should speculate about themselves first and firmly face the absurdities of society that cause the contradictions of the age. Thus we declare that we artists will devote ourselves to enhancing human dignity on the basis of the consciousness of this age."[36] In Seoul in 1980, *minjung* art gained its first gallery space for a show by the Reality and Utterance Collective. The government immediately shut it down.

In 1981, the May Poetry Group published their first magazine, and they included visual media like Hong Sung-dam's prints. One of the country's best-known poets, Ko Un, expressed a sentiment similar to visual artists in Gwangju: "The role of a poet in Korea is not just to write about sentiment, but also to write about movements in history. Poetry is the song of history."[37] Gwangju poet Mun Byong-ran's book of poems, *My Voice Calling for the Dawn*, was so popular it went into its fifth edition.

In December 1981, Hong helped organize an outdoor show, this time on the outskirts of Gwangju in Songjongri. The statement for the show reflected *minjung's* art values: "All we have to do these days is to verify the essence of people's lives. Artists should get out of their studios and get involved."[38] While conducting outdoor shows, Hong and the Gwangju Artists' Council collaborated with theater groups.

The wide net cast by censors meant artists' portrayals of the uprising became larger than life, expressing as they did in images what could not be legally clarified in words. Since journalistic and historical accounts of the uprising were illegal, music, literature, paintings, poetry, and plays became subversive media for expression of the truth about Gwangju, adding another dimension to the movement's vitality.[39] Art was no longer confined to galleries, museums and boutiques but burst onto public space with a vital presence. Illegal plays, banned novels, subversive poetry, and censored songs—to say nothing of antidictatorship paintings—helped forge the *minjung* as a reality at the same time as the normal audience for art expanded. Activists organizing protests made easy targets, but cultural workers were more elusive. Theater teams performed in public places without announcement before melting back into crowds; posters were hung when police were not around; films were shown in homes; visual artists privately exhibited their work; and poems were sold under the counter in bookshops or simply passed around at bus stops. Woodblock prints became a vital medium capable of producing hundreds of copies that could be made at home and distributed informally—beyond the censors' reach.

Puppet Show by Hong Sung-dam. Woodblock print 270x305 mm. 1986

Sometimes, reproductions of art could be shared by neighbors, like a bowl of food being the cover to spread information from door to door as had been practiced for centuries in the past—a legacy of traditional civil society (사발통문). As an expressive vehicle, visual art was able to bring attention to the U.S. role in Gwangju and focus energy on "American cultural colonialism," issues that could be better portrayed in art than in photography. Although many people intuitively knew the United States had abetted Chun, Hong Sung-dam's woodblock prints were able to confirm that suspicion and give people a visceral means to point it out.

In 1985, artists organized a Popular Culture Research Center with a Visual Media Center, which was able to involve dozens of people in ongoing production of insurgent themes. By collaborating across media, artists overcame academic specialization. Not only was the effect of their new combinations of forms exhilarating, they learned from each other and reinvented Korean identity. Banners for rallies became more intense and didactic through a formal adopting of Buddhist and shamanistic expression. Elements of shamanistic ritual were grasped as a means to invoke powers not of this world, while *pungmul* and mask dance (*talchum*) punctured the gravity and danger of many demonstrations. Artists invigorated movement events through indigenous forms of sublimation that expressed essential features of Korean life, especially *han* (longstanding grief, suffering, and sorrow). Artists' ritualistic expressions helped make demonstrations a release of *han* through the forging of collective solidarity and *shinmyong* (group joy and festiveness).[40] Eros and revolution mingled joyously in the midst of police attacks and severe repression. In moments of quiet, dancers often participated in demonstrations with no fixed stage, with no barrier between them and the participants, helping break down structures of hierarchy in spontaneously created collective space.

The elegance of *minjung* art was lost on the dictatorship. In 1985, the show Power of the Younger Generation was confiscated and some of its artists imprisoned.[41] Korea's most famous poet, Kim Gi-ha, was repeatedly arrested and even sentenced to death—although he was later released. Despite police presence, the Association of *Minjung* Artists (*Minmihyup*) and a Seoul film collective brought art into the streets and helped create a vibrant video scene tied to political movements. By November 22, 1985, a Council of Peoples' Artists had been established, "bringing together artists and activists to consolidate a cultural revolution."

Korea's Student Movement

In much of the world, Korean student movements in the 1980s became the stuff of mythology. Poorly understood but widely worshipped, college activists led the nation in achieving democratic reform. More than anyone else, they became the carriers of the new subaltern interpretive frame, bringing the message to workplaces and rural areas. As in so many other countries, students also provided the frontline troops needed to defeat dictatorship. At the same time as the Gwangju Uprising revolutionized subjective forces, Korea's material conditions of existence were being transformed. As South Korea industrialized, universities became central to the economy, providing research and development as well as the off-line workers needed for the country's economic development. Concentrated on campuses with a chance to discuss ideas critically and more time to do so than people with full-time jobs, students are an ideal protest constituency. In Korea, Confucian respect for scholars affords them a sense of pride and duty to lead the country forward.

Since the fifteenth century, when Korea was undergoing a transition to a neo-Confucian system, students have played an important role in Korean politics. At that time, nearly all students were sons of the elite nobility, and they served as the extreme cutting edge of the new order, even daring to protest against King Sejong for his compassion to Buddhism. In 1519, they barged through the palace gates and brought their protest to the doors of the king's home. As Gregory Henderson observed, "Probably nowhere else in the world is there so ancient and continuous a tradition of student demonstrations, memorializing, and active participation in national politics as in Korea."[42]

In the late twentieth century, three factors contributed to a bulging student population. The country's post–Korean War baby boom was huge; the literacy

TABLE 8.1 **College Students in South Korea, 1945–1993**

Year	Number
1945	7,800
1952	34,000
1971	195,000
1986	1,242,000
1993	2,100,000

Sources: Christopher J. Sigur, *Democracy in Korea: The Roh Tae Woo Years* (New York: Carnegie Council on Ethics and International Affairs, 1992), 62; Mi Park, *Democracy and Social Change: A History of South Korean Student Movements, 1980–2000* (Bern: Peter Lang, 2008), 65.

rate was 98 percent; and one-third of all high school graduates went on to college. From 1965 to 1985, Korean young people were increasingly conferred the opportunity for formal education. From only 35 percent of youth attending secondary schools in 1965, 90 percent did so in 1985,[43] and they were concentrated in the large cities, especially Seoul. From 1945, the number of university students grew exponentially—particularly in the period leading up to the June Uprising, as illustrated in TABLE 8.1. The economy had grown an average annual rate of 8.4 percent from 1962 to 1987, and per capita income had soared from $86 in 1960 to $2,800 in 1987.[44] Korea's phenomenal economic transformation meant dislocations and periods of adjustment as well as opportunities. In 1987, the country's unemployment rate was low, but one estimate placed the number of college graduates who could not find jobs in 1987 at more than 40 percent.[45]

In the same period, the country went from being overwhelmingly rural to an urbanized society in which, by 1987, fewer than one in five citizens resided in the countryside.

After Gwangju, the military government strictly disciplined the entire country—especially the campuses. Agents flooded into universities to spy and arrest anyone they caught speaking out against the government, organizing protests, or distributing leaflets. At Yonsei University alone, there were about three hundred undercover agents in 1978; by 1982, their number had grown to about eight hundred—to infiltrate and report on a student body of ten thousand.[46]

Although student mobilizations in 1983 were small, seldom reaching more than a thousand participants, underground organizations bore fruit as the post-Gwangju movement increased in size. A notable protest came on March 22, 1983, at Sungkyungkwan University, where two thousand students used sticks and stones from a construction site to battle police. Their leaflet placed Gwangju squarely at the center of their actions. They reiterated the demand first articulated in rallies in liberated Gwangju—that Chun Doo-hwan be brought to trial: "In 1980, some 2,000 people of Gwangju who were yearning for democracy were mercilessly massacred. Those lives were sacrificed for democracy. Who will compensate for their lives? Our brothers and sisters who were mercilessly beaten and raped by Chun's soldiers—who will heal them? Student Body! We proclaim we are the makers of history. Our only way to survive is to bring down the Chun Doo-hwan regime. Let us all participate in bringing Chun Doo-hwan to trial before history."[47]

Around the same time, feminism informed the movement and deepened its self-understanding. Already in the 1970s, Christian women had protested Korean male sex tourism (although few people had shown interest in the issue), and a Women's Studies Program had formed at Ewha University. In the 1980s, progressive women theologians came together inside *minjung* theology, and in 1983, the first hotline and rape crisis center made its appearance in Seoul. Around the same time as the feminist group Equality and Friendship formed, the Christian Women's Grassroots Organization began to work with poor and marginalized women. These groups' varying ideologies reflected the specialization and complexity in Korean society. Like in Germany, as noted by Chong-Sook Kang and Ilse Lenz, women began to articulate new forms of subjectivity and autonomy.[48] In so doing they set an example that a variety of movement groups would soon follow. Women were nearly 27 percent of college students in 1985 (and the majority of people studying art and to become teachers.).[49] In 1984, a national Women's Studies Association formed, and two other progressive women's organizations emerged that would help women play significant roles in the democracy movement: Alternative Culture (whose name implies their focus on transformation of patriarchal everyday life) and the Women's Bureau of the Youth Association for Democracy (which focused primarily on the struggles of marginalized women and the democratization movement).[50]

While students continued to mobilize, the truth about Gwangju was being revealed, and workers were increasingly restive. In 1984, Buddhists created a national organization to work for democracy, the Buddhist People's Movement Federation. A farmers' movement emerged in 1985 in response to a cattle price crisis precipitated by Chun's favoring U.S. beef imports—among more than three hundred agricultural and livestock products he permitted to be imported. Korea became the U.S.'s fourth-largest trading partner for such goods and the country's food self-sufficiency index fell to 47.7 percent. In response, farmers organized, and by the end of 1986, they published more than fifty county-based newspapers. Faced with stiffening resistance, Chun did what came best to him: he clamped down even harder.

On the campuses in 1984, as soon as Chun ordered the army to withdraw, activists revived student governments and protests flared up. "The main thing right away was Gwangju."[51] In late October, after the university expelled the elected student president, 80 percent of Seoul National University students refused to take their midterm exams. More than six thousand riot police occupied the campus for two days to restore order. On November 20, activists organized the National Federation of Student Councils (*Chonhaknyon*) at Korea University. One of the group's first actions was to sit-in at the headquarters of Chun's ruling Democratic Justice Party (DJP). Police moved in and arrested 264 students.[52] Three weeks earlier, on November 3, representatives of forty-two colleges had formed the United Students for Democratization Movements. The two groups developed an organic division of labor in which United Students took over demonstrations, while the Federation took care of coalition networking.

As the number of protests grew (see TABLE 8.2), they also became increasingly sophisticated. The brutality meted out in Gwangju and Chun's apparatus of campus repression compelled students to better organize themselves. Rather

TABLE 8.2 **Student Protests in the 1980s**

Year	Number of Protests	Number of Participants
1980	70	258,322
1981	39	21,950
1982	70	70,846
1983	143	36,585
1984	1,499	144,126
1985	2,138	469,000
1986	1,270	288,102
1987	1,821	930,644
1988	1,603	605,856
1989	1,772	644,554

Source: Chulhee Chung, "Social Movement Organization and the June Uprising," in *Korean Politics: Striving for Democracy and Unification*, ed. Korean National Commission for UNESCO (Elizabeth, NJ: Hollym, 2002), 246.

than simply gathering at one big demonstration where they could be confronted by massed police, activists formed affinity groups of four to seven people that went to demonstrations together and engaged in a variety of hit and run tactics suited to overcoming the concentrated power of riot police. Informal communication networks of "posts" (demonstration teams and leafleting teams) formed, and councils of posts coordinated them. Difficulties in harmonizing actions then led to "lines"—generally four groups, each with an overall headquarters on campus: political struggle, "propaganda," support of labor movements, and the local student association. Each working line could have as many cells as needed, while student governments had departmentally organized groups.[53]

In the early 1980s, many different attempts were made to form a national federation of student groups, but none succeeded in uniting all sectors. Students were clearly activated by Gwangju. As the conscience of the nation, they took seriously their responsibility for the country's future. Korean students studied their protests during Seoul Spring and concluded that "one of the main causes of the failure of 1980 was that the movement then did not lay its base on the *minjung*" and was "overlooking the essence of the opportunistic conservative political groups" (by which they meant politicians like DJ and YS).[54] The National Alliance of Student Associations, formed on April 17, 1985, at Korea University, expressed "unshakeable faith in the *minjung*" (whom they defined as "the class coalition at the core of labor, peasantry, and the urban poor").[55] Basing itself on radical interpretations of forbidden Marxism, the group fundamentally opposed the United States, which it considered to be primarily responsible for Chun's regime. The next month, on the fifth anniversary of the Gwangju Uprising, they sponsored spirited demonstrations of nine thousand students from thirty-six universities on May 15; more than twenty thousand the next day from thirty-nine universities; and finally, on May 17, some thirty-eight thousand students from eighty universities.[56]

On May 23, the group organized seventy-three students to occupy the USIS Cultural Center in Seoul and demanded an apology from the United States for its complicity in the Gwangju massacre as well as withdrawal of American support for

TABLE 8.3 **Student Rallies, 1984–1986**

Dates	Number of Rallies
First semester 1984	949
Second semester 1984	1,136
First semester 1985	1,883
Second semester 1985	792
First month of first semester 1986	71
Total, March 1984–April 1986	**4,831**

Source: Manwoo Lee, "Anti-Americanism and South Korea's Changing Perception of America," in *Alliance Under Tension: The Evolution of South Korean–U.S. Relations*, eds. Manwoo Lee, R.D. McLaurin, and Chung-in Moon (Boulder: Westview Press, 1988), 16. First semester begins in March, the second in September.

Chun. This action captured great media attention and led in the next few months to at least five other attempted occupations at places like the U.S. embassy, the U.S. Chamber of Commerce, the DJP's training institute, the Ministry of Labor offices in Suwon and Gwangju, and the Federation of Industries. The subsequent trial of defendants in the occupation of the USIS Cultural Center so politicized the country that the Minister of Legal Affairs was fired for his incompetence. In the wake of the trial, the government arrested sixty-three key student leaders and effectively banned their organizations, but new ones were quickly established. Students' success in activating protests in the first semester of 1985 is reflected in TABLE 8.3.

The flexibility in the activist milieu—its ever-changing alliances, coalitions, and leaders—made it both difficult for the police to identify key activists and easy for like-minded students to align with each other. While short-lived, these groups prepared the ground for the formation of the next ones. Thousands of activists gained valuable organizational experiences in the movement's continual reorganization and nurtured each other's development. As they built up organizational strength, they simultaneously encouraged each other to make lifetime commitments.

The extraparliamentary opposition (*chaeya*) of activists from 1970s movements (among students, laborers, dismissed professors, feminists, and banned journalists) organically united many of the constituencies that were becoming even more energized in the 1980s. One of the first formations that broke with *chaeya* activists' reluctance to tinge themselves through association with radical students in the 1980s was the Youth Alliance for Democratization Movement (YADM, or 민청련), which formed on September 30, 1983. Their founding manifesto of September 30, 1983, emphasized four key points:

1) To achieve a truly democratic political system for unification of the nation.
2) To achieve an independent and democratic economic system for the equal and humane life of people, and to abolish corruption and politics for/of/by the privileged.
3) To achieve an independent and creative culture and educational system for the dynamic and healthy life of people.
4) To abolish the Cold War and nuclear weapons for international peace and survival of the nation.[57]

Uniting a variety of organizations, the alliance selected former student activist Kim Gun-tae as its first chairperson. They held one of the first memorials in Seoul for victims of the Gwangju massacre, and set about connecting students with workers and Christians. While Protestant groups were generally aloof, YADM worked closely with Young Catholic Workers, (*Jeunesse Ouvrière Chrétienne* or JOC).

YADM's paid staff members included people responsible for federations with other movement sectors as well as an action branch that helped pull together the March 23, 1985, occupation of the USIS Cultural Center. Besides their own alliances and coalition, YADM and radical students were part of a broader movement of federations advocating reunification that began to appear with great frequency, such as the Federation of *Minjung* Culture and the Council of *Minjung* Buddhism. In October 1984, some 23 organizations formed a broad coalition, the National Council (국민 회의), whose members included the Seoul Federation of Labor Movements, the Workers' Welfare Council, and the Korean Federation of Christian Workers. Like the student alliances that were continually dissolving and reconstituting themselves as a way to break the stranglehold of government suppression, similar attempts were made to reorganize broad bases among workers, farmers, and the democratic movement. With so many different groups rising up against Chun's rule, citizens needed a coordinating group. Korean peoples' strong civil society was a resource that facilitated their efforts. People's capacity to form unified communal forms and large coalitions was a great advantage in their endeavors to overthrow the dictatorship.

On March 29, 1985, the United Minjung Movement for Democracy and Reunification (UMMDR or 민통련) formed at the initiative of YADM and became one of the most inclusive organizations yet to appear with a national roster of key activists (including students). UMMDR soon became a leading force of the entire movement, spawned twenty-five regional branches, and published a national journal, *Voice of the People*. UMMDR urged activists to promote cultural reform as well as political revolution as steps toward reunification of the country. As the group grew in influence, on September 20, they coalesced with religious leaders and politicians in campaigns for constitutional revision. Before being declared illegal on November 11, 1986 (when its offices were closed and its leaders went underground), UMMDR facilitated movement ties across sectors and put reunification squarely at the center of the movement's agenda.

Soon after its formation, key YADM activists became involved in an internal strategic debate. Some felt it best to organize laborers as the key constituency, while others wanted to mobilize as many people as possible in street protests and political actions.[58] Divergent perspectives soon emerged in movement circles everywhere. They remain to this day a source of division and discussion.

Tendencies within the Movement: PD and NL

As the movement grew by leaps and bounds, activists' viewpoints by 1985 clustered around "national democratic revolution," or NL, and "civil democracy," or CD, which had all but disappeared by 1987 as "people's democracy," or PD, emerged. The largest of these tendencies, NL drew great inspiration from Kim

Il-sung's essay, "On Juche Ideology." They felt the main contradiction was between U.S. imperialism and the Korean nation, while PD conceived the main contradiction was capital vs. *minjung*. As NL's focus was on U.S. imperialism, they led the impetus against compulsory military training for male college sophomores and organized actions like the occupation of the USIS Cultural Center in Seoul. The "Iron Letter" by Kim Young-hwan in 1985 became the basis for NL's positions on many questions. In the fall of 1985, a well-known NL pamphlet clarified the group's position: "The main agent of the fascist domination of the Korean people is U.S. imperialism. Conservative bureaucrats, monopoly capitalists, and the military in South Korea are only servants of the U.S."[59]

A few months later, NL's campaign against campus military training began. On April 28, 1986, SNU students Lee Jae-ho and Kim Se-jin committed suicide. As they set themselves aflame, they shouted, "No to Nuclear Weapons!" and "Yankee Go Home!"[60] Lee and Kim's sacrifice spurred greater intensity in movement actions, the most significant of which was organized by the combined forces of PD, NL, CD, the labor movement, and the UMMDR. On May 3, 1986, in Incheon, more than ten thousand people militantly fought with the police. Demonstrators carried signs reading, "Oust the Yankees!" They set fire to an office of Chun's DJP as well as to a car belonging to the opposition NKDP. By attacking both the dictatorship and the liberal party, people in the streets anticipated how "opposition" politicians would subsequently sell out demands for substantive democracy. The protest was "on the verge of becoming a Kwangju-style popular uprising before it was brought under control by a massive riot police force."[61] Despite many arrests, the Incheon action showed the potential power of united forces of *minjung*.[62]

Both for its militancy and for the unity of workers and students, the Incheon action frightened Korean and American elites, greatly fueling efforts at the top to change Chun's obstinate refusal to permit direct elections. Refusing to compromise, Chun instead clamped down. When NL organized a huge meeting at Seoul's Konkuk University in October, he sent in seven thousand riot police with orders to surround the campus. Water, heat and electricity services were cut off.[63] Students held out without food or water for three days and nights, until police finally arrested 1,525 people from twenty-six universities on October 28. Among those arrested for the "crime" of attending a meeting to organize a national organization was a member of the National Assembly.

In the aftermath of the Incheon action and Konkuk University arrests, opposition forces regrouped. Forced to close their offices, UMMDR leaders went underground. Civil Democracy (CD), which advocated a people's constitution as a means to create a better system, soon disappeared. While many different positions were advocated, many activists congealed around PD's call to build a worker-student alliance and to expand organizations among workers. Activists lived the slogan, "Building people's power through the working class struggle."[64] Some counted as many as ten thousand students who went to work in factories as "disguised workers" (*hakchool*) in the 1980s, although it appears that three thousand is a more accurate estimate.[65] Unlike traditional Leninist vanguards, PD sought to become one with workers.[66]

TABLE 8.4 **Tendencies in the South Korean Movement**

Tendency	Main Contradiction	Character of ROK	Main Goal	Slogan
NL National Liberation (Jamintu 자민투)	Imperialism	Semi-capitalist neocolony of the United States	United States out of Korea; Reunification	United States Out of Korea! Nation, People, Struggle
PD People's Democracy (Minmintu 민민투)	Class	State monopoly capitalism	*Minjung* Democracy	Against Imperialism, Comprador Capitalism, and Fascism

While activists worked together, ideological struggles between NL and PD continually emerged, as with the Flag and Anti-flag debate and the Declaration of Anti-imperialist and Anti-fascist Struggle.[67] One indication of the movement's intense thirst for revolutionary theory was the formation of at least twenty-four different radical publishing companies by 1987. While internal differences and severe repression meant large coalitions encountered difficulties holding together, they nonetheless played significant roles in preparing the groundwork for student leadership of the 1987 June Uprising. While both streams were Leninist in orientation, they differed on the question of whether or not North Korea was a free country. For NL activists, South Korea was a semicapitalist neocolony of the United States and could be free only through reunification. The strategic implication of that position meant building an alliance with all Koreans—including bourgeois democratic forces. PD, on the other hand, understood the need for a revolutionary transformation of South Korea and advocated overthrowing both the military dictatorship and *chaebols* (as well as expelling the United States). For PD, North Korea was no workers' paradise and decidedly not a model for how a reunified Korea should be structured.

After Gwangju, activists' discussions were animated by intense exchanges involving levels of analysis previously marginalized: were the comprador bourgeoisie the main problem or was U.S. imperialism the principal enemy? According to NL's analysis, the Gwangju Uprising starkly represented the contradiction between U.S. imperialism and the people of Korea. Imperialism had divided the country, and the United States was primarily responsible for the massacre since the CFC command was in the U.S. hands of U.S. General Wickham. Neocolonialism was the chief problem plaguing Korea, and removing international capital and U.S. troops was the solution. The PD perspective, while noting the urgent task of fighting imperialism, understood Gwangju as a contradiction between the fascist dictatorship of the military, which served the interests of the *chaebol*, and the democratic aspirations of the Korean people. Flowing from this analysis was the conclusion that the first task of the movement was to liberate South Korea, necessitating a base among workers. Building *minjung* democracy was a step toward reunification of a free Korea.

These movement tendencies were not abstract formulations of political beliefs but carried with them practical repercussions. In 1986, each tendency organized its own networks and actions, although they also came together beautifully during the June Uprising. In 1986, NL won most campus elections. No one has exact numbers, but something like ten thouand activists were affiliated with PD groups while perhaps twice that number were in NL groups of one kind or another. Ranging from Leninist activists to academics, PD was more diverse than NL, which was far more disciplined. Within NL, three subgroups eventually emerged, each with its own interpretation of *juche* (the self-reliance ideology of Kim Il-sung)—one dogmatically worshipping Kim Il-sung, one called "love of humanity," and one with its own interpretation of *juche* but believing the base for the revolution was North Korea.

Since NL groups generally support the DPRK as the leadership of the anti-U.S. struggle, they do not seek to build a new party in the South, but instead to promote national unity. By contrast, many PD activists believe independent struggle in the South is necessary for liberation and democratization of the entire country. With a strictly hierarchical orientation in which members follow the line of national (and international) coordination, NL has far greater organizational strength than PD, and had continually outmaneuvered PD in every instance from the 1980s to the present—from student organizations to unions to political parties.

Applauded by the country, students overwhelmingly became the regime's most tireless opponents—and its political prisoners. From little more than one-third of political prisoners in 1978, students became more than 80 percent by 1986, as indicated in TABLE 8.5.

Police arrest statistics are certainly problematic. If anything, it appears the below numbers understate the number of prisoners. *Joongang Ilbo* reported on August 31 and October 4 that the NKDP claimed 1,229 political prisoners were held on September 30, 1986.

Repression may have been difficult to focus on the right people, but it was not for want of trying. At least 813 students were arrested during spring semester of 1986—more than four times the number during the first half of the previous year. More disturbing is that frustration with continuing regime intransigence led six student activists to commit suicide during that time. Chun could have cared

TABLE 8.5 **Occupations of Political Prisoners in South Korea, 1978–1986, by Percentage**

Occupation	1978	1982	1986
College Students	35.2	73.4	83.0
Workers and Farmers	9.8	14.0	13.9
Other	55.0	12.6	3.1
Church Leaders	44.5	3.1	
Writers and Journalists	4.3	0	
Politicians	3.6	0.4	
Professors	2.6	3.6	
Unemployed	0	5.5	
Total	100.0	100.0	100.0
Total Number of Cases	**778**	**417**	**978**

Sources: World Council of Churches, ROK Ministry of Legal Affairs, as reported in Wonmo Dong, "University Students in South Korean Politics: Patterns of Radicalization in the 1980s," *Journal of International Affairs* 40, no. 2 (Winter 1987): 239.

less; surprise night raids at all major universities were massively orchestrated on February 4, February 14, July 11, August 4, and August 11.[68] The student movement remained intense throughout 1986: of 3,400 people arrested at antigovernment rallies, 2,900 were students—more than three times more than the 901 arrested in 1985. Significantly in 1986, 250 factory workers were among those arrested. While nearly every young man had military training, surprisingly few people even considered an armed struggle of small guerrilla groups. A general consensus existed that massive and militant struggles needed to be waged for many years in order to overthrow the regime. One exception was the National Liberation Front in the 1970s, most of whose members were arrested soon after it formed, among them poet-activist Kim Nam-ju. Several were executed in Soedaemun Prison, the same venue where eight falsely accused members of a nonexistent People's Revolutionary Party had been murdered by the state in 1975.

Despite the repression of the regime, students found ways to get their message out. They pulled fire alarms to get students out of class and distributed leaflets among exiting students; they used masked dance to call for actions; they went into movie theaters and distributed their pamphlets; and they did five minute drills in which they would unfurl banners, give out leaflets, and leave before police could arrive to arrest them.

Building a Workers' Movement

At the same time as hundreds of students languished in the nation's prisons, thousands more secretly entrenched themselves in the nation's factories, where conditions were abysmal—dangerous and dirty, with twelve-hour shifts and six-day workweeks. Employers and the police grilled job applicants to weed out potential organizers but still, for every suspected one rejected, others stepped forward—and those refused employment at one plant simply went to the next and tried again. Many workers had little difficulty recognizing the new recruits. Although initially greeted with distance, as people respected their sincerity and commitment, organizing among the workers came naturally. Although some were able to find employment in heavy industry in Busan, Masan and Ulsan, most activists' jobs were in light industry in the Seoul-Incheon region.

The proletarian character of the Gwangju Uprising had a profound effect. As Choi Jungwoon understood: "The so-called 'labor-student alliance' in the 1980s was born in the wake of the Gwangju uprising and subsequent experiences. Only after the Gwangju uprising did intellectuals understand the importance of physical action, while workers and citizens learned language, organization, and social analysis."[69] These young former students were a different and more radical current than the religious–based Urban Industrial Mission. Inspired by Central America's theology of liberation and Martin Luther King Jr., UIM sent organizers into factories. They claimed to have placed people inside 20—the government counted 130.

By the mid-1980s, South Korea was very different than it had been a few decades earlier. From 1966 to 1985, the number of nonfarm wageworkers more than tripled—from 2.1 million to 7.7 million. From half of total employment in 1970, agriculture accounted for only 20 percent in 1987. A handful of *chaebol* controlled as much as 45 percent of GNP, and they kept unions out—a selling point to foreign investors who poured money into Korea as restrictions on them were lifted. As the countryside emptied, people moved to urban shantytowns and felt lucky to find work so they could send money home to their families, even though many urban working-class families could barely make ends meet. Economist Byung-Nak Song calculated the basic poverty level by considering the subsistence budget for a typical household. He found that 60 percent of family units fell below that line in 1980, as did 44.5 percent in 1985.[70] Other groups had even higher estimates of people trapped in dire conditions. Workers were compelled to put what was touted to be the "world's longest workweek: 54.7 hours/week in 1986 (compared to 47.3 in Sri Lanka, 46.0 in Japan, 45.2 in Hong Kong, and 40.7 in the United States). Workers were also grossly underpaid: they made an average of $1.69/hour in manufacturing (compared to $13.46 in the United States, $11.34 in Japan, $2.23 in Taiwan and $2.11 in Hong Kong).[71] For such meager rewards, people risked life and limb: in Korea, an astonishing 2.6 percent of the workforce was killed or injured in 1987; by comparison, in Taiwan it was only 0.7 percent and in Japan, 0.61 percent.[72]

The first-generation of urbanized workers proved a fertile ground for taking action once an opening was provided. Chief among those exploited in Korean industry were women. In the Masan Free Export Zone, more than three-fourths of the workers were female, and more than half of them were teenagers. What few "yellow" unions that did exist were used to discipline the women through a system that privileged males. Strikes and autonomous unions were illegal. Even so, by 1985, movement efforts bore extraordinary results. In the first six months, the Labor Ministry reported a doubling of the number of labor disputes from the previous year to 146.[73]

As workers and students merged into a common milieu, the seeds of organizing efforts, although always facing difficulties, found fertile grounds. As activists patiently continued their efforts, success came step-by-step. At Daewoo Motors, one of South Korea's big-three automakers, more than half of the elected union delegates in the company's yellow union were democracy activists. From below, they led an effort to pressure the union's company-friendly leaders. When bargaining on a new agreement broke down, a six-day strike ensued on April 16, 1985. Police sought to break the strike, but workers armed themselves with sticks and occupied the Technology Center. Surrounded by eight thousand police, three hundred workers threatened to destroy the computers if the police attacked. Food and water were cut off. Two thousand workers rallied in support of their colleagues. Finally Daewoo president Kim Woo-jung arrived, and after negotiations, he agreed to meet most of the workers' original demands.

The Daewoo struggle, the first major strike by male production workers, was costly in terms of subsequent repression at the plant, but it inspired others to take militant, autonomous action. Movement conservatives were shocked by the occupation tactic and argued to build up organization before engaging in such struggles. Grassroots groups continued to move to a higher level. In the Guro Industrial Park, hundreds of factories employed thousands of young women who dubbed their crowded living quarters "beehives." Student activists helped organize a giant women's rally with the theme, "Women's Movement in Unity with the National Democratic *Minjung* Movement." Thousands of women workers attended.[74] Subsequently, union drives proliferated. Overworked and underpaid, they were also tyrannized at the workplace, so much so that when over seven thousand women members of the FKTU were asked what their ideal job looked like, the most popular response was "humanitarian treatment." By comparison, only 8 percent said higher wages, even though women made on the average less than half of men with similar jobs. No less than twenty-six support groups were active for workers rights. Used to getting their way, the companies in the area resisted even minimal changes, and a bitter contest ensued. After three union leaders were fired, workers at five different firms organized a ten-day solidarity strike. Street demonstrations, vigils, refusal of meals, and sit-ins involved thousands of workers from ten unions. Although significant for the interunion solidarity it helped spawn, the strike itself was shut down by hired goon squads who were called in to occupy buildings and attack sit-ins. More than seven hundred workers were fired.[75]

Police spies and raids netted hundreds of union organizers. In a one-year period, 1985–1986, police arrested 671 such disguised worker "agitators."[76] In June 1986, Kwon In-sook was one of the students arrested for working in a factory. She was taken to a Bucheon police station, sexually assaulted, and tortured with electric shocks. In shame, she tried to kill herself, but her fellow prisoners stopped her. Once she was released, she courageously went public with her story— leading to public disgust with the regime. On February 18, 1987, spurred on by the sexual torture case and by more than a decade of women workers' struggles, activists came together and formed the Korean Women's Associations United (KWAU). Many of its founding members grew out of struggles at Control Data, YH Trading Company, Bando Trading, and other firms. The Seoul Women's Workers' Association formed in 1987, after years of organizing in factories and against the dictatorship. In their founding statement, they articulated the desperate situation of women: "women workers earn less than half what men workers earn and are forced to work the longest hours in the world. Hence women workers' livelihood and maternity are endangered. In addition, they bear the double burden of housework and suffer from beating, sexual violence, and harassment, and even sexual torture."[77]

Beginning in March 1987, female workers on the production lines serving Adler Corporation—one of Germany's most successful profit-making activities in Korea—tried without success for their union to negotiate better wages, more free time, better food and more buses to transport them to the distant location of the firm. On April 1, the company announced that the FKTU union had agreed to a new contract that did not include any real changes, and the workers turned it down. The company fired all who opposed the agreement. In response, more than seven hundred women went on strike, and a bitter contest ensued. After one woman tried to take her life in protest, church groups in Germany and Korea mobilized to support the workers, but the company remained stubbornly intransigent. In mid-August, a little known group, the Red Zoras, carried out arson attacks on several Adler outlets in Germany.[78] At first, Adler threatened to move its production to Sri Lanka, but within a month of the arson attacks, they settled: all the fired women were reinstated, wages were raised 23.5 percent, and for the first time, the women could freely elect a union.[79]

Politicians Take the Lead

At the same time as diversity can strengthen insurgent movements by stimulating fresh thinking and propelling people to act resolutely, the NL-PD division also enervated the radical impetus and created space for pro-American politicians to lead the democratization impetus. In this venture, Chun's repressive measures were only too cooperative, legitimizing as they did, mainstream politicians and making them seem like saviors of democracy. Since movement circles had grown so radical in relation to ordinary citizens, a huge gap existed, and the regime painted all students with the stigma of being Communists. Even within the movement, students were increasingly viewed with suspicion. A bulletin of the Christian Institute, a stalwart of the movement, reported that on August 9, 1986, some forty people calling themselves professional revolutionaries formed a Leninist organization that was "training for an armed struggle in order to destroy the present government and to set up an interim revolutionary government for establishing the Democratic *Minjung* Republic. For this they insisted on conducting revolutionary change of the constitution—not the reformist type of revising the constitution."[80] Some Christian activists viewed NL groups with suspicion for holding high regard for the *juche* theory of Kim Il-sung. Even though they agreed with the boycott movement against military training, war, and nuclear power, and admired the stridency of NL demands for direct elections in the first half of 1986, they disapproved of NL's anti-Americanism.[81]

Among the many voices expressing concern with students' "extremism," Cardinal Stephen Kim exhorted the students to distance themselves from "left-leaning radical ideology and the cry of the revolution."[82] Step-by-step, the student movement became revolutionary as its members were radicalized by the cycle of repression and resistance. Police brutality and hefty prison sentences for those unlucky enough to be caught hardened activists and propelled their friends on the outside to redouble their efforts. Many prepared to overthrow the system through massive people's uprisings. Despite their radical positions, more than 60 percent of Koreans polled in 1986 regarded students' demonstrations as contributing to democracy, a positive evaluation constructed by years of skillful student interventions.[83] A manifesto signed by 265 professors on June 2, 1986, also positively evaluated students' impact: "The student movements . . . contain a severe critique of our university education which is compelled to produce intellectual technocrats of a colonialist mentality in service to our nation as a mere bulwark of the anti-communist world power."[84]

As their base of supporters turned to more radical avenues of protest, liberal politicians grew alarmed. From their seats in the National Assembly, they thought if only they were in power the situation could be resolved. They stepped up their drive to amend the constitution (which Chun had railroaded through in the months after Gwangju to allow him to name his own successor). "Direct presidential elections" became their mantra, a slogan for which it was all too easy to gather supporters. DJ had returned on February 2, 1985 after a two-year exile. Like Ho Chi-minh, DJ's life was saved twice by the United States (although comparisons should end there), and his followers greeted his return to Korea as if he had returned from the dead. In the legislative elections of that year, the opposition's combined total stunned Chun's ruling DJP, which received only 35 percent of the vote but retained its hold on the National Assembly because of the 1980 constitution's rigged system of allocating seats. With Chun's term set to expire in 1988, hopes ran high for direct presidential elections. By 1985, public opinion polls secretly conducted by a progovernment newspaper showed 65 percent of Koreans were dissatisfied with Chun's rule—and the number climbed to 85 percent for college grads.[85] Chun remained obstinately opposed to constitutional revision, but after all major cities had large anti-Chun rallies sponsored by the New Korea Democratic Party (NKDP) in February 1986, he decided to permit debate on revising the constitution.[86]

At this point, the liberal opposition became hegemonic, particularly after DJ and YS merged their parties into the NKDP and began in earnest a campaign for constitutional revision. On February 12, 1986, the first anniversary of the opposition's electoral victory, they kicked off a petition drive to gather ten million signatures. Chun responded by arresting hundreds of people who simply sought signatures on the streets. When organizers went into people's homes, they were also arrested.[87] In response to the arrests, more than nine hundred professors publicly signed a statement supporting the constitutional revision drive of NKDP. More and more, opposition forces grew in number—while radicals raised the intensity level of protests (as with the May 3, 1986 near-insurrection in Incheon). On May 31, at least 350 public school teachers publicized a Declaration of Democratization of Education, and on September 7, about two thousand Buddhist monks demonstrated for democracy at Haein temple in Kyongsang.

On November 28, 1986, the NKDP sought to conduct peaceful nationwide rallies, but more than thirty-two thousand combat police mobilized in Seoul to stop them. Across the country, some seventy thousand police were brought into the streets. The only place where people fought back in unison was in front of the Seoul Theater where about five hundred PD students from eight universities refused to be dispersed.[88] PD currents were progressively more militant on the streets and more active inside the nation's workplaces. As Gwangju had proletarianized the democratization movement, the workers' movement transformed human rights struggles into class confrontations. We will see how this incipient movement exploded in the summer of 1987.

U.S. Squeezes Chun

Frightened by the prospect of a radical turn in South Korea, the U.S. embassy organized a series of night meetings with opposition figures, even including the editors of twenty-three Seoul area student newspapers on January 17, 1987. Guests were requested to keep secret the content of the discussions, but underground reports carried in the Christian media noted that the U.S. ambassador "only responded to questions concerning economics, focusing on the basic issue of free trade."[89] When one professor encouraged Deputy Secretary Dunlop to intervene against the dictatorship, Dunlop retorted, "And why does the Korean government not liberalize imports?"[90]

These meetings marked the first time since 1980 that a U.S. ambassador met opposition figures. Urging restraint, the new U.S. ambassador was longtime CIA operative James Lilley, fresh from Taiwan where he had helped prod Chiang Ching-kuo's democratic reforms. Born to missionary parents in China, Lilley worked at CIA stations in Cambodia, Laos, Japan, Hong Kong, the Philippines, Thailand, and China. Around the same time as Lilley was sent to Korea, CFC Commander and U.S. General Luis Menetret sought to encourage and support reform-minded elements in the military. Across the world, the United States understood that the corrupt and dictatorial regimes it had supported for decades had become liabilities—and easier targets of insurgencies and revolutions than elected governments.[91]

In early February 1987, President Ronald Reagan's friend and advisor, Gaston Sigur, spoke to an audience of New York bankers, telling them, "The main force of change in Korea is the development of its dynamic economic system of the past decades. Thus a new dynamic political system is necessary in order to solve problems occurring during this process."[92] Coming to Seoul, Sigur praised Chun for having begun the process of political renovation. Speaking on behalf of the U.S. government, he noted that Chun was going to serve out his term in 1988 and encouraged the opposition to support the peaceful transition according to the constitutional provision providing for Chun to appoint a suitable successor. For years, Chun had made clear he had no intention of loosening his stranglehold on the country. We know now that a secret 1984 Blue House report, "Study of the Peaceful Turnover of Political Power," considered a four-phase plan to permit elections only in the year 2000.[93] When U.S. Secretary of State George Schultz visited Seoul in early 1986 and again in 1987, he supported a delay in the transition. Clearly, at the beginning of 1987, U.S. policymakers thought their Korean assistants would be able to manage to stay in power for many years to come.

Massive protests would soon cause the American position to change, but in February the United States refused to support the opposition's demand for direct presidential elections. Despite public utterances that the United States did not want to interfere in Korea's internal affairs, it kept up the pressure to appreciate the value of the won and expand markets for U.S. imports. The Reagan administration pressured Chun to open markets for beef, cigarettes, and insurance and threatened to invoke sections of trade acts to remove Korean producers from the general system of preference.[94] Even though economic liberalization had proceeded rapidly since 1980, American policymakers squeezed Chun for every last concession they could get out of him, and his government repeatedly signaled its willingness to grant the United States its every wish. Lifting of import restrictions were scheduled on a wide range of goods—some six hundred in total over a three-year period—and enhanced operations of U.S. banks and insurance companies in Korea were made possible. It seemed the old "magic of the marketplace" continued to make Chun's U.S. benefactors nod their heads in approval. Korea was a great place for U.S. investors. An aggregate figure published in 1986 by the U.S. embassy in Seoul calculated remittances from Korea to American businesses at $368 million or about 45 percent of total U.S. investments.[95]

Beneath everyone's radar screens, on January 13, 1987, SNU student Park Jong-chol was taken to a special anti-Communist police interrogation building, and as subsequently revealed by journalists and religious leaders, tortured to death. Two days later, an obscure reference in the papers noted his death as if nothing out of the ordinary had happened. A large coalition of religious leaders, activists groups, and opposition politicians called for protests against torture for February 7. Rallies were planned across the country, but riot police mobilized everywhere. In Seoul alone, seventy thousand rode their armored buses around the city. Although services had been planned for fifty cities, police broke every one of them up with clubs, tear gas, and mass arrests. In dozens of places, people conducted services in the streets, and the only confrontation was Chongno Samga where PD members used Molotovs and stones to assert their right to be in the streets.[96] Some sixty thousand peaceful people gathered at Myongdong, and in Busan and Gwangju tens of thousands stayed in the streets until early the next morning. After the rallies had been suppressed, many aimed criticism at the NKDP's failure to provide strong and assertive leadership. At a press conference marking the two-year anniversary of their electoral victory in the February 1985 national elections, Kim Young-sam and Kim Dae Jung responded by repeatedly reiterating their "Three Anti's": anti-violence, anti-Communism, and anti-anti-Americanism.

The coalition of groups who had called for the February 7 protests turned their frustration into action, announcing a month of activities "for democratization and elimination of torture" that would culminate in a national mobilization on March 3, the forty-ninth day after Park's death (and thus, the time for his reincarnation). Buddhist groups volunteered spacious Chogyesa temple in the middle of Seoul for the gathering. In response, all movement circles called for "the simultaneous utilization of all open 'legal spaces' and secret 'illegal' spaces, i.e. the mixing and unification of indirect, symbolic political struggles mixed with systematic, mass actions."

The array of participating organizations included Korean Women's Associations United (KWAU). The sexual torture case of Kwon In-sook had made the entire nation aware of women's vulnerability. The women's movement changed from being a support group for working-class women's struggles to encompassing broader demands and issues for the liberation of women altogether.[97] Female activists also went on to play a significant role in the national movement. Immediately after revelations of Park's torture death, some fifty women wearing purple scarves went to the site of his murder and protested. Although this special building was regularly used to brutalize activists, this time the police were unable to beat elderly females who had peacefully assembled.

On March 3, all over the country people from every walk of life gathered solemnly for memorials. When the police attacked in Seoul, fierce street battles ensued. Hundreds of people were arrested, universities raided, and homes invaded by the police. People refrained from using Molotovs and stones, but as the day ended, the city's streets were covered with posters and spray-paint. At the time, few people realized that nearly all ordinary Koreans—not only the Cardinal and leading politicians—had distanced themselves from Chun's repressive regime. Within three months, when practically the entire country would rise up against the dictatorship, long-time activists were among those most taken by surprise.

NOTES

1   Lee Jae-eui, *Kwangju Diary*. Originally published under the pseudonym, Hwang Seok-young.
2   See Lewis, *Laying Claim*. Many survivors still suffer mental health problems and have experienced high rates of divorce and suicide. For grim figures on Gwangju veterans' fates, see Na Kahn-chae, 항쟁은 계속되고 있다, 전대신문 1437호, 9. At least 375 of the wounded have committed suicide, and 120 still suffer from severe mental illness.
3   Cho Hee-Yeon, "A Study on the Radicalization of the Opposition Ideology by the Impact of the Gwangju Uprising," in May 18th History Compilation Committee of Gwangju City, *History of the 5.18 Democratic Uprising*, vol. 2 (Gwangju: The May 18 Memorial Foundation, 2008), 592–93.
4   Scott-Stokes and Lee Jae-eui, *The Kwangju Uprising*, 35–37.
5   On December 20, 1988, the *Chosun Ilbo* reported that former Chief of the Army Lee Hee-sung testified before the Korean Parliament that the United States had requested a delay in the army's entering Gwangju in order for the carrier and advance warning aircraft to arrive from Okinawa and the Philippines.
6   See Jameson, "U.S. Support Claimed for S. Korea's Chon."
7   Chong Hyun-ay testimony in 박병기 엮음 , 5.18연구소 자료총서 3, 5.18항쟁 증언자료 집 3 (2003) 전남대학교 출판부, 205.
8   Interview with Na Kahn-chae, Gwangju, April 1, 2009.
9   Matsui, *Women's Asia*, 140.
10 Na Kahn-chae, "A New Perspective on the Gwangju People's Resistance Struggle, 1980–1997," in *South Korean Democracy: Legacy of the Gwangju Uprising*, eds. George Katsiaficas and Na Kahn-chae (London: Routledge, 2006), 171.
11 Cited in Wonmo Dong, "Student Activism and the Presidential Politics of 1987 in South Korea," in *Political Change in South Korea*, eds. Ilpyong Kim and Young Whan Kihl (New York: Paragon House, 1989), 171.
12 Christian Institute for the Study of Justice and Development, *Social Justice Indicators in Korea* (Seoul: Minjungsa, 1988), 55.
13 *Documents of the Emergency World Assembly for South Korean Democracy* (Tokyo: Secretariat of ASKOD, 1982), 199.
14 See Baker, "The International Christian Network for Korea's Democratization," 133–63. Besides the overt support provided by overseas Christians, Baker points out that self-government within the churches provided critical experience for many Koreans to become active in the movement.
15 Huntington, *Third Wave*, 73.
16 Lee, *The Making of Minjung*, 6.
17 Wells, *South Korea's Minjung Movement*, 11.
18 Choi, *The Gwangju Uprising*, 268.
19 Ibid., 28.
20 Wells, *South Korea's Minjung Movement*, 19, 32.
21 Jiseok Jung, "Post-modern Interpretation of Ham Sokheon's *Minjung* Pacifism," paper

presented at the World Conference on Philosophy, Seoul National University, August 4, 2008.

22 Chulhee Chung, "Structure, Culture and Mobilization: The Origins of June Uprising in South Korea," unpublished doctoral dissertation (SUNY Buffalo), 92.

23 See Jung Keun-sik, "The Experience of the May 18 Uprising and the Communal Imagination," in *South Korean Democracy*, 134–57, for discussion of different theories of the uprising.

24 See the work of Kim Sang-bong, especially "The Resistant Commune and Sublated Nation," a talk delivered at the International Conference Commemorating the 30th Anniversary of the Gwangju Uprising in May 2010.

25 Nancy Fraser, "Rethinking the Public Space," in *Habermas and the Public Sphere*, ed. Craig Calhoun (Cambridge, MA: MIT Press, 1996).

26 Han Sang-Jin, "The Public Sphere and Democracy in Korea," in *Korean Politics: Striving for Democracy and Unification*, ed. Korean National Commission for UNESCO (Elizabeth, NJ: Hollym, 2002), 266–67.

27 I am indebted to Professor Kim Jin-ho for this insight.

28 Lee, *The Making of Minjung*, 207–9.

29 Frank Hoffmann, "Images of Dissent: Transformations in Korean Minjung Art," *Harvard Asia Pacific Review* 1, no. 2 (Summer 1997): 44–49.

30 Choi, *The Gwangju Uprising*, 285.

31 See Herbert Marcuse, *The Aesthetic Dimension: A Critique of Marxist Aesthetics* (Boston: Beacon Press, 1978).

32 Frank Hoffmann, "Images of Dissent: Transformations in Korean Minjung Art," 44–49. Although he is mistaken with regards to the origin of *minjung* art, Hoffmann's otherwise excellent work has much to offer.

33 Birgit Mersmann, "Minjung-Kunstaktivismus zwischen sozialistischem Realismus and democratischem Aufbruch," http://www.geocities.com/tack_pr/Minjung.html.

34 Hong Sung-dam, email, July 23, 2008. As we have seen many times, social movements produce an amazing energy that creates similar innovations in many different places simultaneously, and this dynamic was probably at work. That Japan is cited as the original source of Korean *minjung* art is, however, quite problematic given Japan's history of colonialism and propensity to claim what is Korean for its own. To take another example from social movement history, even Korea's 1919 Declaration of Independence is said to have been first organized in Tokyo's YMCA. See the map in Nishi Masayuki, "March 1 and May 4, 1919 in Korea, China and Japan: Toward an International History of East Asian Independence Movements," http://www.japanfocus.org/products/topdf/2560. Contrary evidence was discussed in Chapter 2, namely that *Chondogyo* leader Son Byeong-heui prepared the event for a decade. While many streams flow into every great river, Japanese propensity to claim their leadership of Koreans—even of Korea's movement for independence from Japan—is a striking indication of a larger problem.

35 Kim Kwang-ok, "The Role of *Maddangguk* in Contemporary Korea's Popular Culture Movement," *Korea Journal* 37, no. 3 (Fall 1997): 5–21.

36 Lee Tae-ho, "May 18 Kwangju Democratization and the Art Movement: 20 Years of the Formation of the Kwangju Civil Uprising," in 5–18관련 논문과 작품 영역 및 저술 사업: 2001. 5–18 20주년 기념 학술연구사업 연구소위 (Gwangju: 전남대학교 5–18 연구소: 2001), 134.

37 Nicholas D. Kristof, "Voice of Dissent in South Korea Speaks in Verse," *New York Times*, July 31, 1987, A2.

38 Lee Tae-ho, "May 18th Kwangju Democratization and the Art Movement" (Gwangju, Chonnam National University Museum), 3.

39 Ibid., 131.
40 See Koo, *Korean Workers*, 143–44.
41 Queen's Museum of Art, *Global Conceptualism: Points of Origin, 1950s–1980s* (2000), 120.
42 Henderson, *Korea: The Politics of the Vortex*, 201.
43 Dong Won-mo, "The Democratization of South Korea: What Role Does the Middle Class Play?" in *Korea Under Roh Tae-Woo: Democratization, Northern Policy, and Inter-Korean Relations*, ed. James Cotton (Canberra: Allen and Unwin, 1993), 75.
44 See Hang Yul Rhee, "The Economic Problems of the Korean Political Economy" in *Political Change in South Korea* (New York: The Korean PWPA Inc., 1988).
45 *Robert P. Kearney, The Warrior Worker: The History and Challenge of South Korea's Economic Miracle* (New York: Holt, 1991), 19.
46 Lindstrom, *Accumulation, Regulation, and Political Struggles*, 85.
47 Quoted in Dong, "University Students in South Korean Politics," 240.
48 Kang and Lenz, *Wenn die Hennen krähen*, 81. See chap. 2 and 3 of my book *The Subversion of Politics: European Autonomous Movements and the Decolonization of Everyday Life* (Oakland: AK Press, 2006) for discussion of how Italian and German feminists did much the same thing in their situations.
49 Moon, *Militarized Modernity*, 63.
50 Cho Joo-hyun, "The Politics of Gender Identity," in *Women's Experiences and Feminist Practices in South Korea*, eds. Chang Pilwha and Kim Eun-shil (Seoul: Ewha Womans University Press, 2005), 238.
51 Interview with Im Jong-sok, Seoul, June 4, 2001.
52 Kang Man-gil, *A History of Contemporary Korea*, 212.
53 Chulhee Chung, "Social Movement Organization and the June Uprising," in *Korean Politics: Striving for Democracy and Unification*, ed. Korean National Commission for UNESCO (Elizabeth, NJ: Hollym, 2002), 136–40.
54 Quoted in "University Students in South Korean Politics: Patterns of Radicalization in the 1980s," *Journal of International Affairs* 40 no. 2 (Winter 1987): 249.
55 Ibid., 244.
56 Cho Hyun-Yun, "The Struggle for Inquiring into the Truth of the Gwangju Democratic Uprising," in May 18th History Compilation Committee of Gwangju City, *History of the 5.18 Democratic Uprising*, vol. 2 (Gwangju: The May 18 Memorial Foundation, 2008), 751.
57 Thanks to Lee Jae-won for translation and research.
58 Interview with Kim Gun-tae, Seoul, August 2, 2008.
59 Lee, *The Making of Minjung*, 124.
60 Ibid., 125.
61 "University Students in South Korean Politics: Patterns of Radicalization in the 1980s," *Journal of International Affairs* 40, no. 2 (Winter 1987): 249.
62 Chae-Jin Lee, *A Troubled Peace: U.S. Policy and the Two Koreas* (Baltimore: Johns Hopkins University Press, 2006), 122.
63 Tun-jen Chang and Eun Mee Kim, "Making Democracy: Generalizing the South Korean Case," in *The Politics of Democratization: Generalizing East Asian Experiences*, ed. Edward Friedman (Boulder, CO: Westview Press, 1994), 134.
64 Dong Won-mo, "The Democratization of South Korea: What Role Does the Middle Class Play?" in *Korea Under Roh Tae-Woo: Democratization, Northern Policy, and Inter-Korean Relations*, ed. James Cotton (Canberra: Allen and Unwin, 1993), 7.
65 Kim Young-soo, 한국 노동자 계급정치운동 (Seoul: 현장에서 미래를: 1999), 88.
66 See the discussion in Lee, *The Making of Minjung*, 244.
67 Ibid., 163.

68 Dong, "University Students in South Korean Politics," 253.

69 Choi, *The Gwangju Uprising*, 283.

70 Byung-Nak Song, *The Rise of the Korean Economy* (Hong Kong: Oxford University Press, 1990), 179.

71 Kearney, *The Warrior Worker*, 20–22.

72 Karl Schoenberger, "Korea Shaken by Job Accident Rate," *Los Angeles Times*, July 25, 1988.

73 Hart-Landsberg, *The Rush to Development*, 273.

74 Louie, "*Minjung* Feminism," 125.

75 Koo, "The State, *Minjung*, and the Working Class," 151; Won Young-su, "History of South Korean Labor and Student Struggles Since the End of World War II," in *The International Encyclopaedia of Revolution and Protest: 1500–Present*, ed. Immanuel Ness (London: Wiley Blackwell, 2009), 13.

76 George Ogle, *South Korea: Dissent Within the Economic Miracle* (London: Zed Books, 1990), 99.

77 Moon, *Militarized Modernity*, 151.

78 For more on the Red Zoras, see *Subversion of Politics*, 132–35.

79 Michael Denis, Esther Dischereit, Du-Yul Song, and Rainer Werning, *Südkorea: Kein Land für friedliche Spiele* (Hamburg: Rowohlt, 1988), 148–51.

80 Christian Institute for the Study of Justice and Democracy, *Korean Situationer* (January–February 1987), 29–30.

81 Ibid., 31–32

82 Quoted from *Sae Gae Ilbo*, April 1, 1987, in Dong, "Student Activism and the Presidential Politics of 1987 in South Korea."

83 See *Korean Politics: Striving for Democracy and Unification*, ed. Korean National Commission for UNESCO (Elizabeth, NJ: Hollym, 2002), 388–89.

84 Dong, "Student Activism and the Presidential Politics of 1987 in South Korea," 251.

85 See *Dongrip Sinmun*, September 26, 1986.

86 Doh C. Shin, *Mass Politics and Culture in Democratizing Korea* (Cambridge: Cambridge University Press, 1999), 2.

87 Christian Institute for the Study of Justice and Development, *Lost Victory*, 40.

88 *Korean Situationer*, 28.

89 Christian Institute for the Study of Justice and Development, *Lost Victory*, 61.

90 *Korean Situationer*, 7.

91 Lee Jae-eui makes much the same point in his *Kwangju Diary*, 40.

92 Christian Institute for the Study of Justice and Development, *Lost Victory*, 63.

93 Denis, Dischereit, Song, and Werning, *Südkorea*, 225.

94 See Hong Nack Kim, "The 1987 Political Crisis and Its Implications for U.S.-Korean Relations," in *Political Change in South Korea*, eds. Ilpyong Kim and Young Whan Kihl (New York: Paragon House, 1989).

95 Ogle, *South Korea*, 38.

96 *Korean Situationer*, 20.

97 Interview with Chung Hyun-baek, Seoul, June 12, 2002.

CHAPTER 9

The June Uprising of 1987

Like volcanoes, let us go forward wholeheartedly!
—Leaflet, June 1987

Twenty billion dollars in trade flows between our two countries,
making South Korea our seventh largest trading partner. South
Korea is, in short, a country we cannot afford to ignore. It is,
therefore, essential that a way be found to reopen negotiations
between the Chun government and the opposition. For it is only
through such a dialogue that national consensus can be achieved
and political stability, continued economic growth, and the
preservation of peace can be assured.
—U.S. Congressman Stephen Solarz, May 17, 1987

CHRONOLOGY	
January 14, 1987	Park Jong-chol tortured to death
April 13, 1987	Constitutional debate suspended by Chun Doo-hwan
May 18, 1987	Cardinal Stephen Kim announces truth about Park Jong-chol's murder by torture
May 27, 1987	National Coalition for a Democratic Constitution (NCDC) formed
May 27, 1987	SNU Student Council votes to boycott classes and calls for constitutional revision
June 9, 1987	Student Lee Han-yol struck by tear gas canister, goes into coma
June 10, 1987	Roh Tae-woo nominated as next president
June 10, 1987	Protests begin with 40,000 students in Seoul and spontaneously continue for nineteen days

June 10, 1987	Myongdong Cathedral occupied by hundreds of people
June 13, 1987	Office workers ("necktie brigade") join protests
June 15, 1987	Myongdong occupiers depart victoriously
June 18, 1987	More than one million people protest, 300,000 in Busan alone; people control the streets
June 18, 1987	Chun orders troops to mobilize and plans for martial law
June 19, 1987	Chun meets U.S. Ambassador Lilley and cancels mobilization order
June 23, 1987	President Reagan's envoy, Gaston Sigur, visits Seoul for second time
June 23, 1987	20,000 students hold an open-air assembly in Seoul
June 25, 1987	Kim Dae Jung released from house arrest
June 26, 1987	Huge nationwide protests; more than one million people demonstrate in thirty-four cities
June 29, 1987	Government capitulates to opposition's call for direct presidential elections and reforms
July 5, 1987	Lee Han-yol dies of tear gas injuries suffered on June 9
July 5, 1987	First union formed at Hyundai
July 9, 1987	More than one million people attend Lee Han-yol's funeral in Seoul
July 10, 1987	Chun Doo-hwan resigns as leader of the Democratic Justice Party (DJP)
July–August 1987	Wave of strikes engulfs heavy industry

ON FEBRUARY 22, 1986 in the Philippines, a military mutiny led to a "People Power" revolution. In less than a week, President Ferdinand Marcos, the country's dictator for more than two decades, was on a U.S. plane bound for Hawaii. Few Koreans failed to read the handwriting on the wall. Within a few days of the Philippine uprising, even conservative newspaper *Chosun Ilbo* remarked: "The ruling party must keep in mind the fact that our countrymen are excited about the Philippine situation as if it were a matter of our own." On February 26, Kim Dae Jung interpreted the events for Koreans: "The most impressive thing is that the Philippines has achieved democracy through non-violence. An epochal change in U.S. foreign policy siding with democracy and the people is also a matter that we must think about."[1]

Less than a month after the outbreak of the People Power revolution in the Philippines, Cardinal Stephen Kim publicly called for democracy in Korea, saying that the people of South Korea had learned a lesson. On March 13, Kim Dae Jung wrote in the *New York Times*: "This is the time of people's power in the developing countries of Asia. We have never been so sure before." The next day, President Reagan sent a message to Congress in which he hailed developments in Haiti, the Philippines, and elsewhere as part of U.S. "promotion of a free, open and expanding market-oriented global economy."[2] He placed special hope in "democratic revolutions" to check the power of the Soviet Union.

Little more than a year later, Korea's remarkable journey from dictatorship to democracy reached a defining moment during June 1987, when for nineteen consecutive days, hundreds of thousands of people illegally stayed in the streets of every major city, refusing to go home until democracy had been won. "Gwangju, Gwangju, Gwangju!" was the word that repeatedly formed on everyone's lips. Police reported an average of more than 110 demonstrations per day *every day* during June—some 3,362 in all. Protest organizers counted more than one million participants on three different days. Historian Kang Man-gil estimated between four and five million people participated in protests during three weeks in June.[3] There were probably two million people in the streets on June 26 alone, when citizens poured into the streets in response to Chun's threat of military intervention. Faced with ever-larger demonstrations and unable to stop the mobilizations, Chun finally capitulated to the opposition's demands for direct presidential elections, release of thousands of prisoners, and greater civil rights.

The June 1987 uprising was the high point of the national movement for democracy. People's presence in the streets was so massive, it posed the possibility of a genuine revolution. While many people were convinced that a new military clampdown was coming, the United States feared another Gwangju Uprising, a mutiny within the military, or the rise of another anti-American regime on the Korean peninsula. In the midst of profound social upheavals, the frantic fear of Korean generals gave way to the cool advice of their American mentors to permit elections and allow democratic reforms. Once the dictatorship acknowledged its defeat, the urban uprising receded into the background as rapidly as it had erupted, but the largest wave of workers' strikes in Korean history engulfed the country. The capitalist accumulation regime survived, but the balance of class power shifted to bring expanded rights and privileges to unionized workers and substantial improvements to the lives of millions of ordinary citizens. Although mythologized, surprisingly little has been written in English about the June Uprising. Bruce Cumings mentions it as a ten-day affair "forcing Chun from office in June."[4] Hagen Koo claims most people arrested were workers. Neither of these statements is accurate.

Insisting that the truth about the Gwangju massacre be clarified and those responsible for it be punished, the opposition kept up the pressure for another decade. Finally in 1997, the process of democratic consolidation was completed when Chun Doo-hwan and his protégé Roh Tae-woo were convicted and imprisoned. While their sentences were later commuted, the modicum of transitional justice enacted when former dictators were sent to prison constituted an electrifying victory for Korean civil society. Both men have spent the remainder of their dishonored lives living behind a cordon of bodyguards and severely restrictive security measures.

Chun's April 13 Declaration: "No Constitutional Debate"
With Chun Doo-hwan's presidential term in office scheduled to end in 1988, the opposition mobilized a united campaign to replace him through direct popular elections, rather than by a constitutionally mandated indirect process. Assured of American support for a smooth transition, Chun believed he could simply anoint his second in command, Roh Tae-woo, as the new president. So confident

was Chun that he would continue to wield power after the transition that he insisted he might even run again someday. Despite opposition attempts to persuade him to change his mind, he unilaterally announced on April 13, 1987, that the coming 1988 Olympics demanded national unity, and no further discussion of constitutional reform would be allowed until after his successor had assumed power.

Chun's abrupt measure stunned the country. Immediately after he announced his decision, giant signs denouncing him were erected at Seoul National University, Korea University, and Yonsei University. The next day, Cardinal Kim criticized Chun in his Easter message, and the National Council of Churches also chastised the dictator. Chun was undeterred. He sent an army of thugs, paramilitaries, and police to clear out the Mokdong neighborhood of Seoul to make room for an urban renewal project aimed at sanitizing the city in preparation for the Olympics. In the following three days, bulldozers and the paramilitaries targeted eight other neighborhoods. Altogether, more than three million people were due to be displaced by Chun's grandiose plans, but residents fought back, and many refused to move. When a falling wall killed a child, the police snatched his corpse on the day of his funeral to prevent the solemn occasion from spawning public protests.

Clearly Chun believed business-as-usual would reign, but he could not have been more mistaken. His arrogance ignited an already militant opposition. As neither he nor the democratization movement would back down, someone would have to give—but no one knew whom it would be. On April 21, thirteen Catholic priests in Gwangju began a hunger strike to call for direct elections. Thirty professors at Korea University signed a public declaration in favor of a popular vote. Soon hundreds of professors signed, and groups of writers, actors, and even the National Association of Pharmacists came out in support of constitutional revision. Buddhists also mobilized as part of the unified campaign. They believed that, "If all people and democratic forces unite into one and work in solidarity to achieve genuine democratization, then we, the people, by our own powers can destroy the conspiracy of the military dictatorship to perpetuate their regime, and can truly establish a democratic government."[5]

On April 22, more than four hundred people from eighteen organizations began a sit-in protest, which lasted until May 11. In their public statement, they called upon past uprisings to define their actions: "The movement of people that is now exploding for constitutional revision follows in the footsteps of the March 1 Movement which arose calling for national independence and the April 19th Revolution which arose for democratization." On May 12, the day after their sit-in ended, over 1,500 ministers and laity from six Protestant denominations gathered to discuss their next steps. To prevent them from doing so, police brutally assaulted them.

Of all the forces in motion, students were the most tightly organized. When the new semester began in March, student councils immediately organized protests. The Ministry of Education counted 452 campus incidents in March and April.[6] In the country as a whole, people joined public protests as never before, as partially indicated in TABLE 9.1.

TABLE 9.1 **Demonstrations and Number of Participants in 1987**

Month	Demonstrations	Participants
January	61	3,400
February	53	1,600
March	131	15,000
April	425	119,400
May	856	200,000
June	3,362	1,000,000
July	427	101,000
August	3,037	566,000

Source: Chulhee Chung, "Social Movement Organization and the June Uprising," in *Korean Politics: Striving for Democracy and Unification*, ed. Korean National Commission for UNESCO (Elizabeth, NJ: Hollym, 2002), 248.

Increasingly seen as powerless, the government sought to punish students who had been arrested months earlier at Konkuk University, but students refused to stand for it. In Busan, a group hijacked midterm exams for freshmen, so the school asked the police to arrest the student council. Once the police moved in, an emergency general assembly of students forced the police and the university to back down, release the detainees, and agree to their demands for campus press freedom. Even inside the halls of the U.S. Capitol, dissenting voices began to be heard. On May 17, Representative Stephen Solarz—fresh from helping the Filipino People Power uprising overthrow Marcos—wrote in the *New York Times* that Chun's decision to end negotiations on constitutional change could "impair vital American interests in Asia."

As the seventh anniversary of the Gwangju Uprising approached, a week of events was organized on campuses across the country. On May 18, Catholic leaders in Gwangju and Myongdong simultaneously released a statement, "Truth of the Murder of Park Jong-chol." With the help of friendly prison guards, incarcerated activist Lee Bu-young had smuggled out a jailer's account of Park's water torture death that contradicted public versions released by police officials.[7] At a special memorial service for Park in Myongdong Cathedral, Cardinal Kim made a declaration of the facts, and his announcement became front-page news. In Gwangju, when over 1,500 people gathered in Mangwoldong to commemorate the uprising, they whispered to each other that the time had come at last for a national upheaval and formed a broad coalition to prepare it.

Time after time, police broke up peaceful gatherings of activists. On May 23, Reverend Park Hyung-kyu and 133 other participants from a wide coalition of groups congregated to plan the movement's next steps. Police attacked the meeting, but not before the group issued a call for national demonstrations on June 10. At Wongak Temple in downtown Gwangju, police used tear gas and clubs to assault Buddhists celebrating a special memorial for victims of the Gwangju massacre. Thirteen people were arrested. The next day, some five hundred faithful congregated in front of Province Hall in Gwangju after their plan to meet in the YMCA gymnasium was blocked by police. When they were tear-gassed, thousands more joined them, until their numbers were twenty thousand. After an hour of prayer, their ranks swelled to fifty thousand people.[8]

Creation of the *Kukbon*

While people all over the country were ready to mobilize, continual police attacks prevented organizers from meeting to create a coordinating group for national actions. In a series of discussions, my friend, older brother (*hyoung-nim*), and eventual leader of the nationwide coalition, Reverend Oh Choong-il, revealed the incredible planning needed to establish the group. At every previous gathering, the police had arrived before people could conduct any business and broken it up. Surveillance on his home was so intense that he did not stay there. Oh went fishing to think up a plan to constitute a nationwide front capable of winning democracy. Suddenly, the answer revealed itself to him: he would announce in advance the time but not the place for the meeting. The venue would be made known only to a well-organized team of trusted runners who would convey it to participants an hour ahead of time. Returning to Seoul, Oh announced that the meeting would take place at 8 a.m. on the morning of May 27 (the anniversary of the fall of Gwangju).

At 6 a.m. that morning, he went out for a walk in the park near Seoul's Chongno YMCA where he was staying. Even though he happened to run into another activist, he did not tell him the place but waited according to plan. At 7 a.m., he told his messengers that he had selected Hyang Lin Church. He recounted for me his reasons. Since the police were continually hovering around the Anglican Cathedral, Myongdong Cathedral, and the main offices of the National Council of Churches, they were all out of the question. Near Hyang Lin Church, however, a fifty-meter curve made it difficult for police surveillance.

At the appointed hour, about two hundred activists arrived on time. Just before the meeting began, Oh made sure the media were telephoned, knowing the police would not be far behind them. As the media and police burst into the hall, Oh banged his gavel and announced the formation of the National Coalition for a Democratic Constitution (NCDC or "*Kukbon*") and also declared that national demonstrations would begin on June 10. In front of the assembled press, everyone agreed by acclamation. This time the story got out. With that single event, the movement against the dictatorship united a diverse range of people—workers, journalists, doctors, women, teachers, actors, and especially religious leaders—around a main demand of constitutional revision and direct presidential elections. Although they didn't know it that day, within a month, the group would help coordinate demonstrations involving over a million people.

As with so many social movement events, simultaneous actions occurred without any planning. My interviews with key activists in Gwangju, Busan, and Seoul revealed that in each city, people believed they had been the first to set up a broad coalition and call for the June 10 demonstrations. Especially in Gwangju, people specifically mentioned the whispered conversation at Mangwoldong cemetery on May 18, 1987, as being the place where the *Kukbon* had been first created.[9] While its name was slightly different, the concept was for a broad coalition for a democratic constitution uniting all forces against Chun Doo-hwan. Subsequently, during a meeting in Gwangju at Namdong Cathedral, with the active guidance of Buddhist monk Gi Son, the name was changed to the one chosen in Seoul.

Through organizations of the arrested and wounded, former members of the Citizens' Army were especially involved in this meeting. At least eighteen of the twenty-four participants had been active in 1980, including farmer Soh Kyong-won and Buddhist monk Song Yon.[10]

"Sustained movement experiences over fifteen years made the *Kukbon* possible," Oh Choong-il told me as we discussed this coincidence of groups forming.[11] As he continued, he noted the central importance of Christians in the June Uprising. "The government could not accuse us of being Communists for we believe in God. I myself had been a refugee from the North when I was a child. This created space for us to organize. Some 80 percent of Koreans are Catholic, Protestant, or Buddhists, and with leaders organized together for democracy, there was no way the government could say we were all Reds." [12] Protected from government repression by belief in God—anathema to communism—mainstream Christian organizations became the organizing center of the movement in which sympathetic citizens threw their full weight into overturning Chun's continuing rule.

As the *Kukbon* organized a structure, Oh was elected chairperson of the thirty-three-member Executive Committee, and fourteen copresidents were selected from regions and constituencies. Significantly, no student groups were formally involved, because of the group's fear they would be suspected of harboring Communists if students were included. Two days after the *Kukbon* formed, the "Student Association in the Seoul Area for Withdrawing the Maintenance of the Present Constitution" was formed—and it immediately set up a preparatory committee for demonstrations on June 10. As we will see, although excluded from formal *Kukbon* membership, students became the key force starting the uprising.

Besides the NCDC's Seoul national headquarters, it had affiliated centers in eight cities, regional offices in counties, and committees in towns and villages—for a total of at least 22 local formations.[13] Its symbolic central body of sixty-seven representatives encompassed people from all walks of life—Christians, Buddhists, workers, farmers, urban poor, women, youth, artists, writers, professors, lawyers, families of arrested activists group, politicians, regional movements, *chaeya* (antigovernment activists), and the reunification movement. Described by a key

TABLE 9.2 **NCDC *Kukbon* Founding Members**

Type	Number	Percentage of Total
Religious Groups	683	31 percent
Regional Leaders/Groups	352	16 percent
Opposition (*chaeya*)	343	16 percent
Politicians	213	10 percent
Farmers	171	8 percent
Workers	39	2 percent
Urban Poor	18	1 percent
Others	372	15 percent
Total	**2191**	**100 percent**

Source: 권혁철,한겨레, June 8, 2007.

Kukbon organizer as a "paper organization," the group included an impressive array of 618 board members, such as 156 politicians from opposition parties, 65 regional representatives, 10 permanent representatives, and 29 permanent executive commissioners.[14] Eight key advisors kept the group aware of concerns of every constituency. An on-line bank account was set up for donations.

Besides calling for an end to the dictatorship and civil liberties, the NCDC also explicitly endorsed a "guarantee of the basic rights of workers, farmers and urban poor" as well as "rectification of monopolized and unbalanced distribution of wealth."[15] Slogans and posters included:

> "Termination of the repression of the workers, farmers and urban poor"
> "Stop torture!"
> "A civilian government will facilitate unification"
> "For a massive national movement to remove the wicked laws of the
> dictatorship"
> "Out with the Americans who support the military dictatorship"
> "Down with the murdering, raping regime"
> "Punish the persons responsible for the Gwangju massacre"
> "Down with the military dictatorship that opposes the three basic labor
> rights"

Although DJ, YS and most major politicians were stridently pro-American, the broad coalition embraced many tendencies, including people whose primary chant was "Yankee Go Home!" Oh felt it was not important to be radical but to unite all the people: "Many people taking one step are more important than one person taking one hundred steps."

The *Kukbon* planned simultaneous, unified nationwide protests for June 10—the same day the ruling party was to name Roh Tae-woo to succeed Chun. A variety of nonviolent tactics were advocated, from publicly singing songs like *Arirang* and the national anthem at 6 p.m.; waving handkerchiefs; honking automobile horns while circling through the downtown; ringing church bells; an 8 p.m. blackout of lights and even televisions (at the same time as Roh's nomination); and telephoning one another for encouragement. *Kukbon* spokesperson Reverend In Myung-jin explained, "We wanted to make it easy for people to participate. We could not ask people to go into the streets."[16]

The human rights committee of the National Council of Churches held its national assembly from June 1 to 3 with the theme of "Achieve Democracy by People Power!"—an echo of previous year's Philippine overthrow of Marcos. Endorsing the June 10 actions, the group announced, "The will of the *minjung* is the will of god." Clearly the country supported advocates of democracy. In one poll, published by *Hanguk Ilbo* on June 9, more than 85 percent of respondents found it "more desirable to protect human rights even at the cost of economic growth."[17]

Excluded from formal membership in the *Kukbon* because of politicians' "red complex," students nonetheless sent one or two "observers" to NCDC meetings and maintained a secret dialogue with its leaders in Seoul. In other cities, student groups participated in the NCDC regional organization or, when it was weak, they substituted themselves for the broad coalition. While many *Kukbon* politicians distrusted the student movement and the government portrayed them as Communists, students nonetheless assumed direct responsibility for the June 10 actions. They were the only ones capable of mobilizing massively in the streets—and willing to risk arrest, tear gas, and beatings. Students were at the center of everyone's hopes, and they set about their task methodically and with great energy. More than any other factor, their remarkable capacity for self-organization is what sparked the June Uprising.

Beginning in April, they formed Associations of Student Representatives by region from the bottom up. The Seoul office was entrusted to send out travelers to help stimulate local organizing and lay groundwork for a national organization. Campus activists watched who spoke well at meetings and later secretly recruited them to organizing efforts. They asked articulate leaders to run for student government offices on a platform of working for democracy. In Seoul, about twenty campuses sent representatives to a council that functioned as a loose leadership after April 13, the day Chun had announced there would be no constitutional revision. Out of the week of commemorations for the "Gwangju Struggle," organizations at campuses all over the country were formed, linked together through citywide associations, which, in turn, sent representatives to the Seoul council meetings.[18] From late May to early June, student leaders at over thirty universities fasted in tents set up for round the clock organizing to persuade students to mobilize.

Although inspired by activists in the Philippines, few believed they could win in Korea. One key activist, Woo Sang-ho, admitted to me in all candor that: "Personally I wondered if I could stand in front of tanks as people in the Philippines did." Students reached out for others to join them in the streets but found little support. Woo explained, "We sent representatives to factories and companies. While the labor movement leadership welcomed us, the rank and file was more distant because of the red complex." Lee Nam-ju, leader of SNU student government, later told me, "I didn't think the June action would go far. I thought we would prepare during the summer for the fall."

On June 2, Korea University activist leader Lee In-young was picked up by police, a severe blow to organizing efforts. Underground leadership remained intact and able to function, despite continuing arrests and internal debates about *juche*. Later that week, Seoul student leaders were asked to give the students' council an estimate of the number of people from their campus that could be expected to participate on June 10.[19] The council allocated specific target numbers of students who needed to attend from each school. They calculated that if 1,000 to 1,500 people from each large university joined, with twenty campuses participating, they could mobilize ten to twenty thousand people. In order for students to assemble into feeder marches to City Hall, Seoul was divided into North-South-East-West quadrants. All over the country, students prepared feverishly for June 10. In Gwangju, Busan, and Seoul, organizers made special efforts to reach high school students.

Student Lee Han-yol was fatally wounded on June 9, 1987. Photographer unknown

On June 8, the Ministers of Internal Affairs and Justice declared the June 10 actions illegal assemblies and the NCDC a "subversive organization." The next day, student councils across the country sponsored rallies to build for "D-Day." Publicly promising to block all demonstrations, police arrested nearly five thousand people in nighttime raids and placed an additional seven hundred opposition leaders under house arrest. Nonetheless, students mobilized on their campuses, where they were confronted by heavy police attacks. At 2 p.m. on June 9, during particularly intense confrontations at Yonsei University in Seoul, Gwangju native Lee Han-yol was shot in the head by a tear gas canister and went into a coma. Carried off by his friends, Lee Han-yol's injury immediately sparked wideranging and deeply felt outrage.

That night, thousands of students at Yonsei stayed up all night marching, singing, and practicing team formations. Carrying flags and banners while chanting slogans, they marched the same route three different times to be ready for "D-Day."

On the morning of June 10, no one knew what to expect. Would many people risk arrest and injury by taking to the streets? If so, would the army be called out? As they made their way to Anglican Cathedral, these were some of the questions in the minds of fourteen leaders of the NCDC, including Oh Choong-il, two Buddhist monks, a Catholic leader, a leader of a women's group, and Kim Young-sam. Finding a path to get inside before police barricades closed off the area, they rang the cathedral bell forty-nine times, the same number as when someone dies. Immediately surrounded by police, they held out for two days before being arrested. With the NCDC under attack, its leaders under arrest or barricaded inside the Anglican Cathedral, few people gave the protests much chance to succeed. Government censors stopped the press from announcing the protests. Although *Kukbon* regional travelers spread the word, their activities were monitored, and police sometimes made it impossible for them to meet their contacts.

June 10: The Uprising Begins

On the afternoon of "D-Day," many campus gatherings assembled before joining marches to City Hall. At 6 p.m., or "H-Hour" as students called it, the ruling party's convention opened in Namsun Hotel, but only four to five thousand students had made it to nearby City Hall. Immediately, police attacked, and dozens of students were injured in what was described to me as a "real war." As they left work in their offices in high-rise downtown buildings, citizens observed the protests with curiosity. While many applauded the students and called for democracy, few joined them. Anyone who stepped into the street was at risk of arrest and beating. Around City Hall, cars incessantly honked horns in support of democracy, and thousands of students continually dispersed and regrouped.

For two hours, students held out on the streets, until their numbers swelled to forty to forty-five thousand as feeder marches arrived.[20] Reinforced by the fresh arrivals, protesters got control of streets around City Hall and Shinsegae department store. Police used huge amounts of CN and CS gas, and people responded with Molotovs. To keep police off balance, protesters scattered when police attacked and regrouped in other parts of the neighborhood—sometimes joined by citizens who happened to be there. Near Shinsegae department store, twenty thousand people assembled spontaneously for a political forum in the streets. When police attacked, people fought back and overpowered them. They stripped the riot police of their shields, body armor, and tear gas guns, and burnt the riot gear in the streets or threw it into fountains. People understood their real enemy was not policemen, so they released the humiliated police.

An American correspondent who drove around Seoul that evening noted that, "Drivers blared their horns as a gesture of support. Police saturated protesters with tear gas. They escaped through alleys and regrouped. Shopkeepers pulled down their shutters but opened them to rescue stragglers spluttering from

Students led the 1987 June Uprising. Photographer unknown

the gas. The battle line kept shifting. The rubble of street warfare was everywhere. Fist-sized chunks of paving stone littered main thoroughfares. But there was an order. No shops smashed, no cars overturned, nothing burned, and miraculously, no one killed."[21]

Beyond everyone's expectations, over four hundred thousand people in more than twenty-two cities protested on June 10.[22] The strong showing in the streets surprised even NCDC leaders inside Anglican Cathedral. As rumors mounted that they would be cleared out and marital law declared, they voted to remain inside, but soon surrendered to the five thousand riot police who surrounded them. Widespread participation all over the country meant police were stretched too thin to maintain control everywhere. In Songnam, the police chief was forced by a throng of people to apologize for his previous harsh words. In Daegu, a busload of captured demonstrators was liberated. In Busan, Daejeon, Gwangju, Jeonju, Chuncheon, Suwon, and other cities, the police blocked the rally sites, but people remained in the streets and refused to be intimidated. By the end of the day, police had arrested a total of 3,831 people. Altogether more than 700 protesters were seriously injured, including two Hanguk University students who were so severely beaten they needed brain surgery. Police reported attacks on three police substations (one set on fire) and five vehicles destroyed. A soccer match between Egypt and Korea had to be suspended after tear gas drifted over the field.[23]

With *Kukbon* leaders in prison, students themselves autonomously made two key decisions: to return to City Hall day after day, and to occupy Myongdong Cathedral. On June 10, hundreds of people fleeing from riot squads and tear gas took refuge in Myongdong Cathedral.

Myongdong Cathedral in Seoul became a focal point of the 1987 uprising.
Photographer: Ko Myung-jin

When the smoke cleared, more than 760 people found themselves inside. Led by students, they spontaneously organized a sit-in, and elected representatives of their various constituencies (workers, urban poor, middle-class, and students). The next day, as 350 demonstrators continued to occupy Myongdong, it became a focal point for the movement, comparable to the occupation of the Sorbonne in Paris in May 1968 or rallies in liberated Gwangju. Part energy center, part public forum for strategy development, part dual power, and all public symbol, Myongdong soon attracted wide support. Amid rumors of martial law and the coming arrest of everyone inside, people debated whether or not to stay. As they argued, outside support grew. A veritable "mountain" of money and supplies poured into the occupied building.[24] Many priests joined the debates, and during a break a wedding took place.[25] A thousand students from seven Seoul universities attempted to get in on June 11, but 750 riot police held their blockade firm and arrested at least 301 people. Underground student leaders at SNU dispatched Kim Young-su to the cathedral. Navigating his way through police lines, he made it inside, where he suggested that each university and citizens' groups choose a representative to form a council. Kim was elected as one of the student representatives.[26] The next day, people evicted from the Sangyedong neighborhood (who were living in tents inside the cathedral since their homes had been destroyed) shared food with the Myongdong insurgents; girls from nearby Gyesong High School donated their school lunches; and two hundred nuns and one hundred priests walked through police lines to celebrate the first of their nightly masses. That night four thousand workers from nearby offices met with students in a public political forum where people traded insights into the possibilities and reasons for action. Outside Myongdong, an effigy of President Reagan was burned because he was seen as being the chief supporter of Chun's dictatorship.[27] The next day, the "necktie brigade" first appeared and went on to become one of the main forces of the June Uprising.

Without the tens of thousands of students who braved the streets that day, it is highly doubtful that the uprising could have started. Not only was the courage of students noteworthy, but their capacity for self-organization carried them back to City Hall the next day at 6 p.m.—and the next. The *Kukbon* had made no plans for June 11, but without anyone's instructions to return, students continued to assemble every day for the next four days.[28] Each time, forty to fifty students were so brutally attacked that they required hospitalization. Finally, thousands of ordinary people—office workers whom students dubbed the "necktie brigade"—joined them. Concentrated in Seoul office buildings near where students were demonstrating, they initially remained aloof. After a few days of watching the fights between students and police just outside their buildings, they began to join the protests. Whether out of shame or desire for democracy, their entry propelled the movement to new levels beyond what anyone thought was possible.

Inside Myongdong, insurgents held out. They issued secret ID cards to keep undercover police out and adopted a strict code of conduct (to reject laziness and individualism, to be thankful for food donations, and to "fight by day and discuss by night.") On Sunday, June 14, a grand citizens' forum attracted hundreds of people to an outdoors meeting. Even though rain began around 6 p.m., no one left. On Monday, as people enjoyed the subversive power of direct democracy inside Myongdong, the government promised to let everyone leave peacefully. After prolonged discussion lasting from 2 p.m. until the next morning and three votes, the group decided to end their sit-in by a vote of 119 to 4. That night, the cathedral was full for Mass. As the rain ended after the service, protesters and worshippers moved outside together, carrying candles—about ten thousand people in all. Young people in the front shoved police out of the way as everyone surged through police lines. Filmed by television, the entire country witnessed the government's failure to evict the protesters from the cathedral. As they exited after five nights and six days of occupation, the demonstrators called on all Koreans to rise against the dictatorship and joined the call of Church Women United for national protests on June 18.

Spontaneously developed, the Myongdong victory, so evident in the inability of the government to punish those who had so publicly defied the government, proved to be a critical event in the unfolding of the June Uprising. On the same day the cathedral was vacated, more than ninety thousand students from fifty-nine campuses took to the nation's streets. In Cheonan, Jinju, and at least four other cities, fierce battles were reported.[29] In Daejeon, more than ten thousand students were joined by thousands of citizens, and in Gwangju, many people joined the ranks of the student-led demonstrations. Newfound freedom of action was everywhere to be seen. On Jeju Island, the student union at Cheju National University held the first public commemorative service for those who had been massacred in 1948.[30] Step by step, the movement in the streets was expanding the rights and freedoms enjoyed by ordinary citizens.

As people in Jeju and Gwangju were again able to walk and talk more freely, in Seoul students became even bolder. Organizing themselves into groups of four to seven people, groups converged where the police were weakest, and when the police massed, teams dispersed, making it nearly impossible for the police to stop demonstrators from assembling.[31] On the campuses, students organized Council of Posts comprised of experienced activists on every campus who were placed in leadership. At Yonsei University, students threw Molotovs and rocks in pitched battles with police who used copious amounts of tear gas.

Protests continued on the next day. At one point, more than five thousand office workers, shopkeepers, and strollers-by held a spontaneous rally near Myongdong. As they chanted slogans enthusiastically, people waved and threw flowers from nearby office buildings. Suddenly police attacked. *New York Times* reporter Clyde Haberman observed one elderly women so angered by the police indecency that she struck an officer on the head with her pocketbook. The government shut down more than fifty major universities two or three weeks before summer vacation, but that only encouraged more students to join the protests.

On June 16, the *New York Times* reported that the Reagan administration "has yet to determine how much leverage it has with South Korean authorities and how to use that leverage." Using typical diplomatic language to indicate a lack of interest in seeing change, Assistant Secretary of State for International Affairs Richard Armitage said, "Frankly, we're really busy. I'm up to my ears in Kuwait and contras and the normal press of business."[32] A senior White House official explained that the president was "reluctant to wade into the issue because he is not convinced that the street demonstrations now under way will push the country toward democracy."[33]

On June 17, more than 50,000 students from seventy universities took to the streets. In Busan, 350 students were trapped inside the Catholic Center. Other marchers tried to reach them but were prevented by massed riot police. By 10 p.m.,

Female students valiantly fought the dictatorship in June 1987. Photographer: Ko Myeong-jin

as the struggle continued, at least thirty thousand people were demonstrating, and for several hours they blocked streets around the U.S. consulate. At midnight, about three hundred taxis led ten thousand candlelight marchers. Jinju was also the site of battles. UPI reported that protesters in Jinju burned buses and hijacked a tanker truck. Behind a thick barrage of tear gas, police retook the truck, but three hundred students then hijacked a train until police forced them to retreat. A *Washington Post* headline declared, "Main Street in Daejon Becomes War Zone."[34] One woman reported that citizens threw cigarettes, soft drinks, and *kimbab* to students before police attacked. She commented: "Before people did not like the students. That has changed in the last few days."

June 18: Chun Prepares the Military

With its leadership languishing behind bars, the NCDC was in no position to call for nationwide mobilizations. Instead, a broad alliance of women's groups, comprising a wide spectrum from KWAU to Christian women's organizations, called for June 18 to be a national "Day Against Tear Gas." They prepared meticulous information sheets detailing the harmful effects of the gas, gently gave riot police red flowers, and pinned ribbons on people pleading with the police not to fire gas. One young policeman wept when he received his flower. Their tactic worked. On June 18, more than a million people protested in sixteen cities throughout Korea. Only three times in June were national demonstrations called—on June 10, 18, 26—and each time, movement groups reported more than a million participants.

Although the day had begun peacefully, street battles erupted across the country, as police were ordered to attack the protesters. Altogether 1,487 people were arrested in sixteen cities at 247 demonstrations,[35] but a turning point was reached that day—no longer could police control the crowds. The *New York Times* reported that, "Downtown Seoul looked like a war zone as tens of thousands of demonstrators took control of the streets, overpowering entire units of riot policemen who had run out of tear gas."[36] In Daejeon, one protester drove a bus into police lines, killing a policeman. In Busan as in other cities, citizens simply refused to go home. They fought the police to standstills or, at times, even defeated them. At about 7 p.m., about three hundred thousand citizens assembled peacefully in Busan. So many people were there that they covered about four kilometers of roadway. Police attacked and used such a huge amount of gas, that they soon exhausted their supplies. People made them pay for their excess. As in Seoul, people were able to disarm riot police and burn their protective gear and tear gas guns. At least twelve police substations were attacked, and many police vehicles were burnt, including three buses used for transporting riot police. As the fighting around Busan train station intensified, citizens commandeered ten trucks. Led by two hundred taxis, they drove to City Hall in a procession of thousands. Demonstrations continued throughout the night, and taxi drivers used their fuel to make Molotovs when heavy fighting there broke out. At dawn, cab drivers lined the streets with their cars to protect demonstrators from the police.[37]

The street victories won by protesters clearly alarmed Chun. He ordered the Army, Air Force, and Navy to be ready to mobilize, and reviewed plans to implement martial law. As early as June 10, the ruling party had labeled the demonstrations "overt violations of basic order" and publicly hinted at the possibility of martial law. U.S. Ambassador Lilley had initially told reporters he would not attend the DJP's convention where Roh would be nominated, but he did, in fact, attend—a clear public signal of U.S. support for Chun's orchestration of Roh's succession. On June 15, Roh Tae-woo—now the dictatorship's official candidate to succeed Chun—told the central executive committee of the ruling party "violent demonstrations that may shake the national principle from its roots cannot be tolerated."[38]

On the other side, protesters refused to be quieted. As Choi Jungwoon noted, once Gwangju citizens had been massacred, the rules changed, since any sacrifice seemed small by comparison: "Before the uprising, it was a matter of course that the university students' demonstrations would come to an end when martial law was declared and troops entered . . . Such a custom could never repeat itself after the uprising, however. Even if stronger and more brutal troops entered, students, the downtrodden, and workers would fight them, risking their lives, and at least they would not allow the troops an easy victory. This expectation worked as a decisive factor leading South Korea's democratization movement in 1987."[39]

Top U.S. officials were plainly worried. One report had Chun ordering the military to march on Seoul—but calling off his orders due to opposition from within the military and because of U.S. pressure.[40] On June 18, Reagan sent Chun a letter cautioning him not to use the military. He urged a resumption of negotiations with opposition parties. The next day at 4:30 in the afternoon, only a few hours before troops were scheduled to deploy, Chun suspended the mobilization plan.[41] Interviewed in his home by a sympathetic analyst in 1998, Chun maintained that U.S. pressure, evident in Reagan's letter and in a personal meeting he had with U.S. Ambassador Lilley on June 19, was the key reason for his cancellation of his order to deploy army units to urban areas.[42] In his meeting with Chun, Lilley warned that martial law might provoke another Gwangju Uprising.[43] Nonetheless, Chun sent his figurehead prime minister, Lee Han-key, onto the airwaves on the night of June 19, to announce that "extraordinary" means would be employed if demonstrations did not cease.

The United States worried that if Chun mobilized the army, he might find himself ignominiously deposed by his own troops.[44] Mainstream historian William Stueck believes that "the army's loyalty to him below the top ranks was questionable. In that situation the United States would actually have assumed *more* risk if it had *failed* to press Chun against using the army to control the civilian population."[45] Although he couldn't have known it at the time, even a majority of the Chun regime's elite did not think a military solution would have worked.[46] The Director-General of the National Police, Kwon Bok-kyung, might be thought to have favored use of the army since his police were outnumbered and often defeated in the streets. He later recalled, "If the army intervened, a bloody incident was expected. It was also plausible that military authorities might decide to support the citizens. In either way, a situation of anarchy seemed unavoidable. I could not find any other way but to depend on the police to the end."[47] Although some top generals favored using the army to secure their power, others—including the National Defense Security Commander—expressed strong objections. Even Chun himself was subsequently reported to have worried about a coup. On June 27, he remarked that: "It will have been easy to solve the problem if we turn to military power, but if the military authorities come out, there is always the risk of a coup."[48]

The situation was impossible to grasp, let alone to control—"*insaisissable*," as De Gaulle had described France in May 1968. With hundreds of thousands of unarmed citizens seizing control of the cities, neither military intervention nor outside force (that is, U.S. troops in South Korea) were thought to be helpful, even by top generals. Apparently in moments of the eros effect, even the military command can be impressed by the power of love.

Concerned that Chun would resort to force to stay in power, U.S. Under Secretary of State Michael Derwinski arrived in Seoul on June 20. To emphasize U.S. concerns, Reagan dispatched Gaston Sigur as a special envoy for the second time on June 22. The following day, Sigur reiterated to Chun in no uncertain terms that the United States would not support a military crackdown as they had in 1980.

Clearly, the struggle had reached a new plateau on June 18. Within the next few days, police made only minimal efforts to stop protests and instead appealed for peace. For the first time, people began to think they might be able to win through mass struggles. On June 19, some forty-six thousand students from seventy-nine universities mobilized in 225 places, attacking and destroying at least thirty-one police substations. On June 20, a large contingent of Buddhist monks were prevented from peacefully marching in Seoul, but when they dispersed, thousands of people joined them, chanting "Yankee Go Home!" and "Down with Chun Doo-hwan!"

Buddhists joined the June 1987 uprising. Photographer: Ko Myong-jin

After 80 students took refuge in a market, about 1,500 sat together in a spontaneous forum. In Gwangju, more than two hundred thousand people went into the streets; at 10 p.m. more than eighty thousand remained, and at midnight, there were still at least twenty thousand. In Jeonju, Daejeon, and Incheon, police were unable to disperse demonstrators, and thousands of people held impromptu street forums to discuss the situation and plan future actions. Thousands protested in Jeonju, Daegu, and Incheon. On Sunday, June 21, demonstrations in Gwangju continued. At least ten thousand people gathered initially, but their numbers swelled to at least three times that, and taxi drivers led a midnight procession through the downtown.

In this period, with people optimistic and the movement in control of the streets, a fierce debate broke out inside NCDC. Key organizers had been confined to their offices at the National Council of Churches building for more than two weeks, where they were surrounded by both the foreign press and police. In that situation, strategic discussions were difficult and had to be held in private spaces. Kim Young-sam, a frequent visitor to the offices, strongly opposed new demonstrations, arguing that martial law would be declared—and as many insisted—that he would pay with his life.[49] No stranger to the democracy movement, Kim had fasted for twenty-three days in 1983 and had long commanded great influence.[50] Nonetheless, younger activists were convinced that the movement was powerful enough to defeat even martial law. In an all-night meeting of some twenty people, *Kukbon* leaders resolved that unless the government agreed to accept four basic points, a "People's Peaceful March" should be organized for June 26. The four points were:

1. Withdrawal of the April 13 Measure halting constitutional revision.
2. Release of all political prisoners of conscience.
3. Guarantee of freedoms of assembly, demonstration, and press.
4. End to the use of tear gas.[51]

On June 22, Presbyterian pastors held a nationwide prayer meeting for the survival of the nation. After the service, thousands of people conducted a candlelight march and pushed through police lines. There were massive protests in many cities.

On June 23, with the new situation permitting people to assemble, twenty thousand people met in an outdoor amphitheater at Yonsei University in Seoul under the auspices of the Association of Student Representatives. This direct democratic forum could have become a critical center for strategic discussion, since the government was powerless to stop the meeting. Leadership managed the stage without facilitating debate on the future direction of the movement. Speakers denounced U.S. imperialism and supported Korea's reunification, thereby setting important long-term tasks for the movement. By acclamation, people endorsed the June 26 national mobilization. Privately, student leaders believed the mobilizations in Seoul were declining in energy while those in other parts of the country were ascending in militancy and spirit.[52]

The next day, Kim Young-sam and Chun Doo-hwan met privately to try and work out a deal to resolve the continuing confrontations. Before the meeting, Kim publicly opposed the mobilization for June 26, but after Chun refused to compromise, he joined NCDC's call for action—as did Kim Dae Jung from house arrest. *Time* magazine reported that on the same day, "crowds laid siege to seventeen police outposts, two Democratic Justice district offices, and two buildings of the state-run Korean Broadcasting System."[53]

June 26: Showdown

On the night of June 25, Korea's future was finally in the hands of its people. The political elite's failure to reach a compromise threw the initiative squarely onto the backs of ordinary citizens. With each iteration of the escalating dynamic of protest and repression, the stakes grew higher. With the government warning that protests would not be allowed and hinting repeatedly at the possibility of martial law, would people again risk life and limb for democracy? How would police and the army respond if called upon to stop them? That night, no one could answer those questions.

The next day, for the third time during the remarkable June Uprising, a national mobilization brought more than one million people into the streets. In fact, NCDC organizers counted more than twice that number in thirty-four cities and four counties.[54] Kim Dong-choon counted 1,400,000 protesters in 270 places on June 26.[55] Across the country, 100,000 riot police blocked rally points, but even the full mobilization of all the regime's repressive powers—with the notable exception of the military—was no match for Korean people's determination to have a democratic system of government. Although the official program of the NCDC in Seoul was blocked by tens of thousands of riot police and massive amounts of tear gas, more than 250,000 people gathered near the train station and fought against police clubs for over three hours. Around Myongdong, another 100,000 took to the streets. As Woo Sang-ho put it: "We controlled the streets, and in our free spaces, there were many discussions, like a Commune."

Gwangju had its largest demonstration since 1980, as some 200,000 people fought against thousands of police for five hours, trying to liberate Democracy Square in order to convene an assembly. Busan once again was the site of serious confrontations. In Suwon, Mokpo, and Yeosu, people outnumbered the police and were able to organize peaceful assemblies. In Jeonju, demonstrators numbered over 100,000; in Songnam over 40,000 people gathered, and more than 20,000 people turned out in Jinju. In what some people described as a generalized national uprising, even in normally quiet cities like Gochang, Muan, Wando, and Gwangyang, people took control of the streets, and major mobilizations occurred in Daegu, Jeonju, Chunchon, Incheon, and Daejeon. All the nation's large cities were filled with clouds of tear gas, as were many smaller cities. Through the night, small groups continually regrouped and fought police for control of the streets. In many places, police were outnumbered so rallies continued late into the night. More than 3,467 arrests were reported nationally, of which 2,139 were in Seoul; many people were injured. Despite copious amounts of tear gas, protesters refused to go home. As indicated in TABLE 9.3, the government fired over 670,000 shots of tear gas during June.

Judging by the amount of tear gas used by the police, protests were most intense in Seoul, Gwangju, and Busan.

On June 27 and 28, as demonstrations continued, few could guess when and how it would end. Most people were unaware that on June 27, a letter was hand-carried to Korea from the International Olympic Committee "expressing the IOC's concern at the civil unrest."[56] With the Seoul Olympics due to open in the summer of 1988, policymakers fretted that the games might have to be moved to another part of the world, and several cities—including Berlin, Los Angeles, and New York—proposed themselves as new sites.[57] IOC Vice President Richard Pound of Canada told the *New York Times*, "You're looking at the kind of convulsions we had in North America and France in 1968, that Japan had in the early 70's. One just hopes it doesn't get out of hand."[58] Many people thought Chun's grip on power was too strong to break and that protests might continue for months. On June 29, *Time* magazine prognosticated that, "Even though people power may not be

TABLE 9.3 **Tear Gas Shots Fired in 1987**

Type	Number
Seoul	266,652
Jeonnam (mainly Gwangju)	95,675
Busan	64,830
Chungnam	42,498
Gyeonggi	38,513
Daegu	35,078
North Jeolla	31,415
Total (including many others)	**673,588**

Source: Figures provided to Representative Yong-gwon Lee, 1988 and reported in Chulhee Chung, "Structure, Culture, and Mobilization," (PhD dissertation, SUNY Buffalo, 1994), 250. See also Chulhee Chung, "Social Movement Organization and the June Uprising," in *Korean Politics: Striving for Democracy and Unification*, ed. Korean National Commission for UNESCO (Elizabeth, NJ: Hollym, 2002), 236.

about to triumph in South Korea, the popularity of the Chun government, never very high, is dwindling fast."

The Junta's June 29 Capitulation

To everyone's surprise, on June 29, Roh Tae-woo issued a sweeping declaration on behalf of the government, in which he capitulated to the NCDC's demands. He announced the ruling party's endorsement of amending the presidential election law to allow for direct elections, freedom of the press, improvement of basic human rights, release of many political prisoners (but not for Communists), restoration of the civil rights of Kim Dae Jung and others, autonomy for universities, and the introduction of local autonomy. Although nothing was said about the rights of labor, clearly a great victory had been won. The showdown on June 26 had convinced Chun and Roh that they simply could not deny people's demands for democracy any longer.

Taken by surprise, elated movement activists were shocked at their victory. In interviews, they all expressed how Gwangju had ended in a bloodbath and that they had expected the June Uprising to end in a similar fashion. Although they had organized for years against Chun, they were among those most surprised by the movement's victory. Evidently, the dictatorship drew the lesson from the Gwangju People's Uprising that if the military were again used civilians, people would make them pay dearly.

While Roh's June 29 speech made many promises, few people trusted him to keep them. Many political prisoners remained in custody, and elections seemed a long way off. On July 4, a direct democratic forum of more than twenty thousand citizens assembled at Yonsei University. In a free-flowing discussion, dozens of speakers raised significant issues, but the group was unable to come to any agreement for future actions. Although wanted by the police, SNU student government president Lee Nam-ju chaired the sessions. In his view, "We didn't have experiences to organize such a rally to discuss future direction for the movement. Before that, we had only gone into the streets. We failed to control the rally."[59] Despite movement leaders' inability to organize for future mobilizations, spontaneous actions by ordinary people is also why the movement could not be controlled by the military—no matter how many "leaders" they arrested. For their part, those who spontaneously protested, who risked arrest, injury, and a possible lifetime of hellish negative consequences, embodied the best of Korean civil society.

Less than a week after Roh's capitulation, on July 5, student Lee Han-yol, in a coma during the entire uprising, died of his injuries. Lee had come to symbolize the virtuous youth who sacrificed for their people. The next day, among the prisoners released was NCDC leader Oh Choong-il. Oh joined more than one million people on July 9 to gather solemnly for Han-yol's funeral in Seoul. (Some estimates were double that.) In his eulogy, Oh Choong-il compared Lee Han-yol to Jesus for having given his life for his people. Dancer Lee Ae-ju added shamanistic ritual to the ceremony.

Afraid that the mammoth crowd might march on the Blue House, police fired volley after volley of tear gas and went on a rampage at the Anglican Cathedral,

More than one million people attended Lee Han-yol funeral in Seoul. Photographer unknown

the same place where NCDC leaders had called for the uprising to begin exactly one month earlier. The police actions indicated that the struggle was far from finished. A funeral procession to Gwangju brought Lee Han-yol home, where he was buried in his Mangwoldong Cemetery.

Elite-led Transition?

Leading up to June 18, American policymakers tried to persuade the opposition of the wisdom of an "orderly" transition and to hold back on constitutional revision, but when the *minjung* stubbornly stayed in the streets, the United States switched positions. As with a host of other petty dictators who outlived their usefulness (from Diem to Noriega), Washington officials chose for Chun to exit rather than for U.S. investments to be threatened. Since both Kim Dae Jung and Kim Young-sam continually promised in public to oppose anti-Americanism, free elections posed no problem for the United States. Between U.S. sanctioning of the suppression of the Gwangju Uprising in 1980 and U.S. support for democratization in the Philippines (1986) and Korea (1987), a shift in policy occurred. Explanations of this watershed transition abound.

Understanding U.S. human rights agenda as an awakening to ethical and moral concerns is an idealistic explanation that ignores U.S. support for the Indonesian junta and Chun's suppression of Gwangju (to name only a partial list). A more realistic assessment of the policy shift involves less a change of perceived U.S. interests than in the transformation of the conditions under which such interests can best be maximized. Anti-Americanism in South Korea, the bitter fruit of the U.S. support of Chun's suppression of Gwangju insurgents, caused concern among policymakers in Washington about the safety of U.S. investments.

American human rights advocates' often-hidden agenda is precisely economic interests. Between 1980 and 1987, U.S. banks had made substantial investments in South Korea that would have been jeopardized if the nationwide uprising had brought a radical regime to power. Fearing the reality of a social revolution in South Korea, U.S. policy shifted. If Korea entered a prolonged period of protests and instability—or worse, a military coup and civil war—huge U.S. investments would have been put at risk. Furthermore, American executives needed a favorable investment climate and stable political situation in order to have access to Korean markets and financial resources.

U.S. Congressman Stephen Solarz, spokesperson for People Power in the Philippines and critic of dictatorship in Korea, helped New York bankers ensure lower risks on their ponderous investments in Asia. On May 17, 1987, Solarz wrote in the *New York Times*, "Twenty billion dollars in trade flows between our two countries, making South Korea our seventh largest trading partner. South Korea is, in short, a country we cannot afford to ignore. It is, therefore, essential that a way be found to reopen negotiations between the Chun government and the opposition. For it is only through such a dialogue that national consensus can be achieved and political stability, continued economic growth, and the preservation of peace can be assured." During the 1987 crisis, U.S. senators introduced S.R. 1392 seeking economic sanctions unless progress was made toward democracy in Korea.

Before the consolidation of neoliberal accumulation regimes in Chile and Korea, the United States needed strong dictatorships to suppress insurgent movements that sought indigenous control of local resources and markets. Once this process had occurred and billions of U.S. dollars in corporate investments had been made, the possibility of the emergence of a radical movement that might overthrow the accumulation regime was actually made more likely by dictatorships. Once best friends of the United States, military rulers became threats to economic investments of U.S. corporations and banks, and a transition to a new type of accumulation regime was required to safeguard the investments lucratively made under the military dictatorships. In 1987, fearing a nationwide insurrection against Chun could result in a radical shift in Korea, the United States moved on without him.

The next year, Richard Holbrooke, self-described "chief apparatchik" of the suppression of Gwangju reported to the Trilateral Commission: "The Trilateral nations have a clear and substantial stake in the successful political evolution of the East Asian nations. Without such political evolution, economic progress cannot continue for another two decades as it has over most of the last twenty years. This is the central challenge for the region over the next decade. Political structures and institutions must catch up to the economic achievements of the region, before the cushion afforded by economic growth erodes."[60] In Holbrooke's view, if Chun and Roh had not agreed to opposition demands in June, "blocked evolution might well open the door to chaos or revolution."[61]

Financial deregulation and trade liberalization were foremost among the objectives of United States policy in the earlier period of imposed military dictatorships in Chile, Turkey, and South Korea. In the case of Gwangju, political liberalization was rejected while economic liberalization was heavily pushed—even in the midst of the uprising when hundreds of people were massacred. U.S. demands for neoliberal reforms after Gwangju sought to strip Korea's developmental state of its powers to control corporate growth and economic accumulation. As a result, *chaebol* ties to the global economy were strengthened. As the economic elite lost its ability to control the economy, so too did it lose its standing in the eyes of the population. *Chaebol* had been major beneficiaries of Chun's policies; thus they did not support democratization. Neither the country's political elite nor its *chaebol* captains were leading the country forward.

As early as 1980, Muskie had recognized the weakness of Chun's regime: "As in Iran, we are learning that any government which must enforce its legitimacy through the use of troops, widespread arrests of popular political, religious and intellectual leaders, and severe press censorship, will be an inherently unstable government."[62] By 1987, U.S. policymakers understood well that formal democracies provided stronger bulwarks against radical movements—Communist or not—than did pro-U.S. dictatorships, like Somoza (ousted 1979), Shah Pahlevi (ousted 1979), Duvalier (ousted 1979), Marcos (ousted 1986), or Chun Doo-hwan. In the black-white world of Samuel Huntington: "By the early 1980s American policymakers had absorbed the lesson that democracies were a better bulwark against communism than were narrow-based authoritarian regimes."[63] In the same period of time, Kissinger was concerned that the IMF policies were leading to turmoil the United States "could not control."[64] The United States realized that neither a popular revolution nor a civil war, neither continuing unrest nor a return to brutal dictatorship, was a desirable option. Getting rid of Chun was the least costly alternative.

The beginning of the transition to a neoliberal accumulation regime in Korea is often placed long after Chun's presidency ended, either during Kim Young-sam's 1994 *segyehwa* reforms or in 1997, when financial crisis struck East Asia and the International Monetary Fund (IMF) took control of the economy. My understanding of the consolidation of neoliberalism in the early 1980s implies that the U.S. embassy was far ahead of many Korean economists in comprehending the country's economic trajectory. As late as 1999, respected Korean economist Lee Chan-keun indicated he still was pondering this transition: "If the late President Park Chung-hee's development model has lost its utility, then it is certainly time for the country to reach for a new model for its future economic development . . . Korea can certainly no longer ignore the interlinked international economy . . . The days of double-digit economic growth are over, and . . . there is no clear vision of ensuring a promising future."[65] Nineteen years earlier, the U.S. embassy had already enunciated almost exactly these same views—except U.S. policymakers did have a clear vision for the future.

The finding that neoliberalism began to arrive in Korea in the early 1980s is significant for at least one additional reason: it casts doubt on the conventional wisdom, which holds that the United States supported military intervention during the uprising in 1980, but not in 1987, because Washington policymakers "learned something" from the outbreak of anti-Americanism after the Gwangju massacre. Once it is revealed that a neoliberal agenda was initially implemented beginning with Chun's Fifth Republic, it becomes clear that military intervention of the sort sanctioned by the United States in 1980 would have threatened the very investments by New York banks and American financiers which had accumulated in Korea by 1987.

Without the unrelenting pressure of the insurgency, the United States would have continued to assert the need for a "peaceful transition according to the constitution." The fact that the June demonstrations continued for nineteen days was due to the spontaneous decision of many students to return to the streets around Seoul's City Hall on June 11 and 12. After the first protests on June 10, they made the decision to come back the next day . . . and the next. As in Gwangju, students sparked the uprising, and in June, office workers joined in great numbers. Students timed their protests for the same time as office workers were leaving, hoping to spark action among thousands of people in the mammoth downtown office buildings who initially watched as clouds of tear gas were fired at students. By June 13, when many workers finally joined in, the government's weakness in the face of growing numbers in the streets made it easier for new people to participate.

Despite the existence of the NCDC and various student organizations, the autonomous decision-making of thousands of ordinary people in the streets comprised the cutting edge of the June Uprising. We see this autonomous capacity for action continually inspiring the uprising: in the occupation of Myongdong, in students' decision to return to City Hall, and among young activists who outmaneuvered YS leading up to June 26. With movement organizations in disarray and leaders surprised by people's victory, the government was able to manipulate the outcome of the uprising by channeling the population's unleashed energies into the electoral channel of selecting leaders. Hwang In-sung echoed what many key activists told me: "We didn't think the uprising would spread so fast. It developed more dramatically than we anticipated, so politicians were able to take advantage."[66]

Looking back at the June Uprising and Korea's turn to democracy, the prestigious Carnegie Council on Ethics and International Affairs concluded that Roh Tae-woo was the key figure in the transition from dictatorship to democracy. Following a long line of thinking that Great Men of history are its motor force, the transition was analyzed in terms of personalities. They were not alone. *Los Angeles Times* reporter Frank Gibney wrote that Roh was "quite sincerely a democrat. 'There is an old Korean saying,' he once told me, 'that the wishes of the people are the wishes of God.'"[67] (Roh's intelligence agents evidently showed him *minjung* theology leaflets, from which he paraphrased their slogan, "The will of the *minjung* is the will of God.") The widespread misconception among U.S. elite policymakers that Korea's democratic transition was "elite-led" serves to justify the Chun dictatorship as benign, superior to Chinese Communist autocrats,[68] and deems Roh Tae-woo a participant in the democratization movement—rather than his actual position as its enemy.

The Carnegie report believed Korean "civil society was weak," and the Gwangju Uprising of only marginal significance—to say nothing of the June

Uprising. Even the *New York Times* used the phrase "capitulation to major opposition demands"[69] to describe Roh's statement on June 29, but the Carnegie Report gave it a different twist: "President Roh has successfully led the country through these changes."[70] Gaston Sigur, President Reagan's special envoy to Korea in 1987, also contributed an article to the report. He affirmed that, "Roh led Korea toward a full-blown democracy"; Roh "curbed the power of the police"; his policies "included the freeing of labor unions."[71]

As we will see in the next chapter, Roh declared "war" on the working class and arrested more activists than even Chun had, and both were eventually convicted and imprisoned for their roles in the Gwangju massacre. Roh was also compelled to return hundreds of millions of dollars he had embezzled. Yet, still some people consider him benign and remain convinced that Korean democratization was "elite-led." Such experts completely conflate fact and reality: for them, it was not ordinary people who so mightily sacrificed and struggled for direct presidential elections, but Roh Tae-woo who "proposed" them in his "landmark June 29 speech" to "stop the street riots and daily tear gas."[72] Korean democratic activists did not call for the uprising, but Gaston Sigur's February speech was "a call for a popular uprising" and the "finest hour of U.S. diplomacy." There was "no question that June 29 was not only the precipitating factor in the political liberalization" but was needed "to quell the riots."[73] With such genius-level brains at high levels of American society, is it any wonder that the country has declined so rapidly?

With the trials of Chun and Roh in 1995 still to happen, perhaps the Commission made premature judgments.[74] With the perspective of two decades, former National Assembly member Kim Gun-tae considered their conclusion an "insult" when I showed him a written copy of some of their statements.[75]

The Role of Civil Society

While the Carnegie Council believes Korean civil society was weak, empirical history (from the April 19 overthrow of Rhee to the Gwangju and June Uprisings) reveals the critical role of civil society in overthrowing U.S.-imposed military dictatorships. Sunhyuk Kim is crystal clear on this point: "civic groups initiated and led the entire process of democratization by forming a prodemocracy alliance within civil society, creating a grand coalition with the opposition political party, and ultimately pressuring the authoritarian regime to the 'popular upsurge' from below . . . Civic mobilization was extremely important, and the momentum for greater democracy consistently emanated from oppositional civil society, not from the state."[76]

Chalmers Johnson similarly understood that: "South Korea between '61 and '89 was ruled by some of the worst military dictators created during the Cold War. Finally the Koreans got rid of them and have quite a healthy democracy now. But all the credit goes to the Koreans—there is a terrible tendency for Americans to mislead themselves about the good things they have done in East Asia." According to Johnson, since Koreans won their democracy through struggle and it was not something "bestowed by a foreign conqueror (as in Japan) or from above by a liberalizing elite (as in Taiwan)," it might be stronger than in those two countries.[77]

The hard-earned character of Korean democracy was also a source of great pride for Kim Gun-tae. As he explained, "Before the June Uprising, Koreans were thought inferior to Japanese, but afterward Koreans thought they were equal. Japanese people had to open their eyes and rethink their feelings of superiority to us. From that time, Koreans began to talk with Japanese as equals in every field, including economics and psychology. Quite a few people think Korean democracy was won by the people and is therefore deeper than Japanese democracy which was achieved by the dictatorship of MacArthur."[78] Park Won-soon reiterated Kim Gun-tae's feelings about the strength of Korean civil society, telling me how many Japanese colleagues were so impressed with Korean NGOs success in defeating corrupt and conservative politicians in elections simply by publicizing their records.

Whatever their differences, U.S. liberals like the Carnegie Council and conservatives like Huntington share an underestimation of the significance of civil society. Rather than examining the problematic opinions of Samuel Huntington and U.S. policymakers, the Carnegie Council report included statements like, Korean values are "incompatible with democracy"[79] and Korean people are "uncomfortable with democracy"[80] and want "to be ruled by an elite."[81] This diminution of Korean civil society and the blaming of Korean character, present in even some progressive accounts of Korea, follow in the footsteps of a century of subordination of Korea to U.S. and Japanese interests.

For Bruce Cumings, the *minjung* was the driving force of Korean democratization. For Cumings, civil society "began to waken again with the February 1985 National Assembly elections."[82] Like Gregory Henderson, Cumings believes traditional Korea did not enjoy a strong civil society: "in the Republic of Korea strong civil society emerged for the first time in the 1980s and 1990s, as a product and also a gift of the extraordinary turmoil of Korea's modern history."[83] Cumings's understanding of civil society mistakes European images of it for its universal appearance, specifically in the notion of the autonomous individual and Western forms of civil society. Cumings invokes Habermas's ideal speech community, believing "intellectuals are the primary carriers of a self-conscious civil society,"[84] but he somehow fails to consider Korean intellectuals in Gwangju during the 1980 uprising or traditional Korean intellectuals in private academies (*seowon*). For him, like Habermas, a Eurocentric frame leads to hypostasizing the Western individual and developing universal categories based upon the assumption that the historical trajectory of Europe defines that of every society.

In Cumings's notion that civil society exists between the state and the mass of people, not in the actual relationships among people in their daily lives, he ascribes too much power to government: Park Chung-hee's coup was an act of "shutting down civil society" and "civil society began to waken again with the February 1985 National Assembly elections."[85] Like many Western democratization theorists, he believes Japan became a democracy after 1945 and South Korea after 1993.[86] The paths of these two countries to parliamentary democracy were quite different. Great struggles emanating from civil society won democratic reform in Korea—unlike in Japan where the electoral system was mandated from above. Nevertheless, Cumings believes "the ROK still falls short of either the Japanese or American models of democracy and civil society" because of the continuing existence of the National Security Law (NSL)—the 1948 measure derived from a Japanese model under heavy pressure from the United States.[87] Without any doubt, the continuing division of Korea distorts many aspects of its political and economic life. Yet the NSL is an instrument of state power and has little to do with the strength of civil society. Many people consider it today a dead letter, a vestigial remnant of a past never to be revisited. Rather than understanding civil society as something that can be shut down by a dictator or reawakened in elections, civil society is a vast web of relationships in ordinary people's everyday lives, not a dependent variable of government or marketplace.

Once the June struggle had been won, the struggle shifted to another arena. The Korean working class, compelled by the Park and Chun dictatorships to endure the world's longest workweek for wages below the government's own minimum standard of living, exploded in thousands of strikes. While direct presidential elections and increased liberties had been won in June, the country's working class was left out of reforms in the new alignment of power. The process of democratic consolidation in Korea was far from finished. Military men with Gwangju's blood on their hands were in control of the government, and workers in the country's factories remained in uniforms, chafing under harsh conditions of everyday life.

NOTES

1   *Joongang Ilbo*, February 26, 1986, as quoted in Dong, "University Students in South Korean Politics," 248.
2   "Freedom, Regional Security, and Global Peace," March 14, 1986.
3   Kang Man-gil, *A History of Contemporary Korea*, 255.
4   Cumings, *Korea's Place in the Sun*, 387, and "Civil Society," 24.
5   Christian Institute for the Study of Justice and Development, *Lost Victory*, 87.
6   Ibid., 91.
7   Interview with Lee Bu-young, Seoul, December 1, 2001.
8   Christian Institute for the Study of Justice and Development, *Lost Victory*, 278.
9   Interview with Yoon Kang-ok, October 3, 2001.
10 Interview with Lee Kang, May 9, 2001.
11 Interview with Oh Choong-il, Seoul, November 29, 2001.
12 In 1981, official statistics reported that there were 7.6 million Protestants, 1.4 million Catholics, and 11.1 million Buddhists. See Lienemann-Perrin, *Die Politische*, 124.
13 Chung, "Structure, Culture, and Mobilization," 169.
14 Interview with Hwang In-sung, Seoul, March 29, 2009.
15 Christian Institute for the Study of Justice and Development, *Lost Victory*, 117–18.
16 Interview with Rev. In Myung-jin, Seoul, March 29, 2009.
17 Chae-Jin Lee, *A Troubled Peace: U.S. Policy and the Two Koreas* (Baltimore: Johns Hopkins University Press, 2006), 123.
18 Interview with Lee Nam-ju, Seoul, March 27, 2009.
19 Interview with Woo Sang-ho, Seoul, June 5, 2001.

20 Interview with Woo Sang-ho, Im Jong-sok, Kwan Hyok-ki, and Yoon Byong-sam, Seoul, June 4, 2001.

21 Michael Breen, "Democracy Protests," in *Korea Witness: 135 Years of War, Crisis and News in the Land of the Morning Calm*, eds. Donald Kirk and Choe Sang Hun (Seoul: EunHaeng NaMu, 2006), 264–65.

22 Christian Institute for the Study of Justice and Development, *Lost Victory*, 105.

23 "Worst Street Protests in Years Rock South Korea," *New York Times*, June 11, 1987.

24 Korea Democracy Foundation, Newsletter 20, June 1, 2007.

25 Interview with Kim Young-su, Seoul, March 29, 2009.

26 Interview with Kim Young-su, Ilsan, March 29, 2009.

27 John Burgess, "Police Surround Protesters in Seoul Cathedral," *Washington Post*, June 12, 1987.

28 Interview with Hwang In-sung, Seoul, March 29, 2009.

29 Clyde Haberman, "Street Protests by South Koreans Resume and Grow," *New York Times*, June 17, 1987.

30 Chang-sung Hyun, Young-hee Cho, Chan-sik Park, Seok-ji Hahn, and Chang-hoon Ko, "The Resistance of the People and the Government's Countermeasures: The Historical Flow and Significance of Case Studies from 1,000 Years in Cheju," *Journal of Island Studies* 3, no. 1 (Spring/Summer 2000): 27.

31 Chung, "Structure, Culture, and Mobilization," 137–38.

32 Elaine Sciolino, "U.S. Will Not Press Korean Initiative," *New York Times*, June 16, 1987, A1.

33 Ibid.

34 John Burgess, "S. Korean Protests Grow in Provincial Cities," *Washington Post*, June 18, 1987, A25.

35 Chulhee Chung, "Social Movement Organization and the June Uprising," in *Korean Politics: Striving for Democracy and Unification*, ed. Korean National Commission for UNESCO (Elizabeth, NJ: Hollym, 2002), 235.

36 Clyde Haberman, "Fury and turmoil: Days that Shook Korea," *New York Times*, July 6, 1987, 6.

37 Interview with Kim Jae-kyu, Busan, May 31, 2001.

38 Christian Institute for the Study of Justice and Development, *Lost Victory*, 107.

39 Choi, *The Gwangju Uprising*, 284.

40 Cheng and Kim, "Making Democracy," 142.

41 Kim Yong-cheol, "The Kwangju Uprising and Demilitarization of Korean Politics," in 5–18관련 논문과 작품 영역 및 저술 사업: 2001. 5–18 20주년 기념 학술연구사업 연구소위 (Gwangju: 전남대학교 5–18 연구소: 2001).

42 See Jung-kwan Cho, "The Kwangju Uprising as a Vehicle of Democratization," in *Contentious Kwangju: The May 18 Uprising in Korea's Past and Present*, ed. Gi-Wook Shin and Kyung Moon Hwang (Lanham, MD: Rowman and Littlefield, 2003), 76–77.

43 Chae-Jin Lee, *A Troubled Peace: U.S. Policy and the Two Koreas* (Baltimore: Johns Hopkins University Press, 2006), 124.

44 *Essays*, 88 (see chap. 5, n. 102).

45 William Stueck, "Remembering the Kwangju Incident," *Diplomatic History* (Winter 2002): 157.

46 Cho, "The Kwangju Uprising," 75. Besides interviewing Chun in his home, Cho met with sixty former members of the regime elite in 1996.

47 기록□해설 金聲翊; 월간조선 1989년 12월호 p 115. 군 3개 사단을 투입하라. 權榮基 as quoted in *Essays*, 88.

48 Kim Sung-ik (월간조선 1992년 1월호, 386. 전두환, 역사를 위한 육성증언) as quoted in *Essays*, 88.

49   Interview with In Myung-jin, Seoul, March 29, 2009.
50   Edwin Q. White, "Into the 80s," in *Korea Witness: 135 Years of War, Crisis and News in the Land of the Morning Calm*, eds. Donald Kirk and Choe Sang Hun (Seoul: EunHaeng NaMu, 2006), 285.
51   Christian Institute for the Study of Justice and Development, *Lost Victory*, 110.
52   Interview with Lee Nam-ju, Seoul, March 27, 2009.
53   William R. Doerner, "Under Siege," *Time*, June 29, 1987.
54   Christian Institute for the Study of Justice and Development, *Lost Victory*, 113.
55   Kim Dong-choon, "The Gwangju Democratic Uprising, the June Uprising, and Political Democratization," in *History of the 5.18 Democratic Uprising*, vol. 2, ed. May 18th History Compilation Committee of Gwangju City (Gwangju: The May 18 Memorial Foundation, 2008), 630.
56   James F. Larsen and Heung-Soo Park, *Global Television and the Politics of the Seoul Olympics* (Boulder, CO: Westview Press, 1993), 161.
57   Christian Institute for the Study of Justice and Development, *Lost Victory*, 160.
58   George Vescey, "Thinking About Plan B," *New York Times*, June 24, 1987, D31.
59   Interview with Lee Nam-ju, Seoul, March 27, 2009.
60   Richard Holbrooke, Roderick MacFarquhar and Kazuo Nukazawa, *East Asia in Transition: Challenges for the Trilateral Countries* (New York, Paris, Tokyo: The Trilateral Commission, 1988), 51.
61   Ibid., 5.
62   GDMM X: 46; August 1 letter to Gleysteen.
63   Huntington, *Third Wave*, 284.
64   See Paik Nak-chung, "Trials and Historical Choices of the Twenty-first Century," interview with Immanuel Wallerstein, *Creation and Criticism*, December 5, 1998, 7, http://www.changbi.com/english/related/related15.asp.
65   Lee Chan-keun "Korean Economy in Era of Globalization," *Korea Focus* (March–April 1999): 92–3.
66   Interview with Hwang In-sung, Seoul, March 29, 2009.
67   Gibney, *Korea's Quiet Revolution*, 99.
68   See Cho, "The Kwangju Uprising," 70.
69   Clyde Haberman, "Fury and Turmoil: Days that Shook Korea," *New York Times*, July 6, 1987, 1.
70   Ibid., 6.
71   Gaston Sigur, "A Historical Perspective on U.S.-Korea Relations and the Development of Democracy in Korea 1987–1992," in *Democracy in Korea: The Roh Tae Woo Years*, ed. Carnegie Council (New York: Carnegie Council on Ethics and International Affairs, 1992), 9–17.
72   Carnegie Council, ed., *Democracy in Korea: The Roh Tae Woo Years* (New York: Carnegie Council on Ethics and International Affairs, 1992).
73   Ibid, 47.
74   See *Asia's Unknown Uprisings Vol. 2*, chap. 1 for a critique of Huntington.
75   Interview with Kim Gun-tae, Seoul, August 2, 2008.
76   Sunhyuk Kim, "Civic Mobilization for Democratic Reform," in *Institutional Reform and Democratic Consolidation in Korea*, eds. Larry Diamond and Doh Chull Shin (Stanford: Hoover Institution Press, 1999), 281.
77   Chalmers Johnson, "South Korean Democratization: The Role of Economic Development," *Korea Under Roh Tae-Woo: Democratization, Northern Policy, and Inter-Korean Relations*, ed. James Cotton (Canberra: Allen and Unwin, 1993), 107.
78   Interview with Kim Gun-tae, August 2, 2008.
79   Donald S. Macdonald, in Carnegie Council, *Democracy in Korea*, 24.

80   Stephen Kirby, in Carnegie Council, *Democracy in Korea*, 75–76.
81   Ibid., 73.
82   Cumings, "Civil Society," 24.
83   Ibid., 9.
84   Ibid., 17.
85   Ibid., 23–24.
86   Ibid., 22.
87   Ibid., 26.

CHAPTER 10

The Great Workers' Struggle

The Great Workers' Struggle ranks with Polish Solidarność (1980–81), the Iranian workers councils of (1979–1981) and the Brazilian strike wave of 1978–1983 as one of the foremost episodes of working-class struggle of the 1980s. The strike wave shattered the foundations of almost uninterrupted dictatorship following the end of the Korean War, won significant wage increases for large sectors of the Korean working class, and briefly established radical democratic unions in the National Congress of Trade Unions, committed at least verbally to anti-capitalism.

—Loren Goldner

The 1987 Great Workers' Struggle largely represented a spontaneous, unorganized, and uncoordinated explosion of labor conflicts . . . thousands of labor conflicts occurred almost simultaneously nationwide without systematic planning, strategy, or leadership. There was no national or regional organization that could have coordinated this great eruption of labor actions . . . The explosion of labor militancy occurred so suddenly and on such a massive scale, that even many intellectual labor activists who had been working for labor mobilization for a long time seemed to be at a loss and were unable to play a leading role.

—Hagen Koo

CHRONOLOGY	
June 10–29, 1987	June Uprising: direct presidential elections and reforms won
July 5, 1987	Injured student Lee Han-yol dies in Seoul hospital

July 5, 1987	Workers from Hyundai Engine form first Hyundai union in Ulsan disco
July 9, 1987	Lee Han-yol funeral in Seoul; more than one million people attend
July 10, 1987	Chun Doo-hwan resigns as DJP party chairman
August 8, 1987	40,000 Hyundai workers protest
August 8, 1987	Autonomous Council of Labor Unions formed in Hyundai
August 10, 1987	Daewoo autoworkers take over company cafeteria
August 18, 1987	Hyundai workers defeat police, march to downtown Ulsan
August 18, 1987	3,500 students from ninety five universities form new alliance—*Jeondaehyop*
August 22, 1987	Daewoo shipyard worker Lee Suk-kyu killed by tear gas canister
August 28, 1987	Lee Suk-kyu's corpse stolen by police at his funeral; 933 arrests
August 28, 1987	Strike wave peaks with twenty new struggles emerging on one day
September 2, 1987	Workers again take over Ulsan City Hall
September 29, 1987	Government announces it will take steps for workers to become middle class
November 27, 1987	First regional council organized in Masan
December 16, 1987	Roh Tae-woo wins presidency; opposition had 64 percent of vote

FEW COUNTRIES HAVE witnessed the kind of massive outpouring of grievances experienced by Korea in 1987. As significant as the June 29 victory was, expanded civil liberties and direct presidential elections did not alter the daily lives of workers, which remained mired in miserable conditions of poverty and drudgery. Participation of the "necktie brigade," Busan taxi drivers, and urban poor was a visible sign of the entry of the working class into the country's political arena, but their involvement in June demonstrations was a mere presage to the flood that would soon inundate the country. Without warning, the largest strike wave in the country's history broke out in July and August, as factory workers became the epicenter of an eruption that transformed Korea's economic landscape. Built up by decades of frustration and silent suffering, two weeks after the government's acceptance of opposition demands for direct elections, wildcat strikes shut down the country's large factories at a dizzying pace and with prolonged intensity. The June Uprising not only won direct presidential elections and political reforms, it also helped create space for the union movement in the countries' economy.

In July and August, more than three million workers in over three thousand workplaces rose up, demanding substantial wage increases, improved working conditions and, most importantly, autonomous trade unions. Without warning and in the absence of any central organization, wildcat work stoppages, street actions, plant closures, and marches spontaneously broke out. In a ten-week period, the number of labor disputes was double the number in the previous ten *years*. Schooled in the streets of June, inspired by the victories of the democratic movement, and protected by continuing mobilizations, workers claimed their part of the country's expanding liberties. Their capacity for self-organization in this period is a major indication of the ability of ordinary people to take control of their lives—to articulate their own needs and autonomously take action to make sure they are met.

Mainstream democratization theorists have consistently severed this enormous insurrectionary wildcat strike by Korea's working class from the June Uprising, creating a separation that is chronologically contrived. When divided into "political" and "economic" struggles, the popular movement is bifurcated into middle-class and working-class segments, thereby mirroring the class division of society and serving the divide-and-conquer strategy of the dictatorship. Such a conceptualization fetishizes formal democracy (by regarding voting rather than overall well-being as the meaning of freedom); it fails to understand how increasing "democracy" (voting) can lead to neoliberal immiseration, national dependency, and debt crisis. Misery for the poor finds its cause in New York bankers and investors like George Soros, who with the stroke of a keyboard or a telephone order take for themselves the fruits of years of labor by a country's workers. Since electoral regimes facilitate the privileges of international capitalists, is it any wonder that they support "democratic" transitions?

If one considers the wave of insurrectionary strikes in July and August together with the millions of people in the streets during June, a subversive image of Korea's revolutionary potential becomes visible—a frightening prospect for some, while promising for others. Chalmers Johnson considered the 1987 crisis a "revolutionary situation."[1] Bruce Cumings tells us that in June 1987, "The Reagan administration now worried that a full-fledged revolution might topple the regime."[2] No one—not even Chun—called it a Communist movement.

Major support for democratization had come from the "necktie brigade," who had joined the protests in overwhelming numbers. While many analysts interpreted these strata's actions as indicative of a larger critique of the economy's failings—and possibly in favor of a radical redistribution of wealth—others believe their support for political liberalization had little to do with economic concerns.[3] The most radical oppositionists questioned the entire economic development plan, based upon exports and U.S. support that had increased the marginalization of farmers, workers, and the Jeollas. At their most insightful, *minjung* questioned the ties between *chaebol* and American corporations, in effect germinating the seeds of the subsequent massive movement in South Korea against neoliberalism, the FTA, and the WTO. At that time, IMF-sponsored structural adjustment programs was the *nota bene* of these radical strata.[4] Many activists in 1987 rejected U.S. nuclear power plants, wanted U.S. troops to leave (and take their investors with them), and called for reunification of the country. Considered as a unity, the aspirations of the three-month uprising were to thoroughly transform both Korea's political system and economic relations in libertarian and egalitarian directions. In order to appreciate the centrality of the working class in 1987, I reexamine the June Uprising.

The June Uprising's Class Character

Although union leaders were not a visible part of the NCDC, working people were an indispensable part of the June Uprising. While the main initiators were students and the most visibly celebrated new constituency was the "necktie brigade," anecdotally, many participants remarked that workers were central to demonstrations. One reason for the dearth of union leaders in the front ranks of the movement was that yellow FKTU leaders who remained in office in 1987 did so precisely because they were loyal to the government. Unions had been decimated under Chun Doo-hwan's dictatorship, and no legal *independent* unions existed.

Significantly, nearly all English-language analysts analyze the June uprising as middle-class and do not consider the "necktie brigades" as laborers, a questionable assumption. In contrast to claims of lack of working-class participation, Hagen Koo calculated that the largest proportion of those arrested in June were laborers, a clear indication of the participation of workers in the mass protests: "a large number of wage workers, a number larger than the number of white-collar workers and shopkeepers, in fact participated in street demonstrations in June." Koo continues in a footnote: "This is evidenced by the fact that the largest proportion of the people arrested during this period were laborers, although many of them might have been construction workers or casual laborers." Koo's source of information, however, only deals with one city, Songnam in Gyeonggi Province, and during only a short period of time—beginning on June 19, when most of the arrests were workers. There were few university students in Songnam at that time, and the period from June 19 in one city is far from being reflective of the entire country's June Uprising.[5] Moreover, Songnam was a key target area for movement activists who organized at the point of production.

Arrestee backgrounds from a sample drawn over a few days in Seoul and Gwangju reveal a different picture of the class background of participants. As the TABLE 10.1 indicates, nearly 90 percent of people arrested in Seoul in the first days of the uprising were students. That figure fell to 23 percent in Gwangju on June 20 and 21, when about an equal number of workers, students, business people (including merchants), and unemployed were detained.

TABLE 10.1 **Arrested in Seoul and Gwangju in June 1987**

Occupation	Seoul (June 10–13)	Gwangju (June 20–21)
Students	171	19
Business Persons	6	9
Workers	6	4
Movement Activists	2	–
Service workers	3	16
Merchants	1	9
Unemployed	4	21
Farmers	–	1
Other	3	2
Total	**196**	**81**

Source: Chulhee Chung, 한국일보 June 13 and 16; 동아일보 June 16.

These numbers are also very low when compared to the nationwide total. On June 26 alone (the day of the huge culminating demonstration that convinced the dictatorship they could not continue), police reported 3,467 arrests.

Arrest statistics based upon occupations reported by people when they are detained by the police are not the most robust way to evaluate the class background of demonstrators for many reasons, not least of which is that people fighting the dictatorship have no reason to be truthful about how they make a living. Even if someone reports his or her occupation as restaurant worker, it could be a part-time position that obscures the person's class position more than it illuminates it. Furthermore, police may selectively have chosen to arrest more students who were in the streets after 6 p.m. than office workers who would have been on their way home from work; students have more discretionary time in which to participate in demonstrations than people tied to the discipline of factory jobs or offices; and street actions are only one aspect of movement participation. Statistics analyzing arrested people's occupations were also used by Ahn Jeong-chol and Gi-wook Shin to classify Gwangju as a working-class uprising.[6] Many participants in Gwangju were lumpen—shoeshine boys, prostitutes, beggars, jobless, and urban poor—a category that can be misleading because of middle-class bias.

In most countries, massive uprisings like Korea's in 1987 lead to a period of collapse and renormalization. Social movement theorists often consider such a retreat "normal," part of the life cycle of protest movements. Yet, in Korea, the popular movements surged ahead in the years following 1987—winning legalization of unions, expanded civil liberties, and justice for Gwangju: Chun and Roh were ultimately sent to prison for their crimes. Moreover, sweeping changes in institutions and state-society relations occurred. In short, a whole new epoch ensued after the uprising.

The Wave of Autonomous Worker Actions

On July 5, the same day Lee Han-yol passed away from his wounds, a small group of Hyundai workers met in an Ulsan disco. The simultaneity of these dates indicates how intimately related the workers' uprising and the democracy struggle were—and how close South Korea was to a revolutionary situation in 1987. Within a week of the June 29 capitulation by Chun and Roh, the first union formed at Hyundai. With that seemingly simple step, decades in the making, the labor movement moved to the center of social movements. Workers did not simply want higher wages and better working conditions—although those were central needs. They also wanted a change in the relationships of production—of democratization of the country's economy.

In the newly found space won by the June uprising, workers cared little that their strikes were illegal; instead, they moved decisively to deal with longstanding grievances. In the process, they scorned corporate procedures as they asserted their newly found power. They took managers hostage, occupied buildings, and instituted new norms of behavior in the workplace. Despite the bare subsistence they eked out in factory jobs, workers brought grievances to public attention that were not simply wages, but included a shorter workweek, dress and hair codes, mandatory morning calisthenics, and the arbitrary authority of ruthless supervisors. Most importantly of all, workers organized autonomous unions that would represent their real needs. Within one year, some 4,000 new unions representing 700,000 workers were brought into existence.[7] In four years, union membership nearly doubled from 1,040,000 in 1986 to 1,980,000 in 1990; in *chaebols*, the unionization rate went from 38.9 percent in 1986 to 72.9 percent in 1989. In the same period, the total number of local unions tripled from 2,658 to 7,861.[8] In effect, the summation of these actions in the Hot Summer of 1987 amounted to a spontaneous general strike for wage increases, better working conditions, and basic rights of labor.

Leadership positions in this burgeoning movement were almost always rotated (sometimes by choice, but also by necessity, since arrests and firings of visible spokespersons were all too common). The capacity of the working class for self-organization became a remarkable—and lasting—feature of Korea's social landscape. As in Gwangju seven years earlier, people were able to govern themselves without political parties leading them. Workers directly conducted intense struggles against thousands of armed adversaries, articulated grievances with eloquence and clarity, and provided for their basic needs without the leadership of politicians. Feeling the need to create vehicles to carry them through ongoing struggles with management, they organized new unions, responsive to and led by the workers directly.

After the June 29 victory, the NCDC saw its main tasks as preparing for the presidential election, getting political prisoners released, and reinstating civil rights. While the June Uprising and the Great Workers' Struggle were coterminous and workers were deeply involved in the movement for democracy, many movement activists did not view them as identical struggles. Preoccupied as everyone was with the dictatorship's continuing power, the urban middle class was initially unconcerned with factory workers' struggles. Although defeated in the streets, the regime still retained its grip on power. Chun resigned as DJP party leader on July 10, but fellow army general Roh Tae-woo, Chun's handpicked successor and collaborator, had been chosen to make the June 29 concession speech to position him for the coming election. Nine hundred prisoners were quickly released, but thousands more remained behind bars. The cabinet was reshuffled and armed forces officers reassigned, but the military character of the government went unchanged. Most significantly, no public discourse on continuing to expand civil liberties took place—while the media carried numerous public statements by high-ranking generals that Kim Dae Jung would never be allowed to become president. Whispered everywhere, persistent rumors of a coming military coup created an atmosphere of uncertainty and fear—amid hope and joy. The precarious character of the June victory was evident, even though few realized at the time it would take years of subsequent struggles to enact a modicum of transitional justice as part of a transition to formal democracy.

With police called to duty against the democratization movement in big cities, factory workers found new space for actions previously thought impossible.

Without the overwhelming police presence, factory workers quickly mobilized, conducting an average of 44 actions a day from June 29 to September 15.[9] Of a total of 3,492 disputes recorded by the government in this period, the main concentration was in manufacturing (1,802 cases) and transportation (1,248 cases). At least 342 factories, or 65 percent of those with more than a thousand workers, experienced struggles. In August alone, there were 2,577 conflicts recorded. This rapidly expanding "eros effect" peaked on August 28, when 200 new struggles emerged on one day. As the government moved to isolate and repress the workers—and more significantly, as companies settled the disputes in favor of their laborers—the factories quieted.

Unlike the labor movement of the 1970s that consisted primarily of female workers in Seoul-area textile shops, the strike wave of 1987 among mainly male workers originated in large factories in Ulsan and came to Seoul after spreading through peripheral areas. Beside tremendous wage increases that averaged 11.6 percent in 1987, 19.6 percent in 1988, and 25.3 percent in 1989,[10] the eight-hour day was won. From 1987 to 1993, working hours decreased from 51.9 per week to 47.5.[11]

As we can see in TABLE 10.2, workers job actions predominantly generated economic demands.

TABLE 10.2 **Labor Disputes (January 1, 1987–September 11, 1987)**

Cause	Total Number	Work Sabotage	Sit-in Strike	Demonstration	Other
Wage Increase	2,448	794	1,583	69	2
Improvement of Labor Conditions	523	175	342	6	
Others	150	49	100	1	
Collective Agreement	109	44	63	1	1
Unfair Labor Practices	39	10	28	1	
Overdue Wages	36	12	15	9	
Dismissal	18	7	10	1	
Workers' Dues	14	6	8		
Shutdown/Reduction of Business	6	1	5		
Total	3,343	1,098	2,154	88	3

Sources: Christian Institute for the Study of Justice and Development, *Social Justice Indicators in Korea*, 2nd ed. (Seoul: Christian Institute for the Study of Justice and Development, 1988), 119; Ministry of Labor; Federation of Korean Trade Unions, *Guide for Wage Increase Activity* (1987).

For much of the preceding decades, the labor movement had been strongest among female textile workers in small production sites. Heavy industry such as shipbuilding and steel manufacturing were purposely located in remote areas to isolate workers. *Chaebol* had resolutely opposed independent unions, but in 1987, they too were engulfed by the tidal wave of wildcat strikes.

Uprising within the *Chaebol*

By launching struggles for unionization within the *chaebol*, workers overcame decades of patronizing control and patriotic propaganda about sacrificing for the country. With labor unions extremely rare within them, *chaebol* families dominated the economy, received enormous tax breaks, and were at the center of centrally planned government investment schemes. As a percentage of GNP, the top five *chaebol* accounted for more than half of GNP in 1984—the top ten for more than two-thirds.[12] In 1980, the thirty largest *chaebol* accounted for 36 percent of all goods shipped and 22.4 percent of the country's workforce, and in 1987, the biggest five controlled nearly one-quarter of domestic sales and employed more than 10 percent of all workers in manufacturing.[13] When workers rose against these giant companies, they were effectively challenging the entire system.

By comparison to the previous stage of light industry and small factories, Park Chung-hee's policy of developing heavy industry under Fordist industrial conditions produced a class of highly concentrated workers, whose capacity for action organically included the ability to paralyze huge sectors of the economy. Despite capital's increasing concentration, labor relations remained at a primitive level befitting early days of European capital described by Charles Dickens or Émile Zola. Clearly, workers needed major changes.

Workers had long tasted the bitter results of *chaebol*-government rule in the form of wages being kept artificially low, harshly regimented routines, and long workweeks. According to the FKTU (the yellow union controlled by the dictatorship), the minimum monthly living costs for a family were about 629,000 won, but workers made barely half of that (336,908)—even when they worked overtime. (At that time, the dollar stood at about 830 won.) Although they worked an average of 54.7 hours per week, an astonishing 82.4 percent of laborers received less than minimum costs of living.[14] While a boon to a tiny group of families at the top of these firms, the wage freeze and union busting policies of Chun Doo-hwan had exacerbated working people's problems. Even those unions that were legal and government-controlled scarcely counted a million members at the end of 1986.

To understand the depths of workers' grievances and the deeply enforced class character of Korean society, one could begin with the color-coded uniforms they were required to wear at work; the crude and vulgar language thrown their way every day by superiors, to say nothing of the sexual outrages suffered by women; the hair codes; the foul tasting and inadequate food in workers' cafeterias (as opposed to more privileged strata of company employees); and what was commonly understood as the world's longest workweek. All these outrages, however, pale in comparison to unsafe conditions at workplaces, where the industrial accident rate was ten times that of Japan or the United States. A literal sea of blood created South Korea's economic "miracle." For years, activists counted "six truckloads of fingers cut off every year." More than 15,000 workers were killed or injured in industrial accidents every year; in 1978 alone, 1,397 workers were killed on the job, and 13,013 were totally or partially disabled.[15] There was an average of four fatalities per day.[16] In 1986, some 21,923 workers were physically disabled in accidents. As the workers upsurge brought to the fore long-repressed needs of the class, a National League for Victimized Workers formed on September 27 during a rally. The group noted that under Chun's rule, at least 10,295 workers had been killed in workplace accidents and an additional 969,304 had been injured. As draconian as Park Chung-hee had been, Chun's regime was rapacious, as indicated in TABLE 10.3.

TABLE 10.3 **Industrial Accidents, 1970–1990**

Year	Injuries	Deaths
1970	37,752	639
1975	80,570	1,006
1980	113,375	1,273
1985	141,809	1,718
1990	132,896	2,236

In 1987, the entire country mobilized, as factory workers refused to be mollified or repressed any longer. The explosion tore asunder the long entrenched factory regimes, changing in weeks unfair conditions people had been forced to endure for years. Company after company was compelled to settle disputes by giving into workers' demands, and initial wage increase averaged to 13.5 percent. More than one-time wage increases, workers needed to change their conditions of existence, and for that they required autonomous unions. In about seventy days, they organized more than 1,060 new ones, all the while fighting against yellow unions, isolating their leaders, and recruiting their rank and file.

Significantly, the movement emerged first inside Hyundai Corporation, one of the strongest and most conservative institutions in Korea—and probably the most antiunion. Founder Chung Ju-young threw down the gauntlet when he proclaimed that unions would come to his company over his dead body ("only after earth covers my eyes"). He was one of the toughest disciplinarians of all bosses, requiring workers to have short hair, strictly keeping a hierarchy of lunch perks and uniforms, and maintaining military discipline at all levels. Hyundai's home base was an Ulsan industrial park that employed over 150,000 factory workers.

On July 5, when the first union formed at Hyundai Engine, it became the signal for what turned into a nationwide eruption. As the union movement spread to Hyundai Mipo Shipyards, top management quickly organized new yellow unions loyal to the corporation. But it was too late to foil the workers: the strike wave spread from Hyundai to Korea Zinc on August 3, Hyosung Metals and Hyosung Aluminum, and Taehan Aluminum on August 4, Kyunggi Chemical, Lucky Ulsan, and Hansung Enterprises on August 5, and Jinyang on August 6. On August 8, the second wave of struggle was signaled when forty thousand Hyundai workers took to the streets. After Lee Suk-kyu, Daewoo shipyard worker, was killed by a tear gas canister, militancy intensified. In the third week of August, there were 880 strikes and 113 new unions formed.[17] By the end of the month, some 2,552 labor struggles had occurred, out of a total of 3,749 in 1987—more than thirteen times the 276 disputes recorded in all of 1986.[18] This remarkable uprising is illustrated in FIGURE 10.1.

On August 8, insurgents organized an autonomous Council of Labor Unions in Hyundai, consisting of twelve insurgent unions that demanded negotiations. Chung's response was to lock out six factories on August 17, declaring he would never negotiate with an illegal organization. Workers responded immediately, marching tens of thousands strong to downtown and occupying the city for two days. They easily defeated the riot police, who were no match for workers' forklifts,

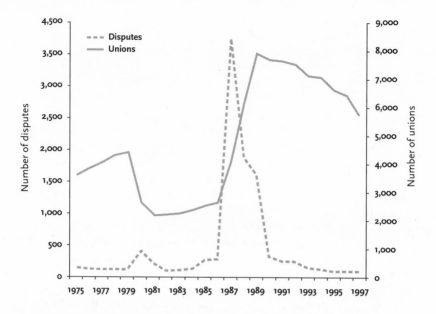

FIGURE 10.1 **Number of Labor Disputes and Labor Unions, 1975 to 1990**
Source: Hagen Koo, *Korean Workers: The Culture and Politics of Class Formation* (Ithaca: Cornell University Press, 2001) 159.

dump trucks, cranes, graders, and steamrollers—to say nothing of their unity. Something like forty thousand workers in gray overalls paraded triumphantly out of the factories. After several hours, the assembly converged on Ulsan Sports Stadium, where thirty thousand family members joined them.

They promised to remain until the conflict was resolved in their favor. While they waited, *pungmul*, the traditional Korean dancing band of drums and gongs, as well as flutes amused them, and trucks full of bread arrived to feed people. While some ate, others sang and chanted, "Down with Chung Ju-yong!" One wife told the *New York Times* that her husband "has worked for the company for fifteen years and earns $1 an hour."[19] The Deputy Minister of Labor flew in from Seoul and gave the government's guarantee that their demands would be met (but no company representative would make the same statement.) The workers had won—but not in the mind of Chung Ju-young, who refused to acknowledge anything promised to the workers by the government. Despite the signing of contracts at three places (Mipo Shipyards, Hyundai Heavy Electric and Hyundai Pipe), the government declared unions across company lines illegal and arrested twenty union leaders including Kwon Yong-mok.

Hyundai was not the only *chaebol* to feel the new power of its workers. All of Goldstar's twenty-seven companies and fifty-seven subsidiaries also were the scenes of strikes and uprisings in 1987. The wave of insurgency spread from Ulsan's epicenter to Masan in the southeast, through larger cities like Busan, Gwangju, Daejeon, and Daegu, until it reached Seoul. From industry to industry and region to region, aftershocks appeared from the earth-shaking movement

Wildcat strikers took over the city of Ulsan. Publisher: Saegil Publisher, 1991

Massive protest by workers won dramatic gains in 1987. Publisher: Saegil Publisher, 1991

in Ulsan. At the peak of the struggle, tens of thousands of workers armed with safety helmets, wooden clubs, and heavy equipment protected themselves from police and company thugs.

At Daewoo, worker Lee Song-yong climbed high on one of the huge cranes he operated and exhorted his fellow workers to form an independent union. Hundreds of workers immediately rallied around him. In the ensuing struggles, strikers fought back against 1,500 police and goons, who attacked everyone including onlookers. In the fighting over the next days, Lee Suk-kyu was killed when a tear gas canister hit him squarely on the chest on August 22, 1987.[20] The day after Lee was killed, about five thousand students and workers gathered at Yonsei University to support workers who had been fired during the struggles. After an all-night student session, they agreed to work in unison but not together, emphasizing the need to strengthen and support the autonomy of workers. Lee's funeral on August 28 became a national mobilization throughout the country. Police moved in, arresting more than 933 people, and they even snatched his corpse as the procession sought to carry it to Gwangju's Mangwoldong cemetery. With the media full of stories about "Communists" in the unions, the next week thousands of police were mobilized to break up protest camps at both Daewoo Motors and Hyundai Heavy Industry. More than a hundred workers were arrested.

Two hundred miles to the north at Daewoo's auto plant, one of the legacies of workers' 1985 victory was a new group of union activists committed to improving the lot of labor. On August 10, 1987, they took over the company cafeteria and demanded significant pay raises, and more importantly, decertification of the FKTU affiliated yellow union, rehiring of fired independent union members, and discontinuation of contracts with U.S. transnational General Motors. Moving around the plant, the three hundred original protesters grew to four thousand workers in one day. The company locked down the plant. Faced with *chaebol* intransigence, workers marched on the management building, seized the president and vice president of Daewoo Motors, and compelled them to bow down to the assembled workers. Despite their moral victory that day, workers were unable to win their demands. Months later, workers were finally granted a 24 percent raise—their first in five years. The next year, as Daewoo remained intransigent, workers used all kinds of tactics to win their struggle. On one occasion, ten thousand workers used the same cafeteria counter resulting in a line more than two miles long and a four-hour lunch break, during which they sang songs and discussed their situation. To express defiance, they wore work uniforms inside out, all took allowed breaks at the same time, and all left early on the same day—not a violation, as the rules permitted occasional early departures.[21] Finally, two workers, Lee Song Mo and Pak Shin Suk, set themselves afire to protest the suffering of workers. After burying their martyrs in Mangwoldong, the union organized a strike for June 22, 1988. The company mobilized fifteen thousand police to retake the occupied plants, but at the last minute a deal was struck with retroactive pay raises and a reduced workweek.

At Hyundai, Chung refused to recognize the new unions. By September 2, when workers had failed to receive any of the concessions promised by the government, laborers again occupied downtown Ulsan. Riot police attacked more than twenty thousand people, but the crowd swarmed past them. They took over City Hall and trashed company shipyard offices, while the police stood by helplessly and watched. Two days later, however, a massive riot squad attacked at dawn and arrested 508 union members. Eight thousand workers mobilized, but this time the police were ready with tear gas and water hoses. Hyundai Heavy Industries eventually settled for more than a 15 percent pay raise, and that figure became the standard for other unions.

In early September, hundreds of strikers were arrested whenever new disputes arose. Alarmed by the growing militancy, the government orchestrated a concerted campaign aimed at swinging public opinion against the workers by inventing stories of worker brutality that were given wide play in the press. In an extraordinary cabinet meeting televised on September 5, the director of the Korean Federation of Industries (FKI) was invited to present his case against the workers. When his blatant stories were broadcast, thirty-five pastors in Seoul and Incheon went on hunger strike in protest of media mendacity. They occupied the FKI offices, but hundreds of riot police removed them.

On November 27, 1987, the first regional labor council was organized in Masan; fifteen other regions soon organized. Occupational councils also were called into being from below among clerical, service, and hospital workers. Alongside factory workers, unions appeared in banks and insurance companies, government investment firms, in the mass media, universities, and schools. In Masan, industrial workers united with women textile workers who had themselves organized about a hundred plants in the Free Export Zone. Parts of Masan were described as a "liberated zone" as workers from different factories marched in unison during each other's strikes in significant shows of solidarity. In April 1989, their united forces battled police and maintained their struggle for weeks, until finally the Goldstar president directly intervened and reached a settlement with the unions.

Of the many streams that flowed together to become the torrent of change in 1987, we must include the "necktie brigade"—the strata of off-line office workers, health care employees, teachers, proletarianized professionals, technicians, researchers, financial services workers, sales personnel, and low-level administrators. Variously known as white-collar workers, the new working class, and the new middle class, these wageworkers are essential to advanced economies like that being built in Korea. By 1980, one estimate classified 38 percent of employees as white-collar workers.[22] While other statistics are lower, they nonetheless indicate growing numbers of such workers.

Throughout East Asia's newly industrializing countries, these strata steadily increased as the economies developed. From the early 1960s to the early 1980s, new working class (or new middle class) strata went from 6.7 to 16.6 percent of the workforce in South Korea, 11.0 to 20.1 percent in Taiwan, and 14 to 21 percent in Hong Kong.[23] Unlike the history of European and U.S. capital formation,

TABLE 10.4 **Korean Occupational Structure, 1960–1985**

Year	1960	1970	1980	1985
Business Owners and Top Executives	0.5	0.6	1.1	1.4
Non-manual workers	5.2	8.9	13.8	17.1
Managers	2.4	3.3	5.3	7.2
Professionals	1.9	2.5	3.4	3.7
Clerical Workers	0.9	3.1	5.1	6.2
Manual Workers	14.6	23.7	30.3	34.0
Industrial Workers	7.1	15.8	24.0	25.7
Sales/Service Workers	2.5	4.5	5.3	7.7
Personal Service Workers	5.0	3.4	1.0	0.6
Non-farm self-employed	10.5	13.6	17.1	21.0
Farmers	65.2	51.7	33.5	23.9
Unemployed	4.0	1.6	4.3	2.6
Total (percent)	100.0	100.1	100.1	100.0
Total (number of workers)	7,522,000	10, 543,000	12,708,000	15,350,000

Sources: Hagen Koo, "Middle Classes, Democratization, and Class Formation: The Case of South Korea," *Theory and Society* 20 (1991): 485; original data from Korean Population Census.

these strata developed before a bourgeois class could fully become hegemonic and simultaneously with the formation of an industrial working class. Korean factory laborers were concerned with job safety and inadequate food, while office workers were more motivated to challenge unnecessary hierarchy; all workers were united by the need for decent wages, autonomous unions, and curbing abusive authority. One dimension of the necktie brigade's attributes is its capacity for self-organization. Another is its integration into the middle class. The government's Economic Planning Board found that 41 percent of people identified themselves as middle-class in 1980 and 53 percent in 1985. Estimating the size of the middle class can be very problematic. Using data from the Economic Planning Board from November 22, 1988, Dong Won-mo estimated only 35 percent of Koreans were middle-class.[24]

Farmers were also greatly affected by the ripples of energy emanating from the great labor struggles of 1987. When workers returned to their hometowns for the August harvest festivals after their strikes and union drives, they boasted, "we fought for ourselves and were given raises, and it is because of our struggles that the labor laws were reformed."[25] In the same month, hundreds of tenant farmers sat-in for weeks at Samyang Company in Seoul to demand the return of their lands. Others took action at Hyundai.[26] Farmers' organizations evolved rapidly in this period. Merger of many regional groups produced the National Federation of Farmers' Association in April 1990 with more than a hundred chapters. Its chairperson, Kwon Chong-tae, called for an end to "economic exploitation by monopoly capitalists at home and abroad."[27] The group protested corporate globalization with visionary critiques and demonstrations against the Uruguay Round that led to the creation of the WTO. Ironically, the rapid changes led to a role reversal of sorts. Nancy Abelmann reported on a visit she made to North Jeolla Province in 1993. Years before, movement circles (or *undongkwon*) was a word associated by farmers with North Korean sympathizers; by 1993, these same farmers were complaining that students sent to their villages to learn and help out "don't seem like *undongkwon* students—they don't seem sufficiently moral or upright."[28]

Workers' culture developed into a diverse and significant source for class consciousness. Workers now addressed each other using the strident term, "*nodongcha*" (노동자), while the government continued to use the more antiquated, "*kunrocha*" (근로자).[29] Newspapers, magazines, night schools, dance, and theater all stimulated new self-confidence and encouraged participation in struggles for better working conditions and improvements in people's standard of living. Many workers lived in inadequate housing. As available housing was 40 percent below the number of households, it was estimated that 20 percent of the urban poor were squatters.[30] Along with a revival of May First gatherings, Korean workers began assembling at annual commemorations of Chun Tae-il's sacrifice on November 13, 1970. Tens of thousands of workers gathered on both occasions, giving movement activists an opportunity to exchange experiences and renew friendships, and for various groups to distribute materials and recruit new members. Workers' culture grew by leaps and bounds. Theater, art, and especially poetry conveyed the sensibility of expanded consciousness and beautiful possibilities. In these lines penned by labor activist Park No-hae, workers' new-found optimism was evident:

Maybe

Maybe I'm a machine
Absorbed in soldering subassemblies
Swarming down the conveyor,
Like a robot repeating,
The same motions forever,
Maybe I've become a machine.

Maybe we're chickens in a coop.
Neatly lined up on our roosts,
Hand speed synchronized in dim light,
The faster the music,
The more eggs we lay,
Maybe we've become chickens in a coop.

They . . .
They who extract and devour
Our pith and our marrow,
Maybe they are barefaced robbers,
Turning humans into machines,
Into consumables,
Into things buyable and sellable.
Maybe they are dignified
And law-abiding barefaced robbers.

Those gentle smiles,
That refined beauty and culture,
That rich and dazzling opulence,
Maybe all of that is ours.[31]

As an observer remarked, "Last year [1988], the focus was better wages and the right to organize unions, but now workers want a say in how their companies are run. They're calling for equal control over personnel management and profit distribution. No longer do they think of business as a personal asset subject to an owner's whim."[32] Yet, although workers often overwhelmed the government forces arrayed against them and were determined to transform their workplaces, they never contested political power. Many of their handmade signs read: "Head of the Company, Submit to Negotiations." This slogan was itself a concession that the company head was in charge, that the paternalism of the executives would be allowed to continue albeit under more humane conditions. While hundreds of new unions formed and won significant improvements in the lives of their members, theirs was not a movement for revolution. Even when workers occupied

Ulsan, the signs on their banners called for independent trade unions, radical enough in its context, but they asked the mayor to help them achieve this goal. Like millions of Koreans, many accepted Roh Tae-woo's June 29 declaration as proof of his benign character. Confucian patriarchy militated against the formulation of revolutionary aspirations that broke with the existing system. In April 1992, working class Ulsan overwhelmingly voted in National Assembly elections for candidates from the party led by Chung Ju-young—the most reactionary *chaebol* boss.

For their part, the *chaebol* were not deterred by any respect for their class adversaries. The companies organized *"kusadae"*—strikebreakers of managers and paid paramilitaries—and sent them to attack workers. In Dongil Industry, a machinery company run by Sun-myung Moon (the Moonies Unification Church), more than five hundred *kusadae* attacked workers who were peacefully sitting-in, injuring many. In this period, the Anti-Communist Federation and the Moonies staged rallies and whipped up sentiment against the "Communist" influence in the labor movement. On July 30, about a thousand female laborers sat in at ICC Corporation in Busan, then one of the world's largest shoe manufacturers. Six hundred thugs wielding iron pipes, hammers, and sticks assaulted them. The women were forced into their dormitory, where they were assaulted again. Even the yellow FKTU organized a thousand-man armed crew to attack autonomous unions. Worst of all was the government's special riot squad, the white-helmeted "White Skull Corps," which viciously attacked workers. At the same time, hundreds of leaders were summarily fired or transferred to more difficult and dangerous jobs. In Gangwondo, when coal miners fought against the FKTU for its complicity with the police, activists were reassigned to the most difficult jobs. After one—Song Won-hee—committed suicide, the union leaders resigned, and ultimately an autonomous union was won.

Student activists recognized the new hegemony of the working class when hundreds attended an August 2 meeting at Yonsei University. Although they convened around a main focus of the coming election, they vowed to support the strike wave. A reporter summarized their orientation as, "we should not weaken the autonomy of the workers or cause resentment toward students by workers."[33] Less than three weeks later, student council leaders formed a powerful national organization on August 19, 1987—*Jeondaehyop*, the National Association of Student Representatives. Somewhere between four to five thousand students representing ninety-five colleges and universities gathered to build this alliance of elected student government presidents. Breaking with prior student groups that were necessarily secretive, *Jeondaehyop* held open conventions, a bold move that helped to ensure coverage of their views in the media and to assure more moderate Koreans of their honest intentions. Significantly, among their goals were a U.S. apology for complicity in the Gwangju tragedy and an end to the increasing amount of U.S. imports into South Korea. Their founding statement included the following objectives:

1. Immediate end of the Chun regime.
2. End of government repression of workers; "common struggle and solidarity with striking workers."[34]

3. Distance from the Unification Democratic Party for its ineffectiveness.
4. Political neutrality of the military.
5. U.S. public apology for Gwangju complicity and for pressure for imports.

Their structure called for one voting representative from each of about 130 campuses in the country. Meetings were flexible enough to include several students from each university student government, and one-year term limits ensured that many activists would gain organizing experience at the national level. Even though only semilegal, one participant described their operation as "complete democracy" balanced evenly between NL and PD groups. While others insisted NL was predominant, both NL and PD tendencies were represented inside the organization—along with their debates and divisions—but also with unity in actions. *Jeondaehyop* was able to keep its activist base until 1992.[35] A central committee of fourteen leaders met every two weeks (or sometimes monthly), but no women were part of this central group since none had been elected presidents of their campus student government. Perhaps one-third to one-quarter of all local representatives was female. Later, a National Association of Female Student Representatives formed. In addition to the national central committee, regional ones formed in Seoul and elsewhere.

After the unprecedented outpouring of grievances in July and August had surprised the government, the police began to conduct a wave of arrests to stem the labor movement. By the end of September, the state had gained the upper hand, and the strike movement receded. When the government announced on September 29 that they were taking steps to make laborers "a middle class," it was clear the movement had won substantial gains—and would not be permitted to expand further. Preoccupied with the exigencies of the struggle for democracy, the democratization movement had failed to mobilize significantly in support of workers. Convinced that the NCDC had failed them, laborers occupied its Busan offices on October 15 and in other cities as well on October 20, 21, and 22, compelling the democratic forces to reevaluate their trajectory. By including politicians like YS and DJ in its ranks and aligning itself with political parties—no matter how progressive—the NCDC had sacrificed its autonomy and now paid the price. Both DJ and YS refused to allow support for strikes—let alone workers' illegal actions—nor even to countenance their endorsement by the broad coalition. When the NCDC's Labor Committee finally organized a rally against the repression of the labor movement at Myongdong Cathedral on October 27, it was already too late for the labor and democratization movements to unite on a radical course. The NCDC's weakened power was evident four days later, on October 31, when police easily blocked its national demonstrations.

Lessons and Legacy
The great victory of the Korean people over the military dictatorship resulted in greater economic prosperity. Wage increases in 1988 and 1989 averaged an astonishing 22.6 percent and 18.8 percent for blue-collar workers (and 11.9 percent and

15.3 percent for white-collar workers).[36] In the ten years after 1987, real incomes doubled, and nearly two million full-time jobs were added to the economy. By 1991, the percentage of Koreans who considered themselves middle-class rose to 61.3 (with only 1.6 percent regarding themselves as upper-class and 37.1 percent as lower-class.) up from 53 percent in 1985. The union movement proliferated in factories and among white-collar workers in banking, health care, and mass media.[37] Another indication of the ways in which political liberalization is good for wealth is the increase in profits of the fourteen largest Japanese banks by 57 percent and U.S. banks by 24.5 percent from 1987 to 1988. With the financialization of South Korea, total stock market value went from 9 percent of GNP in 1985 to an astonishing 56.6 percent in 1988. Two years later, the world's ninth-largest stock market in terms of capitalization was in Seoul.[38] In the same period, real estate prices skyrocketed, appreciating more than 50 percent from 1987 to 1989.[39]

With its "miraculous" economy and newly won liberties, South Korea became an inspirational model for people around the world: from Sri Lanka (where more than forty thousand people have "disappeared") to Cambodia and Burma; from African countries looking to develop to Latin American states seeking high-tech industries, all eyes turned to Korea. Koreans' remarkable historical praxis offers humanity insight into our own future.

In the aftermath of the 1987 uprising, a host of lessons can be gleaned from this praxis, including the issue of who are the subjects of change. When we pause to consider that in the summer of 1987, the multitude then in motion brought South Korea close to a revolutionary situation (if not enmeshing it in one, as Johnson and Cumings maintain), then we need to ask: who created that situation? Surveying the crisis—comprehended as lasting from the contestation of the dictatorship's political power in June through the transformation in the factory regime in July and August—the answer is the *minjung*. Yet within the bifurcated logic of existing categories of existence, factory workers' motion is entirely separate from "middle-class" reformism—a position that disregards considerable historical evidence of the radicalism of the "necktie brigade."

So long as the division in the working class between the "necktie brigade" and blue-collar laborers is salient, the new working class's political orientation toward democratization must be severed from the industrial working class's unionization drive. In this partition, the radical impetus remains latent. When combined, however, the possibility of a thoroughgoing restructuring of society becomes visible—and not in only theories of erudite scholars but in the actions of millions of people who changed their conditions of existence. In the last half of the twentieth century, significant social movements in Europe, the United States, and East Asia were centrally generated by marginalized minorities and students. Members of the lumpenproletariat contributed significantly to the most radical dimensions of movements, from the Black Panther Party to the Gwangju Uprising. When workers at the point of production and proletarianized white-collar workers got involved (as in France in May 1968, Italy's Hot Autumn, Poland's Solidarność, and China's Tiananmen Uprising), they generally did so after the initial waves of protests by students. Not an idle matter, the answer to the question of the composition of the working class—and who is the subject of change (the "multitude" or "proletariat")—will determine activists' strategy for finally bringing an end to the miserable system that degrades human beings and all forms of life in the name of corporate profit. We owe it to ourselves to consider this matter soberly in light of the enormous changes wrought during the twentieth century if we are to succeed in the twenty-first.

Despite its tactical defeat, the *minjung* significantly altered South Korea. Alongside ending military dictatorship, the situation of women and young people underwent positive changes: a broad cultural shift produced new opportunities for millions of people; the working class was transformed; wages and working conditions immediately improved for millions of workers; and the labor movement and its organizations were greatly strengthened. Even the FKTU changed, and after another decade of struggles for legalization of autonomous unions, a new confederation was established. Workers in South Korea are now widely recognized as the leading force of social change and play central roles in continuing struggles for justice.

Significantly, the strike wave followed the crest of the June Uprising. In the second volume of this book, a similar relationship between political uprisings and workers' strikes emerges from empirical histories of uprisings in 1986 in the Philippines, 1988 in Burma, 1989 in China, 1990 in Bangladesh and Nepal, and 1992 in Thailand. This pattern is significant and indicates the hegemonic ascendancy of the working class in the array of forces unleashed as the whole society moves forward. In all these cases, superexploitation of working people under dictatorships functioned to enrich the 1%. Compelled by severe repression to delay for years their struggles for decent standards of living, workers immediately moved forward as soon as democratic breakthroughs provided openings to improve conditions of everyday life. While similar to other struggles, Korean workers' remarkable capacity for self-organization and militancy has recent parallels, among them *Solidarność*, Brazil's strike wave from 1978 to 1983, and Iranian workers' councils from 1979 to 1981.[40]

As the Gwangju Uprising developed into a proletarian struggle in 1980, the working class in July 1987 grew out of the democratization struggles in which the universal interests of the whole society were at stake. Previous Korean factory strike waves were relatively synchronized with more general cycles of protest. In October 1946, workers began the more general uprising, and three other times— on the heels of the April 19 overthrow of Rhee in 1960, the killing of Park Chunghee, and ousting of Chun Doo-hwan—strike movements were able to congeal. Their direct relationship to political change is different than in Europe and the United States, where industrial disputes are more often related to economic cycles and changing productive relations rather than to political dynamics.

At a time when the world is changing more rapidly than ever before, analyzing and interpreting this praxis of millions of people has only begun. Generations of thinkers have articulated answers in reference to objective, economic categories of people's relationship to the forces of production, and manual workers aggregated in large-scale production facilities have been understood as central to the revolutionary project. Marx's most powerful revolutionary pamphlet, *The Communist Manifesto*, was written in response to a request from workers for him to craft a statement of their movement's aims, and for the remainder of his lifetime, he championed the proletariat as the antithesis of bourgeois society and future destroyer of capitalism. After the 1917 October revolution in Russia, factory workers were among its most ardent urban supporters. Organized in workplace formations, they marched *en masse* to the front lines against Euro-American invasion forces, where the vast majority perished in defense of the Bolshevik government. The Chinese revolution was successful only after Mao asserted the peasantry as its leading force—a proposition that initially led his comrades to regard him as a heretic and expel him from the Party. Nevertheless, once in power, Chinese Marxists also enshrined industrial workers in a privileged place as the leading force in constructing socialism. The praxis of Korean movements reveals the *minjung* as a force of change.

A recent theoretical attempt to grapple with the composition of the working class in economically advanced countries was undertaken by Michael Zweig in *The Working Class Majority: The Best Kept Secret in America*. Zweig posed a proletarian majority based upon his understanding of power relations in the workplaces, not simply upon categories of production. While mainstream U.S. commentators glorify the middle class as the bastion of democracy and seek to portray everyone as middle class, Zweig offers an important alternative, insisting workers are the central forces of progress and the majority of society. Developing a rubric of "working class" based upon power relations, he makes significant insights into the reality of workers' lives within the capitalist behemoth.

Zweig provides convincing data of the impoverishment of many working people and the often-vanishing line between the urban poor and workers. He believes some subsets of urban laborers are working class—and thus of great importance—while others are not. In a repetition of nineteenth-century thinking, Zweig regards the new working class as middle class; he subsumes the lumpenproletariat (the chronically unemployed, often criminally involved and impoverished) into the working class; and he remains confined within the parameters of nationalist discourse. While he acknowledges that working and middle class people in the United States share roughly the same levels of income, take similar vacations, live in similar houses (which they often own), Zweig makes power in the workplace the central feature of class stratification. His detailed categorization of jobs finds that 82.8 million jobs (62 percent of the total) are working class, which is the basis for his belief in "a working class majority."[41] Yet his understanding of the working class does not include public school teachers, computer programmers, nurses, librarians, social workers, and many other off-line office workers with little power and no stock ownership built into their jobs—all of whom he considers middle class. While he acknowledges that many professionals have been proletarianized (in a process similar to that undergone by skilled handicraft workers at the end of the nineteenth century), he refuses to consider them as working class. One telling example of his inconsistency is when United Airline Workers became stockholders in their corporation but nonetheless organized a union, Zweig considers that proof of their working class character, but when white collar workers unionized, he considers it only a sign of their "feeling" working class.

For Marx, philosophical categories preceded his enunciation of economic ones. In his schema, the proletariat was a vast majority of capitalist society, had "nothing to lose but their chains," and was the bourgeoisie's determinate negation. Following in that tradition, analysis based upon people's praxis in social movements ("class-for itself") reveals the new working class as a force often opposed to dictatorships of all kinds in one society after another. Is their history of subjective antisystemic mobilization based upon these strata's objective proletarianization? For his part, Zweig discounts the role of "middle class" students even though universities have long since moved to the center of the process of production, and students occupy a subaltern power position within them. Remarkably, students all over the world have opposed dictatorship and imperialism, and they are some of the few constituencies to object to the application of the productive forces in their institutions to warfare. Moreover, their noteworthy class solidarity with workers in the global south who are paid pennies a day to produce university sweatshirts and other college memorabilia indicates a growing class consciousness of apprentice workers (as college students should be understood). A similar problem exists with Zweig's rigid analysis of the lumpenproletariat, which excludes even brief consideration of positive and negative features of its role in social movements.

The main form of power differentials in the world's workplaces today are internationally constituted through imperial relations, an architecture of power in which the U.S. corporations remain preeminent. Like most analysts, Zweig accounts for the dramatic rise in American workers' living standards in the twentieth century solely with reference to higher productivity, making no mention of exploitation of the Third World. His brief chapter on globalization discusses pros and cons of trade and NAFTA without any consideration of the Zapatistas and anti-WTO movements (arguably the most significant form of anti-capitalist world mobilization in the latter part of the twentieth century). Zweig never once mentions imperialism. To analyze "class" solely within the United States and ignore the reality of a global system fails even to acknowledge international perspectives on class formulated decades ago. Zweig's nationalist framework also leads him to ignore economic determinants of the new place of universities at the center of the economy. Rather than developing appreciation of the role of technology in changing production and altering the character of the working class to include "educated" laborers (the new working class), Zweig concludes without much insight into larger economic issues. He notes that, "after Sputnik, the Cold War race against the Soviet Union created a demand for scientists."[42] Compounded by traditional categories of class, nationalism leads Zweig to miss the significance of the widely experienced proletarianization of millions of professionals and office workers.

Beginning with the 1987 mobilization of Korean workers—whether in factories, offices, universities or rural areas—a glimpse was revealed of the proletarian majority's capacity for self-guided action. From the insurrectionary wildcat strikes of 1987 to the struggle against neoliberalism, Korean workers moved to the forefront of social change. In so doing, they positioned the country for the possibility of genuine social transformation.

NOTES

1   Chalmers Johnson, "South Korean Democratisation: The Role of Economic Development," in *Korea Under Roh Tae-Woo: Democratisation, Northern Policy, and Inter-Korean Relations*, edited by James Cotton (Canberra: Allen and Unwin, 1993).
2   Cumings, *Korea's Place in the Sun*, 388.
3   Haggard and Kaufman, *Political Economy*, 96.
4   Ibid., 94.
5   See Koo, *Korean Workers*, 156. The Korean language source Koo gives is Kim Young-soo, 한국 노동자 계급정치운동 (Seoul: 현장에서 미래를: 1999), 207.
6   See Jong-chol Ahn, "The Citizens' Army during the Kwangju Uprising," in *Contentious Kwangju: The May 18th Uprising in Korea's Past and Present*, eds. Gi-Wook Shin and Kyung Moon Hwang (Lanham, MD: Rowman and Littlefield, 2003); and Shin's own analysis in the introduction.
7   Koo, *Korean Workers*, 161.
8   *Hard Journey*, 249 (see chap. 5 n. 68).
9   Christian Institute for the Study of Justice and Development, *Lost Victory*, 131.
10 See Hart-Landsberg's insightful *The Rush to Development*, 157.
11 Dae-oup Chang, "Korean Labour Relations in Transition: Authoritarian Flexibility?" *Labour, Capital and Society* 35, no. 1 (April 2002): 19.
12 Amsden, *Asia's Next Giant*, 116.
13 Koo, *Korean Workers*, 31.
14 Christian Institute for the Study of Justice and Development, *Lost Victory*, 214.
15 Ogle, *South Korea*, 77.
16 Christian Institute for the Study of Justice and Development, *Lost Victory*, 230.
17 See Won Young-su, "History of South Korean Labor and Student Struggles Since the End of World War II," in *The International Encyclopaedia of Revolution and Protest: 1500–Present*, ed. Immanuel Ness (London: Wiley Blackwell, 2009).
18 *Hard Journey*, 247.
19 Susan Chira, "Seoul, in Switch, Moves to Resolve Labor Dispute," *New York Times*, August 19, 1987.
20 Ogle, *South Korea*, 134.
21 Park, *Democracy and Social Change*, 153.
22 Ogle, *South Korea*, 149.
23 Hagen Koo, "Middle Classes, Democratization, and Class Formation: The Case of South Korea," *Theory and Society* 20 (1991): 485.
24 Dong Won-mo, "The Democratization of South Korea," 77.
25 See Nancy Abelmann, "Reorganizing and Recapturing Dissent in 1990s South Korea," in *Between Resistance and Revolution: Cultural Politics and Social Protest*, eds. Richard G. Fox and Orin Starn (New Brunswick, NJ: Rutgers University Press, 1997), 258.
26 Christian Institute for the Study of Justice and Development, *Lost Victory*, 258–59.
27 Hart-Landsberg, *The Rush to Development*, 259.
28 Abelmann, "Reorganizing and Recapturing Dissent," 262.
29 Since North Korea uses "*nodong*" for workers, southern conservatives employed "*kunro*," a term that is only marginally different.
30 Bello and Rosenfield, *Dragons in Distress*, 39.

31 Translated by Kyung-ja Chun. See Koo, "The State, *Minjung*, and the Working Class," 154–55.
32 Quoted in Bello and Rosenfield, *Dragons in Distress*, 44.
33 Quoted in Dong Won-mo, "The Democratization of South Korea," 33.
34 Han Sung-joo, "South Korea in 1987: The Politics of Democratization," *Asian Survey* 28, no. 1 (January 1988): 58.
35 Interview with Im Jong-sok, Seoul, June 4, 2001.
36 Hagen Koo, "Middle Classes, Democratization, and Class Formation," 497.
37 Byoung-Hoon Lee, "Militant Unionism in Korea," 157.
38 Jung-un Woo, *Race to the Swift: State and Finance in Korean Industrialization* (New York: Columbia University Press, 1991), 200–201.
39 Hart-Landsberg, *The Rush to Development*, 239.
40 See Loren Goldner's 2007 article on the Korean working class from 1987 to 2007 at http://home.earthlink.net/~lrgoldner.
41 Michael Zweig, *The Working Class Majority: The Best Kept Secret in America* (Ithaca: Cornell University Press, 2001), 30. The population of the U.S, in 2001, when the book was published, was 278 million, so only about 30 percent of U.S. residents were workers according to Zweig.
42 Ibid., 30.

CHAPTER 11

From *Minjung* to Citizens

With South Korea's transition to parliamentary democracy, and with the disintegration of 'actual living socialism' in East Europe in the late 1980s, the underlying logic of the *minjung* movement had dissolved as well.

—Namhee Lee

Minjung is no longer a useful framework for understanding Korea today.

—Charles Armstrong, 2002

CHRONOLOGY

August 19, 1987	Some 3,500 students from ninety-five universities form a new student alliance
August 22, 1987	Daewoo shipyard worker Lee Suk-kyu killed by tear gas canister fired by police
December 16, 1987	With the opposition divided, Roh Tae-woo wins the presidency
April 26, 1988	Opposition gains a majority in National Assembly elections
May 15, 1988	SNU student Cho Seong-man commits suicide at Myongdong, demanding release of dissidents
May 16, 1988	Committee for Gwangju Uprising Memorial demands investigations, compensation
June 10, 1988	Police thwart meeting between North and South Korean students
September 8, 1988	Primary school teachers in Yeosu form the first primary school teachers association
September 17, 1988	Seoul Olympics open

October 17, 1988	Family members in Gwangju of killed and disappeared people begin sit-in for justice
November 17, 1988	More than ten thousand farmers in Seoul protest opening of markets to U.S. products
November 21, 1988	About ten thousand teachers demand democratic education laws
November 26, 1988	National Union of Media Workers formed at forty-one companies
December 28, 1988	Roh announces a rollback of liberalization measures enacted after June Uprising
May 3, 1989	Dongeui University protests: six police killed
May 18, 1989	854 professors from Jeollanamdo demand punishment for Gwangju massacre
May 28, 1989	Yoon Young-kyu becomes first president of National Teachers Union
June 10, 1989	U.S. State Department releases still controversial White Paper on Gwangju
January 22, 1990	*Jeonnohyop* (forerunner of Korean Confederation of Trade Unions) organized
January 22, 1990	Kim Young-sam merges his party with ruling parties to form *Minjadang*
July 17, 1990	Ruling party (*Minjadang*) passes twenty-six repressive bills in thirty seconds without hearings
October 13, 1990	Roh declares "war" on "crime and violence"—i.e., the working class
April 26, 1991	Student Kang Kyong-dae killed by police; in ensuing struggles twelve more people die
May 19–20, 1991	Battle of Unamdong to bring Kang Kyong-dae to rest in Mangwoldong
May 26, 1991	Two hundred thousand attend Park Seung-hui's funeral in Gwangju
June 3, 1991	Students throw flour and eggs on acting premier; media assault on movement begins
August 19, 1991	Collapse of Soviet Union accelerates; older Korean activists recant positions
September 17, 1991	Both North and South Korea separately join United Nations
Spring 1992	Busan National University: major fights with police; students use iron pipes
May 29, 1992	First public student activist organization appears
December 18, 1992	Kim Young-sam (YS) elected as first civilian president
May 27, 1993	*Hanchongryun* (Korean Confederation of University Student Councils) formed
July 1, 1993	"Cultural turn" in student movement begins

THE KOREAN DEMOCRATIZATION movement's breakthrough in 1987 resulted in a torrential sea change in the country's institutions, norms, and values. After decades of dictatorships, the country transmuted rapidly in the weeks and months after June. While the industrial working class moved squarely to the center of insurgent actions, other groups also mobilized in the newly liberated space, and a broad range of reform movements emerged. With sweeping changes in state-society relations and within institutions, a whole new epoch ensued in which the quality of life improved for tens of millions of Koreans.

This was a remarkably upbeat time. The great victory won by the *minjung* brought political rights and liberties many Koreans had only dreamed of attaining. People no longer glanced over their shoulders when expressing viewpoints critical of government. They were no longer tortured and killed for their political views. Gone were the gulags (*Samchongkyoyukdae*). No more did police arrest people *en masse* for being in the wrong place at the wrong time. At the same time as autonomous trade unions formed, so did a farmers' association, a teachers union, Lawyers for a Democratic Society, and the National Association of Professors for Democratic Society (*Mingyohyop*). South Korea's antinuclear movement began in 1987.[1] In the new climate, free expression flourished. Journalists banned from writing by the dictatorship organized an opposition daily newspaper, *Hankyoreh*, with small contributions from more than sixty thousand people. Selling shares at about five dollars apiece—and, to ensure its democratic base of supporters, with no one allowed to own more than two thousand shares—*Hankyoreh* for more than twenty years has been a reliable source of information. Within four years, the number of the country's daily papers tripled—from thirty to ninety—and more than six thousand magazines were publishing.[2]

As activist circles became professionalized and specialized, a plethora of NGOs arose with specific foci, such as to help prevent environmental degradation, to win increased rights for women, and to mitigate the military madness of the Cold War's tragic continuation on the peninsula. The wanton impunity with which U.S. service members commit crimes against South Koreans was brought onto the public radar screen. Alongside institutional changes, social relations were greatly transformed. The uprisings in Jeju and Gwangju began to be publicly understood and compensation was eventually paid to victims. After a decade more of struggle, dictator Chun Doo-hwan and his underlings were sent to prison for their crimes. Revelations about the 1950 No Gun Ri massacre brought forth dozens of similar cases in which U.S. troops and their ROK allies had wantonly slaughtered tens of thousands of innocent civilians. The Yeosun uprising first entered public consciousness after decades of "willed amnesia."[3] The "comfort women" issue was raised for the first time in 1987 by an alliance of feminists.

Christian organizations were also greatly transformed by the tumultuous events of 1987. In the wake of the national uprising, nearly a hundred *minjung* churches opened in various parts of the country, especially focusing their work on industrial and poor areas. In the energy of June, Kim Gi-ha developed a notion of "collective ecstasy" as a means of transforming society.[4] Paik Nak-chung wrote a careful analysis of Korean literature and concluded that in the aftermath of the

June Uprising, "Korean literature entered a new stage."[5] He sought to engage with North Korean literature, especially the opera, *Sea of Blood*, a bold attempt at literary criticism that got his passport confiscated. Despite the many positive developments in 1987, there were still limits the dictatorship would impose, and it remained far from clear in which direction South Korea was headed. Thousands of political detainees still languished behind bars, the country's restive working class was still in a state of semifeudal bondage, and most importantly, Chun Doo-hwan remained president.

The First Elections

After the June 29 capitulation of the dictatorship to opposition demands, nothing was more vital than electing a president who was committed to democracy. As Koreans focused on the upcoming presidential election, the opposition was lured into the electoral system. Roh's apparent concession on June 29 cleverly changed the dictatorship from an "object of overthrow" into an "object of competition."[6] The National Assembly quickly rubber-stamped a constitutional amendment requiring direct elections, which were scheduled for December 16, 1987. The opposition's failure to field a unified candidate spelled disaster. As the two Kim's (YS and DJ) campaigned against each other, they fomented regional antagonisms. Rallies of hundreds of thousands of people sometimes ended in violent confrontations when their supporters clashed. In mid-September, the United States gave its endorsement for president, when President Reagan received a visit from Roh Tae-woo. U.S. support for the candidacy of the military dictator turned politician could not have been clearer. No other candidate was invited to Washington.

Movement groups did all they could to unite behind one—and only one—progressive candidate. Until the very end, many people believed YS and DJ would reach some kind of accommodation with each other and field a single candidacy. In this period, the NCDC met twice a month—once on a regional level and once with representations of the entire country. So great was its popular support that regional organizers who traveled during the election campaign were routinely not charged toll fees by collectors. At that time, 123 cities and towns were represented in the organization as Oh Choong-il tirelessly traversed the country. He never doubted that YS and DJ would unite, and when they ran against each other, he was haunted for a decade by the decision not to have the NCDC select a unified candidate.

On November 29, only a few weeks before the election, Korean Airline flight 858 disappeared off the coast of Burma with 118 passengers aboard. Although many people today suspect the involvement of ANSP (the Agency for National Security Planning—formerly the KCIA), North Korea was blamed for placing an explosive device on the plane (correctly, as it turns out). The attack helped swing thousands of votes to Roh, who won even though he got four million votes less than the combined total received by YS and DJ. At the end of the day, although the two Kims received well over half of all votes, Roh Tae-woo was elected with a plurality of 36.6 percent. The opposition's failure to unite behind a single candidate, a reality dictated by the political ambitions of two leaders, handed victory to the dictatorship.

TABLE 11.1 **1987 Presidential Election Results**

Candidate	Roh Tae-woo	Kim Young-sam	Kim Dae Jung	Kim Jong-pil
Percent of vote	36.6	28.1	27.1	8.1
Votes	8,282,738	6,337,581	6,113,375	1,823,067

Source: James Cotton, ed., *Korea Under Roh Tae-woo* (Canberra: Allen and Unwin, 1993), 18.

Among voters over fifty years old, Roh won more than 55 percent, while DJ garnered more than 80 percent of the Jeollas and about a third of Seoul. At the time, the failure of the opposition to unite and the North Korean plane bombing were overshadowed by substantial claims of electoral fraud. DJ's party charged the government had fabricated nine hundred thousand votes. The government's list of eligible voters included 25,870,000 people—almost a million more than the number they had previously published. More than 90 percent of absentee ballots (numbering almost a million people) went to Roh, a proportion greatly different than the popular vote. In districts of Seoul and Busan with a substantial number of voters born in the Jeollas, Kim Dae Jung surprisingly received only a modicum of votes. Most revealingly, on the evening of December 16, witnesses observed officials smuggling ballots out of Seoul's Kuro-gu district office by hiding them under loaves of bread in a delivery truck.[7] Thousands of people immediately sat-in at the Kuro-gu district offices to prevent the ballots from being taken away. People—and the ballots—remained in place overnight, until thousands of riot police attacked behind a barrage of tear gas. More than nine hundred people were arrested, and many were injured before the ballots disappeared.

DJ publicly protested the fraud, but his concerns were minimized in the media. So complete was the government's cover-up that a year later, as American journalist Joe Manguno (Seoul bureau chief for the *Asian Wall Street Journal*) was working on a story about how massive computer fraud had stolen the election for Roh Tae-woo, agents from the Korean National Security Planning Agency (the successor to the KCIA) broke into his house and stole his diskettes containing interviews and research materials. In addition, they wiped his hard drive clean of any traces of the files dealing with election fraud.[8] Fraud used to swindle the Korean electorate in 1987 is all too reminiscent of the 2000 election in the United States, when George W. Bush was able to win by the narrowest of margins by having hundreds of Floridians stricken off the eligible rolls or simply refused admittance to polling places. Apparently, Malcolm X was right when he observed that the chickens come home to roost.

Isolated and unpopular, Roh Tae-woo described his own administration as one of "total crisis." Many political prisoners were released, but thousands remained incarcerated. Press freedoms were observed, although within the limits set by the National Security Law (NSL)—and sometimes within even tighter constraints than legally justifiable. Freedom of assembly was sharply circumscribed, and even artists were not immune from censorship. In September 1987, Chosun University students Jun Jung-ho and Lee Sang-ho had their painting confiscated, and they were subsequently arrested. The controversial piece, set on Mount Paekdu in North Korea, depicted farmers', laborers', and students' (*minjung*) struggles on the left and Chun and Roh (along with nuclear arms) as puppets controlled by the United States on the right. Although the two were released on parole after a few months, their treatment reminded many people how much work remained. Movement activists redoubled their efforts against the military.

With massive pre-Olympic spending and "the three lows" (low interest rates, low oil prices, and low won-dollar exchange rate) economic progress helped somewhat to quiet protests. Following in the footsteps of Chun's market-oriented reforms of financial capital and trade, Roh steered the economy in the same pro-business direction it had been going for decades. He immediately opened Korean markets to U.S. beef, activating a nascent farmers' movement in early 1988. On January 8, more than twenty thousand livestock farmers protested the new policies, some even bringing their cows to Seoul to emphasize their opposition to the regime's policies.

In National Assembly elections on April 26, 1988, the ruling DJP lost its majority—the first time ever that opposition parties had won control. With seventy seats, *Pyongmindang* (the Peace and Democracy Party set up in 1987 by Kim Dae Jung) won the most seats. One of the first major items of business of the National Assembly was to convene hearings on Gwangju. Not only was the opposition inside the National Assembly actively pursuing the villains responsible for the massacre, but forces outside the government were mounting pressure as well. A group formed to demand investigation of Chun's "Samcheong Education Camps." Buddhists demanded investigation and punishment of those responsible for police use of excessive force at a temple in 1980.

In the post-June enthusiasm, university students optimistically claimed 1988 as the "first year of unification." In May 1988, more than ten thousand students assembled at Korea University and, as in 1961 (prior to Park Chung-hee's coup), sent a letter to their northern counterparts requesting a meeting to discuss unification. Students in the DPRK immediately agreed, but Roh mobilized more than fifty thousand troops to prevent students from meeting with thirteen North Korean representatives in Panmunjom. Some eight hundred students were detained, and many were prosecuted under the NSL.[9] While Roh clamped down on grassroots diplomacy with North Korea, he declared his own "Northern Policy" in July 1988 and went on to open relations with the Soviet Union, China, and Eastern Europe—but not with Pyongyang. On April 19, 1990, Roh met Soviet leader Gorbachev in Jeju, but he took more than two more years to normalize relations with China.

From the point of view of mainstream political scientists, the first two years of the Roh government were characterized by "continual strikes and student demonstrations."[10] That was only part of the tumultuous times. Besides continuing student and workplace protests, many other groups mobilized. On October 17, 1988, families of deceased activists (the Council of Bereaved Families of Suspicious Death Victims) began a monumental 1,350-day sit-in calling for investigations of secret police atrocities.[11] On November 15, (in the first massive commemoration of Chun Tae-il's suicide), more than forty thousand workers and students assembled at Yonsei University in a campaign for abolition of repressive labor laws. Farmers mobilized near the capitol in Yeuido about ten thousand strong on November 17 to protest U.S. goods flooding the domestic agricultural market. Four days later, thousands of teachers assembled in Yeuido and demanded revision of undemocratic education laws.

The regime's response to this outpouring of long pent-up frustration with government violence was to use the dreaded NSL, just as the Rhee regime had done beginning in 1948, by claiming opposition elements harbored favorable sentiments for North Korea. Coupled with repressive labor laws Chun had railroaded through his rubber-stamp parliament, thousands of activists were arrested and hundreds prosecuted. Public sector unions remained prohibited, and employees were placed on notice that even attendance at demonstrations would have serious repercussions. Autonomous organizations were restricted from organizing at private workplaces, and the legal right to strike was all but denied.

Roh's War on the Working Class

Despite the regime's repression, workers continued to bravely fight for their share of the country's wealth and power. As in 1987, the conflict was centered on the *chaebol*. At Samsung, Korean-American James Lee was hired to bust incipient unions. The company registered phony pro-Samsung unions to prevent any new unions from forming, and when workers attempted to register a new union, they were soundly beaten. In April 1988, as shipyard workers went on strike, Samsung sent in its *kusadae* thugs. Heavy fighting went on for several days, but in the end, the company proposed a "company-friendly union" to split the rank and file, a shrewd move that helped it escape independent unionism. White-collar unions were formed in the financial sector, among journalists, and for a wide array of office workers. In December, continuing intransigence led to a new strike at Hyundai. That same month, laborers convened the first national conference of regional and occupational councils.

As workers organized, Roh waited until after the Olympics closed to unleash ruthless repression on them. On December 28, 1988, in what he called measures aimed at "maintaining civic security," Roh announced a rollback of liberalization measures enacted after the June Uprising. Hundreds more labor leaders were arrested and their illegal unions offices attacked and closed down. A similar fate met thousands of others, including members of the National Democratic Movement Federation—the successor coalition to the NCDC that focused on unification.[12] In 1989, the daily average of arrests was twice that of 1988—and three times that of the Chun Doo-hwan years.[13] Some observers compared Roh's repression to that of Japanese colonial administrators in the 1920s or to the United States from 1945 to 1948. During Roh's first three years in office, some 4,300 people were imprisoned for political infractions—compared to 4,700 during all of Chun's eight years.[14] In July 1989, it was reported that over 6,500 people were detained in June alone—700 of whom went on to face formal charges. There was little the National Assembly could do. Its powers were restricted to budgetary matters, and it watched as the NSL was continually used to intimidate and arrest peaceful protesters.

The centerpiece of the collision between Roh's forces of suppression and insurgent workers was the strike at Hyundai Heavy Industry that began on December 12. Workers with stones and firebombs dueled police with tear gas and water cannons as strikers held firmly onto the plant. On January 8, 1989, in a dawn attack with baseball bats and clubs, company-hired thugs led by James Lee beat union leaders savagely, breaking Kwon Yong-mok's leg and destroying the organizers' office. In response, tens of thousands of workers rallied, and they burnt owner Chung Ju-yong in effigy. Student groups arrived and demonstrated in solidarity. For 108 days, the occupation continued. On March 30, 1989, the government mobilized an army of police to attack the gigantic Hyundai complex in Ulsan.[15] At dawn more than thirteen thousand police launched a coordinated land, sea, and air assault. When advance elements of the police reached the factories, however, they found them empty. Workers had secretly retreated to their dormitories. Hours later, when the police regrouped and attacked once more, savage fighting erupted and quickly spread to nearby Hyundai plants. Parts of Ulsan became battle zones. The next day, family members and campus supporters arrived to help. Intense fights continued for ten days. After hundreds of injuries and dozens of arrests, workers straggled back to work. Key leaders were dismissed and many remained imprisoned. Despite the tactical defeat, workers had won important gains: their organization became more disciplined and united, and their control of the plant floors was vibrant. The crucible of the struggle had amalgamated a hard core, and many newcomers joined the union.

That same month, two thousand riot police disrupted a strike by Seoul subway workers, in what would the first of many job actions by transportation workers. In May, the National Teachers and Educational Workers Union formed. In its first year, 1,636 teachers were dismissed for being members of an illegal union, and 120 were arrested under provisions of the NSL.[16] On the campuses, intense struggles also erupted. On May 3, six riot policemen were killed at Dongeui University in Busan when they were called upon to suppress protests. The university was shut down. On May 10 in Gwangju, Chosun University activist Lee Chol-kyu was found dead in the city's reservoir after he had been chased by the police at a traffic stop.

Even artists were tightly controlled. In 1989, the first May Exhibition about Gwangju became a venue for artists to circumvent the government's censorship of gallery space. Working together, they produced gigantic street murals in Gwangju depicting the history of *minjung* struggles. The epic proportions (one mural was 2.6 meters by 77 meters) involved hundreds of artists. When four artists sent slides of their work to the Pyongyang Youth Festival, they were arrested and their work destroyed.[17] While imprisoned, Hong Sung-dam endured water torture and other assaults before winning release as an Amnesty prisoner of conscience. On May 17, 1990, the first monument to the Gwangju Uprising was unveiled. Funded privately, it was followed by a mural depicting the armed struggle at Chonnam National University. Artists resisted authorities' attempts at censorship by creating autonomous artists' organizations and sponsoring counterexhibitions as part of a subaltern counterpublic space. In 1990, shows focused on the "10-day uprising and

During the Roh Tae-woo presidency, police were given free rein to suppress demonstrations. Student Kang Kyong-dae, beaten to death by police on April 26, 1991, was buried after militant funerals in both Seoul and Gwangju. Photographer unknown

the 10 years since," followed by the "American Show" at Mangwoldong Cemetery the following May.

Roh offered no apologies for his government's continuing use of violence against citizens. In a cabinet meeting, he was quoted as saying, "Democracy, as well as the future of this country, will depend upon our capability to crush the violent revolutionary forces that attempt to destroy democracy."[18] As part of his smooth campaign talk, Roh had promised to seek popular approval of his presidency halfway through his term, and to step down if people opposed him. The scandal resulting from revelations about Gwangju should have sealed his fate. With DJ's party serving as his main opposition, public hearings on Gwangju gripped the nation's attention like few other modern political events. Roh needed a political fix, and he got it when YS and the conservative opposition aligned with him to create a grand coalition. On January 22, 1990, the ruling Democratic Justice Party and two opposition parties (Kim Young-sam's Unification Democratic Party and Kim Jong-pil's New Democratic Republican Party) merged to create the Democratic Liberal Party (*Minjadang*). With that realignment of forces, the Roh government became the ruling party in the National Assembly. Not only could he claim overwhelming support for his presidency, he quickly pushed through legislation further restricting union activities and strikes. On July 17, 1990, the *Minjadang* rammed twenty-six bills through the National Assembly in thirty seconds. With no hearings or even vote counts, state control over the media was increased, and civilian control of the military was decreased. The parliamentary opposition resigned in protest, but the measures stood. As the government's offensive against labor intensified, over four hundred people were incarcerated under the auspices of the NSL, unions were attacked, and publications closed down.[19] The unification movement was branded anti-state. Not by coincidence, 1990 was the only year since 1980 when real wages of workers fell.

Faced with such extreme repression, movement groups tightened their organizations and moved toward explicit endorsement of revolution. Following the student movement's model of alliances of local groups, more than a hundred different groups merged to form the National Alliance of Farmers' Movements (*Jeonnong*). On January 22, 1990, the same day of the *Minjadang* merger, former student activists who had become union organizers successfully united in a militant and radical National Council of Trade Unions (NCTU or *Jeonnohyop*), with slogans "Build an Egalitarian Society!" and "Achieve Working Class Emancipation!"[20] Initial membership included fourteen regional blue-collar union councils and two occupational federations, for a total of 456 unions representing 160,000 laborers—8.6 percent of total union members in Korea.[21] Significantly, the new alliance did not formally include white-collar workers (about one hundred thousand of whom had organized) or *chaebol* unions, especially at Hyundai and Daewoo—although those unions offered solidarity statements and had close links with NCTU.

Jeonnohyop was the first major organization to raise the issue of labor emancipation and oppose capitalism. Since provisions of the NSL prohibited use of words like "socialism" under pain of imprisonment, "labor emancipation" and "opposition to ruling class power" were coded means of expressing essentially the same message. So severely did the state seek to prevent the new organization from consolidating itself that at the time of its founding, most NCTU leaders were in prison or in hiding. Reflecting a desire to be legally viable, the founding declaration of *Jeonnohyop* read: "We will struggle to achieve economic rights and unite with all democratic peoples' movements which fight for economic and social reform, achieve fundamental changes in the current situation of workers, and pursue our struggle for democracy, self-reliance, and peaceful national reunification." Committed to ending capitalism, such a radical formation was targeted by Roh's administration. As soon as it formed, the government outlawed

TABLE 11.2 **Number of Labor Disputes, 1986–1995**

Year	1986	1987	1988	1989	1990	1991	1992	1993	1994	1995
Number	276	3,749	1,873	1,616	322	234	235	144	121	88

Source: Hagen Koo, *Korean Workers: The Culture and Politics of Class Formation* (Ithaca: Cornell University Press, 2001) 159.

Jeonnohyop, declaring it was "leading a vicious conflict with an ideology of class struggle for the liberation of the labor." More than 300 undercover agents were dispatched to factories.[22] The next year, 294 labor leaders were incarcerated in long-term confinement and another 200 were underground and hunted by police.[23] As years of state repression exacted a toll on the new union, it lost members rapidly while emergent leaders languished in prison. At the same time, the government favored *Jeonnohyop's* reformist leaders and soon *Kukminpa* ("labor together with the nation"), a reformist faction aligned with NL politics, appeared within its ranks.

Jeonnohyop formed from thousands of struggles between 1987 and 1990, but soon after it formed, the number of struggles declined, as indicated in TABLE 11.2. The number of strikes may have decreased, but they became ever more political. On April 12, 1990, government-owned Korean Broadcasting System (KBS) workers stopped the station's signal as a protest against Roh's appointment of a friend of Chun Doo-hwan as president of the company. In so doing they launched a struggle for democratization of media that turned into a nationwide media strike, when MBC and Christian television workers also stopped work in solidarity. The nineteen-day KBS strike ended only after 2,400 riot police broke into the building and evicted the strikers.[24]

Union members defended their occupation of Hyundai Heavy Industries in Ulsan in April 1990.
Unknown Photographer

Union members fought the police in Ulsan in April 1990. Unknown Photographer

In the same month, renewed struggles broke out at Hyundai shipyard when arrested union leaders were given heavy jail sentences for the 108-day strike that had ended the previous March. As the government wielded its heavy club, workers at Hyundai Heavy Industries refused to submit.

One of the grievances articulated from the grassroots was a feeling that broadcast workers from KBS who were detained during their strike were subsequently released, while factory workers were forced to endure trials and imprisonment. A union leaflet expressed it: "this time we must correct, once and for all, their attitude that pen and broadcasting are to be feared but workers with hammer and welding machine are to be ignored."[25] The government's divide and conquer tactics were evidently reaping benefits.

On April 28, Roh again sent more than ten thousand police to the shipyards to crush the takeover by workers. This struggle became known as the Goliath struggle because seventy-eight workers climbed to the top of the giant Goliath crane—nearly a football field high—when riot police massed to clear out the strikers. As fighting raged between police and thousands of strikers, eastern Ulsan once again became a battle zone.

Strikes raged at other sites where new unions were strong, and on May 4, *Jeonnohyop* called for a general strike. More than 120,000 workers at 146 plants responded in a political strike resisting the government's repression of their leaders.[26] Although fifty-one people remained atop the Goliath crane until May 10, they descended after a majority of workers returned to their jobs. Despite their defeat, laborers were increasing radical and militant, and their newfound capability to act in solidarity with each other produced regional councils that went beyond plant or industry organizing.

In the early 1990s, as momentum appeared to swing to the government, white-collar unions organized in earnest and became a significant part of union drives. Teachers were especially heroic and inspirational. Although hundreds were dismissed for union membership—losing pensions and secure jobs—they persevered. Health-care workers, financial service workers, publishing employees, researchers, workers at foreign-owned firms, and communications workers all formed autonomous organizations. Unions in manufacturing had won such huge gains that skilled workers' salaries approached those of university professors. As various streams of autonomous unions formed into rivers, they soon merged. Thousands of struggles produced big steps toward the ultimate goal of an alternative to the FKTU.

After October 13, 1990, when Roh declared war on the working class, workers and students organically formed their own semiarmed self-defense squads to defend themselves from *kusadae* and police attacks. By the late 1980s, every major university had autonomous organizations of student fighters. At CNU, the May Brigade had four divisions: Bamboo Spear, Flame, Flying Tiger, and Azalea. These squads trained and drank together, read texts and studied political economy, and coordinated actions regionally and nationally. They guarded front and rear entrances during meetings and patrolled in case of police attacks. Many citizens gave money, food, water, and drinks. Founded in 1988 to protect the newly won student unions, they had four hundred members in their first year.[27] As early as 1984, informally organized groups of fighters came together in Gwangju, but this new level of organization was systematic. Chosun University had a Nok Du Brigade, Gwangju University a Fighters' Platoon, Honam University a One Star Unit, Dongshin University had Innovation, the Teachers' College formed Paek-Du Mountain, Mokpo University called its squad Loyalty to Nation, and Sunchon's was the June Platoon. Besides serving as strike forces for actions and protests at police stations, these self-organized fighting units also took responsibility for leafleting and keeping student morale up.

On April 30, 1988, about five hundred May Brigade fighters went to Mudeungsan, trained in Molotovs, cutting and using iron bars, and building barricades. Later they went to Girisan and trained in the use of sticks, Molotovs, and teamwork. Although few were women, females were integrated into the units as equals. As within *Jeondaehyop*, "older brother" (or "*hyoung*") was used to address both men and women within the teams. In the 1990s, many universities outside Gwangju also organized groups of fighters. The Bull Troops formed at Konkuk University and Storm Brigade at Chongan University. More radical organizations also began to find strength. The League of South Korean Socialist Workers (*Sanomaeng*) claimed that it had positioned itself in sixty-nine factories in five regional structures and had five hundred core members and thousands of supporters.[28] At its height in 1990, its projects included a workers' college and Institute for Scientific Socialism, and its college and high school branches had significant strength as well. The shock value of the group's explicit endorsement of socialism pushed the movement to formulate its own vision no matter what the regime's laws and society's "red complex" prohibited. For their efforts, many *Sanomaeng* members landed in prison.

The breakthrough of 1987 had produced working-class hegemony within the movement, and workers' power seemed just the force needed to create Korea's new landscape. Reaching the limits of enterprise unions, workers systematically organized themselves at higher levels in pursuit of their quest to form an alternative structure to the FKTU. On November 22, 1990, some four hundred workers met at Sungkongkwan University. Together they represented fourteen regions, two occupational-based unions, and six hundred democratic labor unions including clerical and production workers—but their ranks still did not include big industrial unions because they had been unable to contact them due to government repression. As their leaders worked on organizing, the potential power of workers' actions was evident in militant actions. In September 1992, a fifty-day MBC strike for democratic media spread to hospitals, universities, steel mills, and shipyards.

At the same time as laborers asserted their place in the country's changing constellation of power, victims of the military's long history of brutality—especially people in Gwangju—refused to abandon their calls for justice. On January 18, 1989, Gwangju students raided the local USIS and stormed local prosecutors' offices to demand action. The following May 18, 1989, some 854 professors in Jeolla demanded punishment for those responsible for the massacre. Efforts to enact justice—first enunciated at the rallies in liberated Gwangju—refused to die. On March 15, 1992, more than twenty-seven different memorial groups gathered one hundred thousand signatures on petitions calling for investigations. When Roh ignored them, one mother gave up her life in frustration and grief.[29]

Students Point to Reunification

Throughout this period, the student movement militantly opposed government repression of workers, while continuing to focus energy on reunification—for which they suffered many arrests. In March 1989, Reverend Moon Ik-hwan surreptitiously made his way to Pyongyang, where North Korean leader Kim Il-sung welcomed him. A few months later, Im Soo-kyung, a student representing South Korean activists, traveled to Pyongyang as a delegate to the annual World Youth and Student Festival hosted by the DPRK. Her visit clearly violated the NSL, whipping up hysteria among conservatives and intensifying police pressure on activist circles. U.S. troops detained both Moon Ik-hwan and Im Soo-kyung when they crossed the DMZ back into the South. Both were subsequently imprisoned, joining dozens of incarcerated students and reunification activists—many more of whom, wanted by police, lived a furtive underground existence.

TABLE 11.3 **Political Affiliations of Presidents of Student Councils, 1991**

Political Affiliation	Number of Student Councils
NL	64
PD	11
Other Revolutionary Organizations (RMO)	5
NL-PD Alliance	4
Non-RMO	11

Source: *Mal* (January 1991): 209, as cited in Park, *Democracy and Social Change*, 119.

Intense ideological debates began to reveal schisms within the movement. In 1990, tendencies oriented to "*juche*" (pro-DPRK) split into multiple factions. Large numbers of PD activists had gone into workplaces to organize, while NL regenerated its ranks on the campuses. Clearly, the majority of campus governments were NL oriented—meaning they more or less thought North Korea to be a friendly government—not an "enemy state" as defined by the NSL. In 1991, nearly two-thirds of all elected student council leaders were affiliated with NL.

The 1991 Struggle: Defeat and Adjustment

At the beginning of 1991, demarcation lines were evident between system supporters and advocates of a qualitatively different society. With progressive politicians marginalized in the National Assembly, the movement in the streets assumed even more importance to democratic consolidation. In the midst of Roh's intransigence, extraparliamentary forces assembled in a loose alliance against his government. In the ensuing confrontation, student protests against tuition hikes were answered with deadly force on April 26, 1991, when riot police killed Kang Kyung-dae, a Gwangju freshman attending Seoul's Myongji University. Kang was beaten to death with iron pipes wielded by the police, and his killing touched off the largest wave of protests in years. Two months of intense demonstrations ensued, reaching their high point on May 29, when at least two hundred thousand people in forty-four cities and counties protested. From April 26 to June 29 (when protest organizers left their headquarters in Myongdong Cathedral), more than a million people demonstrated in 2,361 rallies across the nation.[30] In five weeks of protests, official estimates counted more than seven hundred thousand protesters in seventy-five cities.[31]

May is the month of unions negotiating new contracts, and a general strike was called for May 18. Although a hundred thousand workers from 156 firms responded, the strike lacked a unifying theme and became understood as a struggle for wage increases.[32] It soon dissipated.

Kang's funeral in Seoul was also on May 18, in the midst of significant street protests against Roh's government. In his hometown of Gwangju, over a hundred thousand people took to the streets, as did twenty thousand people in Busan, twenty-two thousand in Seoul, and large crowds in Daegu, Incheon, and dozens of other cities. In Seoul, over three hours of intense fighting at Yonsei Universities ended only when protesters agreed to a police proposal for a truce. After negotiations, Kang's funeral rites were permitted in Mapo-gu instead of Seoul Station. That day, two activists committed suicide. After the procession in Seoul, thousands of people joined together in a caravan to escort Kang's corpse to Gwangju for burial. The government insisted Kang Kyong-dae could not be buried in Mangwoldong, and a massive police roadblock on the highway into Gwangju was fortified to ensure the caravan could not pass. In a surprise counteroffensive, the city's well-organized student brigades attacked the police from the rear, and a fierce battle lasted until 4 a.m. on the morning of May 19, some sixteen hours in all. During the "Battle of Unamdong," local residents made food for the fighters and gave them water and money. Clearly the radical antistate movement had enormous popular support in Gwangju. As the fighting continued, the caravan was able to take back roads, and it finally arrived on Geumnamno in front of Province Hall, where tens of thousands of people gathered to pay their last respects.

People believed they could force Roh out of office. Besides "Yankee Go Home!" one of their main slogans was "Finish State Terrorism." At the funeral for Kim Kwui-chong, a Sungkwungkwang University coed killed at a demonstration on May 25, Reverend Moon Ik-hwan's eulogy closed by declaring, "Let's bury the Roh government with Kwui-chong!" Disturbingly, thirteen lives were lost in the struggle—all of whom were laid to rest in Mangwoldong Cemetery. Most were suicides, touching off a soul-searching debate in the media and within movement circles. The first self-immolation occurred on April 29, when CNU student Park Seung-hui set herself on fire to protest continuing U.S. domination of Korea. Although she survived until May 19, within days of her attempt other suicides followed. By the end of the struggles, ten people had taken their own lives, including Kim Young-gyun, Chon Se-young, Kim Gi-seol, Yoon Yong-ha, Lee Jeong-soon, Kim Chul-soo, Jeong Sang-soon, Lee Jin-hee, and Seok Gwang-soo. The total number of movement martyrs that month was thirteen, if we include Park Chang-soo, imprisoned chairperson of the union at Hanjin Heavy industries, who was found lifeless in Seoul's Anyang prison on May 6. Poet Kim Ji-ha and other intellectuals harshly criticized students and publicly called on them (even using the pages of conservative newspaper *Chosun Ilbo*) to stop their sacrifices. The Korean movement suffered hundreds of martyrs in the three decades from Chun Tae-il's suicide in 1970, including 431 people who died from torture, injuries from tear gas or clubs, and falls from buildings.[33] That figure does not include hundreds killed in Gwangju during the 1980 uprising. A calendar published in 2008 documented the suicides of at least 119 people during the democratization movement.

So bitter were people's feelings in this time of polarization and death that some took it upon themselves to strike against the enemy without thinking carefully about their target and tactics. On June 3, 1991, angry students at Hanguk University of Foreign Languages set upon new Prime Minister Jung Won-sik, who had fired hundreds of teachers for joining the union in 1989. The students threw flour and eggs on him and beat him. Sensing a chance to isolate the radicals, the conservative media blew the incident out of proportion and railed against a democracy "infested with the evil ghosts of disorder." So long as union leaders were murdered and student activists imprisoned, the *Chosun Ilbo* had scarcely covered the stories, yet when a government minister was slightly manhandled, the editors went hog wild with outrage. Like the Springer Press in Germany, *ChoDongJoong* (a combination word for the three conservative mass-circulation newspapers, *Chosun Ilbo*, *Dong-a Ilbo*, and *Joongang Ilbo*) sensationalized their offensive against the movement. The bitter feelings aroused by *ChoDongJoong's* coverage isolated activists from ordinary Koreans, who felt the affront to Confucian norms embodied in the attack on an old man was too great. As the media made the story the lack of respect of the young, the movement suffered a tactical defeat.

In July 1991, three large underground socialist organizations publicly repudiated the Leninist vanguard party as an appropriate organizational model and announced their creation of an open public Workers' Party. The next month, as the collapse of the Soviet Union and real existing socialism in Eastern Europe accelerated, internal debates among South Korean activists, which previously concerned the character of the *minjung* and "social formations," were replaced by discussion of reified concepts like Althusser's ideological state apparatuses and Gramsci's notion of hegemony. With the turn away from practical involvement in massive struggles, so-called "waves of confessions and repentance" on the part of older activists shocked younger activists.

After the movement had lost its moral authority among the broad public because of the beating of an old man, a turning point was reached, a pivot around which the impetus toward increasing democracy and rising expectations for continuing social transformation was rolled back. Combined with the fall of the Berlin Wall and collapse of existing European Communist regimes, the Left reeled from the global setback suffered by forces opposed to corporate capitalism. On September 17, 1991, as if to acknowledge the intractability of the nation's division, both South and North Korea were admitted as separate members of the United Nations.

On November 10, 1991, more than seventy thousand workers rallied at Yeuido to commemorate the death of Chun Tae-il and to call for revision of the ever-tightening labor laws.[34] As companies hired more and more part-time workers, expanded subcontractor inputs, and shipped off labor-intensive jobs to China and Southeast Asia, further pressures were brought on the working class. The country's progressives regrouped, forming into a more disciplined alliance of fifty-eight organizations on December 12, 1991, the National Coalition for Democracy and Reunification of Korea (*Jeonkukyonhyop*). Excluding any political party, the alliance included among its dozens of member organizations five "jeons"— *Jeonnohyop* (workers), *Jeondaehyop* (students), *Jeonnong* (farmers), *Jeonbinhhyop* (urban poor and street vendors), and *Jeonchunghyop* (youth). As soon as it formed, police declared it illegal, but organizers were able to elect Yoon Young-gyu as chair and to use the organization as a significant means of national coordination.

Abandoned by YS and the right wing of the democratization movement, and with the student movement paralyzed by its mistakes and lack of orientation, the Korean working class suffered defeat in 1991. In the aftermath of this turning point, parallel struggles among feminists, ecologists, and citizens' movements moved to the center of many people's attention, a transition to a new phase of struggles in which the politics of identity signaled the transition from *minjung* to citizens.

Citizens' Movements

Centuries in formation, Korean civil society has always had a plethora of groups, but in the late 1980s, as the energy of the 1987 insurrection thoroughly permeated relationships of everyday life, a remarkable activation of NGOs took place. Civil society's autonomous organizations grew by leaps and bounds among teachers, farmers, street-vendors, artists, journalists, women, ecologists, peace advocates, and gay people. From only 68 NGOs in 1986, the number tripled in a

Workers rallied on November 10, 1991, to commemorate Chun Tae-il's 1970 self-immolation.
Photographer unknown

decade—and continued to multiply. In the late 1990s, more than seven hundred South Korean social movement organizations were counted, approximately three-fourths formed after 1987.[35]

The rise of professional activism began within two years of the 1987 insurgency. In July 1989, about five hundred activists (primarily white-collar employees and professionals) came together as the Citizens' Coalition for Economic Justice (CCEJ), the first split of the *minjung* movement.[36] They believed that problems like economic inequality, speculation, and unfair taxes could only be solved by the "organized power of civil society." Within two years, their membership was more than ten times the number of their founders. Although 80 percent lived in Seoul, they worked with farmers' organizations opposed to marketing of foreign goods inside Korea, assisted migrant workers, endorsed the Buddhist Coalition for Economic Justice, supported unions, and helped with an innovative "Forest for Life" tree-planting project for unemployed people.[37] At one point, CCEJ sued the National Assembly for being "brain dead" after the body did not meet for two months during a time of economic crisis.

In the new atmosphere of democratic transition, a broad array of citizen coalitions arose to influence policy. In 1994, attorneys, former student activists, and professors created People's Solidarity for Participatory Democracy (PSPD). PSPD worked closely with unions and Lawyers for a Democratic Society in seeking *chaebol* reform. In a creative campaign for minority shareholder rights to disrupt excessive corporate greed, about 150 people with less than one percent of the stock of Korea First Bank attended a shareholders' meeting to contest loans made by the bank. Not allowed to participate, they sued and subsequently won annulment of the board's decisions at that meeting as well as hefty fines of board members.

The citizens' movement is often middle-class, legal, nonviolent, and works toward gradual institutional reform, in contrast to the *minjung* movement, which was characterized by participation of the lower classes using militant tactics and calling for structural changes. As Kim Dong-choon noted, citizens' movements were reformist, while *minjung* movements of the 1980s were against the regime and wanted Chun and Roh out of office.[38] In the 1990s, citizens' movements endorsed both YS and DJ.

Probing the impact of NGOs on social movements, James Petras argues persuasively that they represent the depoliticization of insurgencies, that activists are integrated into the dominant political system through receiving jobs that create upward mobility—rather than social transformation.[39] In 1999, he counted more than fifty thousand NGOs in the Third World that received over $10 billion in funding. In his view, "The real boost in NGO mushrooming however, occurs in time of rising mass movements that challenge imperial hegemony. The growth of radical socio-political movements and struggles provided a lucrative

TABLE 11.4 **NGOs in Korea**

Year Founded	Number	Percent
Pre-1960	34	4.0
1961–1970	36	4.3
1971–1979	47	5.6
1980–1986	68	8.1
1987–1992	179	21.2
1993–1996	246	29.2
1997–2000	217	25.7
Unknown	16	1.9
Total	**843**	**100.0**

Source: Hyuk-Rae Kim and David K. McNeal, "From State-Centric to Negotiated Governance: NGOs as Policy Entrepreneurs in South Korea," in *Civil Life, Globalization, and Political Change in Asia: Organizing between Family and State*, ed. Robert P. Weller (London: Routledge, 2005).

commodity which ex-radical and pseudo popular intellectuals could sell to interested, concerned and well-financed private and public foundations closely tied with European and U.S. multinationals and governments. The funders were interested in information—social science intelligence—like the 'propensity for violence in urban slum areas' (an NGO project in Chile during the mass uprisings of 1983–1986), the capacity of NGOers to raid popular communities and direct energy toward self-help projects instead of social transformations and the introduction of a class collaborationist rhetoric packaged as 'new identity discourses' that would discredit and isolate revolutionary activists."

Currents of professionalization and specialization, so strongly developed throughout the society, greatly affected the *minjung* movement. In line with Petras's argument, the radical impetus in Korea was blunted by the movement's transformation, so much so that by 2002, Charles Armstrong maintained that *minjung* is "no longer a useful framework for understanding Korea today."[40] In the new constellation of citizens' activism, workers became one strand among many— and not even the most radical—in the rainbow of opposition currents. While leftists often bemoan the loss of universality when labor's centrality to social movements is replaced by "identity politics," another perspective is to locate the universal in the particular—to comprehend feminism as in the interests of all humans, and to understand ecology as a common need.[41] The concrete enactment of a species-universal necessarily needs to pass through identity politics. The function of a revolutionary perspective under conditions of contemporary capitalism is not to negate attempts to challenge fragmentary forms of oppression, but to elicit the immanent concrete universals within these many strands of resistance, to unite a diversity of people around our common interests to create an economy based upon human needs—not corporate profits—and a democracy in which ordinary people have substantive voices—not simply a formally democratic regime limited to ritualized voting every four years.

Rejuvenation of the Women's Movement

Crucial to understanding the historical unfolding of freedom for millions of people is the role of uprisings in stimulating and accelerating the growth of feminist movements. After the 1987 uprising, activist women realized that neither the democratic movement nor the labor movement by themselves would solve problems facing women. Unlike the 1970s, when female workers had been in the forefront of the labor movement, the great strike wave of 1987 was composed mainly of male factory workers. The new union movement born out of this wave reflected gender hierarchies: although women were 27.4 percent of union members, only 3.6 percent of local union leaders were female.[42] As men in heavy industry fought for gains for themselves, women's organizations became gradually distant and more autonomous. Korean women who work outside the home account for about 40 percent of the workforce, but 95 percent of them were concentrated in low-paying jobs (such as clerical, sales, and manual labor). Women were a majority of teachers (by 2000, over 60 percent of the teachers' union members were female), and they comprised significant proportions of other white-collar unions as well: in 1989, they were 37 percent of banking and clerical workers, 44 percent of tourism, and 39 percent of office workers.[43] In healthcare unions, well over half of all employees were female.[44] Yet women were only 3.2 percent of the chairpersons of 6,142 enterprise unions in 1988, and no women were members of twenty-two industrial union executive committees affiliated with the FKTU. Women responded by stepping up autonomous organizing. Women's associations formed consciousness-raising groups among female unionists and advocated women's trade unions to deal with issues like layoffs of women, pay disparities, female exclusion from leadership, and repression by unions of women workers.[45] In 1992, the Korean Women Workers Associations Council was created as the national outgrowth of six local associations.

In September 1987, radical feminists—some of whom thought of themselves as young cultural guerrillas—protested at the Miss Korea contest by organizing an alternative contest involving intellectual and manual abilities. One of their slogans was "Women Who Play Sports Are Beautiful." Greatly influenced by U.S. feminism, these young women published a visionary newspaper, "*If.*" Although initially isolated, their voices soon resonated widely in one of the world's most patriarchal societies. They were part of a growing cultural women's movement that included *minjung* feminist artists, creators of posters, music, and theater that supported women workers. At least one feminist film group, Barito, formed.

The feminist movement—like other citizen movements—went from the "one great wave that moved us all in the 1980s" to specialization and professionalization in the 1990s.[46] While much of the movement was focused on national power, women's marginalization organically led them to focus on issues of everyday life, and they went about systematically seeking to create preconditions for the next generations of women to grow up under more liberated circumstances. In 1988, the first Women's Workers' Festival in Seoul was a spirited event, and more arenas of everyday life traditionally dominated by men were opened. In 1990, 37 women's organizations formed the "Council for Comfort Women." From December 7 to 12, 2000, the Women's International War Crimes Tribunal convened with more than a thousand people, including seventy "comfort women" from eight countries. Korean women took the issue to the United Nations and appealed to the world body to consider it a human rights issue.[47]

Women won changes in family law in 1990, but *hojuje*—the household registration system and mainstay of Confucian patriarchal order in which only men could be head of the family, remained intact for more than a decade longer. In the 1970s, the Korean National Council of Women had tried without success to change family law. Once they had succeeded in winning reforms in 1990, they set their focus on abolishing *hojuje*. Under its provisions, women could not inherit money nor be granted custody of children if divorce occurred. *Hojuje* was retained until women's groups' continual challenges abolished it in March 2005, an action dubbed part of a "social revolution" by the *Financial Times.*[48]

In arenas of everyday life, traditional domination by men is persistent. In the mid 1990s, one study found that wives worked an average of 72.4 hours per week at home—against only 9.2 hours per week for husbands.[49] In addition to this disparity, many Korean women work outside the home (accounting for some 40 percent of the workforce) but 95 percent of them in 1998 were "concentrated in lower echelons of occupational hierarchy such as clerical, sales, services, agricultural and manual labor." These statistics only begin to give us a picture of patriarchy's pervasive power in shaping daily life. In one case of rape, a woman who bit off the tongue of her rapist was sentenced to three years in prison for "excessive self-defense." Feminist groups rallied to her side and succeeded in getting the verdict overturned. In the process, they helped change public and legal perceptions of the problem of rape—including spousal rape. In 1990, two out of every three wives reported being beaten by their husbands.[50] With increasing opportunities for women, is it any wonder that the divorce rate nearly tripled from 5.8 to 16.8 per hundred between 1980 and 1995? As a "second wave" of the Korean women's movement consolidated, evident in a Sexual Politics Cultural Festival at Yonsei University from October 11–13, 1995, an indigenous gay and lesbian movement emerged.

Ironically with more democracy, women's political participation as measured by the number of female representatives fell. In the 1988 and 1992 parliamentary elections, no women were elected from individual districts, and only two were able to win in 1996. In 1985—under the dictatorship—there were eight congresswomen (two elected); in 1988, six congresswomen; in 1992 only four. (These results are similar in Latin American and Eastern European experiences of democratization.) In the first local elections in thirty years in 1991, women won less than 1 percent of county and provincial seats and only 1.5 percent in 1995.[51]

Ecology Movement
The origins of many environmental organizations can be traced to the 1980s, but democratization brought them legal status, thereby facilitating unity among previously marginalized groups. More than twenty environmental groups merged after 1987 into the Korean Anti-Pollution Civil Movement Council (KAPMA). Korea's antinuclear movement dates to 1987, when residents in Youngkwang sought compensation for their fishing losses from two nuclear plants in operation and two more under construction. With the opening of public deliberation, the conflict quickly drew in both extraparliamentary forces and the National Assembly. By 1989, more than twenty organizations coalesced in the National Headquarters for Eradication of Nuclear Power, bringing together scattered antinuclear groups.[52] As public awareness grew, monitoring of the plants increased. By 1990, at least 193 accidents had been reported in seven reactors. Protests soon expanded into the issue of nuclear waste disposal. Hearing about the German movement's contestation of the end site at Gorleben, activists like Choi Yol, who spent six years in prison during the Park Chung-hee era, drew inspiration.[53] For two decades, regional movements successfully halted planned disposal sites. In 1990 in Anmyondo (off the west coast in Chungnam Province), residents were outraged when the antinuclear movement informed them of deception in the government's announcement of a "research facility." The struggle drew participation from more than twenty thousand residents, some of whom attacked and set on fire

several police stations and public buildings. Children boycotted schools to join the fight. Finally, the Minister of Science and Technology resigned and the site was deselected. People mobilized against U.S. nuclear weapons on the peninsula, compelling the United States to withdraw them in 1991. Repeated mobilizations in Uljin and Puan also successfully stopped nuclear waste sites. In Uljin in 1994, residents blocked highways with burning tires. Over a four-day period, people threw firebombs as ten thousand residents outfought five thousand riot police. The plan was withdrawn. In Puan, people united against a proposed waste site in militant confrontations. The area's governor was bruised by citizen attacks and many buildings burnt before that plan was shelved.

The ecology movement was not limited to nuclear threats alone. In August 1988, when plans were announced for a golf course in Kyungbuk Province, residents began a campaign to stop it. When the government ignored their petition, they camped for four months on the grounds in alliance with Buddhist monks. Clashes with golf course goons were widely publicized, leading to similar struggles in at least thirty other sites slated for golf course construction.[54] In 1993, these many struggles from the grassroots resulted in the formation of the Korean Federation of Environmental Movements (KFEM), which began with two thousand members mainly drawn from white-collar employees and professionals—professors, doctors, lawyers, and journalists.[55] In 1997, KFEM successfully campaigned to stop Taiwan from exporting its nuclear waste to North Korea.

Students Continue to Struggle

On May 29, 1992, at *Jeondaehyop's* sixth annual inauguration ceremony, student activists broke new ground when they publicly revealed the existence of their organization. Previously underground to mitigate police repression, this bold move by *Jeondaehyop* was a bid to reenter the battle for the country's hearts and minds. Within a few months, the conservative media developed a new label for the young activists, labeling them the "Orange Tribe," a negative moniker that stuck. With the pressures from conservatives compounding internal divisions, progressive activists searched for models in the European and American New Left and developed the notion of "sector affiliation movements" through which students could unite with ecological, feminist, cultural, and class-based movements—a different direction than *Jeondaehyop's* orientation to student councils. In July 1993, a new book, *The New Generation: Do What You Want!*, stirred debates that drew in a wide variety of people and became the starting point of a "cultural turn" in the student movement.

As its base of support gravitated to new initiatives, *Jeondaehyop* broke up in 1993, and *Hanchongryun* (the Korean Confederation of University Student Councils) emerged to replace it, but with two major differences. Within *Jeondaehyop*, presidents of student councils had been voting representatives, but *Hanchongryun* included representatives by departments, so every college sent many student delegates to national meetings. Gwangju's CNU alone had more than 20 members. (See FIGURE 11.1.) Instead of 130 student council presidents, *Hanchongryun* included ten times that number of students. *Jeondaehyop*

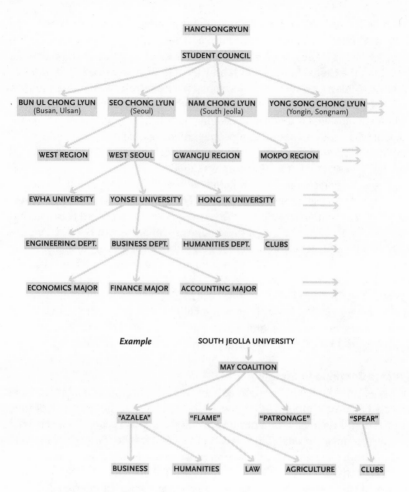

FIGURE 11.1 **Organization of Hanchongryun**
Source: Christopher D. Yoon, "The Kwangju Democratization Movement: U.S. Role During the 1979–1980 Period: Its Impacts and Ramifications," (Master's thesis, Yonsei University, 1994), 43.

had included both PD and NL groups, but *Hanchongryun* was almost purely NL adherents.

At its high point in 1997, *Hanchongryun* was registered at over two hundred universities, and had a membership of more than ten thousand—with even more supporters. One analyst optimistically reported as many as one million members (from two to five hundred at each university).[56] Founded with stridently pro-DPRK language, *Hanchongryun's* platform included opposition to gender oppression and environmental destruction:

1. We will keep our country free from unjust political, military, and cultural domination of foreign powers like the United States, to realize independent democracy in the truest sense.

2. We will firmly unite with all patriotic grassroots forces such as laborers and farmers.

3. We oppose all ideological and cultural plunder from imperialist culture that boosts consumption and manipulates individualism and submission to the stronger powers.

4. We oppose every element of segregation, repression and inhumane treatment of women, the disabled, sexual minorities, both on campus and in society. We also try to bequeath a beautiful land and reunified nation to our descendants, keeping the environment safe from the destruction arising from the use of capital.[57]

On March 29, 1996, Yonsei University student Roh Su-sok suddenly died during fights with police at protests against tuition increases. Soon thereafter, three students committed suicide in protest. The National Professors' Union exhorted students "not to strive to resolve social problems by opting for such an extreme method as suicide. To kill oneself to oppose injustice is the most passive way of struggle and must be avoided by all means." The suicides were an indication of activists' commitment and their frustration with the continuing failure to reunify the nation.

From 1996 to 2000, a newly elected leadership brought *Hanchongryun* members to consider themselves part of a "Community of Life, Study, and Struggle"—a new slogan that reflected an expansion of the student movement's self-understanding from *Jeondaehyop's* focus solely on fights and struggle. Although many activists initially hoped the new civilian government under YS would be liberal in its attitude toward the group, YS interpreted the group's actions as a sign of North Korean influence, and continued to consider the organization dangerous.

Under *Hanchongryun's* leadership, the student movement put reunification at the top of its agenda. One of the group's most famous actions was a reunification festival in August 1996 at Yonsei University. Confrontations with the police occurred when students claimed to be starting on a walk to North Korea. They tried to send faxes to their counterparts in Pyongyang, and prepared to welcome home two students returning from a rally there. Thousands of students were trapped in two buildings for almost a week by thousands of riot police. After the standoff, some twenty thousand riot police, twenty-three helicopters, and a water cannon vehicle assaulted the campus.[58] Police arrested all of the students they could find—5,848 students in all. Arrested people were compelled to exit through a gauntlet, and many were severely beaten. Many females reported being sexually assaulted in the massive overreaction to their peaceful protest. Afterward, 465 leaders were identified by police and kept in custody. During these confrontations, Gwangju fighters were in the front lines—on both sides. When the fights first broke out, riot police brought in from Gwangju found themselves facing the same Gwangju students whom they had just finished fighting at home. "I saw you in Gwangju" exclaimed one to a student activist. "Good job, man" was the student's reply. During a lull in the fighting, police gave students bread, water, and cigarettes. In Gwangju, many student spies were sent into campus groups. Those that were exposed underwent intensive interrogation and were made to sign a confession—followed by public humiliation and ostracism.

After the Yonsei struggle, *Hanchongryun* was defined as "an organization benefiting the enemy," therefore in violation of the NSL. Under attack and increasingly infiltrated, the group became desperate. At Hanyang University on May 31, 1997, a suspected police informant was killed—beaten to death with iron pipes—and a riot policeman was killed during particularly severe fights when he was run over by a police van. Blaming *Hanchongryun* for the deaths, students on major campuses like Korea University, SNU, and Kookmin University left the organization, and a steep decline in membership set in. In October 1997, high-ranking underground member Kim Joon-bae was killed in Gwangju, and at least 357 others languished in prison serving long sentences. *Hanchongryun* shrank from an organization that could mobilize twenty thousand hard-core supporters to a marginal group barely able to muster half that number. In 2003, its membership was only 1,500—15 percent of its size only six years earlier.[59] Nonetheless, the group was not without dedicated members, dozens of whom remained underground in 2010. Generally, *Hanchongryun* positions are increasingly out of step with the public.

The First Civilian Government
After more than three decades of rule by the military, the first civilian administration was elected in 1992. Although his career had been facilitated by his alliance in 1990 with Roh Tae-woo, President Kim Young-sam took significant steps to reduce the power of the military. Like Chun Doo-hwan, Roh Tae-woo had supported Park Chung-hee's coup in 1961. Chun and Roh served together in Vietnam and helped create a secret military organization *Hanahoe*, a secret association of military academy graduates that seized power on December 12, 1979. YS broke up *Hanahoe* and other such secret associations. He forced the resignations of a number of leading generals and helped publicize the role of the military in denying Koreans their democracy for so long.

President Kim promised a "New Korea" where "justice will flow like a river" and a "higher quality of life will flourish."[60] He released 5,823 political prisoners and instituted a real-name accounting system to prevent corruption. Banned for three decades, provincial and local elections again took place. In 1991, local representatives to regional assemblies began to be elected on a regular basis.[61] Under the YS administration, the high technology sector of the economy burgeoned—democracy was evidently good for business—but uneven regional standards of living continued to be a problem. In 1991, per capita gross regional development was over $6,000 in South Gyeongsang but hovered at about half that in the Jeollas and South Chungcheong.[62]

Although YS's presidency was the first civilian government in decades and many people prospered under it, movement mobilizations continued to pressure it to punish Chun and Roh for their murderous spree in Gwangju. Initially YS tried to deflect calls for a trial, but the issue refused to die. Transitional justice for Chun and Roh became a rallying cry for democratic forces.

NOTES

1 Su-Hoon Lee, "Environmental Movements in South Korea," in *Asia's Environmental Movements: Comparative Perspectives*, eds. Yok-shiu F. Lee and Alvin Y. So (Armonk, NY: M.E. Sharpe, 1999), 97.

2 Gibney, *Korea's Quiet Revolution*, 92.

3 Lee, *The Making of Minjung*, 60.

4 See Choi Chungmoo, "The Minjung Culture Movement and Popular Culture," in *South Korea's Minjung Movement: The Culture and Politics of Dissidence*, ed. Kenneth Wells (Honolulu: University of Hawaii Press, 1995), 116.

5 Paik Nak-chung, "The Reunification Movement and Literature," in *South Korea's Minjung Movement: The Culture and Politics of Dissidence*, ed. Kenneth Wells (Honolulu: University of Hawaii Press, 1995), 181–82.

6 Christian Institute for the Study of Justice and Development, *Lost Victory*, 189.

7 Christian Institute for the Study of Justice and Development, *Lost Victory*, 200–210.

8 Joe Manguno, "Memories, First and Last," in *Korea Witness: 135 Years of War, Crisis and News in the Land of the Morning Calm*, eds. Donald Kirk and Choe Sang Hun (Seoul: EunHaeng NaMu, 2006), 296–97.

9 Hart-Landsberg, *The Rush to Development*, 294.

10 Haggard and Kaufman, *Political Economy*, 232.

11 *Hard Journey*, 49.

12 Hart-Landsberg, *The Rush to Development*, 296.

13 See Stephen Kirby's article in *Democracy in Korea: The Roh Tae Woo Years* (New York: Carnegie Council on Ethics and International Affairs, 1992).

14 Hart-Landsberg, *Korea*, 200.

15 Koo, *Korean Workers*, 169–71; Hart-Landsberg, *Korea*, 199.

16 Interview with Yoon Young-kyu, April 10, 2001.

17 Lee Tae-ho, "May 18 Kwangju Democratization and the Art Movement," 140.

18 *Hard Journey*, 48.

19 Haggard and Kaufman, *Political Economy*, 123.

20 Baik Tae-ung, for example, served time in prison simply for refusing to renounce his socialist beliefs. Adopted by Amnesty International as a prisoner of conscience, he was ultimately freed.

21 Koo, *Korean Workers*, 179.

22 Bello and Rosenfield, *Dragons in Distress*, 45.

23 Won Young-su, "History of South Korean Labor and Student Struggles Since the End of World War II," in *The International Encyclopaedia of Revolution and Protest: 1500–Present*, ed. Immanuel Ness (London: Wiley Blackwell, 2009).

24 Hart-Landsberg, *The Rush to Development*, 279.

25 Quoted in Koo, *Korean Workers*, 173.

26 Ibid., 174.

27 Interview with Park Chol-ho, Gwangju, July 11, 2003.

28 Mi Park, *Democracy and Social Change*, 116–17.

29 *Hard Journey*, 55.

30 See Sungmoon Kim, "Confucianism in Contestation: The May Struggle of 1991 in South Korea and Its Lesson," *New Political Science*, March 2009.

31 The Korea Church Coalition for Peace, Justice, and Reunification, *Korea Update* 104 (May–June 1991).

32 Park, *Democracy and Social Change*, 167.

33 Lee, *The Making of Minjung*, 294.

34 *Korea Update* 105 (January 1992): 9.

35 Seungsook Moon, "Women and Civil Society in South Korea," in *Korean Society: Civil*

Society, Democracy and the State, ed. Charles Armstrong (London: Routledge, 2002), 123.

36   Su-Hoon Lee, "Activation of Civil Society in Korea," *Pacific Affairs* 66, no. 3 (Autumn 1993): 364; Ilcheong Yi, "Bowling by the Professional: Development of Civic Advocacy Groups in Korea," paper presented for the IPSA, Fukuoka, July 9, 2006, 6.

37   Carmel Abao, "Beyond Bread and Butter: The Demand for Democracy in South Korea," in *Transitions to Democracy in East and Southeast Asia* (Quezon City: Institute for Popular Democracy, 1999), 136.

38   Kim Dong-choon, "Growth and Crisis of the Korean Citizen's Movement," *Korea Journal* (Summer 2006): 99–128.

39   James Petras, "NGOs: In the Service of Imperialism," http://www.neue-einheit.com/english/ngos.htm.

40   Armstrong, *Korean Society*, 2.

41   For further discussion, see *The Subversion of Politics*, 248–54.

42   Koo, *Korean Workers*, 182.

43   Kang and Lenz, *Wenn die Hennen krähen*, 49.

44   Moon, *Militarized Modernity*, 157.

45   Ibid., 151.

46   Suh Jong-suk, quoted in video, *The Struggle for South Korean Democracy*, 1997.

47   Cho Joo-hyun, "The Politics of Gender Identity," 246.

48   Anna Fifield, "South Korean Registers the End of Male Superiority," *Financial Times*, March 5–6, 2005, 5.

49   Cited in *Asian Women* 4 (Spring 1997): 240.

50   Carl Byker, *The Pacific Century: The Fight for Democracy*, 1992, PBS.

51   Chin, "Self-Governance," 101.

52   Su-hoon Lee, "Environmental Movements in South Korea," in *Asia's Environmental Movements: Comparative Perspectives* eds. Yok-shiu F. Lee and Alvin Y. So (Armonk, NY: M.E. Sharpe, 1998), 98.

53   Interview with Choi Yol and Kim Choony, Seoul, June 22, 2002.

54   Norman Eder, *Poisoned Prosperity: Development, Modernization, and the Environment in South Korea* (Armonk, NY: M.E. Sharpe, 1996), 103.

55   Su-Hoon Lee, "Activation of Civil Society in Korea," *Pacific Affairs* 66, no. 3 (Autumn 1993): 361.

56   Yoon, "The Kwangju Democratization Movement," 41–42.

57   Excerpts taken from *Joongang Daily*, July 9, 2003.

58   Carl J. Saxer, *From Transition to Power Alternation: Democracy in South Korea, 1987–1997* (London: Routledge, 2002), 175; Korea Chun Su-jin, "For an ideal world, a life of isolation," *Joongang Daily*, July 9, 2003, 8.

59   Interview with Choi Song-wook, Gwangju, January 22, 2009.

60   Quoted in Shin, *Mass Politics and Culture*, 200.

61   See Hyug Baeg Im, "South Korean Democratic Consolidation in Comparative Perspective," 30–31; and Kyoung-Ryung Seong, "Civil Society and Democratic Consolidation in South Korea," 104, in *Consolidating Democracy in South Korea*, eds. Larry Diamond and Byung-Kook Kim (Boulder, CO: Lynne Rienner, 2000). In the same volume, Byung-Kook Kim says these elections were reinstituted in 1993 ("Party Politics in South Korea's Democracy: The Crisis of Success," 53).

62   See Kyoung-Ryung Seong, "Civil Society and Democratic Consolidation," 109.

CHAPTER 12

The Struggle Against Neoliberalism

It was only when the military government collapsed in 1987 that the discourse of reunification and anti-Americanism could come out freely, and this might question the consolidated bulwark of South Korea's anti-Communist regime. But the conditioning of genuine "liberal democracy" in political circumstances paradoxically was accompanied by the logic of globalism and market fundamentalism on which the discourse of democracy became obscured by the "dire competition" for survival in a global market.

—Kim Dong-choon, 2006[1]

In Asia, investment returns will be a complete steal.

—Ray Hood, State Street Bank

CHRONOLOGY	
April 15, 1994	Uruguay round of negotiations establishes World Trade Organization
August 30, 1994	May 18 Memorial Foundation established, begins campaign to punish Chun Doo-hwan, Roh Tae-woo, and eight others responsible for the 1980 massacre
June 27, 1995	First local elections
October 11–13, 1995	Sexual Politics Cultural Festival at Yonsei University; second wave of feminism appears
December 19, 1995	Special Law on Gwangju Uprising
March 11, 1996	Chun Doo-hwan and Roh Tae-woo trial begins
Summer 1996	Thousands of students favoring reunification occupy Yonsei University for one week

December 26, 1996	Restrictive new labor laws railroaded through National Assembly
December 26, 1996	General strike against new labor law involves 145,000 workers on first day
December 28, 1996	More than 350,000 workers strike
December 31, 1996	Thousands of workers and citizens in candlelight procession at Myongdong
January 16, 1997	President Kim Young-sam promises to send new labor laws back for revision
April 17, 1997	Chun receives sentence of life imprisonment, Roh seventeen years' imprisonment
May 14, 1997	Foreign speculators led by George Soros begin massively selling off the Thai baht
May 16, 1997	New Mangwoldong Cemetery in Gwangju opens
June 30, 1997	Thai Premier promises not to devalue baht
July 2, 1997	Thai baht allowed to float on international currency market and plunges in value
November 21, 1997	IMF crisis hits Korea: ROK requests $57 billion IMF bailout
December 18, 1997	IMF bailout plan announced
December 18, 1997	Kim Dae Jung elected president
December 22, 1997	YS pardons Chun, Roh, and seventeen others convicted for roles in the Gwangju massacre
January 20, 1998	KCTU agrees to accept layoffs
February 25, 1998	Kim Dae Jung becomes president, declares government of the people
June 15, 2000	Kim Dae Jung meets Kim Jong-il in Pyongyang
December 10, 2000	Kim Dae Jung wins Nobel Peace Prize
April 10, 2001	1,500 riot police viciously attack Daewoo workers

ONCE THE MILITARY dictatorship had been overthrown in 1987, the Korean movement's monumental victories left many people too exhausted to celebrate. Having won direct elections and expanded civil liberties, struggles for autonomous trade unions and better conditions of existence continued, but a fundamental problem nagged at people's consciences. Would former presidents Chun and Roh be brought to justice? Would the murders in Gwangju and the injuries and blemishes on families' names be compensated?

First enunciated in the rallies in Democracy Square in 1980, the struggle to bring Chun and Roh to justice took seventeen long years. As soon as the newly elected National Assembly convened in 1988, it scheduled hearings on Gwangju. In 1989 representatives of the United States were officially requested to testify in person, but they refused to attend. Instead, the State Department drafted written answers to very specific questions related to whether or not the United States had secretly collaborated with Chun Doo-hwan and the new military authorities in overthrowing the government and suppressing the Gwangju Uprising. The State Department's still-controversial White Paper on Gwangju,[2] issued on June

19, 1989, claimed the United States "had neither authority over nor prior knowl-edge of the movement of the Special Warfare Command units to Gwangju" and deflected any criticisms of American actions. Given the widespread feeling that the White Paper failed to acknowledge U.S. responsibilities, it provoked renewed anti-American sentiment. Confucian decorum notwithstanding, Donald Gregg, while U.S. ambassador to the ROK from 1989 to 1993, never made a publicized address at a Korean university because of expected protests.[3] Beyond the specific details so vital to lawyers' language, the issue to many Koreans is the clear histori-cal fact of U.S. support for the Chun regime from 1979 to 1987.

This is not the place to ascertain the guilt or innocence of U.S. officials in the killings in Gwangju in May 1980.[4] For many Koreans, the answer is already clear. A 1996 survey found that 82.5 percent of Gwangju people believe the United States was involved (50.8 percent for the rest of South Koreans).[5] In the same poll, 44.5 percent of Gwangju residents expressed the need for a U.S. apology and 21.8 percent thought the United States should pay reparations. On May 18, 2002, a tel-evised and well-attended Peoples' Tribunal there found former President Jimmy Carter and seven other U.S. officials guilty of "crimes against humanity" for viola-tion of the civil rights of the people of Gwangju.[6] A few months later, on October 11, 2002, Carter was awarded a Nobel Peace Prize. The Nobel Committee praised Carter's decades of "untiring effort to find peaceful solutions to international conflicts, to advance democracy and human rights, and to promote economic and social development." Clearly, contradictory notions of "human rights" prevailed.

When the first civilian government came to power, people thought the time had finally come, but in October 1994, the YS government announced it would not prosecute Chun and Roh to "avoid damaging national unity." An opportun-ist politician within the ranks of the democratization movement, YS had jumped ship and united with conservatives to gain a modicum of power—and he was not about to grant the people of Gwangju their share of justice. On March 18, 1993, angered by YS's comment to "Let the truth stay in the care of history," protesters blocked President Kim from going into Mangwoldong Cemetery. Organizations in Gwangju formed among the wounded and the arrested, while families of deceased and missing all mobilized. On August 30, 1994, the May 18 Memorial Foundation was created to campaign for truth and justice—as well as to take care of numerous victims whose lives were still in shambles. On October 19, National Assembly member Kim Sang-hyun and twenty-two bereaved family members formally requested that the government file murder charges against Chun, Roh, and eight accomplices. The next year, a petition drive was launched to collect one million signatures in support of a special law to prosecute Chun, Roh, and all those who bore responsibility.

As the movement spread throughout the country, a sit-in of 150 people at Myongdong Cathedral in July 1995 demanded punishment for those responsible, and Lawyers for a Democratic Society filed perjury charges against Chun for his untruthful responses to parliamentary questions. University professors led a national mobilization. On July 31, 1995, more than 131 Korea University professors protested the decision to dismiss charges against Chun and Roh. Two weeks later, on August 14, about 150 professors participated in a sit-in to protest; the Korean Council of Professors for Democratization soon released a similar statement and, together with PSPD, formally petitioned the government to suspend statute of limitations for the events surrounding the Gwangju massacre. Over 211 SNU professors signed onto a statement supporting a special law, the third time in as many decades that SNU professors had raised their voices publicly. (The first two times were during the April 19 uprising against Rhee and during the June Uprising.[7]) Soon thereafter, on August 25, 1995, some 3,560 professors from 78 universities signed onto a similar statement.[8]

Under the leadership of *Hanchongryun*, students soon mobilized. Many boycotted classes and used that time to circulate petitions. On September 30, there were major demonstrations in thirteen cities calling for a special law. The next month, as the National Assembly revealed that Chun had secreted away 950 billion won (almost a billion dollars) and Roh had acquired more than $600 million in illegal funds, public opposition mounted.[9] On November 1, more than 3,200 members of three hundred trade unions marched in Seoul, demanding justice for Gwangju. By the end of the month, more than seven hundred thousand signatures had been gathered, and more than a million people signed their names to the campaign by the time it ended.[10]

No finer mobilization of civil society for transitional justice can be found in recent memory anywhere in the world. As Koreans are so remarkably adept at doing, they created an all-inclusive national coalition, in this case, the National Emergency Committee On Enacting a Special Law to Punish the Perpetrators of the May 18 Massacre. In its first meeting, 297 groups were represented. By late November, at least 6,549 people from eighty-nine universities signed on to the petition to prosecute.[11] Finally on November 24, unable to withstand the popular upsurge any longer, YS personally ordered his ruling party to draft a special law.

The "trial of the century" began on March 11, 1996. Eventually all sixteen defendants were found guilty on charges ranging from mutiny to treason for their roles in the 1979 military coup. Chun was found guilty of murder, corruption, treason, and mutiny and received a death sentence and Roh received a life sentence for mutiny, treason, and corruption, but on appeal, their sentences were reduced to life imprisonment for Chun and seventeen years for Roh. In addition, Chun was fined $276 million and Roh $350 million. Pleading poverty, Chun never paid anywhere near that, insisting he had less than three hundred dollars to his name.

With the imprisonment of the former dictators, Gwangju activists' long struggle for justice had finally been won. Korea had a new democratic government, Chun and Roh were behind bars, and victims were being compensated. The YS government paid homage to Gwangju by erecting a new national cemetery adjacent to the original resting place at Mangwoldong, and it opened at almost the same time as Chun and Roh were imprisoned. The Gwangju special law of 1995 became a precedent to establish a similar act for Jeju in 1999.[12] While many movement groups spoke of the compartmentalization of the uprising and the "memorial industry," Gwangju's winning struggle for justice made it an example not

Former presidents Chun Doo-hwan and Roh Tae-woo were arrested and convicted of capital offenses. Credit: Korea Democracy Foundation

only to Koreans but to the entire world. Their remarkable seventeen-year struggle would continue to "globalize" the uprising, sponsoring youth camps, and assisting democratic movements throughout Asia. The example of Gwangju's ultimate victory turned many people's tears of sadness and despair into joy and hope. When survivors of the horrific toll taken by death squads in Sri Lanka first came to Mangwoldong Cemetery, they said, "We must build a memorial for our dead." With the help of Gwangju artist Hong Sung-dam, they did just that. The May 18 Memorial Foundation established a Gwangju International Human Rights Award, and its first recipient was José Alexandre Gusmão, leader of East Timor. On November 3, 2000, Gusmão explained that: "It is a great privilege to come to Gwangju feeling that we are in our home. It is because what happened here in this beautiful city was, since then, an inspiration to us in our difficult struggle."

On December 22, 1997, YS pardoned Chun, Roh, and seventeen others convicted of crimes related to Gwangju. Although DJ had agreed to the decision, many people in Gwangju were angered. In winning transitional justice for the citizens of Gwangju, even temporarily, the *minjung* transformed themselves into citizens of the republic. By compelling the government to do their bidding and bring Chun and Roh to justice, the existing judicial system was unwittingly legitimized. Once again, however, transitional change left out the country's laborers, its poor and dispossessed citizens, and the task of national reconciliation remained unfinished. Under the new "democratic" regime, new forms of struggle emerged to contest these continuing problems.

The Dictatorship of the Market

Once Chun and Roh had been imprisoned and military dictatorships made a thing of the past, many Koreans hoped for a new kind of politics. No one guessed that the country's integration into the structures of "democratic" market systems would so negatively impact millions of lives as they did during the IMF crisis of 1997. To be sure, the economy was always a nagging worry, but after years of strong growth, its importance receded into the background of a more general-ized anxiety, a flux of *han* and fear produced above all by the militarized DMZ. Corruption was still a lingering problem—some people even insisted it was worse than before democratic reforms. Kim Young-sam welcomed neoliberalism, bring-ing intensified economic pressures on everyone. Manufacturing jobs were sent to China and Southeast Asia, and farmers were especially hard hit by U.S. imports. So badly did they feel the pinch in 1993 that they refused to sell their rice, instead blocking government offices with sacks of it. Staging a mock funeral for farmers, thirty thousand people in Seoul mobilized.

Like farmers, unions also opposed the Uruguay Round's creation of the World Trade Organization in 1994, but the YS government happily embraced it. Despite widespread protests, YS stepped up Korea's integration into the global economy. In November 1994, his *segyehwa* reforms, often seen as the beginning of neoliberalism in Korea, promised to "make the life of future generations better."[13] (While some economists place the beginning of neoliberalism in Korea here, the origins are much earlier—in fact, during the Gwangju Uprising, as I portray in Chapter 7). In 1994, subway and railroad workers led the movement against pri-vatization of state-owned enterprises and cutbacks in government subsidies. On June 11, 1994, telecom workers went out on strike. As YS stepped up his globali-zation initiatives, the country's foreign debt skyrocketed from $44 billion in 1993 to $120 billion in November 1997. Of total foreign debt, 58 percent was short-term debt that required continual refinancing—leaving the country at the mercy of lenders' willingness to extend new terms when loans became due.[14]

Faced with a growing autonomous union movement, conservative unions affiliated with the FKTU sought to negotiate a bigger place for themselves by agreeing with the Korean Employers Federation to work together to reduce wages. In response, three major union alliances created a democratic union associa-tion to oppose the FKTU/KEF attempt to roll back workers' salaries. Within the FKTU, thousands of rank-and-file members protested their organization's accom-modationist policies. As a decertification movement spread, new independent unions merged with the recently formed democratic union alliance to finally create an alternative to the FKTU. In November 1995, the autonomous Korean Confederation of Trade Unions (KCTU or *Minju Nochong*) was created from more than eight hundred unions with about half a million members. Although the KCTU remained illegal, their newly elected leader, Kwon Young-gil, reflected the new organization's moderate wing, and he signaled a willingness to work with the government.

While grassroots forces consolidated, the YS administration's corruption emerged as a pressing national issue. In 1996, several top officials—includ-ing a key member of the Blue House staff, the head of the Security Oversight Commission, the Defense Minister, and president of Seoul Bank—were all arrested on corruption charges. The Health and Welfare Commissioner resigned after sus-picions surfaced about a bribe, and in early 1997, the president's son, the Interior

Minister, and a key YS funder were all indicted on graft or bribery charges.[15] Suddenly, even some of the country's *chaebol* were in trouble: in January 1997, Hanbo Steel declared bankruptcy, and KIA, the country's eighth-largest corporation, announced it was also in trouble. The government's response was to clamp down on workers.

At 6 a.m. on the day after Christmas 1996, President Kim Young-sam was in church, being photographed as he said his morning prayers. On the other side of Seoul, his party held a secret meeting in the National Assembly and voted eleven times in seven minutes to pass two new labor laws—even though other parties had not even been notified of the legislature's special session. Kim's maneuvers to pass these already controversial new labor laws amounted to a sneak attack on the rights that workers had so heartily struggled for since 1987. Among other provisions, the new measures gave companies more power to fire workers and hire strikebreakers. Even in the worst of times, Korean workers had been guaranteed a modicum of job security—a safety net that the new legislation sought to destroy. The ruling party also passed laws that resuscitated the national police's capacity to spy on domestic dissidents—activities outlawed since 1994.

General Strike of 1997
Within hours of the new legislation, the biggest strike in decades was workers' response. From the shipyards of Ulsan to offices of Seoul, laborers walked off their jobs, and unions mobilized their emergency response network. At 7:30 that morning, a mass meeting of 17,000 KIA workers decided to go out, and twenty key national union leaders took refuge at Myongdong Cathedral. By the end of the day, more than 145,000 workers from ninety-five unions in heavy industry responded to the call for a general strike. Hospital workers and the mainly white-collar Korean Federation of Professionals and Technicians voted to strike. The next day, some two hundred trucks organized by the Korean Federation of Truck Drivers and a car caravan of about two thousand automobiles joined together to drive to Seoul. Although the strike was spearheaded by the KCTU, even the yellow FKTU joined it. By the third day, more than 350,000 workers shut down Korea's large industries—the first nationwide general strike since the anti-American strike of 1946.[16]

All over the country, workers fought back when riot police attacked rallies. On New Year's Eve, thousands of citizens joined workers at Myongdong Cathedral for a candlelight vigil.[17] On January 3, a second phase of the strike was declared when FKTU leaders visited KCTU leaders (who still had arrest warrants pending) inside Myongdong. Although the government tried to entice the FKTU to relent, their leaders declared themselves and their 1.2 million-member federation in solidarity with the strike. Communications, insurance, clerical, transportation, and university workers all joined the action, as did the National Council of Churches. Buddhist monks formed an emergency task force. Here was the largest and best-organized response to neoliberalism in the world—a political strike directed by a high-tech and militant labor movement equipped with video, film, e-mail, fax, web sites, and mobile phones interlaced into a network of resistance with multiple organizing centers. Besides the symbolic epicenter at Myongdong, Hyanglin

Church was a "revolutionary nerve center." To many people, it appeared the insurrectionary Korean working class was finally becoming a force capable of leading the entire society in a new direction. Labor News Production video caught images in both Masan and Changwon Export Zones depicting protesters disarming riot police and stripping them of their clubs, tear gas, and shields—all the while treating them humanely—as protesters had done in June 1987.

By the third week, the "necktie brigade" in insurance, finance, broadcasting, and hospitals joined. Polls recorded a record 88 percent of people voicing regret for having YS as president. For twenty days, a stop-and-go pattern was repeated. More than 3,500 SNU professors and students signed a statement affirming that, "What President Kim is trying to restore is not the economy but dictatorship." When riot police blocked a January 10 demonstration in Ulsan, worker Chung Jae-sung killed himself. The high point was reached on January 15, when nearly a million workers stayed off the job, and more than four hundred thousand citizens participated in demonstrations across the country.[18] Police rounded up hundreds of strikers and key leaders. Finally, on January 16, YS promised to send the bills back to the National Assembly for revision—the first time workers had defeated the capitalist state in a national confrontation.

Rather than continuing the strikes until the laws were scrapped, the reformist leadership of the KCTU relented at this critical moment and shifted to a Wednesday-only strike that lasted into February. When even conservative newspapers were joining in the chorus calling for YS to give up, the KCTU leadership ended the general strike without even consulting the members of the national coalition that had formed. On February 17, as parliament reopened, hundreds of teachers sat-in at opposition party headquarters to ask for help in legalizing their union. On February 27, the last day of full strike actions, 131,448 workers from 107 unions were counted as participants. From then on, half-day strikes occurred, citizens demonstrated, and rolling strikes of one-hour duration affected many offices and departments, but the main force of the strike had been dissipated from within. Before it was called off, the KCTU counted more than 3,878,000 people and 3,422 unions as having joined the strike, and an additional 1,400,000 people who attended solidarity protests from December 26 to January 15, 1997.[19] Other estimates ranged to five million workers who took part in twenty days of general strikes from December 1996 to February 1997.[20] On average about 190,000 workers from 168 unions participated every day. In at least twenty-two countries, support rallies took place, and more than two hundred labor groups signed letters of support.

In March, when the labor law was revised, the KCTU was made semilegal. While the issue of layoffs was deferred, provisions of the revised legislation differed little from what had set off the strike, such as the continuing outlawing of teachers' and public sector unions. The manner in which the strike had ended portended problems yet to come. Political activity by unions would be legally permitted, but in exchange, "labor market flexibility" (companies' right to lay off and fire workers at will) would become part of the new social contract agreed to by the KCTU.

As we have seen repeatedly in contemporary social movements, grass-roots protests create insurgent organizations and thrust them into the political arena, where professional organizers sell-out their movements of origin for modest gains within the power structure. This is a continuing dilemma faced by insurgencies: they crystallize leadership that then becomes the regime's most potent force for stability and a return to order. A union movement that had braved arrests, beatings, firings, and imprisonment, that had spawned major strikes among subway, railroad, and hospital workers, closed down auto plants and occupied shipyards, endorsed leaders who chose to accede to government needs in exchange for their own legalization. By ending the general strike in exchange for promises of the KCTU's decriminalization (a concession of little consequence for the powers-that-be), the working class lost the autonomy of its organization, the key issue for which it had sacrificed for years. Once it becomes legally part of the prevailing system, any party or organization must obey prevailing laws, which inevitably blunt a more radical questioning of the system as a whole. With legalization of the KCTU, workers' open contestation of power ended.

As early as 1980, U.S. policymakers had grappled with the problem of somehow bringing the insurgent Korean working class to accommodate neoliberalism. They fretted that Chun's repression steered workers to reorganize unions in ways that might involve a "drastic move away from an American-model free trade union."[21] They believed that "when unions are forced into national structures based on industrial unions, the prestige and resources of government and business then can be applied to responsible union leaders to control the union movement for national objectives and maintain stability in the work force. Without the safety valve provided by a reasonably responsible union organization, workers at the enterprise level now will have even fewer alternatives to direct job action or political agitation to gain redress for their economic or social grievances."[22] For American policymakers, unions were simply a pressure release valve on an overheated social network. Just as modest regime change was expected to release the pent-up frustrations of people's aspirations for democratic reform, unions were supposed to ameliorate economic frustrations.

At the end of 1996, the self-formation of the Korean working class, its galvanization as the leadership of society, was embodied in the massive nationwide strike against new labor laws. A decade after the Great Workers' Struggle of 1987, the Korean proletariat moved from demanding economic gains to insisting upon long-term job stability, from contesting managerial tyranny in factories to challenging national policy. Led by militant automotive and shipbuilding workers, some three million people in the major industries, hospitals, and broadcast media ultimately compelled the government to revise hastily passed labor laws.

Despite the national strike against "flexibility" of the labor market, the neoliberal accumulation regime, whose wheels were initially greased by Chun Doo-hwan, rolled over the country. If the process of economic deterioration were gradual, few protests may have been mounted, but within a year, the entire country was engulfed by the East Asian financial crisis, or IMF crisis as it is

Millions of Koreans oppose the Free Trade Agreement with the U.S. Photographer unknown

known in Korea. Overnight, crisis in the world system jeopardized the economic well-being forged by decades of people's hard work.

The 1997 IMF Crisis

In the space of two short decades after Korea's economy was subjected to American-led neoliberal imperatives, billions of dollars of U.S. investors' money flowed into the country. The imposition of a neoliberal accumulation regime on Korea meant replacing military dictatorships with the dictatorship of the market. The country's indebtedness and dependency upon international currency transactions were major factors in the economic crisis of 1997. In a few weeks, the *won* lost more than half its value,[23] two million workers lost their jobs, the stock market index fell from over 1,000 to 350, and some thirty thousand homeless people appeared on the streets as the country went bankrupt.[24] Asked to bail Korea out, the IMF demanded structural adjustments, and when Korea faithfully followed their prescriptions, the income of the highest brackets rose, while that of the lowest 20 percent decreased by 17.2 percent.[25] Wages overall fell by 2.7 percent;[26] small farmers' ability to be economically viable was further undermined; fire-at-will legislation undermined job security and about 30 percent of the workforce was fired;[27] the household poverty rate more than tripled from 1996 to 1999,[28] resulting in dozens of "IMF suicides"—all features of the Americanization of Korea.

While Koreans suffered, foreign capital used the opportunity to siphon billions of dollars out of the country and into the pockets of coupon clippers and hedge fund managers. Buying up financial assets at bargain basement prices, investors flipped them in a few years' time with remarkable rates of return. For American and Japanese corporations, Korea remains a great place to do business.

Korean workers continue to oppose neoliberalism. Photographer unknown

As the dust settled from the stampede of international investors scurrying to maximize billions of dollars poured into lucrative purchases, only belatedly did the country's grim reality settle in. Besides having emptied the coffers of many leading financial institutions, the consolidation of the next phase of the neoliberal accumulation regime meant that about 50 percent of all Koreans would become part-time employees—with no job security and significantly lower wages and benefits. A new labor aristocracy emerged, as unionized industrial workers were able to negotiate for themselves significantly better material rewards for their hard work than their part-time colleagues. Before the crisis, workers were guaranteed lifetime employment, but after the country had sold off some of its best banks and corporations to weather the storm, the majority of working people could only find part-time jobs.

The crisis began in Thailand. On May 14 and 15, foreign currency speculators led by George Soros initiated a massive sell-off of the Thai baht, then pegged to the U.S. dollar. Although the Thai government fought to keep its currency stable, on July 2 it was compelled to let it float on international markets, and its value plunged, wreaking havoc on Thailand's economy and causing South Korean banks to suffer losses of an estimated $2 billion.[29] Japanese banks, which also risked huge amounts through heavy investments in the region, demanded repayment of short-term loans made to Korean banks. As foreign banks refused to refinance short-term loans, Korea's entire financial infrastructure was dealt a body blow. In less than two weeks, Moody's twice lowered Korea's credit rating from A1 to B2. In late November, with credit markets essentially frozen, the government made a $57 billion bailout request from the IMF.

When Korea desperately needed short-term help, the IMF insisted upon harsh conditions for new loans: government services would have to be cut, and leveraged buy-outs of Korean banks and industries permitted. The ceiling on foreign ownership of assets was lifted to 50 percent at the end of 1997 (and raised again to 55 percent in February 1998). Trade was further liberalized and domestic bond markets opened to foreign investors. Decision-makers initially demanded 50 percent of bank workers be laid off, a figure later reduced to 30 percent. All four candidates for president in the 1997 elections were required to sign statements promising to honor the terms of the agreement before funds could be disbursed. As the IMF required tight money, interest rates rose to about 30 percent by the end of 1998. Joblessness tripled, scores of major businesses failed, and incomes dropped. By mid-February 1998, more than a hundred firms were going bankrupt every day in Korea.[30] Altogether in 1998, a total of 22,828 firms went bankrupt, real wages fell by 9 percent, and GDP fell 5.8 percent.[31] By 2000, the size of the middle class had shrunk by nearly 5 percent (from 70.2 percent of households in 1994 to 65.3 percent), and the ratio of government debt to GDP more than doubled (from 13 percent to nearly 30 percent).

While institutions of international capital demanded their pound of flesh, exacerbating the crisis as part of their "tough love" cure, ordinary Koreans stepped forward with generosity and selfless devotion. They lined up to donate gold teeth to help the country raise foreign exchange.[32] People dug out their wedding rings and *dol* (a baby's first birthday ring) and joined in the "gold collection campaign" by the thousands. While that spirit of sacrifice defines the inner kernel of a new value system—the very kind needed in the twenty-first century—structural change is another matter. Not a few Western economists love to credit Park Chung-hee's developmental state and the *chaebol* for the "miracle on the Han" while blaming working-class intransigence for the 1997 crisis (refusing even to call it the IMF crisis). Conservatives seldom mention the many attributes of Korean workers that aid economic growth—attention to detail, discipline, Confucian subservience to hierarchy, diligence, and literacy.

Dynamism continues to characterize Korea's economy, but after 1997, it is dominated by foreign financial capital, all along the objective of U.S. policy. All over the region, global capital mobilized its forces to overthrow and supplant protectionist regimes. American and Japanese banks and corporations had long been blocked from expanding into regions of the world where national developmental states privileged indigenous corporations and "crony capitalism" protected friends and associates of "corrupt" leaders. As barriers to its penetration of markets and labor forces long denied them fell, transnational capitalism created bubble after bubble, lending billions that only made borrowers more dependent upon financial centers in New York and Tokyo, which for their part, subsequently drew in monies from around the world, thereby creating global liquidity crises.[33]

Neoliberalism as Global Capital's Response to Falling Rates of Profits

With massive concentration of planetary wealth in giant corporations, a key structural problem of their capitalist organization is the falling rate of profit. As previous accumulations fund technological innovation and capital expands ever more, the system's very success means future profits constitute a declining percentage of total investments. Capital thereby subverts its own ability to please investors' need for high rates of profit, a source of systematic instability and unbridled quest for growth—no matter what the cost to humans or Nature. One short-term solution for giant corporations has been to extinguish smaller competitors and take over their assets, whether in countries like Korea or at home.

In Korea, concentration of capital was aided by the national development state's guidance of the country's *chaebol*. By 1988, four *chaebols'* revenues— Hyundai, Samsung, Daewoo and Lucky-Goldstar—comprised 60 percent of South Korea's GDP ($80 billion out of $135 billion.)[34] In April 1997, *Le Monde Diplomatique* estimated the *chaebol* share at 80 percent of the economy. Before the late 1980s, net profit of South Korean manufacturing was higher than that of Japan, the United States, or Europe, giving the country a clear advantage in its drive to industrialize. As everywhere else, the rate of profit fell substantially over time. An index devised by Philip O'Hara calculated the falling profit rate of the *Fortune* 500 from 7.15 percent in 1960–1969, 5.30 percent in 1980–1990, 2.29 percent in 1990–1999, and finally to 1.32 percent in 2000–2002.[35] Although higher in manufacturing, rates declined substantially in that sector as well, as indicated in TABLE 12.1.

The overall pattern in Korea is quite similar to global trends. According to the Bank of Korea, the average rate of ordinary profit to total liabilities and manufacturing net worth declined dramatically from the 1970s to the 1990s:

1971–1979	4.42 percent
1980–1989	2.70 percent
1990–1995	2.23 percent[36]

Led by New York bankers in the 1970s, global capital's response to falling profitability was a "new American revolution" to free corporations from "onerous" government control. Recycling petrodollars into loans to Third World regimes—many of whom bought arms to prop up corrupt dictatorships—Chase Manhattan Bank's David Rockefeller (the same man who embraced Chun Doo-hwan soon after the massacre in Gwangju) helped create a financial superstructure that brought in billions of dollars in revenues. So greedy were the wizards of high finance to control global capital that financial crisis after financial crisis elsewhere was the result. Especially noteworthy are crises in Mexico in 1994, East Asia in 1997, the

TABLE 12.1 **Average Rate of Net Profit in Manufacturing (percent)**

Years	South Korea	Japan	U.S.	Europe
1963–1971	39.7	48.2	28.4	16.4
1972–1980	27.7	22.9	17.4	12.7
1981–1990	16.9	14.4	12.6	13.4

[*Japan, America, and Europe: 1981–1987.]

Sources: R. Armstrong, A. Glyn, and J. Harrison, *Capitalism Since 1945* (Oxford: Blackwell, 1991); H.W. Jang, "Phases of Capital Accumulation in Korea and Evolution of Government Growth Strategy, 1963–1990," (PhD dissertation, University of Oxford, 1995); Shin Gyoung-hee, "The Crisis and Workers' Movement in South Korea," *International Socialism* 78 (March 1998): http://pubs.socialistreviewindex.org.uk/isj78/gyounghe.htm, accessed August 14, 2008.

Russian default in August 1998 that affected South Africa, Brazil, and Argentina, and the Nordic and Japanese banking crises of the 1990s. From 1995 to 2003, the IMF, World Bank and U.S. Treasury bailouts of Asia, Mexico, Russia, and Brazil subtracted $250 billion of bad loans from giant banks and corporations and added them to governments' indebtedness.[37] No wonder world economic elites favored "democratization"!

Apparently caused by shortfalls in the U.S. secondary mortgage market, the near collapse of the global financial architecture at the end of 2008 indicates the system's structural instability—and its lack of reasonability. The capitalist system's looming debacle was only averted through trillions of dollars in governments' bailout monies. While the Obama administration plundered the public treasury to prop up giant corporations and banks, to rescue the "free market" system, taxpayers once again lifted the burden of bankers' overstretched loans from their balance sheets—and made the public responsible for trillions of dollars in new debt (and not only in the United States). So quickly did giant corporations recover by 2010 (while smaller companies went bankrupt by the thousands and tens of millions of workers experienced declining standards of living) that Exxon-Mobile reaped over 100 percent growth of profits, and banks and auto companies reported their biggest profits in recent years.[38]

In the name of "free markets," neoliberalism results in takeover of medium-sized firms by giant ones, lower corporate taxes, privatization of public companies, increases in public debt, attacks on trade unions, a widening gap between rich and poor, and an increase in the number of poor people. While Keynesian solutions to the Great Depression of 1929 involved massive national spending programs, beginning in 1979 with stagflation (high unemployment and simultaneously high inflation), world bankers devised a post-Keynesian "neoliberal" solution through which global corporations and banks could reinvigorate profits through penetration of new markets and incorporation of previously unincorporated parts of the world. The "magic of the marketplace" and gutting of government programs were in actuality the empowerment of norms of corporate profitability as the mechanism to allocate humanity's accumulated wealth.

Two examples help explain how neoliberalism hurts poor countries. In 1975, Haiti grew all the rice required to feed its people. The IMF loaned its government $24.6 million on condition that it reduce import tariffs on rice and other agricultural products—that is, to open its market to outsiders. Within two years, local farmers could not compete with "Miami rice" and stopped growing it. Soon, poor people in Haiti ate "mud cookies." Similarly, Kenya became a net importer of corn, the country's most important food, after IMF structural adjustment and trade liberalization in the 1990s. Today, hunger continues to spread in Kenya.

Neoliberalism generates greater class polarization: the UN tells us that the net worth of the world's 358 richest people in 1996 was equal to the combined income of the poorest 2.3 billion people—45 percent of the world's population. The world's two hundred richest people more than doubled their net worth in the four years to 1998, to more than $1 trillion.[39] By 2010, the richest three men in the world held more money than the poorest forty-eight countries.[40]

All these crises flow directly from the structures of the world system—and the solution to these problems requires a very different set of institutional rules by which humanity's vast wealth is governed. Like the Korean *minjung*, whose wisdom we encountered in Gwangju, people throughout the world comprehend the systematic problems of global capital's rule and seek an alternative. As in the past, war looms as the economic engine that could provide a solution to capitalism's failure to find peaceful, steady-state economic prosperity for the vast majority of humanity. Even short of new military disasters, the impoverishing effects of IMF and World Bank programs continue to ravage millions of people's lives. IMF "assistance" to Greece in 2010 meant people's retirement ages were raised, pensions and wages slashed, and national wealth sold off at bargain prices. German suggestions that Greece sell off its islands were no idle desire. Greek resistance to investors' greed follows a long tradition from the 1980s and 1990s, when a global counteroffensive to neoliberal programs was mounted from the grassroots in Jamaica, Venezuela, Ghana, Indonesia, Argentina, and dozens of other places.

In the 1980s and 1990s, throughout East Asia, uprisings swept away entrenched regimes. As I discuss in Volume 2, grassroots insurgencies in ten places led to reforms that helped to accelerate the unfolding logic of capital's rule. Although popular movements and sacrifices resulted in great improvements in millions of people's lives, insurgencies were used by political parties for the benefit of elites, which stole the fruits of people's efforts. Very frequently, progressive politicians served to legitimate new forms of capital's domination. Korea was no exception to this pattern. Within the parameters of "democracy," as the market became the chief means of imposing rule by capital, gains won since the great struggle of 1987, such as higher wages and shorter workweeks, were reversed. Koreans' apparent victory of "democratization" led to massive defeat through the IMF crisis of 1997, with a resultant large number of temporary or part-time workers (now about 50 percent of all jobs in South Korea) and increasing class polarization.

The DJ Government to the Rescue

With Korea's economy under IMF control in 1997, presidential elections in December brought long-time democracy advocate Kim Dae Jung into office. Often spoken of in the same breath as Nelson Mandela, DJ stepped forward to lead the country, promising a "participatory economy" and prosperity with freedom. His inaugural address was optimistic and called upon Koreans to step forward. As DJ put it, "Participatory democracy must be put into practice; the people must be respected as masters and must act like masters." Soon after he became president, he prepared to visit Pyongyang, a trip none of his predecessors had risked making. DJ's historic June 15, 2000 meeting with Kim Jong-il won him the Nobel Peace Prize and guaranteed him a place of honor in history. His Sunshine Policy broke with decades of his predecessors' intransigent hostility to the North and ushered in Koreans' first real period of peace and prosperity in the twentieth century.

As we have seen repeatedly in the history of insurgencies, however, heroic figures from previous episodes are subsequently used by elites to impose strict conditions upon subaltern groups. So it was with DJ—"the Mandela of Asia." During his first four years in office, the man who promised to be a president that would be the "champion of workers and ordinary people" imprisoned an average of five workers per week. In Kim Young-sam's five-year term, 632 union leaders languished behind prison bars, but DJ outpaced even that sad record by imprisoning 686 leaders in his first four years. Under the guise of "progress," DJ built a Tripartite Commission (composed of representatives of business, labor unions, and government) to better manage the economy, in his first months in office. At the same time, he invited billionaire George Soros (blamed by many in Thailand for that country's economic disaster) into his home to discuss solutions to the IMF crisis.[41]

The Tripartite Commission, the first time autonomous trade unions were allowed to participate in the government, resulted in a February 1998 accord by which the KCTU agreed to mass layoffs.[42] A new division of labor in a cooperative labor/management/government council of state enrolled unions to discipline the workforce. The new legal framework for a post-Fordist accumulation regime legalized unions and political activity by workers, while simultaneously guaranteeing employers "flexible workforce rules"—under which thousands of workers were laid off. As union representatives negotiated the new accord, an extraordinary meeting took place in January 1998, when angry KCTU members compelled their entire national leadership to resign as a result of an internal rebellion, during which rank-and-file workers armed with iron pipes shut union officials out of their offices. Although union leaders withdrew from the Tripartite Commission, they eventually returned to it. The IMF crisis compelled many unions to give up collective bargaining and the right to strike in exchange for attempts to maintain jobs. While most workers organized within the KCTU were able to defend their jobs, millions of others had no choice but to accept part-time work with no benefits. That winter, when the IMF crisis hit in full force, dozens of suicides—desperate acts of private surrender to the impersonal force of market profitability—followed closely behind massive layoffs, wage reductions, longer workweeks, and declining living standards.

During retrenchment in the public sector from 1998 to 2000, more than 130,000 workers lost their jobs. In state enterprises, 40,000 workers were made redundant after 20 of 109 public state-owned enterprises were sold off, including Korea Telecom and Korea Electric Power Corporation. An additional 26,000 government employees lost their jobs through cutbacks. In 1998 alone, the top five *chaebol* laid off 80,000 workers. Union activists who were hired back were first made to promise in writing not to cause any more industrial troubles. After 68,000 bank workers were fired in 1998, their protests were answered with helicopters spewing tear gas and riot police clubs. Subsequently, about two-thirds of these workers were reemployed as irregular or part-time workers at greatly reduced rates of pay.

Besides the wave of tragic suicides, the defeat suffered by the working class was measured in deteriorating working conditions. The work hours sharply increased from 207 hours/month in 1997 to 226 hours/month by 1999—a reversal

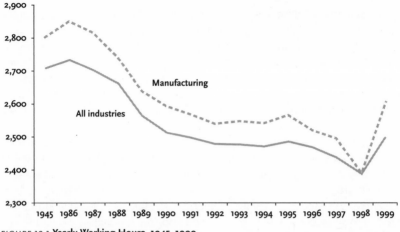

FIGURE 12.1 **Yearly Working Hours, 1945–1999**

of years of decline from a weekly average of 54.7 hours in 1986 to 49.3 in 1991.[43] The annual number of hours worked had steadily fallen since 1987 from a high of 2,720 in all industries (2,850 in manufacturing) to a low of about 2,400 before the IMF crisis—after which it sharply increased, as indicated by FIGURE 12.1. Korea is the only OECD country in which work hours exceeded two thousand hours per year: in 1999, it averaged 2,500 hours annually. In August 2009, Swiss financial group UBS reported that Seoul's workers toiled 2,312 hours per year, second only to Cairo among seventy-three major world cities.[44]

Although Korean laborers were compelled to toil longer hours, their incomes fell. By 2000, the income of the top 20 percent of the population rose 11 percent while the bottom 20 percent saw their incomes fall more than 5 percent. From 5.7 million part-time workers in 1998 (or 47 percent of the workforce), by August of 2001, the government reported 7.4 million—about 56 percent of the workforce— were part-time employees, an even greater percentage than when "democracy" was won in 1987. Korea turned into a "20/80 Society" (where the majority lived below the level of the upper 20 percent of the population, who enjoyed stand-ards of living similar to Australians).[45] The "free" market, not the iron fist of the dictatorship, was now regulator of social wages, and both economic inequality and union density fell to below their levels during the dismal reign of Chun Doo-hwan.[46] When previous methods of authoritarian discipline had become unac-ceptable, companies came to rely on softer, "democratic" means—the market and technological innovation—to discipline their workforces.[47]

DJ's Assault on Labor

Worker resistance to DJ broke out almost as soon as he took over the reins of power. A major challenge was launched on July 20, 1998, when Kim Kwang-sik, president of Hyundai Motors Workers Union, and 300 shop stewards shaved their heads to protest management plans to layoff thousands of workers. Beginning with a chimney protest by three former union presidents, the plant was occupied for over two months. More than 3,000 workers supported them, as did 7,000 family members who lived in tents near the smokestack. Management shut down production. On August 17, some 4,500 police tried to evict the strikers, but they were forced to retreat. Finally, union leaders negotiated a guarantee that layoffs would only be temporary, except for 300 cafeteria workers—all female. Even though 64 percent of union members voted against the settlement, the government and company enforced it. By 2002, more than 10,000 casual workers—many of them in the most dangerous and undesirable jobs—were working at Hyundai Motors.[48]

As market discipline failed to stifle workers' struggle, DJ's neoliberal policies were enforced by brute force. On March 20, 2000, police watched while dozens of gangsters with iron pipes beat striking rail workers. Enduring more than a year of intense struggles, Korail unionists finally won the right to elect their leaders—some fifty-four years after they first demanded it. Months of struggle at Daewoo ended on April 10, 2001, when 1,500 riot police viciously attacked 300 half-naked workers. While workers' lawyers held up a court order giving them the right to assemble, union members were peacefully sitting down, rather than fighting back with Molotov cocktails as had been the norm. Three hours of beatings left fourteen workers hospitalized with broken ribs, partial paralysis, broken noses, and a variety of other injuries.[49] Less than three weeks later, promanagement workers attacked contract workers at Carrier. Remcon Concrete was next. Thugs even attacked women cosmetics workers. By August, with KCTU leader Dan Byung-ho in prison, the workers movement announced a campaign for the five-day workweek and began to fight back with its own weapons—Molotov cocktails—an effective means of blunting police violence.

As unions became more hard-line, by January of 2001, when a vote was taken inside the KCTU, the NL faction captured a majority.[50] Afterward, the new Democratic Labor Party emerged with both PD and NL activists within it (but, as in past joint efforts, NL eventually came to control the organization).

With the spiral of police violence and union resistance threatening to explode, DJ and the Tripartite Commission produced a compromise agreement. In exchange for workers giving up Molotovs, the government promised to refrain from using tear gas. New managerial techniques of control were also implemented: team-based organization and personalized approaches to individual workers marked the change from despotic to hegemonic control, a regime under which employers were aided by constant surveillance technologies. In the words of one union member: "All workers should be in exactly the same uniforms

TABLE 12.2 **Number of Molotov Cocktails Used**

Year	Number of Molotovs
1998	170
1999	613
2000	746
2001	2,453

Source: Government Information Agency; *Korea Herald*, December 10, 2001.

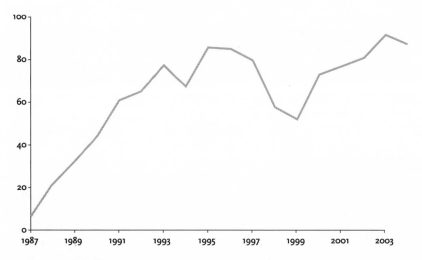

FIGURE 12.2 **Legal Strikes as a Percentage of All Strikes, 1987–2004**

without exception. Smoking is prohibited, and we cannot even imagine having a cup of coffee on the way back from the toilet. We cannot do anything but work. I feel as if my imagination is being supervised . . . the workers in this company are now like slaves."[51]

As union density rates fell precipitously, the cause of labor disputes dramatically shifted from wage increases to contracts.[52] Fatal injury rates at work were abominable, standing at 1.8/10,000—almost ten times higher than in Singapore (0.19) and significantly above Hong Kong (0.57), Argentina (0.8), Mexico (0.8), the United States (0.11), and Japan (0.05)—but strikes were about jobs for union members, not safety issues or the massive transition to part-time employees.[53] In this same period, strikes became increasingly regulated by the state.[54] In 1987, less than 5.9 percent of strikes were legal; by 2003 the number of legal strikes was around 90 percent, as portrayed in FIGURE 12.2.

Under DJ, although strikes became legalized and workers were integrated into the system, class polarization increased, especially involving "irregular workers." By 2005, industrial workers accounted for 40 percent of union memberships—up from 10 percent in 1996.[55] Their pragmatism and self-interestedness fed directly into divide-and-conquer elite strategy. While the number of temporary and daily workers surpassed that of full-time employees in 1999, "informal workers" actually toiled longer hours than did their unionized counterparts—46.5 hours/week as compared to 45.9.[56] As the wage gap grew, so did other indications of inequality. More than 90 percent of regular workers had pensions and health insurance, while fewer than 25 percent of irregular workers did. A casual workers' union was launched but, to this day, it has yet to make significant inroads in altering the status of more than half of all workers.[57] Most tellingly, workplace inequality occurs around gender lines: in 1999, less than 30 percent of women employees were fulltime, while the corresponding figure for men was 69 percent.[58]

Women's Autonomy

Within systems of capitalist patriarchy, women's fate is typically to be "last hired and first fired." After the IMF crisis, a study determined that 73 percent of women workers were part-timers, and women were paid substantially less than their male counterparts. In industrialized countries, only in Japan do women make less in relation to men (44 percent) than in Korea (52 percent). As women mobilized to deal with such gender discrimination, three groups formed—one inside KCTU, one for informal women workers, and one for female clerical workers. In struggles at Hyundai, unions had sacrificed women kitchen workers. One estimate placed the number of women inside KCTU unions at 20 percent while the number of leaders was below 10 percent. In early 1999, after women found that the "patriarchal hierarchy within the present unions became an obstacle to organizing women workers," autonomous unions formed the National Federation of Women's Trade Unions with nine regional unions.[59] The independent union, autonomous of the KCTU, was created for the sole purpose of organizing women workers. Simultaneously, Korean Women's Associations United (KWAU) grew in size to encompass more than twenty-eight organizations and forty thousand individuals.

The 1990s were largely a decade of institutionalization for women: women-related bills were introduced in the National Assembly, as were laws against sexual violence. After a study by KWAU found monthly salaries of women at $243—only 50.9 percent of male earnings—a 1990 Labor Equality Law was passed. Despite the new legislation, Korean women's earnings were only 58 percent of their male counterparts in 1997, a rise from the 44.5 percent given by Amsden for 1980.[60] Data from 2005 put the ratio at 72 percent for regular workers, but overall at 65.4 percent for all women to all men.[61] In 2006, the Korea Economic Institute calculated that the average working woman made 42 percent of what men in comparable jobs made in the 1970s; this number was 63 percent in 2002.[62] Other measurements were lower. In 2009, *Hankyoreh* calculated that women made barely half (52 percent) of male income.[63] An important dimension of women's economic marginalization is their disproportionate share of irregular jobs, which included more than half of all employed females in 1995 (57.5 percent), a number that rose to 67.6 percent in 2006.[64]

These statistics only begin to give us a picture of patriarchy's pervasive power in shaping daily life.[65] Studies consistently place Korea near the bottom

TABLE 12.3 **Elected Female National Assembly Members**

Year	# Females (Directly Elected)
1985	8 (2)
1988	6
1992	3
1996	9
2004	16

Source: Seungsook Moon, "Redrafting Democratization through Women's Representation and Participation in the Republic of Korea," in *Korea's Democratization*, ed. Samuel S. Kim (Cambridge: Cambridge University Press, 2003), 111.

TABLE 12.4 **Proportion of Female Legislators in 2000**

China	21.8 percent
Philippines	12.9 percent
Japan	9.0 percent
Singapore	4.3 percent
South Korea	4.0 percent

Source: Young-hee Shim, *Sexual Violence and Feminism in Korea* (Seoul: Hanyang University Press, 2004), 24.

of the world in terms of gender equality. In a 2000 UN Development Program report, South Korea ranked sixty-three out of seventy—similar to Swaziland or Fiji. By 2008, out of one hundred world nations, South Korea fell to sixty-eighth. In universities, fewer than 20 percent of professors are women, many ghettoized in Home Economics departments. In 2009, women were a scant 13.7 percent of all legislators—an improvement over previous periods. In the 2008 elections, only 2 percent of those elected nationally were women (and in local elections only about 5 percent). Among 299 members of the National Assembly, women scarcely got elected—a situation that has persisted for decades. In comparison with other Asian countries, South Korea ranks near the bottom, as illustrated in TABLE 12.4.

Women's subservient political status is a mirror of their sexual exploitation. An Ewha study found that 83 percent of Korean men had had relations with a prostitute—many during their military service years—but about half of the 83 percent also used prostitutes after getting married. In 2006, the *San Francisco Chronicle* reported that sex work accounts for 4 percent of South Korea's economy—over $21 billion per year, more than electricity and gas combined. According to their data, more than 330,000 people toil as sex workers in eighty thousand brothels and sixty-nine red-light districts.[66] In 2009, evidence of U.S. government complicity in the sex industry emerged in the pages of the *New York Times*.[67]

Wages of sex workers under neoliberalism are determined by the market rather than through dictatorship. Where brute force had been used to abduct "comfort women" and postwar poverty had compelled others to work in the sex industry, today the glitz of consumer goods and a dearth of reasonable alternatives for high paying jobs within the market system provide a stream of women into brothels. Some estimates place the number of prostitutes in Korea at two million. A significant recent development has been the self-organization of sex workers. Women in Gwangju held the first organizing meeting in the mid-1990s, and a cooperative bakery was set up. In February 2002, when two bars burnt in Kunsan, fifteen women were killed. Although the second fire was only five hundred meters from the police station, the police did nothing. When activist Kim Hyun-son began organizing, gangs who profit from the sex trade threatened her life. Demonstrations in Seoul and Kunsan demanded the police chief in Kunsan be arrested. Some female activist groups filed charges while others took direct action: in Ulsan, three women were rescued from a small room where they had been held for four years. Even within the movement, women activists (백인회) began to become stridently opposed to sexism. One group published several lists of male activists deemed sexually oppressive, but male reaction was intransigent and regarded women's going public as a problem. In 2009, after an attempted rape of a female KCTU unionist by a leading member, the entire national board resigned for its role in a subsequent cover-up.

Foreign Investors Make a Steal

Long blocked by the national development state, the floodgates on global capital opened wide after the IMF crisis made its way into Korea. Bargain basement prices on industries and banks made Korea an attractive investment. As the military dictatorship was replaced by the dictatorship of the market, the spiraling dialectic of liberation and enslavement reached a higher level. Using newfound freedoms, capital was able to favorably restructure its relationship with workers. While millions of hard-working Korean workers and farmers suffered under the lash of neoliberal austerity, the men who presided over the bloody suppression of Gwangju were rewarded. Although convicted of treason and imprisoned briefly, Chun Doo-hwan kept hundreds of millions of dollars he had embezzled; Richard Holbrooke made a fortune as an advisor to Hyundai and U.S. banks before being named U.S. ambassador to the UN; and Jimmy Carter won a Nobel Peace Prize. Simultaneously, the U.S. embassy's long-term focus "to protect the interests of U.S. investors" paid off handsomely.

The IMF crisis necessitated devaluation of the Korean won, allowing investors like the Carlyle Group to acquire Korean capital assets at greatly reduced prices, only to sell them off with astonishing profits after markets recovered. From a mere 13 percent share in 1996, foreign investors acquired 40.1 percent of the market value of Korean corporations soon after the IMF crisis hit the country.[68] In 2004, foreigners controlled 43.7 percent of the country's stock values.[69] In the financial sector, the trend was even higher, with foreign control of key banks rising from 12 percent in 1998 to 64 percent in 2004. Foreign direct investment was less than a billion dollars in 1990, but with the astonishing values created by the IMF crisis, it jumped to $15.5 billion in 1999 as international investors poured into the ravaged country to pick up its loot. For years, George H.W. Bush (the first president Bush) chaired the annual meeting of Carlyle Group's Asian Advisory Board. In 2000, when the IMF warned of dire consequences if South Korea did not "shore up financial institutions burdened with bad loans,"[70] he met with Kim Dae Jung's prime minister and other government and business leaders. Soon thereafter, Carlyle's $145 million bid won control of KorAm Bank. A few years later, when KorAm was sold in what *Business Week* described as "the single-largest private-equity exit in Asia to date," Carlyle netted a profit of $675 million on that single transaction.[71]

Other U.S.-based private equity funds have done even better: Newbridge Capital "earned" more than $1.2 billion in five short years by buying and selling Korea First Bank. Lone Star Fund flipped a forty-five-story building in Seoul making a $240 million profit, and its $1.2 billion stake in Korea Exchange Bank, which it acquired in 2003, was reportedly worth more than triple that when it tried to sell it off in early 2006.[72] In the blunt and prophetic words of Ray Hood, State Street Bank's director of Asian investments, "In Asia, investment returns will be a complete steal."[73] According to ROK government statistics, foreign funds' assessed stock investment gains totaled $100 billion between 1998 and 2003; by May of 2005, foreigners held 47 percent of the shares of the top 10 *chaebol* and 42 percent of the entire stock market (up from 9.1 percent in 1997).[74]

Lone Star's attitude toward Korean workers is embodied for many people in the story of Jang Wha Sik, one of 160 workers at Korea Exchange Bank Credit Service (then under the control of Lone Star) who received a text message on February 27, 2004, at 3:20 a.m. announcing that he would be laid off the following day in a cost-cutting measure. In Jang's words: "They are siphoning astronomical amounts of national wealth out of the country. What did they do in return? They laid off workers. Talk about injustice!"[75] But Lone Star was not finished with its demonstration of American friendliness: they balked at paying even a "trifling" amount in taxes since their investments were made through paper companies registered in tax havens.[76] So great was profiteering that the Korean government was compelled to investigate Lone Star and hold up its sale of Korea Exchange Bank. In 2008, Lone Star was convicted of fraud, and the director of its South Korean operations was taken into custody to serve a five-year sentence.[77]

The conflict between Asian and Western values exists at many levels. Western political scientists have long claimed Confucian values are incompatible with democracy, while Western greed appears unsavory from the perspective of Confucian tradition, according to which a successful bargain occurs when both buyer and seller are satisfied that a fair exchange has been achieved. As Mencius wrote, "Why must you speak of profit? . . . Superiors and inferiors will try to seize profit from another. And the state will be endangered."[78] If someone sells cheap products at a high price, thereby hoodwinking unsuspecting buyers, it is actually the seller who has lost face, an egregious error in a society where fairness and ethical behavior are more valuable than making money. In the West (and increasingly everywhere today), the person who bargains "successfully" is someone who buys low and sells high—no matter whom is hurt in the process.

Divergent understandings of the norms of fairness and ethical transactions are a material basis for sustained anti-Americanism. The gap between U.S. and Korean perspectives, readily apparent in a comparison of statements by U.S. officials with voices from Gwangju, has widened in the epoch of the neoliberal accumulation regime, when the preponderant role of finance capital dwarfs other areas of economic activity, and the role of the IMF and World Bank are vital to countries' economic development. Unlike decades past, when Korean values such as hard work, sacrifice, and national solidarity played a primary role, in the neoliberal era, national treasuries can be emptied overnight by the financial wizards of international speculation and corporate domination.

In the current architecture of the world economy, it is "natural" that nations and individuals single-mindedly seek to maximize their profits. Although often rationalized as the "invisible hand" of the market, Adam Smith had only contempt for unbridled profit-taking: "All for ourselves and nothing for other people, seems, in every age of the world, to have been the vile maxim of the masters of mankind."[79] To many Koreans, it appears that the "ugly American" has returned:

As Lee Chan-keun expressed it: "In his *Analects*, Confucius writes that a man of virtue neither pushes others to follow him nor blindly follows another's lead . . . Seen from Confucius's viewpoint, the United States seems to fit the description of the lowly man. Washington demands that other countries adopt its ways and practices."[80]

It is at this point that the very success of U.S. officials making "every effort to protect the interests of U.S. investors" stokes the embers of anti-Americanism in South Korea and undermines the strategic alliance between the ROK and the United States. Many Koreans express outrage at what they perceive as foreign investors' looting of their national wealth, while they become the 20/80 society. Will Korea continue down the path of Americanization? Or will it turn and face toward the EU, perhaps Scandinavia, or, as is more likely, China. For the first time, South Korea exported more to China than to the United States in 2003, and a year earlier, China had become the main place where Korean capital was invested. Manufacturing in Korea is now declining as jobs and industries are being moved out of the country. Under the neoliberal accumulation regime, the greater capacity for financial boondoggles increases anti-Americanism in the ROK. There may be more visible issues driving U.S.-Korea relations, but under the surface, U.S. officials' single-minded pursuit of the interests of American investors—no matter what the cost to Koreans—may well mean the long-term undoing of the U.S.-ROK alliance.

NOTES

1   Kim Dong-choon, "The Great Upsurge of South Korea's Social Movements in the 1960s," *Inter-Asia Cultural Studies* 7, no. 4 (2006): 631.

2   Embassy of the United States, "Statement on the Events in Kwangju," http://seoul.usembassy.gov/p_kwangju.html.

3   See his article, "The United States and South Korea: An Alliance Under Stress—A Reassessment," *Korea Policy Review* 1 (2005): 35–44. Gregg cites a "shocking" poll that revealed widespread anti-Americanism in 2003.

4   For discussion of the details of U.S. involvement in the suppression of the Gwangju Uprising, one could begin with Tim Shorrock's articles, especially "Debacle in Kwangju: Were Washington's cables read as a green light for the 1980 Korean massacre?" *Nation*, December 9, 1996, available at http://base21.jinbo.net/show/show.php?p_docnbr=20896 and the longer version available at http://www.kimsoft.com/korea/kwangju3.htm. See also Sangyong, Simin, et al., *Memories*, 268–77.

5   See Shin and Hwang, *Contentious Kwangju*, xxx.

6   Held in Province Hall auditorium in front of a live audience of several hundred people, the tribunal was simultaneously broadcast throughout the Jeolla region. Dozens of witnesses testified, including victims of the military's violence, family members of the deceased, and a former U.S. soldier who had been stationed near the Gwangju airport during the uprising. A jury composed of people of many different occupations from various parts of South Korea found Carter, former Ambassador Gleysteen, and former U.S. Commander Wickham as well as the following U.S. officials guilty of "crimes against humanity:" former Deputy Secretary of State Warren Christopher, former Assistant Secretary of State for East Asian and Pacific Affairs Richard Holbrooke, former National Security Advisor Zbigniew Brzezinski, former CIA Director Stansfield Turner, and former Defense Secretary Harold Brown. The above named individuals

were asked to apologize for their role in the suppression of the democratic uprising. The U.S. government was asked to send defense counsel but never responded
to the tribunal's request; none of the above named individuals has apologized. For
further information, see: http://news.naver.com/news/read.php?mode=LSD&office_
id=002&article_id=0000001053&section_id=102&menu_id=102.

7   Kim, "Civic Mobilization," 287.

8   *Essays*, 117 (see chap. 5, n. 102).

9   *Facts on File World File Digest*, February 15, 1996, 90.

10   Interview with Rev. Kang Shin-seok, April 22, 2001; Yong Cheol Kim, "The Shadow
     of the Gwangju Uprising in the Democratization of Korean Politics," in *South Korean
     Democracy: Legacy of the Gwangju Uprising*, eds. George Katsiaficas and Na Kahn-chae
     (London: Routledge, 2006), 130.

11   Kim, "Civic Mobilization," 286–87.

12   See Keun-sik Jung, "Has Kwangju Been Realized?" in *Contentious Kwangju*, eds. Shin
     and Hwang, 47.

13   Davis B. Bobrow and James J. Na, "The Globalization Push in Korea," in *The Politics
     of Democratization and Globalization in Korea*, eds. Chung-in Moon and Jongryn Mo
     (Seoul: Yonsei University Press, 1999), 182–83.

14   Chang Ha-joon, "South Korea: The Misunderstood Crisis," in *Tigers in Trouble* (London:
     Zed Press, 1998), 223.

15   Doh C. Shin, *Mass Politics*, 10.

16   See chap. 3.

17   Ann Cook, "South Korea: The Tiger Strikes," http://www.socialistalternative.org/
     literature/southkorea/.

18   C. Jay Ou, "South Korean Workers Resist Labor Law Reform," *Multinational Monitor* 8,
     no. 3 (March 1997).

19   Won Young-su, "History of South Korean Labor and Student Struggles Since the End
     of World War II," in *The International Encyclopaedia of Revolution and Protest: 1500–
     Present*, ed. Immanuel Ness (London: Wiley Blackwell, 2009).

20   Byoung-Hoon Lee, "Militant Unionism in Korea," 163.

21   GDMM X: 670.

22   Gleysteen telegram to Secretary of State, September 15, 1980. GDMM X: 410.

23   Irma Adelman and Song Byung Nak, "The Korean Financial Crisis of 1997–98,"
     http://72.14.207.104/search?q=cache:AcRsVU4f_LcJ:are.berkeley.edu/~adelman/crisis.
     pdf+1997+Korean+currency+devaluation&hl=en&gl=us&ct=clnk&cd=2.

24   Su-Dol Kang, "Labour Relations in Korea Between Crisis Management and Living
     Solidarity," *Inter-Asia Cultural Studies* 1, no. 3 (2000): 396.

25   National Statistics Office as quoted in Economic, Social, and Cultural Rights in the
     Republic of Korea, *Korea NGO Report to the United Nations* (April 2001): 10.

26   Byoung-Hoon Lee, "Militant Unionism in Korea," 159.

27   James Crotty and Kang-Kook Lee, "Korea's Neoliberal Restructuring: Miracle or
     Disaster?" (Amherst: Political Economy Research Institute, 2001), 3, http://www.peri.
     umass.edu/Publication.236+M5db02174714.0.html.

28   James Crotty and Kang-Kook Lee, "The Causes and Consequences of Neoliberal
     Restructuring in Post-Crisis Korea," in *Financialization and the World Economy*, ed.
     Gerald Epstein (Cheltenham, UK: Edward Elgar, 2005).

29   As a result of the IMF crisis, Thailand's stock market dropped by as much as 75 percent,
     its currency lost more than half its value, hundreds of thousands of urban workers
     returned to their villages, and more than half a million foreign laborers left the country.

30   Chang Ha-joon, "South Korea: The Misunderstood Crisis," in *Tigers in Trouble* (London:
     Zed Press, 1998), 229, 299.

31   Chang, *Labor in Globalizing Asian Corporations*, 43.

32   Bill Austin, "Glory, Shock, and Scandal," in *Korea Witness: 135 Years of War, Crisis and News in the Land of the Morning Calm*, eds. Donald Kirk and Choe Sang Hun (Seoul: EunHaeng NaMu, 2006), 326.

33   See Beverly Silver and Giovanni Arrighi, "The End of the Long Twentieth Century," paper presented at the International Conference on the 30th Anniversary of the Gwangju Uprising, May 26, 2010.

34   Bello and Rosenfield, *Dragons in Distress*, 63.

35   Walden Bello, "Afterthoughts: A Primer on the Wall Street Meltdown," http://walden-bello.org/content/view/100/30/.

36   Shin Gyoung-hee, "The Crisis and Workers' Movement In South Korea," *International Socialism* 78 (March 1998): http://pubs.socialistreviewindex.org.uk/isj78/gyounghe.htm.

37   Kristin Dawkins, *Global Governance: The Battle Over Planetary Power* (New York: Seven Stories Press, 2003), 59.

38   See James Petras, "Crisis, What Crisis? Profits Soar!" August 14, 2010, http://www.globalresearch.ca/index.php?context=va&aid=20620. Unlike the American crisis beginning in 2008, when a slump in the housing market precipitated financial insolvency of smaller sized companies and led to huge corporations taking them over, the East Asian crisis of 1997 began as financial problems of large manufacturing corporations weakened banks and credit markets in a "compound slump" of industrial and financial systems, requiring an IMF rescue package that benefited giant multinationals.

39   United Nations Development Program, *Human Development Report*, 1996 and 1999.

40   In 2010, 2 percent of humanity owned more than half the world's household wealth, and the richest 10 percent owned 85 percent of total global assets, while the bottom half of humanity owns less than 1 percent of the wealth in the world. Maude Barlow, *Democracy Now!*, July 2, 2010, http://www.democracynow.org/2010/7/2/maude.

41   Sang-young Rhyu, "Kim Dae Jung's Ideas and Documents: A Perspective of Political Economy," in *Democratic Movements and Korean Society: Historical Documents and Korean Studies* (Seoul: Yonsei University Press, 2007), 186.

42   Dae-oup Chang, "Korean Labour Relations in Transition: Authoritarian Flexibility?" *Labour, Capital and Society* 35, no. 1 (April 2002): 22.

43   *Democracy in Korea: The Roh Tae Woo Years* (New York: Carnegie Council on Ethics and International Affairs, 1992), 85.

44   The August 23 report also noted that workers in Lyon, France clocked only 1,582 hours per year on the job, while Asians averaged 2,119, Africans 2,063, South Americans 1,950 and North Americans 1,890. As a whole, Western Europeans enjoyed the shortest annual working hours with 1,745.

45   South Korea's government support for individuals placed the ratio of welfare spending to total government budget at an abysmal ranking of 132 in the world in 1997. Hochul Sonn, "The 'Late Blooming' of the South Korean Labor Movement," *Monthly Review* (July-August 1997).

46   See Sonn Hochul, "Neoliberalism and Democracy in South Korea," *Korean Political Science Review* 43, 75–92.

47   See Su-Dol Kang, "Information Technology and Labor Relations in South Korea," paper presented at the International Conference, LaborTech 2000, December 2, 2000, University of Wisconsin-Madison.

48   Dae-oup Chang, "Korean Labour Relations in Transition," 29.

49   See Asia Human Rights Commission, *Human Rights Solidarity* 11, no. 5 (May 2001): 14.

50   Interview with Kwak Tak-sung, Seoul, June 6, 2001.

51   Dae-oup Chang, "Korean Labour Relations in Transition," 31.

52   Kevin Gray, *Korean Workers and Neoliberal Globalization* (London: Routledge, 2007), 77. From 1987 to 2004, the cause of labor disputes dramatically shifted from wage increases (69.7 percent of all disputes in 1987 but only 12.1 percent in 2004) to contracts (from 27.7 percent in 1987 to 83.4 percent in 2004). During these same years, service sector strikes rose from 11.4 percent of the total to 34 percent. Union density (members as percentage of workforce) fell from a high of 19.8 in 1989 to just 11.0 in 2003.

53   Holger Heide, ed., *Sudkorea—Bewegung in der Krise* (Bremen: Atlantik, 1999), 105.

54   Byoung-Hoon Lee, "Militant Unionism in Korea," 165–66.

55   Ibid., 160.

56   Dae-oup Chang, *Labor in Globalizing Asian Corporations*, 45.

57   On November 9, 2009, the Korean government released figures claiming 34.9 percent of all employees were part-time, up from 32.6 percent in 2003. The reliability of these figures is uncertain. Most labor activists use the higher estimate of more than half of all employees being part-time.

58   Hagen Koo, "Engendering Civil Society," in *Korean Society: Civil Society, Democracy and the State*, ed. Charles Armstrong (London: Routledge, 2002), 89.

59   Koo, *Korean Workers*, 209.

60   The average wage of Koreans was 1,210,00 won; men made 1,390,000, and women averaged 810,000. See Mun-cho Kim, "Informatization and the Transformation of Women's Social Status in Korea," *Asian Women* 7 (December 1998): 141. Also see Amsden, *Asia's Next Giant*, 204.

61   Namhee Park, "Korean Women Workers' Activism," *Peace Review: A Journal of Social Justice* 18 (Winter 2006): 491–98.

62   *Korea Insight* 8, no. 5 (May 2006).

63   *Hankyoreh*, March 10, 2009.

64   Song-Woo Hur, "Mapping South Korean Women's Movements During and After Democratization: Shifting Identities," in *Gwangju Asian Human Rights Folk School* (Gwangju: 5.18 Memorial Foundation, 2009), 202.

65   See Mun-cho Kim, "Informatization and the Transformation," 141.

66   Meredith May, "A Youthful Mistake," part 2 of a 4-part report on global sex trafficking, *San Francisco Chronicle*, October 8, 2006, A6, http://www.sfgate.com/sextrafficking/.

67   Choe San-hun, "Ex-Prostitutes Say South Korea and U.S. Enabled Sex Trade Near Bases," January 7, 2008. The article reported that, "American military police and South Korean officials regularly raided clubs from the 1960s through the 1980s looking for women who were thought to be spreading the diseases. They picked out the women using the number tags the women say the brothels forced them to wear so the soldiers could more easily identify their sex partners. The Korean police would then detain the prostitutes who were thought to be ill, the women said, locking them up under guard in so-called monkey houses, where the windows had bars. There, the prostitutes were forced to take medications until they were well."

68   Hart-Landsberg, Jeong, and Westra, *Marxist Perspectives*, 17.

69   Sonn Hochul, "Neoliberalism and Democracy in South Korea," 81.

70   Don Kirk, "Bad Loans Imperil South Korean Growth, IMF Warns," *International Herald-Tribune*, November 16, 2000, 19.

71   "Carlyle Group's Asian Invasion," *Business Week Online*, February 14, 2005, http://www.businessweek.com/magazine/content/05_07/b3920143_mz035.htm.

72   William Sim and Michele Batchelor, "Lone Star to sell its stake in Korea Exchange Bank," *International Herald-Tribune*, January 13, 2006, http://www.iht.com/articles/2006/01/12/business/bxlone.php.

73   Tim Shorrock, "Crony Capitalism Goes Global," *Nation*, April 1, 2002. Carlyle's Asia advisory board also includes former Philippine president Fidel Ramos, former U.S.

national security advisor Frank Carlucci and former Korean prime minister Park Tae Joon.

74 Choe Sang-Hun, "Seoul Grows Wary of Foreign Investors," *International Herald-Tribune*, May 12, 2005, 18.

75 Ibid.

76 See "Will Lone Star, Other Foreign Funds Hit Back?" *Korea Times*, September 30, 2005.

77 Choe Sang-Hun, "Lone Star Convicted of Stock Fraud in South Korea," *International Herald Tribune*, February 1, 2008.

78 Mencius, "Humane Government," in *The Works of Mencius*, ed. James Legge (New York: Dover, 1970), 92. In Bruce Cumings's view, "Since both China and Korea share Confucian values, they have been able to maintain friendly relations for centuries. China gave more than it received" (*Korea's Place in the Sun*, 91).

79 Adam Smith, "How the Commerce of the Towns Contributed to the Improvement of the Country," *The Wealth of Nations*," http://www.econlib.org/library/Smith/smMS.html. Smith's critique of what we today name "neoliberalism" was first pointed out to me in Noam Chomsky, "Democracy and Education," Mellon Lecture, Loyola University, Chicago, October 19, 1994, http://www.zmag.org/chomsky/talks/9410-education.html.

80 Lee Chan-keun, "Korean Economy in Era of Globalization," *Korea Focus*, March–April 1999, 94.

CHAPTER 13

The Democratic Dilemma

There exists a broad consensus that the 'regime of 1987' (if we call by that name the general political, economic, and social order created by the June Struggle and its immediate aftermath) constitutes an order much superior to what preceded it, but that it was from the beginning an unstable structure based on a number of make-shift compromises, and has by now almost reached the end of its tether . . . All in all, one rarely hears a voice claiming the health of the '87 regime and its warrant for continued existence.

—Paik Nak-chung, 2007

The June struggle won procedural democracy, but that has grown empty as time goes on. Until now, we have been satisfied with the fact that we have come to choose our presidents through democratic procedures such as direct elections and the secret ballot, but now people want to go beyond those formal procedures and see the realization of substantive democracy.

—*Hankyoreh*, 2008

CHRONOLOGY	
June 13, 2002	Two schoolgirls killed by U.S. military vehicle
November 22, 2002	American servicemen found not guilty in U.S. military court
November 30, 2002	Candlelight vigils protesting U.S. presence in Korea begin
February 25, 2003	Noh Moo-hyun becomes president; calls for participatory government
October 31, 2003	President Noh Moo-hyun officially apologizes twice for 1948 Jeju massacre
November 11, 2003	Our Open (*Uri*) Party founded

March 15, 2004	Despite massive candlelight gatherings, Noh is impeached by National Assembly
April 15, 2004	Noh's *Uri* Party wins a majority in National Assembly elections
May 14, 2004	Noh's impeachment overturned by the Constitutional Court
July 1, 2006	Riot police attack legal strike of POSCO steelworkers; one killed
November 23, 2006	Further anti-FTA protests banned by Noh's government
April 12, 2007	FTA approved
October 4, 2007	Noh Moo-hyun meets Kim Jong-il in Pyongyang
December 19, 2007	Lee Myung-bak (2MB) elected
April 9, 2008	Lee's Hannara Party wins majority in National Assembly
May 2, 2008	High school girls hold first candlelight protest against U.S. beef
June 10, 2008	High point of candlelight vigils: more than one million people protest
June 30, 2008	Police raid PSPD and other NGO offices for first time
June 30, 2008	Dozens of Catholic priests hold outdoor mass at candlelight protest
December 10, 2008	Riot police prevent comfort women from assembling at Japanese Embassy
January 12, 2009	Lee government chooses Japanese company to launch ROK satellite
January 20, 2009	Six people killed and twenty-three injured when police attack Yongsan building occupation
May 22, 2009	Ssangyong Motors workers begin seventy-seven-day occupation
May 23, 2009	Former President Noh Moo-hyun commits suicide
November 10, 2009	Despite widespread disapproval, Lee government begins Four Rivers Project
March 26, 2010	South Korean Navy ship Cheonan sinks
May 24, 2010	President Obama gives ROK "unequivocal" support and orders U.S. military "readiness"
July 21, 2010	U.S. Secretary of State Clinton threatens North Korea with "serious consequences"
July 25, 2010	Massive flotilla of U.S. and South Korean ships conduct drills off the Korean coast

WITH THE DEMOCRATIC movement's many victories, South Koreans enjoyed greater liberties. Once the country recovered from the IMF crisis, it continued to make significant economic gains. In 2003, the "world's first Internet president," Noh Moo-hyun, was inaugurated. A decade under progressive presidents ensured the expansion of the economy and improvement of relations with the North. Simultaneously, as activists from social movements were incorporated into the government, conservatives mobilized a counteroffensive. In 2008, "New Right"

President Lee Myung-bak swept into office and immediately began to bulldoze away many of the gains made since the dark days of military dictatorship.

Enduring Power of Anti-Americanism

While many people thought that anti-Americanism would fade away, its enduring power continues to define the political landscape. In 2000, after several ugly incidents, the State Department advised Americans to refrain from traveling to South Korea.[1] On May 8, 2000, in Maehyang-ri (long used for machine gun and artillery practice by U.S. fighter planes), misplaced five-hundred-pound bombs put seven residents in hospital. Later that year, reports surfaced that illegal chemicals were dumped on a U.S. base into the Hangang River (the main water supply for Seoul's twenty million inhabitants)—a black mark subsequently popularized in the movie, *The Host*. In 2002, so serious was the threat of violence against Americans that President Kim Dae Jung decided to cancel his attendance at the World Cup game between the United States and South Korea in Taegu. A few days later, on June 13, 2002, two fourteen-year-old Korean schoolgirls on their way to a birthday party, Shim Mi-sun and Shin Hyo-sun, were run over and killed by a U.S. military vehicle, igniting a massive anti-American outcry.

People's anger at the killing of Mi-sun and Hyo-sun grew in a context of American service personnel committing thousands of illegal actions for which they were never prosecuted. The death of the two girls was a tragedy made all the worse because it symbolized a veritable crime spree committed by individual GIs (to say nothing of the division of Korea). According to the Korean government, from 1967 to 1987, the number of crimes by U.S. service people was 39,452—an average of 1,972 per year or five per day. In 1991, only 18 of 1,373 reported crimes committed by Americans serving in uniform were prosecuted.[2] From 2000, the number of such reported crimes decreased significantly to about five hundred per year.

In the case of Hyo-sun and Mi-sun, the soldiers responsible refused to stand trial in a Korean courtroom but instead were tried by the U.S. military under the auspices of the bilateral Status of Forces Agreement (SOFA) treaty. The two men had immediately taken shelter on a U.S. base, and not until days had passed did the United States identify them by name. In September 2002, as the trial approached, an altercation on a Seoul subway occurred after three low-ranking U.S. soldiers refused to take a leaflet offered to them about the killings. Although Privates Eric Own and Shane Tucker ran away, John Murphy was taken to a stadium and forced to agree publicly at a memorial gathering that the two GIs who had killed the girls should be tried in a Korean court, not in a U.S. military court. Murphy was then handed over by *Hanchongryun* members to police.[3] When the Korean police finally got involved, they charged the soldiers with assault and did nothing to those accused of kidnapping the American.

To no one's surprise in late November, the U.S. military courtroom found the drivers not guilty, even though another U.S. serviceman testified that he had screamed at them to slow down just before the accident. After their acquittal, the Korean media was finally given a first opportunity to speak directly to them,

On June 13, 2002, a U.S. military vehicle ran over and killed two 14-year-old schoolgirls, Shin Hyo-sun and Shim Mi-sun. After the U.S. soldiers responsible for their deaths were acquitted by a U.S. military court, months of candlelight vigils continued to protest. Photographer unknown

and, politely enough, reporters asked how they felt. The two GIs stated how glad they were to be going home but failed to express any remorse, an omission that shocked Koreans. Rather than offer the families any kind of sympathy, the men were completely self-absorbed.[4]

The acquittal set off more than six months of nightly candlelight vigils and protests at U.S. military installations. Although overwhelmingly peaceful, the candlelight protests also became the scene of burning of American flags and scuffles with riot police.

Public indignation became so intense that President Bush issued a formal apology in November. As awareness of rapes, burglaries, and other crimes committed by American soldiers grew, many Koreans questioned the viability of SOFA, especially since it exempts U.S. troops from local prosecution. In 2006, conflicts about the relocation of the U.S. base from Yongsan to Pyongtaek (about fifty miles south of Seoul) involved weeks of continuing protests and hundreds of arrests and injuries. More than fifteen thousand police were needed to subdue Pyongtaek residents and their supporters as houses were demolished to make room for the expansion of the U.S. base.

The above incidents reflect a much deeper problem—the very real possibility of another U.S. attack on Korea. Although most Americans remain completely unaware of it, in June 1994 the United States came close to bombing North Korea unilaterally. Only a last-minute trip by former president Jimmy Carter to Pyongyang averted a war that in the estimation of the U.S. military commander in Korea would have killed more than three million people.[5] In early 2002, President

George W. Bush not only labeled North Korea part of an "axis of evil," he also threatened to use nuclear weapons against it.[6] Even under the Obama administration, the United States maintains a crippling blockade and continues to threaten the North.

Since the ROK provided one of the largest contingents in support of the U.S. war in Iraq, many Americans assume that South Korean anti-Americanism is a negligible phenomenon. A poll of seven hundred people conducted by the Korean firm KSOI (Korean Society Opinion Institute) on September 13, 2005, indicated the opposite.[7] When asked what respondents thought the government of South Korea should do in the event of a U.S. attack on North Korea, nearly as many people responded that the ROK should help North Korea (40.9 percent) as felt their government should assist the United States (41.3 percent). Similarly, nearly half the respondents felt the U.S. military should withdraw from Korea (47.3 percent), while 51.6 percent thought the U.S. presence should remain intact; and the country named as most opposed to Korean unification was the United States (35.3 percent), followed by Japan (35.2 percent) and China (13.4 percent). Finally, more than half of those polled (53 percent) held the U.S. responsible for the division of Korea.

In this context, DJ's Sunshine Policy of engagement with North Korea drew wide support. Despite the political elite's best efforts to endear the United States to Koreans, anti-Americanism remains an enduring feature of the social landscape. An incongruous cultural and political alignment sometimes confuses people's perception. South Korea appears to be one of Asia's most philo-American lands, yet beneath the surface, great distrust exists. The ROK was created with an enormous amount of indispensable U.S. aid, and for decades, its economy benefited from privileged U.S. ties. Even progressive Presidents Kim and Noh fought to expand economic ties with the United States through a U.S.-ROK Free Trade Agreement (FTA). With the United States weakened in the era of globalization, however, several factors have negative consequences on Koreans' feelings toward the United States: Korea's vulnerability to world economic downturns, Americans' avaricious appetites, and continuing U.S. failure to resolve the lingering state of war with North Korea.

Korea's Coming Unification?

Reunification could well be a big part of the solution for Koreans on both sides of the DMZ. The South would gain an internal market, opportunities for expansion of production, and a disciplined workforce, while the North would benefit from new investments, high technology, and an end to the stifling U.S. blockade. Both countries would save untold billions of dollars in unnecessary defense expenditures. If the state of military preparedness were ended, enormous spiritual as well as material benefits would accrue. Tiny North Korea, the first country to hold its own in a war with the almighty United States, has been compelled to suffer more than half a century of continuing hostilities.

Koreans' traditional self-understanding as a shrimp among whales preconditions the involvement of outsiders in determining Korea's future through the

Six Party Talks, yet reunification can only be accomplished if Koreans themselves act to accomplish it. It is up to Koreans *to be independent* if they are to realize that goal. The superpowers surrounding Korea offer little support for unification. While Russia might gain better access to South Korean markets from a unified Korea, China benefits from North Korea acting as a buffer against U.S. ground troops and the possibility of renewed Japanese and American aggression. Mired in a lost decade of economic stagnation, Japan has no desire to see a reunified Korea that might surpass its own population and economic size. With a unified Korea, the United States would probably lose its last remaining military foothold on the East Asian continent. Already American policymakers have lobbied for a continuing U.S. presence even if the country were to reunify.

So long as the ROK ruling elite collaborates with Japan and the United States to split the country and mobilize against the DPRK, Korean independence will be compromised. Progress under Presidents Kim Dae Jung and Noh Moo-hyun was substantial, yet after Lee Myung-bak took office in 2008, relations with Pyongyang have become severely strained. The ominous possibility that Japan and the United States might again sacrifice Korea for the sake of their own economic well being, as both did in the twentieth century, remains real. A new Korean War would provide enormous opportunities for Japanese businesses to rebuild and for U.S. corporations to earn renewed profits.

A 2006 survey found that 85 percent of college students in South Korea desired the country's reunification.[8] Although more than half a century has passed since the nation's division, many Koreans continue to express a heartfelt desire for reunification of the country. Families continue to be divided with no possibility of even communicating with each other. Much more than in divided Germany—where I lived for seven years—people yearn for reunification, and some struggle desperately to achieve it. The Korean road to unification will be unlike Germany's "big bang." Part of the reason is their long-term perspective and inauguration of a step-by-step process that has already begun. Mount Kumgang tourism, the Kaesong industrial complex, family visits, rail link, sports competitions, and cultural exchanges are all part of a strategy worked out in 2000 at the summit between DJ and Kim Jong-il that would lead to a confederal structure (in which there would not be compulsion to observe decisions made by either state).[9] In contrast to German, Korean unification will be relatively progressive, in part because the country has been tragically and unjustly beset by the brutality of both Japanese and American imperialism, and the peninsula, united as a small nation for more than a millennium, was devastated, divided by foreign powers' rivalries, and its people dispersed.[10] Unlike Germany, which is a giant in its own region, Korea would remain a shrimp among whales.

The Noh Moo-hyun Presidency

Using the Internet, NGOs mobilized against conservative politicians. On January 12, 2000, the Citizens' Solidarity for General Elections was formed by 412 NGOs. Their blacklist of eighty-six candidates deemed resistant to democratic reform resulted in fifty-nine out of eighty-six politicians on the list losing in the 2000 general election. Success breeds expanded membership, and NGO networks grew extensively. One almanac counted 4,023 NGOs in 2000—more than twenty thousand if branches were also tabulated.[11] Hearing of this success in Korea, Japanese activists tried to replicate it without success. As Park Won-soon explained to me, "Years of struggle against the military dictatorship created many activists who know how to work together."[12]

DJ emphasized the need for everyone to learn English and have access to the Internet, thereby setting Korea on a torrid pace to become the "world's most wired society." One of the dividends of DJ's IT investments came when Noh Moo-hyun, former labor lawyer and long-time democratization activist, was elected to succeed him. Right after the presidential election, numerous domestic and international news media declared the victory of the world's first "Internet president." The *Guardian* in Britain reported, "South Korea will stake a claim to be the most advanced online democracy on the planet with the inauguration of a president who styles himself as the first leader fully in tune with the Internet." The *New York Times* observed, "People will be debating what made South Korea go from conservative to liberal, from gerontocracy to youth culture and from staunchly pro-American to deeply ambivalent—but for many observers, the most important agent of change has been the Internet."

Promising to continue DJ's Sunshine Policy of positive engagement with North Korea, Noh replaced DJ's "government of the people" with a "participatory government." Along with Noh, the 386 generation—those who were in their thirties after having been active in the 1980s and born in the 1960s—came to power with the 2002 elections. *OhmyNews*, with more than one million online readers per day and twenty-six thousand citizen-reporters at election time, played a major role, as did dozens of web portals and thousands of netizens. Although presidential candidates drawn from workers' organizations received surprisingly few votes, in 2002 (only two years after it formed), the Democratic Labor Party (DLP)—containing many long-time labor activists—became the first leftist party in ROK history to win seats in the National Assembly.

With Noh's defeat of his conservative opponent, a wide spectrum of progressive Koreans celebrated. So popular was Noh that a fan club grew from the grassroots, "People Who Love Noh" (*NohSaMo*) during the campaign. The campaign followed on the heels of massive peaceful gatherings during the 2002 World Cup co-hosted by the ROK, when hundreds of thousands of Red Devils fans wore bright red shirts (a clear swipe at the "red complex)." The country was deliriously happy with newfound freedoms and stability on the peninsula, and Noh's election promised to be the realization of many people's dreams. Not only did he swear to extend democratic liberties and bring Korean-American relations to a more even level, many people thought he might even reunify the country.

How quickly were Noh's supporters disappointed! Shortly after he took office in 2003, Noh Moo-hyun visited President George W. Bush in Washington, where, in true Korean fashion, Noh unnecessarily humbled himself and promised to send troops to Iraq. Upon his return to Korea, when he sought to visit Mangwoldong cemetery for the annual May 18 commemoration, radical students blocked the front entrance, making him walk the back path through old Mangwoldong. Later, at Chonnam National University, Noh made a short speech to hundreds of professors, after which he opened the floor to questions. I happened to be there, and was pleasantly surprised when the first questioner called upon was one of the radical students who had earlier confronted his caravan. Coming from the United States, where dissident students who get anywhere near the president are tasered rather than permitted to ask a question, I was somewhat impressed with Korean civil society's polite directness. Speaking with a quiet intensity, the student came directly to the point. Why had Noh failed to confront Bush about possible U.S. instigation of a second Korean War? Why did he agree to send troops without first letting the National Assembly debate? After all, the president's interrogator continued, Noh had run for office promising to bring ROK-U.S. relations to a new level. Thanking the student for his question, Noh rambled at length. He compared himself to Galileo, who recanted his views on heliocentrism in order to avoid torture for violating the church's teaching that the earth was the center of God's created universe. Noh pointedly exclaimed that without U.S. support, Korea's economy would collapse. For the sake of Koreans' well being, he was compelled to prostrate himself in front of Bush and agree to send troops to Iraq. He was on a slippery slope, and his slide saw his administration also approve National Defense Reform 2020, a plan to build a more high-tech armed forces and achieve military "cooperative, self-reliance" through increasing the annual defense budget between 6.3 and 9.9 percent, acquiring more than twenty new weapons systems, and maintaining standing armed forces of five hundred thousand. Estimates of the plan's total cost ran over $660 billion.

In fairness, Noh was an honest and decent man, a self-taught lawyer who valiantly defended workers for decades and compared himself to Abraham Lincoln (long before Barack Obama did the same). Although widely misunderstood as president, he made many important breakthroughs. He apologized twice to the people of Jeju for the 1948 massacre and officially changed the status of many victims of past military dictatorships into "heroes of the democracy movement." After his government found innocent the eight men executed by Park Chung-hee in the fabricated People's Revolutionary Party case in 1975, he apologized to the families and paid compensation. (The families created a foundation for activism with much of the proceeds.) Under Presidents Kim Dae Jung and Noh Moo-hyun, per capita income doubled and doubled again. They legalized autonomous trade unions, worked out a tripartite system (of business, unions, and government) to manage industrial relations, and permitted a wide range of protests. With Noh as president, the stock market increased 173 percent in value, real estate prices soared, and per capita income climbed above the $20,000 mark.

Despite glowing macroeconomic indicators, however, the economic conditions of many ordinary citizens worsened. As economic polarization increased, Korea remained a 20/80 society. The graph below indicates the growing divide between the income of the top 20 percent and the poorest 20 percent. Despite half the country's bitter opposition to it, Noh ratcheted up pressure to approve an FTA with the United States. So severely skewed did wealth distribution become, that

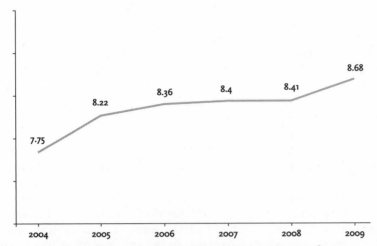

FIGURE 13.1 **Income Ratio of the Richest 20 Percent and Poorest 20 Percent of Koreans**
Source: National Statistics Office, as reported in Sonn Hochul, "Neoliberalism and Democracy in South Korea," *Korean Political Science Review* 43, no. 5, 87.

in 2006, *Hankyoreh* reported that only 1 percent of ROK population owned nearly 60 percent of the land.[13]

After years of overwhelmingly progressive policies and a long history as an advocate of labor, President Noh heavily repressed workers. In 1987, as Korea emerged from the wilderness of the Chun Doo-hwan years, only 18.5 percent of the workforce was unionized. By 2005, after years of progressive, civilian administrations, union density rate dropped to 10.3 percent.[14] In March 2006, the Korean Government Employees Union was declared illegal, and nearly a hundred trade union organizers were serving heavy prison sentences. At POSCO, Korea's largest steel producer, subcontractors employed 90 percent of workers, an arrangement that made it difficult for unions to negotiate. When workers went on strike on July 1, 2006, Noh sent in thousands of riot police to attack their legal protests, and dozens of strikers were arrested or injured. One worker, Ha Jung-keun, died from being beaten by police metal shields. On a separate occasion, family members were attacked, causing one wife to miscarry. More than a month after the strike started, sixty-three union members were in prison, two hundred had been injured, and one lay dead.

Alongside his misguided labor policies were other equally enormous political mistakes. Before his election, Noh insisted he would abolish the National Security Law. Although Noh disappointed his progressive base, he frightened conservative opponents even more, and they organized a counteroffensive. On March 12, 2004, President Noh was impeached by the conservative-dominated National Assembly, but thousands of his supporters rallied in candlelight vigils and mobilized the country to resoundingly win the parliamentary elections the next month. Again using the Internet against conservatives, in 2004, NGO groups helped defeat 78 of 106 targeted candidates.[15] When the votes were in, Noh's *Uri* Party held slightly more than 50 percent of the votes in the Assembly (152 of the 299 seats in parliament), an astonishing victory for a party formed six months before the elections. For the first time in sixteen years, the president's party controlled the National Assembly. Moreover, the Far-Left DLP won ten seats (two outright majorities in districts and eight from proportional representation), and altogether, more than ten former officers in the radical students' group *Chondaehyop* held seats.[16]

Incredibly, despite his party's absolute majority, Noh could muster neither the will nor the majority needed to overturn the NSL. There was never a better chance to get rid of the NSL, yet the matter was not even brought to a vote before the full assembly, a fundamental failure that left the door open to rollback of democratic rights. Under Noh, the NSL continued to be used to imprison radical activists. Years of *Hanchongryun* struggles against "democratic" governments compelled more than 180 students, wanted by police, to live as underground members of an increasingly marginalized organization.[17] Their ranks were continually being increased by the police's capricious use of the NSL. In 2003, Kim Yong-chan and Kim Jong-gon, two student members of the DLP, were arrested under the NSL's Article 7. As part of the evidence that these Konkuk University students engaged in "enemy-benefiting" activity, the government cited their possession and use of Marx's *Capital*, Louis Althusser's *For Marx*, and my book, *The Imagination of the New Left: A Global Analysis of 1968*. Apparently, the students quoted sections of these books in a pamphlet they wrote and distributed in a neighborhood slated for demolition. Besides caving in on the NSL and kowtowing to Bush, Noh acquiesced to Chinese pressure and denied a visa for the Dalai Lama to attend a gathering of Nobel Laureates. After massive protests against the FTA in December 2006, polls showed more than half of all Koreans opposed the treaty, yet Noh stood by while Korean police banned all future anti-FTA demonstrations, thereby abrogating people's right of freedom of assembly.

Is it any wonder that by the time he left office, his approval ratings were in the single digits? Under Noh's leadership, an inverse relation of progressive government and social movements' strength was noteworthy. By incorporating so many progressive activists into his administration, his administration dampened street protests. As professionalized NGOs replaced street protests, the movement was depoliticized. At the same time, by disillusioning nearly all progressive forces in the country through his obstinate drive to get the FTA approved before he left office, Noh not only lost his base of support, he transformed many people into drop-outs from passionate *NohSaMo* partisans. His *Uri* Party disappeared as a significant force, and its remnants merged into other parties. The depoliticization of the student movement was an ironic by-product its own achievements in the 1980s. Here lies proof that even the most mundane "laws" of history are not universally valid. Although Charles Tilly preached that democracy is always good for social movements, in Korea's case, the reverse has also been true.

Despite his many shortcomings, Noh's presidency shines in comparison to his predecessors in office. Although Noh had been singularly unpopular while in office, in retirement, he became remarkably loved, and for months in 2008, thousands of people visited him in his home village. Of Noh's fellow ex-presidents, Chun Doo-hwan was disgraced for his role in the Gwangju massacre and considered publicly mendacious for having secreted away hundreds of millions of dollars in defiance of court orders to return the money. Although he returned nearly half a billion dollars, Roh Tae-woo lived a furtive existence. YS and DJ, Noh's two immediate predecessors, saw their names tarnished in the public eye by way of their children's corruption: one son of YS went to prison for bribery, and all three of DJ's sons were convicted of corruption. For well over a year after he left office, Noh basked in the affection of his supporters.

2MB Government

Under presidents Kim Dae Jung and Noh Moo-hyun, per capita income doubled and doubled again. Nonetheless, the conservative media felt the economy was not performing well enough, and many people agreed. As the presidential elections of 2007 approached, progressive forces failed to produce either a meaningful alternative or a charismatic candidate. Although half the country was against the FTA, no major candidate emerged to oppose it. With progressives divided, conservatives put forth several well-known political leaders. When the dust settled on their selection process, Park Gun-hye (daughter of Park Chung-hee) was narrowly edged out by a former mayor of Seoul, Lee Myung-bak (born in Japan and known as the bulldozer from his days as a Hyundai construction executive under founder Chung Ju-young). As mayor, Lee modernized Seoul's bus system—no small feat—and restored a stream through the city center that had long been covered by concrete and steel. His "747" election program promised that the country's growth rate would be 7 percent per year, per capita annual income would double once again to $40,000, and Korea would be the world's seventh-largest economy.

Lee's promises seduced many voters, and with 48.7 percent of the tally, he won the 2007 presidential election. Despite text-message voting being allowed for the first time, voter turnout was a record low of only 62.9 percent, well below the 70.1 percent in 2002—and far below the participation rates of 89.2 percent in 1987, 81.9 percent in 1992, and 80.7 percent in 1997. Regional differences, a major factor in past elections, were evident again. Yet the main story was the low turnout. With fewer than 31 percent of eligible voters affirming him as their choice, Lee became president.

A few months later, in National Assembly elections, Lee's *Hannara* Party won an outright majority with 153 seats in the 299-member parliament. If we add the Right's total, they captured more than 200 seats, while the opposition Unified Democratic Party, which formed as Noh Moo-hyun's *Uri* Party disintegrated, won only 81 seats, and the DLP received five. (With 5.6 percent or 973,345 votes, the DLP's five seats were half their previous total. NL forces had taken control of the party, compelling PD members—who had founded it in the first place—to split off into a new party, the Progressive New Party, in order to distance themselves from North Korea. Formed only a few weeks before the election, the party won 2.94 percent, just below the 3 percent threshold for proportionally allocated seats.) As in the presidential elections, the real story was voter apathy. In 2008, more than half of voters abstained as only 46 percent of those eligible bothered to cast ballots.[18] Looking at TABLE 13.1, we see a clear pattern of falling voter turnout.

TABLE 13.1 **Voter Participation in National Assembly Elections**

Year	Participation Rate	Comments
1988	76 percent	Soon after June Uprising
1992	72 percent	
1996	64 percent	
2000	57 percent	
2004	60 percent	One month after Noh Moo-hyun impeached
2008	46 percent	17,389,206 out of 37,795,035

The trend of declining electoral participation reflects a lack of interest in government, a feature of Korea's Americanization. While intense political struggles in 1987 and against Noh's impeachment in 2004 produced jumps in voter participation rates, voter apathy was the response to routinization of politics in 2008 when both major parties accepted the FTA. One key reason why conservatives came to dominate the vote is declining interest in mainstream politics after the Noh Moo-hyun presidency. Reflected in the historically low turnout of only 46 percent, the depoliticization of the public opened the door for the New Right's rollback of democratic gains.

The Lee Myung-bak (2MB) administration wasted little time in seeking to roll back the clock of progressive democratic reforms won by South Koreans through decades of arduous struggles. Fifteen days after Lee's inauguration in January 2008, officials forcibly removed members of a part-time workers' union from an ongoing sit-in demonstration. Simultaneously, the new government released imprisoned leaders of *chaebol* (the giant corporations that control much of the Korean economy) who had been convicted of corruption under President Noh Moo-hyun; they stepped up prosecution of immigrant workers who overstayed their visas; and policymakers announced a design for a new Seoul police unit of 1,700 specially trained riot police. President Lee announced plans to replace the forty-thousand-strong police force filled with military conscripts with a more streamlined version—to which he will add fourteen thousand more elite men. For many people, this policy, like many others of the 2MB government, resembles those of disgraced former dictator (and Lee's friend) Chun Doo-hwan. (In this case, Lee's plan resembles the *Baekgoldan*—white skull corps—established by Chun.)

An ardent admirer of former U.S. president George W. Bush, Lee visited Bush at Camp David on April 19, 2008, only a few months after he became president. After driving Bush's golf cart around the compound, Lee promised that evening to lift Seoul's five-year ban on U.S. beef. Although in much of the world, President George W. Bush is rightly understood as having swept away all remnants of the Washington Consensus (even celebrated in some places for his role as a "second Lenin" in nearly destroying capitalism), Lee and the South Korean New Right viewed Bush sympathetically and emulated some of the same Bush-era policies that proved disastrous for the United States and the world economy. Grassroots people proved more insightful about the direction the country should take. Despite Lee's easy win in the election for president in 2007, his decision to

Massive candlelight protests in 2008 compelled the government to renegotiate a beef deal with the United States. Photographer unknown

open the floodgates on American beef set off months of candlelight vigils that subsequently compelled him to modify his capitulation to U.S. demands for unlimited exports. "What he did was little different from an ancient Korean king offering tribute to a Chinese emperor," commented homemaker Kim Sook-yi. "This time we give tribute to Washington?"[19]

2008 Korean Candlelight Protests

On May 2, 2008, hundreds of teenage girls suddenly demonstrated in downtown Seoul against new unlimited importation of American beef—taking the country (including police and movement activists) by surprise. Using text messages and the Internet, high school girls organized themselves without any apparent leaders. They demanded an end to new policies implemented by their government, especially those allowing U.S. "Mad Cow" beef to be imported with almost no restrictions. Innocently enough, Internet fan sites for television personalities were the forums that initially helped create the mobilizations. Once Korean youth acted, they found a populace ready to respond. An anonymous high school student began a petition on *Agora* (a popular online forum) calling for President Lee's impeachment. Within a week, it gathered 1.3 million signatures. Lee was seen as so brainlessly pursuing his own misplaced agenda that after the high school girls who led the first candlelight protests dubbed him "2MB"—the slowest operating speed of a modern computer, as well as a play on his family name, which can also mean "two"—the nickname stuck.

As if out of thin air, a dazzling surge of protests erupted. For more than two months, daily candlelight vigils were organized around the country. By June 10, more than a million Koreans had protested in the streets. Despite continual government raids on offices, confiscation of computers, arrests, and travel bans on "key" individuals, the candlelight vigils went on until August 15—one hundred times in all.

As during the 1987 June Uprising, people spontaneously returned day after day in front of Seoul City Hall. A hastily assembled coalition of NGOs formed to coordinate the logistics for the gathering, and took the name People's Countermeasure Council Against the Full Resumption of Imports of U.S. Beef Endangered with Mad Cow Disease. Within a few weeks, more than 1,700 civic groups endorsed the council.

Despite NGO help, autonomous protesters were the ones who set the agenda and improvised the slogans. In their size and content, the rallies grew larger and more militant. By the end of May, the most popular sign people carried called for 2MB to resign. On May 31, the crowd swelled to a hundred thousand (Seoul police officials estimated half that number), and in at least ninety other cities, tens of thousands of citizens took to the streets. After 8 p.m. that night, people in Seoul spontaneously set off in the direction of the presidential office. For the first time in the month of rallies, riot police used water canons and fire extinguishers against unarmed demonstrators and arrested at least 165. Another sixty-three people were detained when they again tried to march toward the Blue House. At dawn, protesters were sprayed by water cannons near the entrance to the Blue House. Dozens of injuries were reported on both sides. About a thousand college students from Gwangju and Busan arrived in Seoul to join the rallies, and the Korean Confederation of Trade Unions announced a general strike.[20]

In response to the government's escalation of violence, people created a seventy-two-hour festival of resistance the next weekend. Bands played, families and groups of workers wore similar outfits, while students danced in precisely

The author and fellow activists spoke out at a candlelight rally on June 10, 2008.
Photographer: Choi Seong-uk

synchronized movements. Without anyone organizing it, many people shared food with their neighbors in the gathering. A group of children with water guns laughingly attacked police buses, bringing smiles even to the faces of young riot policemen. People's festivities successfully prevented the government from isolating protesters from families. Although the Lee administration remained deaf to the outcry, more than one millon people mobilized on June 10. The next weekend, the president's entire cabinet offered to resign.

Despite a renegotiation of the beef deal with the United States, people continued to congregate in the streets, using the Internet to mobilize, and coordinating their actions in cyberspace. Police sought to contain the protests, but people's diffuse energies were difficult to control. At one point, when rope was needed to pull police buses out of the way, someone posted a real-time request for rope using a cell phone. With a few minutes, many ropes appeared, and the buses were moved. When police brought in cargo containers filled to capacity as barricades, people climbed atop them with banners and microphones, thereby turning them into stages from which the people of "free" Korea could be protected from their "domineering" counterparts. Dubbed "street protests 2.0" and the cyberactivism of "H-generation" (Hyperspace), teenage girls had quickly mobilized the entire nation. Union members, progressive military veterans, Catholics, Protestants and Buddhists all began to march. Even one contingent of women wearing miniskirts took to the streets. Dozens of ordinary people who broadcast live coverage of the protests became overnight television celebrities. "Embedded" citizens using camcorders and Internet broadcasts became a more reliable source of information than the mainstream media. When police beat a Seoul National University student, video footage posted on the Internet caused several officers to be dismissed. Even the conservative press began quoting citizen reporters. Via websites, the president's new nickname found its way into the mainstream.

The new form of leaderless protests empowered people directly. Looking at the "candlelight revolution" in Korea, the same elements of direct democracy that emerged in Gwangju appeared, but this time in demilitarized space as an "eros effect" set off by a national crisis. Leaderless rallies featured open-mics with participants from all walks of life. Rotation of the rallies' main organizers encouraged participation of many different groups rather than the stifling control of a central coterie of prominent citizens. New sectors of the population—from middle school girls to religious leaders, progressive military veterans, mothers pushing baby carriages and unionized workers—brought dynamism to the protests as they joined in. Marching to their own beat, people's diversity of tactics and slogans was remarkable. The wide variety of forms of protest revealed inner tensions and differences in the movement. Far from being reflective of weakness, these differences spring from diversity—and hence strength—a vibrant inner dialectic which motivated development and progress. The Professors' Union summed up a common sentiment: "We think the current situation is similar to that of June 1987, but the government appears not to recognize this."

On June 11, *Hankyoreh* newspaper editorialized that "The June struggle won procedural democracy, but that has grown empty as time goes on. Until now, we have been satisfied with the fact that we have come to choose our presidents through democratic procedures such as direct elections and the secret ballot, but now people want to go beyond those formal procedures and see the realization of substantive democracy. In other words, people are not going to let a president have his way with the country, while ignoring the will of the people because the election is over." The paper concluded by noting that the most popular song at the demonstrations is "Article One of the Constitution: South Korea is a democratic country, and power comes from the people."

On June 10, police conducted an early morning raid on the offices of PSPD—the first time the NGO had been searched. The administration launched a media campaign blaming PSPD for the protests, yet despite the major media echoing police fabrications, most people knew the actions began with teenage girls—not the established veterans of decades of street protests. While PSPD had helped organize a coalition of over 1,700 civic groups who worked together after the protests began, citizen participants were none too friendly to existing organizations. One PSPD organizer related to me that people had booed their spokesperson off the stage. On June 29, the government warned people not to attend rallies, saying police were going to break them up using force. Netizens reported that already police were attacking isolated groups on June 28, when fifty-three people were arrested and more than three hundred injured by riot police. Even when protesters lay down peacefully, riot police trampled them, beat them with their shields, and used their truncheons on them causing many serious injuries.[21] That night, police and demonstrators grappled in the streets. People snatched fire hoses away from police, hooked them up to hydrants, and won temporary control. When it appeared that the weeks-long festival-like atmosphere would become violent, dozens of Catholic priests converged in the streets on June 30 to conduct an open-air religious service amid tens of thousands of people. There was nothing the police could do to stop that day's gathering since it was clearly a religious ceremony and could not to be banned as a public protest. Protests continued until August 15, but as the government increasingly used violence against peaceful protesters and arrested dozens of people identified as organizers, they came to an end. On July 7, six organizers wanted by police took refuge inside Jogye Temple. The police response was to stop all vehicles leaving the temple—including that of one of Korea's most venerable monks—setting off massive protests by two hundred thousand Buddhists.

All in all, during more than a hundred days, a total of 1,332 people were arrested, and thirty-two were convicted and sentenced to prison. Some short-term changes were won: the beef deal was altered and top officials forced to resign. Twice 2MB apologized, but most people doubted his sincerity since he insisted on continuing U.S. beef imports. In the course of the protests, longer term issues emerged: Gwangju high school students threatened to go on strike if teachers continued to beat and swear at them; around the country, students began to publicly question the pressures they face to study around the clock and the consequent denial of adolescent playtime; tens of thousands of auto workers went on strike because of U.S. beef imports and job related issues. Most significantly, high school girls became the inspirational leaders of the world's most Confucian society. Their protests transformed a demoralized and despondent populace, giving people renewed hope. While the government tried to blame protesters for everything including the economic crisis, it became increasingly clear to ordinary Koreans from all walks of life that these girls had people's health interests at heart, while 2MB, George W. Bush, and their associates were leading the world to disaster.

The schoolgirls who led the first protests deserve more than simply a verbal acknowledgment. If it were in my power, I would build a monument to them so that future generations will continue to be inspired by their example. The 2MB administration had another tribute in mind: criminalization and crackdown in cyberspace. Lee was so angered by people's protests that he fell in with his most conservative supporters. Among them was a right-wing coalition formed that enlisted the government's aid in combating demonstrations. Among other measures, the government encouraged lawsuits against NGOs, claiming merchants suffered losses as a result of protests and, since protesters never received permits for using Seoul Plaza (they were denied by the government), that NGOs should pay for garbage cleanup. PSPD activists also faced arrest for their roles, creating a crisis for the group. It is not only PSPD that came under attack, but the very idea of democratic dissent.

President Lee's Rollback of Reforms

Under Noh Moo-hyun's leadership, a Truth and Reconciliation Commission made enormous strides in investigating tens of thousands of state-sanctioned murders during the Cold War. The 2MB government marginalized the commission and limited its purview and longevity. Its final report refused to place blame for tens of thousands of victims massacred half a century ago by the U.S. and Rhee regime. On Jeju, the 2MB government reopened old wounds by insisting some of the 1948 victims were, in fact, Communists—who presumably should not be considered part of the democratization movement. Additionally, 2MB has abolished the official commission investigating Korean collaborators during Japanese colonial rule and cut the budget of the country's Human Rights Commission.

In August 2008, the government announced its decision to build eleven more nuclear power plants by 2030 and proposed a Grand Canal to cut across the peninsula—both of which are widely considered to be ecological nightmares. After popular protests against his canal scheme forced Lee publicly to promise not to build it, he nonetheless continued the project through a revised "Four Rivers Plan." After 2MB's first Minister of Economics was compelled to resign for incompetence, his replacement has been even more forceful in pushing tax cuts for the rich, privatizing the public sector (including in education and health care), expanding labor market "flexibility" (that is, part-time work with no benefits), and relaxing business and financial regulations. "MB-nomics" has slashed wages for new employees and seeks to extend the two-year cap for temporary workers as well to shrink current restrictions on hiring of part-time employees.

Of all the troubling initiatives undertaken by the 2MB government, none is more unsettling than its offensive against the media. In July 2008, MBC television producers were taken to court for alleged exaggerations in a documentary on

U.S. beef imports, and when they refused to show up, over the next ten months, they were arrested one by one as they went about their daily lives (including a bride-to-be planning her wedding). In August, the KBS president was forced to resign—even briefly detained—and replaced with Lee's crony. A friend of the president was named to head Arirang, Korea's English channel. The twenty-four-hour all-news cable station YTN was sent a new president. When union leaders and members sought to block him from coming to work, police intervened. Union leaders were repeatedly summoned for questioning. Even though they complied four times, they were arrested. The Internet also came under close scrutiny. On July 24, Google Korea confirmed it had been pressured to delete two pieces of video footage showing the brother of the National Police Commissioner managing a hotel that allowed prostitution.[22] Minerva, a blogger who had correctly reported on the global crisis and embarrassed the government by revealing its incompetent handling of the economy, was tracked down and prosecuted (although subsequently exonerated). After the government implemented new restrictive requirements for real name Internet postings, in early May 2009, Internet writer and poet Yang Hyung-ku was arrested on charges of violating the National Security Law. Yang had posted hundreds of articles, including a few dozen advocating a federation model for Korean unification and *Juche* thought.[23]

The president and his cronies may be free to pressure the media, but when ordinary citizens do so, it is evidently a crime. A citizens' boycott against the country's conservative newspapers (*Chosun Ilbo*, *Joongang Ilbo*, and *Dong-A Ilbo*) was declared illegal, and charges filed against its Internet organizers, whose passports were seized even before proceedings began. The government's attempt to control the media is so intense that it has criminalized even citizens who hold press conferences. "New Right" ideologues are delighted. Fashioning themselves after U.S. neoconservatives, they revised newly rewritten textbooks that broke ground by denying the role of the democracy movement in the country's progress. The New Right helped produce an "updated" government Korean history video, distributed widely to schoolteachers, which did not include mention of the Gwangju Uprising as part of Korean democratization. Ahead of a formal investigation, 2MB's New Right supporters have already labeled the entire 1948 Jeju Uprising "Communist" as part of their more general campaign to revive the "red complex."

Besides bolstering Lee's tarnished image, another reason for the 2MB government's attacks on media and revision of history is to cover its new close relations with Japan. For ten years, progressive administrations cultivated ties with China—now Korea's main trading partner. 2MB seeks to undo that legacy and reorient the country closer to Japan—following in the footsteps of dictators Park Chung-hee and Chun Doo-hwan. Born in Japan where he used the name, Akihiro Tsukiyama, 2MB personally met an average of once every month during his first years in office with Japan's prime minister. He refuses to tolerate even mild protests against his Japanese friends. On December 10, 2008, the sixtieth anniversary of the UN Universal Declaration of Human Rights, his government sent six police buses of riot police to dismantle a peaceful protest by former "comfort women" and their supporters in front of the Japanese embassy in Seoul. Although the weekly one-hour vigils have gone on since 1992, the government declared the rally illegal because no one had applied for a permit. Furthermore, the police now insist no demonstration can take place within three hundred meters of the Japanese embassy.

On January 12, 2009, at his monthly summit with Japanese Prime Minister Aso, Lee announced that Mitsubishi Heavy Industries, a Japanese company that has ignored demands of hundreds of Korean women to be paid for forced labor during the period of Japanese colonization, was selected to launch a South Korean satellite in 2011. Although Mitsubishi rejected technology transfer as part of its offer, Lee personally ordered the change in the contract from a Russian company, which had included technology transfer. Lee was reported to favor "strengthening South Korea's economic relationship with Japan to shake off its blow from the global financial crisis."[24] At a time when China is the region's rising economic powerhouse and Japan has been mired in economic doldrums for a decade, Lee rivals Inspector Cousteau in finding clues on how to carry the Korean economy forward. Of course, he is not alone in his adulation of Japan. Others see in Korea a "facsimile" of Japan, "a superior, homogeneous nation uniquely fit among Asians to the tasks of the modern world."[25] Cooperating with Japan against North Korea is a shameful action for any Korean patriot, but the president makes no apologies—leading many people to question his loyalties.

Not only did 2MB alienate North Korea (which nullified the contract for the Kaesong Industrial Complex and accelerated its nuclear program), but also his stubborn imposition of his cronies in high positions has opened a wide split within conservative ranks. True to his nickname, "the bulldozer," 2MB refuses to compromise with critics—even within his own party. Instead he and the New Right are opening a new era in Korean politics, in which forceful implementation of unpopular and questionable policies runs roughshod over dissent and chews up anyone standing in its path. On May 20, 2009, during a press conference presided over by Prime Minster Han Seung-soo, the government announced its unilateral decision to discontinue permits for large demonstrations in cities and empowered police to arrest anyone committing the now illegal act of meeting in public. In Prime Minister Han's words, "The government intends to counter illegal strikes and violent demonstrations that could have negative effects on the nation's economy. To reach the level of an advanced nation, it is necessary to correct the backwardness of our demonstration culture."[26]

With the country in crisis, the value of the Korean currency fell by more than 50 percent against the dollar in 2009—a boondoggle for *chaebol* sales abroad but hardship for many others. Lee Myung-bak's hard-line policy against the North caused relations to deteriorate far more than anyone had expected—especially since he promised to deal with the DPRK pragmatically before he was elected. Instead of an even-handed policy, he has continually united with Japanese leaders to marginalize and isolate the DPRK—a shameful betrayal of the national interest in the eyes of many Koreans. Indeed, it was reported in major Japanese newspapers that he agreed in principle that Dokdo Island should become part of Japan, but that the time was not yet "ripe" for him to publicize his position.

Noh Moo-hyun's Suicide

In the United States, it is often thought that presidents make wars to divert hostile public opinion. In Korea, faced with widespread opposition to his presidency, Lee ordered his prosecutors to seek corruption charges against former president Noh Moo-hyun. When it was publicly revealed that his wife had taken a small sum of money from a businessman, Noh voluntarily met with investigators and openly discussed his finances, but prosecutors used the mainstream media to portray his wife's indiscretion as somehow indicative of the former president's corrupt character. As the combined assault of the government and mainstream media refused to relent, Noh Moo-hyun took his own life in protest on May 23, 2009, leaving South Korea in shock. All over the country, tearful people sought to eulogize and memorialize him—to find ways to express their grief and anger. Conservative government politicians were blocked by local residents from joining tens of thousands people who made the journey to Noh's small hometown the day he died. Not only were they refused admittance, many people splashed them with water and screamed at them to get out—shaming them into leaving. Opposition party spokesperson Kim Yu-jeong expressed what was in many people's hearts when he blamed Noh's tragic death on the conservative government's relentless and disrespectful offensive against him: "The people and history know what made the former president do something so tragic."

During his presidency, Noh had often compared himself to Abraham Lincoln (about whom he wrote a book). Both men owed their education to diligent home schooling and sought to bring new progressive policies to their countries. While Lincoln's life was taken by an assassin's bullet, Noh's tragic fate was no less tied to vengeful attackers. A former aide declared, "The late President Noh had appeared to be exhausted from the prosecutors' investigation."[27] As Lee's government tightened its stranglehold on the nation's democracy, police buses encircled a memorial site for Noh at Seoul's Deoksugung Palace. Riot squads refused to open a cordon of buses blockading the memorial, compelling thousands of people bringing incense and prayers to line up through subway stations. Nearly a thousand police were deployed at Deoksugung; altogether over eight thousand police were sent into the streets for crowd control.[28]

In 2008, South Korea's suicide rate was already counted as the highest among OECD members. Although Noh's suicide resulted directly from Lee Myung-bak's pursuit of all who did not march in lockstep with his new conservative government's programs and policies, he was not alone. On May 3, 2008, union leader Park Jong-tae, head of Korea Cargo Transport Workers' Union (KCTWU) in Gwangju, killed himself to protest the unilateral firing without discussion of 78 delivery drivers for Korea Express's Gwangju branch (which has the largest number of labor union members in the company). The government refused to agree to engage in dialogue with the KCTU and KCTWU. After Park took his own life, Labor Minister Lee Young-hee publicly ridiculed his suicide, saying at a press conference that he did not think the labor conflict was significant enough to end one's life over.[29] Adding that the government would not hold talks with groups engaging in such "illegal acts" as demonstrations, the Labor Minister's remarks were echoed by President Lee's similar refusal to speak directly with trade union leaders. The hard-line intensified when police announced arrest warrants for seven union leaders who led the memorial rallies for Park Jong-tae on May 6. Ten days later, at least 457 workers were arrested at a demonstration in Daejeon when fifteen thousand union members gathered to mourn Park and demand reinstatement of fired delivery drivers. According to the legal director of the KCTWU, after police recklessly attacked the dispersing demonstrators, they even arrested people who were eating dinner or on their way home.[30]

Seeming to have no concern for the downtrodden, police moved resolutely against citizens in Yongsan who occupied their businesses after the buildings were slated for demolition. As riot police swarmed over the building on January 20, 2009, fires suddenly exploded, killing six people (including one policeman) and injuring twenty-three others. When investigators sought to determine the cause of the tragedy, police lied about using hired thugs as part of their assault team, and the government was caught manipulating polls indicating disapproval of their actions. For five months, the government stonewalled bereaved family members, who were compelled to wait nearly a year for the corpses of their loved ones to be released from police custody.

The Yongsan tragedy was overshadowed by rising tensions with North Korea. On March 26, 2010, the South Korean Navy ship *Cheonan* split in two and sank, killing forty-six sailors. Although South Korea and the United States quickly blamed the DPRK for the attack, this incident was part of more than a decade of firefights along the contested "Northern Limit Line" in the sea between the two Koreas. In 1999, at least seventeen North Korean sailors lost their lives in a firefight there, and in 2002, six South Korean and thirteen North Korean sailors perished in another confrontation. Continuing American pressure was ratcheted up by President Obama on May 24, 2010, when he asserted "unequivocal" support for the Lee government and ordered heightened U.S. military "readiness." On July 21, 2010, as U.S. and South Korean navies conducted massive shows of strength in both the East and West Seas, U.S. Secretary of State Clinton threatened North Korea with "serious consequences" if it interfered with the American naval build-up on its borders.

The Korean Wave

During the sunshine decade of progressive presidents, the number of workers' disputes went down, and activists seemed to lose interest in politics, while Korean culture suddenly became internationally popular. A Korean Wave (*hallyu*) swept forth from the country's shores. Throughout much of East and South Asia, Korean music, television, and movies became even more demanded than domestic productions. Even in parts of Africa and the Americas, new installments of Korean television series were eagerly awaited, and movie theaters featured Korean films in which surprisingly robust civil relationships were revealed. The gentle depth of traditional civil networks and subtle Confucian values helped create a human-centered value system that had universal appeal in a world yearning for alternatives to the individualistic cultures of "rationally" seeking to maximize private gains and profits. Korea's bloody history during the long twentieth century apparently steeled survivors to rebuild and strengthen their material and cultural infrastructures. Long before the more recent *Hallyu* Wave, North Korea's *Juche* Wave in the 1970s elicited enthusiasm in Africa, the Middle East, and even among activists in the United States. The Black Panther Party widely accepted Kim Il-sung's theories and required members to study his ideas, *juche* (self-reliance) in particular. In Cambridge, Massachusetts, in 1970, an organization emerged that named itself *Juche*. The group worked closely with the Panthers, published a newspaper called *Juche*, started the first Cambridge food co-op, and supported a movement bookstore ("The Red Book"—today the anarchist Lucy Parsons Center).

Alongside *hallyu's* enormous cultural impact, the inspiration for democratic uprisings in other parts of Asia provided by Gwangju and the June Uprising is another dimension of Korean energy breaking upon distant shores. Korean farmers' prominence at international protests against the WTO in Cancun in 2003 and Hong Kong in 2005 were examples of Koreans' global leadership in the struggle against neoliberalism. From 4.19 to 5.18, from the Great June Uprising and Great Workers Struggle to the conviction and imprisonment of Chun Doo-hwan and Roh Tae-woo, the self-formation of the Korean *minjung* is one of the great accomplishments of the last half of the twentieth century—perhaps even surpassing Korea's spectacular economic growth. While many commentators have already announced the decline of *hallyu*, powerfully creative cultural forces and grassroots political dynamics have yet to run their course.

The interplay of contemporary aesthetic forms (movies, television, and music) with traditional social values is what gives the Korean wave its exhilarating power. In the view of actress Jung-Sook Park, *hallyu* functions as a kind of grassroots diplomacy, a consumer-driven people-to-people form of international relations.[31] Unlike state-to-state hierarchies and elite-driven forms of relationships, *hallyu's* political potential includes the proliferation of *minjung* activist experiences to other countries. At the same moment, *hallyu* functions as a vehicle for international legitimation of *chaebol* expansion to markets and domains previously untouched by Korean industry. Without the *chaebol* to produce and market *hallyu's* cultural products, it would hardly have had the kind of international popularity it enjoys in Vietnam, China, Japan, the Philippines, and elsewhere. Directly and indirectly, Korean conglomerates profit greatly from the new popularity of Korean culture.

While the end of the Cold War may have been a precondition for the opening of Chinese and Vietnamese markets to South Korean products, the attractive gentleness of Confucian culture is essential to *hallyu*'s success. Besides behavior patterns rooted in traditional civil society, another significant factor contributing to *hallyu's* formation is the self-confidence Koreans derive from the experience of winning their own democratic transformation. Decades of struggles to change their political system have left a residue evident in people's capacity to transform their own self-understanding in film, music, and television. Contemporary South Korea produces golf and figure skating stars as part of the culture's renaissance.

Gwangju's Continuing Centrality

Much of the credit for the 1990s Korean Wave must be attributed to the human beings created by the democratization movement, whose apex occurred during the Gwangju Uprising. Decades of social movements constructed political freedoms and cultural confidence without which no Korean cultural wave would have been possible. As a result of the dictatorships' attempt to suppress the truth, the Gwangju Uprising animated cultural resistance for more than a decade. After the successful June 1987 uprising, the subsequent process of democratic con-solidation and transitional justice was once again led by Gwangju's citizens, and led to the construction of a proper memorial cemetery for the uprising's victims. After a long grassroots struggle, the Korean Legislature passed a Special Law about Gwangju in 1995. The May 18 Memorial Foundation was established to aid the victims and their families with scholarships for children and compensation. On Jeju, the provincial government led a successful struggle for a law similar to Gwangju's to help heal the wounds from the 1948 massacre there.[32]

Not content merely to build monuments to their martyrs, Gwangju activ-ists fought for international justice, and the South Korean movement became a model for insurgencies throughout Asia.[33] Beginning in 1993, Gwangju people organized more than five international conferences on the May Uprising, and the 5.18 Memorial Foundation has worked continually to build its international solidarity programs. Annual events like the human rights award for activ-ists on the front lines, a yearly International Peace Forum, and a Folk School have brought hundreds of activists to Gwangju to learn about its history and to reflect upon and share their own experiences. In addition, NGO grants facilitate projects throughout Asia, including a Day of the Disappeared in Sri Lanka. In 1997, Gwangju Citizens' Solidarity organized a reunion of foreign correspondents who had been present during the uprising, and a book was published based on their experiences.[34]

Activists from Gwangju conducted peace camps in East Timor, Cambodia, and Thailand to educate new generations. They brought together bereaved family members from Thailand, Korea, Indonesia, and Sri Lanka whose loved ones had been killed during uprisings. They held conferences exploring parallel and diver-gent patterns of movement development among activists and scholars from Nepal, Burma, the Philippines, Bhutan, China, Taiwan, Vietnam, Malaysia, Pakistan, and other parts of Asia. On the fiftieth anniversary of the Universal Declaration of Human Rights in 1998, they declared an Asian Human Rights Charter that had been drafted over four years of meetings in Hong Kong, India, Nepal, and Korea with direct involvement of over two hundred NGOs. When the Charter was announced, the conference agreed that, "The Kwangju Massacre and the response of the Kwangju people as well as the South Koreans to this event is a landmark in the development of the human rights movement in Asia . . . The whole experience has taught many valuable lessons."

After parents of some of the tens of thousands of disappeared people in Sri Lanka visited Gwangju, they were inspired to build a Memorial to the Missing at Raddolugama (Seeduwa) Colombo in 1999 with help from Gwangju activists. "They drew strength from the inspiring experience of family members in Korea. They went to the Gwangju Memorial Cemetery and the old Mangwoldong cemetery. This experience led to their monument for the disappeared."[35] Gwangju's inspiration spread throughout the region. Anya-orn Khiewboriboon, a member of Thailand's Relatives Committee of the May 1992 Heroes (those killed in the 1992 uprising there), visited Gwangju in 1996 and remarked that, "The united movement of Korean people is a model we should follow." On May 18, 2004, Win Khet, member of the central committee of the National League for Democracy, accepted the Gwangju prize for Human Rights on behalf of Aung San Suu Kyi. He summarized the impact of Gwangju on his movement: "We appreciate the Gwangju Democratic Movement, the cornerstone of Korea's democracy, very much and firmly believe it is a role model for all the fighters for the institution of a genuine democratic federal union based on equality and self-determination in Burma." In 2009, Nepalese Prime Minister Madhav Nepal told me he had visited Gwangju before the uprisings in his country and was "inspired by people's heroic struggle."[36]

From the Gwangju Uprising to anti-globalization protests, Korea now provides inspiration to people worldwide. During anti-WTO protests in Seattle in 1999, spirited Korean participants set an example noted by many people in the streets. At the WTO Ministerial meetings in Cancun in 2003, Koreans' unity and Lee Kyung-hae's suicide became the stuff of legends among indigenous peoples of the Americas. When police barricades blocked thousands of protesters from approaching the meeting site in Cancun, dozens of Korean farmers sat down and communally wove rope in the street. Growing up in the countryside, Korean farmers learned rope-making from childhood during annual village games that include a tug of war with precisely such handmade ropes. Patiently singing and weaving, the farmers looped their rope around the barricades and, with everyone's help and encouragement, were able to pull police obstructions aside. Here was a concrete example of how traditional civil society provides tools for mobilizations.

In Hong Kong at the WTO meetings in December 13, 2005, dozens of Korean farmers broke away from a snake dance, put on orange life vests, and jumped into the cold harbor waters to swim around police blockades to protest at the Convention Center. Through such actions, the Korean movement has helped to educate many people around the world about the power of united people's movements—of how the multitude can win huge victories. Korean activists' capacity for creative and courageous action inspired thousands of people to refuse to permit police to dominate them. In the future, Koreans are poised to play an enormously important role in the international movement.

Dialectic of Tradition and Liberation

South Korea's social networks of communication are one of its great historical resources. A rich tapestry of civil society includes meso- and micromobilizations in everyday relations, and the value of human relationships is omnipresent in the mutual respect exhibited in daily life. In the yin and yang of contemporary Korea, however, that same sociability, the strength of which overthrew dictatorships and won liberties denied for decades, simultaneously militates against the free individual, particularly against the liberation of women. Structures of patriarchal Confucianism strictly prescribe patterns of behavior and life opportunities. Youth are duty-obligated to serve the old, women to cater to men, and the poor to defer obsequiously to the rich. Hierarchy is embedded in Korean language and customs. Men who are close commonly address each other as older bother (*hyongnim*) and younger brother (*aunim*); people refer to classmates and colleagues at work as "my junior" or "my senior" depending upon their age. Conveyed in titles and declensions of verbs as well as in myriad rituals and observances, vertically structured relationships exist in forms of politeness only an insider can comprehend. Yet since these forms of embedded hierarchy have the comforts and caring of family, they provide a safe refuge from the cold cash nexus increasingly affecting us all. Strangers commonly address each other as uncle (*ajoshi*) and "older sister" (*ohnee*) with a gentleness that makes hierarchy both easier to tolerate and more difficult to challenge.

Korea's civil society is both a resource to mobilize protests and a brake on developing revolutionary consciousness, a means of enabling collective action and a barrier to decisive breaks with engrained patterns. Clearly a communal form of great promise in comparison to the isolating individualism of Western competitive behavior, it is also a means of confining individuals to fixed places in social networks. Patriarchal power is so pervasively present within these structures that women are systematically mistreated. In 2009, the suicide of actor Chang Ja-yon, who was tormented and used by sex-crazed men who controlled the media, was a result. Social movements are infected with the same problems. In the same month that Chang Ja-yon took her life, the previously mentioned sexual harassment scandal inside the KCTU compelled all its national leaders to resign. Although the working class continued to exhibit militancy beyond other parts of the world—as during the Sangyong seventy-seven-day plant occupation in 2009, during which unionists unsuccessfully fought layoffs using huge catapults, Molotovs and other weapons—the union movement has been gravely wounded by internal dynamics, and many affiliates are breaking ties with the KCTU.

Alternative Movement

As the civil movement spread in the late 1980s, many activists set off in a new direction loosely called the "alternative movement." While the movement's main energies were directed at the shift in political power, the alternative movement sought to transform everyday life. Koreans' struggle for greater freedoms led many people to involve themselves directly in projects that could liberate themselves from hierarchical relations and profit-oriented institutions. Especially during the IMF crisis, when people experienced ill effects of neoliberalism, many moved to rural areas and initiated intentional communities. Drawing from roots in traditional forms of communal endeavor like *ture*, cooperative agricultural communities sprang up alongside community-based nurseries and workers' takeover of idle production sites (deemed unprofitable by corporate owners). Especially in poorer areas, activists' desires for greater self-determination resonated with local people's survival needs.

In 2009, I visited Cloud Mountain Village an hour's drive from Gwangju, where former union activists, tired from years of intense labor struggles, moved into an all but abandoned village in South Jeolla in 2000. Influenced by a similar network in Suncheon, some eighty families in South Jeolla joined together, including some living on the margins. They began to produce organic tofu, soybean paste, and red pepper sauce—key ingredients of traditional Korean food. Building a cooperative involving seven extended families, more people became involved in communal and nonhierarchical production endeavors in which 2 percent of profits go back to the village.[37] Alongside their cooperatives, they have become a safe area where festivals are organized and labor activists can take a rest and get rejuvenated. Historically, the area was a rich source of recruits for the 1894 Farmers revolt (or *Tonghak* Uprising), and key organizers of Cloud Mountain Village expressed to me a hope to create the preconditions for "another Righteous Army" in the future.

In contrast to the established educational system, which emphasizes competition and is aimed at producing passive and compliant employees, a diverse assortment of free schools sprang up all over the country. In at least thirty places, alternative forms of currency, ranging from work credits to barter coupons, have begun to be used.[38] As alternative economic institutions begin to gather momentum, a network of "Beautiful Stores" (recycled clothing and household goods) provides jobs and helps to find recruits for like-minded projects. Importing fair trade coffee from Nepal, the Beautiful Store stimulated an alternative trade movement in Korea. In 2008, profits were used to make $2.5 million of distributions to medical care and housing for indigents and to take special care of the elderly and children.

With the proliferation of high-speed Internet, alternative media appeared on regional and national levels, and in many areas, the most outstanding changes were wrought in media. Founded in 2000 by a fired journalist, *OhmyNews*, an online alternative newspaper, opened a new chapter in reporting. With a slogan, "Every citizen a journalist," *OhmyNews* created "news guerrillas" (citizen reporters) and its impact soon inspired the mainstream media to initiate citizen journalist sections. With people's support, alternative media based in the Internet have continued to be effective after scoring two significant victories: the posting of an apparently isolated netizen led to more than six months of daily candlelight protests against the U.S. Army's killing of Mi-sun and Hyo-sun in 2002;[39] and netizens helped get Noh Moo-hyun elected. In the aftermath of these breakthroughs, hundreds of locally based newspapers and dozens of radio stations emerged as part of an alternative media consciously seeking to transform the global system run by the G-8 and IMF.

By pursuing everyday lives outside mainstream imperatives of profits, passivity, and competition, the alternative movement at its best can be conceived as parallel to Latin American endeavors to oppose neoliberalism. Standing against the established powers in arenas of government and everyday life, the alternative movement presents the possibility of genuine change. While many endeavors are easily co-opted and remain patterned by male domination and hierarchy, others are able to maintain activists' vital needs for life-affirming projects.[40]

Finding the Cost of Freedom

The near collapse of the U.S.-led neoliberal accumulation regime in late 2008 created a worldwide recession, after which U.S. hegemony will never again enjoy the supremacy it attained in the twentieth century. With the world financial crisis, capitalism's instability—its essential need for booms and busts, and its delivery of illness and pain—has become increasingly evident—as has the need for systemic change. The world system's irrationality is visible in bankers' huge bonuses taken at a time when their policies result in increasing world poverty. As the financial crisis began, the UN's Millennium Development Goals Report announced that one billion people will go hungry, another two billion will be malnourished, and because of the rise in food prices in 2008, another hundred million will be pushed into "extreme poverty." For their skill and drive, bankers received billions in bonuses, while hundreds of millions of people faced starvation.

The U.S. and European nations continue to insist upon protecting domestic agribusiness with billions of dollars in annual subsidies, payments that allow rich corporations to drive poor countries' farmers out of business. Starvation is thereby increased at the system's periphery while profits accrue at its center. This is only one dimension of the systematic redistribution of money from the periphery to the center—that is, from the world's poor to the rich. Is it any wonder that the UN reports that "every five seconds a child dies because she or he is hungry; hunger and poverty claim 25,000 lives every day"? Such statistics can disable us—unless we are lucky enough to have the energy of youth, like that of protesting Korean schoolgirls, to inspire us.

The change we need is structural. We need structures in which the simple needs of ordinary people, not the profit needs of giant corporations, are centrally important to science, to politics, and especially to economics. We need fresh foods, ones that are locally grown (thereby reducing their carbon footprint). We need governments that love peace, that don't need wars (or constant preparation for them) as part of their policies to stimulate the economy. We need local, grass-roots democracy and cooperation—exactly like the kinds practiced in liberated Gwangju or during the candlelight protests of 2008. The current system offers us corporate delivery of unhealthy food, unending wars, and systemic starvation; it delivers "democratically" elected leaders like 2MB and George W. Bush, fine illustrations of the routine promotion of dumbed-down men to high positions of leadership. The hundreds of middle and high school girls who led the first protests in Seoul revealed this dilemma of democracy. They embodied a "collective intelligence" superior to their country's elite—elected or not. By seeking deliberation of key issues rather than bulldozing their resolution through elected officials' fiat, these girls were part of a worldwide grassroots initiative that seeks to put direct decision-making by citizens at the center of what democracy means.

As the twenty-first century began, many people complained that Korean students were apathetic, yet with the sudden eruption of candlelight protests, dozens of ordinary people were overnight turned into veteran activists. They distanced themselves from old-time activists who sought to frame the protests. The new activists were criticized for being invisible and transitory, for not being class-based, but they nonetheless mobilized for universal interests. Like all autonomous movements, they were independent of political parties and guarded their precious autonomy by refusing to join any central organization. Is their nomadic migratory character a virtue that leads them to avoid ossification? Or does it make them more easily co-opted by the powers that be? Rather than merging into old activist (*undongkwon*) circles, they used cyberspace to synthesize a new form of collective intelligence. Many people understand that the problem is not just one president, however avaricious he may be, but the capitalist world system that places corporate profits above human needs.

Like European autonomous movements, what began as single-issue protests produced a more generalized system critique. Like the New Left more generally, these movements did not take political power, but the cultural shift they helped produce means far more freedom for millions of people. Except for minor incidents of militant confrontations, street actions were largely festive and expressive, rather than militantly instrumental.

In contrast to European autonomous movements, the festival-like atmosphere in Korea emanated from participation by families, especially mothers with young children and teenagers who brought their parents along with them.

The Korean movement's crystallization from decades of struggles explains why candlelight protests grew so quickly. Korea's candlelight demonstrations were more about human will and imagination than new technology. As a tactic, candlelight vigils began to be used in 1976 when DJ, Oh Choong-il and others carried them against the dictatorship, but fire has remained a continuing means of fueling movements, from the farmers of 1894 who held torches to Gwangju's torchlight parade. Candlelight demonstrations appeared during the 1987 June Uprising in both Seoul (June 15) and Busan (June 17), and they were central means of expression during weeks of daily candlelight vigils for Hyo-sun and Mi-sun in 2002 as well as in 183 days of candlelight struggles in Puan, which defeated a planned nuclear waste site. Tens of thousands of people used candles to challenge the impeachment of Noh Moo-hyun in 2004, and more than two years of daily candlelight vigils in Pyongtaek rallied people against the new U.S. military base. Despite their festival-like appearance, recent protests rekindled the *minjung* movement's opposition to authoritarian regimes (rather than reproducing the reformism of citizens' movements). Candlelight protests embrace the purity of human beings in contrast to our pollution by genetic engineering, industrial foods, hormones, pesticides, and all the other "marvels" of modern technology. Eros and the human heart—not cyborgs and Machiavellian power games—are at their core.

Looking at South Korea's long twentieth century of uprisings discussed in this book, one recurrent theme becomes clear: ordinary people's collective intelligence far surpasses that of existing elites. In all of the uprisings from the 1894 revolt against the Lee dynasty and their Japanese protectors to teenage schoolgirls challenging President Lee and his ties to the United States, hundreds of thousands of ordinary citizens have risked life and limb for well-conceived goals they deem in their hearts to be worth the sacrifices they have been compelled to make.

One of the most significant products of Korea's long and bloody twentieth century is its people's belief in their own power, in their intuitive comprehension of themselves as the subjects and objects of history, and in their rekindled imaginations. People's capacity for collective action stands out as a great legacy of their past struggles. They have won huge and hard-fought victories, and the next generations have incorporated lessons and carry in their hearts the spirit of freedom. They have already eased the military out of power without great loss of life. They have won trade unions and began a cultural transformation that elevated high school girls to leaders. While much remains to be done, the gentleness of Confucian civil society lubricated these transitions. Compared with the barbarity of El Salvador in the 1980s or Indonesia and East Timor in the 1990s, South Korea seems much better off. Koreans' unity—starkly evident in the voluntary giving of gold to the government in 1997 or the hundreds of thousands of people who went out into the flesh-freezing cold and scrubbed clean the coastline after an oil spill near the Taehan Peninsula in 2008—will continue to amaze and instruct. In 2009, despite all the confrontations between labor and management that have occurred, the *New York Times* called communal civility on the job "one of the strongest assets of the South Korean economy."[41]

Unlike in the nineteenth century, it is generally understood today that history is not unilinear. Progress yesterday does not guarantee it tomorrow. We can move backward all too easily. Witness Hitler's rise after the period of Weimar democracy. To take a more recent example, the people of the Philippines successfully expelled U.S. troops from their country in 1992, yet today, American service members are back there as the U.S. "war on terror" replaces the Cold War as the rationale for wasteful militarism. South Korea's democracy and prosperity today is no guarantee that future generations will continue to enjoy them. Unless people resist government officials more interested in "national security" than in peace and restrain the rich who incessantly seek an ever-increasing share of wealth, freedom will be diminished, and prosperity will vanish.

Those who criticize Korea for the demise of its movements before complete liberation would be well advised to consider two contradictory propositions:

1. The lives of millions of its citizens have been remarkably improved by the country's social movements.
2. The existing world system's capacity to absorb and blunt the thrust of all forms of insurgency against it is one of its most significant strengths. The American and French revolutions, the Russian Revolution, the May 1968 uprising in France, and the wave of Asian democratic movements at the end of the twentieth century have all been made into instruments of system rationalization—into means for the expansion of markets and control of greater resources.

The creation of a *reasonable* system remains a work in progress. Whether or not we let our planet's fate be determined by a small coterie of corporate executives and their politician friends is a choice before all of us. While rollbacks are a reality, so too are many freedoms won during the long twentieth century. In 1894, as the

Farmers' War broke out, power-hungry Koreans—who in their own minds were "modernizers"—collaborated with Japan and produced disastrous results for the country. After Japan's defeat in 1945, these same people transferred allegiance to the United States and were able to retain their privileges under the American-led accumulation regime. More than a century later, while a stratum of collaborators still remains ensconced in positions of power (especially in control of the major media), ordinary Koreans are far better off. Prosperity has reached many in the South, and repression is far reduced from the days of Japanese control or military dictatorships. Although foreign military threats remain present and global economic powers control much of the country's future, political power is largely in indigenous hands. If the will can be mobilized, Koreans could finally determine their own future in the twenty-first century. In so doing, they would ennoble all of us. As the elegance and sacrifice of the U.S. civil rights movement elevated the entire society, Koreans' struggles for dignity through their long and bloody twentieth century helped make the world more gentle and participatory.

NOTES

1   Kim Jinwung, "From 'American Gentlemen' to 'Americans': Changing Perceptions of the United States in South Korea in Recent Years," *Korea Journal* 41, no. 4 (Winter 2001): 172.

2   Louie, "*Minjung* Feminism," 130.

3   Don Kirk, "Korean Mob Briefly Detains U.S. Soldier After Subway Fight," *New York Times*, September 17, 2002.

4   U.S. service personnel subsequently blamed poor roads in Korea for the accident. I can only imagine how American people would react if Korean sailors in the United States drove an oversized vehicle and killed two U.S. schoolgirls, took refuge on a Korean ship, got a slap on the wrists when their case was heard by an all-Korean panel, did not apologize when they met the media, and then had Korean people write public letters saying that the *real* problem was that there were too many traffic fatalities in the United States.

5   See Jimmy Carter, "Engaging North Korea," *New York Times*, October 27, 2002, 13. Another U.S. study estimated that within the first weeks, there would be 100,000 U.S. casualties, 490,000 South Korean military, and several million Korean civilians.

6   In March 2002, a Pentagon review of U.S. nuclear policy recommended that the United States threaten to use nuclear weapons against seven countries—including North Korea

7   http://news.naver.com/news/read.php?mode=LOD&office_id=121&article_id=0000001865.

8   The survey was conducted by the National Unification Advisory Council and released in June 2006.

9   Already diversity thrives in the reunification movement. In 2006, four coalitions were working for reunification: Unity Solidarity (통일연대), Korean Council for National Reconciliation (민화협—DJ's coalition plus religious leaders), and People's Confederation for Unification (범민련) as individuals. Interview with Paik Nak-chung, Seoul, July 3, 2006.

10   For discussion of this contrast, see Paik Nak-chung, "Habermas on National Unification in Germany and Korea," *New Left Review* 219 (September/October 1996) 14–22.

11   Civic Organizations, *Almanac 2000* (Seoul).

12   Interview with Park Won-soon, Seoul, July 31, 2003. Park's Beautiful Foundation has

established a series of thrift stores and fair trade items that he developed after learning about them in the United States.

13 *Hankyoreh*, October 3, 2006.

14 "A Look at South Korean Society, 20 Years after Democracy," *Hankyoreh*, June 8, 2007.

15 Hyuk-Rae Kim, "The Paradox of Social Governance in South Korea Reform Politics: Dilemmas and Challenges," paper presented at the Eighth Pacific and Asia Conference on Korean Studies (PACKS), New Delhi, December 15–17, 2006.

16 Lee, *The Making of Minjung*, 302.

17 *Hard Journey*, 334 (see chap. 5 n. 68).

18 Doh C. Shin, *Mass Politics*, 9; Balbina Hwang, "The Elections in South Korea: A Victory for the Electoral Process," http://www.heritage.org/research/asiaandthepacific/wm484.cfm; Angus Reid Global Monitor, "Election Tracker South Korea," http://www.angus-reid.com/tracker/view/1472.

19 Choe Sang-hun, "Protests in Seoul Galvanize Koreans," *International Herald-Tribune*, June 12, 2008, 4.

20 *Hankyoreh*, June 2, 2008.

21 "Protesters Trampled, Beaten by Police," *Hankyoreh*, June 30, 2008. More than a year later, courts ruled the police had used excessive force and ordered minor compensation to the victims.

22 "NPA Orders Google to Remove Video from YouTube," *Hankyoreh*, http://english.hani.co.kr/arti/english_edition/e_national/300711.html.

23 "Police Arrest Another Internet Writer," *Hankyoreh*, http://english.hani.co.kr/arti/english_edition/e_national/355242.html.

24 *Yomiuri Shimbun*, January 13, 2009, as reported in *Hankyoreh*, accessed on January 15, 2009.

25 Meredith Woo-Cumings, "Market Dependency in U.S.-East Asian Relations," in *What Is in a Rim?* ed. Arif Dirlik (Lanham, MD: Rowman and Littlefield, 1998), 166, 184.

26 "Government Announces a Ban on Assemblies in Urban Centers," *Hankyoreh*, http://english.hani.co.kr/arti/english_edition/e_national/356066.html.

27 "Former S. Korea President Roh Commits Suicide," *Hankyoreh*, http://english.hani.co.kr/arti/english_edition/e_national/356455.html.

28 "Police and Citizens Conflict over Roh's Memorial," *Hankyoreh*, http://english.hani.co.kr/arti/english_edition/e_national/356813.html.

29 "Government's Head-On Collision with Labor," *Hankyoreh*, http://english.hani.co.kr/arti/english_edition/e_editorial/355642.html.

30 "Excessive Use of Force by Police During KCTU and KCTWU Labor Rally," http://english.hani.co.kr/arti/english_edition/e_national/355443.html.

31 Presentation at Harvard University, Kennedy School of Government, February 16, 2007.

32 See Ko Chang-hoon, "The U.S. Government's Responsibility for the Jeju April Third Uprising and Massacre: An Islander's Perspective," paper presented at the international conference, The Jeju Sasam Uprising and East Asian Peace: International Legal Issues and Human Rights in Twenty-First-Century Korea, Harvard University, April 25, 2003; see also Na Kahn-chae, "The Revival Movement of the Two Uprisings in Korea: Jeju and Gwangju," 2006.

33 For analysis of the long struggle of the May Movement, see Na Kahn-chae, "A New Perspective."

34 Scott-Stokes and Lee Jai-eui, *The Kwangju Uprising*.

35 Sanjeewa Liyanage, "Memory, Missing People and Hope for Peace in Sri Lanka," *Fourth International Conference on the Anniversary of the Gwangju Uprising: Historical Memory and Cultural Representation, May 15–17, 2003*, 117.

36 Interview with Madhav Kumar Nepal, Kathmandu, April 12, 2009.

37 Interview with Yoon Young-min, Cloud Mountain Village, November 2, 2009.

38 윤수종, 대안운동의 현황과 방향, (사회 이론, 2007 가을 / 겨울).

39 When it was later revealed that the "lone" netizen had worked for *OhmyNews*, many people criticized the lack of transparency.

40 See Park Ju-hee's doctoral work in sociology at Chonnam National University, 주민주도형 농촌 마을 만들기에서 여성 참여에 대한 연구—전라남도 마을 만들기 사례를 중심으로, 박주희(전남대 사회학과 박사수료).

41 Choe Sang-hun, "South Koreans Band Together to Save, and Create, Jobs," *New York Times*, April 1, 2009.

INTERVIEWS WITH CITIZEN-ACTIVISTS

Lee Jae-won	이재원	November 22, 1999
Paik Nak-chung	백낙청	November 27, 1999
Chun Yong-ho	전용호	November 27, 1999
Soh Eugene	서유진	November 27, 1999
Park Byong-ki	박병기	November 29, 1999
Na Kahn-chae	나간채	May 19, 2000
Yoon Soo-jong	윤수종	March 11, 2001
Jung Keun-sik	정근식	March 12, 2001
Yoon Young-kyu	윤영규	March 13, 2001 / April 10, 2001
Na Il-sung	나일성	March 15, 2000
Lee Jae-eui	이재의	March 17, 2000
Jung Keun-sik	정근식	March 18, 2000
Kim U-kon	김우곤	March 21, 2001
Kim Dong-choon	김동춘	April 1, 2001
Ko Chang-hoon	고창훈	April 2, 2001
Kim Sang-jib	김상집	April 6, 2001
Seo Chae-won	서채원	April 6, 2001
We Sung-sam	위성삼	April 13, 2001
Yang Seong-hee	양승희	April 13, 2001
Kim Sang-yoon	김상윤	April 15, 2001
Choi Wan-uk	최완욱	April 16, 2001
Kim Jun-bong	김준봉	April 18, 2001
Kim Ki-kwang	김기광	April 19, 2001
Yang Dong-nam	양동남	April 20, 2001
Kang Shin–seok	강신석	April 22, 2001
Jeong Hae-jik	정해직	April 23, 2001
Kim Dae-sung	김대성	April 24, 2001
Oh Kyong-Min	오경민	April 25, 2001
Na Il-sung	나일성	May 7, 2001
Jung Hyang-ja	정향자	May 9, 2001
Lee Kang	이강	May 9, 2001
Park Nam-son	박남선	May 11, 2001
Park Haing-sam	박행삼	May 2001
Kim Young-jib	김영집	May 2001
Hong Young-ki (Yeosu)	홍영기	May 23, 2001
Kim Kwang-su	김광수	May 24, 2001
Lee Kwang-young	이광영	May 28, 2001
Ko Ho-seok	고호석	May 30, 2001
Kim Ha-gi (Kim Young)	김하기	May 30, 2001
Lee Chin-gol	이진결	May 31, 2001
Song Ki-in	송기인	May 31, 2001
Chung Kwan-min	정관민	May 31, 2001
Kim Jae-kyu	김재규	May 31, 2001
Kim Jung-ho	김정호	May 31, 2001
Son Man-ho	선만호	June 1, 2001
Im Jong-seok (Seoul)	임종석	June 4, 2001
Kwan Hyok-ki	강혁기	June 4, 2001

Yoon Byong-sam	윤병삼	June 4, 2001
Woo Sang-ho	우상호	June 5, 2001
Park Hyung-kyu	박형규	June 5, 2001
Kwak Tak-sung	곽탁성	June 6, 2001
Kim Dong-choon	김동춘	June 7, 2001
Hwang In-sung	황인성	June 7, 2001
Hang Sang-jin	한상진	June 7, 2001
Shim Gue	심구	June 10, 2001
Kim Gyol	김결	June 14, 2001
Kim Son-moon	김선문	June 15, 2001
Lee Kwang-young	이광영	June 21, 2001
Lee Yang-hyun	이양현	June 22, 2001
Yoon Suk-tong	윤석동	September 26, 2001
Yoon Gang-ok	윤강옥	October 3, 2001
Ku Song-ju	구성주	October 3, 2001
Hur Gyu-jung	허규정	October 12, 2001
Lee Sung-suk (Mokpo)	이성숙	October 15, 2001
Chung Sangyong	정상용	October 17, 2001
Lee Song-jin	이성진	October 19, 2001
Suh Kyong-won	서경원	October 20, 2001
Yang In-hwa	양인화	October 24, 2001
Kim Chang-gil	김창길	October 25, 2001
Chong Hyun-ay	정현애	October 28, 2001
Yoon Han-bong	윤한봉	October 29, 2001
Kim Young-jib	김영집	October 30, 2001
Kim Hyo-sok	김효석	November 6, 2001
Kim Jang-gil	김장길	November 7, 2001
Kang Hyon-ah	강현아	November 7, 2001
Kim Tae-chan	김태찬	November 22, 2001
Lee Heong-chol	이홍철	November 24, 2001
Oh Choong-il	오충일	November 27, 2001
Kim Jeong-bae	김종배	November 27, 2001
Chun Choon-sim (Okju)	전춘심	November 28, 2001
Oh Choong-il	오충일	November 28, 2001
Song Yon	성연	November 30, 2001
Lee Boo-young	이부영	December 2001
Oh Choong-il	오충일	December 2001
Kim Ye-hyan (4.19)	김예환	December 13, 2001
Lee Young-il (Yeosu)	이영일	December 14, 2001
Yoon Young-kyu	윤영규	December 18, 2001
Im Chun-hee	임춘희	December 21, 2001
Hyun Ki-young	현기영	April 29, 2002
Bak Tae-bong	박태봉	May 31, 2002
Jung Hyun Baek	정현백	June 12, 2002
Jung Yong-hwa	정용화	June 19, 2002
Choi Yol	최열	June 22, 2002
Lee Young-il	이영일	May 17, 2003
Kim Sun-chool	김선출	May 20, 2003
Oh Gil-jae	오길제	May 29, 2003
Lee Sang-sung	이상승	July 7, 2003
Hong Gun-soo	홍근수	July 7, 2003

Soh Il-hwan	서일환	July 11, 2003
Lee Sung-chol	이승철	July 11, 2003
Sin Jong-ho	신정호	July 11, 2003
Park Chol-ho	박철호	July 11, 2003
Park Won-soon	박원순	July 31, 2003
Lee Young-il	이영일	August 2, 2003
Byun Ju-na	변주나	August 3, 2003
Park Young-soon	박용순	August 3, 2003
Yoon Yeo-yon	윤여연	August 3, 2003
Beh Un-shim	배은심	August 3, 2003
Jo Chan-bae	조찬배	August 3, 2003
Choi Gee-ok	최기옥	July 20, 2003
Kim Dok-ho	김덕호	July 21, 2003
Park Jae-hong	박재홍	July 22, 2003
Hong Sung-dam	홍성담	October 16, 2003
Lee Jae-eui	이재의	April 15, 2008
Kim Pyong (Haenam)	김평	April 21, 2008
Yang Hae-mo (Haenam)	양해모	April 21, 2008
Yoon Shik (Haenam)	윤식	April 21, 2008
Kim Byong-yong (Haenam)	김병용	April 21, 2008
Park Nam-son	박남선	April 23, 2008
Jeong Hae-jik	정해직	April 30, 2008
Na Il-sung	나일성	April 30, 2008
Chun Yong-ho	전용호	June 4, 2008
Kim Eun-chong	김은총	June 16, 2008
Ryu Hyoung-kyong	류형경	June 20, 2008
Chong Hyun-ay	정현애	July 14, 2008
Kim Dong-choon	김동춘	August 1, 2008
Kim Gun-tae	김근태	August 2, 2008
Chang Doo-sok	장두석	August 31, 2008
Ahn Hyo-sun	안효순	February 20, 2009
Lee Nam-ju	이남주	March 27, 2009
Kim Young-su	김영수	March 29, 2009
In Myung-jin	인명진	March 29, 2009
Hwang In-sung	인성	March 29, 2009
Paik Han-gi	백한기	October 29, 2009
Jung Song-gi	정성기	October 29, 2009
Yoon Won-chol	윤원철	October 29, 2009
Choi Kap-soon	최갑순	October 29, 2009
Chang Il-sun	장일순	October 31, 2009
Kwak Dong-hyo	곽동효	October 31, 2009
Kim Ha-gi	김하기	October 31, 2009
Cha Song-hwan	차성환	October 31, 2009
Yoon Young-min	윤용민	November 2, 2009
Chung Oong	정웅	December 4, 2009

CREDITS

Woodblock prints preceding the chapters were generously supplied by artist Hong Sung-dam.

Earlier versions of parts of this book appeared as:

South Korean Democracy: Legacy of the Gwangju Uprising (London: Routledge, 2006) edited with Na Kahn-chae.

Interviews with the Shimingun, 2 volumes of my interviews with participants in the Gwangju Uprising published by May 18 Institute, (Gwangju, South Korea: Chonnam National University Press, 2003) in Korean. 역사 속의 광주항쟁, 5·18 민중항쟁에 대한 새로운 성찰적 시선, 조희연·정호기(서울: 한울, 2009) "The Gwangju Uprising in History."

"Comparing Uprisings in Korea and Burma," *Socialism and Democracy* 23, no. 1, #49 (March 2009): 58–76.

"Asia and South Korean Social Movements," conference book, Pacific and Asia Conference on Korean Studies (PACKS), Hanoi, November 24–26, 2008.

"Korean Candlelights in History," *Jumeokbab*, September 2008, 10–15 (in Korean and English).

"Why Did the US Support Suppression of the Gwangju Uprising?" *Gwangju News*, May 2008.

"Toward a Global Uprising Against Neoliberalism and War," *Voices of Resistance from Occupied London* 2 (October 2007): 10–13.

"Neoliberalism and the Gwangju Uprising," *Korea Policy Review* (Cambridge: John F. Kennedy School of Government, Harvard University) Vol. 2, 2006.

"The System is the Problem," in *Forum: Civilian Massacres* (Gwangju: The May 18th Memorial Foundation, 2004), in Korean and English.

"Impressions of North Korea," *Socialism and Democracy* 18, no. 1, #35 (January–June 2004): 235–48.

"Comparing the Paris Commune and the Gwangju Uprising," *New Political Science* 25, no. 2 (June 2003): 261–70.

"The Real Axis of Evil," in *Masters of War: Militarism and Blowback in the Era of American Empire*, edited by Carl Boggs (New York and London: Routledge, 2003), 343–56.

"North Korea Holds a Peace Conference," *Korean Quarterly* 7, no. 1 (Fall 2003): 1.

"Liberty and National Security," in *Hangyoreh*, August 12, 2003, 10 (in Korean).

"Remembering the Kwangju Uprising," *Socialism and Democracy* 14, no.1 (Spring–Summer 2000): 85–107.

"The Kwangju Commune: 20 Years Later," *New Political Science* 22, no. 2 (June 2000): 281.

ABOUT THE AUTHOR

George Katsiaficas is author or editor of eleven books, including ones on the global uprising of 1968 and European and Asian social movements. Together with Kathleen Cleaver, he coedited *Liberation, Imagination, and the Black Panther Party*. A longtime activist for peace and justice, he is international coordinator of the May 18 Institute at Chonnam National University in Gwangju, South Korea, and teaches at Wentworth Institute of Technology in Boston.

Index

ABOUT PM PRESS

PM Press was founded at the end of 2007 by a small collection of folks with decades of publishing, media, and organizing experience. PM Press co-conspirators have published and distributed hundreds of books, pamphlets, CDs, and DVDs. Members of PM have founded enduring book fairs, spearheaded victorious tenant organizing campaigns, and worked closely with bookstores, academic conferences, and even rock bands to deliver political and challenging ideas to all walks of life. We're old enough to know what we're doing and young enough to know what's at stake.

We seek to create radical and stimulating fiction and non-fiction books, pamphlets, T-shirts, visual and audio materials to entertain, educate and inspire you. We aim to distribute these through every available channel with every available technology — whether that means you are seeing anarchist classics at our bookfair stalls; reading our latest vegan cookbook at the café; downloading geeky fiction e-books; or digging new music and timely videos from our website.

PM Press is always on the lookout for talented and skilled volunteers, artists, activists and writers to work with. If you have a great idea for a project or can contribute in some way, please get in touch.

PM Press
PO Box 23912
Oakland, CA 94623
www.pmpress.org

FRIENDS OF PM PRESS

These are indisputably momentous times—the financial system is melting down globally and the Empire is stumbling. Now more than ever there is a vital need for radical ideas.

In the four years since its founding—and on a mere shoestring—PM Press has risen to the formidable challenge of publishing and distributing knowledge and entertainment for the struggles ahead. With over 175 releases to date, we have published an impressive and stimulating array of literature, art, music, politics, and culture. Using every available medium, we've succeeded in connecting those hungry for ideas and information to those putting them into practice.

Friends of PM allows you to directly help impact, amplify, and revitalize the discourse and actions of radical writers, filmmakers, and artists. It provides us with a stable foundation from which we can build upon our early successes and provides a much-needed subsidy for the materials that can't necessarily pay their own way. You can help make that happen—and receive every new title automatically delivered to your door once a month—by joining as a Friend of PM Press. And, we'll throw in a free T-shirt when you sign up.

Here are your options:

- **$25 a month** Get all books and pamphlets plus 50% discount on all webstore purchases

- **$40 a month** Get all PM Press releases (including CDs and DVDs) plus 50% discount on all webstore purchases

- **$100 a month** Superstar—Everything plus PM merchandise, free downloads, and 50% discount on all webstore purchases

For those who can't afford $25 or more a month, we're introducing **Sustainer Rates** at $15, $10 and $5. Sustainers get a free PM Press T-shirt and a 50% discount on all purchases from our website.

Your Visa or Mastercard will be billed once a month, until you tell us to stop. Or until our efforts succeed in bringing the revolution around. Or the financial meltdown of Capital makes plastic redundant. Whichever comes first.

Asia's Unknown Uprisings
Volume 2
People Power in the Philippines, Burma, Tibet, China, Taiwan, Bangladesh, Nepal, Thailand, and Indonesia, 1947–2009

George Katsiaficas

ISBN: 978-1-60486-488-5
$26.95   448 pages

Ten years in the making, this book provides a unique
perspective on uprisings in nine places in East Asia in the 1980s and 1990s. While
the 2011 Arab Spring is well known, the wave of uprisings that swept East Asia
in the 1980s became hardly visible. This book begins with an overview of late
20th-century history—the context within which Asian uprisings arose. Through a
critique of Samuel Huntington's notion of a "Third Wave" of democratization, the
author relates Asian uprisings to predecessors in 1968 and shows their subsequent
influence on the wave of uprisings that swept Eastern Europe at the end of the
1980s. By empirically reconstructing the specific history of each Asian uprising,
significant insight into major constituencies of change and the trajectories of these
societies becomes visible.

It is difficult to find comprehensive histories of any one of these uprisings, yet
this book provides detailed histories of uprisings in nine places (the Philippines,
Burma, Tibet, China, Taiwan, Bangladesh, Nepal, Thailand, and Indonesia) as well
as introductory and concluding chapters that place them in a global context and
analyze them in light of major sociological theories. Richly illustrated, with tables,
charts, chronologies, graphs, index, and footnotes.

*"George Katsiaficas has written a majestic account of political uprisings and social
movements in Asia—an important contribution to the literature on both Asian studies
and social change that is highly-recommended reading for anyone concerned with
these fields of interest. The work is well-researched, clearly-argued, and beautifully
written, accessible to both academic and general readers."*
— Carl Boggs, author of *The Crimes of Empire and Imperial Delusions*

*"George Katsiaficas is America's leading practitioner of the method of 'participant-
observation,' acting with and observing the movements that he is studying. This study
of People Power is a brilliant narrative of the present as history from below. It is a
detailed account of the struggle for freedom and social justice, encompassing the
different currents, both reformist and revolutionary, in a balanced study that combines
objectivity and commitment. Above all, he presents the beauty of popular movements
in the process of self-emancipation."*
— James Petras, professor of sociology at Binghamton University

Fire and Flames: A History of the German Autonomist Movement

Geronimo
with an Introduction by George Katsiaficas
and Afterword by Gabriel Kuhn

ISBN 978-1-60486-097-9
$19.95   256 pages

Fire and Flames was the first comprehensive study of the German autonomous movement ever published. Released in 1990, it reached its fifth edition by 1997, with the legendary German *Konkret* journal concluding that "the movement had produced its own classic." The author, writing under the pseudonym of Geronimo, has been an autonomous activist since the movement burst onto the scene in 1980–81. In this book, he traces its origins in the Italian *Autonomia* project and the German social movements of the 1970s, before describing the battles for squats, "free spaces," and alternative forms of living that defined the first decade of the autonomous movement. Tactics of the "Autonome" were militant, including the construction of barricades or throwing molotov cocktails at the police. Because of their outfit (heavy black clothing, ski masks, helmets), the Autonome were dubbed the "Black Bloc" by the German media, and their tactics have been successfully adopted and employed at anti-capitalist protests worldwide.

Fire and Flames is no detached academic study, but a passionate, hands-on, and engaging account of the beginnings of one of Europe's most intriguing protest movements of the last thirty years. An introduction by George Katsiaficas, author of *The Subversion of Politics*, and an afterword by Gabriel Kuhn, a long-time autonomous activist and author, add historical context and an update on the current state of the Autonomen.

"The target audience is not the academic middle-class with passive sympathies for rioting, nor the all-knowing critical critics, but the activists of a young generation."
— *Edition I.D. Archiv*

"Some years ago, an experienced autonomous activist from Berlin sat down, talked to friends and comrades about the development of the scene, and, with Fire and Flames, *wrote the best book about the movement that we have."*
— *Düsseldorfer Stadtzeitung für Politik und Kultur*

Portugal: The Impossible Revolution?

Phil Mailer
with an afterword by Maurice Brinton

ISBN: 978-1-60486-336-9
$24.95   288 pages

After the military coup in Portugal on April 25, 1974, the overthrow of almost fifty years of Fascist rule, and the end of three colonial wars, there followed eighteen months of intense, democratic social transformation which challenged every aspect of Portuguese society. What started as a military coup turned into a profound attempt at social change from the bottom up and became headlines on a daily basis in the world media. This was due to the intensity of the struggle as well as the fact that in 1974–75 the moribund, right-wing Francoist regime was still in power in neighboring Spain and there was huge uncertainty as to how these struggles might affect Spain and Europe at large.

This is the story of what happened in Portugal between April 25, 1974, and November 25, 1975, as seen and felt by a deeply committed participant. It depicts the hopes, the tremendous enthusiasm, the boundless energy, the total commitment, the released power, even the revolutionary innocence of thousands of ordinary people taking a hand in the remolding of their lives. And it does so against the background of an economic and social reality which placed limits on what could be done.

"An evocative, bitterly partisan diary of the Portuguese revolution, written from a radical-utopian perspective. The enemy is any type of organization or presumption of leadership. The book affords a good view of the mood of the time, of the multiplicity of leftist factions, and of the social problems that bedeviled the revolution."
— Fritz Stern, *Foreign Affairs*

"Mailer portrays history with the enthusiasm of a cheerleader, the 'home team' in this case being libertarian communism. Official documents, position papers and the pronouncements of the protagonists of this drama are mostly relegated to the appendices. The text itself recounts the activities of a host of worker, tenant, soldier and student committees as well as the author's personal experiences."
— Ian Wallace, *Library Journal*

"A thorough delight as it moves from first person accounts of street demonstrations through intricate analyses of political movements. Mailer has handled masterfully the enormous cast of politicians, officers of the military peasant and workers councils, and a myriad of splinter parties, movements and caucuses."
— *Choice*

Also from ▓SPECTRE▶ from PM Press

Capital and Its Discontents: Conversations with Radical Thinkers in a Time of Tumult

Sasha Lilley

ISBN: 978-1-60486-334-5
$20.00   320 pages

Capitalism is stumbling, empire is faltering, and the
planet is thawing. Yet many people are still grasping
to understand these multiple crises and to find a way
forward to a just future. Into the breach come the essential insights of *Capital
and Its Discontents*, which cut through the gristle to get to the heart of the matter
about the nature of capitalism and imperialism, capitalism's vulnerabilities at
this conjuncture—and what can we do to hasten its demise. Through a series
of incisive conversations with some of the most eminent thinkers and political
economists on the Left—including David Harvey, Ellen Meiksins Wood, Mike Davis,
Leo Panitch, Tariq Ali, and Noam Chomsky—*Capital and Its Discontents* illuminates
the dynamic contradictions undergirding capitalism and the potential for its
dethroning. At a moment when capitalism as a system is more reviled than ever,
here is an indispensable toolbox of ideas for action by some of the most brilliant
thinkers of our times.

"*These conversations illuminate the current world situation in ways that are very useful
for those hoping to orient themselves and find a way forward to effective individual and
collective action. Highly recommended.*"
— Kim Stanley Robinson, *New York Times* bestselling author of the *Mars Trilogy* and
The Years of Rice and Salt

"*In this fine set of interviews, an A-list of radical political economists demonstrate
why their skills are indispensable to understanding today's multiple economic and
ecological crises.*"
— Raj Patel, author of *Stuffed and Starved* and *The Value of Nothing*

"*This is an extremely important book. It is the most detailed, comprehensive, and best
study yet published on the most recent capitalist crisis and its discontents. Sasha Lilley
sets each interview in its context, writing with style, scholarship, and wit about ideas and
philosophies.*"
— Andrej Grubačić, radical sociologist and social critic, co-author of *Wobblies and
Zapatistas*

Love and Struggle: My Life in SDS, the Weather Underground, and Beyond

David Gilbert
with an appreciation by Boots Riley

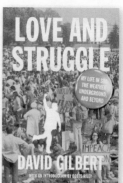

ISBN: 978-1-60486-319-2
$22.00   384 pages

A nice Jewish boy from suburban Boston—hell, an Eagle Scout!—David Gilbert arrived at Columbia University just in time for the explosive Sixties. From the early anti-Vietnam War protests to the founding of SDS, from the Columbia Strike to the tragedy of the Townhouse, Gilbert was on the scene: as organizer, theoretician, and above all, activist. He was among the first militants who went underground to build the clandestine resistance to war and racism known as "Weatherman." And he was among the last to emerge, in captivity, after the disaster of the 1981 Brinks robbery, an attempted expropriation that resulted in four deaths and long prison terms. In this extraordinary memoir, written from the maximum-security prison where he has lived for almost thirty years, David Gilbert tells the intensely personal story of his own Long March from liberal to radical to revolutionary.

Today a beloved and admired mentor to a new generation of activists, he assesses with rare humor, with an understanding stripped of illusions, and with uncommon candor the errors and advances, terrors and triumphs of the Sixties and beyond. It's a battle that was far from won, but is still not lost: the struggle to build a new world, and the love that drives that effort. A cautionary tale and a how-to as well, Love and Struggle is a book as candid, as uncompromising, and as humane as its author.

"David's is a unique and necessary voice forged in the growing American gulag, the underbelly of the 'land of the free,' offering a focused and unassailable critique as well as a vision of a world that could be but is not yet—a place of peace and love, joy and justice."
— Bill Ayers, author of Fugitive Days and Teaching Toward Freedom

"Like many of his contemporaries, David Gilbert gambled his life on a vision of a more just and generous world. His particular bet cost him the last three decades in prison, and whether or not you agree with his youthful decision, you can be the beneficiary of his years of deep thought, reflection, and analysis on the reality we all share. If there is any benefit to prison, what some refer to as 'the involuntary monastery,' it may well look like this book. I urge you to read it."
— Peter Coyote, actor, author of Sleeping Where I Fall

"This book should stimulate learning from our political prisoners, but more importantly it challenges us to work to free them, and in doing so take the best of our history forward."
— Susan Rosenberg, author of An American Radical

Also from ■SPECTRE▶ from PM Press

Global Slump: The Economics and Politics of Crisis and Resistance

David McNally

ISBN: 978-1-60486-332-1
$15.95   176 pages

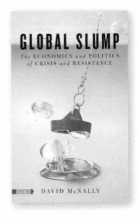

Global Slump analyzes the world financial meltdown as the first systemic crisis of the neoliberal stage of capitalism. It argues that—far from having ended—the crisis has ushered in a whole period of worldwide economic and political turbulence. In developing an account of the crisis as rooted in fundamental features of capitalism, *Global Slump* challenges the view that its source lies in financial deregulation. It offers an original account of the "financialization" of the world economy and explores the connections between international financial markets and new forms of debt and dispossession, particularly in the Global South. The book shows that, while averting a complete meltdown, the massive intervention by central banks laid the basis for recurring crises for poor and working class people. It traces new patterns of social resistance for building an anti-capitalist opposition to the damage that neoliberal capitalism is inflicting on the lives of millions.

"In this book, McNally confirms—once again—his standing as one of the world's leading Marxist scholars of capitalism. For a scholarly, in depth analysis of our current crisis that never loses sight of its political implications (for them and for us), expressed in a language that leaves no reader behind, there is simply no better place to go."
— Bertell Ollman, professor, Department of Politics, NYU, and author of *Dance of the Dialectic: Steps in Marx's Method*

"David McNally's tremendously timely book is packed with significant theoretical and practical insights, and offers actually-existing examples of what is to be done. Global Slump urgently details how changes in the capitalist space-economy over the past 25 years, especially in the forms that money takes, have expanded wide-scale vulnerabilities for all kinds of people, and how people fight back. In a word, the problem isn't neo-liberalism—it's capitalism."
— Ruth Wilson Gilmore, University of Southern California and author, *Golden Gulag*

Also from ■SPECTRE▶ from PM Press

In and Out of Crisis: The Global Financial Meltdown and Left Alternatives

Greg Albo, Sam Gindin, Leo Panitch

ISBN: 978-1-60486-212-6

$13.95   144 pages

While many around the globe are increasingly wondering if another world is indeed possible, few are mapping out potential avenues—and flagging wrong turns—en route to a post-capitalist future. In this groundbreaking analysis of the meltdown, renowned radical political economists Albo, Gindin, and Panitch lay bare the roots of the crisis, which they locate in the dynamic expansion of capital on a global scale over the last quarter century—and in the inner logic of capitalism itself.

With an unparalleled understanding of the inner workings of capitalism, the authors of *In and Out of Crisis* provocatively challenge the call by much of the Left for a return to a largely mythical Golden Age of economic regulation as a check on finance capital unbound. They deftly illuminate how the era of neoliberal free markets has been, in practice, undergirded by state intervention on a massive scale. In conclusion, the authors argue that it's time to start thinking about genuinely transformative alternatives to capitalism—and how to build the collective capacity to get us there. *In and Out of Crisis* stands to be the enduring critique of the crisis and an indispensable springboard for a renewed Left.

"Once again, Panitch, Gindin, and Albo show that they have few rivals and no betters in analyzing the relations between politics and economics, between globalization and American power, between theory and quotidian reality, and between crisis and political possibility. At once sobering and inspiring, this is one of the few pieces of writing that I've seen that's essential to understanding—to paraphrase a term from accounting—the sources and uses of crisis. Splendid and essential."
— Doug Henwood, *Left Business Observer*, author of *After the New Economy* and *Wall Street*

"Mired in political despair? Planning your escape to a more humane continent? Baffled by the economy? Convinced that the Left is out of ideas? Pull yourself together and read this book, in which Albo, Gindin, and Panitch, some of the world's sharpest living political economists, explain the current financial crisis—and how we might begin to make a better world."
— Liza Featherstone, author of *Students Against Sweatshops* and *Selling Women Short: The Landmark Battle for Workers' Rights at Wal-Mart*

Wobblies and Zapatistas: Conversations on Anarchism, Marxism and Radical History

Staughton Lynd and Andrej Grubačić

ISBN: 978-1-60486-041-2
$20.00   300 pages

Wobblies and Zapatistas offers the reader an encounter between two generations and two traditions. Andrej Grubačić is an anarchist from the Balkans. Staughton Lynd is a lifelong pacifist, influenced by Marxism. They meet in dialogue in an effort to bring together the anarchist and Marxist traditions, to discuss the writing of history by those who make it, and to remind us of the idea that "my country is the world." Encompassing a Left libertarian perspective and an emphatically activist standpoint, these conversations are meant to be read in the clubs and affinity groups of the new Movement.

The authors accompany us on a journey through modern revolutions, direct actions, anti-globalist counter summits, Freedom Schools, Zapatista cooperatives, Haymarket and Petrograd, Hanoi and Belgrade, 'intentional' communities, wildcat strikes, early Protestant communities, Native American democratic practices, the Workers' Solidarity Club of Youngstown, occupied factories, self-organized councils and soviets, the lives of forgotten revolutionaries, Quaker meetings, antiwar movements, and prison rebellions. Neglected and forgotten moments of interracial self-activity are brought to light. The book invites the attention of readers who believe that a better world, on the other side of capitalism and state bureaucracy, may indeed be possible.

"There's no doubt that we've lost much of our history. It's also very clear that those in power in this country like it that way. Here's a book that shows us why. It demonstrates not only that another world is possible, but that it already exists, has existed, and shows an endless potential to burst through the artificial walls and divisions that currently imprison us. An exquisite contribution to the literature of human freedom, and coming not a moment too soon."
— David Graeber, author of *Fragments of an Anarchist Anthropology* and *Direct Action: An Ethnography*

"I have been in regular contact with Andrej Grubačić for many years, and have been most impressed by his searching intelligence, broad knowledge, lucid judgment, and penetrating commentary on contemporary affairs and their historical roots. He is an original thinker and dedicated activist, who brings deep understanding and outstanding personal qualities to everything he does."
— Noam Chomsky

Demanding the Impossible:
A History of Anarchism

Peter Marshall

ISBN: 978-1-60486-064-1
$28.95   840 pages

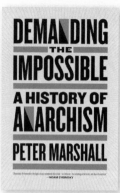

Navigating the broad 'river of anarchy', from Taoism to Situationism, from Ranters to Punk rockers, from individualists to communists, from anarcho-syndicalists to anarcha-feminists, *Demanding the Impossible* is an authoritative and lively study of a widely misunderstood subject. It explores the key anarchist concepts of society and the state, freedom and equality, authority and power and investigates the successes and failure of the anarchist movements throughout the world. While remaining sympathetic to anarchism, it presents a balanced and critical account. It covers not only the classic anarchist thinkers, such as Godwin, Proudhon, Bakunin, Kropotkin, Reclus and Emma Goldman, but also other libertarian figures, such as Nietzsche, Camus, Gandhi, Foucault and Chomsky. No other book on anarchism covers so much so incisively.

In this updated edition, a new epilogue examines the most recent developments, including 'post-anarchism' and 'anarcho-primitivism' as well as the anarchist contribution to the peace, green and 'Global Justice' movements.

Demanding the Impossible is essential reading for anyone wishing to understand what anarchists stand for and what they have achieved. It will also appeal to those who want to discover how anarchism offers an inspiring and original body of ideas and practices which is more relevant than ever in the twenty-first century.

"Demanding the Impossible *is the book I always recommend when asked—as I often am—for something on the history and ideas of anarchism.*"
— Noam Chomsky

"*Attractively written and fully referenced… bound to be the standard history.*"
— Colin Ward, *Times Educational Supplement*

"*Large, labyrinthine, tentative: for me these are all adjectives of praise when applied to works of history, and* Demanding the Impossible *meets all of them.*"
— George Woodcock, *Independent*

Paths toward Utopia: Graphic Explorations of Everyday Anarchism

Cindy Milstein and Erik Ruin
with an Introduction by Josh MacPhee

ISBN: 978-1-60486-502-8
$14.95   120 pages

Consisting of ten collaborative picture-essays that
weave Cindy Milstein's poetic words within Erik Ruin's intricate yet bold paper-cut
and scratch-board images, *Paths toward Utopia* suggests some of the here-and-now
practices that prefigure, however imperfectly, the self-organization that would be
commonplace in an egalitarian society. The book mines what we do in our daily
lives for the already-existent gems of a freer future—premised on anarchistic
ethics like cooperation and direct democracy. Its pages depict everything from
seemingly ordinary activities like using parks as our commons to grandiose
occupations of public space that construct do-it-ourselves communities, if only
temporarily, including pieces such as "The Gift," "Borrowing from the Library,"
"Solidarity Is a Pizza," and "Waking to Revolution." The aim is to supply hints of
what it routinely would be like to live, every day, in a world created from below,
where coercion and hierarchy are largely vestiges of the past.

Paths toward Utopia is not a rosy-eyed stroll, though. The book retains the tensions
in present-day attempts to "model" horizontal institutions and relationships of
mutual aid under increasingly vertical, exploitative, and alienated conditions. It
tries to walk the line between potholes and potential. Yet if anarchist and other
autonomist efforts are to serve as a clarion call to action, they must illuminate
how people qualitatively, consensually, and ecologically shape their needs as
well as desires. They must offer stepping-stones toward emancipation. This
can only happen through experimentation, by us all, with diverse forms of self-
determination and self-governance, even if riddled with contradictions in this
contemporary moment. As the title piece to this book steadfastly asserts, "The
precarious passage itself is our road map to a liberatory society."

"*Writing-speaking differently is part of the struggle for the world we want to create and
are creating, a world that moves against-and-beyond capitalism. These picture-essay-
poems break the existing world both in what they say and how they say it. A fabulous
book.*"
— John Holloway, author of *Crack Capitalism*

"*Paths toward Utopia combines beautiful art, crafted insights, and exemplary stories to
plant inspiring seeds of a better future. What more could one ask for?*"
— Michael Albert, author of *Parecon: Life after Capitalism*

Organize!: Building from the Local for Global Justice

Edited by Aziz Choudry, Jill Hanley & Eric Shragge

ISBN: 978-1-60486-433-5
$24.95   352 pages

What are the ways forward for organizing for progressive social change in an era of unprecedented economic, social and ecological crises? How do political activists build power and critical analysis in their daily work for change?

Grounded in struggles in Canada, the USA, Aotearoa/New Zealand, as well as transnational activist networks, *Organize!: Building from the Local for Global Justice* links local organizing with global struggles to make a better world. In over twenty chapters written by a diverse range of organizers, activists, academics, lawyers, artists and researchers, this book weaves a rich and varied tapestry of dynamic strategies for struggle. From community-based labor organizing strategies among immigrant workers to mobilizing psychiatric survivors, from arts and activism for Palestine to organizing in support of Indigenous Peoples, the authors reflect critically on the tensions, problems, limits and gains inherent in a diverse range of organizing contexts and practices. The book also places these processes in historical perspective, encouraging us to use history to shed light on contemporary injustices and how they can be overcome. Written in accessible language, Organize! will appeal to college and university students, activists, organizers and the wider public.

Contributors include: Aziz Choudry, Jill Hanley, Eric Shragge, Devlin Kuyek, Kezia Speirs, Evelyn Calugay, Anne Petermann, Alex Law, Jared Will, Radha D'Souza, Edward Ou Jin Lee, Norman Nawrocki, Rafeef Ziadah, Maria Bargh, Dave Bleakney, Abdi Hagi Yusef, Mostafa Henaway, Emilie Breton, Sandra Jeppesen, Anna Kruzynski, Rachel Sarrasin, Dolores Chew, David Reville, Kathryn Church, Brian Aboud, Joey Calugay, Gada Mahrouse, Harsha Walia, Mary Foster, Martha Stiegman, Robert Fisher, Yuseph Katiya, and Christopher Reid.

"This superb collection needs to find its way into the hands of every activist and organizer for social justice. In a series of dazzling essays, an amazing group of radical organizers reflect on what it means to build movements in which people extend control over their lives. These analyses are jam-packed with insights about anti-racist, anti-colonial, working-class, and anti-capitalist organizing. Perhaps most crucially, the authors lay down a key challenge for all activists for social justice: to take seriously the need to build mass movements for social change. Don't just read this exceptionally timely and important work—use it too."
— David McNally, author of *Global Slump: The Economics and Politics of Crisis and Resistance*

The Red Army Faction,
A Documentary History
Volume 1: Projectiles For the People

Edited by J. Smith and André Moncourt
Forewords by Russell "Maroon" Shoats and
Bill Dunne

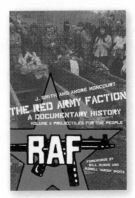

ISBN: 978-1-60486-029-0
$34.95   736 pages

The first in a two-volume series, this is by far the most
in-depth political history of the Red Army Faction ever made available in English.
Projectiles for the People starts its story in the days following World War II, showing
how American imperialism worked hand in glove with the old pro-Nazi ruling
class, shaping West Germany into an authoritarian anti-communist bulwark and
launching pad for its aggression against Third World nations. The volume also
recounts the opposition that emerged from intellectuals, communists, independent
leftists, and then—explosively—the radical student movement and countercultural
revolt of the 1960s.

It was from this revolt that the Red Army Faction emerged, an underground
organization devoted to carrying out armed attacks within the Federal Republic
of Germany, in the view of establishing a tradition of illegal, guerilla resistance
to imperialism and state repression. Through its bombs and manifestos the RAF
confronted the state with opposition at a level many activists today might find
difficult to imagine.

For the first time ever in English, this volume presents all of the manifestos and
communiqués issued by the RAF between 1970 and 1977, from Andreas Baader's
prison break, through the 1972 May Offensive and the 1975 hostage-taking in
Stockholm, to the desperate, and tragic, events of the "German Autumn" of 1977.
The RAF's three main manifestos—*The Urban Guerilla Concept*, *Serve the People*,
and *Black September*—are included, as are important interviews with *Spiegel* and
le Monde Diplomatique, and a number of communiqués and court statements
explaining their actions. Providing the background information that readers will
require to understand the context in which these events occurred, separate
thematic sections deal with the 1976 murder of Ulrike Meinhof in prison, the 1977
Stammheim murders, the extensive use of psychological operations and false-flag
attacks to discredit the guerilla, the state's use of sensory deprivation torture and
isolation wings, and the prisoners' resistance to this, through which they inspired
their own supporters and others on the left to take the plunge into revolutionary
action.

Sex, Race, and Class—
The Perspective of Winning
A Selection of Writings 1952-2011

Selma James
With a foreword by Marcus Rediker
and an introduction by Nina López

ISBN: 978-1-60486-454-0
$20.00   320 pages

In 1972 Selma James set out a new political perspective.
Her starting point was the millions of unwaged women who, working in the home
and on the land, were not seen as "workers" and their struggles viewed as outside
of the class struggle. Based on her political training in the Johnson-Forest Tendency,
founded by her late husband C.L.R. James, on movement experience South and
North, and on a respectful study of Marx, she redefined the working class to
include sectors previously dismissed as "marginal."

For James, the class struggle presents itself as the conflict between the
reproduction and survival of the human race, and the domination of the market
with its exploitation, wars, and ecological devastation. She sums up her strategy for
change as "Invest in Caring not Killing."

This selection, spanning six decades, traces the development of this perspective
in the course of building an international campaigning network. It includes the
classic *The Power of Women and the Subversion of the Community* which launched
the "domestic labor debate," the exciting Hookers in the House of the Lord which
describes a church occupation by sex workers, an incisive review of the C.L.R.
James masterpiece *The Black Jacobins*, a reappraisal of the novels of Jean Rhys and
of the leadership of Julius Nyerere, the groundbreaking *Marx and Feminism*, and
"What the Marxists Never Told Us About Marx," published here for the first time.

The writing is lucid and without jargon. The ideas, never abstract, spring from
the experience of organising, from trying to make sense of the successes and the
setbacks, and from the need to find a way forward.

*"It's time to acknowledge James's path-breaking analysis: from 1972 she re-interpreted
the capitalist economy to show that it rests on the usually invisible unwaged caring
work of women."*
— Dr. Peggy Antrobus, feminist, author of *The Global Women's Movement: Origins,
Issues and Strategies*

"For clarity and commitment to Haiti's revolutionary legacy . . . Selma is a sister after
my own heart."
— Danny Glover, actor and activist

West of Eden: Communes and Utopia in Northern California

Edited by Iain Boal, Janferie Stone, Michael Watts, and Cal Winslow

ISBN: 978-1-60486-427-4
$24.95   304 pages

West of Eden

VTOPIAE INSVLAE FIGVRA

Communes and Utopia
in Northern California
Edited by Iain Boal, Janferie Stone,
Michael Watts, and Cal Winslow

In the shadow of the Vietnam war, a significant part of an entire generation refused their assigned roles in the American century. Some took their revolutionary politics to the streets, others decided simply to turn away, seeking to build another world together, outside the state and the market. *West of Eden* charts the remarkable flowering of communalism in the '60s and '70s, fueled by a radical rejection of the Cold War corporate deal, utopian visions of a peaceful green planet, the new technologies of sound and light, and the ancient arts of ecstatic release. The book focuses on the San Francisco Bay Area and its hinterlands, which have long been creative spaces for social experiment. Haight-Ashbury's gift economy—its free clinic, concerts, and street theatre—and Berkeley's liberated zones—Sproul Plaza, Telegraph Avenue, and People's Park—were embedded in a wider network of producer and consumer co-ops, food conspiracies, and collective schemes.

Using memoir and flashbacks, oral history and archival sources, *West of Eden* explores the deep historical roots and the enduring, though often disavowed, legacies of the extraordinary pulse of radical energies that generated forms of collective life beyond the nuclear family and the world of private consumption, including the contradictions evident in such figures as the guru/predator or the hippie/entrepreneur. There are vivid portraits of life on the rural communes of Mendocino and Sonoma, and essays on the Black Panther communal households in Oakland, the latter-day Diggers of San Francisco, the Native American occupation of Alcatraz, the pioneers of live/work space for artists, and the Bucky dome as the iconic architectural form of the sixties.

Due to the prevailing amnesia—partly imposed by official narratives, partly self-imposed in the aftermath of defeat—*West of Eden* is not only a necessary act of reclamation, helping to record the unwritten stories of the motley generation of communards and antinomians now passing, but is also intended as an offering to the coming generation who will find here, in the rubble of the twentieth century, a past they can use—indeed one they will need—in the passage from the privations of commodity capitalism to an ample life in common.

"As a gray army of undertakers gather in Sacramento to bury California's great dreams of equality and justice, this wonderful book, with its faith in the continuity of our state's radical-communitarian ethic, replants the seedbeds of defiant imagination and hopeful resistance."
— Mike Davis, author of *City of Quartz* and *Magical Urbanism*

On the Ground: An Illustrated Anecdotal History of the Sixties Underground Press in the U.S.

Edited by Sean Stewart
with a preface by Paul Buhle

ISBN: 978-1-60486-455-7
$24.95   208 pages

In four short years (1965-1969), the underground press grew from five small newspapers in as many cities in the U.S. to over 500 newspapers—with millions of readers—all over the world. Completely circumventing (and subverting) establishment media by utilizing their own news service and freely sharing content amongst each other, the underground press, at its height, became the unifying institution for the counterculture of the 1960s. Frustrated with the lack of any mainstream media criticism of the Vietnam War, empowered by the victories of the Civil Rights era, emboldened by the anti-colonial movements in the third world and with heads full of acid, a generation set out to change the world. The underground press was there documenting, participating in, and providing the resources that would guarantee the growth of this emergent youth culture. Combining bold visuals, innovative layouts, and eschewing any pretense toward objectivity, the newspapers were wildly diverse and wonderfully vibrant.

Neither meant to be an official nor comprehensive history, *On the Ground* focuses on the anecdotal detail that brings the history alive. Comprised of stories told by the people involved with the production and distribution of the newspapers—John Sinclair, Art Kunkin, Paul Krassner, Emory Douglas, John Wilcock, Bill Ayers, Spain Rodriguez, Trina Robbins, Al Goldstein, Harvey Wasserman and more—and featuring over 50 full-color scans taken from a broad range of newspapers—*Basta Ya, Berkeley Barb, Berkeley Tribe, Chicago Seed, Helix, It Ain't Me Babe, Los Angeles Free Press, Osawatomie, Rat Subterranean News, San Francisco Express Times, San Francisco Oracle, Screw: The Sex Review, The Black Panther, The East Village Other, The Realist*, and many more—the book provides a true window into the spirit of the times, giving the reader a feeling for the energy on the ground.

"*On the Ground serves as a valuable contribution to countercultural history.*"
— Paul Krassner, author of *Confessions of a Raving, Unconfined Nut: Misadventures in the Counterculture*

"*One should not underestimate the significant value of this book. It gives you real insights into the underground press and its vast diversity of publications, which translated into a taste of real people's power.*"
— Emory Douglas, former Black Panther Party graphic artist and Minister of Culture